INTERNATIONAL CONFLICT AND CONFLICT MANAGEMENT

READINGS IN WORLD POLITICS

Edited by

Robert O. Matthews
Arthur G. Rubinoff
Janice Gross Stein

Department of Political Science
University of Toronto

Prentice-Hall of Canada, Inc., Scarborough, Ontario

Canadian Cataloguing in Publication Data

Main entry under title:

International conflict and conflict management

ISBN 0-13-472739-8

1. International relations — Addresses, essays, lectures.
2. World politics — Addresses, essays, lectures.

I. Matthews, Robert O. II. Rubinoff, Arthur G. (Arthur Gerald), 1942- III. Stein, Janice.

JX1308.I57 1984 327 C84-098027-2

Prentice-Hall, Inc., Englewood Cliffs, New Jersey
Prentice-Hall International, Inc., London
Prentice-Hall of Australia, Pty., Ltd., Sydney
Prentice-Hall of India, Pvt., Ltd., New Delhi
Prentice-Hall of Japan, Inc., Tokyo
Prentice-Hall of Southeast Asia (PTE.) Ltd., Singapore
Editora Prentice-Hall do Brasil Ltda., Rio De Janeiro

ISBN 0-13-472739-8

Production Editor: Bruce Erskine
Designer: Steven Boyle
Production: Barb Almos
Typesetting: ART-U Graphics Ltd.
Printed and bound in Canada by John Deyell Company

1 2 3 4 5 JD 88 87 86 85 84

Contents

Preface

This book emanates from a common desire to make available to students a coherent and comprehensive reader in world politics. The resulting volume is a collection of essays, several of them original, that focus on two of the major themes in international politics — conflict and conflict management. To capture the complexity of conflict and its different, often competing explanations, we have organized the readings according to the major emphasis placed by each author: at the level of the individual, the society, the nation-state, the transnational system, or the international system. We believe that this format is both intellectually coherent and yet sufficiently flexible to allow teachers who employ other organizational schemes to use the materials we have assembled.

While each of us has special interests in the field of international politics, we treated this project as a collective enterprise, working together to select the articles and collaborating in the editing and writing of the introductory sections. As our own perspectives about the discipline differ, the preparation of this volume has truly been an exercise in conflict and conflict management.

In this task we have been assisted by a number of our colleagues. We would like to acknowledge the contributions of Alan Alexandroff, David A. Baldwin, Naomi Black, Aurel Braun, David B. Dewitt, Paul Evans, Franklyn Griffiths, John Kirton, Bennett Kovrig, Charles Pentland, Mike Rubinoff, Edward Safarian, Denis Stairs, Blema Steinberg, Brian Tomlin, and Kenneth Waltz. We owe a special debt of gratitude to William T.R. Fox and Kim Richard Nossal for their thoughtful comments. Gloria Rowe did a superb job, as usual, in typing the manuscript, and Gayle Fraser and Marion Magee proofread the galleys with their customary assiduous care. We are grateful for the support of the staff at Prentice-Hall, but we would like to thank particularly Mary Bruce Grant and Clifford Newman for their interest and encouragement. Finally we dedicate this book to three people whose support has sustained our careers.

September 1, 1983
Toronto

TO

MARTHA
whose support and encouragement are indispensable

WAYNE REYNOLDS MERRICK
teacher, advisor, friend

MICHAEL
who sustains, provokes, and encourages

1 CONFLICT AND CONFLICT MANAGEMENT

World Politics as Conflict Resolution

INTRODUCTION

The central concern of this reader is international conflict and its management. This emphasis is not accidental, for conflict is inherent in world politics; it is an inevitable consequence of relationships and interaction among groups of people who live in a condition of anarchy. But just as conflict is characteristic of international relations, so too is collaboration. Indeed, these two forms of interaction — conflict and cooperation, strife and harmony, war and peace — do not occur in isolation from one another, but are intimately related. Even in wartime, when conflict is most intense, belligerents often collaborate to limit damage to civilians and ensure fair treatment of prisoners-of-war. Conversely, allies who join together to pursue shared objectives often disagree, sometimes quite strenuously, over appropriate strategies, a fair division of labor, and an equitable sharing of burdens. Drawing on a rich and often contradictory body of argument and evidence, this collection of readings examines the impact of the individual, the society, the state, and the system on the processes of international conflict and conflict management.

The terms "conflict" and "war" are sometimes used interchangeably by analysts of international relations. We do not do so. While conflict embraces war, we use conflict in a much broader sense to refer to competition among groups for scarce goods, such as territory and resources, or the pursuit of mutually incompatible values and purposes. This competition need not, and most often does not, culminate in violence. Conflict over goods, services, values, and purposes is as pervasive in international relations as it is in almost all other kinds of relationships, but competing groups, in international as well as in domestic society, often stop short of a use of force in the pursuit of incompatible goals. War is consequently one, but only one, form of broader social conflict. Our concern is with all kinds of international conflict; however, special emphasis will be given to its most coercive and violent form, war.

As long as organized groups resort to force to achieve their purposes and settle disputes, analysts look for less destructive strategies to manage conflict. Indeed, some hope to eliminate conflict, to build a world society of harmony and perpetual peace, free of dissension and strife. However, most of the authors you will read consider a resolution of all conflict improbable and some think it undesirable. In a world of enormous diversity, differing religions, contrasting cultures, diverse ideologies, and policy differences, conflict is not only possible but very probable. Some particularly intense conflicts resist settlement; even after suffering defeat in war, a loser often nurses grievances and awaits the first promising opportunity to engage an adversary again. Some conflicts are settled, others simply fade away, and some are transcended as the participants join together to focus on new issues and new agendas. But as some are settled, new conflicts appear. Conflict is not only a pervasive but also a permanent feature of international political processes.

Not all students of international relations decry the pervasiveness and persistence of processes of conflict. Marxists, for example, see conflict as necessary and positive, as the motor force of history; class conflict in society acts as the midwife to revolutionary change. Others, particularly liberals, consider conflict irrational and undesirable, negative and costly. As we approach the end of the twentieth century, a century dominated by wars unprecedented in their human and social costs, most analysts are more measured in their judgments. They may concur with John W. Burton that "conflict, like sex, is an essentially creative element in human relationships," but fear the enormity of the consequences that may flow from violent conflict today.[1] The likely benefits of a use of force, they argue, may be more than offset by the probable cost, not only to the belligerents themselves, but to global society as a whole. Consequently, they treat non-violent conflict as an essential and even a desirable agent of change, but work actively to control and limit the incidence, the scope, and the level of war.

Since conflict is a recurrent phenomenon, and since the risks of uncontrolled conflict are so great, scholars today pay a great deal of attention to processes of conflict management and regulation.[2] In the opening essay in this collection, William T.R.Fox focuses on the number of parties attempting to resolve international conflict and the different techniques of conflict management they use. He suggests that conflict can be resolved, in whole or in part, by one, two, three, or no parties — that is, by force; through negotiation; as a result of third party mediation, conciliation, or adjudication; or by obsolescence. Kenneth Waltz, in a somewhat different approach, distinguishes between active and passive conflict management. When the parties to a conflict are integrated, either through the creation of common institutions and procedures or through conquest, a conflict is resolved actively. When a conflict is settled passively, the parties reduce their interaction, or even divorce: they withdraw entirely from any relationship. As Waltz notes, Kant dreamt of perpetual peace through a voluntary union of republics, while Rousseau saw utopia as an isolated Corsica. At both extremes, international conflict is eliminated only by abolishing international relations. Since both are extremes, virtually unattainable, Waltz foresees the "ubiquity of conflict and the recurrence of war among states."[3]

Even this brief discussion reveals the richness and diversitv of explanations of conflict, its forms, its processes, its consequences, and its management. In their attempt to explain the sources and processes of conflict and to prescribe effective strategies of conflict management, scholars have worked at quite different levels of analysis and explanation.[4] Although there is some disagreement about the identification and classification of these different levels, in this collection we identify five to organize the analysis of international conflict and its management. We start with the individual and work our way up, through increasingly complex levels, to the international system.

The first level of analysis is the individual: can we explain conflict as a result of leaders' personalities, perceptions, or faulty decision making? If we want to explain, for example, why war broke out in Europe in 1914 and not in 1908 or 1909, do we need to consider the impact of individual leaders charged with responsibility for security? Did these leaders miscalculate dreadfully and provoke a war no one wanted?

Or might we be better off working at the second level, the societal setting or group context which shapes leaders' decisions? Can we explain conflict by the competing demands of powerful groups with privileged access to political leaders, or even by broader patterns of social conflict which spill over into war? Some scholars suggest that intense social conflict within Germany provoked the war in 1914.

Many analysts consider the third level, that of the state, to be the most important. Indeed, they treat the state as the basic unit of international relations. Does the most powerful contribution to international conflict and its management come from the attributes of the state — its sovereignty, territoriality, nationalism, power, and economic structure? Was the war of 1914 an imperialist war? Were differences in military capabilities among the European powers a crucial contributing factor?

Some analysts look to yet a fourth level, the transnational system, as a source of international conflict. Are there conflicts which originate in intersocietal rather than interstate relations and which involve non-state participants?

The fifth and final level is the international system. Do anarchy and the distribution of power within a particular historical system explain the incidence, the form, and the intensity of international conflict? Can we understand the war of 1914, for example, as the consequence of the breakdown of the balance-of-power system? Systems analysts would argue that whether war broke out in 1909 or 1914 is of secondary importance; what does matter is that the collapse of the balance of power made war highly probable, sooner or later. By the same token, do characteristics of the international system contribute to effective conflict management? Those who are skeptical of the capacity of states to manage conflict look to the regulatory capacity of the system, to international institutions and procedures, to manage interstate disputes.

This identification of five important levels of analysis, five sets of explanatory factors, raises obvious questions. As J. David Singer noted in an early and penetrating criticism of many explanations of international conflict, scholars have tended to roam freely from one level to another, without considering the theoretical implications of doing so.[5] He raises the critical question: how do we relate these different levels of analysis to each other and to the problem we are trying to explain? In concluding his volume on the causes of war, Waltz suggests that an adequate explanation of war as well as an appropriate prescription for peace must draw from all levels of analysis; no one level can offer a wholly satisfactory explanation.[6] Similarly, K.J.Holsti argues that a comprehensive analysis of international conflict must examine the contribution of the individual, the state, and the international system.[7] But again, this advice raises more questions than it answers.

First, analysts of international relations, like other social scientists, look for the most economical, the most parsimonious explanation. Is it really necessary to seek evidence of the perceptions of individual leaders, the pattern of domestic pressures, the characteristics of the states engaged in conflict, the constellation of transnational forces and institutions, and the structure and processes of the international system? Is it not more desirable, for reasons of economy, to make choices about the relative importance of different levels? Generally, explanatory knowledge grows because analysts make precisely these kinds of difficult choices which narrow rather than broaden the contributing factors.

Second, when we do consider factors drawn from more than one level of analysis to be relevant, how do we integrate these factors into a coherent and comprehensive explanation? We know how to distinguish among these factors, but how do we add them together? This is an extraordinarily difficult task. Perhaps the international or transnational system shapes the broad probability of conflict and its characteristic forms, while state attributes and social tensions affect the propensity to engage in conflict, and individual leaders determine the precise moment and circumstances of the escalation of conflict. This brings us directly to the third and final issue.

We might best conceive of different levels of analysis as relevant to the different questions we are trying to answer. If we are trying to explain the broad pattern of international conflict over time, then we might be well advised to begin our explanation with analysis of the international system. If we want to know why two states were able to resolve a particular conflict over a specific issue, then we might profitably look at the contribution of individual or societal factors to effective conflict management. Choice among levels depends, at least in part, on what we are trying to explain.

The essays in this collection are grouped according to the level at which the authors cast their explanations. Consider their arguments both in terms of their relevance to the dimensions of conflict and conflict management, and their relationship to explanations formulated at other levels.

ENDNOTES

1 John W. Burton, *World Society* (Cambridge: Cambridge University Press, 1972), p. 136.

2 See Barbara J. Hill, "An Analysis of Conflict Resolution," *Journal of Conflict Resolution,* 26 (March 1982), 109-138.

3 Kenneth N. Waltz, "Conflict in World Politics," in Steven L. Spiegel and Kenneth N. Waltz, eds., *Conflict in World Politics* (Cambridge, Mass.: Winthrop, 1971), p. 474.

4 For a discussion of levels of analysis, see J. David Singer, "The Level-of-Analysis Problem in International Relations," in Klaus Knorr and Sidney Verba, eds., *The International System: Theoretical Essays* (Princeton, N.J.: Princeton University Press, 1961), pp. 77-93; Kenneth Waltz, *Man, the State, and War* (New York: Columbia University Press, 1959); and Robert Jervis, *Perception and Misperception in International Politics* (Princeton: Princeton University Press, 1976), pp. 15-31.

5 Singer, "The Level-of-Analysis Problem in International Relations," p. 78.

6 Waltz, *Man, the State, and War*, pp. 224-238.

7 K.J. Holsti, *International Politics: A Framework for Analysis*, 3rd edition (Englewood Cliffs, N.J.: Prentice-Hall, 1977), pp. 17-18.

World Politics as Conflict Resolution

William T.R. Fox

We live in a world of nation-states. There are about one hundred and fifty of them, more than half born since 1945. A very few are large, rich, and powerful. Most are small or poor or both. World politics is therefore a politics of inequality. Like all politics, it is also a politics of scarcity and uneven change.

In the name of their respective nation-states, political leaders are always advancing more claims than the world political system can possibly satisfy. Wish lists are always longer than the list of available good things to be wished for. "Politics" is the name we give to the process by which it is decided "who gets what, when, and how."[1] World politics, accordingly, is the study of which nation-states get what, when, and how.[2]

One might suppose that in a world in which there is not enough to go around, in terms of whatever scarce things nation-states are competing for, the rich, large, and powerful would always get their way. If they did, that would put an end to international politics; but it is not that simple. The powerful are each other's main competitors, and the main restraint on each other's arbitrary exercise of power over weaker neighbors. The imprudent use of great power against the less powerful can have costly long-run consequences, as Adolf Hitler and other aspirants for hegemony in the international system before him have demonstrated. If for no other reason, the United States would have an interest in a friendly and cooperative Canada because, in a threatening world, both countries seek to keep major threats as far away from North American shores as possible; this very much reduces the relevance of overwhelmingly superior American military power to day-to-day problems of Canadian-American relations.

The rich and powerful states do not automatically have their way for a variety of other reasons. Power is not like money in the bank, equally available to be drawn on, so long as the supply holds out, for all purposes. Iceland is a great fishing power, but otherwise it is not a power at all. Thermonuclear striking power can evidently deter large-scale attack on its possessor, but it cannot be invoked in any direct way in the day-to-day conduct of foreign relations. A prosperous democratic country may be able to develop enormous military power if, after it has been attacked, there is time to mobilize that power, but public opinion will not support an increased level of sacrifice for national defense which threatens social programs that the electorate values more highly than the added security which the proposed new sacrifice is expected to provide. Except for the occasional great aggressor who wishes to overturn the system, such as Napoleon or Hitler, leaders of powerful states have as great a stake in preserving their respective reputations for fair play and in helping to maintain an international order as do the leaders of most other states in the system. Finally, the

---

An original essay written especially for this volume.

rich and powerful are not all-powerful. There is more than one rich and powerful state, and the power of even the very powerful is less and less effective the farther away from home it is to be applied.

In a static world those on top would stay on top even if the system did impose some restraints on their exercise of power. There would be a fixed pecking order, but there would be no politics. In the real world, the world of uneven change, changes occurring in some particular nation-state or some particular part of the world affect the nation-states in the world system unequally. New technologies may confer unequal benefits. New ideas may generate new demands and new willingness to sacrifice and perhaps die for one's country. If the population grows more rapidly in one country than in an adjacent one, if the work ethic makes one group of people more productive than another, if the rate of saving by the people of one country is higher than in that of a traditional competitor, each country's leaders may well make fresh calculations as to what foreign policy demands they can prudently advance.

Because change is uneven and continuous, new opportunities for politicking constantly arise. The political process never stops. Political leaders are always divining new wants, calculating new ways of getting old things long wanted, or mobilizing new strengths in support of long-standing demands. Demands that are not met generate conflict, and there will be conflict as long as there is politics. Peace is not the absence of conflict, but the absence of violence in the process of settling conflicts.[3]

Even if the supply of good things in the world, however the governments of nation-states define what is "good" and therefore worth having, was more than sufficient to meet the most basic human needs of men, women, and children everywhere, and it may well be much more than sufficient, international politics would still be a politics of scarcity. It is not "needs" objectively determined by reference to standards generally agreed to be fair, but "demands" subjectively determined by the governments of nation-states with very unequal ability to make good those claims, that assure that the international politics of tomorrow, like the international politics of today and of yesterday, will be a politics of scarcity.[4]

This most emphatically does not mean that mankind is condemned to an eternal violent struggle between the haves and the have-nots of this world, or to unending cycles of peace and war twice each century among the first-ranking nation-states. Less costly processes of determining who gets what, when, and how may be substituted for more costly ones, as has happened inside well-ordered constitutional democracies. The common interest in some measure of order and predictability in world affairs moderates the intensity and violence of the political competition among states, and may do more. More specifically, the specter of thermonuclear holocaust and the increasing perception that there are pressing world problems that not even the most powerful of today's states can solve by themselves make it possible that the international politics of the future will be in significant respects different from that of the past. It will still, however, be a politics of scarce means, applied in a conflictual process where goals may not be achievable. There will always be politics, it has been said, "except in Heaven, Hell, and other perfect dictatorships." Tomorrow's world, whatever else it may or may not be, will not be a perfect dictatorship. Conflict, and the political processes for adjusting conflicting claims for scarce values, are at the center of the study of international relations.

These things are at the center of the study of domestic politics too, but there are significant differences between typical political processes inside a nation-state and those that adjust competing claims between nation-states. In both cases, if all else fails, force is the ultimate arbiter of conflict. International politics, however, is politics carried on in the absence of government. Governments usually have a near-monopoly, *inside* the state, on the decisive instruments of violence, and constitutional governments ordinarily use that near-monopoly only to put down an illegal resort to violence. Thus, governments characteristically develop peaceful procedures for choosing among competing claimants for the same scarce values. Governments give orderly answers to questions of who gets what, when, and how. The procedures may or may not be fair, and the orderly answers may or may not be just. They may or may not provide strong incentives to increase the supply of good things to be allocated. What gives government authority is that the results of its routinized procedures are accepted and public order is thereby maintained.

Within well-ordered states the expectation of violence is low, and the expectation that the outcome of the state's peaceful political processes will and ought to be respected is high. Those defeated in elections, frustrated in their efforts to get the law changed, or unsuccessful in courts of law, accept unwanted outcomes of legal, political, and administrative procedures peacefully because of the general belief that preserving the peaceful processes of government is more important than changing the outcome of any particular dispute, whether it be electoral, legislative, or judicial.

The well-ordered state provides much more than peaceful procedures for allocating scarce values among its citizens. Modern governments are engaged in the production of "public goods." The most obvious, and the most widely accepted, of these public goods is protection against external threat. Indeed, one cynic has described government as "a group of gangsters organized to sell protection over a limited area at monopolistic prices." Education, public health, water supply, roads and bridges, the provision of recreation areas, and a variety of measures to enhance productivity are all examples of public goods whose production is the consequence of political decisions implemented by governments.

On the international scene, by contrast, absence of government has meant that the role of force as the ultimate arbiter among disputing claimants for scarce values is more clearly and explicitly acknowledged. There is little or no recognition of the existence of a world constitutional order whose preservation is deemed more important than the outcome of a particular dispute. The use of international institutions for the production of public goods on a global scale is still in its infancy, although there are striking examples of coalitions of states in particular parts of the world, or with particular kinds of social systems, developing quasi-governmental institutions for the production of public goods. NATO, the Common Market, OECD, and UNCTAD are examples. Furthermore, a variety of public international organizations reflect some almost inescapable common interests among states. Internationally agreed upon systems of measurement and weight, procedures for assuring safety of life at sea, rules to minimize unintended interference by one state's radio and television broadcasts with those of another, and organizations to promote the accurate exchange of information about epidemic disease are all examples of cooperation between nation-states.

In the governance of the world, the General Assembly of the United Nations, controlled as it is by an overwhelming majority of governments representing states which are relatively poor, small, and weak, may prove to be those states' most effective instrument for promoting international distributive justice. However, the United Nations is still too fragile an instrument to provide the world as a whole with the range of public services which the governments of advanced countries characteristically provide for their citizens.

Given the absence of world government, we may ask exactly what happens when, under conditions of scarcity, states advance competing claims? We can safely assume that there are many wishes of political leaders that do not get translated into foreign policy demands because of the evident impossibility of achieving them. Probably a majority could be found in the General Assembly of the United Nations who would favor the imposition of a world-wide progressive income tax *if* there were any prospect that the machinery of the United Nations could be used to collect the tax and move huge amounts of wealth from Western

Europe, North America, the oil-rich sheikdoms of the Middle East, and Japan to Third World countries. Since there is no such prospect, there will instead be in the years ahead more modest proposals, such as "income transfers," in amounts and under conditions to be established by donor and recipient states. Another example of a wish that is unlikely to be advanced as a claim may be cited. As a result of the secession of Texas from Mexico and its subsequent admission into the United States, and of the American seizure of what is now California, New Mexico, and Arizona as fruits of victory in the United States war with Mexico, some forty per cent of Mexican territory was lost to the United States in the 1840s. No doubt there have been many Mexicans who would have favored demanding the return of the lost territory if there had been the slightest chance that the demand could be seriously considered. But the passage of time and the populating of the lost territory with some forty million citizens of the United States would make any Mexican move to regain what is now the American Southwest implausible.[5]

A slightly, but significantly, different case is that of the British in Gibraltar. Seized in 1703 and for centuries a fortified area critical to Britain's control of the narrow seas around the European land mass, Gibraltar has been a bone of contention between a proud but humbled Spain too weak to push its ongoing claim for Gibraltar to the point of war, and a powerful and determined Britain, unmoved by Spain's protests that the rock of Gibraltar is truly Spanish. Here is an example of a dispute which could be settled only by the two parties agreeing to continue to disagree until time and changed circumstances caused both to forget about it, or by changed circumstances which would incline Britain to negotiate the Spanish claim seriously.

It is not just relatively small disputes about which both sides are intransigent that can only be settled by the passage of time and changed circumstances. The Wars of Religion, the bloody struggles in the sixteenth and seventeenth centuries waged by the forces of the Reformation and the Counter-Reformation, were ideological struggles without clear, fixed goals which, by their very nature, could not really settle anything. The struggles only ended when the wars burned themselves out, and the attention of European rulers was turned toward the consolidation of royal power within the emerging nation-states. What the small case of Gibraltar and the large case of the Wars of Religion have in common with each other and with, for instance, the century-long Anglo-American Fisheries Dispute of the nineteenth century, is that only time and changed circumstances made it possible to remove the matters at issue from the agenda of international conflict.[6] This we may call *no-party settlement*, in order to contrast it with one-party settlement, two-party settlement, third-party settlement, and international community settlement.[7]

Although by their adherence to the Charter of the United Nations, nearly every state in the world has forsworn the use of force as a means of getting what it does not have[8] (though not as a means of keeping what it has), the possibility of violence as the ultimate arbiter if all other means of settlement fail is much more explicitly recognized in the society of nation-states than it is in civil society within well-ordered states. This is another way of saying that if the parties to an international dispute cannot agree, one of them may decide that time has run out in the search for peaceful solutions; it may then either issue an ultimatum, calling for immediate submission to its "final" demands, or go directly to war without even bothering to give the offending party one last chance to yield before commencing hostilities. A successful ultimatum might be described as "winning a war in zero time." Like unconditional surrender at the end of a war, it opens the way to a dictated solution to a dispute, to what we have called *one-party settlement*.

War, we should note, has historically been a legal way of settling disputes between states in our state system. The international law of war and neutrality is as detailed and well-developed as the international law of pacific settlement, and some would say that it has been more regularly observed. Of course, not all wars lead to the kind of clear-cut defeat that ended World War II for Italy, Germany, and finally Japan. Sometimes, as in the case of the Thirty Years' War, which ended in 1648 only after six years of negotiating among two sets of negotiating countries in the Westphalian cities of Münster and Osnabruck, there are no clear victors. Where there is no victory, what war does is make clear to the parties to the original dispute their respective strengths. It also makes clear the probability that further sacrifice in carrying on the war will bring commensurate gain in the peace that sooner or later must follow. Peace is restored at the moment neither side finds it profitable to continue the war.

Ultimatums are not always explicit. A stiff diplomatic note containing a phrase such as "the gravest consequences" if some contingency or other were to occur might be enough to warn off a state whose leaders may be contemplating facing its opponent in a dispute with a *fait accompli*. Leading examples of dictated solutions to disputes in this century that did not involve actual war are those that, in the years before the Second World War, led to the incorporation of Estonia, Latvia, and Lithuania into the Soviet Union, of Austria into Hitler's Third Reich, and of Czechoslovakia into Nazi Germany's *Lebensraum*. Stalin's ultimatum to Finland, on the other hand, led not to Finland's submission but to the Winter War of 1939-40 in which, after inflicting serious and embarrassing losses on the armed forces of its giant Soviet neighbor, Finland was forced to sue for peace but under circumstances that preserved Finland's independence.

More recent examples of dictated solutions without recourse to formal war are provided by events attendant upon the liquidation of the remnants of Portugal's once vast overseas empire. India in 1961 simply announced that the time had come to end Portugal's 400-year control of Goa, a tiny enclave on the Malabar coast of the Indian sub-continent, and two even smaller Portuguese-controlled territories. Portugal was in no position to resist and did not. Neither would Portugal have been in a position to obstruct Indonesia's takeover of the Portuguese-ruled half of the island of Timor, had it been so inclined. On the other hand, Macao, Portugal's historic trading post near Hong Kong, is at least as indefensible as either Goa or Timor, but the Chinese People's Republic has not chosen to occupy it.

The Thirty Years' War in the seventeenth century and the two world wars of the twentieth lasted so long and consumed so many lives and so much treasure that in a very real sense there were only losers, even though in both the twentieth century wars one side was thoroughly defeated. The victory of Germany in the Franco-Prussian War in 1871 is perhaps the last occasion for which a plausible case can be made for saying that in a war between first-ranking powers, the victor actually profited from the war. That there could be a true victor in a Third World War or any other imaginable future war among first-ranking powers appears unlikely.

Lesser wars — including some very large-scale and protracted limited wars such as those in Korea and Vietnam; some very short and decisive ones as in the case of wars involving Israel and its Arab neighbors; some with indecisive outcomes which opened the way to a resumption of fighting whenever one side or the other found it convenient, as in the case of India and Pakistan; and some that were the result of a gigantic miscalculation by the loser, as in the case of the Falkland Islands War — are a feature of the second half of the twentieth century. Except for the few that have been won quickly, the limited wars of recent decades have been terminated after complicated negotiation and, more often than not, only after the active interposition of third parties in their negotiated termination. Thus, while "victory" is a form of one-party settlement, contemporary war is more often a prelude to the resumption of diplomacy, including multilateral diplomacy, i.e., an effort to settle the dispute that engendered the war in a wider forum that involves the active participation of third parties.

Modern governments have a shared interest in the orderly disposition of day-to-day problems that are bound to arise between states as people, goods, capital, information, and ideas move across international boundaries. International law and customary practice give some measure of predictability and reliability to arrangements made to control such movements in an interdependent world. Agreed upon rules, however, have to be applied in particular cases, and consequently there is an unending number of matters to be negotiated involving the raising and lowering of barriers between the countries concerned. Bilateral (and sometimes multilateral) diplomacy deals most of the time with the undramatic problems and conflicts of people living together in a multi-state world. An upstream polluter of an international river and a downstream consumer of fish from that river; the exporting and importing countries when there is an allegation of "dumping"; and finding mutually acceptable formulae to minimize inequitable double taxation are three examples of important but undramatic problems that might be on a diplomatic agenda. Great questions of war, peace, alliances, and coalition politico-military planning are supremely important when they do arise, but they are not on the ordinary agenda of ordinary diplomats on an ordinary day.

Whether the matters for diplomatic negotiation are mundane and ever-recurring questions of trade and finance or dramatic and sometimes dangerous questions of international peace and security, the function of diplomacy is, in the words of one veteran diplomatist, "to establish a firm basis for agreement or disagreement, as the case may be." We may describe the spelling out of a firm basis for agreement as a *two-party settlement*.[9]

When, on the other hand, negotiation has led to the discovery of a firm basis for disagreement, the fact of conflict has been established. There are then several possibilities: (1) The two sides may, after an interval, return to the bargaining table. (2) An open break may be avoided by tacitly agreeing to disagree until enough time has passed and enough circumstances have changed so that the conflict is abandoned and perhaps even forgotten. (3) One of the parties to the diplomatic negotiation might abruptly issue some kind of ultimatum or even proceeds to start a war. Or (4) a crisis may be averted or at least postponed by some form of third-party interposition. In terms of the language of this essay, the four courses of action following the finding of "a firm basis for disagreement" are continued search for two-party settlement; tacit acceptance over a period of years of no-party settlement; force or threat of force leading to one-party settlement; and widening the forum of negotiation and perhaps the balance of contending forces in a way that is meant to produce *third-party settlement*.

Third parties may do little more than pass messages back and forth between parties to a dispute in which direct conversations have broken down. They may suggest ways out of an apparent impasse, as successive American presidents have done in the continuing disputes between Israel and its Arab neighbors. They may recommend a solution with the implication that a party to a dispute that rejects the recommendation may lose the third party's support. Third parties may, if the disputants agree, be clothed with the power to make a binding decision in a process of international arbitration.

The third party may be another state or group of states, e.g., the so-called Contadora group — Costa Rica, Mexico, Panama, and Venezuela — which sought in 1983 to fend off war between Honduras and Nicaragua. It may be an international institution such as the GATT (General Agreement on Tariffs and Trade) making a judgment as to the conformity of Canadian regulations respecting trade between Canada and the United States, with obligations assumed under the GATT. It may be a person, usually one with an exalted or prestigious position, such as Pope John Paul II, called upon to settle lingering boundary problems between Argentina and Chile. If the parties have agreed in advance to accept as binding an international court's decision in any particular class of dispute, that form of third-party interposition is called judicial settlement. Among the more prominent of the relatively few cases referred to the International Court of Justice for judicial settlement is one involving South Africa's legal position with respect to its former League of Nations mandate, Southwest Africa (now called Namibia by those pressing for its full independence).

In the period since the end of the Second World War there has been an enormous increase in the number and activity of international organizations involved in conflict adjustment. One of these organizations, the United Nations, is broad in function and nearly universal in membership. Others are either specialized in purpose, e.g., the Food and Agriculture Organization and the International Atomic Energy Agency, or regional in membership, e.g., the North Atlantic Treaty Organization, the Organization of American States, and the Arab League. The European Common Market and NORAD are both specialized and regional.

The activities of international organizations that have captured the most public attention are those in which bilateral and local disputes involving fighting or the threat of fighting have been moved to a wider forum, most often the United Nations, for what Ernst Haas has called "collective conflict management." Professor Haas reports on a tabulation of 217 disputes between 1945 and 1981 in which some fighting occurred. 103 were rated "serious" and almost three-quarters were referred to some international organization or other.[10]

Establishing new patterns of rights and duties among nation-states by international conferences, multilateral diplomacy, or binding resolutions of the quasi-legislative organs of public international organizations may be viewed as a form of third-party interposition leading to conflict resolution, but in this category it is resolution between classes of states with shared, though not identical, interests. Thus, for example, interest in regulating whaling to prevent the extinction of the species may be universal, but there may be acute disagreement as to what proportion of the permitted kill should be allocated to each country's whalers. The protracted law of the sea negotiations are another example in which the interest of countries now possessing advanced technology for exploiting marine and sea-bed resources, and the interest of those concerned to assure themselves of some future sharing of "the common heritage of mankind," are clearly different.

A final word needs to be said about the four modes of conflict adjustment or settlement here described. It is analytically useful to think of a single mode of conflict management; the no-party method of letting time obsolesce it *or* the one-party method of coercive threat and actual war *or* the two-party method of normal diplomacy *or* any of the bewildering variety of third-party methods. In the real world, however, it is not that simple. Diplomats are aware when they negotiate that if all other methods of conflict adjustment among sovereign states fail, war or the threat of war may force the weaker party to yield. Well publicized speeches and military demonstrations meant to be noticed in a particular foreign country may or may not be regarded as efforts to dictate one-party settlements. Governments contemplating the use of force on an obviously weaker opponent must consider what third-party states or action, through what international organization, may interfere. International organizations may, in the case of a particular dispute, be more important as a cooling-off device, i.e., for allowing the passage of time to lead to "no-party settlement," or as a face-saving device for the side that would have ultimately had to yield. As for war, the so-called ultimate method of settlement, it often leads back to the bargaining table (a bargaining table where the bargaining capacities of the two sides are more clearly understood than before the fighting).

By whatever method peace is restored or preserved, only one thing is certain. Conflict and conflict adjustment — which, as we said earlier, is another name for politics — will go on as long as there are human beings to conflict with each other. In a world of nation-states, international politics and the need for international conflict adjustment will remain an essential part of human interaction.

ENDNOTES

1 Harold D. Lasswell coined the phrase in his *Politics: Who Gets What, When, How* (New York: McGraw-Hill, 1936). Note that the "what" is not necessarily a pie of fixed size. It is not necessarily true that if X gets a larger slice, some Y (or Y's) must get a smaller slice, nor is it true that if X gets a smaller slice, some Y or other must have benefited. A political process may be so wasteful that everybody loses or so useful that everybody wins. World War III would be the limiting case, a conflict in which all participants lose (though the "victor" might be marginally less devastated than the vanquished). A comprehensive set of arms control arrangements, no matter how intense the conflict which had to be resolved on the way to achieving the arms controls, might well allow all participants to win if it provided an increase in security for all signatories to the agreement and makes possible a release of human and material resources for non-military activity.

2 Strictly speaking, it would be more accurate to speak of "world politics" rather than "international politics," for there are politically significant human associations other than nation-states. Many of them cut across national boundaries, and many of those which do not also powerfully influence "who gets what."

3 On peace and peacefulness as a state of affairs in which conflict is carried on in a relatively mild way, see Kenneth E. Boulding, *Conflict and Defense: a General Theory* (New York: Harper and Row, 1962) and Boulding's essay "Toward a Theory of Peace" in Roger Fisher, ed., *International Conflict and Behavioral Science* (New York: Basic Books, 1964), pp. 70-87. One must distinguish between mild or slumbering conflict and conflict which is so visible, acknowledged, and defined that it is a "dispute." A "crisis" occurs in international politics when a dispute is so serious as to involve the threat of war. On crises, see Glenn H. Snyder and Paul Diesing, *Conflict Among Nations* (Princeton, N.J.: Princeton University Press, 1977).

4 One of the valued objects of political activity that may be in short supply is the sense of winning. If the opportunities to compete were greatly increased, the pressure of domestic opinion on national leaders to be seen as "winning" in international crisis situations might be lessened. See Arthur Waskow, "Nonlethal Equivalents of War" in R. Fisher, ed., *International Conflict and Behavioral Science,* pp. 123-141.

5 Ironically, as persons of Mexican descent grow in numbers and political influence in the once Mexican part of the United States, a kind of re-Mexicanization is occurring.

6 A settlement of sorts in the fisheries dispute was in fact reached in 1909, but only after almost a century and long after the dispute had lost its salience in Anglo-American relations. Ironically, the recent widespread international recognition of a 200-mile economic zone for national exploitation of off-shore marine and sea-bed resources has again made fisheries an international problem for North Americans, this time one between Canada and the United States.

7 The concept of no-party settlement, i.e., disposal of a dispute by letting time and changed circumstances make it obsolete, was developed by the late Quincy Wright as part of his four-way classification of settlement procedures, the classification used in this essay. "International community settlement," which I have here chosen to list separately, may also be viewed as a form of third-party interposition. See Professor Wright's *A Study of War* (Chicago: University of Chicago Press, 1942; rev. ed. 1965) for his major contribution to the study of conflict and conflict adjustment.

8 Article 2(4), but note that Article 51 testifies to the "inherent right of individual and collective self-defense."

9 Conflicts are, almost by definition, two-sided; but there may be more than one state on a side, as in the Triple Alliance-Triple Entente confrontation in the decade before World War I.

10 Ernst B. Haas, "Regime Decay: Conflict Management and International Organization, 1945-1981," *International Organization*, 36 (Spring 1983), 189-256.

THE INDIVIDUAL 2

PERCEPTION A

DECISION MAKING B

INTRODUCTION

It may seem rather curious that we begin with an analysis of the impact of the individual on international conflict and its management. Since international conflict, by definition, deals with conflict among nations, would it not be more appropriate to start with an analysis of nation-states or the relationships among them? Scholars who pay particular attention to the role of the individual in international conflict and conflict management will answer this question in several, often quite different, ways.

Those schooled in rigorous logic will insist that it is not nations that act, but their leaders. Every time we encounter the statement that "the United States warned the Soviet Union" or "Canada expressed its outrage to the United States," we understand it to mean that officials of the United States or representatives of Canada were speaking. Indeed, by writing as if the United States can warn or Canada can express outrage, we are committing the logical error of inappropriately ascribing the properties of the individual to the collective.[1] Nations cannot choose to escalate or reduce a conflict, but their leaders can. One need not be wholly persuaded by this logic, however, to accept the proposition that the basic forces of international relations, sooner or later, all work through the individual. As the UNESCO Constitution put it in a now-famous phrase, since wars begin in the minds of men [or women], it is in the minds of men that the defenses of peace must be constructed. Scholars or policy makers who advance similar arguments will insist that the attributes of the individual are important in a comprehensive explanation of international, as well as interpersonal conflict.

Acceptance of the proposition that the individual is an important component in the analysis of international conflict and its management immediately raises the obvious question: how do we study the impact of the individual? Here we can identify two broad approaches. Some scholars, principally diplomatic historians and biographers, insist that the distinctive and idiosyncratic attributes of an individual are the essence of an explanation. Psycho-historians who have examined the roots of World War II have placed a great deal of emphasis on the idiosyncratic character of Hitler, arguing by implication that if he had not come to power, the long-standing conflict between France and Germany might well have taken a different, less violent course. Indeed, anyone who considers an election an appropriate mechanism to choose a leader implicitly accepts the proposition that individual differences do matter in politics;

otherwise, we might as well choose political leaders by the flip of a coin.[2]

By contrast, philosophers, psychologists, socio-biologists, and social scientists tend to concentrate not on the differences among individuals but on their similarities. Some work at the highest level of generality and focus on characteristics common to all individuals. In an exchange of letters with Albert Einstein, for example, Sigmund Freud traced the roots of war to a basic instinct for aggression and destruction, one of two basic instincts characteristic of human nature.[3] In so doing, he joined a long philosophical and religious tradition which locates the source of conflict, aggression, and war in the propensity of the human being to do violence and evil.[4]

More recently, biologists have turned to the analysis of aggression and war. Extrapolating from evolutionary history and drawing analogies to animal behavior in nature, they suggest that the will to fight evolved through history as an important mechanism of survival and adaptation. Aggression, it is claimed, is genetically programed and whether it manifests itself in the drive for territory or the urge to dominate, aggression is characteristic of the human species.[5]

The socio-biological argument, broadly conceived, raises more questions, however, than it answers. First, can we legitimately generalize from animal behavior to human interaction? The biological argument often ignores the important mediating effects of culture and society except as they affect the pattern of biological evolution. Yet as philosophers and psychologists have long argued, a common culture and shared norms and institutions may have a profound effect on the way individuals behave toward one another. Second, even if we ignore the social environment of human action, can we properly extend an explanation of animal aggression to the management of conflict by leaders charged with responsibility to the collective? Socio-biologists, blind to the role of ideology and history in shaping leaders' attitudes and strategies, pay little attention to cultural and environmental differences. In so doing, they diminish the scope of choice and see war as the performance of a role written thousands of years ago. Finally, socio-biologists do not explain why leaders frequently choose to conciliate, to compromise, to cooperate.

Yet, just as war has been a recurrent theme of human history, so we have known long periods of uninterrupted peace. Our genetic composition, which changed so gradually over thousands of years, and varied so slowly, cannot possibly explain the almost continual oscillation between conflict and cooperation which is so fundamental to the history of international relations. At best, socio-biologists document a tendency toward conflict, a tendency that is frequently counterbalanced by other important human attributes, all mediated by the social and cultural environment in which we live. Religious thinkers and philosophers who emphasize only the human capacity for evil are vulnerable to much the same criticism.

More relevant to the analysis of international conflict and its management by individual leaders is the work of psychologists, who study the way human beings acquire information, organize that information into a set of coherent beliefs, and then adapt these beliefs as new information arrives and the evidence changes. Psychologists assert that our perceptions shape the way we understand and interpret our environment: subjective perceptions always differ from "objective" reality, insofar as "objective" reality exists.[6] We see what we expect to see or what we want to see. It is this assertion which makes a psychological interpretation of leaders' choices imperative. We can only understand why leaders decide to escalate a conflict or make an important concession if we understand the way they perceive and interpret their environment. In this argument, perception becomes the critical proximate cause of decisions that dictate the course of a conflict and its management.

The first series of readings traces the linkage between leaders' perceptions and the strategies of conflict management they prefer. Milburn, Stewart, and Herrmann argue that leaders' perceptions of the intentions of their adversary dictate their strategies of conflict management. They examine three quite different sets of perceptions among both Soviet and American leaders and are able to relate the content of these perceptions to strategies designed to handle the conflict between the superpowers. Their study illustrates nicely how widely leaders may differ in their perception of the same adversary at the same moment in time; different leaders perceive the same "reality" quite differently and it is these perceptions which shape their management of a conflict.

Robert Jervis concentrates not on the content of perceptions but rather on the impact of biased perceptual processes on deterrence, one of the most frequently used strategies of conflict management. A leader who is trying to deter an unwanted action attempts to persuade another that the expected value of the action is less than the anticipated punishment. The central concepts are *expected* value and *anticipated* punishment: it is leaders' perception of the likely benefits and costs, as well as their perception that the deterrer's threats are credible and punishment will be inflicted, which are critical. Deterrence works ultimately through the perceptions of leaders and, as is immediately obvious, deterrence can easily fail if leaders are mistaken in their beliefs about each other. As Jervis demonstrates, leaders generally are mistaken because they fall victim to common psychological errors, errors which we all make. Cognitive error and flawed perception are a species characteristic.

The third essay, by George Quester, looks at the kinds of perceptions which contribute to war and peace, and locates these perceptions within the broader environment of military technology and communication networks. In his examination of the necessary and sufficient conditions of war and peace, he finds at least three perceptual errors which contribute to war even though leaders on both sides may wish to avoid hostilities. Leaders may overrate their own capabilities, overrate their own resolve, or falsely assume aggressive intentions by their opponent. As he points out, however, "stupidity" or, more accurately misperception, is only one among several important factors which may exacerbate conflict and push it toward war. We will return to this point shortly.

All three essays suggest that when leaders make decisions and choose strategies, they do not conform to the rational norms that figure so prominently in Western philosophy and intellectual history. Rational decision makers choose among alternatives, but people tend not to be rational when they are making important choices: in their performance of the critical tasks of decision making, they generally engage in a series of cognitive short cuts which bias their choices in fundamentally important ways.[7] Richard Ned Lebow reviews the debate between the two principal psychological explanations of the source of these errors. Are they motivated or unmotivated?

Psychologists who attend to motivation as a principal source of error assert that individuals deny unpleasant information, ignore inconsistencies in their belief structures, and rationalize conflict among their most important values because they seek to satisfy basic needs. People engage in wishful thinking and see what they wish to see. It is not hard to imagine how wishful thinking can have a malignant impact on the management of international conflict. Leaders who attempt to secure unilateral gain at the expense of an adversary may well underestimate the likelihood that their opponent will respond in kind. A good deal of international conflict may result from the miscalculation which grows out of motivated error. But if errors are largely motivated, the prospects of better conflict management are not bleak. Should leaders be made aware of the motives that drive their choices, they might try to correct them or at least to minimize their impact.

Ole Holsti dramatizes a different source of error in his study of decision making by European leaders in the critical days preceding the outbreak of war in 1914. His documentation of the damaging impact of crisis-induced stress on the quality of decision making is consistent with the disturbing evidence of cognitive psychologists. They too document major errors in the way people draw inferences and make judgments, but trace these flaws to fundamental cognitive processes. People deny inconsistencies in their belief structures, interpret information in the light of existing beliefs, and ignore trade-offs not because they are satisfying important needs, but because they are not equipped to do better. Our basic cognitive processes are impaired and, consequently, we see not what we want to see but what we expect to see. If impaired decision making is largely unmotivated and generally characteristic of all leaders, the opportunities for remediation are alarmingly limited. Global security and the effective management of international conflict hang by a slender thread.

These essays, each in its own way, make a persuasive case for the inclusion of the perceptions of leaders as an important component in a comprehensive explanation of strategies of conflict management. Although their authors would argue that perceptions are a necessary condition and the proximate cause of basic strategic choices, none, we suspect, would insist that perceptions and the related processes of decision making are a sufficient explanation. Quester is explicit on this point when he relates certain kinds of misperceptions to distinctive military and technological environments and looks beyond perception to other factors.

We want to know why the perceptions of leaders working in one kind of environment differ from those of leaders in another milieu. How do the policy-making, national, transnational, and international environments of leaders condition their thinking and their choices? Do these environments set the boundaries of perception and constrain the kinds of choices leaders can make? These questions raise the larger issue of the role of the individual in international processes of conflict and conflict management. The individuals that are central to our concerns do not work alone. They are all deeply entrenched in political processes with wide-ranging responsibilities for the promotion of the collective interest and the protection of national security. Politics is quintessentially a group activity and if we are to understand political decisions, we must look at the policy-making system, at the group context of decisions, and at the broader social environment in which strategies of conflict management are conceived and elaborated.

ENDNOTES

1 When we inappropriately ascribe properties of the individual to the collective, we commit the "individualistic" fallacy in reasoning, the obverse of the better-known "ecological" fallacy, or unjustified inference from a higher to a lower level of analysis. For a discussion of these two logical fallacies, see Hayward Alker, "A Typology of Ecological Fallacies," in Mattei Dogan and Stein Rokkan, eds., *Quantitative Ecological Analysis in the Social Sciences* (Cambridge, Mass.: MIT Press, 1969), pp. 69-86, and W.S. Robinson, "Ecological Correlates and the Behavior of Individuals," *American Sociological Review*, 15 (June 1950), 351-57.

2 Morgan makes this point nicely in his examination of the role of the individual in international politics. See Patrick M. Morgan, *Theories and Approaches to International Politics,* 2d ed., rev. (New Brunswick, New Jersey: Transaction Books, 1977), pp. 49-73.

3 See Sigmund Freud, "Why War?" from *Collected Papers of Sigmund Freud* (New York: Basic Books, 1959), V, 273-87.

4 For an excellent treatment of these traditions, see Kenneth N. Waltz, *Man, the State, and War* (New York: Columbia University Press, 1954), pp. 16-79.

5 See Konrad Lorenz, *On Aggression* (London: Methuen, 1966) and Robert Ardrey, *The Territorial Imperative* (London: Fontana, 1969). For a somewhat different treatment, see M.F.A. Montagu, ed., *Man and Aggression* (London: Oxford

University Press, 1968). For a critical review of this literature, see Anatol Rapaport, "Is War-making a Characteristic of Human Beings or of Culture?" *Scientific American*, October 1965, p. 116; Timothy Colton, "The 'New Biology' and the Causes of War," *Canadian Journal of Political Science,* 2 (December 1969), 434-47; and Ralph Pettman, *Human Behavior and World Politics* (New York: St. Martin's Press, 1975), pp. 153-99.

6 The phenomenological tradition within philosophy, for example, argues that a reality does not exist independently of its perception by the human mind. What exists is what an individual considers to exist. Since an "objective" environment is ultimately unknowable and therefore irrelevant, an understanding of choice must rest on the explanations that individuals themselves offer.

7 The literature on decision making in general and on foreign policy decision making in particular is extensive. See in particular, Michael Brecher, *Decisions in Crisis* (Berkeley: University of California Press, 1980); Ole R. Holsti, *Crisis, Escalation, War* (Montreal: McGill University Press, 1972); John Steinbruner, *The Cybernetic Theory of Decision* (Princeton: Princeton University Press, 1974); and Janice Stein and Raymond Tanter, *Rational Decision Making* (Columbus, Ohio: Ohio State University Press, 1980).

A: PERCEPTION

Perceiving the Other's Intentions, USA and USSR

Thomas W. Milburn/Philip D. Stewart/Richard K. Herrmann

To *intend* means more than to want to have a preferred state of affairs; its meaning includes the idea that the actor can exert control over the means employed and the likelihood of achieving it. Intentions imply decision-based commitments to achieve preferred states of affairs; stronger commitments, more firmly held intentions, imply that an actor will use more effort or make a greater investment of resources to move to a desired objective. Actors' statements of intentions are a prediction that something in their control — that preferred state — will occur. Statements of intentions do not perfectly predict the state of affairs a speaker may have had in mind. Aside from the actors' inclination to deceive, events external to the actors before they achieve their preferred state may greatly increase its cost or difficulty or decrease the expected value of that state, at least as contrasted with others.

We know best our own intentions, but we find it convenient and useful to act as if we know the intentions of significant others; we attribute intentions to others and use these to help us plan our interactions with them. To attribute intentions to others is more than simply to predict their behavior; it is also to indicate that we understand what others are up to, and it may imply that we know how to respond effectively. To attribute intentions to other actors suggests that we have an inkling of the meaning, the direction, the flexibility, maybe even the underlying motives and possible responses they may make, to actions we may take. The concept of intention is widely used by various officials and the media but more rarely by scholars. The concept is an important one, if only because intentions *are attributed* to others: Strategic choices are often based upon the assessment of probable intended actions of both adversaries and allies. It is not prudent to decide upon strategic actions without having made judgments as to the likely choices, responses, and intended directions of others. What intentions actually exist in the minds of other national leaders may be less significant for much national behavior than the perceptions of these others hold. Political leaders and other observers attribute intentions to present acts and to possible future actions in order to provide politically meaningful descriptions on the basis of which they can develop strategic prescriptions.

Thomas Milburn, Philip Stewart, and Richard Herrmann, "Perceiving the Other's Intentions," pp. 51-64 in *Foreign Policy USA, USSR: Sage International Yearbook of Foreign Policy Studies, 1982*, vol. 7, edited by Charles Kegley and Pat McGowan. Retitled. Most footnotes have been removed; those remaining have been renumbered.

"Intentions" of other nations are thus in large part functions of observers and serve as bases for the development of policy responses.

This chapter discusses *global* intentions attributed to the national leadership of the United States and to the Soviet Union by those in the other superpower. We shall not discuss certain other categories of intentions often attributed to the leadership of collectivities. For example, battle commanders, correctly or not, usually attribute likely *tactical* intentions to their opponents. Such attributed intentions serve to influence their analyses of the situation and help them to organize their responses; these may dictate, along with other information, what is an effective response. The Soviets correctly attributed to the German High Command several critical aspects of the German plans for the battle of Kursk, the world's largest tank battle, e.g., initiate the attack on about the fifth of July, 1943, with air superiority, and so on. We shall also not discuss attributed *strategic* intentions, which encompass larger time spans and broader purposes than tactical intentions, if narrower than global intentions. In a most serious error by a national commander and despite many intelligence messages, Stalin believed that a German attack such as Operation Barbarossa (1941) would take place only after an ultimatum from Hitler; so the Soviets were largely unprepared for those assaults when they came.

Global intentions are more nearly a rough equivalent of national aims. However, models or images of global intentions may or may not be testable or verifiable, which means falsifiable, by a variety of observational and analytic methods that are becoming a standard procedure for dealing with scientific propositions. Models may vary in what they include such as descriptions of related motives attributed to or the inferred risk-taking proclivities of an adversary. A model or set of attributions may be clear or unclear, internally consistent or not, supported by evidence or not, and, if supported, then supported by single versus multiple kinds of evidence. Models may assume that an adversary's intentions are largely invariant over time and conditions, or susceptible to influences by the attributor or not. Beliefs about intentions may encompass or neglect statements about motives and such matters as the risk-taking proclivities of the intending party.

Those who attribute intentions clearly vary in their ideological positions, in their functional responsibilities around which the content of attributed intentions is centered, and even as to whether they are likely to suffer loss if their attributions of intentions are in error. Finally, attributed intentions may possess or lack a relation to real behavior: A country may be seen to wish or prefer ideally to dominate the world whether on the basis of economic threat, business and trade, or by means of military force. The degree to which one or another of such factors is asserted to influence its behavior in practical conditions is another matter.

SOVIET MODELS OF U.S. INTENTIONS[1]

Identifying the perceptions of the United States held by important elites in Moscow is difficult because of the closed character of Soviet politics and the limited access afforded to Western scholars. Still, some insight into Soviet models of U.S. intentions can be obtained from the images presented in the Soviet media. Although the fundamental differences evident among American models of Soviet intentions are less visible in the censored Soviet media, important variations are nevertheless discernible. We shall review and consider three treatments of the United States in Soviet literature and in presentations by Soviet spokesmen in their dialogues with Western scholars and public figures.

At a broad level of analysis there is a consistent description among Soviet spokesmen of the primary aims of the United States, which is depicted by Soviet spokesmen as striving to preserve and reassert U.S. "political supremacy" and "imperial" control worldwide. At this general level, the Soviet spokesmen uniformly characterize the United

States as imperialistic and as possessed by a desire to claim the mantle of world policeman. Moreover, the general model of U.S. intentions common throughout most of the Soviet media includes a claim that the United States is bent on undermining the unity and political forces of the "socialist community" in an effort to weaken the key obstacle to U.S. global hegemony. Soviet spokesmen attribute U.S. foreign policy to several motives, but nearly all presentations seem to share a general pattern of attributing its imperialist drive to the nature of mature capitalism and in particular, to the material greed and political power of the "ruling circles." The general Soviet model argues that U.S. imperialism is driven by a complex of military and financial elites that personally and as a class gain from persistent international tension, exploitation of the Third World, and continuing fear of the "Soviet threat" among the American public.

While a general model of U.S. intentions is common among Soviet spokesmen, it is possible to detect differences in formulation and emphasis that may reflect important variations in judgments concerning the immutability of U.S. "imperialistic" intentions and the U.S. capacity to pursue its desires. Careful examination of Soviet sources reveals differences in estimations of susceptibility of the United States to Soviet efforts to produce changes in U.S. politics and so preferred strategic prescriptions for the Soviet Union's foreign policy. The view that now prevails, associated with the late General Secretary Brezhnev, is the most optimistic of the three views to be described here about the mutability of U.S. imperialism and, consequently, Soviet-U.S. coexistence. In his view the United States is depicted as a superpower that has irretrievably lost those advantages in influence that it enjoyed in the early 1950s. The correlation of forces has shifted against the United States according to Brezhnev, and a basic parity or balance of power has been established. In the Brezhnev picture, because of both the development of Soviet might and the growth of national liberation forces in the Third World, the United States has been compelled to restrain its attempts at domination and forgo its imperialist objectives.

The Brezhnev image is fundamentally rooted in the idea that a balance of power, achieved by Soviet military developments "catching up" with the United States and the Soviet political parity stemming from this, prevents the United States from actively pursuing its imperialist intentions. This model recognizes that ruling circles in the United States may try to break free from this restraint by developing political and military superiority through any number of policies including a military build-up, a reassertion of U.S. domination in the North Atlantic Treaty Organization (NATO), the "China card," and the development of client regimes in various regions. Nevertheless, the Brezhnev model leads to expressions of confidence that the development of Soviet might will keep pace, foil these attempts, and force sobriety on the United States that eventually will lead to the ascendance of "realistically minded" elites that recognize the reality of parity, the principle of equal security both globally and regionally, and the limits of U.S. power. Consequently, the Brezhnev model suggests that with a solid and persistent balance of power a mutually advantageous détente can be achieved between the superpowers that will stabilize and make the nuclear era safer and at the same time, provide numerous economic, scientific, and cultural advantages. Highlighting Soviet-U.S. relations as the central dilemma in the contemporary world, this Soviet model also prescribes a conflict avoidance or minimizing approach to superpower contests on the periphery, granting a higher priority to détente. The model, however, does not suggest that détente will be granted a position prior to the maintenance of a balance of power, but just the reverse. Consequently, should the political parity of the superpowers be at stake in a Third World contest, the model calls for Soviet commitment.

A second model of the United States can be identified in the Soviet leadership with the late Mikhail Suslov. The Suslov model, unlike the Brezhnev model, does not envision the likelihood of "sober forces" prevailing in the United States, but rather presents the "interests" and "class" of the ruling elites within the United States as inevitably tied to the existing social system and thus attributes a nearly immutable imperialist drive to U.S. foreign policy.

While the Suslov model does not forecast any lasting success for détente, it does suggest that a Soviet strategy of active anti-imperialism may have some positive effect. Presenting a balance of power between the United States and the USSR founded on a nuclear stalemate, the Suslov model takes no refuge in hopes about U.S. sobriety, but rather looks to an active continuation of the revolutionary struggle against imperialism. In the Suslov model, the struggle against imperialism can still be pursued in the Third World through revolutionary parties that are anti-imperialistic because of the nuclear stalemate. Taking advantage of the rise of national liberation movements and the process of decolonization, the Soviet Union can mobilize anti-American sentiment and effectively undermine imperialism. The Suslov approach, therefore, unlike the Brezhnev model, does not suggest that conflicts in the periphery ought to be subservient to the interest of détente, but rather casts revolutionary struggle in the Third World as a most important theater in the anti-imperialist struggle, indeed, the central axis of Soviet foreign policy.

A third model of the United States and prescription for Soviet foreign policy is associated with Leningrad First Secretary Grigory Romanov. The Romanov image shares the Suslov model's pessimism concerning the immutability of U.S. imperialist designs but does not endorse the Suslov model's optimism concerning the beneficial effects of anti-imperialist revolutions in the Third World. Soviet military might according to the Romanov model is the only effective instrument restraining imperialist ambitions and thus ultimately ensuring the defense of the Soviet homeland. In this view, the United States is presented as an untrustworthy partner that always seeks unilateral military advantage and will never accept a negotiated parity and will forever press for superiority. Presenting the U.S. pursuit of military superiority as stubborn and unchangeable, the Romanov model encourages little confidence in arms control negotiations but persistently emphasizes the centrality of Soviet military might and the importance of continual vigilance in the rapid development of Soviet armed forces. In the Romanov model, U.S. military capability is treated with respect, although not awe: It often highlights U.S. developments as reason for further Soviet military spending. The model does not reflect a similar respect for American society, picturing it as decadent and lacking in disciplined organization.

Designating unilateral Soviet military power as decisive, the Romanov model does not include a clear prescription for a Soviet commitment in the Third World, but rather suggests a preference for severely limiting Soviet contributions to states or movements in the periphery. In the Romanov model, Soviet involvement in the Third World is presented as costly and potentially dangerous because it might entangle the USSR in a conflict the escalation of which would not be controllable by Moscow. The Romanov model grants higher priority to domestic concerns of the USSR and shows less inclination than the Suslov model to prescribe Soviet involvement in the Third World contests. Instead, it suggests investments at home in the development of the armed forces and in military-related industries. The Romanov model treats political gains that might accrue from Third World revolutions as short-lived and unreliable at times, perhaps reflecting a distaste if not contempt for potential allies among the national liberation forces. Focusing on Soviet military power and domestic economic growth, the Romanov model prescribes a "Fortress Russia" strategy for the USSR.

U.S. MODELS OF SOVIET INTENTIONS

One model of the Soviet Union's global aims that is well known to Western analysts posits as its central claim that the USSR is essentially expansionistic and driven to establish its political supremacy worldwide.[2] In this model, what we shall call the expansionist model, the USSR is depicted as striving to eliminate alternative political systems and, through force of arms if necessary, establish a universal communist political order. The expansionist model attributes the Soviet Union's revisionist aspirations to the character and personal power concerns of the communist elite in Moscow. This elite, according to the expansionist model, is imbued with a tradition of Russian imperialism and chauvinistic arrogance and has been socialized in a culture that respects brute power, authoritarian coercion, and deceitful cunning. Moreover, the model explains that in order to preserve its personal power and the "totalitarian" regime, the Soviet elite turns to foreign adventure and expansion as a substitute for domestic progress, and to deflect public dissatisfaction. The model also attributes the expansionistic impulse to the messianic desires of communist ideologues and the imputed need to justify the ideological claims to global validity.

The expansionist model presents the Soviet Union as incapable of addressing its multiple domestic problems and as inherently disadvantaged vis-à-vis U.S. political and economic strength. In the model, the USSR derives strength, however, from the U.S. reluctance to employ its full potential in resisting Soviet probes, from Soviet totalitarian repression at home, and from its resorting to conspiracy and subversion abroad. The communist leadership according to the expansionist model recognizes that the USSR would be incapable of matching the United States in direct competition if the United States mobilized its full potential and, therefore, carried on an indirect assault through a strategy of subversion and incremental attack. The USSR in this model is described as masking its political offensives and efforts to achieve military superiority so as to lull the American public and forestall the mobilization of U.S. potential power. The USSR is seen as conspiring to undermine or subvert U.S. allies and alliance systems in order to weaken the U.S. ability to resist Soviet adventures and thus make the USSR's expansion possible.

Treating the Soviet drive for expansion as nearly immutable, short of the overthrow of the communist regime, this model suggests that the U.S. employ a strategy of active containment. In this strategy, the U.S. is called on to use its potential power to insure its strategic military parity — or superiority — vis-à-vis the USSR, while substantially reinforcing its political and military alliance coalitions in Western Europe, the Middle East, and Asia.

Prescriptions flowing from the expansionist model not only support an actively pursued containment strategy but also include suggestions for cautious rollback policies designed to exploit the inherent weaknesses of the USSR's communist empire. Depicting the USSR as incapable of expansion if met by resolute U.S. power, and as vulnerable to demands for national independence within its empire, this model suggests that the U.S. seeks to deflate the USSR's drive for expansion through strongly enforced and active containment policies (not détente or rapprochement).

A second approach to Soviet foreign policy found among Western analysts posits defense, not expansion, as the best descriptor of the general aims of the USSR.[3] This defensive model presents the Soviet Union as essentially striving to ensure the security of its homeland, people, and political system, and attributes this general aim to a number of motives, the most important of which is a deeply felt, historically conditioned sense of insecurity. Pointing to the Soviet leadership's and population's experience with war, this model suggests that the motive of defense is the primary, albeit not exclusive, determinant of Soviet policy.

In the defensive model, Soviet global aims are attributed primarily to national security. They are seen also as a function of the character and personal power of Soviet leadership. The older leaders are seen as deeply imbued with bureaucratic conservatism, while upcoming careerists are ruled by the requirements of professional and material achievement leading in both cases to a resistance to change and a preference for the stable preservation of the existing political system. Unlike the expansionist model, the defensive model suggests that the bureaucratic and material self-interest of the communist elites is served not through foreign adventure, but rather by stability in foreign relations and the development of international contacts that can promote the economic growth of the USSR and personal access to material benefits for the leadership. The defensive model treats Soviet military elites as essentially conservative, concerned with preserving the security of the Soviet homeland, and pursuing a stable assured deterrent force vis-à-vis the U.S. rather than striving for strategic supremacy with which to pursue revisionist aims.

The defensive model sees the USSR as beset by many internal problems and as limited in its capability, but it does not depict the Soviet leadership as facing an unmanageable crisis situation. While defensiveness is pictured as the main thrust of Soviet foreign policy, the Soviet Union is presented as unlikely to capitulate to U.S. pressure, and as inclined to enforce whatever sacrifice is necessary to mobilize the strength to insist on political equality with the U.S. Picturing the communist elite as less vulnerable to domestic instability, the defensive model, unlike the expansionist model, does not anticipate a Soviet inability to defend its preferences when confronted by resolute U.S. power, but predicts enforced discipline within the USSR and a stronger Soviet commitment externally as probable responses to active U.S. containment policies.

The model suggests that the USSR's strategy is designed to defend its territorial and political sovereignty (including its European empire) and that the Soviet Union is committed to establishing and then maintaining an essential balance of power with respect to the United States. In this model, the Soviet Union is seen as deeply committed to, and capable of, albeit at great sacrifice, maintaining both strategic nuclear parity with the U.S. and a system of alliance coalitions offsetting U.S. political influence. The Soviet Union extends its commitments to Third World allies opposing and offsetting U.S. positions, but it does not support with any significant resources the rollback or undermining of U.S. interests in the Third World. U.S. failures and setbacks in the Third World are not attributable to Soviet actions, but are attributed to U.S. overextension and to an apolitical, overly militarized U.S. policy as well as to events beyond the control of either superpower. The model does not evaluate most changes in the Third World as essentially pro-U.S. or pro-Soviet, but offers instead the judgment that neither superpower will be capable of controlling Third World states as the era of mass participation and nationalism continues to unfold.

The defensive model suggests that policies designed to reinforce the U.S. ability to threaten and punish the USSR and U.S. efforts to exclude the USSR from important Third World regions will most likely produce escalated Soviet resistance and consequently prove ineffective and counterproductive. Rather than endorsing a containment policy, the defensive model prescribes a strategy of limited disengagement for the United States and suggests that U.S. recognition of Soviet security concerns and appreciation of Soviet perceptions of threat may have a more positive effect upon the USSR's actions. In the defensive model, the USSR is described as willing to accept strategic parity and as interested in stabilizing Soviet-U.S. relations, thus suggesting that détente is possible (as is the avoidance of superpower contests in the periphery). The Soviet Union's interest in détente according to the defensive model is sincere but linked to a desire for U.S. recognition of the principle of equal security and political equality along with secondary hopes for economic cooperation. Consequently, the USSR's interest in détente is not expected to supersede its basic security policies of ensuring strategic parity, nuclear deterrence, and comparable alliance coalitions. The model does not expect the USSR to capitulate to U.S. preferences for the sake of détente if doing so undermines the USSR's political parity.

A third model of Soviet intentions advanced by

Western scholars, the opportunistic model, presents a mixed picture, arguing that the USSR is clearly not a status quo power but harbors expansionist ambitions while, at the same time, being profoundly defensive.[4] This mixed model describes the Soviet Union as essentially similar to a traditional great power, determined both to defend its national interests and extend its international influence. In this model, the Soviet Union is described as granting highest priority to protecting the security of its homeland and the stability of its satellite empire. The emphasis placed on security and especially military security in the opportunistic model is explained in terms of the Soviet leadership's experience with war and of the internal bureaucratic dynamics of a Soviet military-industrial complex. The model concludes that the general aims of the USSR are achieving international political parity with the U.S., which the Soviets presume is due it as a superpower, and strengthening Soviet security, primarily through military power.

Despite the recognition of Soviet security concerns, the mixed model does not suggest that the USSR is essentially defensive but rather claims that it is an inherently expansionistic state driven by a desire for increased influence and power in world affairs. The manifestation of Soviet expansionism is said to be most clearly visible in the USSR's policy in the Third World. Although the model attributes some of the USSR's behavior in the Third World to Soviet fear, and describes that behavior as an attempt to build defensive alliance coalitions against a new encirclement, it attributes most of the USSR's actions in the Third World to expansionist desires and revisionist aspirations. As Seweryn Bialer argues:

> The Soviet Union is primarily interested not in a more equitable economic or political distribution of influence in favor of third world countries, but in the growth of its own influences.
>
> To say it simply, the Soviet Union is interested in fomenting conflicts, escalating conflicts, maintaining them at a high level of intensity, and exploiting them, but not in their peaceful solution, especially [not] in their early stages, when they are most susceptible to solution.[5]

The model describes the USSR as aiming to exploit Third World conflicts in order to expand its influence, undermine U.S. influence, and pursue revolutionary change in the international arena. The USSR is described as a superpower but with real limitations on its capability. Suffering economic dilemmas, ideological exhaustion, and bureaucratic paralysis, the USSR neither enjoys nor expects to achieve strategic superiority vis-à-vis the United States; nor does it expect easily to pursue Third World adventures. The model presents the USSR as possessing really only one meaningful instrument of strength — military might. It suggests that the USSR is compelled to rely on military force. This position argues that the Soviet leadership, recognizing that strategic superiority is not obtainable vis-à-vis the U.S., accepts the prospects of parity and so is willing to negotiate and abide by arms control agreements that ensure deterrence and essential equivalence. Although the USSR has accepted the principle of strategic parity with the United States, it has not yet learned that armed force interjected into Third World conflicts will be both costly and ineffective.[6] Consequently, while the model calls for a U.S. policy of détente on bilateral and especially nuclear weapons issues, it simultaneously advocates a strengthened U.S. containment policy in Third World regions.

The opportunistic model does not assume that the USSR's behavior is fixed and unchangeable, but rather suggests that U.S. policy can seriously affect the character of Soviet foreign policy. The model pictures both defensive and expansionistic aims as causal determinants of Soviet policy. It therefore suggests a dual prescription for U.S. policy consisting of both containment and détente. It calls for U.S. recognition of Soviet security concerns and prescribes a policy of détente based on strategic parity aimed at stabilizing the deterrent relationship. In this same vein, the model advises against U.S. efforts to exclude the USSR from regions where it has political and proximate interests, and encourages the U.S. to adopt nonthreatening postures that may strengthen the hand of reformers in Moscow. The model suggests, moreover, that the U.S. should strengthen its containment of Soviet adventurism in the Third World, punishing the USSR for its irresponsible and destabilizing behavior with the hope that such treatment may teach the USSR that its desire for aggrandizement must be restrained in the interests of achieving its more central objectives of security and stability in its relations with the West.

DISCUSSION

These global models of intentions, being highly general and evaluative attributions, have the quality of unproven assumptions. Each is largely untestable. It is difficult to imagine evidence that would persuasively disconfirm any one of these models to someone already committed to that position. None of these attributional models is likely to be regarded as scientific by neutral observers. Each shows impressive congruence with the ideological positions of those who hold them. To some degree, although this is most apparent with the various U.S. models of Soviet intentions, those associated with the ideological positions reflected by each of the models tend to argue from their own favorite kinds of evidence. Pipes and Conquest argue on the basis of historical evidence, arms balance, and ideology that the Soviets are used to being invaded and losing vast numbers of lives in wars so that they would not mind the prospect of losing five or ten times more. Kennan and Cohen employ historically rooted data but attend also to actions not taken, i.e., to restraint exercised and the Soviet avoidance of confrontation in Europe and the Third World. Cohen sees the Soviet Union as a conservative, imperial bureaucracy, defensive and eager to hold on to what it has. Kennan also sees the various invasions of Russia and the Soviet Union, but argues that such events have made war not less meaningful but merely less appealing to the Soviet leadership. Bialer and Legvold address evidence of Soviet behavior in the Third World and of the rather dismal performance of the Soviet economy to make the case that the Soviet leadership is therefore more likely to seek equilibrium, to seek stability rather than its absence in Soviet relations with others. While no one has made the case systematically, it is not unlikely that both right-wing and centrist U.S. scholars rank order similarly the probable locations and kinds of incidents that are likely to lead to wars. It is that their assessments of the underlying Soviet motives and of inclinations to take risks on the part of the Soviet leadership vary considerably.

There are curious mirror image aspects between the attributions made by Americans and the ideological equivalents in the Soviet Union. Pipes and Conquest are analogous in position to Suslov and Romanov: All believe that the leadership of their major adversary is monolithic and that there are essentially no differences among members of the ruling class of their opponents. In other respects, Romanov sounds like a Soviet equivalent of isolationist American hawks with his emphasis upon the need for a noninterventionist "Fortress Russia" analogous to a "Fortress America." It is, of course, possible that, were we to have access to a wider spectrum of unofficial Soviet opinion, we would find Soviet citizens (besides Sakharov) who espouse their equivalent of George Kennan's position, namely that the United States is a conservative, status quo power that acts primarily from defensive motives rather than an imperialistic and expansionist power as those in the Politburo see it.

One dimension upon which there exist parallel differences among the U.S. and Soviet observers of one another concerns the perceived flexibility of their rival. Those on the ideological right in both countries argue for the obstinate, stubborn, immutability of their imperialistic opposite number: You just cannot deal with those people; you cannot influence them or produce change in the way they think and act. Negotiation with them is likely to prove a waste of time and, besides, they cannot be trusted. Such is the position of Suslov and Romanov on the Soviet side, and of Pipes and Odum on the U.S. side. Their attributions are comparable mirror images of one another with respect to their inferences of underlying character and behavior to be expected.

We have not tried to deal with the accuracy of the models.It may be that all of them are a little accurate and that all would be acceptable to some degree as views of the other side by those in power, given only that there are different emphases, maybe as a function of the overall political atmosphere and of the nature of the political leadership in power at a particular moment in history. Careful empirical, multimethod research might provide some evidence of the plausibility of such a hypothesis. It would appear worthwhile to pursue such a line of investigation.

In summary, there appear to be at least three U.S. models that attribute very different global intentions, motives, and character to the Soviet leadership and somewhat comparable, if less dispersed, Soviet models of U.S. motives, character, and global intentions. Each of the superpowers sees somewhat analogous ways appropriate to deal with the other. Each side, perhaps depending upon who is in power, includes leaders and staff who either thoroughly or only moderately and cautiously mistrust the other.

ENDNOTES

1 These models are based, in part, on conclusions from the project on Soviet elite perceptions currently in progress at the Mershon Center of the Ohio State University under the direction of Philip D. Stewart.

2 See R. Conquest, *Present Danger: Towards a Foreign Policy* (Stanford, California: Hoover Institution Press, 1979), and Richard Pipes, ed., *Soviet Strategy in Europe* (New York: Crane Russak, 1976).

3 See Richard Barnet, "U.S.-Soviet relations: the need for a comprehensive approach," *Foreign Affairs,* 57 (Spring 1979), 779-795; S. Cohen, "Common and uncommon sense about the Soviet Union and American policy," in *The Soviet Union: International Dynamics of Foreign Policy, Present and Future,* U.S. Congress, House Committee on International Relations, Hearings Before a Subcommittee on Europe and the Middle East, 95th Congress, 2nd Session (Washington, D.C.: Government Printing Office, 1978), pp. 196-239; and George Kennan, "Two views of the Soviet problem," *New Yorker,* 2 November 1981, pp. 54-62.

4 See Seweryn Bialer, *Stalin's Successors: Leadership, Stability and Change in the Soviet Union* (Cambridge: Cambridge University Press, 1980); and R. Legvold, "Nature of Soviet power," *Foreign Affairs,* 56 (October 1977), 48-71, and "Super rivals: conflict in the third world," *Foreign Affairs,* 57 (Spring 1979), 755-778.

5 See Bialer, *Stalin's Successors,* p. 265.

6 From an unpublished summary report by Philip D. Stewart on the XIII Dartmouth Conference, Moscow, USSR, 17-20 November, 1981.

A: PERCEPTION

Deterrence and Perception

Robert Jervis

In the most elemental sense, deterrence depends on perceptions. But unless people are totally blind, we need not be concerned with the logical point that, if one actor's behavior is to influence another, it must be perceived. Rather what is important is that actors' perceptions often diverge both from "objective reality" (or later scholars' perceptions of it, which is as good a measure as we can have) and from the perceptions of other actors. These differences, furthermore, both randomly and systematically influence deterrence. Unless statesmen understand the ways in which their opposite numbers see the world, their deterrence policies are likely to misfire; unless scholars understand the patterns of perceptions involved, thev will misinterpret the behavior. . . .

In light of the dangers inherent in misperceptions, one might expect that statesmen would pay careful attention to how others perceive them. In fact, this is usually not the case. While they are aware that determining others' intentions and predicting others' behavior is difficult, they generally believe that their own intentions — especially when they are not expansionist — are clear. As a result, they rarely try to see the world and their own actions through their adversary's eyes, although doing so would be to their advantage. If a policy is to have the desired impact on its target, it must be perceived as it is intended; if the other's behavior is to be anticipated and the state's policy is a major influence on it, then the state must try to determine how its actions are being perceived. One would think, therefore, that every government would establish an office responsible for reconstructing the other's view of the world and that every policy paper would have a section that analyzed how the alternative policies would be seen by significant audiences. One theme of this essay is that the failure to undertake this task — and I do not mean to imply that it would be easy to accomplish — explains many cases of policy failure. It is hard to find cases of even mild international conflict in which both sides fully grasp the other's views. Yet all too often statesmen assume that their opposite numbers see the world as they see it, fail to devote sufficient resources to determining whether this is actually true, and have much more confidence in their beliefs about the other's perceptions than the evidence warrants.

Robert Jervis, "Deterrence and Perception," *International Security*, Vol. 7 (Winter 1982-1983), pp. 3-14 and 19-30. Reprinted by permission of the MIT Press Journals. Portions of the text have been deleted. Most footnotes have been removed; those remaining have been renumbered.

MISPERCEPTION AND THE FAILURE OF DETERRENCE

One actor deters another by convincing him that the expected value of a certain action is outweighed by the expected punishment. The latter is composed of two elements: the perceived cost of the punishments that the actor can inflict and the perceived probabilities that he will inflict them. Deterrence can misfire if the two sides have different beliefs about either factor.

(Mis)Perceptions of Value. Judging what constitutes harm is generally easier than estimating whether threats will be carried out, but even here there is room for differences which can undermine deterrence. On occasion, what one person thinks is a punishment another may consider a reward. The model is Br'er Rabbit. Only rarely do states in international politics want to be thrown into a brier patch but Teddy Roosevelt's threat to intervene in the Cuban internal conflict of 1903 comes close. He declared that, if American property were raided in the course of the fighting, he would have to send in troops. Unfortunately, both factions believed that American intervention would work in their favor and busily set to work harassing Americans and their property.[1]. . .

As we have seen, threats of coercive war can misfire if the state does not understand what the opponent values. Threats to use brute force, on the other hand, do not involve this pitfall, but they do require the state to determine how its adversary evaluates the military balance — how it estimates who would win a war. This issue arose in the 1930s as the British leaders debated how to deter Hitler. Some felt that "economic stability" — which required that military spending be kept relatively low — contributed to this goal: "The maintenance of our economic stability...[could] be described as an essential element in our defense system...without which purely military effort would be of no avail.... Nothing operates more strongly to deter a potential aggressor from attacking this country than our stability.... This reputation stands us in good stead, and causes other countries to rate our power of resistance at something far more formidable than is implied merely by the number of men of war, aeroplanes and battalions which we should have at our disposal immediately on the outbreak of war. But were other countries to detect in us signs of strain, this deterrent would at once be lost."[2] On the other hand, Churchill stressed the need for larger military forces: "an immense British army cast into the scales" was a great deterrent "and one of the surest bulwarks of peace."[3] Neither side in the argument, however, tried as hard as it might have to learn exactly how Hitler saw the world and what sort of configuration of forces might have deterred him.

Deterrence can also be undercut if the aggressor does not understand the kind of war which the status quo state is threatening to wage. The Japanese had no doubt that the United States would fight if they attacked Pearl Harbor. But many of Japan's leaders thought that the stakes for the U.S. were not sufficiently high to justify an all-out effort and that the Americans would instead fight a limited war, and, being unable to prevail at that level of violence, would agree to a settlement which would give Japan control of East Asia. Similarly, Hitler expected Britain and France to fight in September 1939 but doubted that they would continue to do so after Poland was defeated. Britain especially, he believed, had sufficient common interest with Germany to conclude a peace treaty after limited hostilities. In neither case did either side understand the other's beliefs or values. Indeed, the German and Japanese perceptions of their opponents would have seemed to the latter so out of touch with reality as to hardly deserve consideration. British and American statesmen knew their own outlooks so well that they thought it obvious that others knew them also. To have recognized that alternative views were possible would have implied that their self-images were not unambiguously correct and that their past behavior might be interpreted as indicating a willingness to sacrifice friends and agree to less than honorable settlements.

Because Britain, France, and the United States did not understand the other side's expectations, their deterrence strategies could not be effective. Their task was not only to convince their adversaries they would fight if pushed too far, but also that they would continue to fight even after initial reverses.[4] Doing this would have been extremely difficult since it would have involved presenting evidence and making commitments about how they would behave a few years later under grave circumstances. But had the statesmen been aware of the German and Japanese perceptions, they might have at least made some efforts. For example, President Franklin Roosevelt could have stressed the American tradition of vacillating between isolation and extreme involvement in international politics, of seeing the world in Manichean terms, of fighting only unlimited wars. Prime Minister Chamberlain might have done better explaining why he had abandoned appeasement, why Britain could not allow any power to dominate the continent, and why it would have no choice but to resist even if the military situation was bleak.

Similarly, throughout the 1960s, the U.S. misjudged how much North Vietnam valued reunification and believed that an American threat to fight a prolonged war and inflict very heavy punishment on the North[5] could dissuade the North from continuing its struggle. American decision-makers paid a great deal of attention to how to make their threats credible, but their misjudgment led them to ignore what was actually the crucial problem — that the North was willing to fight the sort of war the U.S. was threatening rather than concede. The Americans might not have been able to solve the problem even had they been aware of it, but as it was they never even came to grips with it.

(Mis)Perceptions of Credibility. Misperceptions of what the target state values and fears probably are less important causes of deterrence failure than misperceptions of credibility. Conclusions are difficult to draw in this area, however. Although many arguments about deterrence turn on questions involving credibility, scholars know remarkably little about how these judgments are formed and altered. For example, how context-bound are these estimates? Obviously the credibility of a threat is strongly influenced by the specific situation in which it is issued. The threat to go to war in response to a major provocation could be credible when the threat to so respond to a minor insult would not. But there also is a component of credibility that inheres in the threatener, not the situation. In the same circumstance, one country's threat can be credible where another's would not be. Part of this difference of course comes from the country's strength, its ability to carry out the threat, and its ability to defend against the other's response. But there's more to it than this. Some states have reputations for being bolder, more resolute, and more reckless than others. That is, states are seen to differ in the price they are willing to pay to achieve a given goal. But it is not clear how these reputations are established and maintained or how important they are compared to the other influences on credibility. We cannot predict with great assurance how a given behavior (e.g., refusing to change one's position on an issue) will influence others' expectations of how the state will act in the future.

To start with, does reputation attach to the decision-maker, the regime, or the country? If one president acts boldly, will other states' leaders draw inferences only about him or will they expect his successors to display similar resolve? After a revolution, do others think the slate has been wiped clean or does the reputation of the earlier regime retain some life? If one kind of regime (e.g., a capitalist democracy) displays willingness to run high risks, do others draw any inferences about the resolve of similar regimes? How fast do reputations decay?

On these points we have neither theoretically grounded expectations nor solid evidence. In another area, we at least can be guided by a good theory. One of the basic findings of cognitive psychology is that images change only slowly and are maintained in the face of discrepant information. This implies that trying to change a reputation for low resolve will be especially costly because statements and symbolic actions are not likely to be taken seriously. Only the running of what is obviously a high risk or engaging in a costly conflict will suffice. On the other hand, a state with a reputation for standing firm not only will be able to win disputes by threatening to fight, but have the freedom to avoid confrontations without damaging its image. But these propositions, although plausible, still lack empirical evidence.

The question of the relative importance of beliefs about the state's general resolve as compared to the role of other factors is also impossible to answer with any precision. How much do states make overall judgments about the prices others are willing to pay as opposed to looking primarily at the specific situation the other is in? In other words, how context-bound are estimates of how others will behave? The debate over the validity of the domino theory reminds us both of the importance of this topic and the difficulty of coming to grips with it. If others were more impressed by America's eventual defeat in Vietnam than by the fact that it was willing to fight for years for a country of little intrinsic value, they would adjust downward their estimate of American resolve. But by how much? If there is another Berlin crisis, will the Vietnam-influenced reputation be as significant as others' judgment of the value of Berlin to the U.S.? When the new situation closely resembles a previous one in which the actor displayed low resolve, others are likely to expect similar retreat. But when the situation is very different, it is not clear whether a judgment of the state's overall resolve has much impact on others' predictions of its behavior.

Even when these questions are not hypothetical, they are usually hard to answer, as is illustrated by the ambiguous nature of the events that followed the American defeat in Indochina. Has the Soviet Union drawn far-reaching inferences from the American retreat? Have the NATO allies lowered their estimates of the probability that the United States would respond to Soviet pressure or military moves in Europe? Have the Third World countries come to see the U.S. as less reliable? Since 1975, the Soviets have taken a number of actions inimical to American interests, the Europeans have voiced doubts about the credibility of the U.S. promise to protect them, and Third World states have been quite troublesome. But these problems do not present a sharp break from the pre-Vietnam era. It is easy to attribute any behavior contrary to American wishes to the lack of resolve which some observers think the U.S. displayed in Indochina. But it is much harder to establish that this is a better explanation than local conditions or general trends such as the increase of Soviet power. . . .

The crucial question is the degree to which observers make general judgments about others' credibility rather than basing their predictions largely on the nature of the specific situation and, if the situation is a continuing one, on the history of the other's behavior concerning it. To a significant extent, deterrence theory rests on the assumption that such general judgments are important. It is this which makes it both possible and necessary for a state to credibly threaten to react to an attack on an unimportant third country by a response which will involve greater costs than the intrinsic value of the third area. Such a threat can be credible because what the state will lose by not responding is not just the third country, but also its reputation for protecting its interests, a reputation that is more valuable than the costs of fighting. By the same logic, this response is necessary, because to fail to rise to the challenge is to lead others to doubt the state's willingness to pay costs to defend the rest of the status quo. Both prongs of this reasoning depend on actors making relatively context-free judgments of credibility.

Even if they do, the way in which these judgments are made can defeat significant aspects of the theory and practice of deterrence. When an actor either carries out or reneges on a threat, observers can make either or both of two kinds of inferences that will influence his future credibility.

First, they may alter their estimate of what I have elsewhere called his "signaling reputation" — i.e., his reputation for doing what he says he will do.[6] The bargaining tactic of commitment, so well known in deterrence literature, is supposed to be effective because the state increases its cost of retreating by staking its reputation on standing firm. But this tactic will work (and this explanation of actors' behavior will be appropriate) only if actors try to determine how likely it is that others will live up to their promises and threats rather than predicting their behavior solely on the basis of estimates of what they value and the prices they are willing to pay to reach various objectives. This is the second kind of inference actors draw from others' past behavior. It ignores statements and other signals that can be easily manipulated and looks only at whether the other stood firm, compromised, or retreated in the past, irrespective of what he said he would do. If this kind of inference is dominant, then signals of commitment have little impact. . . .

Judging The Adversary's Alternatives. Deterrence works when the expected costs of challenging the status quo are greater than those of accepting it; deterrence may fail and defenders be taken by surprise not only if their threats are insufficiently credible or directed at the wrong values, but also if the defenders fail to grasp the expansionist's dismal evaluation of the alternatives to fighting. Although the deterring state realizes that its adversary has strong incentives to take action — or else deterrence would not be necessary — it usually thinks that the latter has a wide range of choice. Furthermore, the deterring state almost always believes that the adversary is tempted to act because of the positive attraction of the gains he hopes to make. In fact, however, the other state often feels that it has little choice but to act because, if it does not, it will not merely forgo gains, but will suffer grave losses.[7] Status quo powers often underestimate the pressure that is pushing the other to act and therefore underestimate the magnitude of threat and/or the degree of credibility that will be required to make the other refrain from moving. The pressures felt by Japan in the fall of 1941 and by China in the fall of 1950 illustrate why the target state can feel it must act even though it knows some sort of war will result. China and Japan perceived the alternative to fighting not as maintaining the status quo — which was tolerable — but as permitting a drastic erosion of the positions they had established. Because the status quo states did not understand this, they did not grasp the difficulty of the job of deterrence that they were undertaking. This is one reason why they thought that their superior power was clearly sufficient to keep the adversary at bay.

The case of the Chinese entry into the Korean War is especially striking since the United States did not even grasp the Chinese fear that, if the U.S. conquered North Korea, it would threaten China. American leaders had no such intention and thought this clear to everyone, just as they felt that their unwillingness to fight a limited war in 1941 was clear to all. Again, not only was there a major difference in perceptions, but one of which both sides were unaware. Deterrence failed; but more than this, the deterrence strategy could not be adequately crafted since it was not based on a correct assessment of what the other side valued and feared. Similarly, the basic question of whether deterrence was possible was not adequately faced. In neither instance did the United States consider that even a well-developed deterrence policy might fail and therefore that it should balance the costs of war against the costs of making concessions; since deterrence seemed likely to succeed, the painful alternative of sacrificing some values and abandoning some foreign policy goals was not to be taken seriously. . . .

LIMITS TO RATIONALITY

Most arguments about deterrence, including those made above, assume that both sides are fairly rational. Some of the general problems raised by this claim have been treated elsewhere.[8] Here I want to focus on four barriers to accurate perception which reduce actors' sensitivity to new information and limit their ability to respond to unexpected situations. The first three barriers are cognitive; the fourth springs from emotions.

Overconfidence. First, there is solid evidence from laboratory experiments and much weaker, but still suggestive, evidence from case studies that people overestimate their cognitive abilities. For example, people's estimates of facts usually are less accurate than they think. When asked to give a spread of figures such that they are 90 percent certain that the correct answer lies somewhere between them, most people bracket the true figure only 75 percent of the time.[9] Similarly, people generally overestimate the complexity of the way they use evidence. They think they are tapping more sources of information than they are, overestimate the degree to which they combine evidence in complex ways, and flatter themselves by thinking that they search for subtle and elusive clues to others' behavior. Acting on this misleading self-portrait, people are quick to overreach themselves by trying mental operations they cannot successfully perform. Thus, when people are given a little clinical training in judging others' psychological states, they make more errors than they did previously because they incorrectly think they can now detect all sorts of peculiar conditions.[10] Overconfidence is also exhibited in the common rejection of the well-established finding that simple computer programs are superior to experts in tasks like graduate student admission and medical diagnosis which involve the combination of kinds of information amenable to fairly objective scoring.[11] People believe that, unlike a simple computer program, they can accurately detect intricate, interactive configurations of explanatory or predictive value. In fact, their abilities to do so are very limited.

Although a full explanation of this phenomenon is beyond the scope of this paper, overconfidence is probably fed by three factors. First, many of our cognitive processes are inaccessible to us. People do not know what information they use or how they use it. They think some information is crucial when it is not and report that they are not influenced at all by some data on which in fact they rely. This makes it easier for them to overestimate the sophistication of their thought processes. Second, a specific aspect of this lack of awareness is that people often rely more than they realize on analogies with past events, especially recent events that they or their country have experienced first-hand. Since these events seem clear in retrospect, much of this certainty is transferred to the current situation. A third cause of overconfidence, also linked to lack of self-awareness, is that people not only assimilate incoming information to their pre-existing beliefs, a point to which we will return, but do not know they are doing so. Instead, they incorrectly attribute their interpretations of events to the events themselves; they do not realize that their beliefs and expectations play a dominant role. They therefore become too confident because they see many events as providing independent confirmation of their beliefs when, in fact, the events would be seen differently by someone who started with different ideas. Thus people see evidence as less ambiguous than it is, think that their views are steadily being confirmed, and so feel justified in holding to them ever more firmly.

Some of the consequences of overconfidence for deterrence strategies are best seen in light of the two other cognitively rooted perceptual handicaps and so the discussion of them should be postponed. But some effects can be noted here. First, statesmen are likely to treat opposing views quite cavalierly since they are often quite sure that their own beliefs are correct. Cognitive dissonance theory asserts that this intolerance arises only after the person has made a firm decision and has become committed to a policy, but our argument is that it occurs earlier, when even a tentative conclusion has been reached. Second, decision-makers tend to overestimate their ability to detect subtle clues to the other's intentions. They think it is fairly easy to determine whether the other is hostile and what sorts of threats will be effective. They are not sufficiently sensitive either to the possibility that their conclusions are based on a cruder reading of the evidence or to the likelihood that highly complex explanations are beyond their diagnostic abilities. Third, because decision-makers fail to realize the degree to which factors other than the specific events they are facing influence their interpretations, their consideration of the evidence will be less rational than they think it is and less rational than some deterrence strategies require. For example, while people realize that it makes no sense to believe that another country is likely to be an aggressor just because a state they recently faced was one, in fact the previous experience will greatly increase the chance that the state currently under consideration will be seen as very dangerous. Similarly, beliefs about the kinds of deterrence strategies which will be effective are also excessively affected by recent successes and failures. Extraneous considerations then influence both conclusions as to whether deterrence is necessary and decisions as to how they will be sought. Decision-makers, furthermore, do not recognize this fact (if they did, presumably they would act to reduce its impact) and so overestimate the extent to which their policies are grounded in valid analysis.

Not Seeing Value Trade-Offs. The second important cognitive process that influences deterrence is the propensity for people to avoid seeing value trade-offs.[12] That is, people often believe that the policy they favor is better than the alternatives on several logically independent value dimensions. For example, those who favored a ban on nuclear testing believed that the health hazards from testing were high, that continued testing would yield few military benefits, and that a treaty would open the door to further arms control agreements. Opponents disagreed on all three counts. This kind of cognitive consistency is irrational because there is no reason to expect the world to be arranged so neatly and helpfully that a policy will be superior on all value dimensions. I am not arguing that people never realize that a policy which gains some important values does so at the price of others, but only that these trade-offs are not perceived as frequently and as severely as they actually occur.

This cognitive impediment has several implications for deterrence. First, it complicates the task of balancing the dangers entailed by issuing threats with the costs of making concessions. Rather than looking carefully at this trade-off, statesmen are likely to be swayed by one set of risks and then evaluate the other costs in a way that reinforces their initial inclinations. For example, a decision-maker who is preoccupied with what he and his state will sacrifice if he compromises on an issue is likely to convince himself that the danger of war if he stands firm is slight; the statesman who concludes that this danger is intolerably high is likely to come to see the costs of retreating as low. As long as the risk on which he focuses is in fact the greater one, and as long as the situation remains unchanging, this minimization of the trade-off is not likely to lead the decision-maker to choose a policy that differs from the one he would have adopted had he been more rational. But if either of these two conditions is not met, then the quality of the policy will suffer. Thus, if the decision-maker focuses first on the risks of war and finds that it looms large, he may incorrectly judge the costs of retreating as less. He could then abandon a policy of deterrence when rationality would dictate maintaining it.

In other cases, a decision-maker who has decided to stand firm may minimize the value trade-off by failing to take full account of the costs of his position. For example, he may come to believe that, while conciliatory measures would lower the short-run risk, they would increase the danger over a longer period by leading the adversary to think that it was safe to trifle with the state's interests. In this arrangement of perceptions and evaluations, standing firm appears preferable to being conciliatory on both the dimension of prevailing on the issue in dispute and the dimension of avoiding war.[13]

The failure to face trade-offs also helps explain the tendency for states to become overextended, to refuse to keep ends and means in balance, and to create more enemies than they can afford. For example, in the years preceding World War I, Germany added Russia and Britain to its list of enemies. On top of the conflict with France, this burden was too great even for a state as strong as Germany. Although both international and domestic factors were also at work, the psychological difficulty of making trade-offs must not be overlooked. When the German leaders decided to drop the Reinsurance Treaty with Russia in 1890, they perceived minimum costs because they expected that ideological conflict would prevent Russia from joining forces with Germany's prime enemy, France. Similarly, the decision to build a large navy and pursue a belligerent policy toward England was based on the assumption that England's conflicts with France and Russia were so deep that eventually British leaders would have to seek an understanding with the Triple Alliance. German statesmen did not see that their policy involved a greater risk of turning Russia and Britain into active enemies than was entailed by the rejected alternative policy of conciliation and compromise.

This failing was not peculiar to Germany. French policy between 1882 and 1898 sought both to rebuild a position of strength against Germany and to contest English dominance of Egypt. To pursue either objective meant risking war with one of these countries. This might have been within the bounds of French resources; war with both was not. So an effective policy required France to set its priorities and decide whether it cared more about its position in Europe or about colonial issues. For over ten years, however, French leaders refused to choose, instead thinking that the same policy could maximize the chances of gaining both goals. It took the shock of England's willingness to go to war in the Fashoda crisis for French statesmen to realize that they could not afford too many enemies and had to make a hard choice.

President Jimmy Carter's foreign policy provides a final example. To most of the goals of the preceding Ford Administration, the President added an increased concern with preventing proliferation and protecting human rights. He and his advisers did not seem to appreciate that pushing states on one front might diminish their ability to push them on others. Only when crises arose to clarify the mind did they decide to relax the more recent pressures in order to increase the chance of enlisting support for what were taken to be the more important national security goals. But by this time, a large price had been paid in terms of antagonizing others and appearing hypocritical; the overly ambitious initial policy jeopardized America's ability to achieve more limited goals.

Assimilation of New Information to Preexisting Beliefs. The third cognitive process I want to discuss is probably the most pervasive and significant. It is the tendency for people to assimilate new information to their preexisting beliefs, to see what they expect to be present. Ambiguous or even discrepant information is ignored, misperceived, or reinterpreted so that it does minimum damage to what the person already believes. As I have discussed at length elsewhere,[14] this tendency is not always irrational and does not always decrease the accuracy of perception. Our environment presents us with so many conflicting and ambiguous stimuli that we could not maintain a coherent view if we did not use our concepts and beliefs to impose some order on it. Up to a point — which cannot be specified with precision —rejecting or providing a strained interpretation of discrepant evidence is the best way to account for all the available information. It is the way scientists behave in treating their data because science would be impossible if they altered their theories to take account of each bit of discrepant information. As Michael Polanyi puts it:

> The process of explaining away deviations is in fact quite indispensable to the daily routine of research. In my laboratory I find the laws of nature formally contradicted at every hour, but I explain this away by the assumption of experimental error. I know that this

> may cause me one day to explain away a fundamentally new phenomenon and to miss a great discovery. Such things have often happened in the history of science. Yet I shall continue to explain away my odd results, for if every anomaly observed in my laboratory were taken at its face value, research would instantly degenerate into a wild-goose chase after imaginary fundamental novelties.[15]

Similarly, statesmen who miss, misperceive, or disregard evidence are not necessarily protecting their egos, being blind to reality, or acting in a way which will lead to an ineffective policy. The evidence is almost always ambiguous and no view can do justice to all the facts. In retrospect, one can always find numerous instances in which decision-makers who were wrong overlooked or misunderstood evidence that now stands out as clear and important. But one can also note, first, that many facts supported the conclusion that turned out to be wrong and, second, those who were right treated the evidence in the same general way — i.e., they also ignored or misinterpreted information which conflicted with their views.

Even if the assimilation of incoming information to preexisting beliefs is not as pernicious as is often believed, it creates a variety of problems for deterrence strategies, especially since this cognitive process operates in conjunction with the other two just discussed. First, images of other states are difficult to alter. Perceptions are not responsive to new information about the other side; small changes are not likely to be detected. Once a statesman thinks he knows whether the other needs to be deterred and what kind of strategy is appropriate, only the most dramatic events will shake him.[16] The problem is compounded by the common belief to the contrary that, if the initial hunches about what the other side is up to are incorrect, the other's behavior will soon set the statesmen straight. For example, those who see the other side as an aggressor usually argue that if this image is incorrect the other can easily demonstrate that its bad reputation is not warranted. In fact, the ambiguity of most evidence coupled with the absorptive power of most beliefs means that an inaccurate image may not be corrected at a point when the situation can still be controlled.

A second and more general consequence of the cognitive limitations we have discussed is that political perceptions are rarely completely accurate and policies rarely work as designed. Statesmen cannot then afford to develop policies which are so fragile that they will fail very badly if others do not act exactly as expected. A large margin of error must be built in. The statesman who is sure that his beliefs and calculations are correct in all their details is likely to encounter serious trouble, just as defense strategies that are based on the need to receive tactical warning of when and where the other side is planning to move are likely to fail. For example, it was not reasonable to have expected the military commanders to have anticipated an attack on Pearl Harbor or to have kept the base on constant alert. The latter procedure would have greatly disrupted the urgent training program. Instead the decision-makers should have sought a way to gain some measure of insurance against an attack with the lowest possible interference with training. The same principle applies to the construction of deterrence strategies. If they are based on an unrealistic assessment of our abilities to perceive our environment and choose among alternatives, they are likely to attempt too much and to fail badly.

Third, cognitive impediments place sharp limits on the degree to which deterrence strategies can be fine-tuned, limits that are more severe than statesmen generally realize. For example, states commonly try to develop policies that exert just the right amount of pressure on the other — that is, enough to show the other that the state is very serious, but not enough to provoke desperate behavior. Or, they try to indicate a willingness to ease tensions with an adversary without cooperating to such an extent that third parties would feel menaced. At the tactical level, intricate bargaining maneuvers are planned and subtle messages are dispatched. For example, in the discussions within the U.S. government in early 1965 about what sort of troops to send to Vietnam, Assistant Secretary of Defense John McNaughton dissented from the view that the initial deployment should be Marines. The problem, he argued, was that the Marines would bring with them "high profile" materiel such as tanks which would indicate to the North that the U.S. was in Vietnam to stay. It would be better to send the 173rd Airborne Brigade which lacked heavy equipment; this would signal Hanoi that the U.S. would withdraw if a political settlement could be reached.[17]

But even if the actions are carried out as the decision-maker wants them to,[18] precision is often defeated by the screen of the other side's perceptual predispositions. As a result, while subtlety and sophistication in a policy are qualities which observers usually praise and statesmen seek, these attributes may lead the policy to fail because they increase the chance that it will not be perceived as it is intended. It is hard enough to communicate straightforward and gross threats; it will often be impossible to successfully apply complex bargaining tactics which involve detailed and abstruse messages. Decision-makers often underestimate these difficulties and so try to develop plans that are too intricate to get across. Furthermore, because it is very hard to tell what others have perceived, statesmen often fail to see that they have failed to communicate.

Finally, since discrepant information is likely to be misinterpreted, deterrence strategies must be tailored to the other's preexisting beliefs and images, thus limiting the range of strategies that can succeed. Because the inferences which the other draws are largely determined by its initial beliefs, acts which will deter one decision-maker will be ignored or interpreted differently by another. If the perceiver thinks that the state is deeply concerned about the issue and has high resolve, deterrence will be relatively easy. If he has the opposite view, it will take great efforts to make a credible threat. But unless the state's leaders know what the other side thinks, they will neither know what they have to do to deter it nor be able to judge the chances of success. A frequent cause of deterrence failure is the state's misdesign of its actions growing out of incorrect beliefs about its adversary's perspective. For example, American leaders were taken by surprise in October 1962 because they thought it was clear to the Soviet Union that placing missiles in Cuba would not be tolerated. Since the Americans believed — correctly — that the Soviets were not likely to run high risks, they found it hard to imagine that the USSR would try to establish a missile base abroad. U.S. leaders did not think that great efforts at deterrence were necessary because they did not realize that the move would not look risky to the Soviets.[19]

Just as the best way to understand the conclusions a person draws from a "fact-finding" mission is to know his initial beliefs rather than to know what evidence he was exposed to, so one can often make better predictions about how a state will interpret others' behavior by knowing the former's predispositions than by knowing what the latter actually did. Unfortunately, statesmen rarely appreciate this and, to compound the problem, usually have a much better idea of what they think they are doing and what messages they want to convey than they do of what the others' perceptual predispositions are. The difficulty is two-fold and two-sided. The fact that perceptions are strongly influenced by predispositions means that it is very difficult to convey messages that are inconsistent with what the other already believes. And the fact that statesmen do not understand this influence reduces their ability to predict how others will react. Even if decision-makers understood the problem, prediction would be difficult because it is so hard for them to grasp the way in which others see the world. But in this case they would at least realize that many of their messages would not be received as they were sent. Since this understanding is often lacking, decision-makers' messages not only convey different meanings to each side, but each is usually unaware of the discrepancy. Statesmen are then likely to err both in their estimates of what the other side intends by its behavior and in their beliefs about how the other is reading their behavior. Severe limits are thus placed on the stateman's ability to determine whether and what kind of deterrence strategy is called for and to influence the other's perceptions in a way which will allow this strategy to succeed. A failure to understand these limitations imposed by the way people think will make it more difficult for scholars to explain state behavior and will lead a statesman to attempt overly ambitious policies that are likely to bring his country to grief.

DEFENSIVE AVOIDANCE

A final impediment to accurate perception that can complicate or defeat deterrence is affective rather than purely cognitive. In a process known as defensive avoidance, people may refuse to perceive and understand extremely threatening stimuli.[20] For example, the failure to see the value trade-offs discussed above can be motivated by the need to avoid painful choices. At this point we do not know enough about the phenomenon to determine when these errors occur and how influential they are in comparison with other factors. But it seems clear that on at least some occasions powerful needs, often arising from domestic politics, can produce badly distorted perceptions of other countries. Thus Paul Schroeder has argued that the British images of Russia in the period leading up to the Crimean War cannot be explained either by Russian behavior or by long-standing and deeply imbedded cognitive predisposition but rather were caused by shifting British needs to see Russia as threatening or accommodating.[21] Whether England tried to deter Russia or conciliate it then depended on internal factors that were neither rationally related to foreign policy goals nor susceptible to Russian influence. Similarly, states may come to think that it is relatively safe to challenge the adversary's deterrent commitments when a modicum of rational analysis would indicate that the risks far outweigh the slight chances of success if domestic or foreign needs for a challenge are very strong.

This is not only to argue that the costs of forgoing gains and accepting the adversary's deterrence can be so high as to rationally justify a challenge that the statesman knows is likely to fail; this may be unfortunate but it is not troublesome in terms of perceptions. Rather the knowledge of the high costs of accepting the status quo can lead statesmen to ignore or distort information about the costs of challenging it. Thus Lebow shows that the reason why India in 1962, the United States in the fall of 1950, and the Soviet Union before the Cuban Missile Crisis were not able to see that their adversaries would inflict painful rebukes if they persisted was that they were preoccupied with the costs they would pay if they did not.[22] To return to a case mentioned earlier, the American attempts to deter Japan failed because Japan thought that the war would be limited. This error may have been at least in part a motivated one. The feeling that acquiescing in the American demands was intolerable led the Japanese to adopt an unrealistically favourable view of the alternative — the only way they could avoid facing the need to sacrifice very deeply held values was to believe that the U.S. would fight a limited war. That their conclusion was driven by this need rather than by objective analysis is indicated by the quality of their deliberations: "Instead of examining carefully the likelihood that the war would in fact be a short, decisive one, fought under optimum conditions for Japan, contingency plans increasingly took on a strangely irrational, desperate quality, in which the central issue, 'Can we win?' was shunted aside. Rather, it was as if Japan had painted itself into a corner."[23] The result is that deterrence can be difficult if not impossible. Threats that should be credible and effective, even when the cognitive impediments discussed above are not operating, may be missed or misread. It usually will be hard for the deterrer to realize that it is facing this danger and even an understanding of the situation will not easily yield an effective policy since the other's perceptual screens are often opaque.

ENDNOTES

1 Allan Millet, *The Politics of Intervention* (Columbus, Ohio: Ohio State University Press, 1968) The point is nicely made in an anecdote about a British General made by B.H. Liddell Hart: "Jack Dill was a delightful man for any enthusiast to meet or serve. But he was quite unable to understand that the average officer did not share his burning ardour for professional study and tactical exercises. An illuminating example of that incomprehension occurred in his way of dealing with the major commanding a battery attached to his brigade who had failed to show the keenness Dill expected. To emphasize his dissatisfaction Dill told his officer that he would not be allowed to take part in the remaining exercises — a punishment, drastic in Dill's view, which was a great relief to the delinquent, who had been counting the days until he could get away to join a grouse-shooting party in Scotland."

— *The Liddell Hart Memoirs, 1895-1938* (New York: Putnam's, 1965), p. 72.

2 Sir Thomas Inskip, Minister for Coordination of Defense, quoted in Martin Gilbert, *Winston S. Churchill, Vol. 5 1922-1939* (London: Heinemann, 1976), p. 891.

3 Quoted in ibid., p. 945.

4 Churchill had a better understanding of the problem. In 1938 he stressed to a German diplomat that "a war, once started, would be fought out like the last to the bitter end, and one must consider not what might happen in the first few months, but where we should all be at the end of the fourth year." Quoted in ibid., p. 964. For a related argument, see Alan Alexandroff and Richard Rosecrance, "Deterrence in 1939," *World Politics,* 29 (April 1977), 404-424.

5 As Walt Rostow put it, "Ho has an industrial complex to protect; he is no longer a guerilla fighter with nothing to lose." Quoted in Department of Defense, *Pentagon Papers,* Senator Mike Gravel, ed., (Boston: Beacon Press, 1971), III, 153. That North Vietnam absorbed almost unprecedented punishment is shown by John Mueller, "The Search for the Single 'Breaking Point' in Vietnam: The Statistics of a Deadly Quarrel," *International Studies Quarterly,* 24 (December 1980), 497-519.

6 Robert Jervis, *The Logic of Images in International Relations* (Princeton: Princeton University Press, 1970), pp. 20-26, 66-112.

7 Ole Holsti, "The 1914 Case," *American Political Science Review,* 59 (June 1965), 365-378; Richard Ned Lebow, *Between Peace and War: The Nature of International Conflict* (Baltimore: Johns Hopkins University Press, 1981).

8 See, for example, Philip Green, *Deadly Logic* (Columbus, Ohio: Ohio State University Press, 1966); Patrick Morgan, *Deterrence* (Beverly Hills: Sage, 1977); Robert Jervis, "Deterrence Theory Revisited," *World Politics,* 31 (January 1979), 299-301, 310-312.

9 Baruch Fischhoff, Paul Slovic, and Sara Lichtenstein, "Knowing with Certainty: The Appropriateness of Extreme Confidence," *Journal of Experimental Psychology: Human Perception and Performance,* 3 (1977), 522-564.

10 Stuart Oskamp, "Overconfidence in Case-Study Judgments," *Journal of Consulting Psychology,* 29 (1965), 261-265.

11 For a review of this literature, see Lewis Goldberg, "Simple Models or Simple Processes? Some Research on Clinical Judgments," *American Psychologist,* 23 (July 1968), 483-496.

12 For a further discussion of this, see Robert Jervis, *Perception and Misperception in International Politics* (Princeton: Princeton University Press, 1976), pp. 128-142.

13 Jack Snyder, "Rationality at the Brink," *World Politics,* 30 (April 1978), 345-365. But for the phenomenon to fit the analysis here, the value dimensions must be logically independent. This will not be true if both the perceptions of the need to stand firm and evaluations of the costs of not doing so are produced by a coherent image of the adversary.

14 Jervis, *Perception and Misperception,* pp. 143-172.

15 Michael Polanyi, "The Unaccountable Element in Science," in *Knowing and Being, Essays by*

Michael Polanyi, ed. Marjorie Grene (London: Routledge and Kegan Paul, 1969), p. 114.

16 Glenn Snyder and Paul Diesing, *Conflict Among Nations* (Princeton: Princeton University Press, 1977), pp. 389-404.

17 *Pentagon Papers*, p. 421.

18 Most studies of policy implementation reveal that this rarely happens. For a nice analysis that combines bureaucratic and perceptual factors that complicate attempts at coercion, see Wallace Theis, *When Governments Collide* (Berkeley: University of California Press, 1980).

19 Klaus Knorr, "Failures in National Intelligence Estimates: The Case of the Cuban Missiles," *World Politics*, 16 (April 1964), 455-467. For an alternative argument, see Richard Ned Lebow, "The Cuban Missile Crisis: Reading the Lessons Correctly," *Political Science Quarterly*, 98, 3 (Fall 1983), 431-458.

20 The fullest discussion is in Irving Janis and Leon Mann, *Decision Making* (New York: Free Press, 1977).

21 Paul Schroeder, *Austria, Great Britain, and the Crimean War* (Ithaca, N.Y.: Cornell University Press, 1972).

22 Lebow, *Between Peace and War* and "Soviet Risk Taking." Also see Richard Cottam, *Foreign Policy Motivation* (Pittsburgh: University of Pittsburgh Press, 1977); Alexander George and Richard Smoke, *Deterrence in American Foreign Policy* (New York: Columbia University Press, 1974); and Jack Snyder, *Defending the Offensive: Biases in French, German, and Russian War Planning, 1870-1914* (Ph.D. dissertation, Columbia University, 1981), which does a particularly fine job of separating motivated from unmotivated errors. Sharp-eyed readers will note a shift from some of my earlier views on this point. For further discussion, see Robert Jervis, "Political Decision Making: Recent Contributions," *Political Psychology*, 2 (Summer 1980), 89-96.

23 Robert Scalapino, "Introduction," in James Morley, ed., *The Fateful Choice: Japan's Advance Into Southeast Asia, 1939-1941* (New York: Columbia University Press, 1980), p. 119. Also see Gordon Prange, *At Dawn We Slept* (New York: McGraw-Hill, 1981), pp. 16, 21.

A: PERCEPTION

War and Peace: Necessary and Sufficient Conditions

George H. Quester

I. CAUSES OF WAR

Any discussion of the "causes of war" intertwines itself interestingly with parallel discussions of the prerequisites of deterrence, or the "causes of peace." Debates about whether deterrence can succeed are buffeted by memories of wars that broke out, but also by memories of wars that never happened.

Such discussions of the causes of war and peace often become more fastened than is justified on one specific factor. Was a particular war caused by external structure, or by domestic irrationalities? Both may have contributed to the war that occurred; but an improvement in either category might have maintained peace. "Did the riverboat hit the bridge because the bridge was too low, or was the river too high?"

In stricter logic, one must distinguish between necessary and sufficient conditions. A *necessary* condition of a war is one that would have to be present, or war could not break out. The availability of weapons perhaps provides a trivial example; without weapons there could not be a war. A *sufficient* condition is one that guarantees a war whenever it is present. If both parties prefer war to peace, for example, war would have to occur.

A condition can be necessary without being sufficient and vice versa. Weapons, as noted above, are necessary to war, but they do not guarantee it. A love of war on both sides might guarantee war, but such love of battlefield carnage is not, per se, necessary for wars to happen.

A condition may also be neither necessary nor sufficient for war, and still be quite important. Miscommunication between two states involved in a confrontation may not be necessary for war, and may not be sufficient per se, but may play a key role in many outbreaks of violence.

It is important to bear some of these logical distinctions in mind, lest we confuse the issue when we discuss the causes of war, or the prerequisites of peace. When linking war and peace, defined as antonyms, we must remember how logic treats such antonyms. *Eliminating what is a necessary condition* for war is a *sufficient* condition for peace. *Eliminating what is a sufficient condition* for war is a *necessary* condition for peace.

What will follow is a discussion of some plausible models of the outbreak of war, models which command our intuitive attention. We must examine these models carefully to discover

---

An earlier version of this article appeared as George H. Quester, "Six Causes of War," *Jerusalem Journal of International Relations*, Vol. 6, No. 1 (1982), pp. 1-23. Reprinted with the permission of the *Jerusalem Journal of International Relations* and the author.

whether they incorporate alternative explanations and whether they show necessary or sufficient conditions. We will follow this examination with a transformation of these explanatory models of war into explanations of deterrence and other modes of maintaining peace.[1]

A. Simple "Folly". Our first candidate cause for warfare is often attacked in Sunday sermons and in more general analyses of the problem of peace; namely, foolishness on the part of man. This is often an argument, in the end, that war *necessarily* presupposes such folly, i.e., that human error is a necessary condition for war (which would mean that wisdom is a sufficient condition for peace).

Isn't war always caused by some sort of foolishness? Many of us might be quick to conclude that it is, that only stupidity could lead two nations into the mutually disadvantageous payoffs of war, when they could both have peace. But when is folly in fact the problem, and when is it not?

Some wars are indeed directly caused by a straightforward mistake, by the simple misanalysis of battlefield outcomes. Greek generals in 1940 told their prime minister that they could hold back Italian armies; Italian generals at the same time told Mussolini that Italian armies could easily plunge from Albania into Greece. The Italian staff officers were wrong, and the war may have simply resulted from their folly. Perhaps there is a tendency everywhere for foolish mortals to overrate their own military prowess. Perhaps all losing generals should be fired, or even shot.

There are at least two problems, however, with this interpretation of folly as the cause of war. First, some miscalculations might be very difficult to avoid; if this is so, we cannot conclude that war is pathological, that it is an avoidable tragedy. The scientific accuracy of attempts to predict the outcome of wars has not yet become so great that we, as neutral bystanders, can always ascertain who has judged correctly the battlefield possibilities.

It would be a more peaceful world if one could trust outside experts to settle the outcomes of wars in advance, much as good lawyers can settle legal cases "out of court," sparing both sides the costs of litigation by their expert predictions of the results of a court trial. One could thus imagine teams of experts from the RAND Corporation being flown into every crisis, to make predictions that would spare all sides the grief and expense of a war. Yet neither RAND nor the accumulated military professional research agencies of the world seem as yet to have this sort of prescient competence.

Second, and a larger problem for an analysis of folly as the cause for war, we may be able to find cases where no such mistake occurred, where this kind of miscalculation (or *any* kind of miscalculation) was not a necessary condition for war. Human error can increase the chances for war, and at times be a sufficient condition; there are also cases, however, where error would have prevented war, while accuracy would have made it more likely. But, as we shall see, other causes for war can intrude to threaten peace, even in a relatively error-free atmosphere.

B. Tug of War. If it is difficult for opposing sides to predict probable war outcomes when they overrate their states' military capabilities, predictions may be just as difficult, and even more important, in our next model of war. Here, each side does not necessarily overrate its own military capability, but rather its own resolve. Each wagers that its opponent will soon surrender, if only the war can be prolonged for a few more months; each is thus overrating and misreading its opponent's aversion to war. In a sense, therefore, this is also a situation where error produces or prolongs war. Which side would surrender first in World War I? Lloyd George and the Kaiser each bet that the other would have to give in first.[2] Similarly, mutually contradictory bets were made by Lyndon Johnson and Ho Chi Minh.

The error here is not so much about each side's military capability (e.g., Nasser's calculations prior to the 1967 Sinai War), but about each side's ability to endure punishment (e.g., Nasser's calculations prior to and during the 1968-70 "war of attrition";

the exchanges of artillery fire and air strikes back and forth across the Suez Canal, intended by each side to impose enough military casualties so that the other would have to cry "uncle").

The war of attrition here, or "tug of war," closely resembles the game of "chicken," where young men drive automobiles directly at each other to see who will first veer off the collision course.[3] The major difference in chicken is that the material costs of the confrontation are not borne minute by minute, but rather in a continually increasing risk of disaster, which of course imposes a psychological cost on the two drivers minute by minute. The persistence of each side in such a costly and dangerous exercise is rooted consequently in the same kind of calculation: each side assumes that the other will be the first to buckle under the strain.

This pattern of an endurance contest shows up frequently in interdependent politics, apart from war. In any situation which is less than ideal, a spectrum of moves is possible which would improve the position of both sides. Since each side knows this, each may be tempted to hold out at the position least favorable to both, continuing to veto and frustrate the ambitions of the other, in an attempt to win the largest gains for itself. The failure to reach the "optimality frontier" becomes an endurance contest where each side is betting that the other will give up first.[4] One side, of course, is wrong in its bet, but is hardly pathologically stupid in its error.

This situation does not determine any behavior. It dictates peace when the other side chooses war, and war when the other side chooses peace. Seeking to predict the ultimate outcome, each side may watch for supposed asymmetries in value patterns, whereby, for instance, one side is perceived to hate war more than the other. While this involves an interpersonal comparison of utility which is of questionable logical validity, it will nonetheless be a factor in driving the sides on.

Such a contest is possible only because each side can impose some substantial pain or hardship on the other, making moves which, while benefiting neither, may lead to a situation where concessions are ultimately offered by one. Where two parties are less interdependently subject to each other's potential vetoes, they might then engage in conflict for other reasons, but not in this kind of endurance contest or war of attrition.

C. Prisoners' Dilemma. A third kind of war may not depend on either of these two mistakes, but may simply be a function of a strategic situation, the "prisoners' dilemma," which allows each side to gain by double-crossing the other, and gives neither side any warning of a double-cross.

The prisoners' dilemma may explain a great deal about war. What if the geographic and strategic situation between two nations is such that whoever strikes first comes out ahead? And what if there is no way for either side to tell in advance whether the other is striking until the blow is felt? The gains of a double-cross in this case always turn out to be greater than those of cooperation, and while the costs of a mutual double-cross are severe, they are less so than the costs of foolish unilateral cooperation, when the other side has decided on a double-cross.[5] In effect each side knows that the other must betray the peace by shooting; because one knows the other will shoot, it is better off shooting first. Indeed, it would be better even if the other were to stop.

Each side might prefer peace to the wasteful war which would follow, a war in which both armies actively defended themselves while attacking each other. Yet each would rather a war in which it alone attacked, while the other lay down its arms. When peace is preferred to bilateral war, but unilateral war is generally preferred to peace, the result is almost inevitably bilateral war.

The error here lies in the absence of a reliable and reassuring communications and monitoring system, one that would let each player know if he were about to be double-crossed in time to allow retaliation. The outcome of the prisoners' dilemma situation is not directly a result of the wisdom or stupidity of the "prisoners," but rather of the presence or absence of devices which assure each side that it will know in time if the other is about to cheat, devices which would make cooperation both safe and advisable. Yet, achieving this kind of warning device can often be very difficult.

The real-life international equivalent of the prisoners' dilemma may be exemplified by the outbreak of World War I and the decisions of the Kaiser and Czar to mobilize their armies.[6] Each side was better off mobilizing, no matter what the other side did. If the other failed to follow suit, one could win a decisive victory; if the other side also mobilized, one could at least prevent a decisive defeat. The result was a war that neither side may have wanted. If observers could have been posted to the barracks and railway terminals of the major European powers, it might have served as the equivalent of a warning device or "window" between prisoners' cells, and the war of 1914 might have been avoided.

D. Mirror-Image Misunderstanding. A fourth version of war is not quite a prisoners' dilemma, but has much of the same instability. In this case, each side actually prefers peace to double-crossing the other side, but each is deeply afraid of the consequences, should the other side commit a double-cross.

Here, each side cannot be sure that the other prefers peace to attacking. Moreover, one side cannot be sure that the other knows it prefers peace to unilateral attack. For either reason, both sides must prepare to defend, preparations which will be indistinguishable from preparations for attack. Hence any slight increase in the perceived probability of war becomes self-confirming. What we have here is merely a "security dilemma," rather than a prisoners' dilemma. We have two nations that are satisfied with the status quo rather than inclined to imperialism, but are nevertheless driven by the international structure to plunge into a war which benefits neither.

Unlike the previous case, peace here does not require that both sides know they could not *get away with* a sneak attack. In fact, neither side would want to get away with it, even if it could. Instead, peace depends on convincing each other that neither side would *want* to get away with a sneak attack. This may seem easier than installing a monitoring system, but in fact it may be more difficult. Technology has given us reconnaissance satellites which can warn us of Soviet missile deployment, but it is far more difficult to persuade American policy-makers that the Soviet Union has never been tempted by war or aggression.

This model has often been put forward as the explanation of the Cold War between the United States and the Soviet Union after 1945, and of World War III, if it ever were to happen; perhaps because bombers or accurate missiles heavily favor whoever attacks first in nuclear war.[8] Proponents of the model presume no real hostility between the powers, no real intent to achieve world conquest for communism or capitalism by "surprise attack"; in this model, it is only the false assumption of aggressive intentions on the other side that threatens war.

The reader should note that the proximate cause for war here is in some sense precisely the opposite of our second model, the tug of war. War occurs here because each side underrates the other's attachment to peace; in the tug of war model, each side overrates the other's attachment to peace, i.e., bets that the other will surrender first. Because the causes are opposite, the "antidotes" would have to be inverse as well. Here, peace is served by teaching each side that the other really is peaceful; in the earlier war situation, we served peace by teaching each side that the other was determined and bellicose, and unlikely to give in easily.

The difference between our third and fourth models of war lies in the reading of the intentions of the parties. Are the belligerents intent on conquest, or is each merely concerned to avoid conquest by the other? This is primarily a question of national motivation rather than of soundness of analysis, although error may nonetheless intrude as each side may *falsely* suspect the other of intent to conquer.

We have identified at least four independent

variables floating through these first four models: the degree of accuracy in analysis shown by each side (either about capabilities or about intentions); the degree to which each side is physically capable of reducing the welfare of the other side (imposing "countervalue" damage on the other); the intentions of each side with regard to possible conquest of the other; and the extent to which nature, in the form of military technology and broader political opportunity, rewards an offensive initiative (presumably this is what is meant by a "counterforce capability").

None of these, per se, can be shown to be a *necessary* condition for war, since war, as the dependent variable, can always be produced by some combination of the other independent variables as sufficient conditions. And at least two more models of war need to be discussed.

E. Zero-Sum Total Hostility. The kinds of war situation discussed so far have in some sense been based on mistaken predictions of the outcome of war (the first two), or on the inability to establish sufficient mutual trust between potential adversaries (the next two). Yet not every kind of war is based on mechanisms of these kinds. To turn to perhaps the most depressing social relationship imaginable, in a symbiotic conflict one side might actually prefer war, rather than offering the minimum required for the other to surrender.

A game-theory-oriented reader will quickly note that this symbiotic incompatability would hold for a "zero-sum" game, i.e., a set of outcomes such that one side cannot gain in any shift without the other side losing an equal amount.[9] But international politics is never a zero-sum game; indeed the concept may be meaningless, since one cannot devise a meaningful interpersonal comparison of utility. This leads to the discovery that possibilities for cooperation are likely to exist. Yet the strict notion of zero-sum is not as necessary for war as we might have hoped. All that is required for this kind of conflict is that the two sides disagree on every possible choice between two outcomes. Since either side can start a war, war instead of peace is guaranteed when at least one side prefers the outcome in mutual war to the outcome in mutual peace. In such a case, it would be impossible for the loser to offer sufficient payment to the winner to make him peace-minded (impossible, that is, without first making the loser war-minded). The weaker side thus can never sue for peace, can never deliver enough "ransom" to make surrender an alternative.[10] Each side most prefers to fight and have its opponent offer no resistance. Can it really be possible that the net utility for the two sides is greater if they both fight than if they both consent to peaceful coexistence? Unfortunately it can.

Perhaps the two populations severely cramp each other's life-style by their existence in the same region, so that "A" could not easily offer "B" life and peace, even in exchange for B's surrender. For an illustrative case, one might look to the treatment of American Indians by white pioneers. People usually have the option to surrender and agree to the governance of new rulers in their territory. As a captive people, they could at least earn their keep, perhaps hoping for rebellion and political victory in the future. If the conqueror has no desire or need for their labor, however, he may not feel able to offer them the option of staying. In such horrible instances, both sides prefer war to peace even if they are fully aware of all the consequences. For at least one side, the war becomes one of extermination or eviction; for the side that is resisting, armed struggle is no more terrible than peace, for peace entails death or eviction from one's home.

If such zero-sum preferences were more often the case, war would more often be totally rational, far more common, and life would be grim indeed. Such a pattern of payoffs and preferences is, happily, rare. Peoples do not normally dislike each other so much that they find the costs of war straightforwardly less than the costs of coexistence.

F. Love of War. As a final discrete model of war, it is possible that one side (or both) will actually prefer war to peace. Such a positive desire for war could emerge because of special interests which stand to gain from war and can ignore the contrary preferences of the masses who must suffer. Or it could emerge because of deep economic, social, or psychological problems in society, problems which can be eased only by the diversion of battles abroad. One can also imagine a society so "naturally" warlike that most of its citizens genuinely prefer combat to peace; for example, the Huns or the Mongols (to omit any more recent examples of this extreme militarism).

It only requires that one side prefer war to peace to make war happen (unless the other side spoils the game by preemptive surrender, forfeiting the contest). If *both* sides loved war, this surely would be a sufficient condition for war, such that no other cause would be necessary.

It is difficult to decide how much, or how little, of war is explainable by such a direct preference. All of our previous models of war assumed that men generally preferred some form of peace to war, other things being equal, but here we see war as preferable to peace, other things being equal. Some of us like a little violence, or else no one would play football, yet how many of us like the violence of a modern battle? Statistics on suicide show that such self-directed violence usually declines at the outbreak of war, suggesting that some disturbed individuals find value for their lives only when their country commits itself to an armed struggle. In a well-functioning society, however, we would arrange for such persons to receive therapy, and, hopefully, to lead happy lives without battlefield carnage.

Marxist and radical economists sometimes argue that the needs of modern capitalism can similarly not be satisfied without substantial expenditures on weapons and without a positive predisposition to war or at least preparations for war. Again, in the Marxist view, a well-functioning society would find other ways to balance aggregate demand and provide full employment; however, without a fundamental rearrangement of domestic society, the lust for war will persist.

There is a different version of the Marxist argument which is much more like the zero-sum model of war we just outlined, namely that advanced capitalist societies are so desperate for overseas markets that they are driven to war, not because they have come to like war itself, but because none of them can stand a peace where they do not control these markets. Such analysis sees World War I, the Spanish-American War, or even the Japanese-American portion of World War II, as a life-and-death struggle among capitalist economies. These capitalist economies may have no particular desire for war, but they are in the grip of an unbridgeable incompatability; what one economy needs for its health competes directly with what another needs. If two nations or societies were to approximate this "zero-sum" hostility, where either felt so irritated, bothered, or deprived by the other in any state of peace, this would constitute a sufficient condition for war.

Love of war or zero-sum hostility are thus *sufficient* conditions for war. Our practical question is whether they occur very often. Does the occurrence of war indeed indicate that one or the other of these conditions *had* to be in place, making them *necessary* conditions? At times, the radical and Marxist analyses come close to this contention. Just as clergymen sometimes reject any explanation for war but error, these analysts reject any explanation but inherent systemic conflict, and thus transform an important causal possibility into a necessary condition.

These radical indictments of a link between capitalism and war are not easy to prove. While we have some evidence that defense industries favor war preparations, other forms of industry typically do not, and even the defense industry has shown no particular lust for fighting, as opposed to preparations. With regard to the competition for markets, the radical analysis must show more than that markets are attractive, for everyone assuredly welcomes a regular customer; it must show rather that the overseas markets involved in possible political conflict loomed so large in the economies of the advanced capitalist states that war became the necessary instrument to secure economic advantage. The data for World War I, or the Spanish-American War, or World War II in the Far East, do not suggest any such dominant role, any zero-sum game.

Summary of Section I. The reader might conclude that, by setting up six models of situations which can explain a war, we have generated six yes-no questions about the world, which would thus give us $(2)^6 = 64$ possible complicated combinations of causes of war. But this is not the case.

The causal model of war we started out with, simple stupidity, can of course coexist with all the others. Foolishness can increase the chances of war in any of the situations. The intent of outlining the next five models was to examine whether ignorance must *necessarily* be required for a war to break out. Each of these models produces an explanation which does not necessarily attribute war to simple foolishness and error. If there is an error, for example, in the tug of war, it is an error that each side is making; the "right answer" does not exist until the two adversaries determine it by their behavior.

Each of the last five models of war is, moreover, discrete from, and incompatible with, each of the others. The models reflect significant threshold crossings on international interdependence; offensive or defensive inclinations in military technology; attitudes toward war; and attitudes toward fellow men.

Moreover, enough *sufficient* conditions for war have been identified to vitiate the claim of any of these causes to be the *necessary* condition for war. We can also see a number of combinations in which changes in two or three causal categories can combine to cause war when peace would have otherwise prevailed.

II. STEPS TOWARD PEACE

If these six discrete transformations of models of international relationships can lead to war, what can one propose to prevent war? What changes in the nature of the situation can one seek in order to increase the chances of peace?

A. Eliminate Love of War. A first change that would be a priority almost by definition and a *necessary* condition for peace would be the elimination of situations where states actually prefer war to peace, where they actually enjoy war. If one accepts any theory which blames war on psychological, sociological, economic, or political pathologies of domestic societies, or which blames individual human beings, one must work for peace mainly "at home." Changing our domestic arrangements would strike some readers as a desirable goal in its own right; often reforms are needed for domestic reasons. Domestic reform is not always easily achieved, however. Fortunately, domestic, social, and economic ailments may not be typical of international problems or the cause of war.

B. Eliminate Disagreement. A second comparably basic ("necessary condition") approach to peace would be to eliminate the total ("zero-sum") hatred which amounted to our fifth cause for war; a situation where each side finds unacceptable what the other finds acceptable, where neither side prefers war to peace, but each prefers war to a peace where the other side is left to live in peace.

Again one must begin by stipulating how little leverage one may have over the preferences of societies and individuals; if men choose to hate each other, and to be uncomfortable in each other's presence, what can be done? We can at least reassure ourselves that such zero-sum hatred is still rare as a cause for war, for it is altogether unusual for men to disagree so totally about their goals in life. The Arab-Israeli conflict is perhaps the closest approximation we have to this kind of conflict today. But other examples are hard to find, and the ideological conflict between capitalism and communism is clearly of a different form.

Continuing with our effort to eliminate causes of war, many might advise emphasizing cooperation and agreement in general; thereby not only eliminating zero-sum conflict, but perhaps eliminating conflict altogether. If nations agreed on their first choices so that what was optimal for one was optimal for the other, wouldn't peace become likely? This might lead to a world where all parties agree totally on their ranking of preferences. Perhaps less demanding, but with the same benefit to a reduced likelihood of war, the two sides could at least agree on their first choices, even if they differed in their evaluation of their second, third, and fourth.

Eliminating disagreements about first choices would do far more than eliminate the possibility of zero-sum conflict. It would also eliminate three of our other models of war; the prisoners' dilemma situation, the tug of war, and the simple operations-analysis-error. (Perhaps in a curious way it would not rule out love of war. What if both sides agreed in enjoying war for its own sake, just as two gangs of boys may enjoy playing football?; an unlikely, but not unimaginable, situation.)

Wouldn't it be a fine world if no one could improve his own lot without improving that of fellow members of the community, and if no one could worsen anyone else's lot without simultaneously adversely affecting his own? How much war would be possible, if substantive disagreement between nations could be eliminated?

C. Eliminate Counterforce Potential. Unfortunately, there is at least some risk of conflict and counterproductive behavior, and of war, even when the two sides agree on their first choices. Here, we would have to return to the mirror-image misunderstanding presented as our fourth model for war. If there is imperfect mutual communication and understanding between the two sides, so that they do not comprehend each other's preferences and mistakenly assume disagreement about first choices and mutual hostility, then a stampede into war may occur.

This is to argue that even where hostility over goals has been largely eliminated, a reduction in the likelihood of war will hinge on eliminating the preemptive counterforce capability, what is sometimes called the offensive in warfare. We are now addressing military *capabilities* instead of intentions, the kind of capabilities that permit each side to take the initiative in inflicting damage on the other side in order to ward off damage to itself. The misunderstanding of the other side which produces precautionary preparations for possible war and, in turn, cycles into matching preparations, would not occur if neither side could make such preparations, if neither side seemed capable of achieving advantage from seizing the military initiative.

Reducing the capability to initiate a counterforce military offensive is thus a valuable contribution to peace, because it lowers the risk of a mirror-image-misunderstanding kind of war; but its contribution goes considerably beyond this. As noted, we cannot normally hope to be very effective in getting all states to share first choices about important issues and interests. An identity of interests would rule out the prisoners' dilemma and operations-research errors as causes of war, but what if an identity of interests cannot be achieved? Where it cannot be achieved, the reduction of offensive weapons potential again becomes an excellent substitute, making the prisoners' dilemma and the operations-analysis error much less likely. A world in which military technology severely penalizes whoever sends troops, ships, or airplanes charging forward is a world where the stampede psychology of the prisoners' dilemma or the mirror-image misunderstanding is very unlikely, and where far fewer generals will ignorantly and foolishly leap to the conclusion that their forces are sure to win.

In a number of the cases described above, peace becomes more likely, and perhaps attainable, if one simply restructures force exchange rates and battlefield outcomes to favor the side on the defensive, rather than the side initiating action. This might lead to the replacement of multiple-warhead missiles with single-warhead missiles, or tanks with pillboxes and minefields and precision-guided anti-tank weapons, or torpedo boats with Dreadnoughts.

In such cases, political crises or even declarations of war might be followed by "phony wars," as happened when troops in the Siegfried and

Maginot Lines sat waiting for the opposition to attack,[11] or the two major fleets waited on opposite sides of the North Sea in 1914. Military systems that punish initiative rather than reward it are, by and large, good for peace.

D. Add Mutual Verification Capabilities. Where the capabilities for military initiatives cannot be eliminated, an important contribution to peace can still be made if one develops and institutes mutual means of monitoring and surveillance, whereby each side will have advance warning if the other is about to attack or about to purchase new weapons. Prisoners' dilemma situations are unlikely to culminate in horrible consequences when the two sides can watch each other. Mirror-image misunderstandings similarly become easier to defuse if each side is reassured that the other does not want to launch an attack. Wars and arms races, which might otherwise develop, can thus be avoided.

A great deal of verification capability can be achieved through such technology as reconnaisance satellites which let each superpower know how many missile silos the other has built. Some can be achieved by human means, a positive result of what otherwise is seen as espionage. At other times, of course, such mutual surveillance becomes impossible, as each side develops or stumbles into ways of concealing its activities; the result is a resumption of the prisoners' dilemma or mirror-image misunderstanding and a greater likelihood of arms races and war.

E. Reduce Countervalue Capabilities. Agreement among powers about first-choices would also eliminate tug of war situations. Neither side could improve its own position by imposing penalities on the other. Where such agreement on goals has not been achieved, however, the risk of this form of war grows and we must then turn to yet another change in the environment that might promote peace.

Our discussion of preemptive offensive advantages referred largely to the counterforce aspect of war, namely the crippling of an enemy's forces by preemptive moves and the protection of one's own forces. The tug of war situation in many ways relies more heavily on the mutual imposition of pain rather than on the incapacitation of forces; more heavily on what could be called the "countervalue" aspect of war. Destroying an enemy's landing fields by an air raid is counterforce; destroying his cherished cathedrals and cultural monuments is countervalue. Blockading and destroying his commerce is largely countervalue.

But what if this countervalue capability were to be reduced? At certain stages of history, defenses against air raids or coastal raiders have been so effective that no damage to cities or cathedrals was likely. At certain stages, the trade and economic well-being of nations have become so autarchic and independent that warfare could not be used to impose much pain on either side. When very little pain can be inflicted on each of the two sides, wars of endurance are not likely.

However, there is a very important qualification that must be attached to this endorsement of the shielding of countries against each other's countervalue efforts. The contribution to peace of such a change will depend very much on whether the offensive military capabilities on the counterforce side have been trimmed back first. Where they have not been trimmed back, where one or both sides see a chance for grand victory in moving to the offensive, the probable countervalue costs of war may well serve to reinsure, rather than threaten peace. As long as the modern weapons of missile warfare remain in place, peace is best served by leaving intact, and reinsuring, the ultimate threat of *nuclear* second-strike countervalue retaliation, while at the same time, reducing *conventional* capabilities for inflicting countervalue pain.

F. Eliminate Folly. Last, but not least, we can hope to reduce the incidence of foolish planning, avoiding bad predictions about who will win any future war or who will give up first. As noted, such kinds of error would make no difference, would cause no wars, if the two sides agreed about the ideal arrangements of a peaceful world. When two sides do not agree, however, the significance of such errors is considerable. Errors about who will win increase as counterforce capabilities increase, and decrease as they recede. Errors about who will give up first are similarly less likely to cause a war when conventional countervalue capabilities recede, and more likely when they reappear.

What was said at the outset, however, must be repeated. We can do what we can to avoid miscalculations on the outcomes of future battles, but our skill at predicting such outcomes is limited, far more so than lawyers, for example, who nevertheless frequently go to trial because they are unsure of who will win. Moreover, if predicting the outcome of battle is difficult, it is even harder to accurately predict who will give up first, whose resolve is less. History shows that we are continually tempted to put in a little more effort, to endure war for a little while longer, in the hope that this will convince the other side that we are not about to give up first.

The question of human folly is equally difficult. Folly can cause wars, as can love of fighting or hatred for one's fellow men. We do what we can to change people so that they will not be foolish, or warlike, or hateful. Yet people tend to resist change. It may be far easier to change our capabilities than to change the way we deal with one another.

Overall Recapitulation. The following chart recapitulates the six models of war we have outlined, set opposite the six kinds of ameliorative turning points in the progress toward peace. The arrows running from right to left suggest how improvements in the international environment are tied to characteristic sources of war.

This analysis suggests that we cannot conclude that any one of these independent variables in particular causes war, or that manipulating any one will produce peace. Successful deterrence probably will depend on a combination of some wisdom, some aversion to war, some moderation of offense, some verification capabilities, and some tolerance of coexistence. Each of these becomes a necessary condition for peace, even as a major absence of any one of them become a sufficient condition for war. Yet the history of international politics demonstrates that the combination is not unattainable.

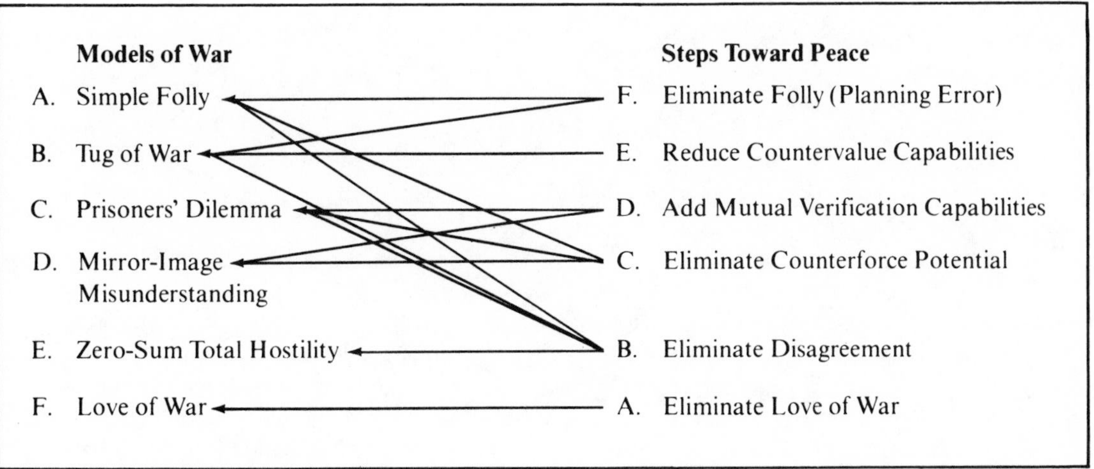

ENDNOTES

1 An earlier, somewhat longer, version of much of this argument, utilizing game-theoretical matrices to compare war situations, was presented in an article on "Six Causes of War," *Jerusalem Journal of International Relations*, 6 (No. 1, 1982), 1-23.

2 For a valuable discussion of the motivations prolonging World War I, see Fred Charles Iklé, *Every War Must End* (New York: Columbia University Press, 1971).

3 The relationship of "chicken" to "prisoners' dilemma" is spelled out in Glenn Snyder, " 'Prisoner's Dilemma' and 'Chicken' Models in International Politics," *International Studies Quarterly*, 15 (March 1971), 66-103.

4 An analysis of the motivations at the heart of the endurance contest is presented in Robert Jervis, "Bargaining and Bargaining Tactics," in J. Roland Pennock and John Chapman, eds., *Coercion* (Nomos XIV) (New York: Aldine, 1972), pp. 272-288.

5 Extended discussions of the workings and implications of "prisoners' dilemma" can be found in Anatol Rapoport and A.M. Chammah, *Prisoner's Dilemma: A Study in Conflict and Cooperation* (Ann Arbor: University of Michigan Press, 1965), and Anatol Rapoport, *Fights, Games and Debates* (Ann Arbor: University of Michigan Press, 1960).

6 For a most detailed account of the real life playing out of the mutually preemptive beginnings of World War I, see Luigi Albertini, *The Origins of the War of 1914* (New York: Oxford University Press, 1957), Volume III.

7 See Robert Jervis, "Cooperation Under the Security Dilemma," *World Politics*, 30 (January 1978), 167-214.

8 For examples, Charles E. Osgood, *An Alternative to War or Surrender* (Urbana: University of Illinois, 1962) on the origins of the Cold War, and Thomas C. Schelling, *The Strategy of Conflict* (Cambridge: Harvard University Press, 1960), pp. 207-209, on a World War III wanted by neither side.

9 A comprehensive and formal analysis of zero-sum games can be found in Anatol Rapoport, *Two-Person Game Theory: The Essential Ideas* (Ann Arbor: University of Michigan Press, 1966).

10 See Paul Kecskemeti, *Strategic Surrender* (Stanford, California: Stanford University Press, 1958) for a fascinating discussion of the underlying rational basis of surrender.

11 See Vivian Rowe, *The Great Wall of France* (London: Putnam, 1959) for an interesting account of the impact of the defensive bulwark of the Maginot Line on French preferences and war plans.

B: DECISION MAKING

Cognitive Closure and Crisis Politics

Richard Ned Lebow

> The Austrians should move, *the sooner the better*, and the Russians — although friends of Serbia — will not intervene.
> *Theobald von Bethmann-Hollweg, July 5, 1914*

> If war does not break out, if the czar is unwilling, or alarmed, if France counsels peace, we shall have the prospect of splitting the Entente.
> *Theobald von Bethmann-Hollweg, July 6, 1914*

> We have not willed war, it has been forced upon us.
> *Theobald von Bethmann-Hollweg, August 4, 1914*

Traditional social science theory depicted decision-making as an essentially rational process. This paradigm assumed that policy-makers processed information in a relatively straightforward and honest manner in order to discover the best policy alternative. To do this, they identified the alternatives, estimated the probability of success of each, and assessed their impact upon the values they sought to maximize. Policy-makers were thought of as receptive to new information. As they learned more about a particular problem they were expected to make more complex and sophisticated judgments about the implications of the various policy alternatives they considered. The rational actor paradigm also assumed that policy-makers confronted trade-offs squarely, that they accepted the need to make choices between the benefits and costs of competing alternatives in order to select the best policy.

Considerable research points to the conclusion that decision-making in practice differs considerably from the rational process we have just described.[1] This finding has prompted efforts to develop alternative paradigms of decision-making, several of which have already been formulated in

---

Richard Ned Lebow, *Between Peace and War* (Baltimore: The Johns Hopkins University Press, 1981), pp. 101-119. Reprinted by permission of The Johns Hopkins University Press. Portions of the text have been deleted. Some footnotes have been removed; those remaining have been renumbered.

considerable detail. Each of these several paradigms claims to represent a more accurate description of the decision-making process than that of the rational actor model.

The variety of models and approaches to decision-making that have been developed in recent years has added immeasurably to our understanding of the decision-making process. The models have made us aware of the complexity of this process and the multiplicity of personal, political, institutional, and cultural considerations that can shape decisions. For this very reason no one perspective provides a satisfactory explanation of decision-making. Each offers its own particular insights and is more or less useful depending upon the analytical concerns of the investigator and the nature of the decision involved.

For our purposes the psychological perspective on decision-making appears to be the most relevant by virtue of the insights it offers into the causes and effects of misperception. Use of the psychological approach is complicated by the fact that there is as yet no integrated statement of psychological principles and processes that could be considered to represent a paradigm of decision-making.[2] There are instead several different schools of thought, each of which attempts to explain nonrational processes in terms of different causation. The state of psychological theory therefore mirrors that of decision-making theory as a whole. As it is often necessary to employ more than one decision-making perspective to understand the genesis of a policy so one must exploit more than one psychological theory or approach in order to explain the nonrational processes that are involved. In the pages that follow we will accordingly describe two psychological approaches, one cognitive, the other motivational...

COGNITIVE CONSISTENCY AND MISPERCEPTION

The cognitive approach emphasizes the ways in which human cognitive limitations distort decision-making by gross simplifications in problem representation and information processing. Some psychologists have suggested that human beings may be incapable of carrying out the procedures associated with rational decision-making. Whether or not this is actually the case, there is growing evidence that people process and interpret information according to a set of mental rules that bear little relationship to those of formal logic....

One principle of psycho-logic that has received considerable empirical verification is the principle of "cognitive consistency." Numerous experiments point to the conclusion that people try to keep their beliefs, feelings, actions, and cognitions mutually consistent. Thus, we tend to believe that people we like act in ways we approve of, have values similar to ours, and oppose people and institutions we dislike. People we dislike, we expect to act in ways repugnant to us, have values totally dissimilar from ours, and to support people and institutions we disapprove of. Psychologists have theorized that cognitive consistency is an economic way of organizing cognition because it facilitates the interpretation, retention, and recall of information. While this may or may not be true, our apparent need for cognitive order also has some adverse implications for decision-making because it suggests the existence of systematic bias in favor of information consistent with information that we have already assimilated.

At the present time considerable work is being done to analyze the various ramifications of cognitive consistency for decision-making. To date, the most comprehensive effort is that of Robert Jervis whose work is especially relevant for our purposes, because he has made the foreign policy process the specific focus of his study.[3]

Jervis contends that it is impossible to explain crucial foreign policy decisions without reference to policy-makers' beliefs about the world and the motives of other actors in it. These beliefs, organized as "images," shape the way in which policy-makers respond to external stimuli. He suggests that the primary source of images is stereotyped interpretations of dramatic historical events, especially wars and revolutions. These upheavals have a particularly strong impact upon the thinking of younger people whose opinions about the world are still highly impressionable. Images formed by adolescents and young adults can still shape their approach to international problems years later when they may occupy important positions of authority. Jervis believes that this may explain why "generals are prepared to fight the last war and diplomats prepared to avoid it."[4]

Lessons learned from history are reinforced or modified by what policy-makers learn from first-hand experience. Jervis finds that events that are personally experienced can be a "powerful determinant" of images. This too may be a source of perceptual distortion because personal experiences may be unrepresentative or misleading. As with historical lessons, events experienced early in adult life have a disproportional impact upon perceptual predispositions.[5]

The major part of Jervis' study is devoted to analyzing the ways in which images, once formed, affect foreign policy behavior. From the outset he makes an important distinction between what he calls "rational" and "irrational" consistency. The principle of consistency, he argues, helps us to make sense of new information as it draws upon our accumulated experience, formulated as a set of expectations and beliefs. It also provides continuity to our behavior. But the pursuit of consistency becomes irrational when it closes our minds to new information or different points of view. Even irrational consistency can be useful in the short run because it helps to make a decision when the time comes to act. However, persistent denial of new information diminishes our ability to learn from the environment. Policy-makers must strike a balance between persistence and continuity on the one hand and openness and flexibility on the other. Jervis marshals considerable evidence to indicate that they more often err in the direction of being too wedded to establish beliefs and defend images long after they have lost their utility.[6]

Irrational consistency can leave its mark on every stage of the decision-making process. Most importantly, it affects the policy-maker's receptivity to information relevant to a decision. Once an expectation or belief has taken hold, new information is assimilated to it. This means that policy-makers are more responsive to information that supports their existing beliefs than they are to information that challenges them. When confronted with critical information, they tend to misunderstand it, twist its meaning to make it consistent, explain it away, deny it, or simply ignore it.

To the extent that a policy-maker is confident in his expectations, he is also likely to make a decision before sufficient information has been collected or evaluated. Jervis refers to this phenomenon as "premature cognitive closure" and sees it as a major cause of institutional inertia. As all but the most unambiguous evidence will be interpreted to confirm the wisdom of established policy and the images of reality upon which it is based, policy-makers will proceed a long way down a blind alley before realizing that something is wrong.[7]

When policy-makers finally recognize the need to reformulate an image, they are likely to adopt the first one that provides a decent fit. This "perceptual satisficing" means that images change incrementally, that a large number of exceptions, special cases, and other superficial alterations will be made in preference to rethinking the validity of the assumptions on which the image is based. It also means that tentative beliefs or expectations, often made on the basis of very incomplete information, come to exercise a profound influence on policy because once they are even provisionally established incoming information is assimilated to them. This in turn lends credence to their perceived validity.

The tautological nature of information processing is further facilitated by the "masking effect" of preexisting beliefs. As information compatible with an established belief will be interpreted in terms of it, the development of alternative beliefs that the information might also support is inhibited. Thus, the belief that the other side is bluffing, as Jervis points out, is likely to mask the perception that it means what it says because the behaviors that follow from these two intentions resemble each other so closely.[8]

The second way in which irrational consistency influences decision-making is by desensitizing policy-makers to the need to make value "trade-offs." Instead of recognizing that a favored option may advance one or even several valued objectives, but does so at the expense of some other valued objective, policy-makers are more likely to perceive the option as simultaneously supporting all of their objectives. As they come to favor an option, policy-makers may even alter some of their earlier expectations or establish new ones all in the direction of strengthening the case for the favored policy.

The failure to recognize trade-offs leads to "belief system overkill." Advocates of a policy advance multiple, independent, and mutually reinforcing arguments in its favor. They become convinced that it is not just better than other alternatives but superior in every way. Opponents on the other hand tend to attack it as ill considered in all its ramifications. In this regard, Jervis cites Dean Acheson's description of Arthur Vandenberg's characteristic stand: "He declared the end unattainable, the means harebrained, and the cost staggering." Cognitions ordered in this way facilitate choice as they make it appear that all considerations point toward the same conclusion. Nothing therefore has to be sacrificed. But, as Jervis points out, "the real world is not as benign as these perceptions, values are indeed sacrificed and important choices are made, only they are made inadvertently."[9]

The final way irrational consistency is manifested is in the form of postdecisional rationalization, a phenomenon described by Leon Festinger in his theory of cognitive dissonance.[10] Festinger argues that people seek strong justification for their behavior and rearrange their beliefs in order to lend support to their actions. Following a decision they spread apart the alternatives, upgrading the attractiveness of the one they have chosen and downgrading that of the alternative they have rejected. By doing so they convince themselves that there were overwhelming reasons for deciding or acting as they did. Festinger insists that people only spread apart the alternatives *after* they have made a decision. The decision must also result in some kind of commitment and the person making it must feel that it was a free decision, i.e., that he had the choice to decide otherwise.

Subsequent research indicates that decisional conflict is positively correlated with the appeal of the rejected alternatives, their dissimilarity from the chosen alternatives and the perceived importance of the choice. In other words, the more difficult the decision the greater the need to engage in postdecisional rationalization. According to Jervis, foreign policy decisions are often characterized by these criteria, and statesmen respond by upgrading their expectations about their chosen policy. By making their decision appear even more correct in retrospect they increase the amount of negative feedback required to reverse it. Postdecisional rationalization therefore makes policy-makers less responsive to the import of critical information.

DECISIONAL CONFLICTS AND DEFENSIVE AVOIDANCE

Whereas Jervis stresses the ways in which cognitive processes distort decision-making, another school of psychology emphasizes the importance of motivation as a source of perceptual distortion. They see human beings as having a strong need to maintain images of the self or the environment conducive to their emotional well-being. This need interferes with their ability to act rationally....

The work of Irving Janis and Leon Mann represents one of the most thought-provoking attempts to construct a motivational model of decision-making. They start from the assumption that decision-makers are emotional beings, not rational calculators, that they are beset by doubts and uncertainties, struggle with incongruous longings, antipathies, and loyalties, and are reluctant to make irrevocable choices. Important decisions therefore generate conflict, defined as simultaneous opposing tendencies to accept and reject a given course of action. This conflict and the psychological stress it generates become acute when a decision-maker realizes that there is risk of serious loss associated with any course of action open to him. More often than not, he will respond to such situations by procrastinating, rationalizing, or denying his responsibility for the decision. These affective responses to stress detract from the quality of decision-making.[11]

Janis and Mann present their "conflict model" of decision-making in terms of the sequence of questions policy-makers must ask when confronted with new information about policies to which they are committed. Their answers to these questions determine which of five possible patterns of coping they will adopt.

The first of the questions pertains to the risks to the policy-maker of not changing his policy or taking some kind of protective action. If he assesses the risks as low, there is no stress and he can ignore the information. Janis and Mann refer to this state as "unconflicted inertia." Sometimes this is a sensible appraisal as when policy-makers ignore warnings of doom from critics motivated by paranoia or partisan advantage. It is dysfunctional when it is a means of avoiding the stress associated with confronting a difficult decision head on.

If the perceived risks are thought to be serious, the policy-maker must attempt to identify other courses of action open to him. If his search reveals a feasible alternative, Janis and Mann expect that it will be adopted without conflict. "Unconflicted change," as this pattern of coping is called, may once again reflect a realistic response to threatening information although it can also be a means of avoiding stress. Unconflicted change is dysfunctional when it mediates a pattern of "incrementalism." This happens when the original policy is only marginally changed in response to threatening information and then changed slightly again when more trouble is encountered. Such a crude satisficing strategy tends to ignore the range of alternative policies, some of which may be more appropriate to the situation. Janis and Mann suggest that this is most likely to occur when a policy-maker is deeply committed to his prior course of action and fears that significant deviation from it will subject him to disapproval or other penalties.

If the policy-maker perceives that serious risks are inherent in his current policy, but upon first assessment is unable to identify an acceptable alternative, he experiences psychological stress. He becomes emotionally aroused and preoccupied with finding a less risky but nevertheless feasible policy alternative. If, after further investigation, he concludes that it is unrealistic to hope for a better strategy, he will terminate his search for one despite his continuing dissatisfaction with the available options. This results in a pattern of "defensive avoidance," characterized by efforts to avoid fear-arousing warnings.

Janis and Mann identify three forms of defensive avoidance: procrastination, shifting responsibility for the decision, and bolstering. The first two are self-explanatory. Bolstering is an umbrella term that describes a number of psychological tactics designed to allow policy-makers to entertain expectations of a successful outcome. Bolstering occurs when the policy-maker has lost hope of finding an altogether satisfactory policy option and is unable to postpone a decision or foist the responsibility for it onto someone else. Instead, he commits himself to the least objectionable alternative and proceeds to exaggerate its positive consequences or minimize its negative ones. He may also deny the existence of his aversive feelings, emphasize the remoteness of the consequence, or attempt to minimize his personal responsibility for the decision once it is made. The policy-maker continues to think about the problem but wards off anxiety by practicing selective attention and other forms of distorted information processing.

Bolstering can serve a useful purpose. It helps a policy-maker forced to settle for a less than satisfactory course of action to overcome residual conflict and move more confidently toward commitment. But bolstering has detrimental consequences when it occurs before the policy-maker has made a careful search of the alternatives. It lulls him into believing that he has made a good decision when in fact he has avoided making a vigilant appraisal of the possible alternatives in order to escape from the conflict this would engender.

If the policy-maker finds an alternative that holds out the prospect of avoiding serious loss he must then inquire if he has sufficient time to implement it. If his answer to this question is no, his response will be one of "hypervigilance." This pattern of coping is also likely to be adopted if the time pressures are such that the policy-maker does not even believe it possible to initiate a search for an acceptable alternative. Hypervigilance is characterized by indiscriminate openness to all information and a corresponding failure to determine whether or not that information is relevant, reliable, or supportive. Decisions made by persons in a hypervigilant state are likely to be unduly influenced by the will and opinions of others. In its most extreme form, panic, decisions are formulated in terms of the most simple-minded rules, e.g., "Do what others around you are doing." This is why a fire in a theater may prompt the audience to rush irrationally toward only one of several accessible exits.

The patterns described above — unconflicted inertia, unconflicted change, defensive avoidance, and hypervigilance — are all means of coping with psychological stress. But they are hardly likely to lead to good decisions as each pattern is characterized by some kind of cognitive distortion. "High quality" decision-making occurs when a policy-maker is able to answer "yes," or at least "maybe," to all four questions. "Vigilance," the pattern of coping that leads to good decisions, is therefore associated with the following conditions: the policy-maker realizes that his current policy will encounter serious difficulties; he sees no obvious satisfactory alternative but believes that a good alternative can probably be found and implemented in the time available to him.[12]

The preceding argument makes it apparent that Janis and Mann believe that stress can facilitate good decision-making but only under circumstances so specific that they are not likely to recur very often. In less than ideal circumstances stress can be so acute as to compel the policy-maker to adopt a decision-making strategy to protect him from it. Any of these patterns of coping will impair the quality of the decision.

COGNITIVE PROCESSES AND DECISION-MAKING PATHOLOGIES

The studies we have just described represent two of the most provocative and comprehensive attempts to apply psychological insights to the study of political behavior. Unfortunately for those concerned with developing a psychological paradigm, the principal arguments of these two works are derived from sufficiently different premises to preclude their reformulation into an integrated model of decision-making. For Jervis, the starting point is the human need to develop simple rules for processing information in order to make sense of an extraordinarily complex and uncertain environment. Janis and Mann take as their fundamental assumption the human desire to avoid fear, shame, and guilt. Jervis describes cognitive consistency as the most important organizing principle of cognition. Janis and Mann contend that aversion of psychological stress is the most important drive affecting cognition. Whereas Jervis concludes that expectations condition our interpretation of events and our receptivity to information, Janis and Mann argue for the importance of preferences. For Jervis, we see what we *expect* to see, for Janis and Mann, what we *want* to see.[13]

Despite the differences between these scholars they are in fundamental agreement about the important implications of cognitive distortion for decision-making. Each in his own way emphasizes the tendency of policy-makers to fail to see trade-off relationships, engage in postdecisional rationalization, and remain insensitive to information that challenges the viability of their commitments. In essence, they are advancing competing explanations for some of the same observable behavior,

behavior they both describe as detrimental to good decision-making.

The several kinds of cognitive distortions Jervis and Janis and Mann refer to result in specific kinds of deviations from rational decision-making. These deviations might usefully be described as decision-making "pathologies." To the extent that they are present they diminish the probability that effective policy will be formulated or implemented. For the purpose of analyzing crisis performance the most important of these pathologies appear to be: (1) the overvaluation of past performance as against present reality, (2) overconfidence in policies to which decision-makers are committed, and (3) insensitivity to information critical of these policies. These pathologies warrant some elaboration.

Overvaluation of Past Success. Policy-makers, according to Jervis, learn from history and their own personal experience. Their understanding of why events turned out the way they did constitutes the framework in terms of which they analyze current problems. It facilitates their ability to cope with these problems and provides continuity to their behavior.

Lessons from the past can discourage productive thinking to the extent that they represent superficial learning and are applied too reflexively. Jervis makes the case that this is a common occurrence because people rarely seek out or grasp the underlying causes of an outcome but instead assume that it was a result of the most salient aspects of the situation. This phenomenon gives rise to the tendency to apply a solution that worked in the past to a present problem because the two situations bear a superficial resemblance. Jervis observes: "People pay more attention to *what* has happened than to *why* it has happened. Thus learning is superficial, overgeneralized, and based on *post hoc ergo propter hoc* reasoning. As a result, the lessons learned will be applied to a wide variety of situations without a careful effort to determine whether the cases are similar on crucial dimensions."[14]

Examples of this kind of learning abound in the political and historical literature. A good case in point is the lesson drawn by the British military establishment and most military writers from the allied disaster at Gallipoli in World War I. Because Gallipoli failed, they became obdurate in their opinion that an amphibious assault against a defended shore was impractical and even suicidal. It took the United States Marine Corps, which undertook a detailed study of *why* Gallipoli failed (e.g., faulty doctrine, ineffective techniques, poor leadership, and utter lack of coordination), to demonstrate the efficacy of amphibious warfare.

Success may discourage productive learning even more than failure as there is much less incentive or political need to carry out any kind of postmortem following a resounding success. If this is true, the greatest danger of superficial learning is that a policy, successful in one context, will be used again in a different and inappropriate context. The chance of this happening is enhanced by the strong organizational bias in favor of executing programs already in the repertory. The Bay of Pigs invasion is a case in point. The CIA, ordered to overthrow Castro with no overt American participation, resurrected the plan they had used successfully in 1954 to topple the Arbenz government in Guatemala. Although the two situations had only a superficial similarity, this plan was implemented with only minor modifications, with results that are well known. Some critics of American foreign policy have suggested that a similar process occurred with the containment policy. Due to its apparent success in Europe it was applied to Asia with consequences that now appear disastrous.[15]

Overconfidence. Jervis theorizes that irrational consistency encourages overconfidence at every stage of the decision-making process. Before a decision is made policy-makers attempt to avoid value trade-offs by spreading the alternatives. In doing so they tend not only to make the favored alternative more attractive but also to judge it more likely to succeed. As policy decisions often hinge on estimates of their probability of success it is not surprising that Jervis finds that people who differ about the value of an objective are likely to disagree about the possibility of attaining it and the costs that this will entail. Those who favor the policy will almost invariably estimate the chances of success as high and the associated costs as lower than do their opponents.[16]

After a decision is made, postdecisional rationalization enters the picture. It too is a means of minimizing internal conflict by providing increased support for a person's actions.For by revising upwards the expected favorable consequences of a policy and its probability of success, policy-makers further enhance their confidence in the policy. By this point their confidence may far exceed whatever promise of success would be indicated by a more objective analysis of the situation.

Janis and Mann also describe overconfidence as a common decision-making pathology but attribute it to different causes and specify a different set of conditions for its appearance. For them it is a form of bolstering, the variety of psychological tactics that policy-makers employ to maintain their expectations of an outcome with high gains and minimal losses. Policy-makers will display overconfidence and other forms of defensive avoidance to the degree that they (1) confront high decisional conflict resulting from two clashing kinds of threat and, (2) believe that they will not find a better alternative for coping with this threat than their present defective policy. Janis and Mann write: "Whenever we have no hope of finding a better solution than the least objectionable one, we can always take advantage of the difficulties of predicting what might happen. We can bolster our decision by tampering with the probabilities in order to restore our emotional equanimity. If we use our imagination we can always picture a beautiful outcome by toning down the losses and highlighting the gains."[17]

Insensitivity to Warnings. An important corollary of cognitive consistency theory is that people resist cues that challenge their expectations. They may misinterpret them to make them supportive, rationalize them away, or ignore them. Jervis finds that resistance to critical information increases in proportion to a policy-maker's confidence in his course of action, the extent of his commitment to it, and the ambiguity of information he receives about it. Under these conditions even the most negative feedback may have little impact upon the policy-maker.[18]

For Janis and Mann, insensitivity to warnings is a hallmark of defensive avoidance. When this becomes the dominant pattern of coping "the person tries to keep himself from being exposed to communications that might reveal the shortcomings of the course of action he has chosen." When actually confronted with disturbing information he will alter its implications through a process of wishful thinking. This often takes the form of rationalizations which argue against the prospect of serious loss if the current policy is unchanged. Janis and Mann find that extraordinary circumstances with irrefutable negative feedback may be required to overcome such defenses.[19]

Selective attention, denial, or almost any other psychological tactic used by policy-makers to cope with critical information can be institutionalized. Merely by making their expectations or preferences known, policy-makers encourage their subordinates to report or emphasize information supportive of those expectations and preferences. Policy-makers can also purposely rig their intelligence networks and bureaucracies to achieve the same effect. Points of view thus confirmed can over time exercise an even stronger hold over those who are committed to them. Some effort has been made to explain both the origins and duration of the Cold War in terms of such a process.[20] The danger here is that perceptual rigidity will impair personal and organizational performance. It encourages a dangerous degree of overconfidence which reduces the probability that policy-makers will respond to information critical of their policies. Karl Deutsch warns: "If there are strong tendencies toward eventual failure inherent in all organizations, and particularly governments — as many pessimistic theories of politics allege — then such difficulties can perhaps be traced to their propensities to prefer self-reference symbols to new information from the outside world."[21]

DEFENSIVE AVOIDANCE AND UNCONSCIOUS CONFLICT

One further decision-making pathology must be considered; the paralysis or erratic steering that can result when defenses, erected to cope with anxiety, break down.

The human mind is particularly adept at developing defenses against information or impulses that threaten the attainment of important goals or the personality structure itself. Some of the more common defenses include repression, rationalization, denial, displacement, and acting out.[22] These defenses are not always effective. Fresh evidence of an unambiguous and unavoidable kind may break through a person's defenses and confront him with the reality he fears. This can encourage adaptive behavior. But it can also prompt him to adopt even more extreme defense mechanisms to cope with the anxiety this evidence generates. This latter response is likely to the extent that there are important causes of decisional conflict at the unconscious level. Even these defenses may prove transitory and ineffective. As a general rule, the more intense and prolonged the defense the greater the probability of breakdown when it finally collapses. In the words of a famous pugilist: "The bigger they are the harder they fall."...

The implications of the preceding discussion for crisis management are obvious. Defense mechanisms are most likely to break down when the policy-maker is inescapably confronted with the reality he has hitherto repressed. Such a situation is most likely to develop during the most acute stage of international crisis when the decision for peace or war hangs in the balance. A breakdown in the policy-maker's defenses at this time may result in erratic behavior or his actual paralysis. Either condition is likely to "freeze" policy and contribute to the outbreak of war to the extent that it leaves the protagonists on a collision course....

ENDNOTES

1 For example, Herbert A. Simon, *Administrative Behavior* (New York: Free Press, 1946); Charles E. Lindblom, "The Science of 'Muddling Through," *Public Administration,* 19 (Spring 1959), 74-88; Richard Cyert and James March, *A Behavioral Theory of the Firm* (Englewood Cliffs, N.J.: Prentice-Hall, 1963); Graham T. Allison, *Essence of Decision: Explaining the Cuban Missile Crisis* (Boston: Little, Brown, 1971); John D. Steinbruner, *The Cybernetic Theory of Decision* (Princeton: Princeton University Press, 1974).

2 Donald R. Kinder and Janet A. Weiss, "In Lieu of Rationality: Psychological Perspectives on Foreign Policy Decision Making," *Journal of Conflict Resolution,* 22 (December 1978), 707-35, offer a thoughtful analysis of the prospects for a psychological paradigm of decision-making. Following a review of the relevant literature the authors identify four common themes they believe will be central to any paradigm. These are (1) the striving for cognitive consistency and its conservative impact upon perception and information processing, (2) systematic biases in causal analysis, (3) distorting effects of emotional stress, and (4) the cognitive construction of order and predictability within a disorderly and uncertain environment.

3 Robert Jervis, "Hypotheses on Misperception," *World Politics,* 20 (April 1968), 454-79, and *Perception and Misperception in International Politics* (Princeton: Princeton University Press, 1976). For other analyses by political scientists of the implications of cognitive processes for decision-making, see Robert Axelrod, *Framework for a General Theory of Cognition and Choice* (Berkeley: Institute of International Studies, 1972), and Robert Axelrod, ed., *Structure of Decision: The Cognitive Maps of Political Elites* (Princeton: Princeton University Press, 1976).

4 Jervis, *Perception and Misperception in International Politics*, pp. 117-24, 187, 262-70. Jervis' argument is reminiscent of V. O. Key's thesis that dramatic historical events like the civil war and

the great depression significantly influenced the formation of party identification which then endured long after the event and the party's response to it. "A Theory of Critical Elections," *Journal of Politics,* 17 (February 1955); 3-18.

5 Ibid., pp. 239-48.

6 Ibid., pp. 17-42, et passim.

7 Ibid., pp. 187-91.

8 Ibid., pp. 193-95.

9 Ibid., pp. 128-43.

10 Leon Festinger, *A Theory of Cognitive Dissonance* (Stanford: Stanford University Press, 1957), and Leon Festinger, ed., *Conflict, Decision, and Dissonance* (Stanford: Stanford University Press, 1964); also Jack W. Brehm and Arthur Cohen, *Explorations in Cognitive Dissonance* (New York: Wiley, 1962); Elliot Aronson, "The Theory of Cognitive Dissonance," in Leonard Berkowitz, ed., *Advances in Experimental Social Psychology* (New York: Academic Press, 1967), IV, 15-17; Robert A. Wicklund and Jack W. Brehm, *Perspectives on Cognitive Dissonance* (Hillsdale, N.J.: Erlbaum, 1976). For a discussion of the literature, see Jervis, *Perception and Misperception in International Politics*, pp. 382-406; Irving L. Janis and Leon Mann, *Decision Making: A Psychological Analysis of Conflict, Choice, and Commitment* (New York: Free Press, 1977), pp. 309-38, 437-40.

11 Janis and Mann, *Decision Making*, p. 15.

12 Ibid., pp. 62-63.

13 Not only do the authors advance different explanations for cognitive failures, they also minimize the importance of the psychological principles upon which the opposing explanation is based. Jervis, *Perception and Misperception in International Politics,* pp. 356-81, devotes a chapter to analyzing the influence of desires and fears upon perceptions and concludes that "the conventional wisdom that wishful thinking pervades political decision-making is not supported by the evidence from either experimental or natural settings." For their part, Janis and Mann, *Decision Making,* p. 85, insist that cognitive consistency may be "a weak need" in many individuals. The effort by these analysts to discredit the principles underlying a different approach is certainly consistent with the principle of cognitive consistency.

14 Jervis, *Perception and Misperception in International Politics*, pp. 227-28.

15 See, Hans J. Morgenthau, "The Unfinished Business of United States Foreign Policy" and, "Vietnam: Another Korea?" in *Politics in the Twentieth Century*, vol. 2: *The Impasse of American Foreign Policy* (Chicago: University of Chicago Press, 1962), 8-16, 265-75; John Lukacs, *A New History of the Cold War*, 3d rev. ed. (Garden City, N.Y.: Doubleday, 1966), pp. 69-71, 161, 167; Robert E. Osgood, *Alliances and American Foreign Policy* (Baltimore: Johns Hopkins University Press, 1968), pp. 75-77; Stanley Hoffmann, *Gulliver's Troubles, or the Setting of American Foreign Policy* (New York: McGraw-Hill, 1968), pp. 140, 153-54; James A. Nathan and James K. Oliver, *United States Foreign Policy and World Order* (Boston: Little, Brown, 1976); John Lewis Gaddis, *Russia, the Soviet Union, and the United States: An Interpretive History* (New York: Wiley, 1978), pp. 187-89, 193-200, 207-13; Leslie H. Gelb with Richard K. Betts, *The Irony of Vietnam: The System Worked* (Washington, D.C.: Brookings Institution, 1979), pp. 78-79, 181-82.

16 Jervis, *Perception and Misperception in International Politics*, pp. 128-30.

17 Janis and Mann, *Decision Making*, pp. 79-80, 91-95.

18 Jervis, *Perception and Misperception in International Politics*, pp. 187-202.

19 Janis and Mann, *Decision Making*, pp. 74-79.

20 See D. F. Fleming, in *The Cold War and its Origins, 1917-1960*, 2 vols. (Garden City, N.Y.: Doubleday, 1961), Walter La Feber, in *America, Russia, and the Cold War, 1945-1966* (New York: Wiley, 1968), and Nathan and Oliver, in *United States Foreign Policy*, all of whom stress the importance of initial American images of the Soviet Union in shaping subsequent policy. For an interesting theoretical analysis of this problem, see, Glenn H. Snyder, " 'Prisoner's Dilemma' and 'Chicken' Models in International Politics," *International Studies Quarterly,* 15 (March 1971), 66-103; Jervis, in *Perception and Misperception in International Politics*, pp. 58-111, also stresses the self-fulfilling nature of foreign policy judgements as to the intentions of other nations.

21 Karl W. Deutsch, *The Nerves of Government* (New York: Free Press, 1963), p. 215.

22 The classic description of defense mechanisms is Anna Freud, *The Ego and the Mechanisms of Defense* 1936 (New York: International Universities Press, 1953).

B: DECISION MAKING

Theories of Crisis Decision Making

Ole R. Holsti

In memoirs written some years before he assumed the presidency, Richard Nixon wrote of crises as "mountaintop experiences" in which he often performed at his best: "Only then [in crises] does he discover all the latent strengths he never knew he had and which otherwise would have remained dormant."[1] He added:

> It has been my experience that, more often than not, taking a break is actually an escape from the tough, grinding discipline that is absolutely necessary for superior performance. Many times I have found that my best ideas have come when I thought I could not work for another minute and when I literally had to drive myself to finish the task before a deadline. Sleepless nights, to the extent that the body can take them, can stimulate creative mental activity.[2]

Others have appraised the effects of crisis on decision making in a similar vein, suggesting, for example, that "a decision maker may, in a crisis, be able to invent or work out easily and quickly what seems in normal times to both the 'academic' scholar and the layman to be hypothetical, unreal, complex or otherwise difficult."[3] More important, theories of nuclear deterrence presuppose rational and predictable decision processes, even during intense and protracted international crises. They assume that threats and ultimata will enhance calculation, control, and caution while inhibiting recklessness and risk-taking.[4] Deterrence theories, in short, tend to be sanguine about the ability of policy makers to be creative when the situation requires it — and never is that requirement greater than during an intense international crisis.

These observations appear to confirm the conventional wisdom that in crisis decision making necessity is indeed the mother of invention. Is there any reason to question the universal validity of that view? Fortunately, scenarios of inadequate decision making resulting in a nuclear war are thus far limited to novels and movies, but otherwise the evidence is less than totally reassuring. The recollections of those who have experienced intense and protracted crises suggest they may be marked at times by great skill in policy making, and at others by decision processes and outcomes

---

Reprinted with permission of Macmillan Publishing Company Inc. from *Diplomacy: New Approaches in History, Theory and Policy,* pp. 99-136, edited by Paul Gordon Lauren. Portions of the text have been deleted. Some footnotes have been deleted; those remaining have been renumbered.

that fail to meet even the most permissive standards of rationality. Some recall the "sense of elation that comes with crises,"[5] whereas others admit to serious shortcomings in their own performance during such situations. Indeed, although the definitive history of the Watergate episode remains to be written, available evidence suggests that Nixon's performance during the culminating crisis of his presidency was at best erratic, certainly falling far short of his own self-diagnosis as described above.

But anecdotes do not provide a sufficient basis for addressing the question: How do policy makers respond to the challenges and demands of crises? Do they tend to approach such situations with high motivation, a keen sense of purpose, extraordinary energy, and an enhanced capacity for creativity? Or, is their capacity for coping with complex problems sometimes impaired, perhaps to the point suggested by Richard Neustadt's phrase, "the paranoid reaction characteristic of crisis behavior"?[6]

This paper will address these questions by describing and analyzing several major theories of crisis decision making.... This will be followed by the presentation of several hypotheses concerning some of the effects of intense and protracted crisis on decision making, utilizing recent evidence from several social sciences, especially the field of psychology. Some of these hypotheses of crisis-induced stress will then be examined in the light of evidence from two classic case studies in diplomatic history: the 1914 crisis leading to the outbreak of World War I and, more briefly, the Cuban missile crisis of 1962. Finally, the conclusion will discuss some of the advantages and disadvantages of interdisciplinary research for psychologists, political scientists, and diplomatic historians.

. . .

CRISIS, STRESS, AND DECISION MAKING: SOME EVIDENCE FROM PSYCHOLOGY

One of the more interesting bodies of theory on crisis behavior is that concentrating upon individual stress. This approach, as indicated previously, focuses upon the impact of crisis-induced stress on certain aspects of cognitive performance that are critical in decision making. In assessing the potential impact of crisis on cognitive performance, it is important to do so against realistic standards. Cognitive limits on rationality include, as suggested by evidence from psychology, limits on the individual's capacity to receive, process, and assimilate information about the situation; an inability to generate the entire set of policy alternatives; fragmentary knowledge about the consequences of each option; and an inability to order preferences for all possible consequences on a single utility scale.[7] Because these constraints exist in all but the most trivial decision-making situations, it is not instructive to assess the impact on crises against a standard of synoptic rationality. A more modest and useful set of criteria might include an individual's ability to do the following:

Identify adequately the objectives to be fulfilled;
Survey the major alternative courses of action;
Estimate the probable costs and risks, as well as the positive consequences, of various alternatives (and, as a corollary, distinguish the possible from the probable);
Search for new information relevant to assessment of the options;
Maintain an open mind to new information, even that which calls into question the validity of preferred courses of action (and, as corollaries, discriminate between relevant and irrelevant information, resist premature cognitive closure, and tolerate ambiguity);
Assess the situation from the perspective of other parties;
Resist both defensive procrastination and premature decision;
Make adjustments to meet real changes in the situation (and, as a corollary, distinguish real from apparent changes).[8]

A vast body of theory and evidence suggests that intense and protracted crises tend to erode rather than enhance these cognitive abilities....

An important aspect of crises is that they are characterized by high stress for the individuals and organizations involved. That a severe threat to important values is stress inducing requires little elaboration. The element of surprise is also a contributing factor; there is evidence that unanticipated and novel situations are generally viewed as more threatening. Finally, crises are often marked by almost around-the-clock work schedules, owing to the severity of the situation (high threat), the absence of established routines for dealing with them (surprise), and the absence of extended decision time. Lack of rest and diversion, combined with excessively long working hours, are likely to magnify the stresses in the situation. Moreover, crisis decisions are rarely if ever analogous to the familiar multiple-choice question, in which the full range of options is neatly outlined. The theoretical universe of choices usually exceeds by a substantial margin the number that can or will be considered. Especially in unanticipated situations for which there are no established SOPs (standard operating procedures) or decision rules, it is necessary to search out and perhaps create alternatives. Thus, the decision process itself may be a significant source of stress, arising, for example, from efforts to cope with cognitive constraints on rationality, role factors, small group dynamics, and bureaucratic politics.

Some degree of stress is an integral and necessary precondition for individual or organizational problem solving; in its absence there is no motivation to act. Low levels of stress alert us to the existence of a situation requiring our attention, increase our vigilance and our preparedness to cope with it. Increasing stress to moderate levels may heighten our propensity and ability to find a satisfactory solution to the problem. Indeed, for some elementary tasks a rather high degree of stress may enhance performance, at least for limited periods of time. If the problem is qualitatively simple and performance is measured by quantitative criteria, stress can increase output. Our primary concern, however, is not with the effects of crisis on persons engaged in manual or routine tasks, but with its consequences on the performance of officials in leadership positions during major international crises. These are nearly always marked by complexity and ambiguity, and they usually demand responses which are judged by qualitative rather than quantitative criteria. It is precisely these qualitative aspects of performance that are most likely to suffer under high stress....

To summarize, in situations of high stress, "there is a narrowing of the cognitive organization at the moment; the individual loses broader perspective, he is no longer able to 'see' essential aspects of the situation and his behavior becomes, consequently, less adaptive."[9]

At this point we shall consider in more detail some potential consequences of stress for cognitive rigidity, span of attention, and time perspectives.

Cognitive rigidity. Charles Lindblom suggests that "a serious emergency or crisis often transforms a policy analyst's perceptions (and sometimes galvanizes his energies) with the result that he gets a new grasp on his problem."[10] But there is also evidence that the effects of stress on cognitive performance are often less benign. Persons experiencing intense stress tend to suffer increased cognitive rigidity, and erosion of general cognitive abilities, including creativity and the ability to cope with complexity. As a consequence, the range of perceived policy options may be narrow. The decision maker is likely to establish a dominant percept through which to interpret information, and to maintain it tenaciously in the face of information that might seem to call for a reappraisal. Often this percept is a familiar one transferred from previous situations (e.g., "lessons of history"), even though it may be inappropriate for the circumstances at hand,[11] and it is more likely to be characterized by stereotypes than by subtlety as the complexity of the psychological field is reduced. To change one's beliefs and theories each time some discrepant information is received is neither possible nor wise, but it is at least useful to be aware that evidence about an unfolding situation may be consistent with more than a single explanation.[12] A finding of special relevance for crisis decision making is that tolerance for ambiguity is reduced when there is high stress. Under these conditions individuals made decisions before adequate information was available, with the result that they performed much less capably than persons working under normal conditions. The combination of stress and uncertainty leads some persons to feel that "the worst would be better than this." Finally, caricatures of motivational structures may develop: the anxious become more anxious, the energetic become more energetic, the repressors become more repressive, and so on....

As a result of these effects of stress, search for information and policy options may be adversely affected in several ways. Other actors and their motives are likely to be stereotyped, for example, and the situation itself may be defined in overly simple, one-dimensional terms — such as, that it is a zero-sum situation, or that everything is related to everything else. The ability to invent non-obvious solutions to complex problems may also be impaired. Finally, complex problems are more likely to be defined by "what is already in" (the decision maker's beliefs, expectations, cognitive and emotional predispositions), and less by the "objective" attributes of the situation.

The inception of a crisis usually results in a sharply increased pace of individual and bureaucratic activity and, concomitantly, an increasing volume of communication. Conversely, information overload in a decision-making situation may itself be a source of serious stress. One way of coping with this phenomenon is to *narrow one's span of attention* to a few aspects of the decision-making task. This may be a functional strategy if it permits the executive to eliminate trivial distractions, filter out irrelevant information, and develop an agenda of priorities. However a number of costs may offset or even outweigh these benefits.... Unpleasant information and that which does not support preferences and expectations may fall by the wayside, unless it is of such an unambiguous nature that it cannot be disregarded. "All Presidents, at least in modern times," writes Sorensen, "have complained about their reading pile, and few have been able to cope with it. There is a temptation, consequently, to cut out all that is unpleasant."[13] Thus, more communication may in fact result in less useful and valid information being available to policy makers.

Time perspectives are also likely to be affected by high stress. For example, the ability to judge time is impaired in situations which increase anxiety. Thus, there appears to be a two-way relationship between time and stress. On the one hand, short decision time, a defining characteristic of crisis, is likely to increase the stress under which the executive must operate. On the other hand, increasing levels of stress tend to heighten the salience of time and to distort judgements about it. It has been found in "real life" crisis situations, as well as experimentally, that as danger increases there is a significant overestimation of how fast time is passing.

Perceived time pressure may affect decision making in several ways. A number of studies indicate that some time pressure can enhance creativity as well as the rate of performance, but most of the evidence suggests that beyond a moderate level it has adverse effects. Because complex tasks requiring feats of memory and inference suffer more from time pressure, its effects on the most important decisions — which are usually marked by complexity — are likely to be particularly harmful. In such situations there is a tendency to fix upon a single approach, to continue using it whether or not it proves effective, and to hang on to familiar solutions, applying them even to problems that may be substantially different.

Experimental research has often shown a curvilinear relationship between time pressure and performance. Under severe time pressure, normal subjects produce errors similar to those committed by schizophrenics. Another study revealed that, although a moderate increase in time pressure can increase the productivity of groups, an increase from low to high pressure has an adverse effect. Increasing the number of decisions required in a given period of time by a factor of five led to a fifteenfold rise in decision errors. There is, in addition, evidence that time pressure increases the propensity to rely upon stereotypes, disrupts both individual and group problem solving, narrows the focus of attention, and impedes the use of available information. Finally, both experimental and historical evidence indicates that high stress tends to result in a shorter time perspective and, as a consequence, a reduced resistance to premature closure.

When decision time is short, the ability to estimate the range of possible consequences arising from a particular policy choice is likely to be impaired. Both experimental and field research indicate that severe stress is likely to give rise to a single-minded concern for the present and immediate future at the sacrifice of attention to longer range considerations. The uncertainties attending severe crisis make it exceptionally difficult to follow outcomes from a sequence of actions and responses very far into the future. Increasing stress also tends to narrow the focus of attention, thereby further limiting perceptions of time to the more immediate future....

This brief overview of evidence is suggestive rather than exhaustive. Moreover, the emphasis has been on processes rather than on decision outputs and, just as we cannot assume that "good" processes will ensure high-quality decisions, we cannot assume that erratic processes will always result in low-quality decisions.... There is sufficient evidence, however, to call into question the universal validity of the premise that we always rise to the occasion in crises, drawing if necessary upon hidden reservoirs of strength. The evidence cited here suggests that among the more probable casualties of crises and the accompanying high stress are the very abilities that distinguish men from other species: to establish logical links between present actions and future goals; to search effectively for relevant policy options; to create appropriate responses to unexpected events; to communicate complex ideas; to deal effectively with abstractions; to perceive not only blacks and whites, but also to distinguish them from the many subtle shades of gray that fall in between; to distinguish valid analogies from false ones, and sense from nonsense; and, perhaps most important of all, to enter into the frames of reference of others. With respect to these precious cognitive abilities, the law of supply and demand seems to operate in a perverse manner; as crisis increases the need for them, it also appears to diminish the supply.

Suggestive as these models and theories of crisis decision making may be, they cannot substitute for evidence from actual foreign policy crises. Abstract and theoretical work must be examined and analyzed in terms of specific evidence — in this case, evidence from diplomatic history. Toward this end, the next two sections will utilize the "focused comparison" approach[14] — in which case studies aim not at a full historical description but at developing or testing explicit propositions of theoretical or policy relevance — and will explore several very specific aspects of individual stress in crisis decision making from the 1914 and Cuban missile crises.

DECISION MAKING IN THE 1914 CRISIS

The assassination of Archduke Franz Ferdinand on June 28, 1914, set off a chain of events that, within six weeks, brought all of the major powers of Europe into war. Soon after Prince von Bülow asked German Chancellor Bethmann Hollweg how the war had come about. "At last I said to him: 'Well, tell me, at least, how it all happened.' He raised his long, thin arms to heaven and answered in a dull exhausted voice: 'Oh — If I only knew.'" Another colleague wrote that "since the Russian mobilization the Chancellor gave one the impression of a drowning man."[15] Are these merely the self-serving recollections of war criminals or of fools whose incompetence visited upon the world a war of unparalleled devastation? If the answer is an affirmative one, the 1914 case is of little interest to the student of crisis, and the prescription is relatively simple — keep war criminals and fools out of high office.

But perhaps the answer to "how it all happened" is not quite so simple. The proposition to be explored in this section is that the individual stress model may help to explain the disastrous events of 1914. It should be made clear at the outset that what follows is an illustration and not an attempt at a full-scale explanation. It does not deal with the state of military technology, European alliance commitments, the balance of power, contingency plans of foreign and war offices, historical enmities, economic competition, or imperial ambitions and rivalries. All of these were important in 1914 and nothing in the analysis that follows is intended to deny their relevance. Nevertheless, these were also important in 1911, in 1908, and in other years that featured confrontations among the major powers. But, unless we adopt a deterministic view — as is implied, for example, by the popular metaphor of the assassination as a lighted match thrown into a keg of powder — it is appropriate to consider not only the European context in 1914, but also the decision processes. The focus here is on perceptions of time pressure and of policy options.

Perceptions of Time Pressure. To examine the effects of deepening crisis on perceptions of time pressure,...all documents written by high-ranking foreign policy officials were coded for evidence of time pressure as a factor in policy decisions....Statements of concern about decision time increased steadily (except in the case of Austria-Hungary), not only in absolute frequency, but even in relation to the total number of policy themes....

During the earliest period of the 1914 crisis, approximately two-thirds of the references to time focused on the desirability or necessity of early action by Austria-Hungary against Serbia. Count Alexander Hoyos, Chief of the Cabinet of the Austro-Hungarian Foreign Ministry, for example, wrote on July 7 that "from a military standpoint ...it would be much more favorable to start the war now than later since the balance of power would weigh against us in the future."[16] The view that time was working against the Dual Monarchy was supported, for Germany was exerting considerable pressure on its ally not to postpone a showdown. Gottlieb von Jagow, German Foreign Minister, wrote on July 15: "We are concerned at present with the preeminent political question, perhaps the last opportunity of giving the Greater-Serbia menace its death blow under comparatively favorable circumstances."[17] In contrast, the view in London, Paris, and St. Petersburg was initially one of relative lack of concern. There is no evidence that leaders in the capitals of the Entente nations felt themselves under any pressure of time to react to this latest episode of instability in the Balkans.

Time perceptions from July 21 through July 28 focused predominantly on the necessity of delaying the course of events in the Balkans. Once the content of the Austrian ultimatum became known, the forty-eight-hour time limit within which the Serbian government had to draft a reply became an immediate subject of concern. Some European officials recognized that the conflict in the Balkans might well engulf all Europe if existing alliance commitments were honored. Whereas both German and Austro-Hungarian leaders had frequently expressed the desirability of moving swiftly against Serbia, those in London, Paris, St. Petersburg, and Belgrade were especially concerned with the necessity of gaining the time which might be used to work out a peaceful settlement of Vienna's demands on Serbia. Although they were far from united on the details of policy, the single common theme in their proposals was the fear that precipitate action could lead only to war. Typical of diplomatic messages during this period was the assertion that "the immediate danger was that in a few hours Austria might march into Serbia and Russian Slav opinion demand that Russia should march to help Serbia; it would be very desirable to get Austria not to precipitate military action and so to gain more time."[18] By July 29 it was apparent that war between Austria-Hungary and Serbia could not be prevented. At the same time, it was increasingly evident that a chain reaction was in danger of being set off.

As late as August 1 many European leaders continued to express the belief that if time permitted the concert powers to be reconvened, general war might be avoided. British Foreign Secretary Grey wrote, for example: "I still believe that if only a little respite in time can be gained before any Great Power begins war it might be possible to secure peace."[19] By this time, however, the pressure of time had taken a different meaning for many decision makers. A major concern was that one's nation not be caught unprepared for the war which might break out.

The situation, as perceived by leaders in the major capitals of Europe, posed a terrible dilemma. It was widely recognized that more time would be required if a general European war were to be averted; above all, a moratorium on military operations was necessary. It was equally evident that military preparations could become the justification for similar actions by others. The German ambassador in St. Petersburg warned the Russian foreign minister that "the danger of every preparatory military measure lay in the counter measures of the other side."[20] But, increasingly, these considerations were overshadowed by the fear of disastrous consequences if a potential adversary gained even a momentary head start in mobilizing its armed forces. As early as July 24, the French minister of war, apprehensive about the outcome of the crisis in the Balkans, asserted that, for France, "first military precautions could not be delayed."[21] Although no *official* mobilization orders except those of Austria-Hungary and Serbia were issued until July 29, rumors and suspicions of undercover preparations were not wholly without foundation. On July 25 the Russian government decided to set into motion all of the preparations preliminary to mobilization. Despite a badly divided Cabinet, even the British were undertaking a number of important military preparations. Winston Churchill, First Lord of the Admiralty, for example, mobilized the British navy contrary to a decision of the Cabinet.

In the early hours of the morning of July 30, the Kaiser wrote on the margin of a message from the Czar: "...the Czar — as is openly admitted by him here — instituted 'mil[itary] measures which have *now come into force*' against Austria and us and as a matter of fact five days ago. Thus it is almost *a week ahead of us*. And these measures are for a *defense* against *Austria*, which is *in no way* attacking him!!! I can not agree to any more mediation, since the Czar who requested it has at the same time secretly mobilized behind my back. It is only a maneuver, in order to hold us back and to increase the start they have already got. My work is at an end!"[22] Later, the Kaiser added, "In view of the colossal war preparations of Russia now discovered, this is all too late, I fear. Begin! Now!"[23] On July 30, German Chancellor Bethmann Hollweg was also concerned with the disadvantages of delay: "...the military preparations of our neighbors, especially in the east, will force us to a speedy decision, unless we do not wish to expose ourselves to the danger of surprise."[24]

On the same day René Viviani, French premier, urged Russia to avoid provocative measures that might provide Germany with a pretext for a total or partial mobilization of its own forces. Nevertheless, the Russians decided in favor of general mobilization, German warnings notwithstanding. "In these conditions," according to Foreign Minister Sazonov, "Russia can only hasten its armaments and face the imminence of war and that it counts upon the assistance of its ally France; Russia considers it desirable that England join Russia and France without losing time."[25] In response to what was perceived as a mounting threat against its eastern frontiers, the German Empire proclaimed a "state of threatening danger of war" on July 31, dispatching a twelve-hour ultimatum to Russia demanding a cessation of military preparations along the border. Berlin then ordered mobilization on August 1. "We could not sit back quietly and wait to see whether a more commonsense view would gain the upper hand at Petersburg, while at the same time the Russian mobilization was proceeding at such speed, that, if the worst came, we should be left completely outstripped in a military sense."[26]

The French government simultaneously ordered general mobilization on August 1. General Joffre had earlier argued that "it is absolutely necessary that the government know that from this evening on, any delay of twenty-four hours applied to the calling up of reserves and to the sending of the telegram ordering covering troops will result in a backward movement of our troops, that is to say an initial abandonment of a part of our territory, either 15 or 20 kilometers every day of delay."[27] Although official British naval mobilization was delayed until August 2, many officials in London had advocated such action considerably earlier. Winston Churchill was perhaps the most energetic proponent of early military preparations.[28] Others included Arthur Nicolson, Permanent Under Secretary for Foreign Affairs, who said on July 31: "It seems to me most essential, whatever our future course may be in regard to intervention, that we should at once give orders for mobilization of the army.... Mobilization is a precautionary measure — and to my mind essential." Three days later he added that "we ought to mobilize today so that our expeditionary force may be on its way during the next week. Should we waver now we shall rue the day later."[29]

Thus, ten days after the full-scale mobilizations by Serbia and Austria-Hungary on July 25, each of the major European countries had called up its armed forces. As each mobilization was ordered, it was defended as a necessary reaction to a previous decision within the other coalition. And with each mobilization came assurances that it was a defensive measure, although in 1914 a decision to mobilize was commonly regarded as tantamount to an act of war. In the rush to mobilize no one wanted to be beaten to the draw, even though there was sometimes an awareness of the logical end of military measures and countermeasures.

In some cases the escalation of military actions and counteractions was sustained almost by accident, or by the failure to perceive the effects of one's own acts. The mobilization of the Russian Baltic fleet provides a good example. "On 25 July, when the Czar looked over the minutes and resolutions of the Council of Ministers of the 24th, he not only approved them by adding 'agreed,' but, where it was the question of mobilizing the districts of Kiev, Moscow, Odessa and Kazan and the Black Sea fleet, he inserted in his own hand 'and Baltic' without any of his Ministers drawing his attention to the fact that the mobilization of the Baltic fleet constituted an act of hostility toward Germany."[30] Although the Russian Baltic fleet was no match for the powerful German navy, the Kaiser apparently felt genuinely threatened. In response to Bethmann Hollweg's plea that the German fleet be left in Norway, he wrote: "There is a Russian Fleet! In the Baltic there are now five Russian torpedo boat flotillas engaged in practice cruises, which as a whole or in part can be at the Belts within sixteen hours and close them. Port Arthur should be a lesson! My Fleet has orders to sail for Kiel, and to Kiel it is going to sail!"[31]

This inquiry into time pressures associated with the 1914 crisis supports the hypothesis that one reaction to decisional stress is hypervigilance. Concern for time increased as the crisis deepened, and it is also clear that time pressures were related to the central rather than peripheral issues in the crisis. When there was a conflict between the need to delay action in order to seek nonmilitary means of resolving the crisis and the perceived needs of military preparedness, the latter consideration prevailed, in large part because so many officials throughout Europe felt that the costs of falling behind the adversary's timetable would be catastrophic. Many decisions during the crisis were undertaken in great haste, and the processes by which they were made were at times highly erratic. For example, the initial Russian decision for a general mobilization was followed shortly by an order for only a partial callup of forces, and then by another reversal to the original decision. In the meanwhile, when it became clear that the conflict between Serbia and Austria-Hungary might lead to a general European war, a series of highly contradictory messages was dispatched from Berlin to Vienna. Demands for restraint in some of them were offset by a telegram from Moltke stating that Austria-Hungary should immediately mobilize against Russia, and that Germany would soon follow suit.

Policy Options. One way of coping with decision stress is a form of bolstering, attributing to the adversary sole responsibility for choices and outcomes, while absolving oneself, owing to the absence of real alternatives. Data from the 1914 crisis provide some striking support for the proposition that, in a crisis situation, decision makers will tend to perceive the range of their own alternatives to be more restricted than those of their opponents. That is, they will perceive their own decision making to be characterized by *necessity* and *closed* options, whereas those of the adversary are characterized by *open* choices.

The 1914 documents are filled with such words as "must," "compelled," "obliged," "unable," "driven," "impossible," and "helpless," but these rarely occur except when the author is referring to the policies of his own nation. To students of strategy the assertions of the Kaiser, the Czar, and others that they were helpless once they had set their military machines into motion may appear to be a "real life" application of the tactics of *commitment*, "a device to leave the last clear chance to decide the outcome with the other party, in a manner that he fully appreciates; it is to relinquish further initiative, having rigged the incentives so that the other party must choose in one's favor."[32] This explanation may be valid for messages that were intended for wide circulation among officials in allied or enemy countries. On the other hand, the most "private" documents — those intended only for circulation within the various foreign offices — do not differ materially from the entire set of documents in respect to the findings reported here. The clearest evidence in support of this assertion is to be found in the Kaiser's marginal notations and in the various minutes of Eyre Crowe, Assistant Under-Secretary of State, in the British Foreign Office.

Even a cursory survey of the diplomatic documents reveals that, with the exception of Austria-Hungary, European leaders consistently perceived fewer options open to themselves than to their adversaries. Edward Grey, for example, who took the most active role in seeking mediation, wrote on July 24 that "we can do nothing for moderation unless Germany is prepared *pari passu* to do the same."[33] Until the final hours of the crisis, leaders in Berlin were opposed to mediation of the local conflict, in part because previous conferences called to settle international crises (such as Algeciras in 1906) had, in the eyes of the Kaiser and others, denied them the diplomatic victories to which they were entitled. According to Bethmann Hollweg, "We cannot mediate in the conflict between Austria and Serbia but possibly later between Austria and Russia."[34] Nor were the Russians inclined to mediation because, in the words of Sazonov, "we have assumed from the beginning a posture which we cannot change."[35]

But the same leaders who expressed varying degrees of inability to cope with the situation in the Balkans tended to perceive more freedom of action for members of the opposing alliance. After the outbreak of war between Serbia and Austria-Hungary, Grey wrote: "The whole idea of mediation or mediating influence was ready to be put into operation by any method that Germany could suggest if mine was not acceptable. In fact, mediation was ready to come into operation by any method that Germany thought possible if only Germany would 'press the button' in the interests of peace."[36]

The tendency to perceive one's own alternatives to be more restricted than those of the adversary is also evident in the reaction to the events leading up to general war. The reaction of German decision makers was typical. On the one hand, they asserted repeatedly that *they* had no choice but to take vigorous military measures against the threat to the east. "Then I must mobilize too!... He [Nicholas] expressly stated in his first telegram that he would be presumably forced to take measures that would lead to a European war. Thus he takes the responsibility upon himself."[37] On the other hand, they credited Russia with complete freedom to take the actions necessary to prevent war: "The responsibility for the disaster which is now threatening the whole civilized world will not be laid at my door. In this moment it still lies in your [Nicholas] power to avert it."[38] And Wilhelm, like the Czar, finally asserted that he had lost control of his own military and that only the actions of the adversary could stop further escalation: "On technical grounds my mobilization which had already been proclaimed this afternoon must proceed against two fronts, east and west as prepared. This cannot be countermanded because I am sorry your [George V] telegram came so late."[39] The same theme of a single option open to oneself, coupled with perceptions that the initiative for peace rested with the enemy, is evident in the French and Austrian statements regarding their own mobilizations.

An increasing sense of helplessness and resignation to the irresistible course of events is evident in many of the documents. On the day of the Serbian reply to the Austro-Hungarian ultimatum, Paul Cambon, French ambassador in London, stated that he saw "no way of halting the march of events."[40] In contrast to Edward Grey, who maintained the hope that the European powers would find a way to prevent a general war, Arthur Nicolson asserted on July 29, "I am of the opinion that the resources of diplomacy are, for the present, exhausted."[41] At the same time, in St. Petersburg, Sazonov wrote of the "inevitability of war" while in Berlin, the Kaiser, in one of the most vitriolic of his marginal notes, concluded that "we have proved ourselves helpless."[42]

Significantly contributing to the belief that options were severely restricted was the rigidity of the various mobilization plans. Austria-Hungary and Russia had more than one plan for mobilization, but once any one of them was set in motion, it could be altered only with great effort. The Russians could order either a general mobilization against both Germany and Austria-Hungary, or a partial one directed only at the latter. But, as Russian generals were to argue vehemently during the crucial days at the end of July, a partial mobilization would preclude a general one for months to come, leaving Russia completely at the mercy of Germany. According to General Dobrorolski, "The whole plan of mobilization is worked out ahead to its end in all its detail. When the moment has been chosen, one has only to press the button, and the whole state begins to function automatically with the precision of a clock's mechanism. ...Once the moment has been fixed, everything is settled; there is no going back; it determines mechanically the beginning of war."[43]

France and Germany each had but a single plan for calling up their armed forces and, in the case of Germany, political leaders were ill informed about the rigidity of mobilization and war plans. The Kaiser's last-minute attempt to reverse the Schlieffen plan — to attack only in the east — shattered Moltke, Chief of the German General Staff, who replied: "That is impossible, Your Majesty. An army of a million cannot be improvised. It would be nothing but a rabble of undisciplined armed men, without a commissariat....It is utterly impossible to advance except according to plan; strong in the west, weak in the east."[44]

Finally, all of the mobilization plans existed only on paper; except for the Russo-Japanese War, no major European power had mobilized since 1878. This fact rendered the plans all the more rigid and made military leaders responsible for carrying them out less likely to accept any last-minute modifications. It may also have added to the widely believed dictum that one did not mobilize for any purpose other than war.

Just as European leaders tended to perceive fewer alternatives open to themselves than to their adversaries, so they regarded their allies to be in a similar position vis-à-vis their enemies. On the one hand, German documents are replete with explanations that Austria was pursuing the *only* policy open to her and thus Germany could not play a moderating role in Vienna, although only four months earlier Wilhelm had stated that if Vienna gets into a war against the Slavs through "great stupidity," it would "leave us [Germany] quite cold."[45] On the other hand, the Kaiser appealed to England, apparently convinced that the latter could perform the very role which he felt was impossible for Germany — restraining the most belligerent member of the coalition. "Instead of making proposals for conferences, His Majesty the King should order France and Russia, frankly and plainly, at one and the same time — they were HIS ALLIES — to DESIST at once from the mobilization, remain NEUTRAL and await Austria's proposals, which I should immediately transmit as soon as I was informed of them.... I could do nothing more direct; it was for him to take hold now and prove the honesty of English love of peace."[46] The assumption of British freedom to determine the policy of her allies, coupled with restrictions on German policy, is nowhere as clear as in one of the Kaiser's marginal notes: "He [Grey] knows perfectly well, that if he were to say one single serious sharp warning word at Paris and Petersburg, and were to warn them to remain neutral, both would become quiet at once. But he takes care not to speak the word, and threatens us instead! Common cur! England *alone* bears the responsibility for peace and war, and not we any longer."[47]

This approach to the problem of allies was not confined to Berlin. Adducing arguments that were strikingly similar to those used by the Kaiser, British leaders denied their ability or willingness to dictate a policy of moderation in Paris or St. Petersburg. Nicolson wrote on July 29: "I do not think that Berlin quite understands that Russia cannot and will not stand quietly by while Austria administers a severe chastisement to Serbia. She does not consider that Serbia deserves it, and she could not, in view of that feeling and of her position in the Slav world, consent to it."[48] Grey assessed the requirements of his French ally in similar terms: "France did not wish to join in the war that seemed about to break out, but she was obliged to join in it, because of her alliance."[49] At the same time, however, he believed that Germany could constrain the cause of her ally: "But none of us could influence Austria in this direction unless Germany would propose and participate in such action in Vienna."[50] On July 28 Nicholas had appealed to his counterpart in Berlin: "To try and avoid such a calamity as a European war, I beg you in the name of our old friendship to do what you can to *stop* your allies from *going too far*."[51]

The few attempts made to restrain the militant members of each alliance were either halfhearted or too late. Typical was the advice of Sir Eyre Crowe, who had written on July 25: "The moment has passed when it might have been possible to enlist French support in an effort to hold back Russia. It is clear that France and Russia are decided to accept the challenge thrown to them." He expressed the opinion that it would be both impolitic and dangerous to try to change their minds.[52] Similarly, a last-minute German attempt to hold Austria in check failed. At 2:55 A.M., July 30, Bethmann Hollweg concluded a telegram to Vienna: "Under these circumstances we must urgently and impressively suggest to the consideration of the Vienna Cabinet that acceptance of mediation on the mentioned honorable conditions. The responsibility for the consequences that would otherwise follow would be an uncommonly heavy one both for Austria and for us."[53] A few minutes later, however, Moltke sent a wire to Vienna urging immediate mobilization against Russia, promising Germany's full support for such an action — even if it led to general war.[54]

DECISION MAKING DURING THE MISSILE CRISIS[55]

A single U-2 American surveillance plane took off on October 14, 1962, for a reconnaissance flight over Cuba. Immediately upon returning, its high-altitude cameras were unloaded. After intensive study of the developed films, intelligence analysts uncovered unmistakable evidence of two medium-range ballistic missile (MRBM) sites in areas previously photographed and found to be empty.

Overflights three days later confirmed these reports and revealed nine sites — 36 launch positions — six for the 1,100-mile MRBM and three for 2,200-mile intermediate-range ballistic missiles (IRBM) in various states of readiness. Thus began the most serious international crisis of the nuclear era, a confrontation during which President Kennedy estimated that the chances of a nuclear war between the United States and the Soviet Union were one in three.

The 1914 and Cuban situations were similar in a number of respects and differed in many others. The similarity of present interest is that both episodes conform to the definition of crisis used here. Despite widespread rumors of Soviet missile installations in Cuba, photographic evidence of their presence was a surprise to virtually all officials in Washington, including the President; the rate of construction on the missile sites made it evident that any decision to prevent their completion could not long be delayed; and, with the exception of Secretary of Defense Robert McNamara, all who joined the American decision group interpreted the Soviet move as a serious threat to national security. As one participant in these discussions put it: "Everyone round the table recognized that we were in a major crisis. We didn't know, that day, if the country would come through it with Washington intact."[56]

The most significant difference between these two events is that the 1914 crisis led to a world war, whereas the Cuban confrontation was resolved without recourse to violence. Thus, the situation that confronted national leaders in the two crises shared a number of attributes (surprise, high threat, short decision time), but the decisions they made led to significantly different results: peaceful settlement versus a world war. In an attempt to explain the different outcomes, the remainder of this section examines several aspects of the decision-making process in 1962, again with special attention to time pressure and the search for and appraisal of alternatives.

Perceptions of Time Pressure. Several sources of time pressure impinged on the President and his advisers during the missile crisis. Initially, there was the need to formulate a policy before the Soviets were alerted by the stepped-up U-2 flights to the fact that their launching installations had been discovered. Conversely, once developments in Cuba became public knowledge, there would be no further time for deliberation and debate on the proper response.

An overriding concern throughout the period was the knowledge that construction on the missile sites was continuing at a rapid pace. The first photographic evidence of construction activities in Cuba indicated that they would be operational within a week to ten days. American officials perceived that their task would become immeasurably more difficult once construction on the launching sites was completed: "For all of us knew that, once the missile sites under construction became operational, and capable of responding to any apparent threat or command with a nuclear volley, the President's options would be dramatically changed."[57] Thus, the situation did not compel a reflex-like response — at least, as it was defined by the President. But in relation to the task at hand decision time was indeed short, and all first-hand accounts of decision making during the Cuban crisis, especially that of Robert Kennedy, are replete with indications of time pressure.

Despite the sense of urgency created by these deadlines, the President and his advisers sought to reduce the probability that either side would respond by a "spasm reaction." Efforts were made to delay taking overt actions as long as the situation permitted. Equally important, discussions in Washington revealed a sensitivity for the time pressures under which the adversary was operating. There was a concern that Premier Khrushchev not be rushed into an irrevocable decision; it was agreed among members of the decision group that "we should slow down the escalation of the crisis to give Khrushchev time to consider his next move."[58] Measures designed to increase Soviet decision time included the President's management of the naval quarantine. He ordered American ships to delay intercepting Soviet vessels until the last possible moment, *and had the order transmitted in the clear.* The Soviets, who were certain to intercept the message, would thus learn that they had additional time in which to formulate a response to the blockade. This ploy also revealed a sophisticated understanding of the social psychology of communication; information from a distrusted source is more likely to be believed if it is obtained through the recipient's own efforts. The Soviet decision on October 25 to slow down the westward progress of their ships in mid-Atlantic can also be interpreted as an effort to lengthen decision time.

A comparison of the 1914 and 1962 crises points to the importance of a subjective rather than an objective definition of decision time. Owing to vast differences in military capabilities, time was objectively of far greater importance in 1962 than in 1914. Hence, Soviet and American leaders were no less aware of time pressures and of the potential costs of delaying action than were their counterparts in 1914. But they also perceived the dangers of acting in haste, and they were successful in mitigating the most severe dangers attending such pressures. They resisted the pressures for premature decisions and took a number of actions which avoided putting their adversaries in a position of having to respond in haste. President Kennedy later acknowledged that the ability to delay a decision after receipt of the photographic evidence of missile sites was crucial to the *content* of American policy: "If we had had to act on Wednesday [October 17], in the first 24 hours, I don't think probably we would have chosen as prudently as we finally did, the quarantine against the use of offensive weapons."[59]

Policy Options. During the missile crisis, the search for alternatives was intimately related to time pressures; in the words of Arthur Schlesinger, "The deadline defined the strategy."[60] Pressures of time notwithstanding, American policy makers made efforts to prevent premature foreclosure of options. McGeorge Bundy noted that upon receiving the first news of the photographic evidence, "his [Kennedy's] first reaction was that we must make sure, and were we making sure, and would there be evidence on which he could decide that this was in fact really the case."[61] As late as October 18, a series of alternatives was being considered pending more accurate information, and while the decision to institute a blockade was being hammered out, open discussion of the alternatives was encouraged. The President recalled that "though at the beginning there was a much sharper division...this was very valuable, because the people involved had particular responsibilities of their own."[62] Another participant in the crisis decision group asserted that President Kennedy, aware that discussion of alternatives in the National Security Council would be more frank in his absence, encouraged the group to hold preliminary meetings without him. Thus, the eventual decision was reached by relatively open and frank discussion.

Six alternative responses emerged from the initial discussions between the President's advisers. Ultimately, the choice narrowed down to the blockade and the air strike. Initially, the option of a sudden air strike against the missile sites had strong support among most of the conferees, including that of the President. An informal vote is reported to have revealed an 11-6 majority in favor of the blockade.[63] The United States Air Force could not guarantee, however, that an air strike would be 100 percent effective. The blockade did not necessarily guarantee success; on the other hand, it did not rule out further measures. After much shifting of positions, the blockade option was selected, partly on the reasoning that "the course we finally adopted had the advantage of permitting other steps, if this one was unsuccessful. In other words, we were starting, in a sense, at a minimum place."[64]

The desire to avoid killing Soviet troops also weighed heavily against the air strike option. The blockade shifted the immediate burden of decision concerning the use of violence to Premier Khrushchev and, should the blockade have proved unsuccessful, it did not preclude later employment of a "much more massive action."[65] By adopting that strategy, no irrevocable decisions on the use of violence had been made and multiple options remained for possible future actions by the United States. At the same time, Soviet leaders were given the time and the opportunity to assess their own choices. Thus, unlike several of the key foreign policy officials in the 1914 crisis, those in October 1962 seemed to perceive a close relationship between their own actions and the options of their adversaries. According to Theodore Sorensen, "We discussed what the Soviet reaction would be to any possible move by the United States, what our reaction with them would have to be to that Soviet reaction, and so on, trying to follow each of those roads to their ultimate conclusion."[66]

American decision makers also displayed a sensitivity for the position and perspective of the adversary, trying to insure that a number of options other than total war or total surrender were available to Soviet leaders. An important advantage of the blockade over other strategies was that it appeared to avoid placing Soviet leaders in that situation. An air strike on the missile bases or invasion of the island would have left Soviet leaders only the alternatives of capitulating to the United States or of counterattacking. In that case, the latter might have seemed the less distasteful course. In disagreeing with General Curtis LeMay's optimistic assessment of the likely Soviet response to air raids on the missile installations, the President asserted, "They, no more than we, can let things go by without doing something."[67] A blockade, on the other hand, gave the Soviet government a choice between turning back the weapons-bearing ships or running the blockade.

By October 26 it seemed clear that, Khrushchev's earlier threats to the contrary notwithstanding, Soviet ships would not challenge the blockade. Despite the advent of negotiations, however, it was far from certain that the Soviet missiles would be removed from Cuba; indeed, there was ample evidence of an accelerated pace of construction on the launching sites in Cuba that, it was then believed, would be completed by October 30. Thus, the question of further steps to be taken in case the blockade proved insufficient to force withdrawal of all offensive missiles again confronted American leaders. Among the options considered were: tightening the blockade to include all commodities other than food and medicine, increased low-level flights over Cuba for purposes of reconnaissance and harassment, action within Cuba, an air strike, and an invasion. In the meanwhile, the President's brother delivered an ultimatum to the Soviet ambassador, and both direct and indirect bargaining resulted in a settlement.[68] Just before "the most serious meeting ever to take place at the White House"[69] was to have started, Premier Khrushchev agreed to withdraw all offensive missiles from Cuba in exchange for President Kennedy's pledge not to invade Cuba.

Time pressure and the search for alternatives are key elements in crisis decision making. Data from 1914 indicate that these factors did in fact vary as crisis-induced stress increased, and these changes apparently had serious consequences for critical policy decisions. A more impressionistic analysis of the Cuban confrontation suggests that the ability of American decision makers to mitigate some of the adverse consequences of crisis contributed to its eventual peaceful resolution. In many respects, President Kennedy's behavior during the Cuban crisis appeared consciously designed to avert repetition of the 1914 disaster. Indeed, he frequently referred to the decision processes leading up to World War I as a source of negative lessons. Having read Barbara Tuchman's *The Guns of August*, for example, the President said: "I am not going to follow a course which will allow anyone to write a comparable book about this time, *The Missiles of October*. If anybody is around to write after this, they are going to understand that we made every effort to find peace and every effort to give our adversary room to move. I am not going to push the Russians an inch beyond what is necessary."[70] Even when discussing the Cuban missile crisis some weeks after its conclusion, he asserted, "Well now, if you look at the history of this century where World War I really came through a series of misjudgments of the intentions of others...it's very difficult to always make judgments here about what the effect will be of our decisions on other countries."[71] Yet the ability of American and Soviet leaders to avoid a nuclear Armageddon in October 1962 is not assurance that even great skill in crisis management will always yield a peaceful solution. As President Kennedy said some months later, referring to the missile crisis, "You can't have too many of those."[72]

CONCLUSION

The approach described here suffers from some clear limitations that should be addressed explicitly. Several objections might be raised about the relevance of the individual stress model of crisis decision making.[73] Does it adequately take into account the executive's prior experience in coping with crises? Will not experience, when combined with selective recruitment and promotion, weed out those who cannot stand "the heat in the kitchen" well before they reach top leadership positions? It is true that individuals differ in abilities to cope with crises and stress. The peak, breaking point and slope of the "inverted U" curve may vary not only according to the complexity of the task, but also across individuals. Thus, the point at which increasing stress begins to hamper cognitive performance, and the rate at which it does so, is not the same for all persons. But only the most optimistic will assume that the correlation between the importance of the executive's role and ability to cope with crisis-induced stress approaches unity. Richard Nixon's behavior during the Watergate episode is a grim reminder to the contrary. Perhaps even more sobering is Robert Kennedy's recollection of the Cuban missile crisis: "That kind of [crisis-induced] pressure does strange things to a human being, even to brilliant, self confident, experienced men. For some it brings out characteristics and strengths that perhaps they never knew they had, and for others the pressure is too overwhelming."[74]

A second possible objection is that, whereas the emphasis here has been on the individual's cognitive performance under conditions of crisis-induced stress, foreign policy leaders rarely need to face crises alone. They can instead draw upon support and resources from both advisory groups and the larger organizations of which they are a part. This point is valid, but on further examination it is not wholly comforting. There is some evidence that during crises advisory groups may be vulnerable to such malfunctions as "groupthink." For various reasons, including perceived needs for secrecy, easier coordination, and the like, decision-making groups tend to become smaller during crises. There may be, moreover, a tendency to consult others less as the pressure of time increases, as well as to rely more heavily upon those who support the prevailing "wisdom." Finally, leaders differ not only in their "executive styles" (note, for example, the strikingly different problem-solving styles exhibited by presidents Coolidge, Franklin Roosevelt, and Nixon), but also in their abilities to employ advisory groups effectively — that is, in ways that may help them to counteract some of the potentially adverse consequences of crisis. Even the same executive may demonstrate great skill during one crisis and equal ineptitude in another instance. John F. Kennedy's use of advisers during the missile crisis and the Bay of Pigs fiasco are illustrative in this respect.

Some more specific limitations can also be identified. Certainly, the two cases are not representative of all crises in any statistical sense. Thus, the results described here should be viewed as illustrative rather than definitive. Moreover, the analysis focused on very limited aspects of crises, to the exclusion of many other potentially fruitful comparisons....In any case, the rather different findings for the 1914 and 1962 crises raise a series of additional questions — about the necessary and sufficient conditions for avoiding decision-making malfunctions — that have barely been touched upon here. The individual stress model focuses on a few aspects of crisis and consciously excludes others. By posing some questions and not others, we have limited the range of answers. Every model or theoretical perspective does so, with some inevitable losses and, it is to be hoped, at least some commensurate gains. The proper question to ask, then, is not whether this approach serves as a complete model for all crises — the answer is unquestionably negative — but whether it directs our attention to important phenomena that might otherwise remain beyond our purview.

Variants of the individual stress model of crisis decision making have been employed in other studies and, not surprisingly, the pattern of findings is mixed....In their impressive study of a dozen international crises — including Fashoda (1898), Bosnia (1908-1909), Munich (1938), Iran (1945-1946), and Berlin (1948-1949) — Snyder and Diesing found no evidence of adverse consequences arising from high stress.[75] Yet they did report that misperception, miscalculation, and other cognitive malfunctions were common occurrences during the crises. Because their research was not designed to test for either the existence or consequences of crisis-induced stress, perhaps it is premature to count this study as definitive evidence against the propositions advanced here. On the other hand, drawing on his research on Israeli behavior during the crises of 1956, 1967, and 1970, Brecher found strong support for the hypotheses that time will be perceived as more salient, that decision makers will become more concerned with the immediate rather than the distant future, and that they will perceive the range of alternatives open to themselves to be narrow.[76]...

These mixed results are not surprising, nor should they occasion premature conclusions about lack of significant research progress or the future of this approach for diplomatic history, theory, or even policy. Other studies could be cited in support of and against the individual stress model, but this does not appear to be the most fruitful way of proceeding. Sustained interest in the effects of crisis-induced stress does not depend on finding that *every* crisis from the historical past resulted in substandard decision-making performance, any more than concern for the consequences of smoking must await evidence that all smokers develop lung cancer. The much more interesting and important questions emerge precisely at the point of recognizing that the dangers and opportunities inherent in crises can give rise to various patterns of coping. At that point our attention is directed to a series of further questions — for example, what are the decision-making structures, personal attributes of leaders, strategies of crisis management, and other variables that are associated with more or less successful coping — that have barely been touched upon in this chapter. It is at this point that we can perhaps begin to appreciate the value of interdisciplinary approaches for the study of crises decision making.

ENDNOTES

1 Richard M. Nixon, *Six Crises* (New York: Doubleday, 1962), p. xvi.

2 Ibid., p. 105.

3 Herman Kahn, *On Escalation: Metaphors and Scenarios* (New York: Praeger, 1965), p. 38.

4 The literature on deterrence is enormous. Recent and indispensable are Alexander L. George and Richard Smoke, *Deterrence in American Foreign Policy: Theory and Practice* (New York: Columbia University Press, 1974); and Patrick M. Morgan, *Deterrence: A Conceptual Analysis* (Beverly Hills: Sage, 1977).

5 Chris Argyris, *Some Causes of Organizational Ineffectiveness within the Department of State* (Washington, D. C.: Center for International Systems Research, Department of State Publication 8180, 1967), p. 42.

6 Richard E. Neustadt, *Alliance Politics* (New York: Columbia University Press, 1970), p. 116.

7 Herbert Simon, *Organizations* (New York: Wiley, 1958), p. 138.

8 Somewhat different lists appear in Morgan, *Deterrence*, pp. 102-103; and in Irving Janis and Leon Mann, *Decision Making* (New York: Free Press, 1977).

9 Sheldon J. Korchin, "Anxiety and Cognition," in

Constance Sheerer ed., *Cognition: Theory, Research, Promise* (New York: Harper and Row, 1964), p. 63.

10 Charles E. Lindblom, *The Policy-Making Process* (Englewood Cliffs, N.J.: Prentice-Hall, 1968), p. 22.

11 For relevant historical evidence on this point, see Ernest R. May, *"Lessons" of the Past: The Use and Misuse of History in American Foreign Policy* (New York: Oxford University Press, 1973); and Robert Jervis, *Perception and Misperception in International Politics* (Princeton: Princeton University Press, 1976).

12 Robert Jervis, "Hypotheses on Misperception," *World Politics,* 20 (April 1968), 454-479; and Robert Jervis, *Perception and Misperception.*

13 Theodore C. Sorensen, Decision-Making in the White House (New York: Columbia University Press, 1964), p. 38.

14 See George and Smoke, *Deterrence in American Foreign Policy* (New York: Columbia University Press, 1974), pp. 94-97; Sidney Verba, "Some Dilemmas in Comparative Research," *World Politics,* 20 (October 1967), 111-127; Bruce M. Russett, "International Behavior Research: Case Studies and Cumulation," in Michael Haas and Henry Kariel eds., *Approaches to the Study of Political Science* (Scranton, Pa.: Chandler, 1970); ...James N. Rosenau, "Moral Fervor, Systematic Analysis, and Scientific Consciousness in Foreign Policy Research," in Austen Ranney ed., *Political Science and Public Policy* (Chicago: Markham, 1968); and Glenn D. Paige, *The Korean Decision: June 24-30, 1950* (New York: Free Press, 1968), pp. 3-18. The latter study is also an important contribution to the study of crisis decision making.

15 Prince Bernhard von Bülow, *Memoirs of Prince von Bülow*, 3 vols. (Boston: Little, Brown, 1932), III: 166; and Alfred von Tirpitz, *My Memoirs* (London: Hurst and Blackett, 1919), p. 280.

16 Quoted in Luigi Albertini, *Origins of the War of 1914*, 2 vols. (New York: Oxford University Press, 1953), II, 122.

17 Max Montgelas and Walter Schücking eds., *Outbreak of the World War, German Documents Collected by Karl Kautsky* (New York: Oxford University Press. 1924), #48. [Hereafter this source will be cited as Germany.]

18 Great Britain, Foreign Office, *British Documents on the Origins of the War, 1898-1914*, 11 vols., ed. G. P. Gooch and Harold Temperely, vol. 11, *Foreign Office Documents June 28th-August 4th, 1914*, collected by J. W. Headlam-Morely (London: His Majesty's Stationery Office, 1926), #99. [Hereafter cited as Great Britain.]

19 Great Britain, #411.

20 Germany, #343.

21 France, Commission de Publication des documents relatifs aux origines de la guerre, 1914, *Documents Diplomatiques Français (1871-1914),* 3rd series, vols. 10, 11 (Paris: Imprimerie nationale, 1936), #32. [Hereafter cited as France.]

22 Germany, #390.

23 Germany, #433.

24 Germany, #451.

25 France, #305.

26 Germany, #529.

27 France, #401.

28 Winston S. Churchill, *The World Crisis, 1911-1914* (New York: Scribner's, 1928),p. 211.

29 Great Britain, #368, 446.

30 Albertini, *Origins of the War in 1914*, II: 558.

31 Germany, #221.

32 Thomas Schelling, *The Strategy of Conflict* (New York: Oxford University Press, 1963), pp. 137-138.

33 Great Britain, #103.

34 Germany, #247.

35 Russia, Komissiia po izdaiiu dokumentov epokhi imperializma, *Mezhdunarodnye otnosheniia v epokhe imperializma*; dokument 12 arkhivov tsarkogo i vremennogo pravitel'stv 1878-1917, gg. 3d series, vols. 4, 5 (Moscow and Leningrad: Gosudarstvennoe sotsial'no-ekonomicheskoe izdatal'stvo, 1931, 1934), #118. [Hereafter cited as Russia.]

36 Great Britain, #263.

37 Germany, #399.

38 Germany, #480.

39 Germany, #575.

40 France, #38.

41 Great Britain, #252.

42 Russia, #221; Germany, #401.

43 Quoted in Sidney B. Fay, *The Origins of the World War* (New York: Macmillan, 1930 ed.), II, 481.

44 Moltke, *Erinnerungen*, quoted in Virginia Cowles, *The Kaiser* (New York: Harper and Row, 1964), pp. 343-346.

45 Quoted in Fay, *The Origins of the World War*, II: 207.

46 Germany, #474.

47 Germany, #368.

48 Great Britain, #264.

49 Great Britain, #447.

50 Great Britain, #99

51 Russia, #170.

52 Great Britain, #101.

53 Germany, #395.

54 Quoted in Fay, *The Origins of the World War*, II: 509.

55 The literature on the missile crisis is immense, including memoirs of participants, polemics, descriptive accounts, and explicitly comparative or theoretical studies. Of the latter genre, some of the most interesting are A.L. George, D.K. Hall, and N.E. Simons, *The Limits of Coercive Diplomacy* (Boston: Little, Brown, 1971); George and Smoke, *Deterrence in American Foreign Policy* (New York: Columbia University Press, 1974); G. Allison, *The Essence of Decision* (Boston: Little, Brown, 1971); Roberta Wohlstetter, "Cuba and Pearl Harbor," *Foreign Affairs,* 43 (July 1965), 691-707; G. Snyder and P. Diesing, *Conflict Among Nations* (Princeton: Princeton University Press, 1977); G. Paige, "Comparative Case Analysis of Crisis Decisions: Korea and Cuba," in C. Hermann, ed., *International Crises: Insights from Behavioral Research* (New York: Free Press, 1972); O. Young, *The Politics of Force* (Princeton: Princeton University Press, 1968); J. Snyder, "Rationality at the Brink," *World Politics,* 30 (April 1978), 345-365; and Albert and Roberta Wohlstetter, "Controlling the Risks in Cuba," *Adelphi Paper,* 17 (London: International Institute for Strategic Studies, 1965).

56 Douglas Dillon, quoted in Elie Abel, *The Missile Crisis* (Philadelphia: Lippincott, 1966), p. 48.

57 Theodore Sorensen, *Decision-Making in the White House* (New York: Columbia University Press, 1963), p. 31.

58 National Broadcasting Company, "Cuba: The Missile Crisis" (mimeo. transcript, February 9, 1964), p. 12.

59 Columbia Broadcasting System, "Conversation with President Kennedy" (mimeo. transcript, December 17, 1963), pp. 2-3.

60 Arthur M. Schlesinger, Jr., *A Thousand Days* (New York: Houghton Mifflin, 1965), p. 804.

61 NBC, "Cuba," p. 14.

62 CBS, "Conversation with President Kennedy," p. 4.

63 Schlesinger, *A Thousand Days*, p. 808.

64 CBS, "Conversation with President Kennedy," p. 4.

65 Ibid.

66 NBC, "Cuba," p. 17.

67 Quoted in Snyder and Diesing, *Conflict Among Nations*, p. 301.

68 The important role of the ultimatum in settlement of the missile crisis is discussed in more detail by George, Hall, and Simons, *The Limits of Coercive Diplomacy*.

69 NBC, "Cuba," p. 42.

70 Robert F. Kennedy, *Thirteen Days* (New York: Norton, 1969), p. 127.

71 CBS, "Conversation with President Kennedy," p. 3.

72 Theodore Sorensen, *Kennedy* (New York: Harper and Row, 1965), p. 726.

73 Interesting alternative explanations for the outcome in 1914, for example, may be found in Bruce M. Russett, "Cause, Surprise, and No Escape," *Journal of Politics,* 24 (February 1962), 3-22; and Lancelot L. Farrar, Jr., "The Limits of Choice: July 1914 Reconsidered," *Journal of Conflict Resolution,* 16 (March 1972), 1-24. Other approaches to crisis decision making that have not received attention here include those that emphasize aspects of personality; see, for example, Lawrence S. Falkowski, *Presidents, Secretaries of State, and Crises in U.S. Foreign Relations;* James David Barber, *The Presidential Character* (Englewood Cliffs, N.J.: Prentice-Hall, 1972); and Thomas M. Mongar, "Personality and Decision-Making: John F. Kennedy in Four Crisis Decisions," *Canadian Journal of Political Science,* 2 (June 1962), 200-225. The psychobiological effects of crisis are discussed in Thomas C. Wiegele, "Models of Stress and Disturbance in Elite Political Behaviors: Psychological Variables and Political Decision-Making," in

Robert S. Robins, ed., *Psychopathology and Political Leadership* (New Orleans: Tulane Studies in Political Science, 1977) and in the same author's "Decision Making in an International Crisis: Some Biological Factors," *International Studies Quarterly,* 17 (September 1973), 295-335.

74 Robert F. Kennedy, "Thirteen Days: The Story About How the World Almost Ended," *McCall's*, November 1968, 148.

75 Snyder and Diesing, *Conflict Among Nations.*

76 Michael Brecher, "Research Findings and Theory-Building in Foreign Policy Behavior," in Patrick J. McGowan ed., *Sage International Yearbook of Foreign Policy Studies* (Beverly Hills: Sage, 1974), II, 71.

THE SOCIETY 3

ORGANIZATIONAL AND BUREAUCRATIC POLITICS A

The Future of Crisis Management

The Essence of Decision: Explaining the Cuban Missile Crisis

Bureaucratic Politics and the Westminster Model

External Bargaining and Internal Bargaining

GROUP POLITICS AND SOCIAL CONFLICT B

Domestic Interest Groups and Canadian and American Policy: The Case of the Arab Boycott

Domestic Conflict and the Origins of the First World War: The British and German Cases

INTRODUCTION

Most of the important decisions about conflict and its management are not made by a single individual working in isolation. Even a very powerful president consults with a handful of senior counsellors and solicits advice from the heads of large and powerful government agencies who identify and explore the obvious policy options. At times, policy can be determined by a group which reviews the alternatives collectively as a prelude to choice. In parliamentary systems of government, for example, policy is often brought to cabinet for final decision, and although the prime minister is first among equals and an essential member of any "winning" coalition, not infrequently cabinet votes determine the final outcome. Even in the Soviet Union analysts look increasingly to the collective basis of policy making. Of course, the relative impact of the individual leader and the group will differ substantially, depending very much on the kind of political regime and the nature of the issues in conflict. Scholars have also moved beyond the small inner circle of policy makers to examine the role of large and powerful bureaucratic organizations and the interplay of competing interest groups in the wider social context in which policy is made.

Analysis of the impact of the group context of policy making on conflict and its management raises obvious questions. What kinds of groups are particularly important? How do we study the effect of these groups? What impact do groups have on strategies of conflict management? There is, of course, no agreed set of answers to these questions. Scholars and policy makers conceive the policy making process differently and identify different groups as central. We can distinguish broadly between those who emphasize concentration of political power, focusing on consensus and cooperation among key group members, and those who look to the diffusion of political power, explaining policy as the outcome of conflict among groups. At least four approaches, approaches that differ in scope and in content, treat the impact of the group on international conflict and its management.

The obvious place to begin is with the immediate circle of influential policy makers, sometimes referred to as the "royal court," that surrounds the principal leaders.[1] Social psychologists look to small group dynamics to explain policy outcomes and argue that the impact of the group on policy depends very much on what kind of group it is and the quality of procedures that it uses. A second approach moves outside the small circle of key advisers to look at the institutional context of policy making. It pays particular attention to the diffusion of political power and to the impact of organizational routines and "bureaucratic politics" on the content and coherence of policy. A third approach casts its net beyond formal institutions to explain the fundamentals of strategies of conflict management. Focusing on the concentration of power, this explanation argues that a small elite dominates and controls the policy process, shapes public attitudes toward conflict and its management, and drives policy in the direction that benefits its narrowly defined interests. Basic to the argument is the homogeneity of the elite, whose consensus is interest-based.[2] Finally, some scholars move outside the policy making process entirely and, using a pluralist model, explore the impact of broadly based interest groups in the wider context of a diffusion of power in society. Generally, social psychologists and elite theorists, although they differ on almost everything else, concur that consensus is the enemy of effective conflict management, while the pluralist analysis of competition within governmental institutions and within society as a whole points to conflict as the principal impediment to more rational policy. Let us look briefly at each of these in turn.

Social psychologists pay attention to the dynamics of a group, to the ways it works. Especially important are the procedures it uses, the quality of discussion, and the openness of its methods. Irving Janis argues that small groups of senior policy makers are prone to the pathology of "group think": their overriding objective is to preserve the cohesion of their group rather than to make a rational decision. Consequently, members are intolerant of criticism, likely to ignore important costs of a preferred option, and express impatience with others who refuse to be team players, who do not "get on board."[3] At the extreme, members who are frequently critical are ostracized and excluded from policy deliberations. This pattern of group decision making compounds the individual deviations from rational norms that psychologists document so extensively.

"Group think" was not uncommon in the governments of pre-1914 Europe, where dissident members were often encouraged to leave. It was also characteristic of the Johnson White House in the later years, when a beleaguered president emphasized loyalty and group cohesiveness at the expense of careful and open-ended consideration of policy alternatives. A false unanimity emerged, premised on the superior morality and intelligence of members who had unique access to policy-relevant information. Janis argues that "group think" is a powerful explanation of the repeated escalation of the war in Vietnam. However, pathological policy making is not necessarily a consequence of group decisions. Janis suggests that it is possible for a group to structure its procedures carefully, to extend the search for options and evidence, to build in dissent and a devil's advocate. He considers ExCom under President Kennedy in 1962 an optimal decision making group.

Richard Ned Lebow, in his discussion of strategies of crisis management, is far more pessimistic in his evaluation of the prospects of an improved policy process. Reviewing the same record in 1962, Lebow argues that the ExCom exhibited many of the characteristics of "group think": the process was promotional rather than analytic and careful. Astutely, he points to the paradox inherent in the analyses of those who document pathologies in collective decision making but hope for rational remedies.

Graham Allison, in a classic analysis, challenges the fundamental concept of choice as the deliberate and purposive action of leaders, a concept that pervades Western thinking and informs all the "rational" models of policy making. Government, he insists, is not a unitary actor. Power is not concentrated, but is diffused at the top among a conglomerate of semi-feudal, loosely allied organizations. Leaders who sit at the top of the pyramid perceive policy problems through organizational sensors. The larger political context shapes what we expect to see or even what we want to see: where we sit determines where we stand and what we see. Role and interest are important determinants of preferred strategies of conflict management.

Allison develops two distinct models of policy making as counterpoints to the prevailing rational actor model which assumes a concentration of power and centers on the principal leader. Looking first at the routine operations of large organizations, the "organizational process" model treats choices as the outputs of large organizations functioning according to well-established and deeply embedded standard operating procedures (SOPs). These SOPs have a life of their own, irrespective of the preferences of senior leaders. They shape the definition of the problem, delimit the policy options, and crucially affect the implementation of the strategy of conflict management that is finally chosen. As Allison puts it, they color the face of the issue that is turned to leaders.

A quite different explanation points to the "pulling and hauling" that is endemic in the politics of large bureaucracies. Because power is shared rather than concentrated, the heads of large agencies — for instance, the Department of Defense, the State Department, the Central Intelligence Agency, and the National Security Council in the United States — are all necessary participants in policy making. They will each defend actively the interests of their agency. Bureaucratic rivalry is the norm rather than the exception and the policy that results is not the preferred position of any one "player," but a compromise — and often an illogical compromise — between the positions of the most powerful and persuasive participants. Allison would contend, for example, that escalation of the war in Vietnam can be far better explained by bureaucratic competition and organizational rigidity than by the dynamics of "group think" or a rational model of the policy process. Bureaucratic politics and organizational routines are the enemies of coherence and flexibility in strategies of conflict management.

Critics have expressed reservations about the validity of organizational process and bureaucratic politics as explanations of policy. First, they question its applicability outside the United States. Perhaps bureaucratic competition is a special characteristic of the separation of powers and the checks and balances built into the American system. In the third essay in this section, Kim R. Nossal addresses the issue in his examination of the impact of bureaucratic politics on policy in a parliamentary system. In his analysis of bureaucratic rivalries in Canada, Australia, and Britain, Nossal concludes that bureaucratic politics play themselves out differently when the executive is stronger, the legislature weaker, career civil servants hold the highest appointed positions, and governments function within the rubric of collective responsibility.

More serious is the allegation that "position" does not determine policy preference. In 1962, in sharp contrast to some of his colleagues who headed civilian agencies, the Secretary of Defense, not terribly alarmed by the military threat posed by Soviet missiles in Cuba, did not advocate strong measures. In their comparative historical investigation of international crises, Glenn Snyder and Paul Diesing find that policy preferences of senior officials were determined not exclusively by their bureaucratic interests, but even more so by their ideological predispositions and the policy options inherent in the bargaining situation. They conclude that an analysis of bureaucratic politics alone would be seriously incomplete.

If policy preferences are not largely a function of position, if people from the same agency differ or people from different agencies agree, then the explanation is not only incomplete but seriously compromised. Finally, as Jervis argues, even if we can gauge the policy preferences of all the important players from their positions, we still cannot predict the outcome of the bureaucratic infighting without knowing a great deal more about the relative status, resources, and strategies of all the important participants.[4] We must move beyond bureaucratic politics to explain strategies of conflict management.

Elite explanations look not to the differences among powerful officials but to the larger consensus to explain conflict and its management. Drawing on a variety of intellectual traditions, ranging from neo-Marxist arguments to those developed by Pareto and Mosca and their successors, they examine the social roots of policy making, paying particular attention to class and status.[5] Although there is lively disagreement about who constitutes the elite, how it is formed, and the sources of its strength, there is agreement on the central premise of the argument: power is concentrated in a relatively homogeneous elite which is agreed on its interests and the policies appropriate to these interests. The elite dominates policy making in the critical sectors of defense and trade; its pursuit of narrowly conceived, class-based interests generates high levels of defense spending and restrictive economic policies which culminate in a high incidence of international military and economic conflict.

One of the best-known applications of an elite explanation is the analysis of the workings of a military-industrial complex in the United States and, for some scholars, in the Soviet Union as well.[6] The central premise is the circulation of a limited elite among the key institutions of the military and industrial sector. Richard Barnet suggests, for example, that a class of "security managers" has dominated U.S. policy making on national security in the post-war period. When not employed directly by the government, these people transact business with each other, belong to the same clubs, and review each other's memoirs. In the United States, he alleges, almost all of the crucial bureaucratic appointments since 1945 have been men whose civilian offices are within ten blocks of each other in New York, Washington, Boston, and Chicago; this small group moves easily back and forth between the public and the private sector. Barnet emphasizes the network of personal and corporate ties and the shared experiences of members of the "complex" which stretches into corporations, legislatures, labor unions which benefit from military contracts, and universities which profit from defense-related research.[7]

As a group, this elite has a vested interest in high defense spending, an interest which promotes arms races and discourages meaningful arms control. There is little disagreement among members of this elite: they propound a pessimistic estimate of an adversary's intentions, urge preparedness, and develop worst-case scenarios to justify military expenditure. In the Soviet Union, a comparable complex includes senior officials of the Soviet armed forces, members of the managerial elite responsible for industrial production, and a technocratic elite with careers closely tied to the armed forces. In both countries, the individual leader in power makes little difference. It does not matter whether it is Ronald Reagan or Jimmy Carter, Joseph Stalin or Yuri Andropov; leaders are but ciphers in an elite-dominated political process.

Critics of elite explanations of conflict respond that policy is not uniform over time. Individuals and groups do seem to make some difference within a set of broad policy guidelines. Military spending in the United States has gone up in the last several years, but in the past it has also gone down as a percentage of the budget and as a percentage of the gross national product: at times there have been decreases in real defense spending, given the impact of inflation. It is far harder to assess accurately Soviet military spending, which appears to have risen dramatically in the last two decades, but even so Soviet policy makers have at times displayed considerable caution in their management of international conflict. Most elite-based arguments have some difficulty explaining decreases in defense spending or cautious limitation of the scope of conflict, and even greater conceptual difficulty in explaining shifts in policy even though the same elite remains in control. The framework for policy making they establish is valuable as a baseline, but elite explanations are far too blunt an intellectual instrument to capture the nuances of strategies of conflict management.

We turn now to the last of the four approaches, an examination of the social context of policy from a pluralist perspective. Pluralism treats political power as diffuse, the group as the basic unit of analysis, and politics as competition among organized interests within society. Foreign as well as domestic policy is the result of that competition. Early pluralist analyses tended to give little independent weight to the state itself; the state was treated as a referee among competing interests, a referee that set the rules of the game. Pluralists suggest that those groups that were best organized, commanded the greatest share of the available resources, and had the best access to government networks determined policy. More recently, scholars have paid more attention to the autonomous role of the state and its capacity to determine policy in bargaining with groups and coalitions. Peter Katzenstein, for example, argues that interest groups are not only the originators of policy pressures, but also act as subsidiary agents of the state to build support for its policies. Coalitions of interest groups can shape the policy networks linking the private and public sectors, but their impact will depend ultimately on the strength or weakness of the state apparatus. In strong states, there is little differentiation between that apparatus and society and, consequently, particularistic interests do not predominate over the collective interest as defined by the principal leader. Weak states, in contrast, tend to reflect a more pluralistic set of processes, with a range of interest groups capturing government policy; here, policy reflects the outcome of complex conflicts among varieties of interests.[8]

Howard Stanislawski, in an essay that follows, looks closely at the impact of interest groups and coalitions on American and Canadian strategies of conflict management. In both cases, he documents extensive lobbying activity by a wide range of groups who joined in coalition to shape government policy. The comparison is an interesting one: both governments faced the same policy issue — a strategic response to the Arab boycott — and both faced powerful and opposing coalitions of interests ranged on opposite sides of the policy debate. Yet the policy outcome was very different. To explain the divergence in policy, Stanislawski traces important differences in political culture, in patterns of deference toward government as the authoritative voice of policy, and in the legitimacy of lobbying in the two systems. Even more important, he looks beyond the range of interest group activity to the policy networks that link these groups to the state. The difference in the autonomy of the two states in the face of intense lobbying was critical to the outcome of the policy debate. In the United States, power was decentralized and groups had multiple channels of access to a diffuse set of governmental institutions; the state was relatively weak and society autonomous. In Canada, on the contrary, the state was far stronger: channels of access were limited, power was concentrated and hierarchical, and a tradition of bargaining among coexisting elites enabled the government to use interest group activity to generate support for policy.

Michael Gordon, in the last reading in this section, gives us a brilliant analysis of the group bases of German and British strategies of conflict management in 1914. He examines the impact of economic and political modernization on state institutions in both countries and carefully traces the linkages between a multiplicity of groups, interests, classes, and the state and its policies. The late industrialization in Germany and the consequent emergence of large firms, for example, led to tariff policies sustained by a powerful coalition of interests among government leaders, the Junker class, and captains of heavy industry. These policies put Russia and Germany on a collision course; German hostility to Russia was rooted in the pattern of domestic coalitions and reinforced by the need for diversionary conflict in the face of an increasingly alienated peasantry and middle class. The pattern of political modernization created additional stress: the presence of large ethnic and religious minorities threatened a weak government which was, however, equipped with a strong state apparatus that intervened extensively in German society. In Britain, neither of these two conditions held: assimilation of groups and classes had been gradual, and the state was weak, its scope narrow. These quite different linkages between state and society contributed in large part to an aggressive German strategy and a hesitant, cautious, and even vacillating British attempt at deterrence in 1914.

In the introduction to this volume, we examined the debate about the appropriate level of analysis of international conflict and its management. In this context, it is instructive to look back at Holsti's emphasis on the flawed decision making that preceded the outbreak of World War I and compare it to the explanation offered by Gordon. The two are not mutually exclusive, but complementary: Gordon documents the broad social conditions which created the predisposition to aggression while Holsti details the processes which were the immediate precursor to war. The question we must consider now is the relationship between the two sets of factors in an explanation of conflict and its management. Are the two related at all? Could the flawed decision making have occurred in another kind of socio-political context? Are either of the two conditions necessary? Could war have occurred if either decision making had been better — or social tensions had been less? And, finally, are either of these two sets of factors sufficient as an explanation of war? Could war have occurred if – and only if – stress had distorted the process of decision, or if – and only if – the German regime had faced the kinds of socio-political challenges it did? We leave these questions with you until we have explored the impact of the state on conflict and its management.

We have gradually broadened our perspective to include an ever-widening range of activity by a variety of participants, inside and outside government. But, as we saw, the impact of these groups was determined in part by the state itself and its autonomy in the face of society. We come directly, therefore, to an examination of the role of the state, traditionally the most important unit of analysis in the study of international conflict and its management.

ENDNOTES

1 See Wilfred L. Kohl, "The Nixon-Kissinger Foreign Policy System of U.S.-European Relations: Patterns of Policy Making," *World Politics*, 28 (October 1975), 1-43.

2 The elite explanation of politics is similar in some important respects to the "instrumental" Marxist argument which we look at when we consider the state in the next section. Classification of these explanations under the rubric of "group" or "state" attributes is very much a theoretical decision, a function of the assumptions different authors make.

3 Irving L. Janis, *Victims of Groupthink: A Psychological Study of Foreign Policy Decisions and Fiascoes* (Boston: Houghton Mifflin, 1972).

4 Robert Jervis, *Perception and Misperception in International Politics* (Princeton: Princeton University Press, 1976), pp. 24-28.

5 The classic study in the United States is C. Wright Mills, *The Power Elite* (New York: Oxford University Press, 1966). See also William Domhoff, *Who Rules America?* (Englewood Cliffs, New Jersey: Prentice-Hall, 1967). In Canada, see Robert Presthus, *Elite Accommodation in Canadian Politics* (Toronto: Macmillan, 1973) and Wallace Clement, *Continental Corporate Power* (Toronto: McClelland and Stewart, 1977).

6 For a neo-Marxist analysis of the military-industrial complex in the United States, see Michael Reich, "Military Spending and the U.S. Economy," in Stephen Rosen, ed., *Testing the Theory of the Military-Industrial Complex* (Lexington, Mass.: Lexington Books, 1973), pp. 85-102. In the same collection, Lieberson uses pluralist assumptions to look at the same evidence and comes to quite different conclusions. See Stanley Lieberson, "An Empirical Study of Military-Industrial Linkages," *ibid.*, pp. 61-84. For an analysis of the workings of the military-industrial complex in the Soviet Union, see Vernon V. Aspaturian, "The Soviet Military-Industrial Complex: Does it Exist?" *ibid.*, pp. 103-134. For a more general examination of the impact of elites in the Soviet Union and China on conflict and its management, see Michael Gehlen, "Political Elites in the Soviet Union and China," in Leroy Gramer, ed., *Systems and Actors in International Politics* (San Francisco: Chandler, 1971), pp. 103-129.

7 Richard Barnet, "The Game of Nations," *Harpers*, November 1971, p. 55. For a more extensive treatment, see his *The Roots of War* (New York: Penguin Books, 1972).

8 Peter Katzenstein, *Between Power and Plenty: Foreign Economic Policies in Advanced Industrial States* (Madison, Wisconsin: University of Wisconsin Press, 1978). Neo-mercantilist arguments which stress the role of the state meet the arguments of "structural" Marxists who also pay increasing attention to the autonomy of the state. We look at this second group of scholars when we examine the impact of the economy of a state on its propensity to engage in conflict. Again, whether we treat explanations as "group" attributes or "state" attributes depends very much on the basic theoretical assumptions authors make.

A: ORGANIZATIONAL AND BUREAUCRATIC POLITICS

The Future of Crisis Management

Richard Ned Lebow

In recent years the concept crisis management has received considerable attention within the government. Crisis action groups have been established in both the State and Defense Departments and also in NATO to assist political and military leaders in managing such confrontations. The Studies, Analysis and Gaming Agency of the Joint Chiefs of Staff designs and administers crisis management games and often draws upon officials at the subcabinet level as players. Similar exercises are run at the four war colleges, whose students are schooled in crisis management techniques.

Much of this interest in crisis no doubt derives from the experience of the Cuban missile crisis which helped to instill the belief within the policy-making community that crisis is the primary means by which nuclear superpowers test one another's mettle and that the peace of the world depends upon the successful mastery of such clashes. After Cuba, Robert McNamara went so far as to claim that "There is no longer any such thing as strategy, only crisis management."[1] This belief has been encouraged by the spate of academic studies on the subject, many of them, including this one, funded by departments or agencies with more than a passing interest in the subject. This research has not entirely fallen upon deaf ears. A surprising number of policy-makers are *au courant* with the latest academic buzzwords that have implications for crisis management. The author has himself heard high officials refer nonchalantly to selective attention, groupthink, and cognitive dissonance — the latter construed as cognitive "dissidents" by one befuddled admiral — with the expectation that these concepts were familiar to their audience. It is doubtful that policy-makers' awareness of such concepts has had any impact upon the quality of their decision-making, but it certainly has made them more self-conscious about the process by which those decisions are reached.

Despite the prominence of crisis management in the political science literature, the concept, as several scholars have observed, is employed in different and even contradictory ways.[2] Everyone agrees that crisis management refers to the detailed control over policy by top leaders, but there is disagreement as to what should be the primary objective of those policy-makers. One school of thought sees the goal of crisis management as the avoidance of war. Advocates of this approach tend

---

Richard Ned Lebow, *Between Peace and War* (Baltimore: The Johns Hopkins University Press, 1981), pp. 291-305. Reprinted by permission of The Johns Hopkins University Press. Portions of the text have been deleted. Some footnotes have been removed; those remaining have been renumbered.

to view crisis as a pathological event that creates dangers the protagonists have a common interest in surmounting. For them, crisis management is or ought to be a joint exercise in tension reduction. Other writers conceive of crisis primarily in terms of the clash of interests and wills that it entails. They see it as an inescapable and even legitimate form of international competition. For them, the goal of crisis management is to win the confrontation. Good crisis management therefore becomes that which results in the attainment of objectives and the denial to the adversary of his.

Several scholars have criticized these formulations as inadequate, because each definition focuses on only one dimension of crisis. They point out that crises among nuclear powers involve both conflict *and* cooperation, the former brought about by the pursuit of clashing interests, the latter by the shared interest in avoiding war. Good crisis management consists of striking a balance between these two concerns. As Snyder and Diesing put it, it is an effort "to coerce prudently, or accommodate cheaply, or some combination of both."[3] Phil Williams offers a more elaborate but essentially similar definition:

> Crisis management is concerned on the one hand with the procedures for controlling and regulating a crisis so that it does not get out of hand and lead to war, and on the other hand with ensuring that the crisis is resolved on a satisfactory basis in which the vital interests of the state are secured and protected. The second aspect will almost invariably necessitate vigorous actions carrying substantial risks. One task of crisis management, therefore, is to temper these risks, to keep them as low and as controllable as possible, while the other is to ensure that the coercive diplomacy and risk-taking tactics are as effective as possible in gaining concessions from the adversary and maintaining one's own position relatively intact.[4]

Students of crisis management, regardless of their conceptualization of the problem, have been motivated by the goal of improving the quality of crisis decision-making. For the most part they have operated on the assumption that knowledge about past decisional failures and the reasons for them will lead to insights and even techniques useful in improving future performance. As Janis and Mann insist, "any theory of decision-making worth its salt should provide valid guidelines for practitioners who want to avoid gross errors when making crucial choices."[5]

Even the most casual review of the crisis literature will reveal the existence of a consensus as to the most widespread and fundamental decision-making problem. This is the failure of policy-makers to consider alternative points of view and seek out the information necessary to assess them. Decision-making theorists have identified a number of ways by which this can occur.... Policy-makers, once they are committed to a policy, become insensitive to information that challenges the efficacy of that policy — also,... subordinates hasten to report information they know would confirm the expectations of their superiors and ignore or suppress information that challenges those expectations. Subordinates may do this when they believe their dissent will prove ineffective or lead to reprisals against them. They may also refrain from criticism for fear of threatening the cohesiveness of the decision-making group.

Irving Janis has commented at length about this latter phenomenon, which he calls "groupthink."[6] He argues that the more cohesive the group the more its members will censor what they think and say in order to adhere to group norms and thereby preserve group unity. Janis attributes this behavior to the important role group unity and the mutual support associated with it play in coping with stress. Group pressures against nonconformity are likely to be particularly great in crisis situations because decisions to threaten or use force may violate the ethical norms of the policy-makers. According to Janis:

> The participant may try to reassure himself with the platitudinous thought that "you

> can't make an omelet without breaking some eggs." Nevertheless, each time he realizes that he is sacrificing moral values in order to arrive at a viable policy, he will be burdened with anticipatory feelings of shame, guilt and related feelings of self-depreciation, which lower his self-esteem.... For all such sources of stress, participating in a unanimous consensus along with respected fellow members of a congenial group will bolster the decision-maker's self-esteem.[7]

"Groupthink" or any of the other decision-making pathologies we have discussed can transform a policy-making session into a kind of ritualized group approval of a predetermined course of action. For this reason many decision-making theorists have argued that some conflict is healthy and even necessary in the decision-making process. This was the theme of Richard Neustadt's pioneering study, *Presidential Power*.[8] More recently, Alexander George has declared that "conflict may help produce better policy *if* it can be managed and resolved properly."[9] Conflict, in the sense of policy disagreements, can compel policy-makers to articulate and defend the unspoken assumptions that underlie their different policy preferences. It may encourage them to debate the pros and cons of several options instead of just one, and to examine all of them in a more realistic and thorough manner. Dissent and criticism can also act as a check on stereotypy and selective attention.

Too much conflict can lead to loss of control.... An ideal decision-making environment would therefore be characterized by the proper mix of consensus and dissent. Dissent is required for the reasons noted above. Consensus within the decision-making elite about fundamental values and objectives is necessary to ensure that a decision is executed faithfully once it is made. Snyder and Diesing, for example, call for a bargaining committee composed of *moderate* softs and hards with a middle-line central decision-maker.[10] A decision-making group must also be sufficiently cohesive to encourage dissent without fear of recrimination. Groups lacking amiability and esprit de corps also tend to make bad decisions because their participants are more likely to fight for their parochial objectives than to work toward a common goal. Janis observes:

> When unlike-minded people who are political opponents are forced to meet together in a group, they can be expected to behave like couples in olden times who were forced to live together by a shotgun marriage. The incompatible members of a shotgun committee often indulge in painfully repetitious debates, frequently punctuated with invective, mutual ridicule and maneuvers of one-upmanship in a continuous struggle for power that is not at all conducive to decisions of high quality.[11]

Most American theorists of crisis management assume that lack of sufficient conflict is a more common cause of decision-making failure than lack of consensus. For this reason they have proposed a variety of techniques that they believe to be useful in helping to overcome this problem. All of these techniques are designed to encourage a meaningful examination of competing policy alternatives. They do so either by attempting to alter the process by which decisions are made or by restructuring the roles of policy-makers, thereby socializing the policy-makers into a new set of decision-making norms. Numerous proponents of the former approach have urged policy-makers to draw up a balance sheet of the pros and cons of the most attractive options and to use it as the starting point for a policy debate.[12] Joseph de Rivera, Alexander George, and Robert Jervis make the case for what George has called the multiple advocacy approach to decision-making.[13] De Rivera would have an office or department *within* an administration obligated to assume the responsibility for making an opposition case. George argues for the creation of a special assistant to the president to act as a disinterested custodian before whom the arguments and options pertaining to a policy issue would be fought over. He believes that this would help to overcome the inevitable inequalities among advocates of differing policy positions that bias the outcome in favor of those with more influence, access to information, and better bargaining skills.[14]

Irving Janis is the best-known proponent of combating decision-making pathologies through efforts to restructure the roles of policy-makers. In his conclusion to *Victims of Groupthink* he offers the following nine prescriptions for counteracting personal and group biases. They are designed to encourage greater impartiality and common effort on the part of participants in group decision processes.[15]

1. The leader of a policy-forming group should assign the role of critical evaluator to each member, encouraging the group to give high priority to airing objections and doubts.
2. The leaders in an organization's hierarchy ...should be impartial instead of stating preferences and expectations at the outset.
3. The organization should routinely follow the administrative practice of setting up several independent policy-planning and evaluation groups to work on the same policy question, each carrying out its deliberations under a different leader.
4. ...the policy making group should from time to time divide into two or more subgroups to meet separately, under different chairmen, and then come together to hammer out their differences.
5. Each member of the policy making group should discuss periodically the group's deliberations with trusted associates in his own unit of the organization and report back their reactions.
6. One or more outside experts or qualified colleagues within the organization...should be encouraged to challenge the views of the core members.
7. At every meeting devoted to evaluating policy alternatives, at least one member should be assigned to the role of devil's advocate.
8. ...a sizable block of time...should be spent surveying all warning signals from the rivals and constructing alternate scenarios from the rivals' intentions.
9. After reaching a preliminary consensus...the policy making group should hold a "second chance" meeting at which every member is expected to express as vividly as he can all his residual doubts and rethink the entire issue before making a definitive choice.

All of these strategies for improving decision-making are based on the assumption that leaders will be willing to make purposeful efforts to structure an environment that elicits and encourages critical thinking and dissent. This seems extremely unrealistic. Certainly, criticism and dissent can increase a leader's authority in the long term by leading to better policies, but they can threaten his authority in the short term by making it more difficult for him to control the decision-making process. In many decision-making groups and political systems, open expressions of criticism may be interpreted as a sign of weakness on the part of the leader. Other leaders may be psychologically unprepared to accept criticism. For one or more of these reasons leaders will probably be more likely than not to discourage the development of the very conditions associated with more open decision-making. A sampling of actual policy-making environments would bear out this contention.

There is an even more fundamental problem associated with efforts to encourage an open decision-making environment. As we have seen, new information and constructive criticism are the last thing leaders seek when they are committed to a policy.... Instead, they act to ignore or suppress dissent. In the Sino-Indian crisis, military officers who warned of the consequences of the forward policy were removed one by one from positions of authority. In the July [1914] and Korea (1950) crises, criticism was simply ignored or brushed aside. Prince Lichnowsky, [German Ambassador in London from 1912 through 1914], who warned of British intervention, was derided as an incompetent fool, while George Kennan and some members of the Policy Planning Staff, who thought that an attempt to unify Korea by force would probably encounter Chinese resistance, were politely dismissed as unduly alarmist.

Social psychologists and political practitioners have noted that advice is unlikely to be listened to unless it is couched in terms of the framework of reality accepted by those a person wishes to influence. DeRivera, for example, finds that "Government policy necessarily operates within a framework of common beliefs. Policy-makers must pay attention to this area of agreement and cannot give real consideration to alternate policies that fall outside of this framework."[16] Describing his own experience as a member of the National Security Staff, Morton Halperin observes:

> By definition, most participants share the images dominant within the government at any one time. However, even those who do not will be constrained by their knowledge that the shared images influence others, and this will affect the kinds of arguments which are put forward.
>
> Participants will have considerable difficulty getting the ordinary administrator or politician to believe facts that go against strongly held beliefs. They either ignore the evidence or reinterpret it so as to change what it seems to mean.[17]

Lichnowsky and Kennan both rejected the analytical framework of their colleagues. Lichnowsky refused to believe that Britain would ever sanction German domination of the continent achieved by force of arms. For his part, Kennan denied the very premise of Acheson's Far Eastern policy: that the Chinese leaders and people had a deep sentimental attachment to the United States and perceived Moscow as posing a greater threat to their security than Washington. Predictably, neither the German nor the American foreign policy establishment was receptive to criticism based on assumptions it did not share. Nor... were Bethmann-Hollweg and Dean Acheson prepared to entertain a challenge of their respective images of reality, given their need to use those images to rationalize the probability of success for policies to which they were committed. Lichnowsky and Kennan were in effect banging their heads against the wall as were the military critics of India's forward policy.

When leaders are committed to a policy, the various techniques advocated by theorists to improve the quality of decision-making have little chance of adoption, even though these are precisely the situations where well informed dissent is most needed as an antidote to irrational consistency or wishful thinking. If any of these techniques are adopted, they may well be applied in a ritualistic manner and used by leaders to convince themselves and others that the decision they have favored all along was reached in the best possible way. George Reedy explains how this was done during the Johnson years: "Of course, within these councils there was always at least one 'devil's advocate.' But an official dissenter always started with half his battle lost. It is assumed that he is bringing up arguments solely because arguing is his official role. It is well understood that he is not going to press his points harshly or stridently. Therefore, his objections and cautions are discounted before they are delivered. They are actually welcomed because they prove for the record that the decision was preceded by controversy."[18]

George, Jervis, Janis and de Rivera are some of the most prominent critics of the rational actor model. They are in the forefront of the effort to construct alternative theories of decision-making. It is remarkable that these same theorists propose antidotes to decision-making failures based, in effect, on the rational actor model. Their advocacy of the several techniques we have just discussed must be seen as evidence of either irrational consistency or of their need to believe that something can be done to improve the quality of crisis decision-making. The latter explanation seems closer to the truth.

The possibility that irrational decision-making

could result in a nuclear war is frightening. Policymakers and social scientists have erected defenses to protect themselves from the anxiety that the recognition of this prospect would almost certainly generate. The doctrine of deterrence is one such defense, and it is for this reason that many strategists are reluctant to recognize its limits. The belief that crises can be managed rationally and techniques developed to facilitate this goal may be another defense. Evidence for this contention can be adduced from the way in which decision-making theorists have treated the Cuban missile crisis. Kennedy's Ex Com...has received the most extensive praise from both practitioners and theorists. Hans Morgenthau, otherwise a critic of the Kennedy administration, called Kennedy's management of the crisis "the distillation of a collective intellectual effort of a high order, the like of which must be rare in history."[19] Britain's Denis Healey, then "shadow" defense minister, declared that it could serve as a "model in any textbook on diplomacy."[20] Henry Pachter, a journalist and academic, wrote that Kennedy's performance was "a feat whose technical elegance compelled the professionals' admiration."[21] Something of an aura has come to surround those thirteen days in October. Decision-making theorists exalt them as a glorious exercise in rational policy-making that should be emulated by other leaders. Alexander George, for one, argues that Kennedy's handling of the crisis is evidence for the feasibility of fruitfully restructuring the roles and norms of policymakers.[22] Janis declares that the Ex Com's deliberations were "at the opposite pole from the symptoms of groupthink" and bases his recommendations for improving crisis decision-making on Kennedy's performance.[23] Just how realistic are these appraisals?[24]

Students of the Cuban crisis point to the various ways in which Kennedy attempted to encourage free-wheeling debate about the various policy options open to the United States: he charged the members of the Ex Com with considering the problem of the Soviet missiles in Cuba as a whole rather than confining themselves to their specific areas of authority or expertise; he purposely included officials in the Ex Com whom he knew were likely to represent differing points of view; he called in outside experts with this end in mind; he encouraged the group to debate the pros and cons of several different options without committing himself to any of them in advance. The president also absented himself from some of the Ex Com's sessions in the hope of encouraging more frankness on the part of his advisors. In his absence, either Robert Kennedy or Ted Sorensen was assigned the role of "intellectual watchdog" in order to ensure that every policy matter was analyzed thoroughly. During some of these sessions the participants engaged in role playing, acting as advocates for positions they did not necessarily support. At one point the Ex Com divided into two subgroups, each assigned with reaching a policy decision and defending it before the other.

Kennedy's efforts were unquestionably innovative and succeeded in bringing about a more thorough evaluation of the various policy options than might otherwise have been the case. It would nevertheless be an exaggeration to describe the Ex Com as an open decision-making environment. The Ex Com's mandate was a narrow one: to consider the pros and cons of the variety of coercive measures that could be employed to get the Soviet missiles out of Cuba before they became operational. From the very outset the president made it clear to the group that he would neither acquiesce to the presence of the missiles nor seek to remove them by purely diplomatic means. He was intent on using force to overcome the threat posed by the missiles and charged the Ex Com with recommending what military option was best suited to the task. In effect, he made the most important policy decision before the Ex Com even convened. The group never debated the wisdom of using force, despite the realization by all of the participants that such a course of action risked triggering a nuclear war. According to Adam Yarmolinsky, "90 percent of its time" was spent on "studying uses of troops, bombers and war ships."[25] Even Janis, one of Kennedy's greatest admirers, reluctantly admits that the "the Executive

Committee could be criticized for conforming too readily with the President's way of defining its mission."[26]

But Kennedy's formulation of the problem did meet with some opposition at first. McNamara believed that Soviet missiles in Cuba made no real difference to the strategic balance. "A missile is a missile," he argued, whether launched from Cuba or the Soviet Union. At best, missiles in Cuba would permit the Soviets to close the missile gap in 1962 instead of a few years later when their second generation ICBMs came on line. Hilsman relates: "The clear implication of McNamara's position was that the United States should do nothing, but simply ignore the presence of Soviet missiles in Cuba and sit tight."[27] Adlai Stevenson was also initially opposed to using force to get the missiles out. On October 16, Kennedy told the ambassador that Soviet missiles had been detected in Cuba, and voiced his conviction that they would have to be taken out by an air strike. Stevenson was shocked by the president's apparent determination to resort so readily to violence and wrote him a note urging caution. In the note, which he personally delivered the following morning, Stevenson warned: "[But] to risk starting a nuclear war is bound to be divisive at best and the judgments of history seldom coincide with the tempers of the moment. ... I feel you should have made it clear that the existence of nuclear bases anywhere is negotiable before we start anything. ... I confess I have many misgivings about the proposed course of action."[28]

Kennedy was annoyed by the note. He brushed aside Stevenson's objections as well as McNamara's, by specifically excluding from the agenda of the Ex Com the possibility of a diplomatic approach to Moscow. By most accounts, McNamara was bludgeoned into accepting the need for forceful action. Along with his deputy, Roswell Gilpatric, he adopted the blockade, which held out the prospect of the least overt use of force, as a fallback position. Stevenson also came out in support of the blockade but continued to voice his concern that everything possible be done to avert war. On October 21, when the National Security Council considered what diplomatic action might accompany the blockade, he raised the possibility of striking a deal with the Russians. Stevenson proposed that the United States give up its base at Guantanamo and guarantee the territorial integrity of Cuba in return for the demilitarization and neutralization of that country. As an alternative, he urged the group to consider offering to withdraw American Jupiter bases in Turkey and Italy as a quid pro quo for a Russian withdrawal of their missiles from Cuba. United Nations inspection teams would subsequently ensure that none of the foreign bases of either superpower were used to mount a surprise attack.[29]

Stevenson's proposals were made in the context of the blockade and would not, he insisted, seem "soft" if they were properly worded. But the president rejected them out of hand.[30] Stevenson was also subjected to a sharp attack by members of the Ex Com led by Lovett and McCone. Allison cautions against drawing too many inferences from this exchange, but there seems little doubt that Stevenson was ostracized by the core of the Ex Com. The president's cavalier treatment of him probably encouraged other members of the group to give vent to their emotions. Allison himself speculates that Kennedy "may have sacrificed the Ambassador to the hawks in order to allow himself to choose the moderate, golden mean."[31] Whatever the explanation, Stevenson, who had been asked by the president to return from New York specifically for this meeting, was deeply wounded by the gratuitously vindictive nature of the attack upon him. According to Abel, "the bitter aftermath of that Saturday afternoon stayed with him until his death."[32]

If Stevenson questioned the overall strategy of the Ex Com, its members had been at loggerheads all week over tactics. Neither advocates of the blockade nor those of the air strike were able to bring about a consensus. The Ex Com's ultimate decision in favor of the blockade was the result of strong presidential pressure. Sorensen reports that "the President was impatient and discouraged" by the fourth day of the Ex Com's deliberations. "He was counting on the Attorney General and me, he said, to pull the group together quickly — otherwise more delays and dissension would plague whatever decision he took."[33] Kennedy made it clear that he wanted to act by Sunday and that to do so he needed a decision in favor of the blockade. When this failed to materialize at the next meeting of the Ex Com, Sorensen invoked the president's authority in order to achieve a consensus. He announced, "we are not serving the president well, and... my recently healed ulcer didn't like it much either."[34] The group got the message and the following day rallied to the blockade. On Saturday, the decision about what response to make to Khrushchev's second cable was brought about in the same way.[35]

The reality of the Ex Com does not measure up to the myth propagated by Kennedy's admirers. The Ex Com proved a relatively pliant tool of the president. Knowledge of his preferences shaped its deliberations at every turn, as none of the participants were prepared to speak out in favor of a position they knew the president would not support. Even when Kennedy did not attend the group's meetings, the prospect of a free-wheeling debate was inhibited by the presence of his brother and Ted Sorensen, whom everyone expected would report what was said back to the Oval Office.[36] Independent thinking was tolerated only within the limits set by the president. Officials who expressed unacceptable points of view were pressured like McNamara to bring their opinions into line or like Stevenson were personally abused.

The attack on Stevenson, one of whose proposals ironically became the basis for the resolution of the crisis, appears to be a classic manifestation of groupthink. The Ex Com had emerged from five days of intensive deliberations with a remarkable degree of group solidarity but a somewhat fragile consensus. It was prepared to defend the blockade option before a wider circle of officials; the National Security Council meeting on Saturday actually marked the group's debut in this respect. Stevenson was an outsider. His proposals challenged the consensus and by extension the solidarity of the Ex Com. This solidarity was unquestionably important to many Ex Com members as a means of coping with the extraordinary stress of a nuclear crisis. Their otherwise uncalled-for attack on the mild mannered Stevenson is best interpreted as a mechanism by which their sense of solidarity could be expressed and strengthened.

In the final analysis the Ex Com could be described as a superb example of promotional leadership. It was brought into being less to make policy than to legitimate it. Kennedy's choice of its members, its restricted agenda, and the use of Robert Kennedy and Ted Sorensen as policemen all point to his intent to use the Ex Com as a means of building a consensus for whatever specific course of action he ultimately decided upon. In practice, the deliberations of the group influenced policy by helping to shift Kennedy away from the air strike in favor of the blockade, although Allison suggests that the Ex Com was only one of several influences in this direction.[37] Kennedy was preparing to initiate a confrontation that he knew risked war with the Soviet Union. To be effective he needed widespread bipartisan support. If something went wrong and the two superpowers moved toward an even more serious confrontation, he knew that he would need this support even more. Kennedy's adroit if not fully conscious manipulation of group dynamics helped to create that political backing. Allowing the Ex Com to debate the pros and cons of the major action-oriented options encouraged them to believe that they were instrumental in making policy, as indeed to a certain extent they were. The group solidarity that developed in the course of these proceedings helped to transform individuals with different political outlooks and bureaucratic loyalties into staunch supporters of the blockade and the other initiatives that accompanied it. The united front they presented impressed other governmental officials and congressmen and helped to widen the scope of support for the president.

The evidence of promotional leadership and

groupthink in the Cuban case raises important doubts in this author's mind about the extent to which leaders are willing and able to take steps to overcome these kinds of decision-making pathologies. As we have noted, Kennedy's handling of Cuba has become a template against which several distinguished decision-making theorists believe the performance of other crisis managers ought to be measured. Holsti, de Rivera, George, and Janis all base their suggestions for improving crisis management on what they describe as Kennedy's superlative performance in this case. But if Kennedy was only partially willing to permit an open decision-making environment, what can be expected of other leaders in other situations? Is it likely that they will be in any way inclined to encourage the dissension and debate decision-making theorists associate with good decisions?

The experience of our cases points to the conclusion that relatively open decision-making environments are largely fortuitous. In the few instances where they existed they were the result of circumstances that policy-makers had done little or nothing to shape and over which they had little or no control. The British experience in the Fashoda crisis...is a case in point. The notable absence of groupthink and other decision-making pathologies in British decision-making can be attributed in the first place to the distribution of power within the British cabinet. The aging prime minister, Lord Salisbury, was quite autocratic by nature but was no longer sufficiently powerful to direct foreign affairs without cabinet participation. His need to develop a consensus within the cabinet meant that his colleagues were brought into the decision-making process. Among them were several strong personalities representing quite different points of view. All of Salisbury's initiatives therefore underwent careful scrutiny from different perspectives before they were adopted as policy. At the same time, the principle of collective responsibility assured that those who had opposed a particular course of action supported its implementation once it became policy.

Another example of relatively open decision-making is that of the Japanese oligarchy at the time of the Russo-Japanese war. Policy during both the crisis and the war that followed was made by a group of fourteen men consisting of the emperor, five elder statesmen (the Genro), five cabinet ministers, and three military leaders. A sense of national mission, similar origins, and shared experience in governing created a high degree of unity and cohesion among this decision-making elite. However, differences in age and political perspective as well as both bureaucratic and personal rivalries guaranteed that a wide range of views was expressed and debated. Of crucial importance in this regard was the declining power of the Genro, who retained sufficient respect and authority to shape the policy deliberations but not enough to govern without a consensus. By virtue of the oligarchical nature of the Japanese government the policy-making elite was also insulated from some of the most bellicose public pressures but at the same time was not altogether immune to considerations of public feeling.

Our evidence indicates that those interested in crisis resolution have probably paid too much attention to crisis management. Their efforts are based on the belief that the quality of crisis decision-making can be improved substantially by manipulating the roles of decision-makers or the format by which their decisions are reached. Certain roles and structures are no doubt better than others, but it is unrealistic to think that leaders can be prevailed upon to make their decision-making processes more open, given the threat this can pose to both their power and policy preferences. The usefulness of efforts for greater openness is further called into question by our finding that the really important preconditions for good decision-making are an expression of underlying conditions. The three most important of these probably are: (1) legitimate central authority, (2) a consensus within the policy-making elite with respect to fundamental political values and procedures, and (3) freedom from domestic political pressures that compel leaders to pursue a particular foreign policy. Unless these conditions are met, the more specific attributes of a good policy-making environment, which Janis and George describe, are hardly feasible objectives. However, policy-makers seem to have little control over any of these conditions; they are almost invariably the result of fortuitous historical and political circumstances. Policy-makers may possess the power to make the decision-making process much worse, but they can make it only marginally better. This is a sobering thought because open decision-making environments are nevertheless necessary to prevent leaders from becoming prisoners of their preconceived notions, which we have seen are so often so dangerously wrong.

ENDNOTES

1 Cited in Coral Bell, *The Conventions of Crisis: A Study in Diplomatic Management* (New York: Oxford University Press, 1971), p. 2

2 Alexander George, David K. Hall, and William E. Simons, *The Limits of Coercive Diplomacy: Laos, Cuba, and Vietnam* (Boston: Little, Brown, 1971), pp. 8-11; Glenn Snyder and Paul Diesing, *Conflict among Nations* (Princeton: Princeton University Press, 1977), pp. 207-9; Phil Williams, *Crisis Management: Confrontation and Diplomacy in the Nuclear Age* (New York: Wiley, 1972), pp. 27-31.

3 Snyder and Diesing, *Conflict among Nations*, p. 207.

4 Phil Williams, "Crisis Management," in John Bayliss et al., *Contemporary Strategy: Theories and Policies* (New York: Holmes and Meier, 1975), p. 157. Reprinted in Williams, *Crisis Management*, p. 30.

5 Irving Janis and Leon Mann, *Decision Making* (New York: Free Press, 1977), p. xvii, citing Kurt Lewin.

6 Irving Janis, *Victims of Groupthink* (Boston: Houghton Mifflin, 1972).

7 Ibid., p. 203.

8 Richard Neustadt, *Presidential Power* (New York: Wiley, 1960)

9 Alexander George, "The Case for Multiple Advocacy in Making Foreign Policy," *American Political Science Review*, 66 (September 1972), 756.

10 Snyder and Diesing, *Conflict among Nations*, p. 310. They nevertheless confess that the closest example they found to such a committee, United States foreign policy-making in 1940-41, "casts doubt on this idea, because this committee was about average in total misperceptions and in initial difference of image."

11 Janis, *Victims of Groupthink*, p. 200.

12 Ralph K. White, *Nobody Wanted War: Misperception in Vietnam and Other Wars* (Garden City, N.Y.: Doubleday, 1970), appendix; Janis and Mann, *Decision Making*, pp. 405-9; Roger Fisher, *International Conflict for Beginners* (New York: Harper & Row, 1969).

13 Joseph de Rivera, *Psychological Dimension* (Columbus: Charles E. Merrill, 1968), pp. 61-64; George, "Case for Multiple Advocacy in Making Foreign Policy," pp. 751-95, which includes a "Comment" by I.M. Destler and a "Rejoinder" by George; Robert Jervis, "Hypotheses on Misperception," *World Politics*, 20 (April 1968), 454-79, and *Perception and Misperception in International Politics* (Princeton: Princeton University Press, 1976), pp. 415-18.

14 De Rivera, *Psychological Dimension*.

15 Janis, *Victims of Groupthink*, pp. 207-19; George, "Case for Multiple Advocacy in Foreign Policy."

16 De Rivera, *Psychological Dimension*, p. 63.

17 Morton H. Halperin, *Bureaucratic Politics and Foreign Policy* (Washington, D.C.: Brookings Institution, 1974), pp. 150-55.

18 George E. Reedy, *The Twilight of the Presidency* (New York: World, 1970), p. 11. Ritualized dissent in the Johnson administration is also commented on by James C. Thompson, Jr. in "How Could Vietnam Happen? An Autopsy," *Atlantic Monthly*, April 1968, pp. 47-53.

19 Hans J. Morgenthau, *Truth and Power, Essays of a Decade, 1960-1970* (New York: Praeger, 1970), p. 158.

20 Cited by Henry M. Pachter in *Collision Course: The Cuban Missile Crisis and Coexistence* (New York: Praeger, 1963), p. 87.

21 Ibid., p. 86.

22 George, "The Case for Multiple Advocacy in Making Foreign Policy," p. 763.

23 Janis, *Victims of Groupthink*, p. 165.

24 The "revisionist" literature is now blossoming although much of it remains polemical. See, for example, I. F. Stone, "The Brink," [review of Elie Abel, *The Missile Crisis*], *New York Review of Books*, 14 April 1966; Ronald Steel, *New York Review of Books*, 13 March 1969; John Kenneth Galbraith, "Storm Over Havana: Who Were the Real Heroes?" [review of Robert Kennedy, *Thirteen Days*], *Book World*, 19 January 1969; Louise Fitzsimmons, *The Kennedy Doctrine* (New York: Random House, 1972), pp. 126-73. James A. Nathan's "The Missile Crisis: His Finest Hour Now," *World Politics*, 27 (January 1975), 265-81, is probably the most thoughtful critique.

25 Adam Yarmolinsky, in *The Military Establishment: Its Impact on American Society* (New York: Random House, 1971), p. 127, relates that although the State Department considered diplomatic negotiation, the Ex Com did not. Nor did the Ex Com contemplate any economic measures.

26 Janis, *Victims of Groupthink*, p. 142. Janis appears to turn a blind eye to practically all of the instances of groupthink and promotional leadership in the Cuban case. The reader cannot help but be struck by his apparent need to portray Kennedy's handling of the crisis in a good light, perhaps in order to prove that it is possible to manage a crisis free of groupthink and other decision-making pathologies.

27 Roger Hilsman, *To Move a Nation* (Garden City, New York: Doubleday, 1967), p. 195.

28 Theodore Sorensen, *Kennedy* (New York: Harper and Row, 1965), pp. 694-95. John Bartlow Martin, in *The Life of Adlai Stevenson*, vol. 2: *Adlai Stevenson and the World* (Garden City, N.Y.: Doubleday, 1977), p. 721, reports that Stevenson attended the Ex Com meeting on the 17th, where he argued in favor of sending a high level emissary to Khrushchev.

29 Sorensen, *Kennedy*, pp. 695-96; Martin, *Life of Adlai Stevenson*, vol. 2, pp. 721-23.

30 Sorensen, *Kennedy*, pp. 695-96.

31 Graham Allison, *Essence of Decision* (Boston: Little, Brown, 1971), p. 209; Martin, *Life of Adlai Stevenson*, vol. 2, pp. 586-87, notes that Kennedy's relationship with Stevenson had always been uncomfortable, even painful, and that the younger men around the president frequently spoke disparagingly of the ambassador. Martin, *Life of Adlai Stevenson*, vol. 2, pp. 587 and 724, asserts that Kennedy admired Stevenson for having the "guts" to speak out for a position he believed in.

32 Elie Abel, *The Missile Crisis* (Philadelphia: Lippincott, 1966), p. 96. Martin, *Life of Adlai Stevenson*, vol. 2, pp. 741-48, describes the attack on Stevenson following the crisis and concludes that his subsequent role in the administration was merely ritualistic.

33 Sorensen, *Kennedy*, p. 692.

34 Ibid.

35 Allison, *Essence of Decision*, p. 227.

36 Ibid.,p. 207.

37 Ibid., p. 202.

A: ORGANIZATIONAL AND BUREAUCRATIC POLITICS

The Essence of Decision: Explaining the Cuban Missile Crisis

Graham Allison

The Cuban missile crisis was a seminal event. History offers no parallel to those thirteen days of October 1962, when the United States and the Soviet Union paused at the nuclear precipice. Never before had there been such a high probability that so many lives would end suddenly. Had war come, it could have meant the death of 100 million Americans, more than 100 million Russians, as well as millions of Europeans.[1] Beside it, the natural calamities and inhumanities of earlier history would have faded into insignificance. Given the odds on disaster — which President Kennedy estimated as "between one out of three and even" — our escape seems awesome.[2] This event symbolizes a central, if only partially "thinkable," fact about our existence.

Although several excellent accounts are now available, the missile crisis remains, as Harold Macmillan has observed, a "strange and still scarcely explicable affair."[3] Even the central questions have eluded satisfactory answers:

Why did the Soviet Union place strategic offensive missiles in Cuba? For what purpose did the Russians undertake such a drastic, risky departure from their traditional policy? Given the repeated American warnings that such an act would not be tolerated, how could Khrushchev have made such a major miscalculation?

Why did the United States respond with a naval quarantine of Soviet shipments to Cuba? Was it necessary for the United States to force a public nuclear confrontation? What alternatives were really available? What danger did the Soviet missiles in Cuba pose for the United States? Did this threat justify the President's choice of a course of action that he believed entailed a 33 to 50 percent chance of disaster? Did that threat require more immediate action to disable the Soviet missiles in Cuba before they became operational?

Why were the missiles withdrawn? What would have happened if, instead of withdrawing the missiles, Khrushchev had announced that the operational Soviet missiles would fire if fired upon? Did

---

From Graham T. Allison, *Essence of Decision: Explaining the Cuban Missile Crisis,* pp. 1-9, 245-263. Portions of the text have been deleted. Some footnotes have been removed; those remaining have been renumbered.

the "blockade" work, or was there an "ultimatum" or perhaps some "deal"? Why did the Soviets remove the missiles rather than retaliate at other equally sensitive points — Berlin, for example?

What are the "lessons" of the missile crisis? What does this event teach us about nuclear confrontations? What does it imply about crisis management and government coordination? Is this a model of how to deal with the Soviet Union?

Satisfactory answers to these questions await information that has not yet come to light and more penetrating analysis of available evidence. This study provides new information about the missile crisis and a more powerful analysis of some aspects of it. But the missile crisis also serves here as grist in a more general investigation. This study proceeds from the premise that satisfactory answers to questions about the missile crisis wait for more information and analysis. Real improvement in our answers to questions of this sort depends on greater awareness of what we (both laymen and professional analysts) bring to the analysis. When answering questions like "Why did the Soviet Union place missiles in Cuba?" what we see and judge to be important and accept as adequate depends not only on the evidence but also on the "conceptual lenses" through which we look at the evidence. Another purpose of this study is therefore to explore some of the fundamental yet often unnoticed choices among the categories and assumptions that channel our thinking about problems like the Cuban missile crisis.

THE GENERAL ARGUMENT

When we are puzzled by a happening in foreign affairs, the source of our puzzlement is typically a particular *outcome*: the Soviet emplacement of missiles in Cuba, the movement of U.S. troops across the narrow neck of the Korean peninsula, the Japanese attack on Pearl Harbor.[4] These occurrences raise obvious questions: *Why* did the Soviet Union place missiles in Cuba? *Why* did U.S. troops fail to stop at the narrow neck in their march up Korea? *Why* did Japan attack the American fleet at Pearl Harbor? In pursuing the answers to these questions, the serious analyst seeks to discover why one specific state of the world came about — rather than some other.

In searching for an explanation, one typically puts himself in the place of the nation, or national government, confronting a problem of foreign affairs, and tries to figure out why he might have chosen the action in question. Thus, analysts have explained the Soviet missiles in Cuba as a probe of American intentions. U.S. troops marched across the narrow neck in Korea because American objectives had escalated as a consequence of easy victories in the South. The attack on Pearl Harbor is explained as Japan's solution to the strategic problem posed by U.S. pressure in the Far East.

In offering (or accepting) these explanations, we are assuming governmental behavior can be most satisfactorily understood by analogy with the purposive acts of individuals. In many cases this is a fruitful assumption. Treating national governments as if they were centrally coordinated, purposive individuals provides a useful shorthand for understanding problems of policy. But this simplification — like all simplifications — obscures as well as reveals. In particular, it obscures the persistently neglected fact of bureaucracy: the "maker" of government policy is not one calculating decisionmaker but is rather a conglomerate of large organizations and political actors. What this fact implies for analysts of events like the Cuban missile crisis is no simple matter: its implications concern the basic categories and assumptions with which we approach events.

More rigorously, the *argument* developed in the body of this study can be summarized in three propositions:

1. *Professional analysts of foreign affairs (as well as ordinary laymen) think about problems of foreign and military policy in terms of largely implicit conceptual models that have significant consequences for the content of their thought.*[5]

In thinking about problems of foreign affairs,

professional analysts as well as ordinary laymen proceed in a straightforward, informal, non-theoretical fashion. Careful examination of explanations of events like the Soviet installation of missiles in Cuba, however, reveals a more complex theoretical substructure. Explanations by particular analysts show regular and predictable characteristics, which reflect unrecognized assumptions about the character of puzzles, the categories in which problems should be considered, the types of evidence that are relevant, and the determinants of occurrences. The first proposition is that bundles of such related assumptions constitute basic frames of reference or conceptual models in terms of which analysts and ordinary laymen ask and answer the questions: What happened? Why did it happen? What will happen?[6] Assumptions like these are central to the activities of explanation and prediction. In attempting to explain a particular event, the analyst cannot simply describe the full state of the world leading up to that event. The logic of explanation requires that he single out the relevant, important determinants of the occurrence. Moreover, as the logic of prediction underscores, he must summarize the various factors as they bear on the occurrence. Conceptual models not only fix the mesh of the nets that the analysts drags through the material in order to explain a particular action; they also direct him to cast his nets in select ponds, at certain depths, in order to catch the fish he is after.

2. *Most analysts explain (and predict) the behavior of national governments in terms of one basic conceptual model, here entitled Rational Actor or "Classical" Model (Model I).*[7]

In spite of significant differences in interest and focus, most analysts and ordinary laymen attempt to understand happenings in foreign affairs as the more or less purposive acts of unified national governments. Laymen personify rational actors and speak of their aims and choices. Theorists of international relations focus on problems between nations in accounting for the choices of unitary rational actors. Strategic analysts concentrate on the logic of action in the absence of an actor. For each of these groups, the point of an explanation is to show how the nation or government could have chosen to act as it did, given the strategic problems it faced. For example, in confronting the problem posed by the Soviet installation of strategic missiles in Cuba, the Model I analyst frames the puzzle: Why did the Soviet Union decide to install missiles in Cuba? He then fixes the unit of analysis: governmental choice. Next, he focuses attention on certain concepts: goals and objectives of the nation or government. And finally, he invokes certain patterns of inference: if the nation performed an action of this sort, it must have had a goal of this type. The analyst has "explained" this event when he can show how placing missiles in Cuba was a reasonable action, given Soviet strategic objectives. Predictions about what a nation will do or would have done are generated by calculating the rational thing to do in a certain situation, given specified objectives.

3. *Two alternative conceptual models, here labeled an Organizational Process Model (Model II) and a Governmental (Bureaucratic) Politics Model (Model III),*[8] *provide a base for improved explanations and predictions.*[9]

Although the Rational Actor Model has proved useful for many purposes, there is powerful evidence that it must be supplemented, if not supplanted, by frames of reference that focus on the governmental machine — the organizations and political actors involved in the policy process. Model I's implication that important events have important causes, i.e., that monoliths perform large actions for large reasons, must be balanced by the appreciation that (1) monoliths are black boxes covering various gears and levers in a highly differentiated decisionmaking structure and (2) large acts result from innumerable and often conflicting smaller actions by individuals at various levels of bureaucratic organizations in the service of a variety of only partially compatible conceptions of national goals, organizational goals, and political objectives. Model I's grasp of national purposes and of the pressures created by problems in *inter*-national relations must confront the *intra*-national mechanisms from which governmental actions emerge.

Recent developments in organization theory provide the foundation for the second model, which emphasizes the processes and procedures of the large organizations that constitute a government. According to this Organizational Process Model, what Model I analysts characterize as "acts" and "choices" are thought of instead as *outputs* of large organizations functioning according to regular patterns of behavior. Faced with the problem of Soviet missiles in Cuba, a Model II analyst frames the puzzle: From what organizational context and pressures did this decision emerge? He then fixes the unit of analysis: organizational output. Next, he focuses attention on certain concepts: the strength, standard operating procedures, and repertoires of organizations. And finally, he invokes certain patterns of inference: if organizations produced an output of this kind today, that behavior resulted from existing organizational features, procedures, and repertoires. A Model II analyst has "explained" the event when he has identified the relevant Soviet organizations and displayed the patterns of organizational behavior from which the action emerged. Predictions identify trends that reflect established organizations and their fixed procedures and programs.

The third model focuses on the politics of a government. Events in foreign affairs are understood, according to this model, neither as choices nor as outputs. Rather, what happens is characterized as a *resultant* of various bargaining games among players in the national government. In confronting the problem posed by Soviet missiles in Cuba, a Model III analyst frames the puzzle: Which results of what kinds of bargaining among which players yielded the critical decisions and actions? He then fixes the unit of analysis: political resultant. Next, he focuses attention on certain concepts: the perceptions, motivations, positions, power, and maneuvers of the players. And finally, he invokes certain patterns of inference: if a government performed an action, that action was the resultant of bargaining among players in games. A Model III analyst has "explained" this event when he has discovered who did what to whom that yielded the action in question. Predictions are generated by identifying the game in which an issue will arise, the relevant players, and their relative power and skill.[10]

A central metaphor illuminates the differences among these models. Foreign policy has often been compared to moves and sequences of moves in the game of chess. Imagine a chess game in which the observer could see only a screen upon which moves in the game were projected, with no information about how the pieces came to be moved. Initially, most observers would assume — as Model I does — that an individual chess player was moving the pieces with reference to plans and tactics toward the goal of winning the game. But a pattern of moves can be imagined that would lead some observers, after watching several games, to consider a Model II assumption: the chess player might not be a single individual but rather a loose alliance of semi-independent organizations, each of which moved its set of pieces according to standard operating procedures. For example, movement of separate sets of pieces might proceed in turn, each according to a routine, the king's rook, bishop, and their pawns repeatedly attacking the opponent according to a fixed plan. It is conceivable, furthermore, that the pattern of play might suggest to an observer a Model III assumption: a number of distinct players, with distinct objectives but shared power over the pieces, could be determining the moves as the resultant of collegial bargaining. For example, the black rook's move might contribute to the loss of a black knight with no comparable gains for the black team, but with the black rook becoming the principal guardian of the palace on that side of the board....

These conceptual models are much more than *simple* angles of vision or approaches. Each conceptual framework consists of a *cluster* of assumptions and categories that influence what the analyst finds puzzling, how he formulates his question, where he looks for evidence, and what he produces as an answer. The three cuts at the missile crisis demonstrate both the complexity of the models and the differences in analysis that they make....

There is an apparent incompatibility between the level of discourse in the Model I account and that of the Model II and Model III accounts. The Model I analyst approached the Soviet installation of missiles in Cuba, the American naval blockade, and the Soviet withdrawal of missiles as strategic choices. By analyzing the strategic problem that the Soviet Union faced, and the characteristics of the Soviet missile deployment, he produced an argument for one goal (rectifying the nuclear balance) that made the Soviet emplacement plausible. The American blockade was explained simply as the U.S. value-maximizing choice. Withdrawal of the missiles was understood as the only option left for the Soviets after the United States signaled the firmness of its intentions. While these explanations were offered without detailed attention to the internal mechanisms of the governments, the Model I analyst's appropriation of statements by officials of the government as "the government view" and his use of fine detail about the Soviet missile deployment as a criterion for distinguishing among Soviet objectives would seem to imply coincidence of perceptions, control of choice, and coordination of movement within the government-as-unitary-actor.

As the Model II and Model III accounts of bureaucratic machinations demonstrate, this was not in fact the case. Many crucial details of implementation followed from organizational routines rather than from central choice. The principal government leaders differed markedly in their perceptions of the problem, their estimates of the consequences of various courses of action, and their preferred solutions. These facts force one to wonder about the Model I account. The explanation proceeds as if it were simply describing the process of governmental reasoning, choice, and implementation. But since, as we have seen this account does not accurately describe the process, what does it describe? To whose objectives and reasons does the Model I analysis refer? In contrast with the Model II and Model III accounts, the Model I version seems somewhat disembodied.

The Model I analyst fastened on particular characteristics of the Soviet installation of missiles, and of the blockade, as signals of central calculations and choices. The Soviet installation of more expensive and more visible IRBMs as well as MRBMs was taken by the Model I analyst as a major piece of evidence against which to test the competing hypotheses about Soviet intentions. He used this fact to disqualify the "Cuban defense" hypothesis on the grounds that MRBMs alone would have sufficed to guarantee the defense of Cuba. But the Model II analyst challenged the presumption that evidence of this sort can be used to identify governmental intentions. He explained the simultaneous installation of IRBMs and MRBMs as a consequence of organizational goals and routines. Similarly, the construction of MRBMs before completion of the SAM network, the positioning of Soviet missiles in the standard four-slice pattern, and the failure to camouflage the sites were explained by the Model II analyst as normal, organizational performance — rather than as occasions for extraordinary puzzlement.

The most glaring conflict between Model I's strategic summary of the event and Model II and Model III's examination of details of the process — organizational or political — reflects the incentives that each model produces for probing the facts. The Model I analyst's explanatory power derives primarily from his construction of a calculation that makes plausible the character of the action chosen, given the problem the nation faced. This construction requires a factual base. But the available, conventional facts usually suffice, since the essential element in the analyst's work is his reasoning, his thinking through the nation's problem....[11]

The alternative interpretations of the Soviet missile withdrawal provide the most suggestive instance of these differences among the models over evidence and interpretation. Our Model I analyst explained the withdrawal as a consequence of the American ultimatum. Most analysts will find this interpretation preferable to explanations that focus on the blockade. This explanation is certainly satisfactory in Model I terms. But the Model II and Model III analysts carry the argument a step further. They are naturally inclined to dig deeper into the evidence about organizations and internal politics. Though the information is incomplete, the Model II analyst uncovered and emphasized the importance of U.S. missiles in Turkey and a Presidential order that they be defused. This led him to hypothesize with respect to the final Saturday that either (1) an American ultimatum forced Soviet capitulation, or (2) while Kennedy was beginning to wobble, Khrushchev folded. From a Model III perspective, a further hypothesis emerged. The argument against a "deal" (i.e., withdrawal of Soviet missiles in Cuba for withdrawal of American missiles in Turkey) has — in Model I terms — been heretofore entirely compelling. In spite of the fact that the Soviets proposed precisely this arrangement in their Saturday letter, the United States simply could not accept such terms: it would shake the alliance; it would signal weakness; it would confuse the issue. No published analysis of the missile crisis has been able to escape this reasoning. But from a Model III perspective, it is hard to believe that John F. Kennedy should have been so insensitive to Khrushchev's problem as to refuse, in private, what he in fact planned — and had previously meant — to do. Robert Kennedy's last account of the crisis, published after our Model III analyst generated this hypothesis, suggests strongly that the Model III analysis is correct.

Between the Model II and Model III versions there are a number of additional differences in emphasis and interpretation. For example, the Model II explanation credited Kennedy's consultation of General Sweeney, the head of Tactical Air Command, on Sunday, October 20, as a *bona fide* last minute reconsideration. But the Model III understanding of this occurrence as "preparation of the record" seems closer to the mark.

More revealing is the divergence between Model II and Model III interpretations of the Air Force estimate of U.S. capabilities for a surgical air strike. From a Model II perspective, that inaccurate estimate — which in its error eliminated the Air Force's preferred course of action — emerged according to the established routines of the Air Force. In contrast, the Model III interpretation of this event highlighted both the overconfidence of the Air Force Chief of Staff, which reduced his suspicion of the estimate, and the willingness of other government leaders not to probe an estimate that served their purposes. The available evidence is insufficient to permit confident judgment between these hypotheses.

A large number of puzzles about this most important event are yet unresolved — leaving a real need for a thorough historical study of this crisis.

SUMMING UP: DIFFERENT ANSWERS OR DIFFERENT QUESTIONS?

Such variance among interpretations demonstrates each model's tendency to produce different answers to the same question. But as we observe the models at work, what is equally striking are the differences in the ways the analysts conceive of the problem, shape the puzzle, unpack the summary questions, and pick up pieces of the world in search of an answer. Why did the United States blockade Cuba? For Model I analysts, this "why" asks for reasons that account for the American choice of the blockade as a solution to the strategic problem posed by the presence of Soviet missiles in Cuba. For a Model II analyst, the puzzle is rather: What outputs of which organizations led to this blockade? A Model III analyst understands the basic "why" as a question about the various problems perceived by relevant players and their pulling and hauling from which the blockade emerged.

Typically, the thing to be explained is designated by a rather vague, summary clause, accompanied by an implicit appendix that specifies the relevant aspects of the occurrence. For a Model I analyst, "blockade" is an aggregate act. The perceived context, formal decision, and implementation are all aspects of one coordinated, rational choice. The Model II and Model III analysts insist on splitting up the blockade into a number of pieces. The Model II analyst focuses on slices like *when* the missiles were discovered, *how* the options were defined, and the *details* of the blockade's execution. The Model III analyst focuses both on the emergence of the blockade decision in the ExCom and on various aspects of implementation.

To explain the blockade, the Model I analyst examines the U.S. strategic calculus: the problem posed by the Soviet missiles, relevant American values, and U.S. capabilities. Explanation *means* placing the blockade in a pattern of purposive response to the strategic problem. For a Model II man, this "solution" emerges as the by-product of basic organizational processes. The analyst emphasizes organizational constraint in choice and organizational routines in implementation. Organizational processes produced awareness of the problem on October 14 (rather than two weeks earlier or later); organizational routines defined the alternatives; organizational procedures implemented the blockade. These features overshadow the "decisions" of the unified group of leaders within these constraints. Explanation starts with existing organizations and their routines at *t* minus 1 and attempts to account for what is going on at time *t*. The Model III analyst accents the action of players in the relevant games that produced pieces of the collage that is the blockade. Bargaining among players who shared power but saw separate problems yielded discovery of the missiles on a certain date in a special context, a definition of the problem which demanded strong action, a coalition of Presidential intimates set on averting holocaust, failure to probe the military estimate, and consequently a blockade. In the absence of a number of particular characteristics of players and games, the action would not have been the same.

The information required by Model II and Model III analysts dwarfs that needed by a Model I analyst. An armchair strategist (in Washington or even Cambridge) can produce accounts of U.S. (or Soviet) national costs and benefits. Understanding the value-maximizing choices of nations demands chiefly an analytic ability at vicarious problem solving. But analyses that concentrate on processes and procedures of organizations, or on pulling and hauling among individuals, demand much more information. Some observers (particularly players in the game) rely on a version of Model III for their own government's behavior, while retreating to a Model I analysis of other nations. Thus *information costs* account for some differences among explanations. The difficulty of acquiring information, however, is no more important than the differential capacity of different models to recognize the relevance and importance of additional pieces of information. For a Model I analyst, information about a split between McNamara and the Joint Chiefs over the proper response to Soviet missiles constitutes gossip or anecdote but not evidence about an important factor. Only Model II analysts are willing to gather information about existing organizational routines. Model III's delineation of positions, and its attention to the advantages and disadvantages of various players, strikes other analysts as an undue concern with subtlety.

Thus while at one level three models produce different explanations of the same happening, at a second level the models produce different explanations of quite different occurrences. And indeed, this is my argument. Spectacles magnify one set of factors rather than another and thus not only lead analysts to produce different explanations of problems that appear, in their summary questions, to be the same, but also influence the character of the analyst's puzzle, the evidence he assumes to be relevant, the concepts he uses in examining the evidence, and what he takes to be an explanation. None of our three analysts would deny that during the Cuban missile crisis several million people were performing actions relevant to the event. But in offering his explanation, each analyst attempts to emphasize what is relevant and important, and different conceptual lenses lead analysts to different judgments about what is relevant and important.

WHERE DO WE GO FROM HERE?

In the last several years it has been remarked with increasing frequency that American academic and professional thought about foreign affairs seems to have reached a hiatus. Strategic thought has made little progress since Schelling's *Strategy of Conflict*. Sovietology is just "more of the same." The arms control literature has been coasting on ideas generated by the time of the summer study of 1960. The new wave of revisionist studies of American foreign policy turns traditional interpretations on their head without really increasing our understanding. Diplomatic history shows little life.

Why should this be the case? My colleagues in Harvard's Research Seminar on Bureaucracy, Politics, and Policy have convinced me that my argument really backs into consideration of these larger issues: namely, where does our thinking about foreign affairs now stand? Where should we go from here? The answer provided by this study is half-baked and rather haphazard, since these are not questions with which it began. Still, the tentative answer it implies should be made explicit.

That most thinking about foreign affairs is dominated by one basic set of categories is hardly accidental. Confronted by a puzzling occurrence in international affairs, we naturally ask why, and try to understand how the nation involved could have chosen the action in question. Without thinking, we immediately begin talking about "Hanoi" or "Peking." We try to "see the problem from the North Vietnamese point of view" — that is, from the point of view of a reasonable leader sitting in Hanoi — and to reason why "he" chose the action in question. The analogy between nations in international politics and a coordinated, intelligent human being is so powerful that we rarely remember we are reasoning by analogy.

The contribution of the classical model (Model I) to our explanations, predictions, and analyses of foreign affairs is considerable. This lens reduces the organizational and political complications of a government to the simplification of a single actor. The array of details about a happening can be seen to cluster around the major features of an action. Through this lens the confused and even contradictory factors that influence an occurrence become a single dynamic: *choice* of the alternative that achieved a certain goal. Thus the Rational Actor Model permits us to translate the basic question, "Why did X happen?" into the question "Why did this nation do X?" The question then becomes: "What problem was the nation solving (or what goal was the nation achieving) in choosing X?" The classical model allows us to deal with the last question in the same way that we would answer a question about an individual's action.

Recall once more the Model I analyst's explanation of Soviet installation of missiles in Cuba. Confronted with the fact, he formulated the puzzle as a question about why the government chose this aggregate action. Explanation then consisted in constructing a calculation according to which the Soviet government reasonably chose to make the move. In producing the explanation, the Model I analyst proceeded as if his assignment had been: make a powerful argument for one objective that permits the reader to see how, given the strategic problem, if he had been playing the Soviet hand, he would have chosen that action. In more technical terms, the game is one of maximization under some set of constraints.[12]

The model employed in this explanation is not only the basic framework used by ordinary men and professional analysts in explaining occurrences in foreign affairs.It is even more essential. Perhaps the most fundamental method employed by human beings in their attempt to come to grips with the puzzling occurrences around them is to conceive of these occurrences not as simple phenomena or events (i.e., things that just happen) but rather as *action* (i.e., behavior expressing some intention or choice). This is the way we explain our behavior to ourselves and to others: "I wanted X." "I chose Y." This is the way we understand the behavior of our fellow men.

For explaining and predicting the behavior of individual men, this general orientation toward purpose and rational choice seems to be the best available. The rationality of man's choices is, of course, "bounded" by things such as the availability of information and the difficulty of calculation. But as a baseline, if one knows how an individual has defined his problem and what resources he has available, his objectives provide a good clue to his behavior.

Difficulties arise when the thing to be explained is not the behavior of an individual but rather the behavior of a large organization or even a government. Nations can be reified, but at considerable cost in understanding. By personifying nations, one glides over critical characteristics of behavior where an organization is the main mover — for example, the fact that organizational action requires the coordination of large numbers of individuals, thus necessitating programs and SOPs. Thinking about a nation as if it were a person neglects considerable differences among individual leaders of a government whose positions and power lead them to quite different perceptions and preferences. Thus where the actor is a national government, a conception of action for objectives must be modified. (Perhaps the organizational and political factors could be formulated as "constraints" within which the government actually chooses, though this would require an analysis quite distinct from Simon's concern with "bounded rationality.")[13]

As we have noted earlier, the Model II and Model III accounts of questions treated ordinarily in standard Model I fashion highlight this difficulty. No longer is it possible to maintain that the Model I explanation is simply *describing* the processes within the national government. We are forced to recognize that in treating happenings as actions, and national governments as unitary purposive actors, we are "modeling." The fact that the assumptions and categories of this model neglect important factors such as organizational processes and bureaucratic politics suggests that the model is inadequate. Careful examination of the model's performance confirms this suspicion. For example, the U.S. intelligence estimate of September 19, 1962, contained a plausible strategic analysis showing that the Soviets would not place missiles in Cuba. If no missiles had been placed in Cuba, a Model I analyst would have explained this fact by reference to these reasons. Given that the Soviets did emplace missiles, the Model I analyst attempts to explain this event by constructing the strategic analysis that makes plausible their choice to do so. But the occurrence or nonoccurrence of the Soviet missile deployment in Cuba must have been determined by something more than these strategic reasons.

The present hiatus in thinking about problems of foreign affairs derives in large part from attempts to pursue Model I reasoning, without much self-consciousness, as the single form of analysis. Model I analysis can be valuable. It does permit a quick, imaginative sorting out of a problem of explanation or analysis. It serves as a productive shorthand, requiring a minimum of information. It can yield an informative summary of tendencies, for example, by identifying the weight of strategic costs and benefits. But it is not itself a full analysis or explanation of an event, and it cannot stand alone. We must understand much more clearly what a Model I analysis refers to, what part of the problem it captures, how we should modify its rules for the use of evidence, etc. Part of "where we should go from here" is to develop Model I as one of several conscious and explicit styles of analysis.

The burden of this study's argument, however, is that larger payoffs in the future will come from an intellectual shift of gears. We should ask not what goals account for a nation's choice of an action, but rather what factors determine an outcome. The shift from Model I to the Model II and Model III forms of analysis really involves a fundamental change in intellectual style. From the basic conception of happenings as choices to be explained by reference to objectives (on analogy with the actions of individual human beings), we must move to a conception of happenings as events whose determinants are to be investigated according to the canons that have been developed by modern science.

Model II and Model III summarize two bundles of categories and assumptions, and two distinctive logical patterns that provide useful, emphatic shorthands in which governmental action can be explained and predicted. The separation of these two models as alternative pairs of spectacles facilitates the generation of hypotheses and highlights features that might otherwise be overlooked. The focus on separable clusters of factors with distinguishable logical thrusts makes persuasive the importance of certain factors that might not otherwise be so. But this argument should not be misinterpreted as an assertion that Model II and Model III are the *only* alternative conceptual models. One of my colleagues in the Bureaucracy Research Seminar, John Steinbruner, has stated a fourth conceptual model.[14] A number of others are clearly possible. Nor should the fact that several are stated, and additional models contemplated, be misunderstood as a denial of the possibility of a grand model that would incorporate the features of all. The basic orientation toward outcomes and their determinants invokes an image of an ideal model in which all determinants and their relations could be specified (at least probabilistically). The only issue here is one of the relative merits of alternative paradigms versus a grand model at the present stage of understanding.

The outline of a tentative, *ad hoc* working synthesis of the models begins to emerge if one considers the general questions that each model leads one to ask of a problem of explanation, analysis, or prediction.

Among the questions posed by Model I are:[15]

1. What is the problem?
2. What are the alternatives?
3. What are the strategic costs and benefits associated with each alternative?
4. What is the observed pattern of national (governmental) values and shared axioms?
5. What are the pressures in the "international strategic marketplace"?

Model II leads one to ask:

1. Of what organizations (and organizational components) does the government consist?
2. Which organizations traditionally act on a problem of this sort and with what relative influence?
3. What repertoires, programs, and SOPs do these organizations have for making *information* about the problem available at various decision points in the government?
4. What repertoires, programs, and SOPs do these organizations have for generating *alternatives* about a problem of this sort?
5. What repertoires, programs, and SOPs do these organizations have for *implementing* alternative courses of action?

The central questions posed by Model III include:

1. What are the existing action channels for producing actions on this kind of problem?
2. Which players in what positions are centrally involved?
3. How do pressures of job, past stances, and personality affect the central players on this issue?
4. What deadlines will force the issue to resolution?
5. Where are foul-ups likely?

Thus we can see how Model I emphasizes, on the one hand, the problem and context that create incentives and pressures for a government to choose a particular course of action, and, on the other, the national (or governmental) values and axioms that create propensities to respond in certain ways. Overarching problems and axioms summarize important differences between behavioral tendencies of nations. Were one ignorant, for example, of the differences between American national attitudes in the mid-1960s and those in

Summary Outline of Models and Concepts

The Paradigm	Model I	Model II	Model III
	National government [Black box] Goals (objective function) Options Consequences Choice	National government [Leaders; A B C D E F G] Organizations (A–G) Goals SOPs and programs	National government [A z y C n x; D t y; B r y E z r F p r] Players in positions (A–F) Goals, interests, stakes, and stands (r–z) Power Action-channels
Basic unit of analysis	Governmental action as choice	Governmental action as organizational output	Governmental action as political resultant
Organizing concepts	National actor The problem Static selection Action as rational choice Goals and objectives Options Consequences Choice	Organizational actors (constellation of which is the government) Factored problems and fractionated power Parochial priorities and perceptions Action as organizational output Goals: constraints defining acceptable performance Sequential attention to goals Standard operating procedures Programs and repertoires Uncertainty avoidance (negotiated environment, standard scenario) Problem-directed search Organizational learning and change Central coordination and control Decisons of government leaders	Players in positions Parochial priorities and perceptions Goals and interests Stakes and stands Deadlines and faces of issues Power Action-channels Rules of the game Action as political resultant
Dominant inference pattern	Governmental action = choice with regard to objectives	Governmental action (in short run) = output largely determined by present SOPs and programs Governmental action (in longer run) = output importantly affected by organizational goals, SOPs, etc.	Governmental action = resultant of bargaining
General propositions	Substitution effect	Organizational implementation Organizational options Limited flexibility and incremental change Long-range planning Goals and tradeoffs Imperialism Options and organization Administrative feasibility Directed change	Political resultants Action and intention Problems and solutions Where you stand depends on where you sit Chiefs and Indians The 51–49 principle Inter- and intra-national relations Misperception, misexpectation, miscommunication, and reticence Styles of play

the mid-1930s, he would miss fundamental factors in the foreign policy of the United States. The shared objectives of national leaders, and the pressures created by strategic problems influence the trend line of any nation's action. Indeed, it is not difficult to see how the factors summarized by Model I affect assumptions of players in the Model III game, the kinds of arguments that these men can make, and even the range of outputs that organizations examined by Model II are prepared to produce. For some purposes, then, Model I may provide a satisfactory summary of the longer-run patterns of a nation's foreign policy.

Model II and Model III analysts, however, assume the influence of Model I factors, focusing within this environment — this set of market pressures — on the mechanism that produced a particular outcome. The problem, according to these analysts, is not to explain, for example, why the United States had 500,000 men in Viet Nam in the mid-1960s, rather than in the mid-1930s. The problem is, given the national values and leaders' objectives in the United States in the 1960s, why did the United States have 500,000 men in Viet Nam? Overarching ideas or the climate of opinion constitute a large part of the explanation of the differences between the 1930s (when the probability that any U.S. leader or governmental organization could have inserted 500,000 men in Viet Nam approached zero) and the 1960s (when the possibility of this outcome was closer to 0.2). But the Organizational Process and Governmental Politics Models assume the context, and focus on the problem of explaining the occurrence of an event that values and objectives made 20 percent probable.

Thus the models can be seen to complement each other. Model I fixes the broader context, the larger national patterns, and the shared images. Within this context, Model II illuminates the organizational routines that produce the information, alternatives, and action. Within the Model II context, Model III focuses in greater detail on the individual leaders of a government and the politics among them that determine major governmental choices. The best analysts of foreign policy manage to weave strands of each of the three conceptual models into their explanations. A number of scholars...display considerable intuitive powers in blending insights from all three models. By drawing complementary pieces from each of these styles of analysis, explanations can be significantly strengthened. But we must pay more careful attention to the points at which the explanations are complementary and the junctures at which implications may be incompatible.[16]

As a final reminder of the importance of the differences in emphasis among the three models, consider the *lessons* that each model draws from the crisis. The most widely believed and frequently cited lessons of the crisis have emerged from Model I analysis. These include: (1) since nuclear war between the United States and Soviet Union would be mutual national suicide, neither nation would choose nuclear war, and nuclear war is therefore not a serious possibility; (2) in a world of rough nuclear parity, the United States can choose low-level military actions with no fear that they will escalate to nuclear war; (3) nuclear crises are manageable — that is, in situations involving the vital interests of the superpowers, the leaders of both nations will have little difficulty in thinking through the problem and its alternatives, finding limited actions (the blockade) that communicate resolve, and thus settling the issue (withdrawal of the missiles). According to these analyses, the missile crisis was one of the Kennedy administration's "finest hours," though the "flap in the White House" — the White House tendency to view the problem in apocalyptic terms — was not only unnecessary but positively dangerous. As we noted earlier, the major departmental post-mortem on the crisis concluded that "this exaggerated concern [about the possibility of nuclear war] prompted consideration of improvident actions and counseled hesitation where none was due."[17]

Model II and Model III analysts caution against confidence in the impossibility of nations stumbling — "irrationally" — into a nuclear exchange, in the manageability of nuclear crises, or in our understanding of the ingredients of successful crisis management. According to Model II's account of the crisis, our success included crucial organizational rigidities and even mistakes. Except for the routines and procedures that produced an inaccurate estimate of our capability for a surgical air strike, the probability of war would have been much higher. Only barely did government leaders manage to control organizational programs that might have dragged us over the cliff. In several instances, we were just plain lucky. The lesson: nuclear crises between machines as large as the United States and Soviet governments are inherently chancy. The information and estimates available to leaders about the situation will reflect organizational goals and routines as well as the facts. The alternatives presented to the leaders will be much narrower than the menu of options that would be desirable. The execution of choices will exhibit unavoidable rigidities of programs and SOPs. Coordination among organizations will be much less finely tuned than leaders demand or expect. The prescription: considerable thought must be given to the routines established in the principal organizations before a crisis so that during the crisis organizations will be capable of performing adequately the needed functions. In the crisis, the overwhelming problem will be that of control and coordination of large organizations.

The lessons that emerge from Model III give one even less reason to be sanguine about our understanding of nuclear crises or about the impossibility of nuclear war. The actions advocated by leaders of the U.S. government covered a spectrum from doing nothing to an air strike. The process by which the blockade emerged included many uncertain factors. Had Cuba II been President Kennedy's first crisis, Robert Kennedy and Sorensen would not have been members of the group, and the air strike would probably have emerged. Had Kennedy proved his mettle domestically in a previous confrontation, the diplomatic track could have prevailed. The lessons in Model III terms, then, are that: (1) the process of crisis management is obscure and terribly risky; (2) the leaders of the U.S. government can choose actions that entail (in their judgment) real possibilities of escalation to nuclear war; (3) the interaction of internal games, each as ill-understood as those in the White House and the Kremlin, could indeed yield nuclear war as an outcome. From this perspective, the "flap in the White House" was quite justified — especially for men aware that the internal politics of the government whose behavior they were trying to influence must have been no less confusing and complex than their own. If a President and his associates have to try to manage a nuclear crisis, the informal machinery, freewheeling discussions, and devil's advocacy exemplified by the ExCom have many advantages. But the mix of personality, expertise, influence, and temperament that allows such a group to clarify alternatives even while it pulls and hauls for separate preferences should be better understood before we start down the path to nuclear confrontation again. On the evidence of the Cuban missile crisis, clarification is scarcely assured....

ENDNOTES

1 Deaths of this order of magnitude would have occurred only in the worst case.

2 Theodore Sorensen, *Kennedy* (New York: Harper & Row, 1965), p. 705.

3 Harold Macmillan, "Introduction" to Robert F. Kennedy, *Thirteen Days: A Memoir of the Cuban Missile Crisis* (New York: Norton, 1969), p. 17.

4 The term *outcome* is introduced here as a technical concept meaning a selectively delimited state of the real world importantly affected by the action of a government. The assertion is that in thinking about problems of foreign affairs, what most participants and analysts are really interested in are outcomes and the specific actions governments take that affect outcomes.

5 In attempting to understand problems of foreign affairs, analysts engage in a number of related but logically separable enterprises: (1) description, (2)

explanation, (3) prediction, (4) evaluation, and (5) recommendation. This study focuses primarily on explanation and, by implication, prediction.

6 In arguing that explanations proceed in terms of implicit conceptual models, this essay makes no claim that foreign policy analysts have developed any satisfactory, empirically tested theory. In this study the term *model* without qualifiers should be read "conceptual scheme or framework."

7 Model I has been variously labeled the rational-policy model, the unitary-purposive model, and the purposive-actor model....

8 Earlier drafts of this argument have generated heated discussion about proper names for the models. To choose names from ordinary language is to promote familiarity and to court confusion. Perhaps it is best to think of these models simply as Model I, Model II, and Model III.

9 Model III might have been labeled administrative, internal, governmental, machine, or even palace politics. "Politics" signifies the subtle pulling and hauling in intricate games that characterize the action. "Bureaucratic" signifies that the action is located in the bureaucratized machine that is the executive, or administration, or (in the United Kingdom) government.

10 In strict terms, the "outcomes" these three models attempt to explain are essentially the behavior of national governments, i.e., the sum of official behavior of all individuals employed in a government, relevant to an issue. These models focus not on a state of affairs, i.e., a full description of the world, but upon national decisions and implementation. This distinction is stated clearly by Harold and Margaret Sprout, "Environmental Factors in the Study of International Politics," in James Rosenau (ed.), *International Politics and Foreign Policy* (Glencoe, Ill.: Free Press, 1961), p. 116....

11 Some Model I analysts go a step further in constructing their explanations: they try to account for a large number of particular characteristics of the action, or to find more subtle reasons for the action. One could imagine a competition among Model I analysts, the point of which would be to construct the most subtle set of objectives that the action maximized. A competition of this sort has developed among economists using a maximizing model to explain the behavior of consumers and firms.

12 Variants of Model I can be produced by changing the constraints, e.g., by changing the assignment to: make a powerful argument for a more complex national objective function, including both foreign and domestic objectives, that permits the reader to see how he could have chosen that action.

13 Herbert Simon developed the concept of "bounded rationality" for individual actors, stressing bounds such as costs of information and calculation. An analogous concept could be developed for governments, though in this case the central problems would be identification of the governmental actor's goals, perceptions, etc.

14 Steinbruner's Model IV emphasizes cognitive processes of individuals. It can therefore be understood as a gloss on Model III or Model II. See his ... *The Mind and the Milieu of Policy Makers.*

15 To make Model I ask questions about determinants requires some translation.

16 Though the explanations produced by analysts relying predominantly on different models reflect differences in emphasis, focus, and collateral purpose, can one satisfactorily account for the seeming conflicts among explanations by noting that different models address somewhat different questions? Is this not analogous to some physicists' attempts to explain the differences between wave and quantum theories of light? Certainly this does not relieve the suspicion that at some level there is a conflict between President Kennedy's explanation of the U.S. imposition of the blockade as the only rational strategic choice and the Model III analyst's explanation of the blockade as the result of a struggle in which the majority of the ExCom's first choice was eliminated by the believed (but inaccurate) assertion that a surgical air strike could not be chosen with high confidence of success. The difficulty in coming to grips with the complementarity or contradiction between explanations produced by different models stems from the problem of unraveling the central propositions implied by these explanations. What basic propositions are entailed by the Rational Actor Model's explanation of the presence of missiles in Cuba by reference to the Soviet Union's objectives? Is this compatible with a diversity of objectives on the

part of central Soviet leaders? Must all have subscribed to the same objective? Diplomatic historians often attribute objectives to nations, though they would allow that no one in the nation at the time appreciated the fact that this was the nation's objective. Proper attention to the question of whether these models simply present partial, alternate, complementary stories (as Gilbert Ryle's philosophical equivalent suggests) or rather permit contradictions will require much more careful definition of the propositions employed and entailed by explanations according to each model. See Gilbert Ryle, *Dilemmas* (Cambridge, England: Cambridge University Press, 1954).

17 Edward Weintal and Charles Bartlett, *Facing the Brink: An Intimate Study of Crisis Diplomacy* (New York: Scribner, 1967), pp. 54-55.

A: ORGANIZATIONAL AND BUREAUCRATIC POLITICS

Bureaucratic Politics and the Westminster Model

Kim Richard Nossal

INTRODUCTION

The bureaucratic politics paradigm, as elaborated by such analysts as Graham Allison and Morton Halperin,[1] has been treated as essentially idiosyncratic and applicable only to the analysis of United States foreign policy. The paradigm was developed within a specific national context, and, it might be argued, using a particularist American framework for explaining state behavior. It features "players in positions" of policy-making authority who jockey along "action channels" for advantage between and among themselves by "pulling and hauling," who have different foreign policy goals and objectives they wish transformed into policy and then action, or who engage in "politics" to gain parochial advantage.[2] But these features of the model suggest that it may be applicable, at least in part, to foreign policy-making in other national systems.

THE UNITED STATES FOREIGN POLICY SYSTEM

There are three important features of the American foreign policy-making system that would suggest the appropriateness of the bureaucratic politics model as a tool for analyzing American foreign policy.

The first, and most important, of the characteristics of the United States foreign policy-making system is the constitutional separation of powers, which assigns both the executive and legislative branches of government in the United States authority over the making of foreign policy. The powers over foreign policy-making given, implicitly or explicitly, to the Congress by Articles I and II of the United States constitution mean that there can be legitimate and authoritative grounds for disputes between the two branches of government. Indeed, in those periods when Congress seeks to assert itself in the making of foreign policy, as in the 1970s, the exercise of its constitutional powers can severely limit presidential freedom of action.[3] For example, the War Powers act of 1973, enacted by Congress over President Richard Nixon's veto, was a legislative response to the conduct of an undeclared war in Vietnam. Inter alia, it prevents the president from using American troops in hostile situations abroad for periods longer than sixty days without congressional approval. This act provides legislative sustenance to the explicit power to make war given to Congress by the constitution.

The assertiveness of Congress in the 1970s was of course a reflection of a contemporary reaction

---

An original essay written especially for this volume.

to the war in Vietnam and the excesses of Watergate; but it is also a good indication of the kinds of tensions built into the system of government of the United States by those who framed the constitution. Their abiding fear of absolutism created a legislature that enjoys a preeminence in the making of foreign policy that is unrivaled in the contemporary international system.

Second, the nature of the bureaucratic system in the United States encourages conflict among policy-makers to be expressed openly and resolved openly. The various departments of government are encouraged by the system to form interlinking alliances with "clients" outside the state apparatus and with congressional committees and other agencies within that apparatus. In this, Washington's bureaucracies are particularly autonomous from each other and relatively autonomous from the White House. Although there is a "cabinet," the cabinet secretaries who head government departments have, in Allison's words, considerable "baronial discretion" over their fiefs.[4] Moreover, since each cabinet-level officer owes his or her appointment to the president, there is only a minimal attachment to the notion of collective responsibility. Further, the executive agencies in Washington are also staffed at the senior levels by presidential appointment, but these "supergrade" appointments include both career civil servants and political appointees.[5] This creates both internal departmental conflicts of interest between career civil servants and those "in-and-outers"[6] whose terms of office tend to correspond, on the one hand, to the president who appointed them and, on the other, to the lack of cohesiveness and continuity that is a mark of any number of other political systems.[7]

Third, the "rules of the game" of the American political system permit the kind of conflictual relationships that recur in the making of American foreign policy. There are few sanctions imposed against those participants in the process who advance their particular views through leaks to a press geared for this kind of bureaucratic combat, or ally with congressional committees, or disagree openly with senior officials of cognate departments.[8] In the last decade, for example, we have seen a running battle between the National Security Council and the Department of State: while there have been lulls, often the fractious rivalry between State and the NSC has produced undesired (and undesirable) outcomes. American policy during the Iranian revolution stands out as but one example of bureaucratic combat producing unintended outcomes.[9] It is because "[t]he central feature of American politics is the fragmentation and dispersion of power and authority,"[10] as Stephen Krasner puts it, that the bureaucratic politics model is a useful and appropriate heuristic framework for the analysis of United States foreign policy-making.

It is also an appropriate framework to use in the American national context, given the explanatory power of pluralism in accounting for the behavior of the state in the United States. As Krasner notes, "Bureaucratic politics applies the logic of pluralism to policy-making within government."[11] In other words, each participant in the policy-making process is treated as an individual actor with particular interests he or she wants to maximize, and those "players," to use Allison's argot, who have what pluralists term the weightiest political resources, will be able to translate their preferences into policy. While Allison does not explicitly suggest the absence of a hierarchy based upon authority, the pluralist perspective does underemphasize the power and authority of the president in relation to other policy-makers.[12]

But are these characteristics of the United States political system — characteristics that I have argued make the bureaucratic politics model so appropriate and useful for the analysis of American foreign policy — in any way unique to the United States?

Certainly no other legislature has the effective power over foreign policy decision-making enjoyed by the United States Congress. In most national systems, foreign policy-making remains solely the prerogative of the executive branch, a twentieth-century vestige of the monarchical systems so studiously avoided by the American founding fathers. In British parliamentary systems, for example, the Crown (the executive branch) has proved unwilling to allow parliament any meaningful role in the making of foreign policy. And there are no comparable constitutional requirements for parliamentary approval of executive initiatives. The executive — in other words the cabinet — can negotiate treaties; declare and wage war; dispatch ambassadors and emissaries — all without the explicit consent of parliament, relying instead on the wide-ranging authority of the Royal Prerogative.

For their part, parliamentarians who are not members of the cabinet have generally proven unwilling to demand a role in the making of foreign policy. While foreign policy issues occasionally become the subject of heated national debate — for example, the testing of the cruise missile in Canada or the admission of South African rugby teams to play in New Zealand — there has traditionally been little willingness to insist on a change in the prerogatives of the executive in shaping foreign policy.[13]

Nor is there evidence in parliamentary systems of the kind of fragmentation at the bureaucratic level evident in Washington. Instead, a greater premium has traditionally been placed on the coordination of policy-making between the various departments with foreign policy responsibilities in states like Australia, Canada, and Britain.[14] Indeed, in Canada, the Trudeau government has spent the last decade and a half searching for the perfect administrative scheme to achieve a more coherent system of policy management by the several foreign policy departments.[15]

Finally, the rules of the policy-making game in parliamentary systems — and indeed most other systems — are far less permissive than they are in Washington. First, the dictates of the collective responsibility of cabinet ministers in parliamentary systems change the nature of conflict in the senior reaches of government. Being part of a collectivity precludes overt and public squabbling between cabinet-level officials. Second, the coherence, cohesiveness, and continuity of a bureaucracy staffed entirely by career civil servants at the upper echelons have a dramatic impact on the incidence of overt conflict between officials at the bureaucratic level. As the report of the British committee struck to examine the Official Secrets Act (the Franks Committee) noted in 1972: "A civil servant who is regarded as unreliable, or who tends to overstep the mark and to talk too freely, will not enjoy such a satisfactory career as colleagues with better judgement and greater discretion."[16] Similarly in Ottawa, as Denis Stairs has noted, because there is a conscious effort among officials to avoid overt conflicts over policy and because bureaucratic exchange is more "casual," bureaucratic politics will be more muted.[17] Finally, the press is considerably more constrained in British parliamentary systems than it is in the United States, and thus does not have the same kind of impact on policy-making. In Britain, for example, the legal sanctions of section 2 of the 1911 Official Secrets Act are reinforced by the system of "D Notices," which are official but non-binding requests to the British press that certain subjects not be disclosed.[18]

In short, the characteristics that make bureaucratic politics an important feature of foreign policy-making in the United States are not found to the same extent or degree in other national systems. This suggests that in other systems there will be fewer opportunities for legitimate conflict over foreign policy issues between officials at either the bureaucratic or political levels.

CONFLICT AND BUREAUCRATIC POLITICS

It is too often assumed that the major contribution that Allison's model makes to our understanding of policy-making is the emphasis it places on conflict between participants in the process, and how that conflict affects policy outcomes. However, as I have argued elsewhere,[19] to think of policy outcomes shaped by bureaucratic politics as involving only those issues where conflict between policymakers is evident and overt is to miss the essence of the paradigm. The basic premise of the model is that when different policy-makers approach an issue, their objectives, their conception of the "best" outcome, or their view of how best to achieve those goals, will differ. However, there is nothing intrinsic in the bureaucratic politics paradigm that suggests the resolution of those differences must always be marked by conflict. There are other ways of reconciling politically divergent interests: by the exercise of authority, by manipulation, by persuasion, or by inducement. Because the analyst may not observe conflict does not mean that the participants in the decision-making process, both political and bureaucratic, were all agreed on ends and means and had developed a unanimous conception of the national interest.

Instead, the bureaucratic politics paradigm suggests that we should look for competing interests within the state[20] and abandon the analytical conception that the state, or government, is a monolithic entity with a single, rational, identifiable interest. It suggests instead that participants in the process of making policy will attempt to maximize their own interests and conceptions of what is "best" for the state. Allison — among others — has demonstrated that officials charged with making United States foreign policy have parochial interests that are shaped by a concern about the health of the organization to which they are attached, or by a concern for their own careers within government. However, one of the criticisms of the bureaucratic politics paradigm is that it reduces officials to little more than a petty species of *homo bureaucraticus*.[21] By contrast, it is important to see that policy-makers are preoccupied with more than budget-maximizing and bureaucratic empire-building.[22] Rather, following Krasner, it might be argued that officials have some conception of the "national interest" that helps shape their policy preferences — and this conception is highly ideological in nature.[23]

BUREAUCRATIC POLITICS IN PARLIAMENTARY SYSTEMS

When analyzing the foreign policy of a parliamentary system, we should thus assume, as Allison does, that the same kinds of parochial concerns — and ideological considerations — will motivate policy-makers. We should assume that those who make policy in other systems will be no less prone to differ among themselves about what is best for them, their department, or the state; what course of action should be pursued in a given situation; what ends to seek; and the means needed to achieve their purposes. While there are differences in political structure, in political culture, and in patterns of bureaucratic and political socialization, it could be argued that foreign policy-makers in other systems will be as prone to engage in bureaucratic politics as their counterparts in Washington. To these natural proclivities should be added two features of parliamentary systems that increase the likelihood of bureaucratic politics in the foreign policy-making process.

First, disagreement is likely when the foreign policy issue cuts across jurisdictions of departments: rarely does one department of government have sole authority over such aspects of foreign policy as trade, development assistance, or the international dimensions of monetary, energy, civil aviation, food or environmental policies. Instead, it is likely that on such issues officials with different departmental perspectives and imperatives will be obligated to interact to formulate policy. It is equally likely that issues which cut across the jurisdictional authority of different departments will prompt officials (at both the bureaucratic and ministerial levels) to pursue parochial interests.[24]

Second, under the Westminster model, government tends to be marked by strong central agencies,[25] whose primary function is to coordinate policy. The initiatives of different departments are subject to strong centralized pressures from such institutions as Canada's Privy Council Office or Britain's Central Policy Review Staff[26] to ensure coherence. If necessary, these central agencies will act as arbiters in disputes between competing departments.[27] But a policy process marked by small but powerful departments at the apex of the bureaucratic structure, endowed with a mandate to rearrange the priorities of program departments, increases the salience of divergent interests, as coordinative agencies often perform their functions at the expense of line departments.

In addition to these two factors, it might be added that in Canada and Australia, there is a third characteristic of the political system that increases the likelihood of conflict over foreign policy between policy-makers: the federal structure. In Canada, in the absence of a prohibition comparable to that in the United States constitution (Art. I, sect. 10 prohibits the various states from engaging in foreign relations without the consent of Congress), there is a powerful incentive for the provincial governments to pursue their own parochial interests. Often these interests are at odds with the interests of the national state, increasing the likelihood of disagreement in the policy-making process.[28] In Australia, although the constitution provides explicitly that the federal government enjoys preeminence in foreign policy, the state governments have on occasion sought to press their political interests on the government in Canberra.[29]

If we can assume these features of parliamentary systems will enhance the likelihood of bureaucratic politics, what we cannot, and should not, assume is that the inevitable result of the attempts of individual policy-makers in other countries to maximize their policy preferences will lead to the same degree of conflict evident in the foreign policy-making process in the United States.

CABINET AND CONSTRAINTS ON CONFLICT: A CASE STUDY

In our study of the acquisition of a new fighter aircraft by the Canadian government,[30] Michael Atkinson and I found that the classical elements of the bureaucratic politics paradigm were present. The cabinet was seeking a high-performance, low-cost aircraft whose manufacturer was willing to invest at least 100 percent of the purchase price in new economic activity (or "industrial offsets") in Canada. Each of these objectives had a sponsor in the bureaucracy — the Department of National Defence, the Department of Supply and Services, and the now-defunct Department of Industry, Trade and Commerce. From their record on past weapons procurements, there was a high expectation not only of a divergence of interests between these three departments, but of overt conflict. Indeed, as the head of the New Fighter Aircraft Program Office admitted publicly at the outset of the program, "Each of the departments quite rightly wants to protect its own ability to carry out its statutory functions and to retain the flexibility to look after its own interests. ... [D]ifficulties could conceivably be encountered in resolving the sort of problem where departments' objectives were at odds."[31]

However, we found that the three-year process of choosing a fighter aircraft was, with one important exception, virtually conflict-free. We attributed the muting of conflict to three factors. First, we confirmed Robert Goodin's observation that divergence of interest will not necessarily lead to overt conflict if the stakes are not high enough.[32] In this case, there *was* a conflict of interest: between the Department of Industry, Trade and Commerce and the other two departments. But the stakes in the New Fighter Aircraft program were so low for DITC that there was little inclination to engage in overt conflict.

Second, we argued that in order for conflict to occur, players have to have formulated clear preferences on the issue. Indeed, the bureaucratic politics paradigm assumes that the policy preferences of the participants will be well defined. In fact, in the NFA decision, we found that in the case of one set of participants — those (again) from DITC — preferences did not emerge until very late in the process; too late in fact to change the decision making process.

Most important, however, we argued that the principal reason we did not see overt conflict in the making of these decisions was that the Canadian cabinet had structured the decision-making process in a fashion that all but eliminated the possibility of legitimate conflict between the bureaucratic participants. It rigorously specified the parameters under which the bureaucrats were to come forward with a recommendation: inter alia, cabinet decreed that no fewer than 130 aircraft with specified capabilities were to be procured for no more than $2.34 billion. These and other "structuring decisions" reduced not the divergence of interest between participants, but rather the propensity to transform divergence of interest into overt conflict. In only one area did cabinet not structure the decision process tightly — that of industrial offsets — and it was on this one issue that conflict emerged.

CONCLUSIONS

One of the recurrent criticisms of the bureaucratic politics paradigm has been that it tends to ignore political authority and the hierarchical relationship of obedience between those at the apex of the power structure of the state and those who are in essence the servants of the political executive. The bureaucratic politics model, it has been argued, relegates the elected official to a position of unwarranted insignificance in the policy-making process, and instead attributes to the bureaucracy a power it does not have.[33]

The criticism would be valid if Allison had intended that the focus be solely on the bureaucracy. Unfortunately, however, nomenclature has muddled the model. Because Allison chose to term it a "governmental (bureaucratic) politics" paradigm (and subsequently used, with Halperin, the term "bureaucratic politics"), the model is invariably interpreted as focusing on bureaucracies and bureaucrats alone. However, Allison makes clear in *Essence of Decision* that the proper focus of the model should be on "players in positions," which includes players in bureaucracies, in the legislative branch, or in the political executive. Similarly, there is no analytical distinction made between "Indians and Chiefs" (to use his term): a "player in position" can be a desk officer in the foreign ministry or the head of government. Thus, looking at the utility and applicability of the "bureaucratic" politics paradigm, one must look further than the bureaucracy, to "governmental" politics and examine the question of political authority.

But such criticism of the paradigm, while it is based on a misreading of Allison, alerts us to an important element in applying the model to parliamentary systems: the concentration of political authority in the cabinet. Cabinet government does not eliminate bureaucratic politics, but rather changes its face. As Richard Rose notes, "Cabinet deliberations bring politics into the center of government. Ministry is set against ministry...and the ambitions of individual politicians are also at war with each other. Political temperatures rise with the importance of the issue. The authority of Cabinet does not eliminate politics; instead, the *Cabinet permits the fusion of government and politics*."[34]

The case study of Canada's new fighter aircraft demonstrates that in parliamentary systems the concentration of political authority in cabinet allows the political executive to impose constraints on legitimate conflict between policy-makers at lower levels in the decision making process. This is not to suggest that there will not be divergences in interests between players in the foreign policy game in parliamentary systems, but rather that their propensities to engage in conflict to ensure that their preferences will be transformed into policy may be sharply reduced by the imposition of centralized authority.

ENDNOTES

1 The basic bureaucratic politics literature would include: Graham T. Allison, "Conceptual models and the Cuban Missile Crisis," *American Political Science Review*, 58 (September 1969), 689-718; *Essence of Decision* (Boston: Little, Brown, 1971); Allison and Morton H. Halperin, "Bureaucratic politics: a paradigm and some policy implications," in Raymond Tanter and R.H. Ullman, eds.,

Theory and Policy in International Relations (Princeton: Princeton University Press, 1972), pp. 40-79; and Halperin, *Bureaucratic Politics and Foreign Policy* (Washington: Brookings Institution, 1974).

2 Allison, *Essence of Decision*, pp. 162-81.

3 See, for example, the articles in John Spanier and Joseph Nogee, eds., *Congress, the President and American Foreign Policy* (New York: Pergamon Press, 1981), particularly Nogee's "Congress and the presidency: the dilemmas of policy-making," pp. 189-200. Also, David Leyton-Brown, "The role of congress in the making of foreign policy," *International Journal,* 38 (Winter 1982-3), 59-76.

4 Allison, *Essence of Decision*, p. 145. See also Richard Rose, "Government against sub-government: a European perspective on Washington," in Rose and Ezra N. Suleiman, eds., *Presidents and Prime Ministers* (Washington: American Enterprise Institute, 1980), pp. 284-347.

5 Hugh Heclo, *A Government of Strangers: Executive Politics in Washington* (Washington: Brookings Institution, 1977).

6 Halperin, *Bureaucratic Politics*, p. 89.

7 By contrast, see Hugh Heclo and Aaron Wildavsky, *The Private Government of Public Money: Community and Policy inside British Politics* (London: Macmillan, 1974), p. 9.

8 For a former operative's account of this problem, see Thomas L. Hughes, "The power to speak and the power to listen: reflections on bureaucratic politics and a recommendation on information flows," in Thomas M. Franck and Edward Weisband, eds., *Secrecy and Foreign Policy* (New York: Oxford University Press, 1974), pp. 13-41.

9 William H. Sullivan, "Dateline Iran: the road not taken," *Foreign Policy,* 40 (Fall 1980), 175-86.

10 Stephen D. Krasner, *Defending the National Interest: Raw Materials Investment and U.S. Foreign Policy* (Princeton: Princeton University Press, 1978), p. 61. Similar observations about the nature of United States politics have been made by Walter Dean Burham, *Critical Elections and the Mainsprings of American Politics* (New York: Norton, 1970) and Samuel P. Huntington, *Political Order in Changing Societies* (New Haven: Yale University Press, 1968), quoted in Krasner, *National Interest*, pp. 61-62.

11 Krasner, *National Interest*, p. 27.

12 Robert Art, "Bureaucratic politics and American foreign policy: a critique," *Policy Sciences,* 4 (December 1973), 467-490, and Amos Perlmutter, "The presidential political center and foreign policy: a critique of the revisionist and bureaucratic political orientations," *World Politics,* 27 (October 1974), 87-106.

13 William Wallace, *The Foreign Policy Process in Britain* (London: George Allen & Unwin, 1976), chap. 4; James Eayrs, *The Art of the Possible: Government and Foreign Policy in Canada* (Toronto: University of Toronto Press, 1961), chap. 4; and Henry S. Albinski, *Australian External Policy under Labor* (St Lucia, Queensland and Vancouver: University of Queensland Press and University of British Columbia Press, 1977), chaps. 8 and 9.

14 See, for example, Richard Rose, "British government: the job at the top," in Rose and Suleiman, eds., *Presidents and Prime Ministers*, pp. 1-99; John J. Kirton, "Foreign policy decision-making in the Trudeau government: promise and performance," *International Journal,* 33 (Spring 1978), 287-311.

15 Gordon Osbaldeston, "Reorganizing the Department of External Affairs," *International Journal,* 37 (Summer 1982), 452-66. See Denis Stairs, "The political culture of Canadian foreign policy," *Canadian Journal of Political Science,* 15 (December 1982), 688-90, for a commentary on what Stairs terms "the relentless preoccupation of [Canada's] governors with refining the administrative machine."

16 Quoted in Anthony Sampson, "Secrecy, news management and the British press," in Franck and Weisband, eds., *Secrecy and Foreign Policy*, p. 222.

17 Denis Stairs, "The foreign policy of Canada," in James N. Rosenau, Kenneth W. Thompson and Gavin Boyd, eds., *World Politics: An Introduction* (New York: Free Press, 1976), pp. 185-86.

18 See Sampson, "Secrecy, news management and the British press," pp. 224-25. The situation in Canada is not dissimilar: see Anthony Westell, "Access to news in a small capital: Ottawa," in ibid., pp. 253-71.

19 Kim Richard Nossal, "Allison through the (Ottawa) looking glass: bureaucratic politics and foreign

policy in a parliamentary system," *Canadian Public Administration,* 22 (Winter 1979), 610-26.

20 Both Krasner and Allison define the state in the narrowest of terms. For a critique of their position, see Eric A. Nordlinger, *On the Autonomy of the* Democratic State (Cambridge, Mass.: Harvard University Press, 1981), p. 124. For his definition of the state, see pp. 9-13.

21 This point is made in a good, if somewhat acerbic, critique of the bureaucratic politics model. See Lawrence Freedman, "Logic, politics and foreign policy processes: a critique of the bureaucratic politics model," *International Affairs,* 52 (July 1976), 434-449.

22 This is the characterization of bureaucrats usually associated with Niskanen: see William A. Niskanen Jr., *Bureaucracy and Representative Government* (Chicago: Aldine/Atherton, 1971).

23 See Krasner, *National Interest*, chap. 9.

24 In an Australian context, disputes over immigration and resource management occurred in the 1970s: Albinski, *Australian External Policy*, pp. 295-97; for an interesting examination of bureaucratic politics in an Australian domestic context that makes no reference to the American literature, see Martin Painter and Bernard Carey, *Politics Between Departments: The Fragmentation of Executive Control in Australian Government* (St Lucia: Queensland University Press, 1979). In Canada, frequent disputes erupted over development assistance: Nossal, "Allison through the (Ottawa) looking glass," pp. 613-14.

25 For example, Mattei Dogan, *The Mandarins of Western Europe: The Political Role of Top Civil Servants* (New York: Wiley, 1975); and Colin Campbell and George J. Szablowski, *The Superbureaucrats: Structure and Behaviour in Central Agencies* (Toronto: Macmillan, 1979).

26 Heclo and Wildavsky, *Private Government of Public Money*, pp. 267-68; Rose, "British government," p. 31.

27 Colin Campbell, S.J., "Political leadership in Canada: Pierre Elliott Trudeau and the Ottawa model," in Rose and Suleiman, *Presidents and Prime Ministers*, pp.63-77.

28 For one overview of the foreign relations of Canada's provinces, see P.R. (Roff) Johannson, "Provincial international activities," *International Journal,* 33 (Spring 1978), pp. 357-378.

29 In 1974, all Australia's state governments, including the Labor governments in Tasmania and South Australia, sought successfully to keep the federal government from inviting representatives of the Palestine Liberation Organization from visiting Australia. For details on this and other federal-state disputes on foreign affairs, see Albinski, *Australian External Policy*, pp. 274-77.

30 Michael M. Atkinson and Kim Richard Nossal, "Bureaucratic politics and the new fighter aircraft decisions," *Canadian Public Administration,* 24 (Winter 1981), 531-62.

31 Brig.-Gen. P.D. Manson, "Managing the New Fighter Aircraft Program," *Canadian Defence Quarterly* 7 (Spring 1978), 8-9.

32 See Robert E. Goodin, "The logic of bureaucratic backscratching," *Public Choice,* 21 (Spring 1975), esp. 65.

33 Perlmutter, "Presidential political center". See also Goodin, "Logic of bureaucratic backscratching," 58: "whenever a 'superpower' (e.g., the President or Congress) is heavily involved, the bureaucratic politics element is likely to be obscured, the reason being that few bureaucrats have the power to bargain seriously with those superpowers."

34 Rose, "Government against sub-government," pp. 292-93; emphasis in original.

A: ORGANIZATIONAL AND BUREAUCRATIC POLITICS

External Bargaining and Internal Bargaining

Glenn Snyder/Paul Diesing

...When more than two persons or agencies are involved, decisions are a result of the differing values, perceptions, and influence of these participants. Here, the "bureaucratic politics" paradigm, or a modified version of it, is useful for explaining decision making. From this perspective, the process and outcomes of crisis bargaining are the result of an interplay between "external" interstate bargaining and internal bargaining. [Our] main purpose... is to analyze this interplay. But first, we wish to mention certain limitations of the bureaucratic politics paradigm[1] when applied to crisis behavior.

First, there is a general tendency in crises to limit participation to a few top officials and to minimize involvement of bureaucracies. Usually, if more than the head of government and foreign minister are actively involved, participation is limited to some sort of inner cabinet or ad hoc committee consisting of no more than four or five persons. (The Cuban missile crisis was unique in the large number of individual participants for the United States.) Thus, while the "pulling and hauling" described in the bureaucratic politics theory does occur in these cases, the "bureaucratic" element is minimal. The degree of lower-level involvement does vary across cases — in general, in inverse ratio to the brevity and severity of the crisis.

Second, the bureaucratic politics theorists emphasize that attitudes of decision makers are strongly role-conditioned: "where you stand depends on where you sit." However, in our cases individuals' views seemed at least as often to be the function of personal predilection toward "hard" or "soft" strategies. These predilections were fairly consistent for given individuals on different issues, though there were a few exceptions. Dulles, for example, was rather moderate on Berlin but tough on Quemoy; Acheson the opposite. Role influences were most clearly seen in the case of military participants. All this suggests that the bureaucratic politics paradigm is useful in crisis studies mainly for its account of the internal bargaining *process* (when such bargaining does occur), not for its explanation of why peoples' attitudes differ.[2]

Third, although the bureaucratic politics paradigm has been developed by empirical reference to

---

Glenn H. Snyder and Paul Diesing, *Conflict Among Nations: Bargaining, Decision Making, and System Structure in International Crisis.* Excerpts, pp. 511-23.

Portions of the text have been deleted. Some footnotes have been removed; those remaining have been renumbered.

the U.S. decision-making structure, it seems less relevant to the United States, where the president holds the ultimate power of decision in foreign policy, than to other kinds of regimes where responsibility is shared.[3] Finally, the theory is more relevant to modern times when agencies other than the foreign office have become involved in foreign policy making, with military participation especially active, than to, say, the pre-1914 period when the foreign office and head of government had virtually all the action with the military more or less waiting in the wings until called upon.

We turn now to the interplay between external and internal bargaining.[4] The most obvious link is that internal bargaining produces decisions about strategies and tactics to be employed by the state in its bargaining with other states. Responses of other states are similarly the product of "pulling and hauling" between individuals and agencies with different interpretations of the first state's move, different interests, different influence bases, etc. From this perspective the process and outcome of international bargaining is more the adventitious result of configurations of attitude and influence *within* states than of the "balance of bargaining power" *between* states. (We shall have more to say below about how these two conceptions may be reconciled.)

There is a further, less obvious link that the bureaucratic politics theorists have missed. This is that the stances taken by individual participants tend to mirror the spectrum of external bargaining options available to the state. The salient options are coercion (offensive or defensive), accommodation, or some mixture of these two. Each of these external alternatives has a coherent logic that makes it a rational choice provided its assumptions are granted, and the proponents of each will of course argue that logic. For example, the soft-liner will argue that conciliation ought to be tried first; if it doesn't work, there will be time later to fall back on the coercive option. If coercion is tried first, this will get the opponent's back up, make him less willing to concede, set off an escalation of threats and counterthreats and block the initiation of a negotiation process through which a mutually satisfactory compromise might be found. The hard-liner will argue that accommodation at the beginning will give an appearance of weakness and make the opponent push harder for his own goals, not a compromise. The correct approach is to be firm from the start; there will be time to make concessions later if one has to. While the soft-liner underrates the danger of looking weak, the hard-liner discounts the risk of provocation and escalation. Thus, the central decision maker's problem of choosing between, or mixing, these external options is paralleled by his internal problem of building a majority coalition or compromising divergent advice so as to keep "on board" as many participants as possible. The alternatives that are "bargained out" internally come from competitive logics that are inherent in the external bargaining situation. The internal power of the proponents of each alternative will tend to vary with the potency of its logic, given the facts of the external situation, and interacting with whatever consensus does exist about the nature of the opponent and the "national interest."

The bureaucratic politics theorists miss this point because of their commitment to the notion that internal bargaining positions stem primarily from agency interests. The external situation appears only as one kind of occasion for decision, a stimulus that triggers the internal struggle, in which the policy preferences of the various participants come chiefly from internal sources[5] — notably agency role and the desire to enhance the status and influence of their agency. Power in the internal bargaining process also is said to flow mainly from internal sources. We do not deny that these internal factors are operative, but assert that the external situation — i.e., what the opposing state is doing and how it affects the interests of one's own state — is at least as important in determining bargaining positions and influence in the internal debate. Even if certain agencies or individuals can be expected regularly to take hard or soft positions, their influence will be greater or less depending on whether the external situation seems to favor an accommodative or coercive strategy, in the eyes of the central decision maker and in terms of the core of consensus in the group.

A few examples...illustrate the point. In...the pre-1914 crises, beginning with Morocco, 1905, Lord Grey faced the external choice between deterring Germany and Austria while supporting France or Russia (the coercive alternative), or conciliating the former while restraining the latter (the accommodative option). This choice was mirrored in the internal division between the foreign office hard-liners and the Radical soft-liners in the cabinet. The foreign office people spoke the logic of defensive coercion: Germany was out to dominate the continent; thus she must be contained and France must be supported at all costs. The Radicals perceived little threat from Germany and felt she had a right to be consulted about and perhaps to share in the control of Morocco; the connection with France was not an alliance, thus Britain had no obligation of support; furthermore, support would encourage French intransigence, which might precipitate war. In 1905-1906, when the entente was still fragile and untested, Grey leaned toward the foreign office view and managed to carry out a tough strategy against Germany by simply not informing his Radical colleagues of everything he was saying to France and Germany, or about the initiation of military staff conversations with the French. In 1911, during the early part of the Agadir crisis, Grey leaned the other way, believing the German demand for compensation to be legitimate. He took the Radicals into his confidence and adopted their preferred strategy of concilation. Later, when it appeared the Germans were after a piece of Morocco rather than just "compensation" in Central Africa, Grey's own preference shifted toward coercion, and he managed to form a new majority coalition around this strategy by gaining the defection of the Radical leader, Lloyd George, who had become enraged by Germany's high-handed behavior. In both these cases the internal division was linked to the international bargaining situation via the competing logical strategies for dealing with it. In 1911, as the situation changed so that British interests seemed threatened, the internal balance of power changed with it, making possible a shift of strategy.

In the 1961 phase of the Berlin crisis, President Kennedy was faced with a situation that did not seem to demand either a purely coercive or purely accommodative strategy. It was necessary that the Soviets understand that the United States would fight for its vital interest, and what those vital interests were; at the same time the United States should be willing to negotiate in search of a settlement that would leave its essential interests intact. These alternatives were reflected in the domestic debate, with the hard-liners, led by Dean Acheson, calling for a refusal to negotiate (and citing the damage to the U.S. reputation for firmness if negotiations were entered into) and simply waiting for the Soviets to carry out their threat if they dared, then putting selective, graduated military measures into play. The soft-line group favored entering into negotiations without threats and considering military steps as a last resort. In resolving his external dilemma in favor of a mixture of those two options Kennedy at the same time settled the internal struggle by giving something to everyone. The United States would negotiate, he announced, but certain things were non-negotiable, the Acheson plan for military measures was put in reserve as a threat in case negotiations failed, and military forces were increased. But it was Kennedy's personal preference for a mixed strategy that most influenced the decision; the concurrent compromise of the internal struggle was incidental.

The bureaucratic politics theorists do not deny, of course, that states can be influenced by external stimuli. However, they argue that if one's influence attempt is to succeed, there must be someone with influence in the opposite government who already wants to do what one desires of that government. Hence the prescription: if you want to influence another government, find out what group(s) in that government are already inclined to do what you want, and shape your moves so as to strengthen those groups in their own government's internal debate.[6] This point is the bureaucratic politics school's most original and interesting contribution to the theory of international politics and bargaining, as distinct from internal decision making. Let us see how it stands up empirically.

This theory implies that the first task of the international bargainers is to assess the internal configuration of attitudes and influence in the other government. Assessment or information-search is indeed... a primary component of bargaining; what the bureaucratic politics theory does is shift the focus of search from the aims, interests, and power of the other state in general to the interests and power of individuals or factions within the state — certainly a more difficult task.

Decision makers... only occasionally attempted such assessments, and when they tried they did pretty miserably. A typical example was Bulow's and Holstein's estimate that the formation of a new Liberal government in Britain in 1905 was a great break for Germany since the Liberals were pro-German and would forsake the entente with France that had been negotiated by the previous Conservative government. The Germans apparently were not aware of the division within the Liberal party between rather hard-line "imperialists" and soft-line "radicals" and that the imperialists held all the foreign policy-related portfolios. On the other hand they did correctly perceive that the French foreign minister was in a weak domestic political position, which could be exploited to get rid of him. But they did not perceive the nuance that the opposition to Delcassé was based mainly on personal animus and domestic issues rather than foreign policy, so they were surprised when the French position on the Morocco issue did not change after he left. The record does not show that either the French or the British had a glimmer of the sharp split in Germany between Holstein and the Kaiser.

Consistent with the typically poor analysis of the divisions and influence patterns within the adversary was the infrequency and usual failure of deliberate attempts to affect those patterns, as prescribed by the bureaucratic politics theory. For crises the prescription boils down to "strengthen the soft-liners" or "avoid strengthening the hard-liners" in the adversary government. The few attempts that were made almost all failed, largely reflecting mistaken estimates of internal politics in the other state.

In some cases, the outline of the internal split was estimated correctly, but an inappropriate strategy was chosen for dealing with it. One of the German motives for staging a naval demonstration at Agadir in 1911 was to help the conciliatory French premier, Caillaux, overcome his hard-line opposition by creating a rationale for concessions. The move merely stiffened sentiment for resistance in the French cabinet. The error here was not so much a failure to perceive the division in the opposite government as a mistaken judgment about how to influence it, and this in turn is attributable, probably, to the peculiar German insensitivity to the emotional "stiffening" effect of tough moves on others, though they were remarkably thin-skinned themselves.

Deliberate attempts to manipulate the adversary's internal balance of power are few, but there are many instances of international bargaining moves having had such effects unintentionally. In 1905, for example, the initial German demands over Morocco were perceived by the dominantly soft-line French cabinet as appeasable by offers of compensation elsewhere. When these offers were spurned and the French leaders perceived that Germany was out to humiliate France at a conference and break the entente with Britain, the hard-line foreign ministry gained influence and the premier, Rouvier, who had taken over the foreign office portfolio, shifted his own position from soft to hard. In the Agadir crisis of 1911 the sudden public British intervention via the Lloyd George speech first produced a spasm of indignation in Germany, but its more important consequence was that the accommodatively inclined Kaiser called his hard-line foreign minister to heel, putting Germany's policy on the road to compromise. After Eisenhower refused to apologize for the U-2 incident in 1960, leading to the collapse of a summit conference, Khrushchev evidently lost standing in the Kremlin. To keep his more militant comrades at bay he was forced to adopt their line and speak in more bellicose terms on the Berlin issue when he opened it up again in 1961.

When the parties are aware of each other's internal divisions, the division in one's own state may be exploited in external bargaining. Delcassé made full use of English apprehensions about the weakness of his government in the Fashoda crisis of 1898 and about the possibility of a military coup if the British pushed too hard. The turbulent political situation in Iran in 1946 enabled the Iranian premier, Qavam, to pose for the Russians the possibility of a more intransigent regime replacing his own if they refused to accept his terms. A variant is to warn, not of the downfall of one's own government, but of a shift in the balance of influence within it toward a harder bargaining position. Hence the Czar's statement to the Kaiser in 1914 that he was under "tremendous pressure" from his military to mobilize. Khrushchev says in his memoirs that at the height of the Cuban missile crisis Robert Kennedy told Ambassador Dobrynin "I don't know how much longer we can hold out against our generals" and even spoke of the president's fear of a military take-over. "We could see that we had to reorient our position swiftly," Khrushchev states, thus implying that concern about the internal power balance in the U.S. government was the most important single factor in inducing the Soviets to retreat.[7]

Another kind of internal-external interaction occurs when an internal faction undertakes independently to influence another state's policy. In one variant of this, the purpose is to persuade the other state to do something that will strengthen the position of the faction in its own state. A well-known example is the attempt by German conspirators in 1938, including some high military figures, to persuade the British government to stand firm against Hitler. This, they argued, would strengthen their own position sufficiently to bring off a coup against Hitler or at least to frustrate his plans. The attempt failed basically because it did not mesh well with the image of the dominant British appeasers — the image of Hitler as a man who could be reasoned with and who had limited aims — and with Chamberlain's desire to achieve a general settlement in Central Europe. More specifically Chamberlain did not wish to risk war to precipitate a revolt that might fail, and the conspirators' report that Hitler intended to attack Czechoslovakia by late September seemed only to increase the urgency of getting a negotiated settlement. A somewhat similar example, this time involving allies, occurred in 1911 during the second Moroccan crisis when Cambon, the French ambassador in London, urged the British government to bring pressure on the French government for a more conciliatory policy toward Germany; this would strengthen the French "peace faction." The attempt succeeded by producing a British statement and a French understanding that there were limits to British support. This example does support the prescription of the bureaucratic politics theory, but it is noteworthy that it required an appeal from a faction of the French government to get the British to act according to that prescription.

Sometimes minority factions in allied governments collaborate to undermine the strategy of their governments. Thus Vansittart and Churchill in 1938 privately encouraged hard-liners in the French cabinet. In turn (but whether as a result of the Britishers' urging is unclear) certain of the like-minded Frenchman telephoned Benes in Czechoslovakia urging him to resist the official Anglo-French "ultimatum," which insisted that he accede to Hitler's demands. At the same time some members of the Agrarian party in Czechoslovakia, apparently including Hodza, the premier, were urging another faction of the French government to exert pressure on Benes to accept the ultimatum.

Sometimes two factions act independently toward the opponent, producing what appears to be a calculated mixed strategy but really is not. Soviet strategy during the Berlin crisis of 1961-1962 appeared at times to be a deliberately mixed strategy, combining elements of the accommodative and coercive, but apparently was the result of two factions following different tracks, or alternatively gaining the upper hand in the Presidium. Khrushchev, the soft-liner, constantly pushed for negotiations and entered into a private correspondence with Kennedy to that end. But Soviet hard-liners who opposed a negotiated settlement apparently were able to take decisions on their own or force them through over the chairman's opposition, e.g., to resume nuclear testing and strengthen the Soviet armed forces, which got in the way of the chairman's accommodative tactics.

During the Iranian crisis of 1946 the conciliatory Iranian premier, Qavam, was often irritated by the insubordinate behavior of his U.N. ambassador, Hussein Ala, who constantly reiterated Iranian grievances against the Soviets in the Security Council. Sometimes this undermined Qavam's strategy by irritating the Soviets, but in a larger sense it contributed to the ultimate settlement by keeping the issue high on the U.N. agenda, thus keeping alive the "stick" of possible U.N. condemnation of Soviet behavior.

Examples of this kind shade over into instances where subordinates not in sympathy with official policy sabotage its implementation. In 1914, Paleologue, the French ambassador in St. Petersburg, ignored directives from his government to restrain Russia from taking precipitate action and instead urged mobilization, pledging unqualified French support. Roosevelt's licensing order of August 1, 1940, which permitted licensing of low-grade gasoline and crude oil exports to Japan, was turned into a complete embargo by hard-liners in the State Department who were in charge of implementing the program.

Summarizing, we can distinguish at least five different ways in which internal bargaining may interact with the external bargaining process: (1) the internal pattern of influence and attitudes affects choices of bargaining strategy and tactics toward the other state; (2) external bargaining moves may either intendedly or unintendedly affect the configuration of influence in the opposite decision-making unit; (3) opposing factions within a state may carry out independent strategies that usually undercut each other, but may also be mutually supportive, in effect constituting a mixed strategy that is objectively more effective than either of the independent strategies alone might have been; (4) dissident individuals may sabotage official policies in implementation; and (5) potential changes in the balance of influence at home may be used as warnings to inhibit the opponent's coercion.

What is one to make of all these examples of external-internal interaction in the light of the bureaucratic politics theory's proposition that other nations can be influenced only "when a clear signal is sent, when someone in the other nation already wants to take the desired action and the action increases that player's influence"?[8] Apparently the situation is somewhat more complicated, at least for crises. In crises the "desired action" that one presumably wants is a concession from the other side. The "someone" most likely to want to concede is the soft-liner; hence one wants to increase his influence. But how is that to be done? Logical reasoning does not provide an unambiguous answer. According to one line of reasoning the influence of the softs in the other state ought to be increased (and that of the hards decreased) by conciliatory gestures and concessions by one's own state; the softs' argument that a satisfactory negotiated settlement is possible would gain credibility. Conversely, a tough strategy by the self would strengthen the hards in the other, either by triggering emotions and status values or by giving credibility to their argument that only firmness can lead us to reason. Following another logic, the softs in the other state would gain power by a strong coercive policy that made clear the necessity to yield, and the hards would gain strength by our own accommodative moves, which show that we are weak and can be pushed farther.

The empirical evidence is highly mixed. The most meaningful thing that can be said about it is that the "logic" that prevails tends to reflect the structure of the crisis itself and the relative bargaining power between the states, and changing perceptions of structure and power relations during the crisis.... In 1914 Lord Grey's tardy declaration of British support for France produced an immediate increase in soft-line strength in Germany. The Kaiser pushed his Halt-in-Belgrade scheme (though its communication to Austria was sabotaged by subordinates) and Bethmann, previously hard-line, switched to soft-line in trying to restrain Austria. But these internal changes were merely ancillary to the fact that the German civilian leadership finally realized they had miscalculated English interest and intentions and hence the structure of the game they were playing with England....

The pattern of an accommodative move strengthening the opponent's soft-liners is found only twice in our cases and both are dubious instances. In 1941 an apparent U.S. conciliatory message may have strengthened slightly the weak "peace group" in Japan — at any rate, it brought a bid for negotiations from Japan. This is a dubious interpretation, however, since the hard-line group in control in Japan also wanted negotiations with the United States if there was any chance of success. Khrushchev, who was soft-line relative to certain others in the Kremlin, may have had his internal position strengthened by Eisenhower's agreement to a summit in 1959. The corollary — tough move strengthens opponent's hard-liners — appears somewhat more frequently. The more intransigent U.S. position in Berlin in 1960, followed by the U-2 incident and the aborted summit conference, apparently lowered Khrushchev's stock in the Kremlin and strengthened his hard-line opponents. In 1914 the Russian partial mobilization greatly strengthened the position of the military in Berlin; then when it became clear that Germany intended to attack France and Belgium as well as Russia, the evenly split British cabinet swung over to a hard-line majority. These 1914 examples again suggest a link between internal shifts and crisis structures....

If these examples show anything, it is that the bureaucratic politics theorists have stated at best a half-truth in their dictum: "Ask who in another government wants to do what you want for his own reasons. If you locate him, strengthen him. If you do not, despair."[9] It is only a half-truth because the ability to influence another government in a crisis depends primarily on the balance of bargaining power, which in turn depends on the balance of interests and military forces and relative disutility for war between the two *governments.* If these things are estimated correctly, one can wield as much influence (or must submit to as much influence) as the state-to-state power relations and one's bargaining skill will permit. The power relations will indeed depend somewhat on who is in charge in each government. And the exercise of the influence may be accompanied by, or may operate through, a change in the internal balance of power in the other government. But the internal change will usually be incidental to a changed perception of general power relations between the governments. Even if no one in the opposite government *wants* to do what you want, you need not "despair," since people can be persuaded to change their minds. And if there *is* someone, "strengthening" him means persuading others to the same view, which may require the same strategy as if there were no one. And what that strategy may be depends greatly on the general context, the structure of power relations between the *states.* The element of half-truth is that it may often help to know something about the distribution of attitudes and influence in the other government in devising an optimum strategy, especially if there is a fairly wide spectrum of opinion in the other state. Then, if one faces a coercive opponent, but the opponent's majority coalition includes a few wavering members inclined to compromise, a compromise proposal that suits their views may cause their defection and the formation of a different majority coalition. Or if the opponent's strategy is accommodative, based on a tenuous soft-line coalition, one knows that care is required in implementing one's own coercive strategy to avoid the opposite kind of shift in the other state. It bears repeating, however, that governments generally do not do well in analyzing each other's internal politics in crises, and indeed it is inherently difficult.[10]

An alternative and more theoretically satisfying way to link up the bureaucratic politics model with international bargaining is descriptive rather than prescriptive. If the analyst knows something about the distribution of internal attitudes and influence, he can explain and predict the outcome of bargaining episodes between states in greater detail and within narrower limits than would be possible with bargaining theory alone. In the usual bargaining model the outcome is indeterminate within a certain range; the internal factors the bureaucratic theory emphasizes provide empirical materials that reduce the range of indeterminacy.

Admittedly, there is usually a core of shared images and values on both sides, and if this core is large relative to what is not shared, an identification of individuals' values and images would not add anything useful to the analysis. In some situations, however, there is considerable divergence. Soft-line actors tend to estimate force ratios more favorably to the opponent than hard-liners, to place a greater disutility on the costs of war, and to estimate their own state's interests lower — especially since, for them, "resolve reputation" is not one of those interests whereas for the hard-liners it is extremely important. Thus, the "balance of forces and interests," i.e., the balance of bargaining power generally between the states, is affected by the relative influence of hard- and soft-line participants within the states. The analyst is able to estimate the balance of bargaining power and hence explain and predict the probable outcomes more accurately if he knows something about the hard-soft lineup in the decision-making units....

ENDNOTES

1 We refer, of course, to recent works on bureaucratic politics that treat the subject in a quite theoretical vein, chiefly those of Graham T. Allison and Morton Halperin. While these writers have made a valuable contribution in systematizing the subject, earlier studies should not be forgotten and are still useful. See, e.g., Roger Hilsman, *The Politics of Policy Making in Defense and Foreign Affairs* (New York: Harper and Row, 1971); Samuel Huntington, *The Common Defense (*New York: Columbia University Press, 1961); Warner Schilling, Paul Hammond, and Glenn H. Snyder, *Strategy, Politics and Defense Budgets (*New York: Columbia University Press, 1962); and Richard Neustadt, *Presidential Power* (New York: Wiley, 1960).

2 Here it must be said the Graham Allison's choice of the Cuban missile crisis as the empirical vehicle for his excellent exposition of the paradigm was unfortunately misleading. His Models II and III are more generally applicable to non-crisis decisions in which agency biases are freer to operate, untrammelled by constant presidential involvement and a shared sense that the "national interest" should take precedence over bureaucratic concerns. Graham Allison, *The Essence of Decision* (Boston: Little, Brown, 1971).

3 See Stephen Krasner, "Are Bureaucracies Important?" *Foreign Policy,* 7 (Summer 1972), 159-179 for a critique of the theory, emphasizing the president's primary role in U.S. foreign policy making. Also see Robert J. Art, "Bureaucratic Politics and American Foreign Policy: A Critique," *Policy Sciences,* 4 (December 1973), 467-490.

4 We follow Allison and Halperin in using the term "bargaining" for collective internal decision making. For them it apparently means the whole process of maneuver and "pulling and hauling" by which decisions get made, a meaning more diffuse and comprehensive than the definition we gave earlier for interstate bargaining. We accept this, but point out that in crises the process of decision or coalition-formation often takes the simpler form of merely discussion and persuasion among top decision makers. See Graham Allison and Morton Halperin, "Bureaucratic Politics: A Paradigm and Some Policy Implications," in Raymond Tanter and Richard H. Ullman, eds, *Theory and Policy in International Relations* (Princeton, N.J.: Princeton University Press, 1972), pp. 50-51.

5 Morton Halperin, *Bureaucratic Politics and Foreign Policy* (Washington: Brookings Institution, 1974), pp.101-112. Halperin and Allison do recog-

nize four categories of "interest" that are held by individual decision-makers: conceptions of the national security interest, agency interest, domestic interests, and personal interests. However, the emphasis is placed on agency interests and the influence of agency role on conceptions of the national interest.

6 Allison and Halperin, "Bureaucratic Politics," pp. 57-66.

7 *Khrushchev Remembers,* trans. by Strobe Talbott, with Introduction, Commentary and Notes by Edward Crankshaw (New York: Little, Brown, Sphere Books Ed., 1971), p. 459. Obviously the statements mentioned, as in any memoirs, must be treated with some skepticism. Khrushchev may have misrepresented, or mis-remembered his ambassador's report of Robert Kennedy's words, or Dobrynin could have mis-transmitted them. There has been no corroboration on the U.S. side that Robert Kennedy ever said anything like this to Dobrynin, much less that the president had any fear of a "military take-over."

8 Allison and Halperin, "Bureaucratic Politics," p. 60.

9 Ibid., p. 72.

10 Halperin recognizes the difficulty: *Bureaucratic Politics,* p. 313.

B: GROUP POLITICS AND SOCIAL CONFLICT

Domestic Interest Groups and Canadian and American Policy: The Case of the Arab Boycott

Howard Stanislawski

Analyses of international conflict and its management traditionally have focused on the impact of interest groups and their political demands on state policy. Particularly in the United States, the roots of policy have long been traced to the competition among political groups that animates the American political process.[1] Indeed, at times pluralists have suggested that the state is only a referee among competing interests. Moreover, they argue, such a limited and neutral role is wholly appropriate: competitive group activity is an effective and equitable method of ensuring public control of policy. Other analysts are far less sanguine and challenge both the description and prescription of the impact of organized political groups on policy. Some argue that interest groups enter the political arena with highly inequitable resources and access and, consequently, some groups are far more influential than others in shaping policy. The high levels of military spending, for example, are frequently traced to the easy access and powerful interests of those who benefit from defense dollars. Strategies of conflict management, this kind of argument suggests, are very much a product of well-organized special interests with easy access who shape the broad outlines, if not the specific details of policy.

Equally to the point, scholars challenge the description of the state as neutral, as an impartial arbiter among competing interests. In an ambitious attempt to identify the important factors which affect policy, Peter Katzenstein looks at interest groups as part of a much larger policy network which shapes policy outcomes.[2] Together with other "political action groups," like bureaucracies and political parties, they constitute the ruling coalitions in advanced industrial states and create the policy networks which define the boundaries of policy. To assess the impact of interest groups, Katzenstein treats them within the broader context of society as a whole and distinguishes between "strong states" and "weak states" in their relationship to society. Strong states are essentially those in which state and society are closely intertwined, in which particularistic interests of specific groups do not predominate over the collective interests as defined by the state; the state is not a referee but the most important participant in the political process, the participant with the deter-

---

An original essay written especially for this volume.

mining influence. Weak states in contrast tend to reflect a more pluralistic set of political processes; different private interests strongly influence and at times determine governmental decisions. Policy reflects the outcome of complex conflicts among varieties of interests.

To assess the impact of organized political groups on strategies of conflict management, we examine the response of two industrialized states, the United States and Canada, to the same policy issue, the Arab boycott. We look first at the range of political and societal factors that affect lobbying in the two countries, then at the role of competing interests in shaping policy toward the Arab boycott, and finally at the impact of different kinds of interests within the wider context of state-society relationships.

I. LOBBYING IN THE AMERICAN AND CANADIAN POLITICAL SYSTEM

Lobbying is carried out differently, within different constraints, and leads to differing types of outcomes in the United States and Canada. In a comparison of interest group activity in the two countries, Robert Presthus has examined their differing political cultures and the forms of interest group activity they promote. In Canada, he claims, interest group activity in general tends to be seen as more legitimate and equitable than it is in the U.S.[3] While this may well be true with regard to large economic or corporate interest groups on issues of domestic policy, it is not so in the foreign policy sector. Generally, suspicion of governmental authority in the United States contrasts with the deference to authority that permeates Canadian politics and society. In addition, channels of access for interest groups differ sharply in the two states. While American society and government are much more open, with multiple channels of access, the Canadian equivalents tend to be relatively closed, with fewer, though closer, relations as the norm, at least for major pressure groups. Certainly, the American system of separation of powers and checks and balances, together with a powerful system of congressional committees, contrasts strongly with the Canadian parliamentary and cabinet system. In Canada, non-cabinet members of parliament (even of the party in power) play a very minor role in policy-making and parliamentary committees wield little effective legislative power. Opportunities for access are far greater in the American than in the Canadian legislature. The power of the bureaucracy is also far more extensive in Canada than it is in the U.S., since the continuing bureaucracy, normally entirely unaffected by changes in government and accustomed to dealing with political ministers unskilled in the portfolios they administer, is much better placed to shape policy outcomes.

Canadian and American approaches toward societal integration are also strikingly different. While the U.S. has adopted a "melting pot" approach, seeking to assimilate divergent ethnic, racial, and religious groups into the American mainstream, Canada has articulated a concept of an "ethnic mosaic," fully supported in recent years by governmental grants — a system that should reinforce social and cultural divisions in Canadian society. In contrast to the theory, however, in practice American politics has proven much more accepting of ethnic, racial, or religious interest group activity than has Canada, which regards such action as illegitimate. Perhaps the "ethnic mosaic" model of social policy, which encourages cleavages, paradoxically perpetuates majority resentment against minorities.

It is not surprising that the bases for overt lobbying by ethnic interest groups differ in the two countries. Ethnic groups in Canada have tended not to employ professionals to act as lobbyists, depending instead upon occasional private meetings between ethnic representatives, more often than not major businessmen, and senior governmental officials. Traditionally, they have relied on "quiet diplomacy" to advance their interests. Beyond this, the representational function in Ottawa is generally met through various "old boys" networks, crossing governmental, business, and special interest lines. This is so to a far greater extent than in the United States. It is also interesting to note that while agents of domestic and foreign groups of course function in Ottawa, there is little or no acknowledgement of their status and no legal requirement (like that in the United States) that lobbyists register with the government. The perceived impropriety of overt lobbying and the absence of professional representation on behalf of ethnic groups have sharply limited the political activity and effect of interest groups in Canada. This has been especially so in the management of international economic conflict, where the power and legitimacy of countervailing economic and bureaucratic interests present even greater obstacles to successful representational activity by ethnic interests.

Looking particularly at Jewish and Arab interest groups in the two countries, it appears that Arab groups in both states have not yet developed major domestic electoral power, either in voting strength or in fundraising, though, of course, the economic power of the Arab lobby, emanating from abroad and allied to domestic corporations, far outstrips that of the Jews. Jewish groups in the U.S., however, have developed political capabilities that make them a far more significant force in electoral terms than the Jews in Canada.

II. THE ARAB ECONOMIC BOYCOTT

The Arab boycott has its origins in the earliest decades of Jewish-Arab strife in British Mandatory Palestine. One of the stated objectives of the Arab League, founded in 1944, was "to frustrate further Jewish economic development in Palestine by means of a boycott against Zionist produce."[4] Arab League states undertook to prevent the introduction into their countries of Jewish-produced goods.[5] A Central Boycott Office (CBO) was soon established, with each Arab League state responsible for its own boycott operation and overall coordination of the boycott of Jewish goods and services assigned to the CBO.

After the establishment of the State of Israel in May 1948, the boycott of Jewish goods and services became a boycott of Israel's goods and services, and soon afterward, the boycott expanded from a direct, or primary boycott, into secondary and tertiary dimensions.[6]

1. The *primary boycott* is a direct boycott of Israel and Israeli goods and services by Arab states, firms, and individuals that refuse to do business with Israel. Countries such as the U.S. and Canada are essentially unaffected by and play no role in the primary boycott.
2. The *secondary boycott* is an attempt by Arab states, firms, or individuals to pressure firms of other countries to refrain from dealing with Israel or Zionists, or to end certain relationships with Israel or Zionists, as a condition of trade with Arab states, firms, or individuals.
3. The *tertiary boycott* is an attempt by Arab states, firms, or individuals to prevent firms of uninvolved third party states from dealing with firms of their own or other similarly uninvolved third party states because of the latter's relationship with Israel or Zionists, as a condition of doing business with Arab states, firms, or individuals. Secondary and tertiary boycott provisions constitute an attempted extraterritorial application by Arab states of their laws within the jurisdiction of the United States, Canada, and other countries.

Firms or individuals seeking to engage in business with Arab states, firms, or individuals are asked to provide information about their activities; alternatively, information about their activities may already have been compiled by the CBO or any of its contributors. Failure to respond to a request for information, the provision of information deemed unacceptable under the boycott regulations, or suspicious evidence that need not be cited can lead to the blacklisting of the third party firm.

III. INTEREST GROUPS AND AMERICAN GOVERNMENTAL RESPONSES TO THE ARAB BOYCOTT

A series of boycott-related incidents in the 1950s and 1960s aroused American popular and governmental concern. By 1956, Congress formally viewed Arab boycott activity as inimical to American interests and values.[7] In 1956, Brown and Williamson Tobacco Company stopped selling its American brands to Israel because of Arab threats. Coca-Cola, Ford, Xerox, Miles Laboratories, and Topps Chewing Gum were all blacklisted in the 1960s because of relations with Israel.[8] In 1956, American Express closed its offices in Israel, allegedly because of commercial considerations. Shortly thereafter, American Jewish organizations protested and American Express reopened its operations in Israel. In 1961, successful resistance to Arab boycott pressures was undertaken by Hilton Hotels Corporation.[9] No punitive action resulted, and Hilton Hotels expanded in both Israel and the Arab world.

Because of the attention focused by American interest groups on the Arab boycott, governmental action followed. In 1960, the State Department protested Kuwaiti requests that American firms clarify their relations with Israel, or face blacklisting.[10] In the same year, Congress stated its opposition to economic boycotts, blockades, and restrictions on the use of international waterways.[11] In 1965, Congress passed an amendment to the Export Administration Act (EAA) of that year, opposing compliance with the boycott in principle and requiring all American exporters to report to the Commerce Department the receipt and nature of any Arab boycott-related request.[12] This principled statement was only a recommendation, however, and Commerce Department personnel continued to disseminate trade information and tender materials containing boycott references.[13]

Despite the enactment of the statute in 1965, in the decade that followed American-Arab trade increased considerably, growing to $5.4 billion by 1975 and then to $8.36 billion by 1978.[14] By 1974, however, it was clear that the 1965 EAA provisions were doing little to prevent American compliance with the boycott. For example, in the final quarter of 1974, companies reporting on boycott issues indicated 80% compliance with boycott clauses.[15] In the aftermath of the Arab oil embargo of 1973-74 and the quadrupling of oil prices, the lobbying activities of American Jewish organizations intensified, and other American groups, including labor unions and human rights groups, actively joined the anti-boycott coalition. In response to these activities, over twenty anti-boycott proposals were introduced in Congress in the 1975-76 session.[16] On November 25, 1975, in an attempt to forestall legislation and still respond to the growing anti-boycott pressure, President Ford tightened the 1965 Commerce Department's monitoring mechanism, requiring all companies to report all requests received and prohibiting compliance by American firms with discriminatory clauses. In subsequent months, presidential directives required banks, freight forwarders, and insurance companies to file reports, opened these reports to public inspection (after October 7, 1976), and required the Commerce Department to cease disseminating notices of trade opportunities requiring boycott compliance.[17] The 94th Congress, moreover, passed a significant piece of limited anti-boycott legislation. The Tax Reform Act (TRA) of 1976 contained within it an amendment, authored by Senator Abraham Ribicoff of Connecticut, which denied to U.S. corporations complying with secondary and tertiary boycott clauses (as defined by Treasury regulations) foreign tax credits, tax benefits for domestic international sales corporations (DISCs), and deferral of taxation on foreign income derived by corporations from business in countries requiring boycott participation.[18]

At the same time as federal institutions were responding, anti-boycott activists, including Jewish organizations, and civil liberties and human rights groups, undertook activity on the state level to encourage state legislatures to enact their own anti-boycott statutes. Since banking is subject to state regulation, state anti-boycott provisions were able to deal with the important letter of credit aspect of boycott compliance in the United States. Between 1975 and 1977, wide-ranging anti-boycott statutes were passed by thirteen American states.[19] Enactment of state anti-boycott statutes constituted a substantive expansion of anti-boycott coverage in the U.S., while at the same time creating an incentive for federal legislators seeking an equalization of anti-boycott coverage across the country. In addition, specific provisions of certain state anti-boycott statutes motivated corporate and interest group action. For example, in response to specific provisions in the California statutes relating to coverage of letters of credit, the California-based Bank of America reportedly began to petition for federal anti-boycott legislation, so that national standardization would prevent the creation of competitive advantages and disadvantages with respect to boycott compliance depending upon the state in which any given corporation was based.[20] Economic data available then and later showed, moreover, that trade had not been affected by previous anti-boycott action, and it was not affected by the new initiatives. American trade with the Arab world continued to increase in proportion commensurate with previous increases, and in a manner consistent with anticipated increases in a context devoid of anti-boycott action.[21]

While the state and municipal initiatives were continuing, federal activity accelerated. From 1976 to 1979, the focus of federal attention was primarily on the enactment of comprehensive anti-boycott legislation under the provisions of the EAA, administered by the Department of Commerce. During the 1976 presidential election campaign, Jimmy Carter declared himself committed unequivocally to anti-boycott legislation. After his election, however, Carter Administration officials argued in favor of a limited anti-boycott approach, only selectively regulating secondary boycott problems.[22] At the same time, business groups began to organize against various proposed anti-boycott bills.

The new administration argued against the strong anti-boycott proposals being considered by Senate and House committees. But Congress affirmed its intention to proceed with these strong versions, despite administration opposition; consequently, the administration argued for the inclusion in the proposed bills of provisions being advocated by business groups, which insisted on the need for broad exceptions for unilateral selection of goods and services, for compliance with host country laws, for limited American extraterritorial reach, for preemption with regard to state laws, and for limited reporting.[23]

It became clear during the early weeks of the 95th Congress that a major battle was looming between those backing Congressional anti-boycott legislative proposals, including Jewish organizations and their allies, and major American corporate interests, supported by officials of the Carter administration. To resolve the major differences between these interests, the administration, national Jewish organizations, and major corporate interests turned to a new and remarkable effort to resolve the problem — negotiations aimed at achieving a joint statement of principles, held between national Jewish organizations and the Business Roundtable, a group composed of the chief executives of 180 of the largest American corporations.[24] In early May 1977, after a period of negotiations between the Business Roundtable and Jewish organizations, a joint statement of principles was carefully developed, satisfying the basic concerns and requirements of the two sides. The agreement supported legislation to prohibit all forms of religious or ethnic discrimination arising out of a foreign boycott, to prohibit all secondary and tertiary boycott conditions involving restrictive trade practices, and to prohibit the provision of boycott-related information.[25] The memorandum of agreement was adopted verbatim by the Congress and received the full endorsement of President Carter, who signed the new EAA into law on June 22, 1977.

The provisions of the new law, implemented by detailed Department of Commerce regulations, prohibit compliance by U.S. persons with secondary and tertiary boycott conditions that are both discriminatory and restrictive in nature. A compulsory, comprehensive reporting mechanism was established, requiring that all cases of boycott requests be reported to the Secretary of Commerce, together with information regarding the disposition of those requests, and that the information thus compiled would be available to the public.[26] On February 22, 1977, prior to the enactment of the EAA but in the midst of its consideration by Congress, the *Journal of Commerce* reported that all the Arab states, with the exception of Iraq, had dropped their requirement for the provision of negative certificates of origin.[27] Other business and banking journals soon reported similar significant changes in Arab boycott demands.[28]

American Jewish organizations played key roles in the lengthy processes which led to the enactment of the state statutes, the TRA of 1976, and the EAA of 1977. They prepared extensive legal memoranda, pursued legal action against various Administration officials in an attempt to obtain public disclosure of boycott-related documentation,[29] engaged in a lengthy and extensive shareholders' campaign on the issue,[30] dealt with the *Fortune* 500 corporations and American university presidents and chairmen to obtain support for anti-boycott action,[31] participated in the negotiations with the Business Roundtable, and engaged in extensive public communication, legislative liaison, and lobbying. Business groups were generally opposed to the legislation but when the public impact of anti-boycott activists became clear, they sought to affect the content of the legislation by entering into negotiations. Even so, some corporate representatives (for example, those from Mobil Oil) refused to endorse the negotiated agreement.

IV. INTEREST GROUPS AND CANADIAN GOVERNMENTAL RESPONSES TO THE ARAB BOYCOTT

The Canadian experience with the Arab boycott of Israel is quite different from that of the United States. The federal government was far less willing to act against the operation of the Arab boycott in Canada. Indeed, although generally political leaders in Canada regarded the boycott as offensive and contrary to Canadian values and practices, senior officials of the federal government repeatedly stymied the development of procedures to control and curtail boycott activities.

For many years, despite acquiescence by Canadian companies in many requirements of the Arab boycott, the Canadian government undertook no response. Canadian policy sought to maximize every trading opportunity, and contracts of all sorts were pursued by Canadian firms with the support of the government. As part of its normal support role, Canadian government personnel abroad forwarded information relating to transactions to Canadian firms, including information known to contain boycott requirements, and government publications provided information to Canadians on how to comply with boycott stipulations.[32]

The Arab boycott became a significant issue of public policy in the period following the October War in 1973 and the ensuing oil price increases and oil embargo. In April 1975, the Hon. Herb Gray (who was not at that time in the federal cabinet) revealed that the Export Development Corporation (EDC), an important federal crown corporation providing both financing and insurance coverage for export transactions, had been giving insurance coverage to export transactions with Arab states that included Arab boycott conditions. On May 8, 1975, Prime Minister Pierre Elliott Trudeau stated in the House of Commons:

> I think it is sufficient to say that this type of practice is alien to everything the government stands for and indeed to what in general Canadian ethics stand for.[33]

However, this statement of principle was not translated into policy guidelines aimed at dealing with the Arab boycott.

For the next eighteen months, Canadian Jewish organizations spearheaded an intensive lobbying campaign. They mobilized support for anti-boycott legislation among the media, human rights and civil liberties associations, and trade unions and discussed the issue with the federal and provincial governments and opposition parties. On October 21, 1976, the federal government announced an anti-boycott policy, to be administered not through legislation, but rather through administrative guidelines. Government services, support, and facilities would be denied to companies for specific transactions containing certain types of boycott clauses, which would,

> in connection with the provisions of any boycott, require a Canadian firm to: engage in discrimination based on the race, national or ethnic origin or religion of any Canadian or other individual; refuse to purchase from or sell to any other Canadian firm; refuse to sell Canadian goods to any country; or refrain from purchases from any country.[34]

The government also stated that it would require all Canadians to report to the government on their experiences with boycott requests and would make public the names of firms signing unacceptable clauses. While initially this policy seemed attractive to anti-boycott activists, its haphazard application by the Department of Industry, Trade and Commerce, its many loopholes that quickly became apparent, and a number of *ex post facto* policy reinterpretations which widened existing loopholes led to intensified lobbying for comprehensive anti-boycott legislation. The January 1977 report of the Commission on Economic Coercion and Discrimination, a citizens' panel composed of distinguished Canadians from all major political parties, provoked large-scale public activity. Editorialists across the country unanimously called on the federal government to enact serious, comprehensive anti-boycott legislation.[35]

On January 21, 1977, the government quietly released brief guidelines implementing its policy. Officials of Industry, Trade and Commerce in Ottawa were to keep track of cases they heard about and prepare semi-annual reports of the information at their disposal. These guidelines weakened considerably the promise inherent in the policy statement. Under these parameters, the majority of boycott clauses requested from Canadian firms continued to be acceptable, and companies that complied would not lose government assistance. In addition, the reporting mechanism called for in the government's policy statement was abandoned in the guidelines.

In June 1977, while controversy swirled around the federal government's guidelines on the boycott issue, the Canadian Association of Statutory Human Rights Agencies passed two resolutions calling for anti-boycott legislation, as did the Canadian Labour Congress in September 1977. In the midst of the growing controversy, Ontario Premier William Davis announced his intention to introduce provincial anti-boycott legislation, should federal inaction continue. After lengthy and careful legislative study, Ontario's anti-boycott legislation was enacted in November 1978.

Throughout 1977 and 1978, the press and the Jewish community pressed the federal government to initiate legislation, while bureaucratic and business groups opposed any significant federal anti-boycott action. Major behind-the-scenes business lobbying had failed to dissuade Ontario from its action, but, on the federal level, business groups joined in coalition with bureaucratic and political forces to prevent new initiatives. Nonetheless, a series of damaging revelations, indicating substantial deficiencies in the federal program's coverage, fueled the controversy. In August 1978, in anticipation of a forthcoming election, the federal government announced a significant tightening of its program and a commitment to legislate a compulsory, comprehensive reporting mechanism. Although the House of Commons reconvened in October 1978, a bill providing for a reporting mechanism was introduced only in mid-December and was never brought back for legislative action. During the 1979 election campaign, the Liberal Party promised to reintroduce the bill and the Progressive Conservative Party and the New Democratic Party forcefully called for the enactment of comprehensive anti-boycott legislation, along the lines of the American and Ontario statutes. The election of a Conservative government on May 22, 1979, created expectations that new legislation would be forthcoming soon after the opening of the new parliament.

Between April 25, 1979, and late October of that year, the Conservative Party and (later) government found itself in the midst of a new controversy. Its leader, Joe Clark, had pledged during the campaign to move the Canadian embassy in Israel from Tel Aviv to Jerusalem. Enveloped in growing controversy, the new government ultimately refused to consider anti-boycott legislation during its brief, nine month tenure in office. On December 14, 1979, the government of Prime Minister Joe Clark was defeated in the House of Commons and, in the election that followed two months later, the Liberals and Pierre Trudeau were returned to power. Under the new Trudeau government, no new investigations of the significance of the Arab boycott in Canada or new anti-boycott policies were initiated.

Throughout the controversy, the Canadian media were virtually unanimous in their continuing criticism of the government and in their support for anti-boycott legislation. But there was strong and effective lobbying against legislative action. In 1979, during the heated debate over the Jerusalem embassy question, officials in the Department of Industry, Trade and Commerce leaked selective, and at times erroneous, information to the press. Arrayed against Jewish interest groups on the boycott and Jerusalem issues were Canadian business groups, Canadian banks, and domestic and foreign Arab representatives who sought to link the two issues and convince Canadians of the likelihood of Arab retaliation, should Canada proceed to move its embassy and/or enact anti-boycott legislation.

The groups opposed to any action against the boycott were closely linked to the Canadian foreign policy-making elite. Members of the bureaucratic elite made consistent efforts first to prevent any governmental initiative; once initiatives were undertaken, to prevent implementation; once implementation began, to forestall rigorous implementation; when public pressure mounted because of limited implementation, to deny information to the public and to distort information, claiming progress where no progress had been made; when forced to deal with public groups interested in the issue, to appear conciliatory despite private opposition to anti-boycott efforts; when asked by political leaders to develop legislative options, to produce proposals that were thin and lacking in substance; and finally, when faced with imminent legislative action, to leak information to the media to undermine the efficacy of the legislative effort.

Members of the corporate elite played a similar role. Beginning with occasional private representations to members of both the political and bureaucratic elites, corporate intervention intensified, still in private, reflecting the traditionally close association of members of the corporate and political elites. Governmental policy at first was an irritant rather than a hardship to the corporate elite. However, as demands for expansion of governmental action against the boycott intensified, and as the government responded with policy initiatives, corporate opposition grew. When the Clark government affirmed its intention to move the embassy to Jerusalem, corporate leaders orchestrated large-scale public representations, and, in unprecedented action, began to voice objections to policy proposals in public. Members of the corporate elite resorted to public advocacy, a search for mass support, and coalition formation in the public arena. Direct communication between leading corporate figures and senior governmental ministers intensified. The battle was joined against both anti-boycott initiatives and the implementation of the government's policy on Jerusalem. The pro-business orientation of the Conservative Party reasserted itself as members of the bureaucratic, corporate, and political elites pressed for a simultaneous and total reversal of both policy commitments. The bureaucratic-corporate alliance succeeded in linking the two issues and after the defeat of the Clark government in February 1980, anti-boycott legislation was no longer regarded as necessary or feasible by political leaders. The issue did not return to the policy agenda.

V. INTEREST GROUPS AND THE ARAB BOYCOTT: COMPARING THE AMERICAN AND CANADIAN EXPERIENCES

American and Canadian policy reactions to the Arab economic boycott were significantly different. In both cases, one coalition of interest groups opposed another — in essence, Jewish organizations, trade unions, human rights and civil liberties organizations in opposition to Arab organizations and powerful corporate bodies. In both cases, the executive branch of government aligned itself with those opposing statutory or regulatory anti-boycott action. In both cases, major governmental leaders sought to respond in as limited a manner as possible to the pressures of the anti-boycott activists. In the American case, however, multiple channels of access to a diffuse set of governmental institutions with decentralized power led to strong congressional and moderate presidential support for anti-boycott action. In the Canadian case, the limited channels of access and the hierarchical and concentrated nature of power constrained the impact of anti-boycott activists.

Differences between American and Canadian political cultures and norms were significant in the divergent policy outcomes. First, while American political leaders reacted negatively to Arab threats of economic retaliation, Canadian politicians and bureaucrats seized upon these threats to alarm the Canadian public. Traditional Canadian patterns of deference to political authority assured public receptivity to governmental estimates and policy preferences. Second, in contrast to the U.S., the absence of independent, powerful parliamentary investigative committees reduced the likelihood of competing, detailed estimates reaching the public. Third, while ethnic and special interest group lobbying on foreign policy issues is suspect in both countries, there is a major difference in degree between Canada and the United States. In the U.S., such intervention may be frowned upon by political, bureaucratic, and corporate elites, but interest aggregation is nonetheless rooted in the American conception of a pluralist democracy. In Canada, despite its model of an ethnic mosaic, there is a very limited tradition of pluralist practices.

While ethnic interest lobbying occurs in both countries, it is more circumspect, much more restrained, and much less effective in Canada than in the U.S. To a significant degree, Canadian groups either instinctively know or have come to believe that they should be less vigorous in their activities as their audience is neither receptive nor politically dependent upon their support. While the size of the Jewish population differs in the two countries (Jews are approximately 2.6% of the American population, less than 1.5% of the Canadian population), Jews are concentrated in important electoral districts in both countries. Because of the difference in electoral systems, however, their electoral impact diverges widely. In Canada, the "Jewish vote" can swing possibly five or six constituencies of the nearly 300 in the House of Commons — a relatively unimportant factor except in very close elections, while in the United States, the nature of the electoral college and the system of checks and balances tends to increase the significance and political leverage of concentrated ethnic groups.

Katzenstein's distinction between strong and weak states is very useful in explaining the divergent outcomes in the two countries. He suggests that an examination of ruling coalitions, the relationship between state and society, and the interactions between ruling coalitions and the policy networks created by state-society relationships will define the limits of the impact of interest groups on policy.

Katzenstein classifies differentiation between state and society as low, for example, in Japan, where compliance with the most restrictive provisions of the Arab boycott is possibly the highest in the industrialized world, as relatively high in

Britain, and as high in the United States. While Katzenstein does not deal with Canada, Canada would likely rank below the U.S. in differentiation and well above Japan. Canadian governmental policy would therefore be less susceptible to interest group intervention from those outside the ruling coalition than would that of the United States. The closer, more intimate, and more integrated the state-society relationship, particularly as it manifests itself in the corporate-banking sector's connectedness with government, the less the legitimacy accorded to intervention by other kinds of groups. In Canada, the scope of state action in society, the deference to authority, and the centralization of much of policy-making enables the state to resist pressures coming from society. Certainly in the contemporary period, the ruling coalitions that have governed Canada, incorporated, through processes of elite accommodation, key members of the corporate, political, and bureaucratic elites who shaped Canada's policy networks and determined policy outcomes. In Katzenstein's terms, the coalition is continuing, consistent, and effective in its governance of the country. The legitimacy of corporate interests is unassailable and is usually articulated from within, as part of the standard process of decision-making. A strong ruling coalition easily resists the demands of other groups which challenge established interests and programs.

In the United States, the state-society relationship is altogether different. The ruling coalition is more diffuse, with undisciplined political parties, a highly politicized bureaucracy, and greater penetration of a multiple-channeled political process by diverse interest groups. The government is consequently more likely to respond to policy demands coming from groups in society. Institutions compete to define the most acceptable and effective statutory or regulatory responses to demands emanating from beyond the corporate sector.

In strong states, breaking through the power of the ruling coalition is a far more difficult political challenge than in weak states. This comparison of the policy responses to the Arab boycott illustrates the complex relationships among institutions and groups that interact to structure political demands and shape policy. If we are to understand why policy differs, we cannot look only at the number of interested and active groups in the field, or even at the effectiveness of their organization, their ease of access, and the resources they command as they try to influence strategies of conflict management. We must situate the activity of interest groups within the broader context of the relationship between the state apparatus and society and the policy networks that set the boundaries and limits of acceptable action.

ENDNOTES

1 Group theory has long been important in the explanation of American politics. See Arthur F. Bentley, *The Process of Government* (Chicago: The University of Chicago Press, 1908), Earl Latham, *The Group Basis of Politics* (Ithaca: Cornell University Press, 1952), and David Truman, *The Governmental Process* (New York: Alfred A. Knopf, 1965). For specific studies of the impact of business groups on public policy, see the classic study by E.E. Schattschneider, *Politics, Pressure, and the Tariff* (New York: Prentice-Hall, 1935). Critics of pluralism include Theodore Lowi, *The End of Liberalism* (New York: W.W. Norton, 1969) and James Q. Wilson, *Political Organizations* (New York: Basic Books, 1973).
In Canada, see Kenneth McRae, ed., *Consociational Democracy: Political Accommodation in Segmented Societies* (Toronto: McClelland and Stewart, 1974), John Porter, *The Vertical Mosaic* (Toronto: The University of Toronto Press, 1965), Wallace Clement, *Continental Corporate Power* (Toronto: McClelland and Stewart, 1977), and Paul Pross, ed., *Pressure Group Behaviour in Canadian Politics* (Toronto: McGraw-Hill Ryerson, 1975).

2 Peter Katzenstein, *Between Power and Plenty: Foreign Economic Policies in Advanced Industrial States* (Madison: University of Wisconsin Press, 1978).

3 Robert Presthus, *Elites in the Policy Process* (London: Cambridge University Press, 1974).

4 Donald L. Losman, *International Economic Sanctions: The Cases of Cuba, Israel, and Rhodesia* (Albuquerque: University of New Mexico Press, 1979), p. 47.

5 Dan S. Chill, *The Arab Boycott of Israel: Economic Aggression* (New York: Praeger, 1976), p. 1, and W.H. Nelson and T. Prittie, *The Economic War Against the Jews* (New York: Random House, 1977), p. 103.

6 Nancy Turck, "The Arab Boycott of Israel," *Foreign Affairs*, 55 (April 1977), 474. Also see Report of the Subcommittee on Oversight and Intelligence of the Committee on Interstate and Foreign Commerce of the U.S. House of Representatives, Chairman, Rep. John Moss (Washington, D.C., U.S. Government Printing Office, n.d.), p. 20.

7 Chill, *The Arab Boycott,* p. 48.

8 Nelson and Prittie, *The Economic War Against the Jews,* pp. 5-54. Also see Turck,"The Arab Boycott of Israel," p. 475.

9 Nelson and Prittie, *The Economic War Against the Jews,* pp. 179-80.

10 Chill, *The Arab Boycott,* p. 48.

11 Ibid., pp. 48-9.

12 Turck, "The Arab Boycott of Israel," p. 484.

13 Chill, *The Arab Boycott,* pp. 50-1.

14 Turck, "The Arab Boycott of Israel" p. 485.

15 Chill, *The Arab Boycott,* pp. 51-2.

16 Turck, "The Arab Boycott of Israel," p. 485.

17 Ibid., pp. 485-86.

18 For provisions of the Ribicoff Amendment, see Tax Reform Act of 1976, Sections 999, 999a, 999b, 999c, 999d, 999e, and 999f of the Internal Revenue Code, amending P-L 95-455. For detailed regulations of the TRA, see *Federal Register*, January 5, 1977, 42, 3; March 1, 1977, 42, 40; August 17, 1977, 42, 159.

19 Beginning with New York whose statute became effective on January 1, 1976, significant measures were enacted in Illinois, Ohio, Maryland, Massachusetts, California, Florida, New Jersey, Minnesota, Washington, Oregon, North Carolina, and Connecticut.

20 For an examination of the banking situation, see *The New York Times*, September 12, 1976.

21 See "Israeli Boycott Losing its Grip," *The New York Times*, June 12, 1978; "Anti-boycott Law: a Quiet Success," *US News and World Report*, June 26, 1978. Also see *Newsday*, May 30, 1978 and *New York Times*, October 12, 1976.

22 Henry J. Steiner, "Pressures and Principles — The Politics of the Antiboycott Legislation," *Georgia Journal of International and Comparative Law*, 8 (No. 3, 1978), 550-51.

23 Ibid., p. 552.

24 See Steiner, "Pressures and Principles," p. 553 for a description of the Business Roundtable.

25 Michael Beasley, "Analysis and Application of the Anti-Boycott Provisions of the Export Administration Amendments of 1977," *Law and Policy in International Business*, 9 (1977), 930-33.

26 For a detailed report on the provisions of the Export Administration Act of 1977 regarding the Arab boycott, see Stanley J. Marcuse, "The Arab Boycott Law: The Regulation of International Business Behavior," *Georgia Journal of International and Comparative Law*, 8 (1978), pp. 559-80.

27 *Journal of Commerce*, February 1977.

28 *American Banker*, April 1978; *Houston Business Journal*, May 29, 1978; *Newsday*, May 30, 1977; and *New York Times*, June 12, 1978. Also see *US News and World Report*, June 26, 1978.

29 For example, see "American Law vs. the Arab Boycott: A Memorandum to the President of the United States," submitted by the American Jewish Congress, May 1975, 29 pp.

30 For an analysis of the American Jewish Congress' shareholders' project see *News for Investors*, III (Washington, D.C.: Investor Responsibility Research Center, January 1976), pp. 1-9. Also see Will Maslow, "The Struggle against the Arab Boycott: A Case History," American Jewish Congress, New York, 1977, 30 pp.

31 For example, see American Jewish Committee, "The Arab Boycott and American Law: A Brief Guide for Companies Active in the Middle East," New York, January 1979, 12 pp.

32 For example, see *Canada Commerce*, June 1973, p. 17.

33 Canada, House of Commons, *Debates*, May 8, 1975.

34 Ibid., October 21, 1976.

35 See Katzenstein, *Between Power and Plenty.*

B: GROUP POLITICS AND SOCIAL CONFLICT

Domestic Conflict and the Origins of the First World War: The British and the German Cases

Michael R. Gordon

For those interested in the First World War, two recent debates loom especially large. The first, inspired by Fritz Fischer, concerns the degree of German responsibility for the war's outbreak and course. The second, which has in part been thrashed out... between Arno Mayer and Peter Loewenberg, concerns the proper way to study international conflict — wars in particular. The present paper joins both debates and tries to show how they interrelate.

I

More than thirteen years have gone by since Fischer first startled the German historical profession[1]... Of his numerous challenges to orthodoxy, not the least provocative lies in the books' methodology. Both, but especially the second, have broken cleanly with the traditional explanatory model (or logic) of diplomatic history.

Briefly, the key assumption underlying this model is about the "primacy of foreign policy." From it three or four postulates follow. The model distinguishes rigorously between domestic and foreign politics; it tends to treat the state as a unified, monolithic actor operating within an external environment of competition and imperatives; and it lays down that these actors are primarily motivated by rational power considerations — by the cold rules of statecraft. The controlling concepts for describing these rules are national interest and national security, power, prestige, and perhaps reasons of state. The explanatory power of the model derives from a pattern of inferences about the relationship between specific situations and the state's adherence to these rules: the state — as a rational, unitary decision maker uninfluenced by domestic politics — will presumably choose the one alternative in the situation that best promises to maximize its security, its power, its prestige, and other interests. The state may turn out to have miscalculated, of course; nevertheless, the grounds for its actions are largely reducible to these considerations. It follows that the crucial

Reprinted with the permission of the author and publisher from the *Journal of Modern History,* 46 (June 1974), 191-226. Published by the University of Chicago Press. Portions of the text have been deleted. Most footnotes have been removed; those remaining have been renumbered.

evidence for a foreign-policy move will be located in the "minutes of bilateral or multilateral negotiations or the texts of foreign office dispatches"; and for the scholarly investigator, the problem is then to reconstruct the motives and other causes behind the move through careful textual analysis.[2]

In the renewed debate over the origins of the First World War, this traditional model has proved diminishingly fruitful. Even some of Fischer's most hostile critics have come to scrap it. Its main drawback is its inability to explain why the same foreign office document can serve to underpin two totally opposed interpretations. Such ambiguity can be overcome, or at any rate delimited, only if the traditional postulates are dropped or relaxed in favor of a wider perspective. On the Fischer side of the debate, for instance, he and his sympathizers have tried to uncover the degree to which German foreign policy was prompted by the logic of domestic bargaining maneuvers — by concern for the social status quo, for the prestige of the imperial regime, for the needs of the economic elites. In Fischer's second book, this domestic impact even becomes decisive. Its argument — stripped to the bone — amounts to a thesis of aggressive war, launched by the principal German policy makers in 1914 to preserve an expansionary future in the belief that expansion alone could preserve the threatened status quo at home. Not for nothing has a younger generation of German historians come to turn Ranke on his head and to speak of the primacy of domestic policy.

All this is extremely thoughtful and stimulating, a major scholarly accomplishment. Nonetheless, two important problems remain.

First, for all his clearing away of old and unfruitful assumptions, Fischer has not been so explicit about the methods and assumptions that he has put in their place. As things stand now, he has clearly effected a productive shift in perspective; whether this perspective adds up to a consistent and realistic pattern of explanatory logic is, however, not too clear. His second book, for instance, uses a mixture of categories and concepts from Marxist theories of imperialism, from elitist theorists like Robert Michels, from standard liberal critiques of German militarism and equally standard conservative critiques of mass society; and therefore, although the resulting argument is massively documented and his findings possibly sound, the criteria governing his choice of materials remain ambiguous — and so does the logical status of his inferences. It is hard to be categorical here, and I wish to stress my uncertainty. But that is also precisely the problem; a greater degree of explicitness seems desirable.[3] And second, as well as being insufficiently explicit, Fischer's work is also inadequately comparative. As a result, he has left himself exposed to the charge that he and his sympathizers have unfairly singled out Germany as the culprit in the war controversy.

It is at this point that the second debate between Mayer and Loewenberg joins the first. Like Fischer, both have broken with the traditional model and argued for an alternative framework of analysis. Mayer, in a series of theoretically bold writings, has developed a completely explicit and comparative model of domestic violence, counterrevolutionary reaction, and precautionary or diversionary war.[4] To Loewenberg, Mayer's model is too structural and macroscopic; he believes that a more psychological approach — especially depth-psychological — would be better.[5] But for reasons that will emerge later, I take exception to both alternatives. Loewenberg seems wrong in regarding psychological and structural explanations as incompatible: handled properly, the two are complementary to one another, not contradictory. As for Mayer, his model — theoretically provocative though it is — strikes me as one-sided and to apply, at most, to one of the two nations under study here.

The model used here is taken from theories of economic development and political modernization. Intended to uncover more of the "why" of things in the Fischer debate, it compares the domestic impact on foreign policy in Britain as well as Germany before and during the July crisis, 1914. The postulates, concepts, and patterns of reasoning that comprise the model are set forth and applied in Section IV below. First, however, two preliminary tasks need attention.

II

The first task is briefly to describe British and German foreign policies before 1914.

As far as German policy is concerned, its readiness to risk war for its own ends — either a local Balkan war fought by its ally in Vienna or a larger, continental-sized war in which it, France, and Russia participated — now seems unshakably established.... By either one of these two wars the German government thought its interests would be served: at a minimum, a successful localized war — kept limited by Russia's backing off in fear — would in the German view probably break up the Franco-Russian alliance, shore up the tottering Austro-Hungarian empire, and clear the way in Central Europe for an eventual German breakthrough to successful *Weltpolitik*. On a more ambitious level, the German government was convinced it could also secure these aims even more emphatically in a triumphant continental war. As for the world war that happened, German leaders did not consciously aim at it, not at any rate in 1914, and for that matter not even Fischer has claimed this. What they hoped was that Britain would remain neutral or at least a nonbelligerent at the outset. Nonetheless, the possibility of British intervention was appreciated at the very outset, even by Bethmann himself; and by risking its occurrence, the German government bore the responsibility for the ensuing worldwide struggle in at least the sense of conditional intent. To this extent the work of Fischer and his sympathizers seems to be unchallengeable. Fischer himself is probably justified, therefore, when he claims that the debate has now moved irretrievably away from any thesis of coequal responsibility or international anarchy, let alone of German innocence, and toward convergence on a thesis of preventive war.

What remains controversial is the precise meaning of a "preventive German war policy" and especially the motives behind it. Fischer started out in his first book with an argument that the motives were coolheaded, deliberate instances of outright expansionist goals. Some of his pupils, however, came to lay less emphasis on such goals and more on "the German mood of 1914, that strange mixture of ideological despair, political bankruptcy and overwhelming economic and military power" as the propellant behind the plunge into war.[6] Most scholars of the subject, it is fair to say, hew closer to the latter interpretation — without, however, necessarily buying the argument that the motives were therefore "defensive." Fischer himself, though willing in his latest book to allow for an explosive bundle of German ambitions and complexes, has persisted in imparting to the motives as "aggressive" a cast as possible. This article will itself have something to say later on about these motives.

As for British foreign policy, it was something much different in the period before and right through the July crisis. Except for prevailing opinion in interwar Germany and some revisionist historians elsewhere, nobody has made a charge of bellicosity stick. On the contrary, if any charge can be levelled at Sir Edward Grey, the foreign secretary, it is that he did not pursue as effective and energetic a policy as he might have during the crisis — that, instead he wavered between two inconsistent courses, backing France and, to a lesser extent, Russia in order to deter Germany on the one hand, and on the other hand playing the role of the disinterested mediator; that, in addition, he never clarified his policy one way or another until the very end, by which point German policy makers had already decided to risk even a world war; and that, consequently, British influence during the crisis fell far short of what British power in the international system warranted at the time.[7]

Judged strictly in terms of the traditional model — that is, from the viewpoint of external pressures and national interests — the ineffectuality of British policy remains an impenetrable puzzle. After all, neither Grey nor Asquith the prime minister had overlooked the multitudinous danger signs hinting at German aims over the years. Just the reverse; the major premise of Grey's diplomacy ever since coming to office, in 1906, had been to avoid a situation in which Britain might face a German menace without any allies. Hence the ententes with France and Russia; hence, too, the reinforcement of ties, especially to France, including recurring staff talks since late 1905 and the important naval arrangements of 1912. These were weighty moves, which nudged Britain away from isolation and toward alliance relationships. Why, accordingly, did the Liberal government not pursue more rigorously the logic behind the effort to reorient British policy? Why settle for a dangerous half-way adjustment, which went far enough to entail uncertain commitments and so a limitation on British freedom, but which stopped short of a full-fledged alliance that might have created both an effective control over French policy and an effective deterrent to German belligerence?

The answer is to be found, of course, in places outside the scope of the traditional model — in domestic politics, especially the resistance to a reoriented policy on the part of the radical wing within the Liberal party and cabinet. A courageous campaign of reeducation might have reduced the ranks of the resisters; the Foreign Office, for one, had long thought so and advised accordingly. Yet Grey and Asquith, far from undertaking to lead such a campaign, shied away from spelling out the implications of their new policy to even the cabinet. It was largely for this reason that British diplomacy remained stuck, when the July crisis erupted, with an "unsatisfactory compromise" as a guide — with a "policy of partisan and unforeseen commitment."[8] The result was widespread confusion on the cabinet level, and also no little self-delusion.

As this last line of argument suggests, British policy cannot be fully accounted for in terms of the traditional model. The same can be said (and will be argued) about German policy. Those scholars who work with a traditional explanatory logic balk at recognizing this; they persist in trying to explain German and British behavior by reference to unified decision makers, objective and perceived threats, and the rules of statecraft. The fact is, however, that international situations of the two countries did not differ enough to justify such contradictory responses to the July crisis — British policy hesitant and wavering, German policy rash and aggressive. If anything, Germany's future prospects in the international system looked brighter by far than Britain's. In industrial productivity, economic growth, and foreign commerce — in literate population, technology, and military weight — Germany had a decisive advantage not only over Britain but over all its European rivals. It is true that Germany's ability to achieve a breakthrough in *Weltpolitik* seemed temporarily hemmed in by several factors in 1914. But it is equally true that Britain's preeminent position was under assault, both from within and from without, at almost every point on the globe. Moreover, these strains soon colored British psychology in several quarters. A spiral of apprehension shook British life in repeated waves after 1900; invasion scares, scares about imperial disintegration, scares even about the quality of the British "race," abounded.[9] Nor were fears about encirclement a German monopoly. Recurringly, after 1880, British policy makers were haunted by the specter of a hostile coalition.

Given these trends, might not the traditional logic of statecraft point to a reversal of policies? Should it not have been British policy makers who were rash and desperate, determined to stave off decline in a bold showdown struggle, and German policy makers who were increasingly buoyant, increasingly confident that their nation was riding a glorious wave of history?

III

If, then, the gap between British and German foreign policy is too great to be explained fully by their international situations, the next task is to inquire whether their domestic situations differed enough to account for it.

At first glance this does not seem a promising

undertaking. What immediately strikes one is the apparent parallel between the two domestic scenes before 1914. Each nation experienced an alarming wave of unsettling events, resulting in social strife, economic dislocation, and left-right polarization. In both a constitutional crisis was emerging and with it the prospect of large-scale violence.

In Germany, the situation heated up in proportion as the enemies of the existing system (*Reichsfeinde* as Bismarck had branded them) advanced in numbers and organizational strength. At one time the Catholic center figured among these enemies; by the turn of the century the term referred almost exclusively to Social Democrats (SPD) and the trade unions. Their advance seemed irresistible. In fact, the more the nation industrialized and modernized, the more the social structure that underpinned the Reich at its founding, in 1871, inevitably altered in their favor. The SPD's revisionism did little to assuage the fears of... the forces of order. On the contrary, the most moderate proposals for electoral and fiscal reforms were denounced as though tantamount to revolution. And, indeed, in a sense they were: for the Bismarckian system, fabricated for a traditional social order, could hardly accommodate strong bourgeois participation — let alone that of the working class. Following the SPD advances in the 1912 Reichstag elections, a precarious situation, latent for years, was thus pushing to the surface. The more the forces of change pressed for reforms, the more the forces of order took fright. Hence the alarming wave of fanatical chauvinism, mass demagogy, and crude racism that enveloped the nation from the right in the years before the war. Hence, too, the revised interest in coup d'état schemes. The whole interrelated but untenable system of power and privilege was moving toward crisis and probably breakdown.

As for Britain, classic home of political stability, it too was undergoing a cycle of internal unrest and tensions. Class conflict was spiraling, unions were growing militant, women suffragettes resorted to violence. Worse, with segments of the army dabbling in mutiny and the Conservative-Unionist party toying with sedition, the prospect of civil war loomed ever likelier in Ireland. Culturally, a jittery mood of unease and dislocation pervaded much of Edwardian England; "decay, decline, fall, and decadence were the language of the time and not of party,"[10] Neither inherited political habits nor tested mechanisms of adjustment could readily cope with the sudden upsurge in strife. The English Constitution was based largely on tacit gentlemanly agreements — implicit rules of the game. On the Tory side, however, these rules were no longer being observed, in fact were being openly flouted, as the ancient props of patrician Britain (land, paternalism, the House of Lords, the Church) came under repeated blows. Even Liberals suffered from the distempers of the time. Divided between Whigs and Radicals over domestic affairs, and between Imperialists and Internationalists over foreign policy — faced also with an emerging Labour party on its left — the Liberal party could not spawn a coherent vision of a new society to replace the one currently under attack. Amidst these circumstances the cabinet itself tended more and more to postpone and to wobble — Asquith, indeed, something of a master at inaction. By July 1914 a sense of national disaster lurked in the air.

In many respects, then, the German and the British situations overlapped. But the parallel between them goes only so far. Dig deeper, and certain crucial differences are found that still separated the two nations — not least, in the strength (or really lack thereof) of the British extreme right as compared with its German counterpart. The fact is that the social base for powerful reactionary or counter-revolutionary mass movements was built into the very structures of Imperial Germany; in Britain, by contrast, it was almost wholly lacking. Again, a strong state but a weak regime reinforced the prospects for such extremist activity in Germany; in Britain no such state apparatus existed. The importance of this contrast cannot be overestimated. Because of it, the quality of politics in the two nations diverged in essential ways.

For decades, and not just after 1912, the elites in Wilhelmine Germany lived in an ambivalent and anxiety-ridden condition regarding modernism. On the one hand the inexorable industrial advance was welcomed by them as a means to national aggrandizement, a step toward successful *Weltpolitik*. On the other hand, few were optimistic about the future of an industrial society, and the social and political changes it created.[11] At the same time the existing ruling groups lacked a political system with built-in mechanisms of political adjustment — indeed, they steadfastly opposed changes that might create such mechanisms; even a moderate like Bethmann Hollweg was no major exception. Finally, Germany was still, for all its advanced industry, predominantly preindustrial in social structure; this meant that millions of threatened peasants in the countryside and more millions of old *Mittelstaende* within the cities were available for political mobilization [by] extremists on the right against the working class or the pitifully small progressive middle class. Edwardian England, by contrast, was simply not fertile ground for right-wing extremism of a mass sort, any more than was depression-laden England in the 1930s. By then there were no peasants to mobilize, and no militaristic aristocrats to lead them. By then, too, the commercial and industrial middle classes were numerous, articulate, and independent minded, putting a liberal stamp on British politics. As for the lower-middle classes, they were, it is true, growing in number, but unlike those caught up in the turmoil of Germany's rapid industrialization, they had long been assimilated to modern life and took it for granted. Moreover, there was no standing army, no powerful state bureaucracy, no large state role in the economy — in fact, despite recent changes, hardly a state in any modern sense at all. Least of all was there, for all the jitters of the time, a potent antimodernist tradition on which an embattled right could draw in order to rally mass support. The contrary was the case: thus, whereas Bethmann was a fatalist and full of forebodings for the future, Asquith remained certain that something good would turn up even over Ireland. For all these reasons, accordingly, even to speak of an extreme right-wing movement is to speak at best of what might have happened, and not what did in fact happen, as a noted left-wing historian concedes.[12] Indeed, Unionist flirtation with extra-constitutional methods, far from mobilizing mass enthusiasm, did not even command widespread support within the Unionist party itself.

The reasons for these contrasting situations remain to be set forth. What is important to note here, before leaving this section, is the hookup with foreign policy. Owing to the divergent political conditions, not only were the domestic crises in the two nations approached in contrary ways by the British and the German governments, but so, too, were the problems of foreign policy that faced each. German political elites (as will be seen) had an overwhelming incentive to use foreign policy as a method of domestic control; in fact, they had been doing so for years. No similar temptation offered itself to British elites, nor is there evidence that they ever used foreign policy to that end. It follows that any effort to explain British and German decisions to wage war in equivalent terms, as comparable cases of diversionary war, seems misplaced.[13]

IV

So far the analysis has been largely descriptive. The remaining task is explanatory, and much the most important: why, for all the internal conflict besetting each, did the British and the German political situations continue to contrast so markedly, and why by extension were their foreign policies influenced in no less contrasting ways?

An answer requires a look at German and British economic and political development over the long haul. Specifically, on the economic level, both the rates and the structural forms of their industrialization need to be probed. In like manner, the various ways each grappled with the three critical problems of political modernity — national identity, authoritative and effective government, and popular participation — need to be dissected.

Together, these categories permit the British and the German routes to the modern world, at any rate down to 1914, to be traced in comparable terms and the consequences for foreign policy, in turn, to be isolated and analyzed.

Economic Development. Economists continue to debate among themselves, and with others, about the key mechanisms of economic modernization. From the recent literature, nevertheless, two pivotal concepts can be extracted and made use of here.

1. *Rate of Industrialization.* — The contrast between Germany and Britain in this respect is pronounced. Britain pioneered the industrial revolution; nonetheless, by international standards, the modernization of its economic structure proceeded at a fairly modest, if steady, pace. "Compared with countries which have industrialized since...the British rate of growth was a slow process."[14] Germany, on the other hand, was largely agrarian even in 1871. Thereafter, however, industrial growth exploded, and by the turn of the century Germany had been propelled to the rank of the second industrial power in the world. The process was anything but a slow-motion exercise.

The unsettling effects of rapid economic growth are well known.[15] For this reason the slower British growth enabled British society to absorb the inevitable dislocations and turmoil much more effectively than was possible in the German case. The compressed pressure of German urbanization — rural dwellers declined from 57 percent to 45 percent during the one decade of the 1890s alone — explains in large part the social and political tensions of the period: the rapid upsurge in agrarian agitation, the growth of right-wing radicalism among peasants and *petits bourgeois*, the cultural gloom among German elites, and the enormous advances of the Social Democrats....As the latter point suggests, these rapid social changes had direct political implications for the stability of the political system. Universal male suffrage was established by Bismarck, back in 1871, as a means of winning the allegiance of the German people to his new Reich and at a time when the working classes were only 20 percent of the total population. By 1882, however, they had swelled to 25 percent, and by 1907 to 33 percent of the total. Not only would they grow in size the faster Germany industrialized; what was more, the franchise seemed more and more rigged against them as time passed and as the Reich's leadership refused to contemplate changes in the electoral districts. By 1907, for instance, it has been estimated that each Conservative deputy required an average of only 18,000 votes for election but a Socialist required about 70,000.

2. *Forms of industrialization.* — The second theoretical concept is a tendency to reject the idea of uniform prerequisites of industrial development.[16] In particular, backward countries that industrialize at later points often substitute in ways that offset their deficiencies vis-à-vis more advanced economies. According to Gerschenkron, the more economically backward a nation is when it begins to experience accelerated growth: (1) the faster its rate of industrial advance; (2) the greater its stress on big plants and enterprise; (3) the more it favors heavy over light industry; (4) the more it borrows technology and finance from abroad; (5) the greater the pressure on consumption standards; (6) the more passive the agricultural sector; (7) the greater the role of banks and State budgets; (8) the more virulent the ideological conflicts that ensue.[17]

With one exception — the sixth factor — the list accounts for the enormous differences between the forms of British and German industrialization. British development started early; was pioneered by a vigorous, self-confident, ever-larger middle class; was mainly "stateless," at any rate after the eighteenth century; and showed a preference for small plants and enterprises. German development, by way of contrast, started late; was pioneered by the state, beginning with the Stein reforms, largely for reasons of state aggrandizement; showed a preference for large plants and enterprises that easily lent themselves to monopolies, cartels, trusts, and syndicates; and led the state, which was also the largest single property owner, onto a course of state socialism as a means of coping with the resulting ideological conflicts.[18] This state, it must be remembered, was authoritarian, bent on preserving the privileges of Junkers, the military, the bureaucratic elites, and — eventually, once the coalition between Junkers and industrial barons was forged by Bismarck in 1879 — the industrial barons in the west.

It is this latter point that explains why Gerschenkron's sixth factor does not apply to Germany. Once American and East European grain began undermining the competitiveness of German grain in the late 1870s Bismarck and the Junkers — free traders until then — swung round in favor of protection and instituted a series of tariffs favouring heavy industry and Junker estates but at the expense of the urbanized middle and working classes. Only in the 1890s did the economic interests of these two elite groups diverge and a "new course" ensue. But the course was short lived, high tariffs were reinstituted in 1902, and an otherwise heavily industrialized nation saw its state pursuing a largely agrarian policy that enabled a "semifeudal" class to maintain its economic basis, its social status, and its political privileges. In the process, the bourgeoisie was itself "feudalized" — abandoning its own values, taking on those of the aristocracy, and in effect becoming the pillars of an authoritarian state. In Britain, it is true, a superficially similar process of aristocratic co-option took place in the late nineteenth century. But only superficially; if the British entrepreneurial classes also grew more conservative, also adopted bit by bit gentry values, also sloughed off their former progressive political ideology, at the same time the aristocrats embracing them had themselves over the generations become in large part "embourgeoisized" — something de Tocqueville had appreciated a generation earlier.[19] It was largely entrepreneurial and liberal ideals that prevailed in mid-Victorian England, not aristocratic ideals, as the collapse of agrarian resistance and the repeal of the Corn Laws in 1846 made clear; and whatever political changes ensued amounted to a genuine compromise of values and privileges, not a sellout of the middle classes to the crown and to the Junkers as in Prussia (and later in the Reich).

3. *International implications.* — The social and economic implications of these two different industrial routes inevitably influenced the foreign policy of each, but in contrary ways.

In Germany the tariff policies, by cutting off the national economy from international competition, hastened the growth of monopolies and cartels, strengthened the impulse to economic expansion abroad, and added to the frictions and tensions shooting up within the international system at the time. Lenin, it is true, later argued that this had happened in all the capitalist nations, but in fact he was wrong. British industry remained overwhelmingly wedded to small-sized firms and avoided monopolistic tendencies throughout the prewar period; what is more, the powerful movement for protection failed, and again throughout the prewar period free trade prevailed. In terms of Schumpeter's imperialist thesis, accordingly, the German economy must be said to have raised international tensions and the British economy — with London the center of a multilateral payments system — to have offset or dampened them.[20]

Nor was this the only serious international spillover of German tariff policies, themselves the outcome of a political deal among the state, heavy industry, and Junkers. Another consequence was built-in hostility both to Britain and to Russia. Concerning Britain, as Eckart Kehr first noted, the complex of cultural pessimism and agrarian antipathy to industrialism led to hatred of that nation among both parties to the protectionist cartel. To the Junkers, England loomed with its weak agricultural sector and antimilitarism as "the advanced capitalist model of Germany's own industrial development." To the feudalized industrialists, it loomed as a painful reminder of how they had betrayed their own earlier liberalism. Concerning Russia,...the accelerating conflicts that overtook the two nations in the last decade before war did not arise from irreconcilable interests in foreign policy or from antagonistic political ideologies, but rather from the economic policies of the protectionist cartel after its restoration in 1902. On the one hand, the Junkers were determined to keep out cheaper Russian grain at any price, and on the other, the industrialists were determined to penetrate the Russian market at almost any price. Since the Russians would not lower their own industrial tariffs without the Germans lowering their grain tariffs, the two goals were irreconcilable, and the only way for the German government to try squaring them was by applying ever greater dosages of political pressure on Saint Petersburg.

Bismarck himself, it is true, endeavored to seal off his diplomacy from these domestic pressures — but in vain. As with imperialist agitation that he himself helped to call into being, so with powerful economic impulses toward Central Europe, the Balkans, and Russia: he discovered, much to his surprise, that he could not turn these forces on or off at will. Toward the end of his reign, he could not even divert them; his options abroad were too constrained by uncontrollable domestic developments. Already, in 1887, at the very moment he was renewing his Reinsurance Treaty with the Russians, the latter were excluded from the German financial markets. From there it was not such a terribly big step, let along a surprising one, for his successors to cold-shoulder the treaty and then to follow this with a tariff war against Russia in 1893. Thus, domestic pressures, and not just a lapse from Bismarckian principles by the German foreign office, explain in large measure the collision course on which Russia and Germany were placed. At its end, the course issued in the dual Junker-industrialist scheme for a German-dominated *Mitteleuropa* as a prelude to *Weltgeltung*. What economic impulses required, but economic leverage alone could not achieve, the "good German sword" would.[21]

For Britain, by contrast, there was nothing inherent in either its pattern of economic development or its pattern of related pressure-group activities that generated similar basic antagonisms toward outsiders. On the contrary, their very absence facilitated the colonial deals behind the ententes with France and with Russia, hitherto Britain's major imperial rivals. As far as Germany was concerned, British resentment of economic competition from that quarter was no doubt strong in the late 1880s and 1890s, but it was a passing phenomenon, and right down to the war the City of London was in fact regarded as a fount of pro-German sympathy.

Finally, it is worth reemphasizing the role of the state in German industrialization. Whereas in Western Europe generally the industrial revolution was either preceded or accompanied by political revolution,this was not true of Germany. The only political revolution that took place in Germany, to the extent it can be called that, was the "emancipation" of the Prussian bureaucracy, especially during the brief reform era after 1807, when it emerged as the most powerful force in Prussian life next to the monarchy and the army. The reform era itself, a prerequisite to economic modernization, was undertaken in response to military collapse at Jena in 1806 and for the express purpose of creating a more powerful nation. Economic development and political reform were not ends in themselves; they were valued mainly to the extent that they would enable Prussia, first to defend itself more effectively, then to attain a position of leadership in Germany and later Europe. Not surprisingly, the political and military considerations of the economy therefore always took precedence in the last analysis; and what was more, the most powerful German businessmen seemed generally happy to acquiesce in their role as quasi state officials.

The international implications of this pattern are easy enough to isolate. A semifeudal, militarist aristocracy survived economic modernization; managed to maintain a privileged role for the military; joined with the heavy industrialists and other middle classes to tame not only liberal internationalist sentiments but the labour force; and — whenever its economic privileges were threatened (as they briefly were during the Caprivi era after 1890) — resorted to mass demagogic, racist agitation among the peasants and lower-middle classes. Not only did such a system require a heavy armaments industry, later expanded to a large naval build-up, both of which created untold frictions with other powers, but in addition, precisely by stimulating racist and aggressive attitudes among the wider middle classes, it gave a powerful impetus to that explosive psychological complex of power yearnings, overweaning ambitions, antagonisms, fears, and neuroses that lay behind the disaster of an erratic, bullying *Weltpolitik* and eventually a desperate bid in 1914 to wage preventive war against overwhelmingly self-created menaces.

In Britain there was nothing comparable: no large military machine, no outmoded and apprehensive upper class manipulating public opinion, no powerful state subsidies for the economy. Indeed, until the war the state hardly penetrated the consciousness of the average British subject. Even the truculent jingoism of the 1880s and 1890s had exhausted itself with the fiasco of the Boer War, as Grey noted shortly after becoming foreign secretary. There was, of course, an armaments industry relating to the navy, but it was not a very powerful component of total industrial output, and neither was it in the least indispensable to the economy's health or to group interests bound up with an untenable economic status quo.

To be sure, the differences between Britain and Germany in these respects were not due wholly to the circumstances of their modernization. Geopolitical factors also mattered. Britain, as an insular power, did not need a large army; Germany, in the heart of Europe, did. But if geopolitical factors should not be slighted, neither should they be exaggerated. The minuscule size of the British army depended just as much, and perhaps more so, on the traditional antimilitarism of the aristocracy — on its fear, rooted in the struggles against the crown, that a large military establishment would invariably come under the control of its rival. At late as 1830-32, despite the tumult of the time, the governing Whigs rejected the repeated urgings by the king to beef up the army; they remained less frightened of rioting mobs than of the prospect of creating a huge coercive state apparatus. If it is impossible to imagine the Junker aristocracy behaving similarly, the reasons are to be found less in geopolitics than in the modernization peculiar to that nation.

National Identity. All modern national societies are plural, comprised of different economic classes and communal groups. For a national government to function effectively, a strong sense of common national identity and shared political community is therefore needed to bind classes and groups together and offset their parochial loyalties. The stronger this sense of subjective identity, the better from the standpoint of long-run governmental authority and stability. With it, the government's ability to cope with conflicts and to weather crises is enhanced. Without it, not only is governmental authority liable to be questioned or rejected in crisis, but governmental leaders — precisely because they cannot always count on the attachments of large numbers of people — may be tempted to fall back on demagogy or repression as tactics for handling major political problems.

In particular, if repression proves unsuccessful, then demagogy may come to include the manipulation of foreign policy for domestic purposes.

With one exception — Ireland — Britain is a classic case of a nation which early developed a sense of common nationhood and experienced a gradual and successful extension of political community among all groups and classes. Citizenship, which can be regarded as an objective sign of this subjective process, spread in the sense of civil rights in the eighteenth century, political rights in the nineteenth, and social rights in the twentieth. As one result, a set of inclusive loyalties already existed among groups and (proto) classes by the time an industrial breakthrough was achieved. As another result, even during the turmoil between 1815 and 1850, when both the emerging working classes and economically powerful middle class agitated for political change, the politically powerful aristocracy eventually responded to appeals for sharing their prerogatives in the interest of the nation. A pattern of conciliation and compromise was thus institutionalized, setting precedents for the future that helped to reconcile the working class with the existing political system, undercut Marxist and other radical notions of class warfare, and enabled the upper classes to weather political crises without fear that concessions might send the system crashing down at any moment. In the upshot, temptations to repression or demagogy were seldom alluring and even less seldom succumbed to.

Imperial Germany, on the other hand, was almost a classic case of the opposite sort — a nation internally fragmented among a host of competing antagonisms.

Not only did no common political system unite the Germans for hundreds of years before the Reich was established in 1871; what was more, there was no large mass basis for the nation-state that emerged. Except for the fairly small entrepreneurial and business middle class and the equally small if vociferous professional class (*Bildungsbuerger*), other groups and classes were either divided in their loyalties or lacked enthusiasm. Aristocrats, despite Bismarck's policies on their behalf, remained suspicious for years. Particularist sentiments remained strong, especially among the masses of the south. There were also intense among the large national groups that found themselves within the borders of the new nation-state: 2.2 million Poles (5.2 percent of the population), more than 80,000 Danes, 60,000 Lithuanians, and 1.5 million inhabitants of Alsace-Lorraine who were treated as second-class citizens. Catholics, too, soon had reasons for dissatisfaction, when they became branded *Reichsfeindlich* during the *Kulturkampf* — to say nothing of the working classes who supported the socialist party. In fact, the *Kulturkampf* and the subsequent antisocialist laws must be understood largely as Bismarck's efforts to deal with the centrifugal forces contained within the nation-state that he created by war. So, too, must the other strong-arm tactics — the "war-in-sight" rhetoric, the heated attacks on the Reich's enemies (at home and abroad), the threatened coups d'état, etc. — with which Bismarck fought every Reichstag election down until his dismissal in 1890. Though the maneuvers of his successors were less muscle ridden, they were no less essentially demagogic — Bethmann Hollweg, for all his moral regrets, no noticeable exception.

The international implications were enormous in the German case. Two sorts can be distinguished. On the one hand were spillovers resulting from deliberate policies. German governments, in struggling with the terrific centrifugal forces at home, were constantly tempted to fall back on their ultimate strategem — the diversion of the conflict outward, the manipulation of foreign and colonial policy as a means of domestic control. This pivotal point will be refined below. For the moment it is enough to note that German Marxists were not the only contemporaries who speculated about this temptation. "Reactionary governments" — as no one less than Friedrich von Holstein observed from behind-the-scenes at the Foreign Office — always try "to divert the internal struggle to the *foreign sphere*." Johannes von Miquel, Prussian minister of finance and the key figure in engineering a new coalition of industrialists and aristocrats in 1897-98 (*Sammlungspolitik*), put the sentiment more verbosely but also more candidly: "national questions," "questions of foreign policy" had to be introduced into the Reichstag to "turn our attention outwards...for in foreign affairs the sentiments of the nation could usually be united."[22] On the other hand was a critical spillover that arose quite irrespective of demagogic calculation, out of the inherent national situation of the Reich. For there was nothing basically solid or enduring about the Reich's boundaries of 1871 — the "Small Germany" that Bismarck had created. Millions of German-speaking peoples continued to live outside them, in the Austrian Empire, Switzerland, the rest of Central and Eastern Europe. At the same time millions of non-German peoples (or, in the case of Alsace-Lorraine, German-speaking but

French-influenced in custom and politics) lived inside them. The result was an inherently uncertain situation in Central Europe — and not only uncertain but also dangerous. In effect Germany's elites and masses were confronted with the choice, over time, of trying: (1) to preserve the Small Germany, which Prussia dominated and millions of whose inhabitants, German-speaking or otherwise, were branded as enemies — in short, a basically unstable German situation; (2) to escape from that instability by creating a Great Germany, with Austria and parts of its empire absorbed; (3) to go further and seek a German-dominated *Mitteleuropa* running from the North Sea to the French Alps, from Alsace-Lorraine into Western Russia, and including as at least economic satellites the former members of not only the Austro-Hungarian but the Turkish empires as well. As Fischer has persuasively argued, *Mitteleuropa* was the choice that most of the elites for converging reasons came to embrace shortly before 1914.

There were no similar spillovers from the British national situation, with the exception of Ireland — itself on the verge of civil war by 1914. But the analogy between Ireland and Germany's national difficulties and borders is incomplete. For the situations to be very comparable in international terms, it would be necessary to imagine Britain no longer an island off Europe but in Europe's heart, surrounded by other powers — all of them uneasy about the rapid growth of British power, its internal stability, its erratic and provocative foreign policy once the British Bismarck had gone. As it was, Britain could keep the Irish problem isolated from its European policies, and the only international implication of the Irish problem for European affairs in 1914 was that it so preoccupied the cabinet during the July crisis, that it was not until July 27 that the cabinet as a whole gave events in Central Europe its attention.

Governmental Institutions. This is a vast subject and only two major aspects of the developmental processes in the two nations will be tackled here.

Britain in this period was a successful unitary state (Ireland always excepted); Germany, a mainly unsuccessful federal experiment. The British state had evolved early; its major problems of executive-legislative relations had been largely, though not entirely, settled by 1725 through an elaborate system of patronage and in the aftermath of the revolution of 1688 — that is, even before the industrial revolution multiplied class conflicts; and the principle of ministerial responsibility was then anchored in 1835. The result was a complex of effective and flexible governmental institutions, which could dampen the struggle for power by diverting it toward the parliamentary arena. The power struggle was dampened at the same time for another, loosely related reason: though government in the sense just mentioned was flexible and adaptable, the "political domain" itself was comparatively narrow. The British never had a statist tradition in the French or the Prussian sense, not even during the era of mercantilism. After 1815 the state played but a minor role in the economy. It had no standing army establishment, no centrally controlled police forces, and hardly the makings of a modern bureaucracy. This dual combination — effective and flexible government but a weak state — produced a situation that enormously influenced the resolution of socio-economic conflict that industrialization heaped up without respite. In effect, even during the turbulent period between 1815 and 1850, that conflict was diverted into political channels, where it took the form of contending over the franchise and the nature of parliamentary rule.

On the one hand the forces of challenge, first the new middle class and later the equally new working class, went along with this diversion because they knew that the parliamentary system was not a fraud, however corrupt the electoral base itself happened to be. Whoever controlled Parliament would be able to control the executive and, by extension, pass laws favourable to their interests. The challengers thus accepted the existing system; they played the parliamentary game precisely because it did not strike them as hopelessly rigged. On the other hand, the existing elites continued to play the game, rather than turn to repression or to demagogy as an answer to the challenges, first because the "stakes of political competition" were limited and second because they confidently calculated that they could exploit the rules so as to survive. Their calculation manifestly paid off. The landed aristocracy dominated local government until the end of the 1880s, and cabinet politics until 1906. The House of Lords itself might not have had its powers curbed in 1911 had it not flouted the rules of the game so blatantly at the time. In short, British policy makers never succumbed to any temptations to manipulate foreign policy for domestic purposes. They had no compelling reasons to do so.

German policy makers, by contrast, did. The enormous, irrepressible inducements here arose from a situation that was the diametric opposite of the British. The German state was powerful, but German government weak and inflexible.

On the one hand Bismarck's Reich inherited the autocratic legacy of the Prussian state and all that this meant. It intermixed bureaucratic absolutism, militarism, and aristocratic privilege; its leadership, from the lowest official to the King Emperor, clung to the Prussian ideology of romantic and reactionary conservatism. At the same time, particularly as compared with Britain, the political domain of the German state was ambitious and wide ranging. The state commanded huge military and police establishments, the former of which, moreover, eluded effective legislative accountability and set the tone for social values. The state also played a dominant role in German industrialization, indeed was the single largest property holder in society, and it also came to erect an ambitious system of social welfare. The result of all this was "high stakes of political competition": whoever controlled the government, and through it the state machine, controlled an enormously powerful, coercive political instrument. Yet, on the other hand, the institutional arrangements and policy patterns of the Reich did little, if anything, to dampen the fierce struggle for power. On the contrary, these arrangements and patterns were unsuited for the politics of a complex, fast-industrializing society, and they became more obsolete each year. Instead of making for effective means of political accommodation, either through normative procedures that were regarded by all politicized forces as basically fair or through log-rolling and other techniques of satisfying completing interests by compromise, they made for fragile political authority, tenuous and uncertain modes of conflict resolution, and almost total rigidity in the face of demands for sharing power with new groups.

This was especially noticeable in the case of the Reichstag. In Britain, Parliament helped to modulate the struggle for power; new groups, first the middle classes and later the working classes, did not see the parliamentary game as hopelessly fraudulent. Their equivalents in Germany, especially middle-class Progressives and Social Democrats, faced an entirely different situation. Since the Reichstag never came to control the executive, let alone the mammoth civilian and military bureaucracies that the executive administered, what were the incentives for the Socialists to accept the political system as legitimate and play the parliamentary game without reservation? Suppose, for instance, they did win an outright Reichstag majority; would this really signal a change of the guard? Far from it, the likely result would either be continued impotence vis-à-vis the executive or a coup d'état, followed probably by a new wave of repression and perhaps an extension of the three-class system of Prussian suffrage to the federal level.

The effect on the quality of politics was inevitable. Because the political system lacked inherent means of accommodation and adjustment, the governing elites resorted to various mixtures of repression and demagogy as the only means of internal control. Moreover, the recurring temptation to use such tactics was reinforced by the stakes of political conflict: the elites, full of cultural despair anyway, were doubly fearful of making concessions to new and clamorous political forces that might eventually capture the powerful state machine and turn it against their former masters. Bismarck himself tried to control these forces through various measures, including the diversion of the conflict outward: hence his colonial policies as a crucial complement to his welfare programs — the whole policy an exercise in "social imperialism." The demagogic pattern here was set by Bismarck even before the Reich was established, during the period of his wars for unification. "The domestic situation does not make a war necessary," he said in 1866 right before the war with Austria, "but it is an additional factor making one seem desirable."[23] The difference between 1866 and 1886 was that the domestic situation now made such tactics necessary, not just desirable; there was no other way to contend with the cyclonic pressures being unleashed by fast industrialization and by equally fast urbanization that were bursting the premises of the political system apart. Bismarck himself was the first to appreciate this. The colonial question, the manipulation of foreign policy, remained for him as much a swindle as ever; nonetheless, they were "needed," he confessed, for the forthcoming Reichstag election of 1887.[24] As before, the ruse paid off — this time with a new war scare; a "cartel" majority resulted. It soon began to fall apart, however; and more and more Bismarck was driven back onto increasingly drastic measures until, in the end, he abandoned all hope of salvaging the system and contemplated an outright coup d'état.[25] This was too much for the new Kaiser, William II, solicitous of popularity at the start of his reign. The autocratic chancellor was dismissed.

Thereafter, the same tactics were refined and elaborated. Gone, however, were the explicit antisocialist measures, the repression of the Reich's "enemies"; gone, too — or at least shuttled into the background — were new schemes of coup d'état. In their place was put increasing reliance on the rigging of foreign policy. "Only a successful foreign policy," according to Buelow, foreign secretary in 1897, "can help to reconcile, pacify, rally, unify."[26] Buelow ought to have known. The elaborate program contrived in the following years for pursuing this course — *Weltpolitik*, a rapid naval build-up, the reformation of the old "cartel" groups, mass agitation, extreme nationalism, and tariff wars — was completed in 1902, and Chancellor Buelow was the man entrusted with its implementation. It was a devious program, a perilous course. "The threat of war in our time lies... in the internal politics of those countries in which a weak government is confronted by a strong nationalist movement," noted Kurt Riezler, Bethmann Hollweg's longtime political confidant and secretary.[27] Precisely so. The Buelow strategy, with its roots in the Bismarckian era, was pursued no less faithfully by Bethmann himself, his successor — though no doubt with greater moral qualms. It was a strategy, it is now clear, that led to: (1) an erratic, bullying diplomacy and eventual diplomatic isolation, (2) fanatical chauvinism, (3) preventive war, and (4) subsequent defeat and the collapse of the Reich that it was intended through demagogic means to prop up.

This is not simply a retrospective indictment. Many German contemporaries appreciated the risks, and in fact the best assessment was made by no one less than Bethmann Hollweg during a particularly anxious moment in the July crisis. Why, he asked himself, was Germany in its current predicament: "The earlier errors: simultaneously Turkish policy against Russia, Morocco against France, the navy against England — challenge everybody, put yourself in everybody's path, and actually weaken no one in this fashion. Reason: aimlessness, the need for little prestige successes and solicitude for every current of public opinion. The 'national' parties which with their racket about foreign policy want to preserve and strengthen their party position."[28]

• • •

V

If the various strings of the argument are now drawn together, the following conclusion emerges.

Domestic conflict had a contrary impact in the

two nations. In Britain, for all the turmoil that erupted before 1914, foreign policy remained moderate and largely defensive; and this was so even though the nation's world position was itself on the decline and under challenge at almost every point on the globe. Nonetheless, internal conflict did take its toll. It added to the defensiveness of Britain's posture, indeed, its increasing reactiveness, by inhibiting Grey's efforts to reorient foreign policy and leaving the nation stuck, therefore, at a dangerous point halfway between isolation and full-fledged alliances. The result was the ambivalent policy of "partial and unforeseen commitment" with which the Liberal cabinet approached the July crisis, uncertain whether it should try to act as a mediator in the old "free hand" sense of Salisbury's days or to act as an ally of France and Russia so as to deter Berlin. In the event, Grey's cautious zigzagging as the crisis unfolded only "reinforced the German hope that England would stand aside."[29]

Grey's advisers at the Foreign Office saw that his policy revisions added up to an unsatisfactory compromise, with consequent confusion both at home and abroad. Again and again, accordingly, they pressed him to clarify his actions and carry his campaign for reorientation through to its logical end; yet again and again Grey balked, well knowing that the Liberal party, and hence the cabinet itself, was too divided to permit such clarification. "I do not know," Arthur Nicolson, the permanent under-secretary, wrote in April 1914, "how much longer we shall be able to follow our present policy of dancing on a high rope and not be compelled to take up some definite line or other."[30] But the high-rope act went on; what else could Grey do in view of the political situation? Mayer argues that he and Asquith could move toward the right, toward the hawkish Unionist party — that, in fact, they did precisely this during the July crisis, overcoming the waverers and the noninterventionists in the cabinet with a threat to create a Liberal-Unionist coalition.[31] There are some scattered indications that Asquith toyed with such a threat. Yet it does not appear to have had nearly the effect that Mayer maintains it did. On the contrary, Asquith himself thoroughly feared the reactionary consequences that would follow from any such coalition. In short, as before 1914, so throughout the July crisis itself: partisan conflict and internal Liberal discord continued to obstruct a clarification of foreign policy one way or another.

In Germany, even though domestic conflict appeared to be more latent than in Britain, it was in fact even more politically far reaching, and its repercussions on foreign policy were pronouncedly of an aggressive sort. Three such repercussions have been distinguished here. First of all, quite apart from deliberate foreign-policy decisions, there was a set of spillovers that arose from the very national situation of the Reich in 1871 and after. Among the most prominent of these were the unsolved problem of national identity, doubts about the viability of the Reich's borders, and the unforeseen consequences of tariff policies that arose out of the bargains struck between industrialists and Junkers. There was a second set of spillovers, on the other hand, that did derive directly from calculated political maneuvers. These maneuvers aimed at trying to control an increasingly impossible domestic situation by ever-greater efforts of social imperialism, mass propaganda, *Weltpolitik*, armaments programs, and diversionary quests for prestige of the quickest and cheapest sorts — in short, the whole complex of foreign adventures and aggressive diplomacy that embittered relations with other great powers and created diplomatic isolation. Finally, somewhere in between there was a third pattern of repercussions, a psychological pattern, by which the fears and grudges that German elites nurtured in domestic politics were turned outward and led them to detect international spectres all over Europe. Bismarck, who had unified the nation, had spoken ominously of his "nightmare of hostile coalitions." By 1914 the whole nation, at any rate to the right of the Social Democrats, was tormented by such nightmares, even if they were overwhelmingly self-induced. The upshot of all three kinds of repercussions was the the calculated gamble in favor of war that was taken in July 1914. With one sudden desperate charge, the Reich's leadership hoped to achieve that ultimate breakthrough in *Weltpolitik* that would safeguard the nation's expansionist future and its conservative order at home. By 1917, to take a date that was uppermost in German thinking at the time, it would be too late. By then, Russian and French military reforms would be completed and the chances of a successful breakthrough, therefore, that much less.

Bethmann Hollweg himself, it has been argued, had doubts that a war would actually strengthen the conservative order. He seemed in fact to fear that it might hasten its decline and lead through mass mobilization to democratic concessions or worse. But one should not make too much of these qualms. For one thing, as Fischer notes, Bethmann's warnings in this respect "only confirm how widespread the contrary view was."[32] For another thing, he clearly embraced the "curious blend of contradictory beliefs — social Darwinism, misunderstood romanticism, and cultural pessimism — all pointing to German expansion as the only alternative to stagnation."[33] In this respect, as Stern also hastens to add, there was really no fundamental divergence of political aims between Bethmann and the other leaders of Imperial Germany; "the general consensus about Germany's national destiny was too broad and the Kaiser's tolerance for dissent too narrow" to permit anyone who dissented too much from continuing in office.[34] For a third thing, finally — as Riezler's diary makes clear — he unequivocally hoped that "if war comes and the veils fall, the whole nation will follow, driven by necessity and peril."[35]

ENDNOTES

1 Fritz Fischer, *Griff nach der Weltmacht: Die Kriegszielpolitik des kaiserlichen Deutschland 1914/1918* (Dusseldorf, 1961); *Krieg der Illusionen: Die deutsche Pollitik von 1911 bis 1914* (Dusseldorf, 1969).

2 Arno J. Mayer, "Internal Causes and Purposes of War in Europe, 1870-1956: A Research Assignment," *Journal of Modern History*, 41 (September 1969), 302. Admittedly, owing to the brevity of formulation, a pretty sharp and simplified picture of the traditional model has been sketched in. Nonetheless, I do not think that it is a caricature. On the contrary, even though many diplomatic historians had come to modify the key postulates long before Fischer was heard of, most have probably continued to use a variant of the traditional model until quite recently.

3 In other words, to paraphrase a general argument of Richard Hofstadter: Fischer's analysis does a better job of accounting for "what" happened and "how" it happened than "why" it did so; yet until the "why" of things emerges more clearly, one cannot be fully confident about the "what" and the "how" (see "History and Sociology in the United States," in *Sociology and History: Methods*, ed., Seymour Martin Lipset and Richard Hofstadter [New York, 1968], pp. 8-18).

4 In addition to the article in n. 2 above, see Arno J. Mayer, "Domestic Causes of the First World War," in *The Responsibility of Power: Historical Essays in Honor of Hajo Holborn*, ed. Leonard Krieger and Fritz Stern (New York, 1967), pp. 286-300; *Dynamics of Counterrevolution in Europe, 1870-1956: An Analytic Framework* (New York, 1971).

5 Peter Loewenberg, "Arno Mayer's 'Internal Causes and Purposes of War in Europe, 1870-1956' — an Inadequate Model of Human Behavior, National Conflict, and Historical Change." *Journal of Modern History*, 42 (December 1970), 628-36.

6 Imanuel Geiss, ed., *July 1914: The Outbreak of the First World War: Selected Documents* (New York, 1967), pp. 367-68.

7 Herbert Butterfield, "Sir Edward Grey in July 1914," *Historical Studies*, 5 (1965), 20.

8 J.A.S. Grenville, *Lord Salisbury and Foreign Policy: The Close of the Nineteenth Century* (London, 1964), p. 436.

9 Samuel Hynes, *The Edwardian Turn of Mind* (Princeton, N.J., 1968), pp. 15-54.

10 Ibid., p. 45.

11 Kenneth D. Barkin. *The Controversy over German Industrialization 1890-1902* (Chicago, 1970), pp. 1-15, 131-32; Ralf Dahrendorf, *Society and Democracy in Germany* (New York, 1967), pp. 9-10; Fritz Stern, *The Politics of Cultural Despair: A Study in the Rise of the German Ideology* (Berkeley, Calif., 1961).

12 E.J. Hobsbawm, *Industry and Empire* (New York, 1968), p. 163.

13 It is precisely for this reason that Mayer's thesis of counterrevolution — diversionary war — illuminating though it is in the German case, goes astray in the British.

14 Phyllis Deane, *The First Industrial Revolution* (Cambridge, 1965), p. 271.

15 Mancur Olson, "Rapid Growth as a Destabilizing Force," *Journal of Economic History*, 23 (December 1963), 529-58.

16 Alexander Gerschenkron, *Economic Backwardness in Historical Perspective* (Cambridge, Mass., 1962), chap.2

17 Alexander Gerschenkron, *Europe in the Russian Mirror: Four Lectures in Economic History* (Cambridge, 1970), p. 99.

18 Dahrendorf, *Society and Democracy in Germany*, pp. 38-48; see, too, Barrington Moore, Jr., *Social Origins of Dictatorship and Democracy* (Boston, 1966), pp. 440-52.

19 Alexis de Tocqueville, *L'Ancien Régime* (Oxford, 1952), p. 105...

20 Joseph A. Schumpeter, *Imperialism and Social Classes* (Cambridge, Mass., 1951), especially pp. 117-29; see, too, Albert H. Imlah, *Economic Elements in the Pax Britannica* (Cambridge, Mass., 1958), pp. 195-98.

21 Something emphasized by Fischer, *Krieg der Illusionen*, pp. 23-39, 65-84, 289-324, 368-84, 636-62, 752-74.

22 Both quoted in J.C.G. Roehl, *Germany without Bismarck: The Crisis of Government in the Second Reich 1890-1900* (Berkeley: 1967), pp. 234, 251, 252.

23 Quoted in Helmut Boehme, *Deutchlands Weg zur Grossmacht* (Cologne and Berlin, 1966), p. 198.

24 Quoted in Dirk Stegmann, *Die Erben Bismarcks* (Cologne and Berlin, 1970), p. 106.

25 Roehl, *Germany without Bismarck*, pp. 45-64.

26 Quoted in ibid., p. 252.

27 Kurt Riezler [J.J. Roedorffer], *Grundzuege der Weltpolitik in der Gegenwart* (Stuttgart and Berlin, 1914), p. 222.

28 Quoted in Fritz Stern, "Bethmann Hollweg and the War: the Limits of Responsibility," *The Responsibility of Power: Historical Essays in Honor of Hajo Holborn*, eds., Krieger and Stern, p. 265.

29 Samuel Williamson, *The Politics of Grand Strategy: Britain and France Prepare for War, 1900-1914* (Cambridge, Mass., 1969).

30 Quoted in Zara S. Steiner, *The Foreign Office and Foreign Policy, 1898-1914* (Cambridge, 1969), p. 138.

31 Mayer, "Domestic Causes of the First World War," pp. 288-89, 298-300.

32 Fischer, *Krieg der Illusionen,* pp. 13, 693.

33 Stern, "Bethmann Hollweg and the War," p. 257.

34 Ibid., pp. 259-60; see, too, Fischer, *Krieg der Illusionen,* p.158; Geiss, *July 1914,* p. 47.

35 Quoted in Konrad H. Jarausch, "Illusion of Limited War: Chancellor Bethmann Hollweg's Calculated Risk, July 1914," *Central European History,* 2 (March 1969), pp 48-77.

THE STATE 4

TERRITORIALITY, SOVEREIGNTY, AND NATIONALISM A

Origins and Characteristics of the Modern State

Rise and Demise of the Territorial State

Why Africa's Weak States Persist:
The Empirical and the Juridical in Statehood

The Paradoxes of Nationalism

POWER, CAPABILITIES, AND THE USE OF FORCE B

Capabilities and Control in an Interdependent World

The Expansion of Force

From Middle to Foremost Power:
Defining a New Place for Canada in the Hierarchy of World Power

To What Ends Military Power?

THE ECONOMY AND IMPERIALISM C

Marxism: An Alternative to the Statist Approach to Economic Policymaking

Foreign Economic Policymaking in the United States

Economic Imperialism as a Reductionist Theory

INTRODUCTION

It is not surprising that, historically, the state has dominated the analysis of international conflict and its management. For the last three hundred years, the state has been the principal actor in international relations and the legitimate employer of force. Because it is society's organizational unit for purposes of security, processes of state formation are of enduring importance. We begin with an examination of three centrally important attributes of the state — sovereignty, territoriality, and nationalism — and consider their impact on international conflict. As we shall see, the linkages among the three are multiple and complex: they are not easily unraveled. To disentangle these linkages, we first analyze the origins of the modern state and then discuss the emergence of the "nation-state" as the preeminent actor in the international system.

Donald Puchala and John Herz date the emergence of the modern state to the Europe of the mid-seventeenth century. The distinguishing characteristics of the modern state are its sovereignty and territoriality. Indeed, it is extraordinarily difficult to separate the two, for sovereignty is defined in part by the capacity of the state to impose order in a territorially delimited area. The second and complementary characteristic of sovereignty is external autonomy, the capacity to act freely in relation to other states. In its external dimension, sovereignty implies juridical recognition by others of the independence, territorial integrity, and inviolability of a state. By the mid-seventeenth century, European states were no longer subjected to the higher authority of the Holy Roman Emperor, who had previously circumscribed their independence. External autonomy derived in large part from the capacity to create internal order within a territorially defined area. As Hans Morgenthau notes in the essay that follows, states freed themselves from the imperial power — above — and the feudal order — below. The roots of the sovereign state are embedded in its control of territory.

Herz and Puchala trace the success in consolidating the state to fundamental changes in technology, wealth, administrative efficiency, and ideology, attributes of the state we will explore in greater detail when we consider power. Most important in the emergence of the territorial state, Herz suggests, was the revolution in military technology, the invention of gunpowder and the development of artillery which permitted monarchs to destroy the baronial castles and walled cities, centralize authority, and create order. Indeed, Herz argues that the modern state is defined by its territoriality; the capacity to protect its boundaries through the exercise of military force. The sovereign state consists of territory organized within a defensible perimeter, internally peaceful, and rimmed by a "hard shell." If we conceive of the sovereign state as the quintessential protector, as the defender of its external independence through the use of force and as the guarantor of internal order through the monopoly of force, then historically the sovereign state is intimately linked to its territoriality through military power. Interstate conflict grows out of the exercise of military force as states struggle to preserve their autonomy and protect their territory in an anarchic international system. This is the argument Herz makes when he links sovereignty to territoriality and power, an argument we will consider again when we look at power as an attribute of the modern state.

Neither Herz nor Puchala would suggest, however, that the process of modern state-building culminated neatly in elegant territorial packages uniformly agreed to by all state actors. On the contrary, throughout the long period of state consolidation in Europe and after, states fought over territory, frequently seeking to expand their own at the expense of others'. It is hardly surprising that it should have been a major source of conflict throughout the eighteenth, nineteenth, and into the twentieth centuries, for territory is the essence of the modern state.

Some of the new states in the third world that gained their independence only in the last few decades have also engaged in bitter conflict over territorial issues, because, here too, the control of territory goes to the heart of the state-building process. Yet, Robert Jackson and Carl Rosberg point to an interesting paradox when they look at the attributes of the newly sovereign states in Africa. Few of the more than forty states have the capacity to ensure internal order and to extend the mandate of government throughout their territory. Indeed, at times, governments have ceased to control substantial segments of their country's territory and population; we need think only of Chad, Ethiopia, Uganda, and Zaire in the last several years. Yet these weak states persist; in some cases, they are kept afloat by the international community to prevent the chaos that would follow their collapse. Jackson and Rosberg conclude that in the Africa that grew out of the anti-colonial revolution, the juridical definition of sovereignty is far more important than its empirical attributes. Even though most African states do not meet the empirical criteria of sovereignty, the legal fiction of sovereignty legitimates the existing territorial order and, in so doing, contains the forces of anarchy. At least in Africa, the widespread recognition of sovereignty and the inviolability of territorial borders has reduced the incidence of interstate conflict.

It is not the state that is generally recognized as the primary actor in international relations, however, but the "nation-state." Very quickly after the consolidation of the territorial state came the growth of modern nationalism, one of the most powerful political forces of the last two centuries. In Europe, nationalism developed partly as a consequence of a centralized state structure and the differentiation of territory. Within territorial borders, inhabitants increasingly spoke a common language, shared a common culture, grew attached to territory held in common, and differentiated themselves from those who lived outside the territorial perimeter.[1] Nationalism expressed itself in a distinction between "we" and "they" in a powerful emotional attachment to territory and group.

The English "nation" was the first to acquire a distinctive identity within the framework of the state. English nationalism developed gradually over time within the framework of common political institutions, an expanding economy, and a diffusion of political power to the new middle classes. In a transformation with profound implications for international conflict and its management, at the end of the eighteenth century the French revolution vested sovereignty not in the monarch, but in the people as a whole.[2] No longer were only the interests of the state at stake in conflict and war, but also the future of the nation. This fusion of nation with state led to the creation of the "nation-state" as the focal point of political loyalty and emotional attachment and, in so doing, frequently, though not always, expanded the purposes and scope of international conflict. In the nineteenth century, for example, nationalism joined with liberalism in Britain to promote individual liberty at home and laissez-faire economics abroad as the basis of international order.

Not everywhere in Europe did the state precede the nation. Morgenthau, in his analysis of the paradoxes of nationalism, traces a second path in Italy and Germany, where the nation preceded the state. In Germany, where no common state institutions existed, nationalism could not draw on shared political traditions. German nationalism, cast in the idiom of romantic thought, emphasized the cultural basis of the nation, its organic unity despite its political fragmentation. Hegel wrote, for example, of the spirit of the nation and its dominance in the world historical process: the nation would create the state to give expression to the syncretic unity of culture, language, and spirit.[3] In this romantic, culturally defined nationalism, devoid of a liberal political tradition, the rights of the individual were far less important than the collective rights of the people and its political expression, the nation-state. Nationalism was thus defined as the demand of an identifiable community for a state. Under Bismarck's conservative leadership, Germany fought several wars to forge the nation-state. In the final war of unification in 1870, by annexing the provinces of Alsace and Lorraine, Bismarck provoked almost a century of conflict with France that culminated in two world wars. In Germany, a conservative cultural nationalism intensified until it spilled over its territorial borders into war.

These consequences of nationalism were not unique to Germany. In Europe and in the Middle East, nations without a state insisted on territorial independence and, in so doing, challenged the multinational empires and embroiled the great powers. For decades, nationalism in the Balkans, a patchwork quilt of ethnic and political loyalties, threatened not only the Austro-Hungarian Empire, but a far wider conflict among the great powers that supported one or another national group. And, as Morgenthau argues, nations have frequently invoked the principle of self-determination in laying claim to a particular territory, while simultaneously denying the same right to others. In part because it is territorially exclusive, modern nationalism often provoked bitter conflict and war when nations competed for the same territory. Only after 1945, in a Europe devastated by the violence unleashed by nationalism and exhausted by the carnage of two wars, has a new generation of leaders tried to tame nationalism and transcend the nation-state by creating supranational institutions. The European Economic Community is one result.

The repudiation of nationalism as the basis of the international order was not shared by the scores of newly independent states that grew out of the anti-colonial revolution after World War II.[4] For many in the third world, an independent, sovereign state was the logical and necessary expression of nationalism.[5] Yet, throughout the third world, the disjuncture between state and nation is even greater than it was in Europe. Although older states like Britain, France, Belgium, Spain, and Canada contain more than one nation, the multinational character of many of the new states of Asia and Africa is far more pronounced. In Africa alone, the fifty or so states must encompass the loyalties of more than 2,000 tribes. Because of the arbitrary borders imposed by the colonial powers, in some instances the nation is divided among several states — the Somali people live today in Ethiopia, Kenya, and Djibouti as well as in Somalia — while in other cases, the state encompasses far more than one nation — Nigeria. The fragmentation of nations, the multi-nationality of states, and the rival claims of competing nationalities to the same territory are major causes of violent conflict in the third world; they threaten the survival of fragile political structures as nationalism explodes into civil war as well as interstate conflict.[6] More generally, throughout the international community today, most of the world's 892 national groups have not secured statehood. Walker Connor, who examined global patterns of ethnicity, finds that less than 10 percent of existing states are ethnically homogeneous, while most include more than five major ethnic groups within their borders.[7] The nation-state as the terminal political community is rare.

For generations, scholars and policy makers have debated the relationship between nationalism and international conflict. Liberal nationalists of the nineteenth century insisted that individual liberty and national self-determination were the foundation of international peace and harmony. Drawing primarily on the European experience, Karl Deutsch looks to nationalism, closely associated with state-building and an expanding economy, to promote common identity and political loyalty. Indeed, Deutsch treats nationalism as inseparable from the state-building process.[8] Connor, who draws on the experience of the third world, reverses this argument and suggests that nationalism escalates conflict and inhibits effective conflict management. Precisely because the state is not coterminous with the nation, Connor argues that state-building in the third world must compete with primordial loyalties.[9] Although neither deals directly with the linkage between nationalism and international conflict, by extension the evidence of this century would give the debate to Connor. The demand of the Ibos for independence from Nigeria, the ongoing war between Ethiopia and Somalia, and the cycle of wars in the Middle East attest to the high price of a modern political identity.

Power, the next attribute we consider, is closely linked to the sovereignty and territoriality of the state. Although it is relevant to every level of social relations, from parapolitical units like families to international organizations, we treat power as a state attribute because the sovereign state is the legitimate employer of force in the international arena. Indeed, since its emergence in the seventeenth century, the territorial state has had as its primary function the maintenance of security. To assure their security in an anarchical world, states have had to rely largely on their own resources. Because resources are scarce and national objectives often in conflict, one state frequently achieves its own purposes at the expense of another. Consequently, power is at the heart of international conflict. Indeed, some would liken its importance in international politics to the centrality that money plays in economics. More properly, power is treated as the currency of international relations, the commodity that helps a state to achieve its goals.[10]

Just as most analysts would accept the proposition that "power" is important, so too they would agree that its meaning is elusive. The confusion arises in part from the different, often competing, definitions of power. Students of international politics have traditionally used power to refer to the resources of a state. Yet, the resources or elements that have contributed to the power of a state have varied considerably over time, and there is little agreement among analysts about the kinds of resources that are important at different times for different purposes.

Historically, a "powerful" state possessed a large territory and a population sizeable enough to support significant military forces. The most powerful were those with the largest military establishments and, as a result, scholars tended to equate power with the capacity to use military force. Even today, the two states who possess a second strike nuclear capability, that is the ability to withstand an initial attack by their adversary and then to inflict an unacceptable level of destruction on their attacker, are called "superpowers." Only the United States and the Soviet Union have such a capacity.

Yet, as Morgenthau argues, the use of force is often the most costly and least sophisticated way for a state to achieve its purposes.[11] In part because unprecedented advances in military technology in the last three decades have depreciated military force as an instrument of conflict management, other resources have become increasingly important. James Eayrs, in his essay on the relativity of power, pays particular attention to the plentiful minerals and energy at Canada's disposal and urges Canada's leaders to design policies commensurate to its rich resource base. If they did so, he insists, Canada would deserve to be treated as a "foremost" rather than a "middle" power.

This treatment of power as a resource has given way gradually to the concept of power as a relationship: a state is powerful if it can achieve its purposes. More particularly, the power of one state is not absolute but relative to that of another, and it is related to specific goals at specific times. If one state can get another to do something it otherwise would not have done, or to refrain from doing something it would otherwise have done, then the first state has "power" for that specific purpose in that particular relationship.[12]

Even though analysts recognize that power is a relationship, there is nevertheless a tendency to revert to the older notion of power as a capability, and to rank states in terms of a given mix of tangible and intangible resources. In part, this is a function of language, of the structure of the word "power," which is rarely used as a verb in the analysis of international politics. As James Rosenau points out in his essay in this volume, "no matter how sensitive analysts may be to the question of how the resources used by one actor serve to modify or preserve the behavior of another, once they cast their assessment in terms of the 'power' employed, they are led...invariably...to focus on the resources themselves rather than on the relationship they may or may not underlie."

What is important is to preserve both meanings of the word "power" while differentiating between them. And this, we believe, Rosenau clearly does. He proposes that we divide the concept "power" into its two component parts: possession and relationship. He employs "capabilities" to designate resources and uses either "influence" or "control" to discuss relationships. This basic distinction is very helpful in clarifying the ambiguities of the concept and in underlining the two critical dimensions of power.

The analysis of international conflict is intimately linked to the evaluation of both these dimensions of military capabilities and the use of force as an instrument of influence. This preoccupation with force is the natural result of the anarchical system in which sovereign states exist. As long as no central authority can enforce binding decisions on states, it is always possible that one state will resort to force to influence another, to achieve its purposes through coercion. Historically, international relations have taken place within the shadow of war. But, is this so today?

The role of force in contemporary international conflict is the subject of vigorous debate. Have the destructiveness, the speed, and the range of nuclear weapons rendered the use of military force obsolete? Robert Osgood and

Robert Tucker, in their essay in this volume, provide the necessary historical background to an analysis of the impact of the nuclear revolution. In describing the expansion of force over the last two centuries, the result of the rationalization, centralization, popularization, professionalization, and modernization of military power, they remind us of the dramatic changes in the nature of warfare and the accompanying transformation in prevailing attitudes toward force. Scholars today challenge the traditional perspective that force is a legitimate instrument of national policy, that war is but the continuation of policy by other means. Indeed, Herz argues that the impact of nuclear technology is so radical that it threatens to make the territorial state obsolete.

It is of course the unimaginable horrors of a nuclear holocaust that have made urgent questions about the continuing utility of military force. After a careful examination of the functions of force in international conflict, Robert Art concludes that the development of nuclear weapons has complicated the exercise of coercive influence. Nuclear weapons have bred moderation and caution in the leaders of nuclear states, both toward one another and toward their respective allies, but they have not eliminated the need for states to develop military capabilities. Nuclear arms have altered the uses of military capabilities: military planning has shifted its focus from defense and victory in a general war to the prevention of war. Deterrence has replaced defense as the primary function of military force. In the nuclear age, unlike earlier periods, a resort to force would signal the total failure of policy. Paradoxically, we develop nuclear weapons not to use them.

While the destructive capability of the major powers has never been more potent, their ability to influence the behavior of others, ironically, is limited. Although the margin of military superiority of the superpowers over others has widened, their inability or unwillingness to use nuclear force against states with no capacity for retaliation has given these states unprecedented scope for action.[13] And in their relationship to each other, parity of strategic weapons has forced them both to settle for marginal gains. It seems that even a large nuclear capability that is immune to destruction does not permit states to achieve even their most important objectives by threatening force.

On the issue of the usefulness of military resources in the nuclear age, Art and Rosenau part company. Although Art recognizes that the threat of force cannot achieve all the goals that states may consider important, he is inclined to stress the overriding importance of military capabilities as a factor conditioning the exercise of influence in relations among states. In contrast, Rosenau argues that the increasing importance of "interdependence issues" will lead, not to the elimination of traditional capabilities, including military resources, but to an emphasis on new capabilities, such as the capacity to develop and apply scientific knowledge, societal cohesion, the ability of public bureaucracies to overcome the policy fragmentation inherent in the management of complex international issues, and the capacity of officials to frame and pursue policies designed to revive old, or build new, international institutions. The agenda of international conflict has broadened to include new issues, which in turn require new resources and new skills.

In part because of the new importance of economic resources and capabilities, recently scholars have again turned their attention to the impact of a state's economic structure on its propensity to engage in international conflict. To what extent are certain kinds of political economies more likely than others to expand, and possibly, to engage in conflict? This is not a new question; it was asked long before military conflict among the great powers became less probable and, consequently, economic conflict grew more likely. The relationship between the economy as a state attribute and international conflict has been argued vigorously for a long time, first by mercantilists, then by pluralists, but principally by neo-Marxists.

Historically, the linkage between political economy and international conflict dates to the mercantilist doctrine of the seventeenth and eighteenth centuries.[14] Mercantilists argued that a positive balance of trade was necessary to increase a state's stock of precious metals, a stock which was an important measure of strength. Since, by definition, all states could not have a positive balance of trade and since, at the time, the supply of precious metals was considered finite, conflict among states was inevitable. Indeed, trade was treated as an instrument of state warfare.[15] The historical or national school of the nineteenth century, represented by Frederick List in Germany and Alexander Hamilton in the United States, refined and adapted mercantilist analysis to the modern international economy.

Pluralists, as we saw in Part II of this volume, look not to the state's economic responsibilities and actions as the source of international conflict, but rather to the preferences of powerful, competing groups within society and the state apparatus. The followers of Marx disagree: all state action, including the propensity to engage in conflict, is determined by the capitalist nature of the state. Before we look in detail at the arguments of those who link capitalism to imperialism, conflict, and war, we will consider very briefly two important schools within a rich neo-Marxist intellectual and political tradition.

David Blake and Robert Walters group a broad range of scholars under the rubric of the "radical" perspective. This perspective treats the process of foreign policy making, Blake and Walters note, as one "in which economic and political interests, as defined and advanced by large business enterprises, dominate the substance of political and economic policy as well as the process by which foreign and domestic policies are made." Within this broad perspective of those who concentrate on the class basis of politics and the privileged role of powerful economic interests, Stephen Krasner distinguishes two strands of neo-Marxist arguments. The "instrumentalists" link the capitalist economy directly to state action; the state is the tool of the dominant, capitalist class. "Structural" Marxists, on the other hand, increasingly treat the state as autonomous from the class struggle; state action reflects the broader structure of society even though its policies are designed to reinforce the capitalist economy. The debate about the autonomy of the state is not trivial. We may get quite different strategies of conflict management if a state is merely the instrument of the dominant class or if it has some autonomy in defining state as well as capitalist interests. But whether or not they treat the state as autonomous, neo-Marxists place state action within the broader context of society. In this sense, this section addresses what Katzenstein refers to as the "externalization" of domestic structures, although within the narrower context of international conflict and conflict management.[16]

It was Lenin, with the publication in 1917 of *Imperialism, the Highest Stage of Capitalism*, who first articulated a fully developed neo-Marxist theory of conflict and war.[17] Drawing on the earlier works of liberal writers like John Hobson as well as other Marxist scholars, Lenin argued that imperialism is essentially an economic phenomenon which results from the latest phase in the growth of capitalism, a stage he termed "finance capitalism." Faced with a declining rate of return, the new monopolies of finance capital were driven to find outlets abroad for the surplus capital they could not invest at home. As a result, tension and conflict increased among the monopolies and their respective national governments, eventually culminating in World War I. Lenin argued, therefore, that conflict and war were the inevitable outgrowth of the capitalist process. Unlike Hobson, who considered that the capitalist system could adapt to increase consumption at home and absorb surplus capital, Lenin was convinced that the flaws were inherent in the system.

This classical theory of imperialism and war provoked a great deal of controversy and criticism. Scholars, drawing on extensive empirical research, have challenged the direction of capital flows and material exports and have raised serious doubts about Lenin's estimates of the rate of return on foreign investment. But even more damaging to Leninist theory, which tied war to the imperative of expansion abroad and territorial control through empire, was the anti-colonial revolution which swept the third world after 1945. Did this process of decolonization not herald the end of imperialism?

Neo-Marxist scholars, writing half a century after Lenin, are not impressed by the "independence" of the new states in Asia and Africa. The independence granted by the metropolises to their colonies, they argue, is independence in name only. Imperialism continues, although now it works informally and subtly, rather than openly through formal control. Contemporary neo-Marxist scholars do disagree on the roots of neo-colonialism — the need of giant multinational firms to protect and enhance their share of the market; the search for scarce raw materials to fuel the advanced industrial economies; the export of production to ensure profits through lower wage costs; or even militarism that grows out of the high defense spending that is functional in a capitalist economy. All emphasize, however, the development of new instruments of control — large aid programs, an unequal system of trade, and, above all, the multinational enterprise, which has given the capitalist economy of the United States unprecedented mobility of capital and technology. It is not surprising, therefore, that a great deal of neo-Marxist scholarship analyzes the international impact of the United States as the leading capitalist state in an integrated world economy. But as Krasner notes, despite differences in analysis, one argument remains constant throughout neo-Marxist writings, classical and modern: capitalist expansion abroad is a necessity. Capitalist societies cannot escape the imperative to expand beyond their borders if they are to survive their contradictions and, forced to expand, they cannot avoid confrontation with other societies and states, as well as competition with each other. Conflict is an inevitable outcome of the political economy of capitalist states.

Kenneth Waltz, in the last essay in this section, critically reviews neo-Marxist theories of imperialism, conflict, and war. He acknowledges that the examination by Hobson and Lenin of the economic attributes of capitalist states at the turn of the century did uncover important linkages between domestic societies and their policies abroad. But they err, Waltz insists, in attempting to generalize from these specific cases to a comprehensive explanation of war. Moreover, their arguments are over-simplified and reductionist: they treat only economic attributes and class relations as the explanation of the far more complex and multi-faceted problem of conflict and war. Finally, he maintains that their arguments are logically unsound. Waltz posits that the system dictates the basic rules for all state action; states behave in similar ways, irrespective of their particular economic systems. If we are to understand international conflict, we must go beyond the state and focus first on the transnational forces and transnational institutions, which are the newest challenge to the autonomy of the state, and then analyze the international system which sets the boundaries of state action.

ENDNOTES

1 Carleton J. Hayes, *The Historical Evolution of Modern Nationalism* (New York: Macmillan, 1948).

2 Hans Kohn, *The Idea of Nationalism* (New York: The Macmillan Company, 1944).

3 Georg Wilhelm Frederick Hegel, *Political Writings*, trans. T.M. Knox (Oxford: Clarendon Press, 1964).

4 In "The Territorial State Revisited: Reflections on the Future of the Nation-State," *Polity*, 1 (Fall 1968), 11-34, Herz reconsidered his original assumption that nationalism was as obsolete as the territorial state.

5 Rupert Emerson, *From Empire to Nation* (Boston: Beacon Press, 1960).

6 Harold R. Isaacs, *Idols of the Tribe* (New York: Harper Colophon Books, 1975), p. 3.

7 Walker Connor, "Nation-Building or Nation-Destroying," *World Politics*, 24 (April 1972), 319-55.

8 See especially his "The Growth of Nations: Some Recurrent Patterns of Political and Social Integration," *World Politics*, 5 (January 1953), 168-95; "Social Mobilization and Political Development," *American Political Science Review*, 55 (September 1961), 493-514; and *Nationalism and Social Communication* (Cambridge, Mass.: The M.I.T. Press, 1953).

9 Walker Connor, "Self-Determination: The New Phase," *World Politics*, 20 (October 1967), 30-53; and "The Politics of Ethnonationalism," *Journal of International Affairs*, 27 (No. 1, 1973), 1-21.

10 David A. Baldwin, "Money and Power," *Journal of Politics*, 33 (August 1971), 578-614.

11 Hans J. Morgenthau, *Politics Among Nations* (New York: Alfred A. Knopf, Inc., 1948).

12 See K.J. Holsti, "The Concept of Power in the Study of International Relations," *Background*, 7 (February 1964), 179-92.

13 Henry A. Kissinger, *American Foreign Policy* 2d ed., rev., (New York: W.W. Norton & Co., 1974), p. 60.

14 Raymond Aron, *Peace and War, A Theory of International Relations*, trans. Richard Howard and Annette Baker Fox (Garden City, N.Y.: Doubleday & Co., 1966), pp. 245-46.

15 Edward M. Earle, "Adam Smith, Alexander Hamilton, Frederick List: The Economic Foundations of Military Power," in Earle, ed., *Makers of Modern Strategy, Military Thought from Machiavelli to Hitler* (New York: Atheneum, 1966).

16 Peter J. Katzenstein, "International Relations and Domestic Structures: Foreign Economic Policies of Advanced Industrial States," *International Organization*, 32 (Autumn 1978), 2.

17 V.I. Lenin, *Imperialism: The Highest Stage of Capitalism* (New York: International Publishers Co., Inc., 1939).

A: TERRITORIALITY, SOVEREIGNTY, AND NATIONALISM

Origins and Characteristics of the Modern State

Donald J. Puchala

A survey of world history reveals that the modern state, as we know it, is of relatively recent origin. Some historians date the emergence of the state in the seventeenth century. Others set this date either somewhat later or somewhat earlier. Even dating the emergence of the state from the early sixteenth century, however, leaves a broad span of time in which world political interaction was between units or forces that could not be called "states" in the modern sense. A long era of European political history, for example, is more appropriately characterized as a period of interactions among cultures, religions, or princes, rather than among states. Similarly, Renaissance and Ancient Greek political history is better characterized as a history of interactions among cities or principalities rather than states. Much of Oriental political history is the story of interactions among great cultures, and Ancient Mediterranean political history is the story of interactions among powerful tribes. Hence, the first questions we must ask about the modern state are: What is it? and What are its origins? These questions answer each other.

The modern state is best defined as "a sovereign territorial political unit."[1] This definition will be derived in a moment. Suffice it to say at this point that *sovereignty* implies external autonomy, and it also implies internal order and control over means for maintaining this order. *Territoriality* denotes a geographic perimeter or unit, and territoriality linked with sovereignty implies that external autonomy and internal order are characteristics of geographically defined units. *Political*...implies interaction in goal-seeking behavior, so that the sovereign territorial political unit — the state — is, in the abstract, an externally autonomous, internally ordered geographic unit that interacts in its goal-seeking behavior with other such units. It becomes more meaningful to talk about states after we place people within the geographic perimeter and charge some of them with responsibility for maintaining external autonomy and internal order. But for the moment let us preserve the abstraction.

Tracing the emergence of the modern state helps both to clarify the meanings of "sovereignty" and "territoriality," and to pave the way for discussing the international political implications of these characteristics of states. The modern state is European in its origin. Its emergence was largely the

---

 Portions of the text have been deleted. Some footnotes have been deleted; those remaining have been renumbered.

product of the related supersession of central government over feudal decentralization and state autonomy over transcendent religious and secular authority in Europe during the sixteenth and seventeenth centuries generally, and during the Thirty Years' War, 1618-48, in particular. R.R. Palmer, in his *History of the Modern World*, descriptively captures the emergence of the modern state system in two passages that amount to a "before and after" comparison of political organization in Europe at the beginning and at the end of the Thirty Years' War. Remarking in the first passage upon conditions at the outbreak of the war, Palmer notes that:

> The Wars of Religion, despite the religious ferocity shown by partisans of both sides, were no more religious than they were political.... [They] were essentially a new form of the old phenomenon of feudal rebellion against higher central authority. "Feudal," when the word is used of the 16th, 17th or 18th centuries, generally refers not to nobles only, but to all sorts of component groups having rights within the state, and so including towns and provinces, and even craft guilds and courts of law, in addition to the church and the noble class. It remained to be seen whether all these elements could be welded into one body politic. If the reader will recall how hard it is in the Twentieth Century to unify an army, navy and air force, or form a tariff union between two states, not to mention the problem of international government, he may be less puzzled as to why the history of Europe, for centuries, seems to consist of struggles between "feudal decentralization" and "central power."[2]

States existed territorially in medieval Europe, but these were seldom political units internally ordered under the authority of central governments or ruling houses. Instead, the predominant units of political organization in medieval Europe were feudal units smaller than medieval states — baronial fiefs, walled towns, monasteries, tradesmen's guilds, secular and clerical social classes, and the like — *and these units were often completely autonomous within their domains within the states.* Central authorities in the medieval states were often deficient in legitimacy, and, consequently, kings and princes could influence or control the activities of autonomous feudal groups only to the extent that they were willing and able to bring force to bear. Medieval history records numerous instances in which the coercive capabilities of central authorities were markedly inferior to the capabilities of feudal groups within their states. Hence, the picture that Palmer paints of feudal groups within states warring with central authorities and with one another for autonomy and aggrandizement is an accurate and vivid picture of relative anarchy within medieval states. This is a far cry from the internal order and central governmental control generally characteristic of modern sovereign states.

Just as internal order was not characteristic of the medieval state, neither was external autonomy. During the medieval era, all states were formally, and from time to time actually, under the transcendent dominion of both a Holy Roman Emperor, charged with the maintenance of European political unity, and a Pope, responsible for the spiritual orthodoxy and unity of Christendom. Therefore, the external autonomy of medieval states was at least formally controlled and constrained by the efforts of temporal and religious authorities charged with overseeing different aspects of interstate relations. Even as internal control in the medieval era depended on force and the ability to use it, the influence of transcendent authority over medieval states depended largely upon the military capabilities of these higher authorities. States maneuvered and fought to thwart external control, and Holy Roman Emperors and Popes maneuvered and fought to impose and exercise overarching control. This struggle between local and transcendent authority became another phase of medieval political interaction. Palmer captures this phase and its outcome in a passage describing the conference at Westphalia that marked the end of the Thirty Years' War in 1648:

> The Peace of Westphalia marked the advent in international law of the modern European system of sovereign states. No one any longer pretended that Europe had any significant unity, religious, political or other. Statesmen delighted in the absence of any such unity, in which they sensed the menace of "universal monarchy." Europe was understood to consist in a large number of unconnected sovereignties, free and detached atoms, or states, which moved about according to their own laws, following their own political interests, forming and dissolving alliances, exchanging embassies and legations, alternating between war and peace, shifting position with a shifting balance of power.[3]

Hence, two developments combined during the sixteenth and seventeenth centuries to destroy the medieval state and feudal system, and to initiate the rise of the modern state and the modern state system. First, central authorities within medieval states succeeded, after decades or even centuries of civil strife, in undermining and dashing the political and military autonomy of feudal units within their domains. Next, and relatedly, these same kings and princes managed ultimately to seal their states against the demands and incursions of secular and religious transcendent authorities.

To elaborate the many reasons why central authorities were ultimately able to gain superiority and impose order within their territorial domains is beyond the scope of this discussion. A deeper treatment, however, would have to take account of such factors as accretions in wealth in central treasuries from exploration and exploitation in the New World, improvements in military technology — in artillery especially — which rendered baronial castles and walled towns vulnerable, improvements in central administrative organization and efficiency, and impacts from religious schism that enhanced the legitimacy of secular authority.

For purposes of this discussion, the impacts of internal consolidation in the medieval states are more important than the causes, because these impacts led directly to the enforcement of external autonomy and the emergence of the modern international system. One of the most important results of the internal consolidation of princely authority in medieval states was greatly increased power in the hands of central governments. In effect, the victory of "central authority" over "feudal decentralization" transferred absolute control over the human and material (and hence military and economic) resources of territorial units to the authorities governing these units. With the exception of the tiny German states, most of the newly ordered territorial units were sizable and therefore usually well endowed with resources that could be transformed into central governmental power.

New power was wielded by governments first to irreversibly complete their internal ascendancy, and then to exert and enforce their independence from transcendent authorities. New capabilities under the control of central governments served to render their territorial domains defensible against, and largely impermeable to, military thrusts directed by Holy Roman Emperors and Popes seeking to extract tribute or to otherwise realize their nominal hegemonic control. The result was that the imperial claims of these transcendent authorities were undermined; and in consequence, the international order of Europe was changed, *de facto*, from mythical unity in a Holy... Roman empire, to fragmentation and a system of internally ordered and externally autonomous territorial political units. By the time the medieval jurists met at Westphalia in 1648, state sovereignty had become a fact. The modern state system had emerged.

IMPACTS AND IMPLICATIONS OF STATE SOVEREIGNTY

A number of important analytical implications follow from this descriptive history of the emergence of the modern international system of sovereign states. These have to do first with the definition of sovereignty as "an objective state of affairs"; second, with the kind of international politics that results when political actors are sovereign units; and third, with relations between citizens or subjects, their governments, and the international order in a system of sovereign states.

First, it must be emphasized that the expression "state sovereignty" is descriptive of an objective state of affairs. The predominant actors in the international system *are* sovereign states. "State sovereignty" therefore is neither a creation of international lawyers, nor simply a phrase in legal jargon. It refers to internal order and external autonomy, and it suggests that international political interaction must be conceived and perceived in terms of a system of ordered, autonomous political actors. Not all states participating in international politics at the time of the Treaty of Westphalia, nor, surely, all states participating in international politics today are fully sovereign in an ideal sense. But if political units were located in two-dimensional space along continua that ran from "ordered" to "anarchic" and "autonomous" to "dependent" respectively, it could be observed that most political units actually participating in international politics are those that cluster in the "ordered-autonomous" quadrant. Units falling into other quadrants would be either unable or unwilling to participate. Hence, sovereignty has an operational meaning; a "sovereign state system" does in fact exist; and international politics acquires a number of notable characteristics as a result of the fact that "players in the game" are sovereign states....

Politics among sovereign states amounts to a politics of anarchy in an arena where violence becomes the only tool ultimately available for exerting influence, and where warfare becomes the ultimately available means for settling disputes. As John Stoessinger tells us, "it is sovereignty more than any other single factor that is responsible for the anarchic condition of international relations."[4] Where each unit is legally autonomous, and where many units are able to preserve and protect their autonomy with military might, there is no reason why any unit should bend to the will of any other *when it does not wish to*. Neither is there any way to make such a unit submit short of demonstrating the inferiority of its military forces or actually defeating them in battle. To be sure, this is a rough and painful way to run a world. But it is the way the world of sovereign states has been running for centuries, despite noble and impressive attempts to change it.

A world of sovereign states and a resultant politics of anarchy suggests a world of jeopardy for citizens residing within states. Since attack remains the ultimate instrument of international political persuasion, citizens may never completely alleviate the dread that a foreign government might attempt to violently exert its will. Moreover, though it is argued that nuclear weaponry and mutual deterrence have lowered probabilities of major war to near zero, few citizens in the West or the East are fully convinced that "the other side" is actually deterred, and few of us can help wondering about our fates in the event of a nuclear war. As Harold Lasswell suggests most eloquently, world politics is a continuing source of personal insecurity.[5]

Furthermore, personal insecurity may be compounded by the internal characteristics of state sovereignty. The state, by virtue of its sovereignty, is, *de facto,* the final arbiter over the life, death, or livelihood of every person residing within its territorial domain. The autonomy of the state means that there is no secular court of individual appeal above or beyond the government of the state. In consequence, citizens may be commanded or otherwise compelled to suffer for their states, to fight for them, and even to die for them. Flight from one state to another amounts simply to movement from one governmental jurisdiction to another, and flight from international politics seems impossible as long as one remains on this planet. For these reasons state sovereignty has traditionally been the target of anarchists, and the system of sovereign states has been a prime object of pacifists' outcryings.

But while "world politics and personal insecurity" is surely a valid theme, it must also be pointed out that the emergence of the sovereign state has, in one important sense, heightened personal security. A world of sovereignties is nonetheless a world of relative order *within* states. History shows that the rise and predominance of the centrally governed state has considerably reduced the scale of world anarchy. As noted earlier, the age prior to the rise of the modern state was characterized — in Europe at least — by continual civil warfare, baronial feuding and by general internal disorder. When every feudal lord thought himself sovereign in his own domain, and when literally thousands of tiny sovereignties were scattered across Europe, the probability of continual violent conflict was extremely high; and the scale of anarchy increased in direct proportion to the expanding number of miniature feudal units. Constant civil turmoil took frightfully heavy tolls of civilian populations. On the other hand, the enforced civil order that followed the consolidation of major states drastically reduced the frequency of internal warfare, and consequently injected an element of relative security into citizens' lives. Hence, a world of sovereign states is at least a world where citizens within states are relatively protected from one another....

ENDNOTES

1 John H. Herz, *International Politics in the Atomic Age* (New York: Columbia University Press, 1959), pp. 39-61.

2 R.R. Palmer, *A History of the Modern World,* 2nd ed. (New York: Alfred A. Knopf, 1957), p. 114.

3 Ibid., p. 130.

4 John G. Stoessinger, *The Might of Nations,* 3rd ed. (New York: Random House, 1969), p. 10.

5 Harold D. Lasswell, *World Politics and Personal Insecurity* (New York: McGraw-Hill, 1935).

A: TERRITORIALITY, SOVEREIGNTY, AND NATIONALISM

Rise and Demise of the Territorial State

John H. Herz

Students and practitioners of international politics are at present in a strange predicament. Complex though their problems have been in the past, there was then at least some certainty about the "givens," the basic structure and the basic phenomena of international relations. Today one is neither here nor there. On the one hand, for instance, one is assured — or at least tempted to accept assurance — that for all practical purposes a nuclear stalemate rules out major war as a major means of policy today and in the foreseeable future. On the other hand, one has an uncanny sense of the practicability of the unabated arms race, and a doubt whether reliance can be placed solely on the deterrent purpose of all this preparation. We are no longer sure about the functions of war and peace, nor do we know how to define the national interest and what its defense requires under present conditions. As a matter of fact, the meaning and function of the basic protective unit, the "sovereign" nation-state itself, have become doubtful. On what, then, can policy and planning be built?

In the author's opinion, many of these uncertainties have their more profound cause in certain fundamental changes which have taken place in the structure of international relations and, specifically, in the nature of the units among which these relations occur. This transformation in the "statehood" of nations will be the subject of this article.

I. BASIC FEATURES OF THE MODERN STATE SYSTEM

Traditionally, the classical system of international relations, or the modern state system, has been considered "anarchic," because it was based on unequally distributed power and was deficient in higher — that is, supra-national — authority. Its units, the independent, sovereign nation-states, were forever threatened by stronger power and survived precariously through the balance-of-power system. Customarily, then, the modern state system has been contrasted with the medieval system, on the one hand, where units of international relations were under higher law and higher authority, and with those more recent international trends, on the other, which seemed to point toward a greater, "collective" security of nations and a "rule of law" that would protect them from the indiscriminate use of force characteristic of the age of power politics.

John H. Herz, "Rise and Demise of the Territorial State," *World Politics*, Vol. 9, No. 4 (July 1957). Copyright © 1957 by Princeton University Press. Reprinted by permission of Princeton University Press. Most footnotes have been removed; those remaining have been renumbered.

From the vantage point of the atomic age, we can probe deeper into the basic characteristics of the classical system. What is it that ultimately accounted for the peculiar unity, compactness, and coherence of the modern nation-state, setting it off from other nation-states as a separate, independent, and sovereign power? It would seem that this underlying factor is to be found neither in the sphere of law nor in that of politics, but rather in that substratum of statehood where the state unit confronts us, as it were, in its physical, corporeal capacity: as an expanse of territory encircled for its identification and its defense by a "hard shell" of fortifications. In this lies what will here be referred to as the "impermeability," or "impenetrability," or simply the "territoriality," of the modern state. The fact that it was surrounded by a hard shell rendered it to some extent secure from foreign penetration, and thus made it an ultimate unit of protection for those within its boundaries. Throughout history, that unit which affords protection and security to human beings has tended to become the basic political unit; people, in the long run, will recognize that authority, any authority, which possesses the power of protection.

Some similarity perhaps prevails between an international structure consisting of impenetrable units with an ensuing measurability of power and comparability of power relations, and the system of classical physics with its measurable forces and the (then) impenetrable atom as its basic unit. And as that system has given way to relativity and to what nuclear science has uncovered, the impenetrability of the political atom, the nation-state, is giving way to a permeability which tends to obliterate the very meaning of unit and unity, power and power relations, sovereignty and independence. The possibility of "hydrogenization" merely represents the culmination of a development which has rendered the traditional defense structure of nations obsolete through the power to by-pass the shell protecting a two-dimensional territory and thus to destroy — vertically, as it were — even the most powerful ones. Paradoxically, utmost strength now coincides in the same unit with utmost vulnerability, absolute power with utter impotence.

This development must inevitably affect traditional power concepts. Considering power units as politically independent and legally sovereign made sense when power, measurable, graded, calculable, served as a standard of comparison between units which, in the sense indicated above, could be described as impermeable. Under those conditions, then, power indicated the strategic aspect, independence the political aspect, sovereignty the legal aspect of this selfsame impermeability. With the passing of the age of territoriality, the usefulness of these concepts must now be questioned.

Thus the Great Divide does not separate "international anarchy," or "balance of power," or "power politics," from incipient international interdependence, or from "collective security"; all these remain within the realm of the territorial structure of states and can therefore be considered as trends or stages *within* the classical system of "hard shell" power units. Rather, the Divide occurs where the basis of territorial power and defensibility vanishes. It is here and now. But in order to understand the present, we must study more closely the origin and nature of the classical system itself.

II. THE RISE OF THE TERRITORIAL STATE

The rise of the modern territorial state meant that, within countries, "feudal anarchy" of jurisdictions yielded to the ordered centralism of the absolute monarchy, which ruled over a pacified area with the aid of a bureaucracy, a professional army, and the power to levy taxes, while in foreign relations, in place of the medieval hierarchy of power and authority, there prevailed insecurity, a disorder only slightly attenuated by a power balance that was forever being threatened, disturbed, and then restored. Such has been the customary interpretation.

It is possible to view developments in a somewhat different light. Instead of contrasting the security of groups and individuals within the sovereign territorial state with conditions of insecurity outside, the establishment of territorial independence can be interpreted as an at least partially successful attempt to render the territorial group secure in its outward relations as well. Especially when contrasted with the age of anarchy and insecurity which immediately preceded it, the age of territoriality appears as one of relative order and safety.

Indeed, the transition from medieval hierarchism to modern compartmentalized sovereignties was neither easy, nor straight, nor short. Modern sovereignty arose out of the triangular struggle among emperors and popes, popes and kings, and kings and emperors. When the lawyers of Philip the Fair propounded the dual maxim according to which the king was to be "emperor in his realm" (*rex est imperator in regno suo)* and was no longer to "recognize any superior" (*superiorem non recognoscens*), it was the beginning of a development in the course of which, in McIlwain's words, "Independence *de facto* was ultimately translated into a sovereignty *de jure*."[1] But centuries of disturbance and real anarchy ensued during which the problems of rulership and security remained unsettled. The relative protection which the sway of moral standards and the absence of highly destructive weapons had afforded groups and individuals in the earlier Middle Ages gave way to total insecurity when gunpowder was invented and common standards broke down. Out of the internal and external turmoil during the age of religious and civil wars, a "neutralist" central power eventually managed to establish itself in and for each of the different territories like so many *rochers de bronze*.

The idea that a territorial coexistence of states, based on the power of the territorial princes, might afford a better guarantee of peace than the Holy Roman Empire was already widespread at the height of the Middle Ages when the emperor proved incapable of enforcing the peace. But territoriality could hardly prevail so long as the knight in his castle (that medieval unit of impermeability) was relatively immune from attack, as was the medieval city within its walls. Only with a developing money economy were overlords able to free themselves from dependence on vassals and lay the foundations of their own power by establishing a professional army. Infantry and artillery now proved superior to old-style cavalry, firearms prevailed over the old weapons.

As in all cases of radically new developments in military technology, the "gunpowder revolution" caused a real revolution in the superstructure of economic, social, and poltical relationships because of its impact on the units of protection and security. A feeling of insecurity swept all Europe. Though a Machiavelli might establish new rules as to how to gain and maintain power, there still followed more than a century of unregulated, ideological "total" wars inside and among countries until the new units of power were clearly established. Before old or new sovereigns could claim to be recognized as rulers of large areas, it had to be determined how far, on the basis of their new military power, they were able to extend their control geographically.

The large-area state came finally to occupy the place that the castle or fortified town had previously held as a unit of impenetrability. But the new unit could not be considered consolidated until all independent fortifications within it had disappeared and, in their place, fortresses lining the circumference of the country had been built by the new central power and manned by its armed forces. If we contrast our present system of bases and similar outposts surrounding entire world regions with what are today small-scale nation-states, perhaps we can visualize what the hard shell of frontier fortifications consolidating the then large-scale territorial states meant by way of extending power units in the age of absolutism. They became, in the words of Frederick the Great, "mighty nails which hold a ruler's provinces together." There now was peace and protection within. War became a regularized military procedure; only the breaking of the shell permitted interference with what had now become the internal affairs of another country.

In this way was established the basic structure

of the territorial state which was to last throughout the classical period of the modern state system. Upon this foundation a new system and new concepts of international relations could arise. And as early as the second half of the seventeenth century a perspicacious observer succeeded in tying up the new concepts with the underlying structure of territorial statehood.

III. THE NATURE OF TERRITORIALITY

It was hardly a coincidence that this connection was established shortly after the end of the Thirty Years' War, when formal sanction had been given to territorial sovereignty in the Westphalian Peace. For here was the turning point, the Great Divide between what were still partially medieval situations reflecting a certain permeability of the rising nation-state (when, for instance, outside powers could still ally themselves with *frondes* within a country against that country's sovereign) and the modern era of closed units no longer brooking such interference.

The clarification of the nature of territoriality to which we referred above is found in a little and little-known essay by Leibniz, written for an entirely pragmatic purpose — namely, to prove the right of legation of the territorial ruler (the Duke of Hanover) in whose service the philosopher then was. Leibniz' problem derived directly from the situation created by the Peace of Westphalia. This settlement, for all practical purposes, had conferred sovereign independence upon those princes who formally were still included in the Empire; yet it had not abolished the long-established, essentially feudal structure of the Empire itself, with its allegiances and jurisdictions, its duties of membership, and even its clumsy and scarcely workable framework of government. Thus some of the factually sovereign territorial rulers in Europe were somehow still under a higher authority. Were they now "sovereign" or not? What accounted for sovereignty?

Leibniz' contemporaries failed to see the problem in this light. The muddled state of affairs was made to order for those jurists and others who argued fine points perennially with the aid of sterile or obsolete concepts. Leibniz, instead, proceeded to study "what actually happens in the world today," and as a result could boast of being "the first to have found the valid definition of sovereignty."[2]

As he saw it, the first condition for sovereignty was a minimum size of territory. Minuscule principalities, at that time still abundant, could not claim to be on a par with those that recognized each other as equally sovereign in respect to peace and war, alliances, and the general affairs of Europe, because, not possessing sufficient territory, they could at best, with their garrisons, only maintain *internal* order. But there remained the chief problem: how to define the status of those rulers who, because of their membership in the Empire, were subjects of the emperor. Could one be "sovereign" and "subject" at the same time? If not, what was the status of these "subject" rulers as compared with that of their "sovereign" European brethren? If so, what did their subjection to the emperor amount to? These questions were further complicated by the fact that at every European court, and in the Empire as well, there were certain high dignitaries, often called "princes," "dukes," etc., who customarily held the rank of "sovereign." It was through this maze of relationships that Leibniz arrived at his definitions.

He elaborated his concept of sovereignty by distinguishing it from "majesty." Majesty, the authority which the emperor has *qua* emperor over the Empire's members, consists of a number of jurisdictions that confer the right to demand obedience and involve duties of fealty, but it is not sovereignty. Why not? Simply because, with all its supreme authority, majesty does not involve an "actual and present power to constrain" subjects on their own territories. Their territory, in other words, is impermeable. The subject, on the other hand, if he is a territorial ruler, is sovereign because he has the power to constrain *his* subjects, while not being so constrainable by superior power. The decisive criterion thus is actual control of one's "estates" by one's military power, which excludes any other power within and without. Contrariwise, the absence of such forces of his own on his subjects' territories accounts for the absence of "sovereignty" in the emperor's "majesty." He can enforce his authority or rights only by applying his own or other sovereigns' forces from the outside, "by means of war." But in doing so, his condition is no different from that of any other sovereign vis-à-vis *his* fellow-rulers, for war is a contest which can be inaugurated not only by majesties but by any sovereign ruler. And force of arms may constrain a sovereign outside the Empire quite as well as one inside; in fact, war constitutes the only way in which even sovereigns can be constrained. By perceiving that the emperor's power to enforce his authority was actually reduced to means of war, Leibniz was in a position to demonstrate that any and all rulers of impermeable territory, whatever their status in regard to imperial authority, were equal in their sovereign status.

This capacity also distinguished them from those dignitaries who were sovereigns in name only. Leibniz, by way of example, referred to the non-sovereign status of certain papal "princes," contrasting it with that of sovereign princes: "Should His Holiness desire to make...[the papal princes] obey, he has merely to send out his 'sbiroos' [bailiffs], but in order to constrain...[the sovereign princes] he would need an army and cannon." Similarly, if the Empire wants to constrain a sovereign member, "what would begin as court procedure in an imperial Tribunal, in execution would amount to a war."[3] In the new age of territoriality, those superior in law no longer could use the machinery of government (courts, etc.) to enforce claims against territorial rulers. In more recent times, this has come to be the relationship between sovereign nation-states as members of international organizations (like the League of Nations or the United Nations) and the organizations as such.

IV. THE TERRITORIAL STATE IN INTERNATIONAL RELATIONS

From territoriality resulted the concepts and institutions which characterized the interrelations of sovereign units, the modern state system. Modern international law, for instance, could now develop. Like the international system that produced it, international law has often been considered inherently contradictory because of its claim to bind sovereign units. But whether or not we deny to it for this reason the name and character of genuine law, it is important to see it in its connection with the territorial nature of the state system that it served. Only then can it be understood as a system of rules not contrary to, but implementing, the sovereign independence of states. Only to the extent that it reflected their territoriality and took into account their sovereignty could international law develop in modern times. For its general rules and principles deal primarily with the delimitation of the jurisdiction of countries. It thus implements the *de facto* condition of territorial impenetrability by more closely defining unit, area, and conditions of impenetrability. Such a law must reflect, rather than regulate. As one author has rightly remarked, "International law really amounts to laying down the principle of national sovereignty and deducing the consequences.[4]" It is not for this reason superfluous, for sovereign units must know in some detail where their jurisdictions end and those of other units begin; without such standards, nations would be involved in constant strife over the implementation of their independence.

But it was not only this mutual legal accommodation which rendered possible a relatively peaceful coexistence of nations. War itself, the very phenomenon which reflected, not the strength, but the limitations of impermeability, was of such a nature as to maintain at least the principle of territoriality. War was limited not only in conduct but also in objectives. It was not a process of physical or political annihilation but a contest of power and will in which the interests, but not the existence, of the contestants were at stake. Now that we approach the era of absolute exposure, without walls or moats, where penetration will mean not mere damage or change but utter annihilation of life and way of life, it may dawn on us that what has vanished with the age of sovereignty and "power politics" was not entirely adverse in nature and effects.

Among other "conservative" features of the classical system, we notice one only in passing: the balance of power. It is only recently that emphasis has shifted from a somewhat one-sided concern with the negative aspects of the balance — its uncertainty, its giving rise to unending conflicts and frequent wars, etc. — to its protective effect of preventing the expansionist capacity of power from destroying other power altogether. But at the time of its perfection in statecraft and diplomacy, there were even theories (not lived up to in practice, of course) about the *legal* obligations of nations to form barriers against hegemony power in the common interest.

More fundamental to the conservative structure of the old system was its character as a community. Forming a comparatively pacified whole, Europe was set off sharply against the world outside, a world beyond those lines which, by common agreement, separated a community based on territoriality and common heritage from anarchy, where the law of nature reigned and no standards of civilization applied. Only recently have the existence and role of so-called "amity lines" been rediscovered, lines which were drawn in the treaties of the early modern period and which separated European territories, where the rules of war and peace were to prevail, from overseas territories and areas. There was to be "no peace beyond the line"; that is, European powers, although possibly at peace in Europe, continued to be *homo homini lupus* abroad. This practice made it easier for the European family of nations to observe self-denying standards at home by providing them with an outlet in the vast realm discovered outside Europe. While the practice of drawing amity lines subsequently disappeared, one chief function of overseas expansion remained: a European balance of power could be maintained or adjusted because it was relatively easy to divert European conflicts into overseas directions and adjust them there. Thus the openness of the world contributed to the consolidation of the territorial system. The end of the "world frontier" and the resulting closedness of an interdependent world inevitably affected this system's effectiveness.

Another characteristic of the old system's protective nature may be seen in the almost complete absence of instances in which countries were wiped out in the course of wars or as a consequence of other power-political events. This, of course, refers to the territorial units at home only, not to the peoples and state units beyond the pale abroad; and to the complete destruction of a state's independent existence, not to mere loss of territory or similar changes, which obviously abounded in the age of power politics.

Evidence of this is to be found not only in a legal and political ideology that denied the permissibility of conquest at home while recognizing it as a title for the acquisition of territorial jurisdiction abroad. For such a doctrine had its non-ideological foundation in the actual difference between European and non-European politics so far as their territoriality was concerned. European states were impermeable in the sense here outlined, while most of those overseas were easily penetrable by Europeans. In accordance with these circumstances, international politics in Europe knew only rare and exceptional instances of actual annihilation through conquest or similar forceful means.

Prior to the twentieth century, there were indeed the Napoleonic conquests, but I submit that this is a case where the exception confirms the rule. The Napoleonic system, as a hegemonial one, was devised to destroy the established system of territoriality and balanced power as such. Consequently, Napoleon and his policies appeared "demonic" to contemporaries, as well as to a nineteenth century which experienced the restoration of the earlier system. During that century occurred Bismarck's annexations of some German units into Prussia in pursuance of German unification. As in Napoleon's case, they appeared abnormal to many of his contemporaries, although the issue of national unification tended to mitigate this impression. Beside these, there was indeed the partition of Poland, and considering the lamentable and lasting impression and the universal bad conscience it produced even among the ruling nations in a century used to quite a bit of international skulduggery, again one may well claim an exceptional character for that event.

What, in particular, accounts for this remarkable stability? Territoriality — the establishment of defensible units, internally pacified and hard-shell rimmed — may be called its foundation. On this foundation, two phenomena permitted the system to become more stable than might otherwise have been the case: the prevalence of the legitimacy principle and, subsequently, nationalism. Legitimacy implied that the dynasties ruling the territorial states of old Europe mutually recognized each other as rightful sovereigns. Depriving one sovereign of his rights by force could not but appear to destroy the very principle on which the rights of all of them rested.

With the rise of nationalism, we witness the personalization of the units as self-determining, national groups. Nationalism now made it appear as abhorrent to deprive a sovereign nation of its independence as to despoil a legitimate ruler had appeared before. States, of course, had first to become "nation-states," considering themselves as representing specific nationality groups, which explains why in the two regions of Europe where larger numbers of old units stood in the way of national unification their demise encountered little objection. In most instances, however, the rise of nationalism led to the emergence of *new* states, which split away from multinational or colonial empires. This meant the extension of the European principle of "non-obliteration" all over the world. It is perhaps significant that even in our century, and even after the turmoil of attempted world conquest and resulting world wars, a point has been made of restoring the most minute and inconsiderable of sovereignties, down to Luxembourg and Albania.

This hypertrophy of nation-states presented new problems — above all, that of an improved system of protection. For by now it had become clear that the protective function of the old system was only a relative blessing after all. Continued existence of states as such was perhaps more or less guaranteed. But power and influence, status, frontiers, economic interests — in short, everything that constituted the life and interests of nations beyond bare existence — were always at the mercy of what power politics wrought. Furthermore, much of the relative stability and political equilibrium of the territorial states had been due to the extension of Western control over the world. When what could be penetrated had been subjugated, assimilated, or established as fellow "sovereign" states, the old units were thrown back upon themselves. Hence the demand for a new system which would offer more security to old and new nations: collective security.

I propose to view collective security not as the extreme opposite of power politics, but as an attempt to maintain, and render more secure, the impermeability of what were still territorial states. To an age which took territoriality for granted, replacing power politics with collective security would indeed appear to be a radical departure. From the vantage point of the nuclear age, however, a plan to protect individual sovereignties by collective guarantees for continuing sovereignty appears questionable not because of its innovating, but because of its conservative, nature. Its conservatism lies in its basic objective: the protection of the hard-shell territorial structure of its members, or, as the core article of the Covenant of the League of Nations put it, its guarantee of their "territorial integrity and political independence" against external aggression. The beginning of air war and the increasing economic interdependence of nations had indicated by the end of World War I that the old-style military barriers might be bypassed. If territorial units were to be preserved in the future, it would be accomplished less by reliance on individual defense potentials than by marshaling collective power in order to preserve individual powers.

But since the idea of organizing a genuine supranational force — an international police force — was rejected, the League had to cling to classical arrangements insofar as the procedures of protection were concerned. The guarantee to the individual states was to be the formation of the "Grand Coalition" of all against the isolated aggressor, which presupposed the maintenance of a certain level of armed strength by the member states. A member without that minimum of military strength would be a liability rather than an asset to the organization — in Geneva parlance, a "consumer" and not a "producer" of security. Thus classical concepts (the sovereignty and independence of nation-states) as well as classical institutions (in particular, hard-shell defensibility) were to be maintained under the new system.

Whether there ever was a chance for the system to be effective in practice is beside the point here. It is sufficient to realize how closely it was tied to the underlying structure as well as to the prevailing concepts and policies of the territorial age.

V. THE DECLINE OF THE TERRITORIAL STATE

Beginning with the nineteenth century, certain trends became visible which tended to endanger the functioning of the classical system. Directly or indirectly, all of them had a bearing upon that feature of the territorial state which was the strongest guarantee of its independent coexistence with other states of like nature: its hard shell — that is, its defensibility in case of war.

Naturally, many of these trends concerned war itself and the way in which it was conducted. But they were not related to the shift from the limited, duel-type contests of the eighteenth century to the more or less unlimited wars that developed in the nineteenth century with conscription, "nations in arms," and increasing destructiveness of weapons. By themselves, these developments were not inconsistent with the classical function of war. Enhancing a nation's defensive capacity, instituting universal military service, putting the economy on a war footing, and similar measures tended to bolster the territorial state rather than to endanger it.

Total war in a quite different sense is tied up with developments in warfare which enable the belligerents to overleap or by-pass the traditional hard-shell defense of states. When this happens, the traditional relationship between war, on the one hand, and territorial power and sovereignty, on the other, is altered decisively. Arranged in order of increasing effectiveness, these new factors may be listed under the following headings: (a) possibility of economic blockade; (b) ideological-political penetration; (c) air warfare; and (d) atomic warfare.

(a) *Economic warfare.* It should be said from the outset that so far economic blockade has never enabled one belligerent to force another into surrender through starvation alone. Although in World War I Germany and her allies were seriously endangered when the Western allies cut them off from overseas supplies, a very real effort was still required to defeat them on the military fronts. The same thing applies to World War II. Blockade was an important contributing factor, however. Its importance for the present analysis lies in its unconventional nature, permitting belligerents to by-pass the hard shell of the enemy. Its effect is due to the changed economic status of industrialized nations.

Prior to the industrial age, the territorial state was largely self-contained economically. Although one of the customary means of conducting limited war was starving fortresses into surrender, this applied merely to these individual portions of the hard shell, and not to entire nations. Attempts to starve a belligerent nation in order to avoid having to breach the shell proved rather ineffective, as witness the Continental Blockade and its counterpart in the Napoleonic era. The Industrial Revolution made countries like Britain and Germany increasingly dependent on imports. In war, this meant that they could survive only by controlling areas larger that their own territory. In peacetime, economic dependency became one of the causes of a phenomenon which itself contributed to the transformation of the old state system: imperialism. Anticipating war, with its new danger of blockade, countries strove to become more self-sufficient through enlargement of their areas of control. To the extent that the industrialized nations lost self-sufficiency, they were driven into expansion in a (futile) effort to regain it. Today, if at all, only control of entire continents enables major nations to survive economically in major wars. This implies that hard-shell military defense must be a matter of defending more than a single nation; it must extend around half the world.

(b) *Psychological warfare,* the attempt to undermine the morale of an enemy population, or to subvert its loyalty, shares with economic warfare a by-passing effect on old-style territorial defensibility. It was formerly practiced , and practicable, only under quite exceptional circumstances. Short periods of genuine world revolutionary propaganda, such as the early stages of the French Revolution, scarcely affected a general practice under which dynasties, and later governments, fought each other with little ideological involvement on the part of larger masses or classes. Only in rare cases — for instance, where national groups enclosed in and hostile to multinational empires could be appealed to — was there an opening wedge for "fifth column" strategies.

With the emergence of political belief-systems, however, nations became more susceptible to undermining from within. Although wars have not yet been won solely by subversion of loyalties, the threat involved has affected the inner coherence of the territorial state ever since the rise to power of a regime that claims to represent, not the cause of a particular nation, but that of mankind, or at least of its suppressed and exploited portions. Bolshevism from 1917 on has provided the second instance in modern history of world revolutionary propaganda. Communist penetration tactics subsequently were imitated by the Nazi and Fascist regimes and, eventually, by the democracies. In this way, new lines of division, cutting horizontally through state units instead of leaving them separated vertically from each other at their frontiers, have now become possible.

(c) *Air warfare* and (d) *nuclear warfare.* Of all the new developments, air warfare, up to the atomic age, has been the one that affected the territoriality of nations most radically. With its coming, the bottom dropped out — or, rather, the roof blew off — the relative security of the territorial state. True, even this new kind of warfare, up to and including the Second World War, did not by itself account for the defeat of a belligerent, as some of the more enthusiastic prophets of the air age had predicted it would. Undoubtedly, however, it had a massive contributory effect. And this effect was due to strategic action in the *hinterland* rather than to tactical use at the front. It came at least close to defeating one side by direct action against the "soft" interior of the country, by-passing outer defenses and thus foreshadowing the end of the frontier — that is, the demise of the traditional impermeability of even the militarily most powerful states. Warfare now changed "from a fight to a process of devastation."[5]

That air warfare was considered as something entirely unconventional is seen from the initial reaction to it. Revolutionary transition from an old to a new system has always affected moral standards. In the classical age of the modern state system, the "new morality" of shooting at human beings from a distance had finally come to be accepted, but the standards of the age clearly distinguished "lawful combatants" at the front or in fortifications from the civilian remainder of the population. When air war came, reactions thus differed significantly in the cases of air fighting at the front and of air war carried behind the front. City bombing was felt to constitute "illegitimate" warfare, and populations were inclined to treat airmen engaging in it as "war criminals." This feeling continued into World War II, with its large-scale area bombing. Such sentiments reflected the general feeling of helplessness in the face of a war which threatened to render obsolete the concept of territorial power, together with its ancient implication of protection.

The process has now been completed with the advent of nuclear weapons. For it is more than doubtful that the processes of scientific invention and technological discovery, which not only have created and perfected the fission and fusion weapons themselves but have brought in their wake guided missiles with nuclear warheads, jet aircraft with intercontinental range and supersonic speed, and the prospect of nuclear-powered planes or rockets with unlimited range and with automatic guidance to specific targets anywhere in the world, can in any meaningful way be likened to previous new inventions, however revolutionary. These processes add up to an uncanny absoluteness of effect which previous innovations could not achieve. The latter might render power units of a certain type (for instance, castles or cities) obsolete and enlarge the realm of defensible power units from city-state to territorial state or even large-area empire. They might involve destruction, in war, of entire populations. But there still remained the seemingly inexhaustible reservoir of the rest of mankind. Today, when not even two halves of the globe remain impermeable, it can no longer be a question of enlarging an area of protection and of substituting one unit of security for another. Since we are inhabitants of a planet of limited (and, as it now seems, insufficient) size, we have reached the limit within which the effect of the means of destruction has become absolute. Whatever remained of the impermeability of states seems to have gone for good.

What has been lost can be seen from two statements by thinkers separated by thousands of years and half the world; both reflect the condition of territorial security. Mencius, in ancient China, when asked for guidance in matters of defense and foreign policy by the ruler of a small state, is said to have counseled: "Dig deeper your moats; build higher your walls; guard them along with your people." This remained the classical posture up to our age, when a Western sage, Bertrand Russell, in the interwar period could still define power as something radiating from one center and growing less with distance from that center until it finds an equilibrium with that of similar geographically anchored units. Now that power can destroy power from center to center, everything is different.

VI. OUTLOOK AND CONCLUSION

It is beyond the compass of this article to ask what the change in the statehood of nation implies for present and future world relations; whether, indeed, international relations in the traditional sense of the term, dependent as they have been on a number of basic data (existence of the nation-state, measurable power, etc.) and interpreted as they were with the aid of certain concepts (sovereignty, independence, etc.), can survive at all; and, if not, what might take their place. Suffice it to remark that this question is vastly complex. We cannot even be sure that one and only one set of conclusions derives from what has happened or is in the process of happening. For, in J. Robert Oppenheimer's words, one of the characteristics of the present is "the prevalence of newness, the changing scale and scope of change itself...."[6] In the field of military policy, this means that since World War II half a dozen military innovations "have followed each other so rapidly that efforts at adaptation are hardly begun before they must be scrapped."[7] The scientific revolution has been "so fast-moving as to make almost impossible the task of military men whose responsibility it is to anticipate the future. Military planning cannot make the facts of this future stay long enough to analyze them."[8]

If this applies to military planning, it must apply equally to foreign policy planning, and, indeed, the newness of the new is perhaps the most significant and the most exasperating aspect of present world relations. Hardly has a bipolar world replaced the multipower world of classical territoriality than there loom new and unpredictable multi power constellations on the international horizon. However, the possible rise of new powers does not seem to affect bipolarity in the sense of a mere return to traditional multipower relations; since rising powers are likely to be nuclear powers, their effect must be an entirely novel one. What international relations would (or will) look like, once nuclear power is possessed by a larger number of power units, is not only extremely unpleasant to contemplate but almost impossible to anticipate, using any familiar concepts. Or, to use another example: We have hardly drawn the military and political conclusions from the new weapons developments, which at one point seemed to indicate the necessity of basing defense on the formation and maintenance of pacts like NATO and the establishment of a network of bases on allied territory from which to launch nuclear weapons "in case" (or whose existence was to deter the opponent from doing so on his part), and already further scientific and technological developments seem to render entire defense blocs, with all their new "hard shells" of bases and similar installations, obsolete.

To complicate matters even more, the changeover is not even uniform and unilinear. On the contrary, in concepts as well as in policies, we witness the juxtaposition of old and new (or several new) factors, a coexistence in theory and practice of conventional and new concepts, of traditional and new policies. Part of a nation's (or a bloc's) defense policy, then, may proceed on pre-atomic assumptions, while another part is based on the assumption of a preponderantly nuclear contest. And a compounding trouble is that the future depends on what the present anticipates, on what powers now think and how they intend to act on the basis of their present thinking; and on the fact that each of the actors on the scene must take into consideration the assumptions of the others.

There then evolves the necessity of multilevel concepts and of multilevel policies in the new era. In this we have, perhaps, the chief cause of the confusion and bewilderment of countries and publics. A good deal in recent foreign policies, with their violent swings from one extreme to another, from appeasement or apathy to truculence and threats of war, and also much in internal policies, with their suspicions and hysterias, may be reflections of world-political uncertainties. Confusion, despair, or easy optimism have been rampant; desire to give in, keep out, or get it over with underlies advocacy of appeasement, neutralism, or preventive war; mutually exclusive attitudes follow each other in rapid succession.

One radical conclusion to be drawn from the new condition of permeability would seem to be that nothing short of global rule can ultimately satisfy the security interest of any one power, and particularly any superpower. For only through elimination of the single competitor who really counts can one feel safe from the threat of annihilation. And since elimination without war is hardly imaginable, destruction of the other power by preventive war would therefore seem to be the logical objective of each superpower. But — and here the security dilemma encounters the other great dilemma of our time — such an aim is no longer practical. Since thermonuclear war would in all likelihood involve one's own destruction together with the opponent's, the means through which the end would have to be attained defeats the end itself. Pursuance of the "logical" security objective would result in mutual annihilation rather than in one unit's global control of a pacified world.

If this is so, the short-term objective must surely be mutual accommodation, a drawing of demarcation lines, geographical and otherwise, between East and West which would at least serve as a stopgap policy, a holding operation pending the creation of an atmosphere in which, perhaps in consequence of a prolonged period of "cold peace," tensions may abate and the impact of the ideologies presently dividing the world diminish. May we then expect, or hope, that radically new attitudes, in accordance with a radically transformed structure of nationhood and international relations, may ultimately gain the upper hand over the inherited ones based on familiar concepts of old-style national security, power, and power competition? Until recently, advocacy of policies based on internationalism instead of power politics, on substituting the observance of universal interests for the prevalence of national interests, was considered utopian, and correctly so. National interests were still tied up with nation-states as units of power and with their security as impermeable units; internationalist ideals, while possibly recognized as ethically valid, ran counter to what nations were able to afford if they wanted to survive and prosper. But the dichotomy between "national self-interest" and "internationalist ideals" no longer fits a situation in which sovereignty and ever so absolute power cannot protect nations from annihilation.

What used to be a dichotomy of interests and ideals now emerges as a dichotomy between two sets of interests. For the former ideal has become a compelling interest itself. In former times, the lives of people, their goods and possessions, their hopes and their happiness, were tied up with the affairs of the country in which they lived, and interests thus centered around nation and national issues. Now that destruction threatens everybody, in every one of his most intimate, personal interests, national interests are bound to recede behind — or at least compete with — the common interest of all mankind in sheer survival. And if we add to this the universal interest in the common solution of other great world problems, such as those posed by the population-resources dilemma (exhaustion of vital resources coupled with the "population explosion" throughout the world), or, indeed, that of "peacetime" planetary pollution through radioactive fallout, it is perhaps not entirely utopian to expect the ultimate spread of an attitude of "universalism" through which a rational approach to world problems would at last become possible.

It may be fitting to conclude this article by quoting two men, one a contemporary scientist whose words on nuclear problems may well apply to other problems of world relations, the second a philosopher whose statement on the revolutionary impact of attitude changes seems as valid today as when it was first made: "It is a practical thing to recognize as a common responsibility, wholly incapable of unilateral solution, the complete common peril that atomic weapons constitute for the world, to recognize that only by a community of responsibility is there any hope of meeting the peril. It would seem to me visionary in the extreme, and not practical, to hope that methods which have so sadly failed in the past to avert war will succeed in the face of this far greater peril. It would in my opinion be most dangerous to regard, in these shattering times, a radical solution less practical than a conventional one" (J. Robert Oppenheimer)[9] And: "Thought achieves more in the world than practice; for, once the realm of imagination has been revolutionized, reality cannot resist" (Hegel).

ENDNOTES

1 Charles H. McIlwain, *The Growth of Political Thought in the West* (New York: Macmillan, 1932), p. 268.

2 "Entretiens de Philarète et d'Eugène sur le droit d'Ambassade"; quoted here from *Werke*, 1st series, III, Hanover, 1864, pp. 340, 342.

3 Ibid., p. 354.

4 François Laurent, as quoted by Walter Schiffer, *The Legal Community of Mankind* (New York: Columbia University Press, 1954), p. 157.

5 B.H. Liddell Hart, *The Revolution in Warfare* (New Haven, Conn:, Yale University Press, 1947), p. 36.

6 *The Open Mind* (New York: Simon and Schuster, 1955), p.141.

7 Roger Hilsman, "Strategic Doctrines for Nuclear War," in William W. Kaufmann, ed., *Military Policy and National Security* (Princeton, N.J.: Princeton University Press, 1956), p. 42.

8 Thomas K. Finletter, *Power and Politics: US Foreign Policy and Military Power in the Hydrogen Age* (New York: Harcourt-Brace, 1954), p. 256.

9 "Atomic Weapons," *Proceedings of the American Philosophical Society*, XC (January 29, 1946), 9f.

A: TERRITORIALITY, SOVEREIGNTY, AND NATIONALISM

Why Africa's Weak States Persist: The Empirical and the Juridical in Statehood

Robert H. Jackson/Carl G. Rosberg

INTRODUCTION

Black Africa's forty-odd states are among the weakest in the world. State institutions and organizations are less developed in the sub-Saharan region than almost anywhere else; political instability (as indicated by coups, plots, internal wars, and similar forms of violence) has been prevalent in the two-and-a-half decades during which the region gained independence from colonial rule. Most of the national governments exercise only tenuous control over the people, organizations, and activities within their territorial jurisdictions. In almost all of these countries, the populations are divided along ethnic lines; in some, there has been a threat of political disorder stemming from such divisions; in a few, disorder has deteriorated into civil warfare. Some governments have periodically ceased to control substantial segments of their country's territory and population. For example, there have been times when Angola, Chad, Ethiopia, Nigeria, Sudan, Uganda, and Zaire have ceased to be "states" in the empirical sense — that is, their central governments lost control of important areas in their jurisdiction during struggles with rival political organizations.

In spite of the weakness of their national governments, none of the Black African states have been destroyed or even significantly changed. No country has disintegrated into smaller jurisdictions or been absorbed into a larger one against the wishes of its legitimate government and as a result of violence or the threat of violence. No territories or people — or even a segment of them — have been taken over by another country. No African state has been divided as a result of internal warfare. In other words, the serious empirical weaknesses and vulnerabilities of some African states have not led to enforced jurisdictional change. Why not? How can the persistence of Africa's weak states be explained? In order to answer the latter question, we must enquire into contemporary African political history as well as into the empirical and juridical components of

---

Robert H. Jackson and Carl G. Rosberg, "Why Africa's Weak States Persist: The Empirical and the Juridical in Statehood," *World Politics*, Vol. 35, No. 1 (October 1982). Some footnotes have been removed; those remaining have been renumbered.

statehood. An investigation of this question has implications not only for our understanding of African states and perhaps other Third World states, but also of statehood and contemporary international society.

THE CONCEPT OF STATEHOOD

Many political scientists employ a concept of the state that is influenced by Max Weber's famous definition: a corporate group that has compulsory jurisdiction, exercises continuous organization, and claims a monopoly of force over a territory and its population, including "all action taking place in the area of its jurisdiction."[1] As Weber emphasized, his definition is one of "means" and not "ends," and the distinctive means for him are force.[2] A definition of the state primarily in terms of means rather than ends — particularly the means of force — emphasizes the empirical rather than the juridical, the *de facto* rather than the *de jure*, attributes of statehood. This emphasis is undoubtedly an important element in the appeal of Weber's sociology of the state to political scientists. To be sure, Weber does not overlook the juridical aspects of statehood. However, he does not explore what many students of international law consider to be the true character of territorial jurisdiction: the reality that such jurisdiction is an international legal condition rather than some kind of sociological given.

By Weber's definition, the basic test of the existence of a state is whether or not its national government can lay claim to a monopoly of force in the territory under its jurisdiction. If some external or internal organization can effectively challenge a national government and carve out an area of monopolistic control for itself, it thereby acquires the essential characteristic of statehood. According to Weber's *de facto* terms of statehood, two concurrent monopolies of force cannot exist over one territory and population. In situations where one of several rival groups — that is, claimant states — is unable to establish permanent control over a contested territory, Weber would maintain that it is more appropriate to speak of "statelessness."

By Weber's definition, a few of Africa's governments would not qualify as states — at least not all of the time — because they cannot always effectively claim to have a monopoly of force throughout their territorial jurisdictions. In some countries, rivals to the national government have been able to establish an effective monopoly of force over significant territories and populations for extended periods — for example, Biafra in Nigeria and Katanga in the Congo (now Zaire). In other countries — such as Chad and Uganda — some of the territories have not been under the continuous control of one permanent political organization, and a condition of anarchy has existed. Furthermore, the governments of many Black African countries do not effectively control all of the important public activities within their jurisdictions; in some, government is perilously uncertain, so that important laws and regulations cannot be enforced with confidence and are not always complied with. If the persistence of a state were primarily the result of empirical statehood, some sub-Saharan African countries would clearly not qualify as states some of the time. Yet it is evident that all of them persist as members of the international society of states; it is also evident that none of the claimant governments that have on occasion exercised *de facto* control over large territories and populations within the jurisdictions of existing states have yet succeeded in creating new states in these areas.

Definitions that give priority to the juridical rather than the empirical attributes of statehood are employed by international legal scholars and institutionally oriented international theorists. One such definition —which shares a number of characteristics with Weber's, but gives them a different emphasis — is that of Ian Brownlie, a British legal scholar. Following the Montevideo Convention on Rights and Duties of States, Brownlie describes the state as a legal person, recognized by international law, with the following attributes: (a) a defined territory, (b) a permanent population,

(c) an effective government, and (d) independence, or the right "to enter into relations with other states."[3]

If the assumption of juridical statehood as a sociological given is a shortcoming of Weber's definition, a limitation of Brownlie's is the tendency to postulate that the empirical attributes of statehood — i.e., a permanent population and effective government — are as definite as the juridical attributes; they are not. What does it mean to say that a state consists, *inter alia*, of a permanent population and an effective government? Our research reveals that within sub-Saharan African states, these empirical properties have been highly variable, while the juridical components have been constant. Kenya's population has been more "permanent" and its government more "effective" than Uganda's; yet both states have survived as sovereign jurisdictions. Moreover, an exclusively legal approach cannot adequately deal with the empirical properties of statehood: "Once a state has been established, extensive civil strife or the breakdown of order through foreign invasion or natural disasters are not considered to affect personality."[4] In the formulation of concepts, empirical properties can be determined only by investigation, not by definition.[5] Although Brownlie recognizes the need to incorporate empirical criteria into a "working legal definition of statehood,"[6] he acknowledges (as do other scholars) that there is considerable difficulty in employing these criteria without specifying them concretely. Nonetheless, his definition enables us to undertake an analysis of the empirical as well as the juridical aspects of statehood — that is, a sociological-legal analysis.

Political scientists do not need to be convinced of the limitations of an exclusively legalistic approach to the state, which is usually summed up as "legal-formalism": an undue emphasis on abstract rules, leading to the neglect of concrete behavior and the social conditions that support or undermine legal rules.[7] What is more difficult is to convince a generation of political scientists whose theories and models were formulated in reaction to legal, institutional, and philosophical studies of the state, of the limitations of an exclusively sociological conception of statehood. However, if one assumes that the state is essentially an empirical phenomenon — as was suggested not only by Weber but also by David Easton in a systems approach that has been very influential — one cannot explain why some states manage to persist when important empirical conditions of statehood are absent, or are present only in a very qualified manner.[8] In sum, one cannot explain the persistence of some "states" by using a concept of the state that does not give sufficient attention to the juridical properties of statehood.

THE EMPIRICAL STATE IN BLACK AFRICA

Weber's and Brownlie's definitions of statehood provide a useful point of departure for examining empirical and juridical statehood in contemporary Black Africa. (Juridical statehood is discussed in the following section.) We shall begin with Brownlie's definition, which is more explicit and current. As we noted above, Brownlie specifies two empirical attributes of the state: "a permanent population [which] is intended to be used in association with that of territory, and connotes a stable community," and an "effective government, with centralized administrative and legislative organs."[9]

Before we can apply Brownlie's empirical attributes to our analysis, we must clarify them. First, what exactly do we understand by "a stable community" and its crucial empirical component, "a permanent population"? In attempting to define these terms in the context of contemporary Africa, we find that political sociology may be of considerably more help than law. In political sociology, societies are seen as integrated or disunited, culturally homogeneous or fragmented — resting on common norms and values or not. If we take "a stable community" to signify an integrated political community resting on a common culture, we must conclude that few contemporary Black African states can be said to possess this attribute. The populations of many Black African countries are divided internally among several — and often many — distinctive ethnic entities by differences of language, religion, race, region of residence, and so forth. Moreover, these ethnic cleavages can reinforce each other, thus aggravating the differences. In Sudan, for example, the racial division between Arabs and Africans is reinforced by geography, religion, and language; it has resulted in bitter conflicts over the control of the state. Furthermore, many ethnic entities are divided by international boundaries, with members residing in two or more countries; however, the social and political boundaries between these ethnic entities may well be more significant in terms of public attitudes and behavior than are the boundaries between the countries. As a result, political tensions and conflicts arising from ethnic divisions can seriously affect national political stability and the capacity of governments to control their territories.

From our discussion, it appears that few African states can qualify as stable communities. Where ethnic divisions have been politicized, the result has been serious civil conflict. Thus, ethnic divisions have been a major factor contributing to extreme disorder or civil war in the following countries: Sudan (1956-1972); Rwanda (1959-1964); Zaire (1960-1965; 1977-1978); Ethiopia (1962-1982); Zanzibar (1964); Burundi (1966-1972); Chad (1966-1982); Uganda (1966; 1978-1982); Nigeria (1967-1970); and Angola (1975-1982). In other countries, ethnic divisions have been sufficiently threatening to prompt governments to control political participation severely out of fear that they would otherwise jeopardize their command of the state. Recent African politics have been characterized by the opposition of most African governments to competitive party systems, their preference for political monopoly generally, their lack of sympathy for federalism, and their attack on political liberties (among other things). All of these can be explained at least in part by the governments' fear of politicized ethnicity. Efforts by African governments to emphasize the "nation" and "nationalism" at the expense of the "ethnos" — efforts that are evident elsewhere in the Third World as well — indicate their concern about the instability of their political communities and the threat posed by that instability not only to individual governments, but to statehood itself.

Second, by "an effective government" Brownlie means exactly what Weber means by "compulsory jurisdiction": centralized administrative and legislative organs.[10] Such a definition is somewhat Eurocentric because it identifies governing not only with administering, but also with legislating. In contemporary Africa, governments do not necessarily govern by legislation; personal rulers often operate in an arbitrary and autocratic manner by means of commands, edicts, decrees, and so forth. To make this empirical attribute more universal, let us redefine it as a centralized government with the capacity to exercise control over a state's territory and the people residing in it. By "exercise control" we mean the ability to pronounce, implement, and enforce commands, laws, policies, and regulations.

The capacity to exercise control raises the question of means. Analytically, the means of government can be considered in terms of the domestic authority or right to govern (legitimacy) on the one hand, and the power or ability to govern on the other. In Michael Oakeshott's terms, the modern state consists, among other things, of both an "office of authority" and "an apparatus of power";[11] the two are analytically different and should not be confused. For example, governmental administration usually involves the (delegated) authority to issue regulations *and* the power to enforce them. A government may possess legitimacy, but have little in the way of an effective apparatus of power; or it may have an imposing power apparatus, but little legitimacy in the eyes of its citizens. Other combinations are also possible.

In our judgment, the capacity of Africa's governments to exercise control hinges upon three factors: domestic authority, the apparatus of power, and economic circumstances. First, political authority in Africa (and in other parts of the Third World as well) tends to be personal rather than institutional. Geertz has commented:

> Fifteen years ago, scholarly writings on the New States... were full of discussions of parties, parliaments, and elections. A great deal seemed to turn on whether these institutions were viable in the Third World and what adjustments in them... might prove necessary to make them so. Today, nothing in those writings seems more *passé*, relic of a different time.[12]

Constitutional and institutional offices that are independent of the personal authority of rulers have not taken root in most Black African countries. Instead, the state and state offices are dominated by ambitious individuals, both civilian and military. Post-independence rulers of Africa and Asia, Geertz writes, "are autocrats, and it is as autocrats, and not as preludes to liberalism (or, for that matter, to totalitarianism), that they, and the governments they dominate, must be judged and understood."[13] Wherever African governments have exercised substantial control, strong personal rulers have been firmly in the saddle. This has been the case in regimes that are primarily autocratic — such as Félix Houphouët-Boigny's Ivory Coast, H. Kamazu Banda's Malawi, Omar Bongo's Gabon, Ahmadou Ahidjo's Cameroon, and Gnassingbé Eyadéma's Togo. It has also been the case where regimes are primarily oligarchic — such as Léopold Sédar Senghor's Senegal, Jomo Kenyatta's Kenya, and Gaafar Mohamed Numeiri's Sudan — and where they are primarily ideological — such as Julius Nyerere's Tanzania and Sékou Touré's Guinea (which exhibits features of despotism as well). Where African governments have not exercised control, it has often been because no personal leader has taken firm command; alternatively, it has been as a result of excessively arbitrary and abusive personal rule, as was the case in Uganda under Idi Amin. In the most unstable African regimes, the military has repeatedly intervened in politics — as in Benin from 1960 to 1972 and in Chad from 1975 to 1982.

Related to the problem of institutional weakness in African states is the disaffection of important elites from the government. The frequency of military coups is perhaps the best indication of elite alienation and disloyalty. Between 1958 and the summer of 1981, more than 41 successful coups had taken place in 22 countries of Black Africa; in addition, there had been many unsuccessful ones.[14] Gutteridge has noted that, "by 1966, military intervention in politics in Africa had become endemic.... Even the smallest armies [had] carried out successful coups."[15] There is little doubt that the internal opponent most feared by African rulers — both military and civilian — is the military. Indeed, military rulers have themselves been the victims of military coups — for instance, Yakubu Gowon of Nigeria, and Ignatius Kutu Acheampong and Frederick Akuffo of Ghana in the 1970s. It should be noted that, although Africa's military formations are called "armies" and their members wear uniforms and display other symbols of state authority, they cannot be assumed to be loyal to the government. A military career is sometimes a promising avenue for political advancement; soldiers in Black Africa have become not only government officials, but also rulers of their countries.

Second, the apparatus of power in African governments — the agents and agencies that implement and enforce government laws, edicts, decrees, orders, and the like — can in general be considered "underdeveloped" in regard both to their stock of resources and to the deployment of these resources. In proportion to their territories and populations, African governments typically have a smaller stock of finances, personnel, and materiel than Asian or Western governments, and their staffs are less experienced and reliable. As a result, the concept of governmental administration as a policy instrument bears less relation to reality. Governmental incapacity is exacerbated by overly ambitious plans and policies that are prepared on the assumption that underdevelopment is a problem of economy and society, but not of government. In fact, it is also African governments that are underdeveloped, and in most countries they are very far from being an instrument of development. The modern "administrative state" image of government is of questionable applicability in many parts of the world, but Black African governments are even less likely than others to be rational agencies.

Undoubtedly the biggest problem of both civilian and military administrations in Africa is the questionable reliability of staffs. In a famous phrase, Gunnar Myrdal characterized the governments of South Asia as "soft states."[16] The term can be applied equally to many governments in Black Africa which must operate amidst corruption and disorder. The problem of inefficient staff has rarely been as candidly exposed as in a 1977 report by Julius Nyerere on socialist progress in Tanzania. He noted that ministries were overspending in disregard of severe budgetary restraints; the Rural Development Bank was issuing loans that were not being repaid; state enterprises were operating far below capacity — sometimes at less than 50 percent; "management" was preoccupied with privilege and displayed little enterprise; and "workers" were slack, incompetent, and undisciplined.[17]

Of course, there is considerable variation in the administrative capacity of African governments, and Tanzania is by no means the country most seriously affected by an inefficient state apparatus. While the comparative effectiveness of the Ivory Coast, Kenya (at least under Kenyatta), and Malawi is striking, Benin, Congo-Brazzaville, Mali, Togo, and Upper Volta are infamous for their swollen bureaucracies and administrative lethargy. Once relatively efficient Ghana and Uganda are examples of marked deterioration, the origins of which are perhaps more political than economic and relate to a failure to establish an effective and responsible ruling class. One of the worst cases of administrative decay is Zaire, where the state's resources have been plundered and regulations abused by government officials at all levels. President Mobutu Sese Seko has identified abuses such as the case of army officers who divert for "their own personal profit the supplies intended for frontline soldiers"; the refusal of rural development officials to leave their air-conditioned offices in Kinshasa; and the "misuse of judicial machinery for revenging private disputes,...selective justice depending upon one's status and wealth."[18] So extreme is the corruption that observers have had to invent new phrases to describe it; Zaire has been referred to as "an extortionist culture" in which corruption is a "structural fact" and bribery assumes the form of "economic mugging."[19] It has been estimated that as much as 60 percent of the annual national budget is misappropriated by the governing elite.

As we have noted, the inefficiency of African governments extends to the military as well as the civilian organs of the state. As in the case of civilian maladministration, military ineffectiveness stems from sociopolitical as well as technical-material factors; the size and firepower of the armed forces can also play a role. Typically, military forces in African countries are small in relation to the size or population of a state; however, they are considerably larger than the colonial armies they replaced. Over the past two decades, the size of African armies has increased (primarily for purposes of internal security), and their equipment has been upgraded. As early as 1970, Gutteridge commented that "there is no doubting a general upward trend in the numbers of men under arms in regular forces";[20] there have been no significant developments since 1970 to suggest any change in what appears to be military "growth without development."

In practice, most African armies are less like military organizations and more like political establishments: they are infected by corruption, factionalism, and patterns of authority based not only on rank, role, or function, but also on personal and ethnic loyalties. The ability of African armies to deal with internal conflicts is dubious. Despite overwhelming superiority in men and equipment, the Nigerian Federal Army had great difficulty in defeating the forces of Biafra in the late 1960s; according to Gutteridge, "there were times when the Federal Army seemed to have lost the will to win."[21] Moreover, the state's apparatus of power may be not only aided and supported by the solicited intervention of a foreign power in the form of troops, military equipment, advisers, and so forth, but such intervention can be essential to the survival of a regime. In a number of French-speaking countries, a French military presence has enhanced the power of the African government; in Angola and Ethiopia, Cuban soldiers and Soviet arms and advisers have made a decisive difference to the power and survival of incumbent African regimes in their conflicts with both internal and external powers. The lethargy of African armies has sometimes been acutely embarrassing. When Zaire's copper-rich Shaba Province (formerly Katanga) was invaded by Katangan forces from neighboring Angola in 1977 and again in 1978, President Mobutu's army proved incapable of stopping them; Mobutu had to call upon friendly powers (Morocco, Belgium, France, and the United States) to save his regime.

Third, governmental incapacity in Black Africa is affected by economic circumstances, which are exacerbated by the small size of the skilled work force. African economies are among the poorest and weakest in the world: in 1978, 22 of them had a per capita GNP below $250; throughout the 1970s, the Black African countries had the lowest worldwide rates of growth. Of the world's poorest countries — those with per capita incomes below $330 — the 28 that were African had the lowest projected growth rates for the 1980s. In many of these countries, absolute poverty is increasing as birthrates continue to exceed economic growth rates.

Many African countries are highly dependent on a few primary exports for their foreign exchange earnings. They are therefore vulnerable to uncontrollable fluctuations in world commodity prices and, in the case of agricultural commodities, unpredictable changes in weather conditions and harvest returns. The countries without petroleum resources have had to face dramatically increased prices for oil imports, resulting in very severe balance-of-payments problems. In some countries, more than 50 percent of scarce foreign exchange had to be used to pay for imported oil. Moreover, 27 countries had a shortfall in their production of food crops — principally maize — in 1980; they were therefore forced to import food, which resulted in a further drain of scarce foreign exchange. (South Africa became an important supplier of food to Angola, Kenya, Malawi, Mozambique, Zaire, and Zambia, among others). Lacking industrial and manufacturing sectors of any significance and being highly dependent upon imports, most African countries are caught between the certainty of their demand for foreign goods and the uncertainty of their ability to earn the foreign exchange to pay for them. In many (if not most) of these countries, inflated and consumption-oriented government administrations — whose members enjoy a standard of living far in excess of the national average — weigh down the already overburdened and sluggish economies; in many, the economy is simply exploited to support the political class. The hope that intelligent government planning might effect a substantial economic transformation has long since faded.

It is evident that the term "empirical state" can only be used selectively to describe many states in Black Africa today. With some notable exceptions — for example, Kenya and the Ivory Coast — it seems accurate to characterize Africa's states as empirically weak or underdeveloped. If we adopted a narrow empirical criterion of statehood — such as Weber's monopoly of force — we would have to conclude that some African countries were not states, and that statehood in others has periodically been in doubt. In 1981, the governments of Angola, Chad, Ethiopia, and Uganda could not claim a monopoly of force within their jurisdictions. Furthermore, these countries and some others — for example, Nigeria, Sudan, and Zaire — have exhibited *de facto* statelessness in the past, and there are reasons to believe that they might do so again. Yet it is unlikely that any of their jurisdictions will be altered without the consent of their governments. Jurisdictional change by consent has happened, however. In 1981, The Gambia was forced to call upon neighboring Senegal for troops to put down an armed rebellion by a substantial segment of its own field force under the leadership of leftist militants. The episode undermined the security of the Gambian government to such an extent that it consented to a form of association with Senegal which resulted in a new confederation: Senegambia.

THE JURIDICAL STATE IN BLACK AFRICA

Before we investigate the significance of the juridical state in Black Africa, let us emphasize that "juridical statehood" is not only a normative but essentially an international attribute. The juridical state is both a creature and a component of the international society of states, and its properties can only be defined in international terms. At this point, it is important to clarify what is meant by "international society." It is a society composed solely of states and the international organizations formed by states; it excludes not only individuals and private groups, but also political organizations that are not states or are not composed of states. The doctrine of "states' rights" — that is, sovereignty — is the central principle of international society. It often comes into conflict with the doctrine of international human rights, but international society does not promote the welfare of individuals and private groups within a country or transnational groups among countries; nor does it protect individuals or private groups from their governments. Rather, international society provides legal protection for member states from any powers, internal and external, that seek to intervene in, invade, encroach upon, or otherwise assault their sovereignty. A secondary but increasingly important goal — one that is linked to the emergence of Third World states — is to promote the welfare and development of member states.

According to Brownlie, the juridical attributes of statehood are "territory" and "independence" (as recognized by the international community). In international law, a demarcated territory is the equivalent of the "property" of a government — national real estate, including offshore waters and airspace; international boundaries are the mutually acknowledged but entirely artificial lines where one government's property rights end and another's begin. Determinate and recognized frontiers are therefore a basic institution of the state system and an essential legal attribute of any state. A government recognized as having political independence is legally the equal of other independent governments, and is not only the highest authority within its territorial jurisdiction but is under no higher authority. It has the right to enter into relations with other states and to belong to the international society of states.

A political system may possess some or all of the empirical qualifications of statehood, but without the juridical attributes of territory and independence it is not a state. Furthermore, these attributes — which constitute territorial jurisdiction — serve as a test of a government's claim to be a state; there is no empirical test. For example, the Transkei, Bophuthatswana, Venda, and Ciskei — black "homelands" in South Africa — are as much empirical states as some other territories in Africa, but they lack statehood because they are not recognized by any state except South Africa and enjoy none of the rights of membership in international society. Since they are creatures wholly of South Africa's apartheid regime, their political survival is probably tied to the survival of apartheid. On the other hand, the former British territory of Lesotho, which is also an enclave within South Africa, but was never ruled by Pretoria and has gained its independence from Britain, is a recognized state and exercises full rights of membership in international society, which are not likely to be threatened in this way precisely because it is independent.

The juridical state in Black Africa is a novel and arbitrary political unit; the territorial boundaries, legal identities, and often even the names of states are contrivances of colonial rule. Only rarely did a colonial territory reflect the shape and identity of a preexisting African sociopolitical boundary, as in the cases of the British Protectorate of Zanzibar (formerly a sultanate) and the

High Commission Territories of Swaziland and Basutoland (Lesotho), which had been African kingdoms. (Under British rule, the *internal* administrative boundaries of a colony were often drawn to conform with indigenous borders where these could be determined.) During the European colonization of Africa in the late 19th century, international society was conceived as a "European association, to which non-European states could be admitted only if and when they met a standard of civilization laid down by the Europeans."[22] With the exceptions of Ethiopia and Liberia, which escaped colonialism and were treated as states, Black African political systems did not qualify as states, but were regarded as the objects of a justified colonialism.

At independence (beginning in the late 1950s), there were therefore very few traditional African states to whom sovereignty could revert. Consequently, there was little choice but to establish independence in terms of the colonial entities; in most cases, a colony simply became a state with its territorial frontiers unchanged. Most attempts to create larger political units — usually conceived as federations — failed, as happened in the cases of the Mali Federation and the Central African Federation.[23] Kwame Nkrumah's vision of a United States of Africa received virtually no support from his counterparts in the newly independent states. Instead, the Organization of African Unity (O.A.U.), formed in May 1963, fully acknowledged and legitimated the colonial frontiers and the principle of state sovereignty within them. As President Modibo Keita of Mali put it: although the colonial system divided Africa, "it permitted nations to be born.... African unity...requires full respect for the frontiers we have inherited from the colonial system."[24]

It is a paradox of African independence that it awakened both national and ethnic political awareness. In almost every Black African country there are ethnic groups that desire to redraw international boundaries in order to form independent states. Self-determination, which accelerated after World War I and reached its peak in the years after World War II with the independence of numerous colonies, came to a halt in Black Africa at the inherited (colonial) frontiers. The movement, which is still alive sociologically among millions of Africans and within many ethnic communities, is unlikely to make further political-legal progress. The opposition of existing African states and of international society has reinforced the legitimacy of the inherited frontiers and undermined that of the traditional cultural borders. One of the exceptions to ethnic Balkanization has been Somali irredentism in Ethiopia and Kenya, which has sought the creation of a greater Somalia defined by cultural rather than colonial boundaries. But so far, Somali irrendentism — as well as Biafran nationalism, Katangan separatism, and Eritrean secessionism — has failed to win international legitimacy. When the claims of Somali cultural nationalists were debated at the founding meeting of the O.A.U. in 1963, the argument advanced by the Kenyan delegation represented the view of the vast majority of African governments: "If they [the Somalis] do not want to live with us in Kenya, they are perfectly free to leave us and our territory.... This is the only way they can legally exercise their right of self-determination."[25] When the Kingdom of Buganda — an administrative region within the colony of Uganda and a traditional African state — declared itself independent in 1960 after realizing that the British authorities were going to give independence to Uganda, no other state recognized the declaration. Buganda failed to achieve juridical statehood; it remained a region — albeit a troublesome one — of the new Ugandan state, which became independent in 1962.

African decolonization — like decolonization elsewhere —demonstrated that it is impossible to have rational empirical qualifications for statehood. Many colonies became states although the viability of their economic bases and their developmental potentiality were questionable. Some of the new states had minuscule populations and/or territories: Cape Verde, the Comoros Islands, Djibouti, Equatorial Guinea, Gabon, The Gambia,

Sao Tome and Principe, the Seychelles, and Swaziland. Empirically these entities are really microstates, but juridically they are full-fledged states. Their independence reveals the assumption of the contemporary international community that even countries of very questionable viability and capacities can be preserved by a benevolent international society. In other words, international society has become a global "democracy" based on the principle of legal equality of members. Even the most profound socioeconomic inadequacies of some countries are not considered to be a barrier to their membership: all former colonies and dependencies have the right to belong if they wish. The existence of a large number of weak states poses one of the foremost international problems of our time: their protection and preservation, not to mention development. The survival of states is not a new issue; indeed, it is the historical problem of international relations, which has served to define traditional international theory as "the theory of survival."[26] What is new is the enlarged scope, added dimensions, and greater complexity and delicacy of the problem in contemporary international society.

INTERNATIONAL SOCIETY AND THE AFRICAN STATE

The juridical attributes of statehood can only be conferred upon governments by the international community. The Transkei is not a state because South Africa alone does not have the right to confer statehood, whereas Lesotho is a state because the international community accepted — indeed encouraged — British decolonization in Africa. Even though a state's jurisdictions and boundaries often appear to be "natural" phenomena and sometimes correspond with natural land forms, they are political artifacts upheld by the international community. Among other things, the international society of states was formed to support the doctrine of states' or sovereigns' rights as a cornerstone of international order. Basically, it involves mutual rights and obligations — for example, the right of a country to exist and not to have its jurisdiction violated, and its duty not to violate the rights of others.

In this section we offer an explanation as to why the existing pattern of juridical statehood has been maintained in Africa. The most important conditions that have contributed to this phenomenon appear to be: the ideology of Pan-Africanism; the vulnerability of all states in the region and the insecurity of statesmen; the support of the larger international society, including particularly its institutions and associations; and the reluctance, to date, of non-African powers to intervene in the affairs of African states without having been invited to do so by their governments. We will briefly discuss each of these conditions.

First, unlike any other continent except Australia, "Africa" is a political idea as well as a geographical fact with a distinctive ideology: African nationalism. This ideology emerged largely as a result of the universal African experience of colonial domination. European colonialism and its practices fostered the reactive ideology of African nationalism, which was directed at political independence and the freedom of the continent from European rule. Colonialism was the experience of Africans not only as individuals or as members of subordinated communities, or even as members of particular colonies; it was also their experience as Africans — a common political experience. As long as any country on the continent remains dominated by non-Africans, Pan-Africanism means the liberation of the continent in the name of African "freedom." Almost without exception, the Pan-Africanists came to realize that freedom could in practice only be achieved within the existing framework of the colonial territories that the Europeans had established. The European colonies were the only political vehicles that could give expression to African nationalism; as a consequence, these artificial jurisdictions acquired a vital legitimacy in the eyes of most knowledgeable Africans. Politicians in particular have maintained that, whatever the size, shape, population, and resources of these jurisdictions, they have a right to exist because they are the embodiment of the African political revolution. The only practical way of realizing the goal of African freedom was through the independence of the colonial territories. By this process, the successor states were made legitimate — not one, or several, or many individually, but all equally. Moreover, it is consistent with the ideology of Pan-Africanism that until Namibia — and perhaps even South Africa — are free, "Africa" is not yet free.

Therefore, however arbitrary and alien in origin the inherited state jurisdictions might have been — and however far removed from traditional African values — they have been endowed with legitimacy. The ideology of Pan-Africanism that has gained historical expression in this way is a fundamental bulwark within Africa against the violation of existing, inherited state jurisdictions. At the same time, Pan-Africanism disposed the new African statesmen to associate in a common continental body whose rules would legitimize existing jurisdictions and specify any international actions that would be considered illegitimate. As a result, the principles of the O.A.U., as set down in Article III of its Charter, affirm: the sovereign equality of member states; non-interference; respect for sovereignty; peaceful settlement of disputes; and the illegitimacy of subversion. In sum, the ideology of Pan-Africanism has been expressed in the acceptance of the inherited colonial jurisdictions and the international legitimacy of all of the existing African states.

Second, there is a common interest in the support of international rules and institutions and state jurisdictions in the African region that derives from the common vulnerability of states and the insecurity of statesmen. This approach would appear to be a variant of Hobbes's explanation of why rational individuals would prefer subordination to Leviathan as against freedom in the state of nature: general insecurity. "Since many are vulnerable to external incitement for secession it was obvious to most of the O.A.U. Members that a reciprocal respect for boundaries, and abstention from demands for their immediate revision, would be to their general advantage."[27] In order to survive, weak African governments had to be assured of the recognition and respect for their sovereignty by neighboring states, as well as any other states in a position to undermine their authority and control. Regional vulnerability and the general apprehension of externally promoted interference and subversion have disposed African governments to collaborate in maintaining their jurisdictions.

From a balance-of-power perspective, it might be objected that, in actual fact, the roughly equal powerlessness of African governments is what upholds state jurisdictions by making violation very difficult and therefore unlikely. But military weakness did not prevent the Tanzanian army from invading Uganda and overthrowing Amin's tyranny, and it did not prevent the Katangan rebels from invading Shaba province in Zaire on two separate occasions. To the contrary, the civil and military weakness of most African governments disposes them to fear international subversion by neighboring states and others who may support their internal enemies. Consequently, it is weakness that induces all of them to support the rules and practices of the O.A.U. which are intended to uphold existing state jurisdictions. African international society — specifically the O.A.U. — is intended to provide international political goods that guarantee the survival, security, identity, and integrity of African states, which the majority of African states cannot provide individually.

The O.A.U. is less an "organization" with its own agents, agencies, and resources than it is an "association" with its own rules: a club of statesmen who are obligated to subscribe to a small number of rules and practices of regional conduct, and to which every state except South Africa belongs. It is evident from the rules of Article III that the O.A.U. is very much a traditional association of states. But the O.A.U.'s effectiveness, like that of other successful international associations, probably owes less to its formal procedures than to its internal political processes. According to a leading student of the association, its main source of strength is the way in which it fosters the peaceful settlement of disputes.[28] Conflict resolution has often taken place outside the Commission of Mediation, Conciliation, and Arbitration — which was specifically set up for the purpose. Most statesmen involved in disputes have resorted to mediation or conciliation by the O.A.U. Chairman, who is elected annually by the members, or by another respected member who is not involved in the disputes. The success of the O.A.U. is indicated by the fact that the majority of the numerous disputes among its members have been contained through its internal political process. Its only significant failures to date have been the wars in the Horn of Africa prompted by Somalia's attempts to claim border territories in Ethiopia and Kenya (challenging the inherited boundaries as well as a fundamental principle of the O.A.U.) and the Uganda-Tanzania war of 1978-1979, which resulted in the overthrow of Idi Amin's tyranny.

Third, the African states all became independent at a time when international society was highly organized and integrated. Its elaborate framework of international associations of both a worldwide and a regional or functional kind includes bodies that are important for African states: the United Nations (and its numerous specialized agencies that deal in whole or in part with Africa), the Commonwealth, Francophonie, the Lomé Convention of the European Economic Community (EEC), and so forth. Membership in such associations is an acknowledgement of the existence of the member states and of their international rights and duties, including the right not to be interfered with. Their membership in international society acknowledges the legitimacy and supports the independence of African states. Indeed, the states' rights that derive from membership in the United Nations and other bodies are commonly used by African governments — sometimes with considerable skill and success — to secure both material and non-material benefits from the international system.

International society is a conservative order. Any international actor that seeks to interfere by force or any other illegitimate means in the affairs of a member state is almost certain to be confronted by a condemnation of its actions by most other states. The only interventions that are acceptable under present international rules and practices are those to which the legitimate government of the target country has consented. Imposed or unsolicited interference is difficult to justify; in Africa, the attempts by Katangan rebels, Biafran secessionists, Eritrean separatists, and Somali and Morrocan irredentists to alter existing jurisdictions by force have to date not only been roundly condemned, but successfully resisted. Moreover, external powers that have been in a position to assist African claimant or expansionist states in their attempts at forced jurisdictional change have usually been loath to do so. For example, in 1977 the U.S.S.R. switched its military support from Somalia to Ethiopia when the Somalis seized Ethiopian territory by force. The Ethiopian army did not invade Somalia after it had expulsed the Somali forces from Ethiopia's Ogaden region (with major Cuban as well as Soviet assistance). When external powers have intervened in Africa, they have usually respected existing state jurisdictions: most such interventions were in response to solicitations by African governments or revolutionary movements fighting against colonial or white minority regimes.

The rare interventions in independent African states that were not solicited by a sovereign government, and thus did not respect existing state jurisdictions, can — with two exceptions involving France — be explained by the intervening power's status as an international outcast. In southern Africa, there have been numerous armed intrusions by the South African army into Angola to destroy, harass, or contain forces of the South West Africa People's Organization (SWAPO), and at least one dramatic raid into Mozambique to punish or destroy anti-apartheid movements in their sanctuaries. They can be accounted for by Pretoria's outcast status and preoccupation with political survival. The military interventions by the Rhodesian armed forces into Zambia and Mozambique toward the end of the Rhodesian conflict can be understood in similar terms, as can the 1970 raid by Portuguese soldiers and African collaborators on Conakry, the capital of independent Guinea. The only interventions that cannot be explained in this way were made by France: in Gabon (1964) to restore a regime that had been overthrown, and in the Central African Republic (1979) to overthrow a government and impose a new regime. In the first case, France had entered into an international agreement to protect the M'Ba government; in the second, it appears that other African states had given their tacit consent to the action, and may even have solicited it.

CONCLUSION

We have argued that juridical statehood is more important than empirical statehood in accounting for the persistence of states in Black Africa. International organizations have served as "post-imperial ordering devices" for the new African states,[29] in effect freezing them in their inherited colonial jurisdictions and blocking any post-independence movements toward self-determination. So far, they have successfully outlawed force as a method of producing new states in Africa.

Membership in the international society provides an opportunity —denied to Black Africa under colonialism — to both influence and take advantage of international rules and ideologies concerning what is desirable and undesirable in the relations of states. The impact of Third World states on those rules and ideologies is likely to increase as the new statesmen learn how to take advantage of international democracy. They have already been successful in influencing the creation of some new ideologies. For example, the efforts of the Third World have led to the formation of the North-South dialogue which would legitimate an international theory of morality based on assumptions of social justice that have heretofore been largely confined to internal politics. The states of the South — supported by some Northern statesmen — have asserted a moral claim on the actions and resources of the North; international society is not only being subjected to demands for peace, order, and security, but for international social justice as well. This radical new development in international relations is associated with the emergence of the Third World. If it succeeds, a revolutionary change in international morality will have been brought about.

The global international society whose most important institutions have been established or expanded since the end of World War II has been generally successful in supporting the new state jurisdictions of independent Africa; thus, the survival of Africa's existing states is largely an international achievement. Still, international effects on empirical statehood are ambiguous. International society has legitimated and fostered the transfer of goods, services, technology, skills, and the like from rich to poor countries with the intention of contributing to the development of the latter. But there are definite limits to what international society can contribute to the further development of the capabilities of African states. A society of states that exists chiefly in order to maintain the existing state system and the independence and survival of its members cannot regulate the internal affairs of members without the consent of their governments. It is therefore limited in its ability to determine that the resources transferred to the new states are effectively and properly used. In spite of a strong desire to do so, there is no way to guarantee such transfers against the wishes of a sovereign government without interfering in its internal affairs. Consequently, the enforcement of state jurisdictions may be at odds with the effort to develop the empirical state in Africa and elsewhere in the Third World. By enforcing juridical statehood, international society is in some cases also sustaining and perpetuating incompetent and corrupt governments. Perhaps the best example in sub-Saharan Africa is the international support that has gone into ensuring the survival of the corrupt government of Zaire. If this relationship is not an uncommon one, we must conclude that international society is at least partly responsible for perpetuating the underdevelopment of the empirical state in Africa by providing resources to incompetent or corrupt governments without being permitted to ensure that these resources are effectively and properly used.

State-building theories which assume that empirical statehood is more fundamental than juridical statehood, and that the internal is prior to the international in state formation and survival, are at odds with contemporary African experience. To study Black Africa's states from the internal perspective of political sociology is to assume that the state-building process here is basically the same as it was in Europe (where the political sociology of the modern state largely developed). In Europe, empirical statehood preceded juridical statehood or was concurrent with it, and the formation of modern states preceded (and later accompanied) the emergence of a state system. European statesmen created jurisdictions over the course of several centuries in Machiavellian fashion — by dominating internal rivals and competing with external rivals — until the international system had attained its present-day jurisdictions. However, as Tilly points out: "The later the state-making experience...the less likely...internal processes...are to provide an adequate explanation of the formation, survival or growth of a state."[30] In Black Africa (and, by implication, in other regions of the Third World), external factors are more likely than internal factors to provide an adequate explanation of the formation and persistence of states. State jurisdictions and international society, which once were consequences of the success and survival of states, today are more likely to be conditions.

Arnold Wolfers pointed out that in the Anglo-American conceptualization of the international system versus the nation-state, the most persistent image has been one of international discord versus internal order and civility.[31] In contemporary Black Africa, an image of international accord and civility and internal disorder and violence would be more accurate. At the level of international society, a framework of rules and conventions governing the relations of the states in the region has been founded and sustained for almost two decades. But far less institutionalization and political order has been evident during this period at the level of national society: many African countries have been experiencing internal political violence and some internal warfare. Insofar as our theoretical images follow rather than precede concrete historical change, it is evident that the recent national and international history of Black Africa challenges more than it supports some of the major postulates of international relations theory.

ENDNOTES

1 Max Weber, *The Theory of Social and Economic Organization*, ed., Talcott Parsons (New York: Free Press, 1964), p. 156.

2 Ibid., p. 155.

3 Ian Brownlie, *Principles of Public International Law*, 3d ed. (Oxford: Clarendon Press, 1979), pp. 73-76.

4 Ibid., p. 75.

5 See Giovanni Sartori, "Guidelines for Concept Analysis," in Sartori, ed., *Social Science Concepts: A Systematic Analysis* (forthcoming).

6 Brownlie (fn. 3), p. 75.

7 See Harry Eckstein's brilliant critique, "On the 'Science' of the State," in "The State," *Daedalus*, 108 (Fall 1979), 1-20.

8 Easton avoids the concept of the "state" in favor of that of the "political system"; see *The Political System: An Inquiry into the State of Political Science* (New York: Knopf, 1953), pp. 90-124.

9 Brownlie (fn. 3), p. 75.

10 Brownlie (fn. 3), p. 75; Weber (fn. 1), p. 156.

11 See Michael Oakeshott, "The Vocabulary of a Modern European State," *Political Studies*, 23 (June and September, 1977), 319-41, 409-14.

12 Clifford Geertz, "The Judging of Nations: Some Comments on the Assessment of Regimes in the

New States," *European Journal of Sociology*, 18 (no. 2, 1977), 252.

13 Ibid., p. 253.

14 There is a wealth of literature on military intervention in Africa. Two outstanding accounts are Samuel Decalo, *Coups and Army Rule in Africa: Studies in Military Style* (New Haven: Yale University Press, 1976), and Claude E. Welch, Jr., ed., *Soldier and State in Africa: A Comparative Analysis of Military Intervention and Political Change* (Evanston, Ill.: Northwestern University Press, 1970). Both have excellent bibliographies.

15 William Gutteridge, "Introduction," in Richard Booth, "The Armed Forces of African States, 1970," *Adelphi Papers*, No. 67 (London: International Institute for Strategic Studies, 1970), p. 4.

16 Gunnar Myrdal, *Asian Drama: An Inquiry into the Poverty of Nations* (New York: Twentieth Century Fund, 1968).

17 Julius Nyerere, *The Arusha Declaration Ten Years After* (Dar es Salaam: Government Printer, 1977), esp. chap. 3: "Our Mistakes and Failures," pp. 27-48.

18 Independence Day Speech of President Mobutu Sese Seko, July 1, 1977, typescript, translated from the French by James S. Coleman.

19 See *West Africa*, No. 3255 (December 3, 1979), 2224; and Ghislain C. Kabwit, "Zaire: The Roots of the Continuing Crisis," *Journal of Modern African Studies*, XVII (No. 3, 1979), 397-98.

20 Gutteridge (fn. 15), p. 1.

21 Ibid., p. 3.

22 Hedley Bull, *The Anarchical Society* (London: Macmillan, 1977), p. 34.

23 At the time of independence in 1960, British-governed Somaliland joined the Italian-administered trust territory to form the Somali Democratic Republic. In October 1961, the Federal Republic of Cameroon came into being, composed of East Cameroon (formerly a French Trust Territory) and West Cameroon (part of a former British Trust Territory). Independent Tanganyika joined with Zanzibar to form the United Republic of Tanzania in April 1964.

24 Quoted in Robert C. Good, "Changing Patterns of African International Relations," *American Political Science Review*, 58 (September 1964), 632.

25 Quoted in Ali A. Mazrui, *Towards a Pax Africana: A Study of Ideology and Ambition* (Chicago and London: University of Chicago Press, 1967), p. 12.

26 Martin Wight, "Why is there no International Theory?" in Herbert Butterfield and Martin Wight, eds., *Diplomatic Investigations* (London: George Allen & Unwin, 1966), p. 33.

27 Zdenek Cervenka, *The Organization of African Unity and its Charter* (New York and Washington: Praeger, 1969), p. 93.

28 Zdenek Cervenka, *The Unfinished Quest for Unity: Africa and the OAU* (New York: Africana Publishing Co., 1977), p. 65.

29 Peter Lyon, "New States and International Order," in Alan James, ed., *The Bases of International Order: Essays in Honour of C.A.W. Manning* (London: Oxford University Press, 1973), p. 47.

30 Charles Tilly, ed., *The Formation of National States in Western Europe* (Princeton: Princeton University Press, 1975), p. 46.

31 "Political Theory and International Relations," in Arnold Wolfers, *Discord and Collaboration: Essays on International Politics* (Baltimore and London: The Johns Hopkins University Press, 1965), pp. 239-40.

A: TERRITORIALITY, SOVEREIGNTY, AND NATIONALISM

The Paradoxes of Nationalism

Hans J. Morgenthau

The Western world faces in the universal triumph of nationalism some extraordinary paradoxes, pregnant with tragic irony. These paradoxes test its political imagination; they challenge its moral judgment; they put in jeopardy not only its own existence, but the survival of civilized life on this planet. Yet it was not the enemy of the West and of civilization that gave the idea of nationalism to the world. That idea, together with Marxism, is the last great original contribution the West has made to the political thought and practice of the world. What has become a threat to civilization, the West has claimed as a condition of civilized life. What has become a source of political anarchy and oppression, the West has offered as the principle of political order and freedom. With what has become a mockery of political morality, the West set out to establish political justice throughout the world.

The idea of nationalism, both in its historic origins and in the political functions it has performed, is intimately connected with the idea of freedom and shares the latter's ambiguity. Nationalism as a political phenomenon must be understood as the aspiration for two freedoms, one collective, the other individual: the freedom of a nation from domination by another nation and the freedom of the individual to join the nation of his choice.

As the aspiration of a collectivity to be free, nationalism originated in the sixteenth and seventeenth centuries from the struggles of the territorial state against its two enemies, one — the feudal order — resisting it, as it were, from below; the other — the imperial power — from above. Both, defeated in the dynastic and religious wars of the age, proved to be incapable of exerting the functions of government in the territories claimed by the territorial princes who, in turn, were able to impose their rule upon the feudal lords and free themselves from the rule of the emperor. Thus the territorial state emerged in the political form of dynastic sovereignty, the monarch being the highest secular authority within his territory.

Dynastic sovereignty found its philosophic justification in its ability to defend the territory under its control against enemies from without and disorder from within. Bodin in the sixteenth century and Leibniz in the eighteenth justified the absolute monarchy in these terms. It remained unchallenged both in theory and practice as long as it met this test in actual performance. Yet when in 1791 the King of France appeared to be plotting

Hans J. Morgenthau, "The Paradoxes of Nationalism," *Yale Review*, 46 (June 1957), 481-91.

with foreign monarchs against his country, the absolute monarchy failed the test as defender of the nation and its territory. First in practice and then in theory, the nation itself was called upon to defend its freedom. Thus nationalism as the collective expression of a nation's political identity was born.

That birth coincided with, and was really an integral part of, the triumph of individual liberty within France. The absolute monarchy was destroyed because it had betrayed the nation abroad and oppressed the individual at home. It left the stage of history as a defeated enemy of both individual and collective freedom. Individual freedom was taken as a precondition of national freedom and the latter, in turn, was regarded as a mere extension of the former to the international scene. The political and legal principles, originally formulated to support and guarantee the freedom of the individual, were applied to the nation. The nation came to be regarded as a kind of collective personality with peculiar characteristics and inalienable rights of its own; and the typically liberal antithesis between individual freedom and feudalistic oppression was transferred to the nation where it was duplicated in the hostility between the national aspirations and the feudal state. The nation should be free from oppression, both from within and from without. Free nations had only one enemy, and he was common to all of them: the dynastic oppressor of their freedom, individual and collective.

Given these assumptions, there could be no enmity among free nations who were united in a solidarity of individual and collective self-interest against the enemies of anybody's freedom. The popular will should decide how and by whom the people were to be governed, and the determination of the state to which a people was to belong was part of this decision. Thus the principle of national self-determination fulfills the postulates of both democracy and nationalism.

The practical political consequences of this new philosophy of nationalism, merging the ideas of individual and collective liberty, were immediate and striking. The Decree of Armed Propaganda of November 12, 1792, proclaimed: "The National Convention declares in the name of the French nation that it shall accord fraternity and aid to all peoples who want to recover their liberty, and charges the executive power with giving to the generals the orders necessary to bring aid to those peoples and to defend the citizens who are or might be persecuted for the cause of liberty." Napoleon conquered Europe in the name of this principle, destroying in the process more than two hundred dynastic sovereignties which were incapable of effective defense and disqualified from ruling in the name of their subjects.

In the struggle, dominating the better part of the nineteenth century, for the national unification of Germany and Italy and the national liberation of the Balkan nations from Turkish rule, the causes of national unity and freedom from oppression merged, for the liberal champions of nationalism as well as for their dynastic enemies. While the German liberals cried, "Through unity to liberty," Mazzini's flag of 1831 bore on one side the words, "Unity and Independence," on the other "Liberty, Equality, Humanity." Metternich's policies, on the other hand, were opposed to the national movements as a manifestation of democratic tendencies. The foreign policy of Napoleon III, who favored the national movements because he saw, according to his Foreign Minister, "a real equilibrium only in the satisfied wishes of the nations of Europe," was ironically called "the diplomacy of universal suffrage."

The First World War seemed to confirm, rather than deny, the assumptions and expectations of nationalism; for was it not caused by the unfulfilled aspirations of the nationalities of the Austro-Hungarian Empire? Thus the Western alliance fought the war in the name of national self-determination, and Germany turned the same weapon against Russia. The result was a peace settlement that reflected to a very high degree the principle of national self-determination. Austria-Hungary and Western Russia were dissolved into their national components, and the new frontiers of Germany followed in good measure the will of the populations concerned, which was either obvious, as in Alsace-Lorraine, or was determined by internationally supervised plebiscites, as in Silesia.

Yet that triumph of the principles of nationalism did not bring a viable order to Central and Eastern Europe. Nor did it bring justice to the populations concerned; it rather made the oppressors and oppressed exchange their roles. Thus what appeared at the time as the consummation of the expectations of nineteenth-century nationalism — peace, order, and justice built on the satisfaction of national aspirations — turned into its first great moral and political crisis. That crisis revealed the insufficient, self-contradictory, and self-defeating nature of nationalism as the exclusive principle of international order and justice and its inevitable subordination in fact, and requisite subordination in theory, to an overriding political system.

Nationalism, taken by itself, is both in logic and experience a principle of disintegration and fragmentation, which is prevented from issuing in anarchy not by its own logic but by the political power which either puts a halt to its realization at a certain point, as did the peace settlement of 1919, or else uses it for its purposes up to a certain point, as did the unifiers of Germany and Italy in the nineteenth century. There are no inherent limits to the application of the principles of nationalism. If the peoples of Bulgaria, Greece, and Serbia could invoke these principles against Turkey, why could not the people of Macedonia invoke them against Bulgaria, Greece, and Serbia? If it was right for the Czechs and Slovaks to free themselves in the name of nationalism from Austrian rule, it could not be wrong for the Slovaks and Sudeten Germans to free themselves from Czech rule in the name of the self same principle. Poland, the very moment she had recovered her national identity from Austrian, German, and Russian rule, felt she had to defend it against the German, Ukrainian, and White Russian minorities within her borders, comprising one-third of her total population. Thus yesterday's oppressed cannot help becoming the oppressors of today because they are afraid lest they be again oppressed tomorrow. Hence, the process of national liberation must stop at some point, and that point is determined not by the logic of nationalism, but by the configurations of interest and power between the rulers and the ruled and between competing nations.

This paradox of B invoking the principles of nationalism against A and denying them to C — both for the sake of his own survival — is accentuated by the practical impossibility of applying these principles consistently to mixed populations. The individual's rights to his property and pursuit of happiness become incompatible with his right to choose his government according to his national preferences when he is a member of a minority which is inextricably intermingled with the majority controlling the government. Not being able to enjoy both rights simultaneously, he must sacrifice one or the other. The treaties for the protection of minorities, to which Bulgaria, Montenegro, Rumania, and Serbia were subjected in 1878 and Czechoslovakia, Poland, and Rumania in 1919, tried to mitigate the dilemma by protecting certain minorities in the enjoyment of a free national life at least in certain fields, such as language, schools, religion.

However, such attempts were largely frustrated by the fact, which constitutes the second manifestation of the crisis of nationalism in the interwar period, that the conflicts between the new national states and their minorities were more intimately interwoven than ever before with the international conflicts among the new nation states and the great powers. This had always been the case within certain limits; Russia, for instance, had always supported the Balkan nations against Turkey and the Czechs and Serbs against Austria-Hungary. Yet as in the interwar period the new nation states competed with each other for power and were at the same time the pawns of the great powers in their struggle for hegemony, the national minorities became to an ever increasing extent, as it were, sub-pawns whose aspirations and grievances the contestants used to strengthen themselves and their friends and weaken their enemies.

All of Central and Eastern Europe from the Baltic to the Mediterranean became the stage for continuous interconnected and overlapping rivalries and conflicts: Poland vs. Lithuania, Czechoslovakia vs. Poland, Hungary vs. Rumania, Bulgaria vs. Greece, Italy vs. Yugoslavia, Germany vs. Poland, and, overshadowing them all, the decline of France, the rise of Germany, the indecision of Britain, and the ever-present threat of the Soviet Union. The instability which from 1878 to 1914 had been confined to the Balkans, always threatening and in the end destroying the peace of Europe, now extended to all of Central and Eastern Europe, for the same causes and with the same results. As the fragmentation of the European part of the Turkish Empire into its national components brought forth the "Balkanization" of the Balkans, so did the fragmentation of the Austro-Hungarian and the Western part of the Russian Empires lead to the Balkanization of that part of Europe. And while the First World War arose from the threat of Serb nationalism to Austria-Hungary, the Second World War became inevitable when Germany succeeded in using the German minority to destroy Czechoslovakia and was started on the pretext that the German minority needed protection against the government of Poland.

Nationalism, far from creating a juster and more viable international order, became the great disruptive and anarchical force of the interwar period. Into the severed members of the empires it shattered, nationalism poured the same passions which, first, as lust for power had created these empires and, then, as aspiration for freedom had destroyed them. The endemic disorder thus created cried out for a "new order," which only the strong could make and maintain. Germany and Russia, the new empire builders, saw their opportunity, and in a series of swift and effective strokes, starting in 1938 and ending in 1941, they seized the new nation states of Central and Eastern Europe, endeavoring to melt them down into new structures of empire.

It is another of the paradoxes of nationalism that its defeat on the eve of the Second World War was achieved in the name of the same principle which brought it victory in the aftermath of the First: national self-determination. Germany justified its use of the German minorities of Czechoslovakia and Poland for the destruction of these nation states with the same principle of national self-determination with which before the Czech, Slovak, and Polish nationalities had justified their attack upon, and destruction of, the Austro-Hungarian Empire. Yet while the words were the same, the passions behind them and the philosophy which roused and justified them were different not only in degree but in kind. The nationalism with which Nazi Germany and the Soviet Union set out to conquer the world has only the name in common with the nationalism of the nineteenth century and the first three decades of the twentieth.

The libertarian goals of the older nationalism were the rightful possession of all nations who wanted to be free; the world had room for as many nationalisms as there were nations that wanted to establish or preserve a state of their own. The international conflicts growing out of this nationalism were of two kinds: conflicts between a nationality and an alien master and conflicts between different nations over the delimitation of their respective boundaries. The issue at stake was either the application of the principles of nationalism or else its interpretation.

The new nationalism has only one thing in common with the old: the nation is the ultimate point of reference for political loyalties and actions. But here the similarity ends. For the old nationalism, the nation is the ultimate goal of political action, the end point of the political development beyond which there are other nationalisms with similar and equally justifiable goals. For the new nationalism, the nation is but the starting point of a universal mission whose ultimate goal reaches to the confines of the political world. While the old nationalism seeks one nation in one state and nothing else, the new one claims for one nation and one state the right to impose its own values and standards of action upon all the other nations.

The new nationalism is in truth a political religion, a nationalistic universalism which identifies the standards and goals of a particular nation with the principles that govern the universe. The few remaining nations of the first rank no longer oppose each other within a framework of shared beliefs and common values which impose effective limitations upon the means and ends of their policies. Rather they oppose each other now as the standard-bearers of moral systems, each of them of national origin and each of them claiming to provide universal moral standards which all the other nations ought to accept. The moral code of one nation flings the challenge of its universal claim into the face of another, which reciprocates in kind.

This transformation of nationalism was foreshadowed by the Napoleonic Wars and the First World War. The Napoleonic Wars were fought in the name of particular principles claiming universal validity: here the principles of the French Revolution, there the principle of legitimacy. For the West, the First World War transformed itself with the intervention of the United States into a crusade "to make the world safe for democracy." "It is our inestimable privilege," said Woodrow Wilson in his Fourth-of-July speech of 1918, "to concert with men out of every nation who shall make not only the liberties of America secure but the liberties of every other people as well." A few months after the democratic crusade had got underway, in October, 1917, the foundations were laid in Russia for another moral and political structure that, while accepted by only a fraction of humanity, also claimed to provide the common roof under which all humankind would eventually live together in justice and in peace.

This well-nigh universal commitment to the principles of nationalism revealed a profound difference between the attitude of the Western democracies and that of their totalitarian enemies. That difference was to have far-reaching moral and political consequences. The West had come to see in the principles of nationalism the revelation of universal truth to be lived up to regardless of political consequences. Totalitarianism looked at those principles as political tools to be used if their use promised results, to be discarded otherwise. Hitler did not hesitate to sacrifice the Germans of Northern Italy for the friendship of Mussolini by transferring the majority of them to Germany. The nationalities policy of the Soviet Union, while committed in theory to national autonomy, has been at the service of the political and economic interests of the central government which, as the instrument of "democratic centralism," has manipulated, controlled, and destroyed their national life without regard to principles of any kind.

Yet when totalitarianism turned the principles of nationalism against the West, the West stood morally and intellectually disarmed. The totalitarian arguments being its own, it could not answer them. The West had welcomed the victory of national self-determination in the aftermath of the First World War on moral and political grounds, and it found itself now incapable, when Hitler used the German minority for the destruction of Czechoslovakia, of defending its interests against its principles. It even lent a helping hand to its defeat and congratulated itself upon its moral consistency. "Self-determination, the professed principle of the Treaty of Versailles, has been invoked by Herr Hitler against its written text, and his appeal has been allowed," wrote the London "Times" on September 28, 1938, commenting upon the Munich settlement.

The Second World War and the Cold War following it have both qualitatively and quantitatively magnified the paradoxes of nationalism which the interwar period had brought to the fore, and they have added a new one which has made nationalism altogether obsolete as a principle of political organization. The new fact that has created that new paradox is the feasibility of all-out atomic war.

The justification of the nation state, as of all political organization, is its ability to perform the functions for the sake of which political organization exists. The most elementary of these functions is the common defense of the life of the citizens and of the values of the civilization in which they live. A political organization which is no longer able to defend these values and even puts them in jeopardy must yield, either through peaceful transformation or violent destruction, to one capable of that defense. Thus, under the impact of the invention of gunpowder and of the first industrial revolution, the feudal order had to yield to the dynastic and the nation state. Under the technological conditions of the pre-atomic age, the stronger nation states could, as it were, erect a wall behind which their citizens could live secure and the weak nation states were similarly protected by the operation of the balance of power which added the resources of the strong to those of the weak. Thus under normal conditions no nation state was able to make more than marginal inroads upon the life and civilization of its neighbors.

The feasibility of all-out atomic war has completely destroyed this protective function of the nation state. No nation state is capable of protecting its citizens and its civilization against an all-out atomic attack. Its safety rests solely in preventing such an attack from taking place. While in the pre-atomic age a nation state could count upon its physical ability to defend itself, in the atomic age it must rely upon its psychological ability to deter those who are physically able to destroy it. The prospective enemy must be induced to refrain from attacking; once he attacks, the victim is doomed.

This psychological mechanism of deterrence operates only on the condition that the prospective atomic aggressor is clearly identified beforehand, that is, that no more than two nations are capable of waging all-out atomic war; for it is only on this condition that deterrence operates with automatic certainty. Today, the Soviet Union knows that if it should attack the United States with atomic weapons, the United States would destroy it, and vice versa; that certainty deters both. Yet the time is close at hand when other nations will have the weapons with which to wage all-out atomic war. When that time has come, nations will have lost even the preventive capacity of psychological deterrence, which they still possess today. For the United States, if then attacked with atomic weapons, will no longer be able to identify the aggressor with certainty and, hence, deter the prospective aggressor with the certainty of retaliation. When this historic moment comes — as it surely must if the present trend is not reversed — the nation state will connote not life and civilization, but anarchy and universal destruction.

It is in the shadow of this grim reality and grimmer prospect that the inherent paradoxes of nationalism have taken on a novel urgency, threatening to overwhelm the remnants of international order. Balkanization, demoralization, and barbarization on a world-wide scale are the result....

B: POWER, CAPABILITIES, AND THE USE OF FORCE

Capabilities and Control in an Interdependent World

James N. Rosenau

In pondering the changing nature of "national power," two recent but contradictory examples come to mind as indicative of profound changes occurring in the nature and dynamics of whatever it is we mean when we refer to the "power" of nations. One example is the "failure" of American "power" in Vietnam. The other is the "success" of Arab "power" in the 1973-74 oil embargo. What kind of changes these examples indicate, however, is obscure. Do they suggest that military "power" has diminished (hence the Vietnam failure) and that economic "power" has become more effective (hence the oil embargo success)? Do they point up the increasing variability of "power" considerations? Do they suggest that generalized characterizations of national "power" are no longer reasonable? Or do they highlight the limitations of the "power" concept, suggesting once again that it is a concept without meaningful content and with misleading connotations?

If the last question is addressed first and the parameters of the concept precisely delineated, all four of these questions can be answered in the affirmative. Such is the thrust of the ensuing pages. The ambiguous and misleading uses of the "power" concept are set forth at the outset and an alternative formulation outlined. The latter is then applied to the changing nature of world politics, to the evolution of economic and other new, nonmilitary types of issues, and to the implications of these issues for the nature of national "power."

THE "POWER" CONCEPT AND ITS LIMITATIONS

To stress that conventional usage of the "power" concept results in misleading ambiguities is not in any way to deny that profound changes have occurred in world politics and that these have greatly altered the dynamics whereby nations employ their "power" to pursue and achieve their foreign policy goals. The changes are independent of the way in which the concept is formulated. Appreciation of their scope and direction, however, becomes difficult if they are traced with imprecise and obfuscating conceptual equipment. Vietnam and the oil embargo can thus be seen as illustrative of both substantive change and conceptual disarray.

Stated differently, the *surprises* that attended the inability of the "mighty" United States to

---

James N. Rosenau, "Capabilities and Control in an Interdependent World," *International Security*, Vol. 1 (Fall 1976), pp. 32-49. Reprinted by permission of the MIT Press Journals. Some footnotes have been removed; those remaining have been renumbered.

prevail in Vietnam and the ability of the "weak" Arab states to induce altered postures in the industrial world regarding their conflict with Israel are but the most recent and dramatic examples supporting a long-standing conviction that the concept of national "power" confounds and undermines sound analysis. Little is accomplished by explaining the surprising quality of these events in terms of the changing nature of "power." Such an explanation merely asserts that surprising events occurred because unrecognized changes had transpired in whatever may have been the sources of the events. Likewise, to stress that military "power" has given way to economic "power" is not to enlarge comprehension of *why* American policies in Vietnam and the Arab oil embargo had such contradictory outcomes. Had the conventional usage of the concept of "power" been more precise, with its empirical referents more accurately identified, there would have been no surprise with respect to Vietnam and the embargo. Indeed, conceivably neither the war in the former nor the crisis surrounding the latter would have occurred if officials had more clearly grasped the "power" concept and disaggregated it into its component parts at the time policies toward these situations were evolving.

The two examples clearly highlight the central problem with the concept because they both suggest that the success or failure of foreign policy efforts is dependent on the possession of appropriate resources in sufficient abundance to prevail in conflict situations. So viewed, the United States "failed" in Vietnam because it lacked the requisite military resources and Middle East countries "succeeded" because they had sufficient economic resources. Nothing could be more misleading. Such an interpretation overlooks the equally crucial facts that while the North Vietnamese were not overly impressed by American military resources, the Western industrial nations were impressed by the oil which Middle East states could or could not make available.

Possessed resources, in other words, are only one aspect of "power"; actions and reactions through which actors relate to each other are another aspect, and neither aspect is alone sufficient. Put even more pointedly, whatever else it may connote, national "power" involves relational phenomena. Whether it be considered in the bipolar period when military considerations predominated, or whether it be assessed in the present era when economic and transnational factors are more salient, national "power" can only be understood in the context of how the actors involved relate to and perceive each other. The resources each "possesses" may well be relevant to the way in which they perceive each other, but the outcome of the way in which they exercise "power" toward each other is primarily a consequence of how they assess, accept, resist, or modify each other's efforts.

Stated in still another way, the "power" of a nation exists and is subject to meaningful assessment only insofar as it is directed at and responded to by other actors. All the possessed dimensions of "power" imaginable will not have the anticipated and seemingly logical outcomes if those toward whom they are directed perceive the possessions otherwise and thereby withhold the expected compliance. This is perhaps the prime lesson of both the Vietnam War and the oil embargo, the lesson that renders the two seemingly diverse situations highly comparable.

Unfortunately, for reasons having to do with the structure of language, the concept of "power" does *not* lend itself to comprehension in relational terms. Without undue violation of language, the world "power" cannot be used as a verb. It is rather a noun, highlighting "things" possessed instead of processes of interaction. Nations influence each other; they exercise control over each other; they alter, maintain, subvert, enhance, deter, or otherwise affect each other, but they do not "powerize" each other. Hence, no matter how sensitive analysts may be to the question of how the resources used by one actor serve to modify or preserve the behavior of another, once they cast their assessment in terms of the "power" employed they are led — if not inevitably, then almost invariably — to focus on the resources themselves rather than on the relationship they may or may not underlie.

The tendency of the concept of "power" to focus attention on possessed qualities is clearly illustrated by the pervasive inclination to rank states in terms of their "power" as defined by these attributes. Indeed, analyzing the attributes and resources of states in such as way as to classify some as superpowers, some as great powers, others as regional or middle powers, and still others as small powers is the standard approach to the concept. Nor have changes on the world scene altered this conventional treatment of the concept. Most analysts tend to account for the changes by assessing how they affect the mix of attributes and resources states possess and then derive conclusions as to whether, say, the United States is still number one, whether China has moved ahead of Western Europe and Japan as number three, and whether all of these plus the Soviet Union form a world of five superpowers that has come to replace the bipolar world of the postwar era.[1]

There is a remarkable paradox in the compulsion to analyze world affairs in terms of rankings of relative strengths and weaknesses. As students of international politics we are primarily interested in what states do or do not get each other to do, and yet we are diverted from concentrating on such relational phenomena by our reliance on a concept that focuses on the secondary question of their attributes and resources.

This is not to say, of course, that the attributes and resources that states bring to bear in their foreign relations are irrelevant. The "power" they possess underlies their officials' estimates of what can and cannot be accomplished abroad, just as the estimates made by those toward whom their actions are directed depend on calculations of the attributes and resources that may be operative. Furthermore, no matter how the possessed or deficient resources may be perceived and assessed, they are likely to shape what happens when states interact with each other. The more a state possesses the attributes and resources appropriate to its goals in a situation, the more its actions are likely to move it toward the objectives sought. So "national power" can have some predictive and analytic value *if* it is estimated in the context of its appropriateness to situations — but to add this condition is to highlight again the significance of relational phenomena. For estimates of how one or another "power" factor may be appropriate to a given situation requires attention to the resources, expectations, and likely responses of other parties to the situation.

How, then, to focus on both the possession and interaction dimensions of "power" without being driven by the structure of language to an overriding preoccupation with the former dimension? My answer to this question is simple, though its simplicity should not be allowed to obscure the degree to which it reduced ambiguity and allows us to concentrate on the prime questions that concern us. For years I have solved this conceptual problem by dropping the word "power" from my analytic vocabulary (thus the use here of quotation marks), replacing it with the concept of capabilities whenever reference is made to attributes or resources possessed and with verbs such as control or influence whenever the relational dimension of "power" is subjected to analysis.

This disaggregation of the "power" concept virtually compels analysts to keep their eyes on the interaction phenomena primarily of interest to them because any assessments they may make of existing or potential resources and attributes are bound to be manifestly incomplete and insufficient. Their conceptual equipment will necessitate that they inquire into how the assessed resources and attributes may or may not contribute to the control of desired outcomes or otherwise influence the attitudes and behaviors of other actors. Stated differently, modifying or preserving events and trends abroad — i.e., controlling them — depends on a wide range of variables, only some of which involve the resources and attributes of the parties to the control relationship; disaggregation of the "power" concept facilitates consideration of the full range of these variables.

Another important virtue of this disaggregated approach is that it facilitates concentration on the capabilities of governments to engage in cooperative action abroad. For historical reasons stemming from the independence of states in the international system, the "power" concept has come to have conflictual connotations. "Power" is ordinarily conceived to be applied *against* potential adversaries or any obstacles that block the path to goal achievement. It is not normally viewed as embracing resources and attributes that are employed *for* the realization of objectives through concerting efforts with other states. Consequently, analysts have long had the tendency to conceive of "power" in military terms, military action being the last resort through which states seek to maintain their independence. Yet, as elaborated below, world politics is increasingly marked by interdependence, by new issues that cannot be addressed or resolved through the threat or use of military capabilities and that instead require cooperation among states if obstacles to goals are to be diminished or eliminated. In addition to the maintenance of physical security and territorial integrity, national "power" today must be exercised with respect to the problems of oceans, exchange rates, pollution, agricultural production, population size, energy allocation, and the many other issues fostered by mounting interdependence. The distinction between capabilities and control, being free of long-standing conflictful connotations, should facilitate more cogent analysis of the role states play in resolving (or sustaining) these issues. At least the distinction should allow for a fuller treatment of those organizational skills and knowledge bases from which spring the dynamics of these newer issues than would be the case if analysts relied on the undifferentiated "power" concept.

To be sure, many of those who are accustomed to the "power" concept stress that they have in mind a broad range of factors that extend well beyond military capabilities. And, indeed, frequently the concept is formulated in ways to include national morale, societal cohesion, leadership development, and many of the other intangible attributes and resources that underlie the foreign policy efforts of states. Even the more sophisticated formulations, however, frequently succumb to the historical tendency associated with the "power" concept and analyze non-military capabilities as if they were designed only to serve conflictual purposes. It is no accident, for example, that the problems of monetary stability, devaluations, and exchange rates are frequently cast as problems of "economic warfare." And surely it is a measure of the extent to which the "power" concept habitually provokes military and conflictual connotations that when the problem of agricultural production and distribution is treated in the context of national "power," it is typically conceived as a "food-as-a-weapon" issue.

THE NARROWING SCOPE OF MILITARY CAPABILITIES

None of the foregoing is to say that military capabilities are no longer available to statesmen or that they have become unwilling to use force as a means of controlling circumstances abroad. To stress mounting interdependence and the emergence of new issues is not to deny that arms races mark the world scene, that weapons production and sales is a global industry, that threats by states to use force are an almost daily occurrence, or that all too frequently states seek to control outcomes by resorting to their military capabilities. Rather it is to say that for a variety of reasons, all of which sum to greater complexity within states and greater interdependence among them, the range through which military capabilities can achieve effective control has narrowed substantially in recent decades and that, consequently, a host of new types of abilities have become increasingly relevant if states are to maintain any control over their environments. Stated in conventional terms, "national power" is today far more multifaceted than ever before.

It is important to appreciate that the narrowing scope of military capabilities is not simply a function of the advent of nuclear weapons and the deterrence systems they have spawned. The ever-present possibility of a nuclear holocaust has made officials more cautious in their readiness to resort to military instruments of statecraft. This caution is especially acute among those who preside over the foreign policies of superpowers, but it probably has also increased among officials of non-nuclear powers in the sense of a heightened sensitivity to avoiding military actions that could escalate to superpower involvement and the subsequent introduction of nuclear weapons.

The advent of the nuclear age, however, is only one reason why military capabilities have declined in relative importance. A seemingly much more crucial reason derives from the many ways in which an ever more dynamic technology and ever growing demands on the world's resources have shrunk the geographic, social, economic, and political distances that separate states and vastly multiplied the points at which their needs, interests, ideas, products, organizations, and publics overlap. Quite aside from the activities of governments, what happens within states would appear to have wider and wider ramifications across their boundaries and these proliferating ramifications have created, in turn, an ever-widening set of external control (i.e., foreign policy) problems for governments. The more societies, cultures, economies, and polities become interdependent, the less do the resulting conflicts lend themselves to resolution through military threats and actions. The threat and use of force is maximally effective, to the extent it is effective at all, when control over territory or compliance with the exercise of authority is at stake. But the new problems of interdependence involve attitudinal and behavioral patterns that have few, if any, territorial or legitimacy dimensions.

To modify or preserve these patterns governments must rely on much more variable and subtle means of control — means which are as complex and technical as the social, cultural, scientific, and economic dimensions out of which the patterns emerged and through which they are sustained. Military forms of control are most applicable in situations where issues cannot be split, refined, or redefined — where compliance gets cast in either/or terms — whereas the newer issues of interdependence are pervaded with so many nuances and subparts that control can be exercised only with respect to limited areas of behavior and can result in compliance that is not likely to be more than partial and incremental.

The narrowing scope of military capabilities can be readily illustrated by some hypothetical situations that once might have seemed logical but that appear patently absurd today. Imagine, for example, one state threatening a resort to force if another did not comply with its demand for a currency devaluation. Or consider the likelihood of two neighboring states going to war over a question of pollutants that flow downstream or downwind across their common borders. Compliance with demands in such situations is clearly likely to result from complex bargaining and the very absurdity of seeking to control them through the use or threat of force is a measure of the degree to which interdependence has fragmented the issues that comprise world politics today. Indeed, one does not have to resort to hypothetical situations to make this point. It will be recalled that during the height of the dislocation that accompanied the Arab oil embargo several analysts proposed that the West threaten, and possibly even undertake, military action in order to sustain the flow of oil from the region if a lifting of the embargo failed to occur.[2] This proposal involved control efforts so manifestly inappropriate to the situation that it failed to generate much support in or out of governmental circles.

Since it also bears on the problem of employing capabilities relevant to maximizing control over the newer issues generated by mounting interdependence, one other reason why military capabilities have become more narrowly circumscribed needs to be noted. It involves the greater self-consciousness of ethnic, racial, linguistic, and other subgroups within nation-states, a sense of identity that has led such groups to become increasingly coherent, articulate, and demanding. Few states are so homogeneous as to have avoided the contention and fragmentation inherent in the world-wide process through which subnational loyalties have come to rival, if not to replace, those directed toward national states. While it may well be that these disintegrative tendencies are both a source and a consequence of interdependence — in the sense that the proliferation of transnational relationships both stems from and contributes to heightened subgroup consciousness — one clearly discernible result of the dispersal of loyalties is that national governments are no longer as capable as they once were of mobilizing the kind of unquestioning support that is necessary for effective military operations. The American effort to effect control in Vietnam, resisted by subnational groups within the United States, not to mention the enormous mobilization problems encountered by the South Vietnamese in Vietnam, is but the most recent example of how the disenchantment of subgroups and their ties abroad have reduced the scope of military instruments available to most states.

Indeed, the declining capacity of national governments to govern is not confined to foreign military undertakings. For most, if not all, governments the decline spans an entire range of issue-areas, both domestic and foreign. The greater internal division, the persistence of severe economic dislocations, the continued depletion of resources, the emergence of interdependence issues that cannot be resolved through unilateral action, the increased competence of transnational actors — these are but a few of the many developments that have resulted in governmental performances that fall short of aspirations and that further diminish the public support most governments once enjoyed. As will be seen, this generalized diminution of the capacity to mobilize domestic support is no less central to the handling of the newer nonmilitary problems of interdependence than to the traditional issues of national security.

THE STRUCTURE OF INTERDEPENDENCE ISSUES

If, as indicated earlier, the newer issues of world politics are unlike those involving military security and do not consist primarily of territorial and legitimacy dimensions, what are their main characteristics? In the answer to this question lies the basis for assessing the changing nature of "national power." Four characteristics seem salient as central features of all the diverse issues of interdependence, from those involving monetary stability to those associated with food-population ratios, from the uses of the ocean to the abuses of the atmosphere, from the discovery and distribution of new energy sources to the redirection of trade and the reallocation of wealth. Perhaps the most persuasive characteristic of all such issues is the large degree to which they encompass highly complex and technical phenomena. To grasp how food production can be increased, ocean bottoms utilized, pollutants eliminated, and solar energy exploited is to acquire mastery over physical and biological processes that involve an extraordinary range of subprocesses, the interaction of which is not easily understood, much less easily controlled. To grasp how monetary stability can be maintained, population growth reduced, and wealth reallocated is to achieve comprehension of social, cultural, and economic processes that are equally complex and no less difficult to control. Most of these issues of interdependence, moreover, overlap so thoroughly that proposed solutions to any of them have important ramifications for the others, thereby further complicating their highly technical character.

Quite aside from the politics of coping with these new kinds of issues, their structures and contents require new kinds of advanced scientific and social scientific knowledge and expertise if efforts to control them are to be undertaken and minimally successful. It is hardly an exaggeration to assert that what weapons and troops are to the traditional problems of national security, so are scientific knowledge and technological sophistication to the newer dimensions of security.

A second major characteristic of interdependence issues is the large degree to which many of them encompass a great number of nongovernmental actors whose actions are relevant to issue management. This decentralized character of most interdependence issues is in sharp contrast to the conventional foreign policy situation — such as a treaty negotiation or a severance of diplomatic relations — in which the course of events is shaped largely by choices that government officials make. Indeed, virtually by definition an interdependence issue involves the overlap of many lives, so much so that the unfolding of the issue depends on decisions (or lack of decisions) made by countless individuals, none of whom is necessarily aware of what others have decided (or not decided). The actions of innumerable farmers, for example, are central to the problem of increased food production, just as many pollution issues depend on choices made by vast numbers of producers, energy conservation on millions of consumers, and population growth on tens of millions of potential parents. To be sure, governmental choices and actions can influence whether the decisions made by the multitude of persons encompassed by such issues are consistent and appropriate — which is precisely why the mobilization of domestic support has become increasingly relevant to foreign affairs. But the very fact of such decentralization renders the handling of interdependence issues very different from the standard means of framing and implementing foreign policy.[3]

A third major feature of interdependence issues arises out of the combination of their decentralized structure and the technical knowledge on which they rest. These two variables interact in such a way as to fragment the governmental decision-making process through which such issues are considered. More precisely, in the United States and other industrial societies with large public bureaucracies the link between most such issues and particular clienteles among the citizenry endows the governmental agencies and sub-agencies responsible for tending to the welfare of the relevant clientele with unusual degrees of authority and political clout. And this clout is further augmented by the fact that such agencies tend to acquire a governmental monopoly of the technical expertise needed to cope with the issues in their jurisdiction. Hence in the American case, for example, units of the Treasury Department tend to carry the day on monetary issues and bureaus within the Agriculture Department tend to monopolize decision making on questions pertaining to the production and distribution of various foodstuffs. Whenever an issue draws on several expertises, of course, the fragmented authority that has evolved with respect to it leads to especially intense bureaucratic wrangling, or at least to the need for elaborate interdepartmental committees to handle it.

In either event, whether an issue is processed by a single bureaucratic unit or by several subunits, a main consequence of the dispersed expertise is to diminish the capacity of top officials to maintain control over it. Whereas the traditional issues of foreign and military policy are founded on nationwide constituencies and can be managed by heads of state and prime ministers through their foreign offices and military establishments, interdependence issues render the politically responsible leadership much more subject to the advice, direction, contradictions, and compromises that emanate from a fragmented bureaucratic structure. They normally do not have the time or expertise to master the knowledge necessary to grasp fully such issues and ordinarily they lack the political fortitude to resist, much less reject, the pressures from the special clienteles that seek to be served by the issues. The role of expertise, of whether the expert is on tap or on top, has long been a problem in the military area,[4] but this problem is miniscule in comparison to the place which scientists, engineers, agricultural economists, demographers, biologists, and many other types of experts have come to assume in the newer issues of interdependence.[5]

Allusion has already been made to a fourth structural characteristic of all interdependence issues that appears to have major consequences for the changing nature of capabilities and control, namely, the large extent to which the management and amelioration, if not the resolution, of such issues requires multilateral cooperation among governments. Any issue is, by definition, founded on conflict, but issues can differ considerably in the degree to which the conflicts that sustain them can be isolated, contained, or otherwise managed unilaterally by governments. The conventional diplomatic and strategic issues of foreign policy, springing as they do from conflicts over territory and legitimate authority, can often be pressed, resisted, or ignored by a government without concurrence by other governments. Hard bargaining and negotiating concessions may follow from the positions which a government adopts on such matters, but these can be broken off, suspended, or otherwise limited — and the issues thereby left unmanaged — if the government finds it expedient to do so. The newer issues of interdependence, on the other hand, do not lend themselves so readily to unilateral action. Many of them spring from conflicts over the uses and abuses of the natural environment — the air (e.g., pollution), the land (e.g., food productivity), the water (e.g., ocean resources) — which do not conform to political boundaries and which most governments can thus neither dismiss nor handle on their own. Instead agreements among governments must be developed even as each presses positions that best serve its own interests. Such is the nature of interdependence issues, be they conflicts over the natural or the socioeconomic environment. Defiance, avoidance, rejection, and other forms of conflict behavior can be temporarily employed for tactical advantage, but the interdependence will not disappear nor will the issues it spawns be contained. Eventually knowledge has to be exchanged and some form of agreement achieved among those states interdependently linked by their shared reliance on the same environment.

The international monetary policy of the United States during John Connally's term as Secretary of the Treasury from 1970 to 1972 illustrates the limits of such strategy. It will be recalled that Connally took a defiant and uncompromising stance toward other states in order to win concessions in the restructuring of the international economic system. The instability of the existing economic order, however, persisted and the United States soon felt compelled to turn to a more accommodative posture. Perhaps an even better example of the way in which interdependence issues tip the balance in the direction of cooperative behavior is provided by the Organization of Petroleum Exporting Countries (OPEC). The members of that organization may have many differences over oil-pricing policies, but they must — and do — bury some of these in order to render OPEC more effective and thereby achieve their individual goals through collective action.

CAPABILITIES AND CONTROL IN AN INTERDEPENDENT WORLD

Given the narrowed scope of military capabilities, the declining capacity of governments to mobilize domestic support, and the technical, decentralized, fragmented, and accommodative structure of interdependence issues, it is not difficult to trace substantial changes in the capabilities that states bring to world politics and the extent and manner of the control they can exercise over events and trends abroad. Indeed, the problem is one of limiting the analysis to the allotted space. An almost infinite number of changes can be identified, thus confining the ensuing discussion to only those changes that seem most profound and enduring.

Turning first to the transformations that are likely to occur (and may have already begun) in the control dimension of national "power," several nonmilitary techniques are available for foreign policy officials to use in their efforts to modify or preserve the patterns that comprise the newer issues of world politics. Bargaining over differences, trading issues off against each other, promises of future support, threats of future opposition, persuasion through appeals to common values, persuasion through the presentation of scientific proof — these are the prime control techniques through which the problems of interdependence must be addressed. They are, of course, as old as diplomacy itself, but they have taken on new meaning in the light of the decline of force as a viable technique and in view of the complex nature of the interdependence issues. In particular, the last two of these non military techniques seem destined to become ever more salient as instruments of statecraft. The inclination to rely on appeals to common values, with a corresponding diminution in the tendency to threaten reprisals, appears especially likely to emerge as central to the conduct of foreign affairs. The fact that interdependence issues cannot be handled unilaterally, that foreign policy officials must engage in a modicum of cooperation with counterparts abroad in order to ameliorate the situations on which such issues thrive, means that the rhetoric, as well as the substance, of control techniques must shift toward highlighting the common values that are at stake.

Nor is this rhetorical shift likely to be confined to the bargaining that occurs behind closed doors. The decline of a sense of national identity and the emergence of more pronounced subnational loyalties seem likely to impel foreign policy officials to refer more frequently to shared international values in their public pronouncements as well as their private negotiations. That is, appeals to national interest and loyalties seem likely to become less compelling as means of mobilizing domestic support, so that positions on interdependence issues will have to be sold internally in terms of their consistency with the aspirations of external parties to situations.

Resort to scientific proof is a second control technique that seems headed for much greater use in the years ahead. The complex and technical nature of most interdependence issues seems likely to lead officials to place heavy reliance on the data and knowledge they have gathered as they seek to persuade counterparts abroad of the soundness of their positions. To be sure, there has always been a knowledge component of sound diplomacy. Statesmen have long preferred to seek desired modifications of behavior abroad through rational argument before turning to coercive techniques of control. If goals can be advanced by persuading others of their inherent logic and validity, the costs of success are much less than is the case when the threat or use of force produces movement toward goals. Historically, however, the technical dimension of issues has not been so pervasive as it is in this era of interdependence, with the result that appeals founded on scientific proof were rarely controlling. Thus, despite their preferences, the practice of statesmen across centuries has been largely one of nonrational argumentation. But today's issues cannot be readily separated from their knowledge bases. To take positions on interdependence issues that ignore their technical and scientific underpinnings is to risk pursuit of counterproductive policies. Hence it seems highly probable that foreign policy officials will become increasingly inclined to achieve and maintain control through efforts to "prove" to adversaries and friends alike the validity of their positions.

This is not to say, of course, that the inherent logic and validity of data bearing on interdependence issues will necessarily, or even frequently, be persuasive and yield the desired modifications of behavior. Such issues are not free of values. They do not rest on an objective reality that speaks with a single and coherent voice to statesmen of all countries. One need only recall the persistent differences between industrial states and those in the Third World over the sources and dynamics of economic progress and dislocation to appreciate that the knowledge bases of even the most complex interdependence issues are subject to varying interpretations, depending on the perspectives and goals of policy-makers. Yet, although future statesmen may thus be prone to bring their knowledge bases into line with their policies rather than vice versa, and even though they are therefore likely to resist and counter "proofs" advanced by adversaries, these tendencies will probably become less and less pronounced as technical knowledge becomes ever more central to the conduct of foreign affairs. The inclination to proceed from and cling to scientific proof as a basis for negotiation would thus seem to be headed for much greater priority in the array of control techniques on which officials depend. And who knows, in more than a few instances perhaps the proofs will seem compelling and serve to modify attitudes and behavior that in the past could have been expected to remain unaffected by this form of control.

It must be stressed that these anticipated changes in the exercise of control are not posited as replacing the conventional practices of statecraft. To highlight tendencies toward greater appeals to shared values and greater reliance on scientific proof is not to herald the dawn of a new era in which rational discourse and harmony mark world affairs. The old issues of territorial jurisdiction and the scope of legitimate authority are not about to pass quickly from the scene and the conflicts and hard bargaining which they generate are not about to disappear suddenly as interdependence mounts. Rather the anticipated changes are seen as extensions of the art of statecraft, as broadening the mix through which officials seek to adapt to their external environments. Whether the long-run alterations in this mix will be sufficient to foster steady progress toward a more rational and orderly world can hardly be estimated at this time. The possibility of such progress is clearly inherent in the changing nature of control and the shifting capabilities of states (outlined below), but one ought not be so naive as to overlook the many variables that can perpetuate or deepen the differences among states and that can even encourage resort to nonrational techniques of control.

The advent and structure of interdependence issues also points to several important changes in the capabilities dimension of national "power." Again these changes are best viewed in the context of a new mix, of long-standing aspects of capabilities continuing to be crucial to the conduct of foreign affairs even as mounting interdependence has made other, previously peripheral aspects relatively more significant. The fertility of the soil, the minerals and other resources possessed, the configurations of geography, the size and skills of populations, the breadth and equipment of the military establishment — these are but a few of the attributes that continue to differentiate the strong from the weak and to shape the extent and direction of the control that states can exercise abroad. Growing interdependence has not diminished the role of such attributes — in some cases (e.g., oil reserves) it has even increased their role — but rather it has enlarged the composite of possessed qualities from which effective control derives.

The capacity to develop and apply scientific and technical knowledge is perhaps the attribute that has undergone the greatest transformation. The complexity of interdependence issues and their close link to the natural environment means that states are likely to be better able to cope with and procure benefits from their external settings the more they possess the ability to comprehend the dynamics whereby land, air, and water resources can be used and abused. The depth, breadth, flexibility, and commitment of a state's scientific establishment has thus come to rival its military establishment as a national resource. And, in turn, this attribute highlights the centrality of a state's educational system and its ability to produce a continuous flow of analytic, wide ranging, and technically competent citizens. The considerable stress states in the Third World place on establishing technological institutes and sending students abroad for advanced training is but one of the more obvious measures of the degree to which the capacity to generate and utilize knowledge has entered the ranks of prime national attributes.

Societal cohesion is another capability that has acquired prime importance. The decentralized nature of interdependence issues and the widening consequences of the attitudes and decisions of subnational groups have made external control efforts ever more dependent on the degree to which these subgroups perceive their interests as shared and served by the policies of their national governments. The greater the cohesiveness in this regard, the more does it seem likely that foreign policy officials will be able to pursue successfully those courses of action they deem essential to the management of interdependence issues. The readiness of American farmers, for example, to harmonize their production schedules with the requirements of proposed international agreements on the distribution and storage of foodstuffs constitutes a critical element in the United States government's ability to undertake successful negotiations on such matters. Of course, the degree of societal cohesion — and the mobilization potential thereby created — has always been a critical factor in the military area, but its centrality to other areas of foreign policy has not been so extensive. The emergence of interdependence issues has changed all this and, combined with the shifting loyalties of subnational groups, has rendered the cohesion attribute a major component of national capabilities.

The capacity of public bureaucracies to overcome — or at least compensate for — the fragmentation inherent in interdependence issues is still another attribute that has become increasingly important in recent years. The readiness of one subagency to inform other relevant subagencies of its activities is not a predisposition that comes easily to units of a bureaucracy. On the contrary, rivalry is probably more securely embedded in bureaucratic structures than coordination, and these structural tendencies seem likely to be exacerbated by the fragmentation, decentralization, and specialization that accompanies interdependence. It follows that states that can continuously adapt their decision-making structure to mounting interdependence — that can train and utilize the relevant expertise, that can sensitize officials to the implications of their choices for other governmental units working on other problems of interdependence, that can find techniques for generating innovative proposals and for transforming destructive rivalries into creative tensions, that can develop scientific proofs which support appeals to transnational values — will bring to the conference tables of the world considerable advantages not accruing to those that conduct bureaucratic politics and diplomacy as usual. The capacity to render large-scale governmental organizations relevant to existing problems has always been an important component of national "power," but its role would appear to be even more central as world affairs become ever more complex.

Closely related to the increasing importance of decision-making variables is the capacity of officials to frame and pursue policies designed either to build new international institutions or to give new directions to long-established patterns. As previously noted, by their very nature interdependence issues tend to require multilateral cooperation among governments for their amelioration. The ability to contribute to the evolution of such institutions and patterns can vary considerably, depending on the readiness of societies, their publics, and their governments to acknowledge that their futures are interdependently linked and to adapt to the changing circumstances which may thereby arise. The adaptation of national societies can take several forms, including maladaptive assessments of the way in which domestic life is interwoven into foreign affairs. Adaptation and maladaptation involve nothing less than the images which citizens and officials hold of themselves in relation to their external environments; and if these images are unrealistic and fail to account for the need to sustain cooperative foreign policies, then burdens rather than benefits are bound to mount with interdependence. Inasmuch as the images underlying the adaptive capacities of states derive from the functioning of their communication systems, the viability of their value frameworks, the flexibility of their political ideologies, and the dynamics of their educational systems, as well as the structure of their public bureaucracies, it seems quite evident that the capability for multilateral cooperation will not come readily to governments. Equally obvious is the fact that those which can enlarge this capability will achieve greater measures of national security than those which do not.

If the foregoing analysis of the changing mix of capabilities that accompany mounting interdependence is accurate, it seems reasonable to generalize that "national power" is on the decline, that the capacity of individual states to control developments abroad is diminishing and will continue to diminish. Some will remain relatively "strong" and others relatively "weak," and some may become relatively stronger and others relatively weaker, but in absolute terms all seem likely to become less able single-handedly to modify or preserve patterns in their external environments. Why? Because it seems unlikely that any state, even the most industrially advanced, can develop a scientific community with sufficient breadth and depth to cope with all the diverse issues of interdependence; because everywhere societies seem destined to become less cohesive and the mobilizing capacities of their governments less effective; and because everywhere bureaucracies seem likely to become more fragmented. Whether the decline in overall capabilities to enhance national security will result in a corresponding diminution of international security, however, is less clear. As interdependence impinges ever more tightly, so may the adaptive capacities of states allow them to evolve a greater readiness for multilateral cooperation.[6] The years ahead may thus be witness to a profound paradox in which the decline of national "power" is matched, and perhaps even exceeded, by the rise of international "power."

ENDNOTES

1 For sophisticated analyses of recent changes on the world scene that nevertheless fail to break away from the tendency to rank possessed attributes and resources, see Seyom Brown, "The Changing Essence of Power," *Foreign Affairs*, 51 (January 1973), 286-99; and Stanley Hoffmann, "Notes on the Elusiveness of Modern Power," *International Journal*, 30 (Spring 1975), 183-206. A somewhat more successful effort to probe systematically the relational consequences of relative changes in the possessed qualities of states can be found in Klaus Knorr, *The Power of Nations: The Political Economy of International Relations* (New York: Basic Books, 1975).

2 This line of reasoning was later developed more elaborately in Edward Friedland, Paul Seaburg, and Aaron Wildavsky, *The Great Détente Disaster: Oil and the Decline of American Foreign Policy* (New York: Basic Books, 1975), and Robert W. Tucker, "Oil: The Issue of American Intervention," *Commentary*, 57 (January 1975), 21-31.

3 For a cogent discussion of this point, see Robert L. Paarlberg, "Domesticating Global Management," *Foreign Affairs*, 54 (April 1976), 563-76.

4 See Burton M. Sapin and Richard C. Snyder, *The Role of the Military in American Foreign Policy* (Garden City, N.Y.: Doubleday & Co., 1954).

5 For a useful essay relevant to this point, see Allan W. Lerner, *Experts, Politicians, and Decision-making in the Technological Society* (Morristown, N.J.: General Learning Press, 1975).

6 For some stimulating discussions relevant to this possibility, see Marvin E. Wolfgang, ed., "Adjusting to Scarcity," *The Annals*, 420 (July 1975), 1-124.

B: POWER, CAPABILITIES, AND THE USE OF FORCE

The Expansion of Force

Robert E. Osgood/Robert W. Tucker

SOURCES OF THE EXPANSION OF FORCE

Between the full establishment of the modern military state in the eighteenth century and the dawn of the nuclear age, military power underwent a transformation as remarkable as its transformation in the nuclear age. As in the nuclear age, the chief impetus of this transformation came from the tremendous expansion in the destructive power available to the most advanced states; but the sources of expansion were rooted deeply in social and political changes.

Materially, this expansion of force began most conspicuously in the middle of the nineteenth century with a sudden acceleration of technological innovation, mass production, and applied science. But material expansion was the product of these developments interacting with the state's mobilization and exploitation of mass enthusiasm for military purposes, its peacetime conscription of manpower, and the co-ordinated utilization of all these human, economic, and technological resources under professional military staffs.

Politically, the expansion of military power resulted first from the state's consolidation of internal order and its development of an efficient administrative apparatus and second from the emergence of popular national governments following the American and French revolutions.

Socially, these political sources of expanding military power were associated with the breakdown of aristocratic privileges and the development of a politically conscious mass, which made possible a professional military leadership and the conscription of manpower from a broad national base instead of a military caste system and an outcast soldiery drawn from the dregs of society.

Psychologically and spiritually, the beginnings of modern military power must be traced to the erosion of esthetic, moral, and cultural constraints upon warfare under the impact of a secular, rational, utilitarian approach to force in international politics; to the more recent injection of popular national and ideological fervor into state policy; and to the depersonalization of warfare that has accompanied military specialization and bureaucratization, the increasingly technical nature of military management, and the increasing remoteness of the inflictors of great destruction from their victims.

Robert E. Osgood and Robert W. Tucker, *Force, Order and Justice* (Baltimore: The Johns Hopkins University Press, 1967), pp. 41-70, 118-20. Reprinted by permission of The Johns Hopkins University Press. Portions of the text have been deleted. Most footnotes have been removed; those remaining have been renumbered.

One can sum up the sources of the expansion of military power in the following terms, arranged in the approximate chronological sequence of their initial impact upon international politics: the rationalization, centralization, popularization, professionalization, and modernization of military power.

In many ways these developments have fostered disorder and complicated the problem of controlling and restraining military power. But since they seem as irreversible as modern Western civilization, we must wonder whether they condemn us to novel and terrible destruction or whether they may provide the foundation of a new international order of unprecedented stability.

THE RATIONALIZATION OF FORCE UNDER THE STATE

The modern state, applying a rational, instrumental approach to power and war in the wake of the relatively disorganized conflict of the Middle Ages, became the primary agent of the expansion of force. Man's approach to war had been highly rationalized in relatively orderly periods before. It did not become entirely divorced from motives of glory, adventure, and mission in the eighteenth century. When transferred to the nation-state after the French Revolution, these motives were more compelling than during the Crusades. Nevertheless, a significant change in man's approach to war took place with the state's establishment of internal order in the eighteenth century. As military power became the instrument of state policy, the religious and messianic, the social or agonistic, and the personal motives of war became subordinate to a utilitarian approach oriented toward using power with studied efficiency. This rationalization of military power has become increasingly comprehensive, calculated, and technical since the last part of the nineteenth century. Although we take this approach for granted as part of our civilization, this was not always the prevailing attitude.

In the Middle Ages, from roughly the eleventh century through much of the fourteenth, war was more a way of life than a calculated instrument of policy. It was virtually a continuous but small-scale activity that men took for granted.[1] The small scale resulted from the smallness of the armies, the short term of service, and the physical difficulty of keeping forces in the field for more than a few weeks at a time. Moreover, armies lacked the weapons and logistics to overcome the defensive advantage of castles and fortresses or to hold territory. The most successful commanders relied on maneuver, while generally avoiding pitched battles, where all might be lost in a day. Strategic direction was weak or entirely missing, although some commanders displayed great tactical skill.

Battles were, in effect, extensions of personal disputes arising primarily from the network of conflicting jurisdictions and loyalties involved in feudal obligations and dynastic claims. They needed no other justification. Except for the Crusades and the later years of the semi-national Hundred Years' War (1338-1452), wars were fought for the security, status, and enrichment of kings and for the emotional and economic gratification of the nobility. They were permeated by the chivalric values of personal honor, glory, and vengeance. We need not enter the controversy over the extent to which these values — especially the gentler ones of magnanimity and fair play — were actually lived up to. There are many examples in the Middle Ages of the mutual observation of rules of fair contest and of ceremonial restraints in the conduct of warfare. There are also many examples of one or both sides violating such rules and restraints. The important point here is that social and personal motives were so pervasive that war was more like a continuing enterprise or recreation than a recurrent political necessity. Consequently, boldness, vengeance, adventure, plunder, and sometimes even generosity frequently overrode tactical or strategic considerations. In the spirit of knight-errantry, kingdoms went to war in the most reckless and unpremeditated way; armies fought in the most amateurish and capricious fashion.

Chivalry as a code of military conduct was largely destroyed during the fourteenth through sixteenth centuries by infantries with crossbows and longbows, by Swiss pikemen, gunpowder, and the growth of national allegiance. Still, the instrumental approach to war remained subordinate to its social or agonistic aspect. The chaotic Religious Wars of the sixteenth and seventeenth centuries dissolved what was left of the old codes of combat and injected a new intensity into warfare. Yet war did not become an instrument of policy in the modern sense.

War was scarcely under the effective control of rulers. Armies were often little more than undisciplined bands of marauders living off the land, since states lacked organizational control of them and were unable to provide logistical support. War was a clash of dynastic and religious sectarian allegiances. Above all, it was, in Sir George Clark's words, a "general melee," a "collision of societies."[2] Even in fifteenth- and sixteenth-century Italy, which saw the origins of modern diplomacy, the formation of military coalitions, and the consolidation of several fairly cohesive political units absorbed in Machiavellian competition, war was governed by feudal and dynastic interests rather than by the interests of nations or modern states.

In the second half of the seventeenth century, as the religious issues waned, monarchs began to construct internal order by establishing effective control over economic and political life. The growing internal power of governments facilitated their control of war and gave war political direction. In the coalitions formed against Louis XIV's drive toward Continental hegemony, diplomacy became absorbed in efforts to shape the configurations of state interest and power. Concomitantly, effective control of the military establishments, marked by improved military discipline, the formulation of military codes restraining plunder and piracy, and the creation of more efficient and larger standing armies, laid the foundation for the war system of the eighteenth century, in which force and the threat of force were to serve as instruments of state policy. Through these developments modern *Realpolitik*, foreshadowed in Renaissance Italy, emerged on a larger scale than ever before, backed by the organized power of the state.

In the eighteenth century kings became identified with modern sectarian states, yet states transcended the monarchy to encompass the people and the land as well. The development of centralized authority and of financial and bureaucratic structures capable of raising revenue enabled the state to create and control professional standing armies in order to enforce civil order and support external policies. In the aftermath of Louis XIV's failure to establish a European order based on French hegemony, the ambitions and rivalries of military states led to a pattern of calculated, circumspect relations based upon alignments of countervailing power. The stakes of politics were predominantly dynastic, turning largely upon marriages and inheritances, territory and commerce, but the common unit of political currency was now more clearly the power of the state to make war. This currency was freely exchanged in limited quantities for limited ends. Yet these limitations were, in a sense, the result of the weakness as well as the strength of the state.

THE CONSTRAINTS ON FORCE

The rulers of eighteenth-century Europe lacked the mobility and firepower and the base of mass enthusiasm that were essential to wage Napoleonic war. Equally important, they lacked the political system and the administrative capacity to mobilize the whole nation and its resources for war. The expensive standing armies and artillery of the period imposed a severe strain on the limited capacity of governments to tax the people and finance protracted campaigns. The stringencies upon seapower were even greater, since no state could afford to train seamen in time of peace, and the quantity and quality of seamen that could be dragged into the service by press gangs were not conducive to large-scale warfare. Throughout the eighteenth century, war on land and at sea had to be attenuated or terminated because it threatened financial ruin, owing to the destruction of commerce at sea and to the expense of keeping armies and navies fighting.

These limiting conditions were in accord with the political necessities of the ruling classes. To have waged war for larger purposes with greater violence would have required popular states (whether autocratic or representative) and, therefore, the end of the Old Regime. Besides, the stilted tactics and clumsy logistics of warfare seemed appropriate to the social differences of the time. They reflected on the one hand the aristocratic and mercantilist outlook of the ruling classes, who liked their battlefield amenities and wished to limit the expenditure of life and money, and on the other hand the apathy and unreliability of the soldiery, who, having been drawn from the nonproductive segments of society and feeling little allegiance to the state, had to be disciplined to the stylized, drill-like maneuvers of the time in order to be kept reasonably efficient.

Yet the social and political constraints upon war would not have been so limiting without the material and technological constraints, which, in fact, persisted for decades after the French Revolution. The military inventions of the eighteenth century did not notably increase the scope, tempo, or intensity of warfare. The important changes in weapons since the Middle Ages — notably the development of muskets and artillery, fortresses, and heavily armed sailing ships — were assimilated only very gradually. The relative strength of the defense continued to retard the pace of war. Indeed, the greater use of artillery further encumbered logistics; and material shortages, especially in metal, fuel, and saltpeter, hampered exploitation of the new technology. The nearest thing to a modern arms race was the competitive establishment and enlargement of standing armies, but this competition was not accompanied by comparable competition in weapons.

European industry, still mainly dependent on craftsmanship, had not yet developed much standardization or mass production, either in civilian or military technology. Transportation and communication did not become significantly faster and cheaper. There was little or no pressure for innovations in military technology from monarchs, and there was considerable resistance to it on the part of the nobility and soldiery: the nobility, because innovations threatened their supremacy as a fighting class; the soldiery, because they feared the destructiveness of new weapons. Military inventions were not the product of a systematic response to military needs; they were largely a by-product of civilian technology. Science was not oriented toward practical invention, even for civilian uses; and scientists were generally hostile to the thought of applying their learning to military uses.

These basic material, technological, political, economic, and social constraints enable us to speak of the eighteenth century before the French Revolution as a century of limited wars. The generalization is too sweeping, since these wars were not notably different from those of the seventeenth century in their number, frequency, scope, duration, intensity, and deadliness to combatants. Indeed, when the typical wars of maneuvers and positions were punctuated with pitched battles, the improved discipline of the armies, together with the continuing low level of medical science, produced extremely high casualty rates. In one important respect, however, the limited wars of the eighteenth century were comparatively moderate: they caused significantly less destruction of civilian life, property, and welfare, with the exception of the devastating Seven Years' War in Prussia. This limitation distinguished them from the *grand mêlée* of the Religious Wars and made them a discriminating tool of statecraft.

In this respect kings and statesmen, anxious to avoid the excesses of the Thirty Years' War and determined to employ no more force than necessary to achieve modest and well-defined objectives, kept war limited. Limited war in turn generally served them as a means of policy commensurate with their ends. Thus the limited scope of land warfare was well suited to the limited territorial goals that states usually sought. War at sea was frequently little more than commercial war with an admixture of violence. Diplomatic bargains resolved what force could not decide.

HARBINGERS OF MILITARY DYNAMISM

Yet even in this century of limited war there were harbingers of a new military dynamism. The rulers of Prussia, despite the many limitations on military power, demonstrated the capacity of the state to improve its relative position in the hierarchy of states by generating military power. By the end of the seventeenth century Frederick William, the Great Elector of Brandenburg-Prussia, had already shown the capacity of an absolute monarch to utilize the material, human, and administrative resources of the state to build a superior standing army.[3] In the eighteenth century his successors, Frederick William I and Frederick the Great, added limited military conscription, intensive tactical training, efficient artillery barrages, and skillful generalship to raise Prussia through conquests and diplomacy to the front rank of states, although France, Russia, and Austria had from ten to twenty times the population and corresponding advantages in wealth, resources, trade, and territory.[4]

England provides the other striking example of an eighteenth-century state capitalizing upon military superiority based on efficient use of natural and human resources. By concentrating on naval power and a merchant marine and keeping military adventures on the Continent to a minimum, England compensated for her scarce native material resources by using her strategic geographical position, her substantial population, and her financial and trading prowess to become the dominant commercial and colonial power, with hegemony on the seas.

As Prussia based its military ascendance on the army and the control of land, England based its hegemony on the navy and control of overseas commerce. Through its army Prussia acquired and controlled land and population, which in turn were major ingredients in strengthening the army. Through its navy England acquired colonies and controlled commerce, which in turn provided the money to hire soldiers and subsidize allies on land while supporting a navy that could strangle the commerce of adversaries. Both were pre-eminent examples of states operating as successful military organizations, although the relatively unobtrusive impact upon domestic life of a standing navy, as compared to a standing army, helped England avoid the conspicuous militarism that arose in Prussia. Both provided impressive examples of the internal expansion of military power, which subsequent generations would emulate in the nineteenth century.

Moreover, in the rationalism of the eighteenth century there was also a harbinger of the technological explosion that transformed the scale of military power in the half century before World War I. In this century modern materialism — faith in the inevitable progressive increase of man's mastery of inanimate things for practical ends — became a sacred standard. The standard eroded the remnants of medieval moral and esthetic constraints upon weaponry and laid the cultural foundation for the uninhibited advancement of military technology. The invention of more powerful weapons was presumed to be a mark of advancing civilization. The perfection of firearms, some hoped, would make wars so destructive that they would be quickly terminated or avoided altogether. Thus Europe was being prepared for a revolution in military technology that would be the counterpart of the industrial revolution — that astonishing explosion of man's ingenuity and productivity ignited in England two hundred years ago.[5]

Yet before the rise of popular nationalism and the onset of the industrial-technological revolution, military power could not approach the volatility, dynamism, mass, and intensity it attained in the nineteenth and twentieth centuries. Consequently, the military managers of the eighteenth century were spared the problems of control which afflicted their successors and were permitted the illusion of mastering the still latent energy of destruction. In the hands of enlightened statesmen and generals, military establishments seemed to be calculable and safe instruments of policy.

Confidence in the calculability of war was consonant with the stress on rigid tactical principles of maneuver and position and with elaborate rules of siege and surrender. It reflected the prevalent faith in the ability of men to rationalize all human activity by discovering the precise, mechanical laws of its operation. Some analysts foresaw a universal military science that would be so exact as to render war futile and unnecessary. There was reason for such confidence, for although the outcome of war depended on many imponderables, the principal elements of military power were sufficiently ponderable to facilitate roughly accurate comparisons in advance of war. In war itself they remained fairly stable, and victory turned upon the most skillful use of largely unchanging weapons and tactical rules known to everyone.

In reality, of course, war was not as precisely calculable as its theorists professed. The vicissitudes of physical environment and human skill on the battlefield and especially at sea, where weather and unreliable communications interfered more with command and control, repeatedly led to miscalculations. The chief significance of the limitations on armed forces was that, together with the rough equality of combinations of opposing forces, they rendered the consequences of miscalculations less serious.

Thus Frederick II, who was increasingly impressed by the role of chance in war and diplomacy as he gained experience, reflected upon the results of the War of the Austrian Succession (1740-48) with a certain melancholy satisfaction: "Since the art of war has been so well understood in Europe, and policy has established a certain balance of power between sovereigns, grand enterprises but rarely produce such effects as might be expected. An equality of forces, alternate loss and success, occasion the opponents at the end of the most desperate war, to find themselves much in the same state of reciprocal strength as at the commencement."

The wars of the French Revolution and Napoleon's military adventures would reveal a dynamism and decisiveness in war that Frederick II could not have imagined. But this new dimension of force also created a new dimension of miscalculation — and new efforts to master force.

The wars of the French Revolution showed what unprecedented concentration of military energy the popularization of war could produce even before the technological transformation preceding World War I. Although Carnot, as Minister of War in 1799, directed the first concerted effort to mobilize scientific talent for war, Napoleon was indifferent to technological innovations. Nevertheless, Napoleon magnified the force of war tremendously by exploiting the new sources of organized violence released by popular nationalism and ideological fervor. Following the course of the revolutionary leaders who preceded him, he transformed warfare into a national crusade, involving not just tactical maneuver and attrition of the enemy's supply lines but annihilation of the enemy's forces, occupation of his territory, and even political conversion of his people. With universal military conscription and comprehensive material and economic mobilization, he created a "nation in arms." To the revolutionary tactics of offensive mobility, surprise, the concentration of overwhelming numbers on a single point, massed artillery fire, and destructive pursuit, he added the extravagant ambition of a bold field commander, to give war a terrible new impact and momentum.

Truly, "The wars of Kings were at an end; the wars of peoples were beginning."[6] The sheer scale of the resulting violence made the impact of war as unpredictable and uncontrollable as it was momentous. In Clausewitz's terms, it made war more nearly "a thing in itself."

Yet, although the potential autonomy and dynamism of popular, massive war had been revealed, the European wars of the following century, from 1815 to 1914, were relatively limited. Indeed, there were fewer significant wars in the European state system than in the period from the defeat of Louis XIV to the French Revolution. There were none of the scope or duration of the Seven Years' War and only one, the Crimean War, that was a general war involving several major powers. In the Crimean and Franco-Prussian Wars the field armies were several times larger than those of the seventeenth and eighteenth centuries — in the hundreds of thousands instead of twenty or thirty thousand — but the percentage of combat casualties was not much different, and civilian destruction was localized. The wars of this period are notable for their short duration and the small number of battles and participating states, as compared to the eighteenth or twentieth centuries. They were fought and settled for limited objectives, they were localized, and they were quickly terminated. Only the Crimean War was a general war involving a number of states, but it did not approach the duration or economic and human devastation of the Seven Years' War. Only the Franco-Prussian War approached the Napoleonic Wars in intensity of battles and numbers of forces involved, but it was far more limited in geographical scope and duration.

The explanation of limited war in the period between the Napoleonic Wars and World War I, as in the eighteenth century, seems to lie in circumstances that were partly fortuitous, partly technological and economic, and partly the result of deliberate restraints upon the political objectives of war. Although the material and technical limits upon war were not so constraining as before the French Revolution, the destructive potential of armies was still sufficiently restricted to enable states to keep combat within bounds in the absence of a political occasion for fighting a general war of annihilation.

The Austro-Prussian War and the Franco-Prussian War were limited chiefly by Prussia's ability to bring superior force to bear quickly and by Bismarck's willingness to negotiate a limited victory consistent with a new equilibrium of power. The Russo-Japanese War of 1904-5 was limited chiefly by Japan's sudden naval victory, by its satisfaction with a local victory, and by the material incapacity of both belligerents to carry the war to the other's homeland. The Crimean War was limited by its location — the same war in Austria might well have become a world war — and by the incompetence and inefficiency of the belligerents. These and other wars in this period remained local largely because the European system of political alignments, as in the eighteenth century, was relatively fragmented and loosely knit before the emergency of the two great alliances that clashed in 1914.

THE NEW MANAGEMENT OF FORCE

Although war itself remained limited in the period after the Napoleonic Wars and before World War I, military power expanded greatly. The professionalization and modernization of military power in the latter half of this period created an unprecedented peacetime war potential. But the success of states in preserving a relatively peaceful and orderly international system while greatly expanding its military basis concealed the latent dangers of the new military potential.

In the latter half of the nineteenth century, military power in Europe came under the systematic direction of a new class of specialists in military organization and planning. Professionally dedicated to maximum military efficiency, these specialists directed their nation's human, material, technological, and economic resources toward the creation in peacetime of military machines capable of inflicting maximum destruction upon the enemy's forces in war. The systematic training of these military specialists, with their highly developed staffs and administrative procedures, codes of professional conduct, formulation of war plans, conduct of war games, and development of strategic and tactical doctrine marked the application to the management of force of those methods of modern production that were transforming private industry.

The outstanding model of military management was the Prussian General Staff. By capitalizing on two great new military resources, universal compulsory peacetime conscription and the railways-and-telegraph system, the Staff led Prussia to two rapid, stunning victories over Austria in 1866 and France in 1871.[7] The quickness and completeness of Prussia's destruction of the fighting capacity of the dominant military power in Europe was particularly remarkable. It convincingly demonstrated to the rest of Europe the necessity of systematically developing peacetime military potential under professional, scientific management. Thereafter all the major states on the Continent created general staffs, railway networks, and systems of universal peacetime military service.

As we shall see in examining the political consequences of the expansion of military power, the new military machines provided statesmen with a powerful political instrument; but, unfortunately, the statesmen permitted the machines to follow a logic of their own — the narrow logic of military efficiency held by the professional managers. Thus instead of becoming a flexible instrument of policy short of war, the new peacetime military potential became, in effect, an independent force largely divorced from political control. Because the military machines were geared so strictly to fighting a war, they tended to foreclose new opportunities for using force short of war.

This fatal deficiency was related to the inflexibility of strategic doctrine. The growing need to concert and co-ordinate the increasingly diverse components of military power gave new importance to strategy. The increased importance of continual planning and the growing dependence of military power on industry and technology expanded the very meaning of military strategy. Strategy outgrew its traditional meaning: the plan for fighting a battle. It became the plan for utilizing all the nation's resources and instruments of war most effectively in order to exert force advantageously in future military contingencies, in the light of a potential adversary's intentions and capabilities. The operational strategy of states in peacetime might have a determining effect upon the character and even the outbreak of war. Strategic doctrine could also become a primary political factor short of war,... e.g., the case of airpower after World War I.

The expanded function of strategy called for a systematic integration of military plans with foreign policy. In the hands of military professionals, however, strategy tended, on the one hand, to exalt the romantic emphasis of Foch on *will* and the all-out offensive and, on the other hand, to emphasize meticulous operational planning for military efficiency measured by the maximum force that could be brought to bear upon the enemy. The result was a kind of strategic monism that simplified planning but did not serve policy.

Thus the war mobilization plans of the general staffs in the years of armed peace after the Franco-Prussian War seriously limited the opportunities for diplomatic accommodation and committed governments in certain contingencies to an almost automatic shift into general war, as though their war machines had only one forward gear and no brakes. The prevailing military assumption that a future war would be swift and decisive like the Franco-Prussian War and that a long war would ruin a nation's economy and incur the danger of revolution put a premium on striking first with superior forces. This requirement in turn led military staffs to commit their governments to plans for total mobilization only and to regard mobilization as an inevitable prelude to all-out war. When mobilization began, diplomacy would stop. For the sake of military efficiency, military plans were directed toward meeting a single contingency with one kind of response. The whole machinery was inflexibly geared to the complicated, exacting logistics of the railway networks, with the object of concentrating the maximum force at a single military point as quickly as possible. Consequently, when Austria declared war against Serbia in 1914, Austria, Russia, and Germany forfeited the diplomatic opportunities for avoiding war that partial mobilization against each other might have afforded, lest they lose precious time in fully mobilizing for the war that their military staffs considered inevitable.[8]

Actually, despite their commitment to full mobilization, each of these governments, at the behest of statesmen, tried to resist and, except in Germany, temporarily succeeded in resisting the prescribed automatic response by undertaking partial mobilization so as not to provoke the potential adversary into war or draw others into war. In the end, however, the military, pleading military necessity, prevailed and full mobilization was instituted, thereby turning military foresight into a self-fulfilling prophecy. In this way the attempt to manage military power more precisely and calculably made it more autonomous and less subject to control.

Thus mobilization plans seriously limited opportunities for diplomatic accommodation and, once they had been put into effect, virtually assured general war. In the end, the ineffective political control of peacetime military preparations proved to be even more dangerous to international order than the tremendous increase of destructive power that accompanied the outburst of industrial and technological energy. On the other hand, the modernization and hence increasing complexity of military power created a far more serious problem of peacetime political control than had existed before.

THE TECHNOLOGICAL REVOLUTION IN MILITARY POWER

Competitive arming in a dynamic military technology further enhanced the role of military power as an autonomous political force. The modern arms race originated in an unprecedented surge of military invention in the last quarter of the nineteenth century.

The rifled gun barrel, together with improvements in gunpowder and firing mechanisms, led to tremendous improvements of range and accuracy. The development of breech-loading rifles and artillery, along with improved recoil mechanisms late in the century, greatly increased rapidity of fire. As significant as the accelerated rate of invention was the reduction of time between invention, mass production, and tactical assimilation of weapons, due to the effective co-ordination of economic and technological-scientific resources and to systematic battlefield experimentation and analysis.[9]

As land warfare was transformed by the utilization of railways and the telegraph, maritime warfare was transformed by the invention of the iron-hulled, steam-propelled warship. The rapid development of the battleship and the profusion of offensive and defensive naval technology to counter it were unprecedented in the history of military innovation. This weapon system changed more in the latter half of the nineteenth century than it had in the preceding ten centuries.

The development of the battleship altered the distribution of power, stimulated far-reaching rivalries, and shaped new political alignments. More than ever before a single weapon became the pre-eminent test and symbol of national greatness.[10] It was integrally linked to foreign policy in the gospel of seapower according to Mahan. Mahan's great popularity as a strategist (particularly in England, Germany, and France) was based on his view that seapower was the royal road to national wealth and prestige. It would enable states to enlarge and protect overseas imperial holdings and commerce with an integrated system of colonies, bases, and merchant marine, supported by a fleet of line-of-battle ships designed to control the sea lanes, not merely to raid commerce and protect ports.

The rapid improvement of battleships created the first modern technological arms races. The arms race is a somewhat misleading metaphor for a competitive advancement of the type, quantity, and quality of weapons between adversaries seeking an advantageous ratio of military strength. In the latter part of the nineteenth century it became a major form of power politics and greatly enhanced the role of military power in peacetime.

From the 1850s through the 1880s France precipitated an arms race with Britain by attempting to offset numerical inferiority in warships with superiority in ironclad battleships, guns, and commerce-destroying torpedo boats and light cruisers.... The resulting competition was most conspicuous in the contest between offensive guns and defensive armor. France eventually abandoned the competition without approaching naval equality chiefly because of disorder in French politics, growing fear of the German army, and friendlier political relations with Britain.

Germany launched another naval race with Britain in 1898, primarily to compete with her as a colonial world power. The British naval program, based on the famous two-power standard, had been designed to offset a Franco-Russian combination. Germany's program, coinciding with an alleviation of the Russian threat by virtue of the Anglo-Japanese Alliance and the Russo-Japanese War, shifted the focus of Britain's naval program to Germany. In October, 1905, Britain laid down the original *Dreadnought* and in February, 1906, launched it. The *Dreadnought* had greater speed and several times greater long-range firepower than previous battleships.Germany soon followed suit, and in 1912 First Lord of the Admiralty Churchill announced a British naval standard of 60 per cent superiority over Germany in dreadnoughts, while threatening to lay two keels for every one German keel unless Germany would reciprocally slow down or freeze construction without any political conditions. By 1914 the German government had abandoned this competition for fear of encouraging further British naval expansion and pressing German taxpayers too heavily, as well as because of more urgent demands imposed by military preparations on land.

The role of dreadnoughts foreshadowed the revolutionary role of submarines and airpower in that they were intended not merely to defeat the enemy's forces but to exert a far-reaching effect upon its livelihood and status. They would do this, moreover, not merely by harassing commerce directly but primarily by securing or denying control of sea lanes vital to a nation's welfare and greatness. What is more, they were admirably suited to sustaining in peacetime a world policy and position through the conspicuous representation of a nation's might in distant places. This had been the more or less conscious strategy of British seapower since the latter part of the eighteenth century, but Mahan made it explicit and popularized it, and the modern battleship dramatized its efficacy.

The development of steamships with screw propellers relieved sea maneuvers from dependence on the vagaries of the wind and currents and completely outmoded sailing vessels. It greatly enhanced the defensive strength of advanced industrial nations, especially such insular powers as Japan and the U.S. It also greatly enhanced the geographical extension of the power of nations that could develop coaling bases and colonies. Therefore it became the mainstay of the great imperial contests and the virtually global struggles for hegemony that agitated international politics in the two decades or so preceding World War I.

In these ways the dreadnought exemplified the momentous impact of technological innovation upon international politics. It demonstrated the growing impact of armed forces, as well as their growing dependence, upon the nation as a whole.

It also posed the question of whether the new technology could be controlled. This question was posed in one form by the new factor of uncertainty in warfare and military planning, injected by the accelerated rate of technological innovation. The dreadnought complicated the calculation of relative military power and made more difficult the control and prediction of the outcome of war. To integrate the new battleships into war plans and production programs, certain assumptions had to be made about their military function. The assumption that a surprise attack with naval forces-in-being would be decisive provided the strategic impetus for naval competition, just as the assumption that the army that struck first with the most firepower would have a decisive advantage impelled the arms race in land weapons. Yet forces-in-being at the moment of a hypothetical war would depend not only on existing weapons but, equally, on future weapons produced by the building programs in the shipyards — programs that were complex and, in the case of challenging states, shrouded in secrecy.

In 1909 official and private British sources indicated that Germany might build 17 or even 21 dreadnoughts by 1912 instead of the officially announced 13. This estimate turned out to be wrong. It was based on information concerning an increase in German shipbuilding capacity; an increase in Krupp's capacity to produce gun mountings; the secret accumulation of nickel for use in guns, armour, and mountings; and an acceleration of contracts for ships. In effect, the alarmists based estimates of production on their view of Germany's capabilities, whereas more moderate advocates of a naval build-up credited Germany's announced intentions. England, unlike Germany, did not keep production details secret. The details of its naval program were publicly debated in Parliament and in the press. On the other hand, the public debate was often a confusing guide to those concerned with estimating the future of England's naval program.

The secrecy, complexity, and dynamism of building programs meant that naval programs had to be based on uncertain estimates not only of an adversary's relative capacity but also of its *intentions* to increase the quantity and quality of its navy. Yet the adversary's intentions could be affected by many imponderable internal and external considerations, including its estimate of one's own capacity and intentions. Therefore one state might try to alter the other's intentions by threatening and bargaining with a construction program and, perhaps, by linking this game with political proposals.

After some controversy, the British built the more powerful dreadnoughts, although they knew that this would lead to expensive and possibly dangerous competition with Germany in a weapon in which British superiority would not be as great as in pre-dreadnought battleships. The decisive argument for doing so was simply that Britain's refraining from building dreadnoughts would not prevent Germany from building them but only give Germany a head start. After competitive building started, however, the British tried to induce the Germans to agree to a reciprocal reduction of the tempo of competition or at least to an exchange of construction information in order to mitigate exaggerated suspicions of rates of construction. But the German government was unwilling thus to concede British superiority without some political *quid pro quo*, such as British neutrality in the event of a Franco-German war. The British government, on the other hand, was unwilling to break the Anglo-French entente. Winston Churchill, First Lord of the Admiralty, tried in vain to get German agreement to proportional reductions or to a joint holiday in construction of dreadnoughts while threatening, otherwise, to outbuild Germany by a precise ratio or number of ships. In the end, Germany defeated its political purpose by driving Britain closer to France. At the same time, it had to concede British superiority in the naval competition.

The difficulties of using the new peacetime power of weapons as a finely calculated instrument of policy were demonstrated in the failure of Admiral Tirpitz's too-clever "risk" strategy, which foundered on miscalculations of British policies and capabilities. Tirpitz developed his "risk theory" as a strategy for advancing Germany's political status and security vis-à-vis Britain by improving its relative naval power without obtaining naval equality. According to this strategy England would prefer to make concessions to Germany in the colonial field or possibly even enter a military commitment with Germany rather than risk a clash with a smaller German navy, if, in the event of such a clash, that navy were strong enough to leave England inferior in the face of a Franco-Russian naval combination. The underlying assumptions of this strategy, if they ever had any merit, were invalidated by the Anglo-Russian entente, the Anglo-French rapprochement, the Admiralty's decision to concentrate the British fleet in the North Sea, and England's decision to build dreadnoughts. But the German government continued to pursue Tirpitz's strategy and brought about the very political result — consolidation of the Triple Entente — that it was intended to prevent, while inciting Britain to enter a competition Germany could not win.

As the Anglo-German naval competition illustrates, the nature of the new technology gave arms races a kind of self-generating impetus based on the interaction of opposing military capabilities and intentions, real and estimated. This interaction produced a mode of peacetime power politics that resembled the maneuvering and bargaining of eighteenth-century wars, except that the stakes of the game were larger, the rules less reliable, and the whole game more volatile and subjective.

Moreover, because the game was expensive, because it impinged upon national pride and affected international tensions and the prospect of war, and because even nondemocratic governments felt the need to elicit popular consent for arms policies, arms races were also deeply involved in the vagaries of public opinion and internal politics — an involvement which the armed services and the armaments manufacturers stimulated and exploited. Thus during both the Anglo-French and Anglo-German naval races there were a number of naval scares in England, causing widespread, although unwarranted, fears of sudden naval attack and invasion. News of French and German naval increases created considerable public apprehension and touched off controversies with political overtones in the government and press. There were lively public disputes over future German naval strength and the proper number of ships to be built in the British program.

In England, as elsewhere, it was widely assumed that the outcome of crises like the two in Morocco depended upon naval superiority. Therefore all governments that could afford a navy, as well as some that could not, pointed to the navy as a symbol of national might and pride. The involvement of the public in military policies through arms races, demonstrations of military prowess, and crises added a further dimension of subjectivity and incalculability to the use of military power short of war.

The difficulties of planning in peacetime for the effective use of military power in war were no less severe. For in addition to all the other complicating factors in arms races, the new high rate of technological innovation and obsolescence deprived the military managers of one of the crucial, though increasingly inadequate, criteria for determining military requirements: wartime experience. Thus the London *Times* of November 19, 1895, noted: "A modern navy is a totally untried weapon of warfare. It is the resultant of a host of more or less conflicting theories of attack and defense. The seaman, the gunner, the torpedoist, the engineer, and the naval constructor each has his share in the creation of the modern man-of-war, each presses the paramount claim of his own department, and the result is a marvel of theory, compromise, and complication."[11]

To some extent, formulation of strategic doctrine, conduct of war games, and mathematical calculations of projected operations compensated for lack of experience,[12] but they also tended to foster a dangerous illusion of precision and predictability. The meticulous planning and rehearsal of complex military operations and the single-minded pursuit of maximum wartime efficiency tended not only to overlook the contingent and unpredictable elements of war; equally important, the inflexibility of military plans had unexpected and often quite adverse political consequences. Germany's Schlieffen Plan, before World War I, is the most notable case in point.

Under Chief of Staff Von Schlieffen's command, this plan followed his predecessor Waldersee's crucial assumption that a full-scale two-front war with France and Russia was inevitable. The elder Moltke had planned a quick war and a settlement with Russia in the East while offering France neutrality or fighting her with a holding action if necessary. But Waldersee, coming into office after the formation of the Franco-Russian Alliance, planned a full-scale war against Russia, preceded by a quick knockout blow against France. This foreclosed the possibility of keeping a Balkan war localized, since even if a war with the Russians were to originate in the Balkans, Germany would have to strike first against France. Moreover, the Schlieffen Plan envisaged an attack through Belgium even if, as proved to be the case, France were to refrain from invading Belgium first and England were to regard the invasion of Belgium as requiring her intervention.

Strategic prognostications in other countries showed the same lack of foresight. On the eve of World War I the general staffs of the major

European antagonists were universally convinced that their forces, with the help of allied forces, would be victorious and that victory would come from a quick, decisive contest like the Prussian victory over France in 1871.[13] They believed in Marshal Foch's mystical doctrine of *l'offensive brutale et à outrance.* Foch's stress on offensive action went along with his advocacy of "absolute" or total war, in opposition to the eighteenth-century limited wars of maneuver and position. It was associated with his belief in the decisiveness of the moral factor in war: the will to victory. It was in accord with the widespread belief that a modern war of attrition would be such a severe strain on industrial economies that nations would have to end a war quickly rather than face bankruptcy and revolution.

The military staffs were, therefore, completely unprepared for the war of stalemate and attrition that ensued when the devastating firepower unleashed by the new weapons, unaccompanied by comparable innovations in tactical mobility, drove troops into the trenches and exacted unimagined casualties for negligible advances.[14]

WORLD WAR I

In World War I the principal object of war was conceived to be the annihilation of the enemy's forces. Yet the British blockade and the German submarine campaign put whole nations under siege as never before. In the end Britain was bankrupted, France and Britain had lost a terrible portion of their youth, Italy was on the brink of political chaos, Russia and Germany were racked with revolution, the Austro-Hungarian Empire had vanished, and the Ottoman Empire was dismembered. Only the American Civil War, the first conflict to reveal fully the momentous destructive power generated by modern technology and the popularization of war, could have prepared the world of 1914 for the protracted, profligate expenditure of lives, homes, and money; but the lessons of that war were largely ignored in Europe.

Thus, contrary to the illusion of precision and calculability conveyed by advanced professional management — but contrary also to the conviction that sheer morale and the will to victory would be decisive — total war proved to be far more intractable to intelligent direction than the managers expected. This was partly the result of unwarranted faith in the simple military axioms that led armies into massive assaults in the expectation of quick, decisive victories and partly the result of the enormous dimensions of force and the immense complexity of military establishments, which multiplied the frequency and repercussions of unanticipated developments.

World War I precipitated a torrent of technological innovations, fostered for the first time by a comprehensive mobilization of scientific talent. These innovations included not only the improvement of previous weapons but also the introduction of new weapons: the airplane, the tank, poison gas, and the submarine. Each of these weapons and the interaction of all of them with other weapons, with tactical innovations, and with new factors of logistics and materiel affected the conflict in unexpected ways. The submarine, which had been only an ineffective novelty in previous wars, came close to being a truly decisive weapon.

Of course, all these innovations provided only a faint foretaste of the proliferation of decisive technology in World War II,[15] in which the participants were as unprepared for mechanized, mobile, blitzkrieg warfare as they had been unprepared for trench warfare in 1914. In the interwar period mechanized mobile warfare had been espoused by a few prophets in England and France — notably, Fuller, Liddell Hart, and de Gaulle — but only the Nazis put it into practice.

The fact that the marvelous ingenuity of technology and military management resulted in such unexpected destruction of life and property produced a deep agony and revulsion in the world, in many ways deeper than that created by World War II. The unprecedented loss of life and the massive devastation of material civilization, compressed into a few years, intensified the psychological shock caused by the sharp contrast with prewar expectations of a quick, decisive, exhilarating contest. The wholesale inhumanity and suffering inflicted by modern nations geared to war seemed like a cruel refutation of the general optimism in the preceding decades that industrial-technological and sociopolitical progress marched together.

It is true that if one measures the destructiveness of war by economic and demographic statistics covering the immediate postwar period of recuperation as well as the war itself, World War I seems much less pernicious as a whole than its reputation — indeed, almost beneficent in some countries. For the same factors of modern civilization that made massive violence possible also facilitated a rapid restoration of population and national incomes. But this measurement, of course, is irrelevant to the lasting psychological and political effect of an immense, violent upheaval in modern civilization inflicted by man's own monstrous military machines running amuck.

A NEW DIMENSION OF FORCE

Man's enthusiasm for war and the whole war system was deeply shaken by World War I, yet his underlying confidence in technological solutions to warfare was not undermined. On the contrary, the war aroused hope that some single new weapon might prove overwhelming, that some technological breakthrough might simplify the problem of exerting calculable, decisive force. This hope centered above all on the strategic bomber, which promised to attain victory by striking directly at the enemy's homeland, avoiding massive, inconclusive encounters on the ground and obviating the travails of attrition.

Actually, although the development of strategic airpower greatly enhanced the peacetime effects of force, it showed as dramatically as World War I the difficulty of controlling the wartime effects of the volatile new technology. Indeed, the very characteristic of strategic airpower that enhanced its political impact short of war complicated its control in war: its capacity to inflict sudden punishment directly upon civilians at a range far beyond the battlefield. This characteristic, although analogous to the indirect punitive effect of the naval blockade, distinguishes airpower from all other kinds of military power.

In the midst of the stalemate during World War I, the development of the military airplane inspired a small but influential group of advocates to propound a doctrine of strategic bombing long before the bomber was technically capable of playing its purported role. The doctrine promised victory by inflicting decisive damage on the basic civilian sources of enemy power without having to defeat the enemy's armed forces or occupy his territory.

In April, 1918, British political leaders, over the opposition of the highest ranking military officers, succeeded in establishing a separate Royal Air Force in their search for an alternative to sending the flower of British manhood to "chew barbed wire in Flanders," as Churchill put it. The public shock over the German attacks on London with Zeppelins, and later Gotha bombers, provided the immediate impetus. The prevailing strategic doctrine at the time contemplated the use of bombers against military targets directly related to the war on the ground, but the general impression that punitive air raids on cities could exert great psychological effects injected a significant ambiguity in the nascent doctrine of airpower. The heavy casualties inflicted by the daylight raids on undefended London raised great popular and professional expectations about the efficacy of strategic bombing. On the basis of these casualties it was calculated that in a future war London might be made almost uninhabitable in the first weeks of bombing. Furthermore, the one-sided emphasis on offensive uses of airpower in World War I fostered the conviction that there was no effective defense against such devastation except bombing the enemy's bases and factories and inflicting reprisal damage upon his cities. These assumptions and the strategic doctrine that was based upon them had a powerful effect upon international politics after World War I.

In the years after the war the writings of the

Italian prophet of airpower, Giulio Douhet, broadcast the doctrine of victory-through-strategic-bombing throughout Europe and beyond. In essence this doctrine held that victory depended first on obtaining "command of the air," which in turn depended on destroying air bases and air factories, and then on shattering the enemy's will to fight by inflicting maximum damage on his cities, transportation centers, and industries. The doctrine assumed that war among major powers must aim at annihilating the enemy before he annihilates you, that there would be no defense against the bomber, and that victory would come quickly (and, incidentally, therefore humanely) to the force that could strike first by surprise and inflict the greatest damage in the shortest time. The logical defense against this danger would be either to strike first in a pre-emptive or preventive attack or else to depend on the threat of reprisal to deter the enemy from striking first.

As in the case of a prospective naval or ground attack, the supposition that a sudden first strike from the air could be decisive added an element of tension to international conflict and a new danger of pre-emptive or preventive attack. It also gave states a mighty instrument of intimidation and deterrence. With the integration of airpower into military establishments, the whole nation became the direct object as well as the source of military power — in peacetime as well as in war. In short, strategic bombing put the nation-in-arms in the front line. This further complicated the problem of calculating and controlling military power.

Success in exploiting military power for its psychological and political effects short of war depended heavily on the credibility of a government's and, indirectly, a whole nation's will to use its power of devastation, especially when the enemy was assumed to have the power of counter-devastation. But what determined credibility? It depended partly on the relative material capabilities of opposing air forces; but, because of the subjective nature of governmental and national will, the relation of capabilities to credibility was less direct and more complicated than in the case of weapons that exerted their effect only against armed forces.

Moreover, the estimate of air capabilities was also uncertain. Not only was the efficacy of untried weapons in doubt, but, as in the case of naval competition, plans and preparations for weapons that would be produced only years hence were a crucial factor in capabilities; yet these plans and preparations were obscured by secrecy and the diffuseness of the production process. Thus after the British decided in 1934 to seek air "parity" as a "deterrent" to German aggression, they discovered not only that parity was difficult to define in quantitative and qualitative terms but that attaining it required a rearmament effort based on quite uncertain and fallible estimates of Germany's rate of production, which in the early stages of German rearmament depended heavily on such obscure auxiliary preparations as the manufacturing of machine tools. In May, 1935, Prime Minister Baldwin publicly confessed that his government had completely underestimated the rate of German rearmament. Britain's task then became to expand her aircraft industry and rate of production so as to obtain parity with the air force that Germany was expected to have by 1940.

Britain's whole air rearmament program was based on the assumption that Germany could deliver a knockout blow against England. Baldwin's pronouncement that "the bombers will always get through" was taken as axiomatic. The fact that the Germans had no intention, plan, or capability for such an attack did not change the significance of the British assumption. Indeed, Germany capitalized on this psychological reality by encouraging British apprehensions of a knockout blow and by exploiting them to paralyze British diplomatic and military resistance to piecemeal aggression. Consequently, Britain's strategic doctrine stressed the deterrent effect of a capability for offensive reprisals against Germany, and her rearmament program stressed heavy bombers. Nevertheless, when the government belatedly discovered the magnitude of Germany's air superiority after 1938, it shifted from a strategy of massive civilian bombing to one of confining bombing to military objectives in the hope that Germany would spare British cities. Then, shortly before the war, the Air Staff, having previously failed to base air strategy on operational possibilities, discovered the limited penetration ability of bombers; so it shifted the strategic priority to defending France on the ground, although there were no concerted plans to fulfill this priority.

War itself was the great school of strategy and tactics, but wartime trial and error provided unexpected lessons. Strategic bombing turned out to be even more volatile and less subject to foresight and control than the contest between massive armies had been in World War I. At first both sides confined bombing to tactical and industrial targets. The air war demonstrated that both sides had unprecedented incentives for contrived reciprocal restraints. And for a while such restraints were practiced. But, contrary to claims of great precision, the inaccuracy of bombing and the collateral civilian damage, combined with the unexpected vulnerability of bombers engaged in precision bombing, eventually broke down reciprocal restraints and led to raids designed chiefly to inflict terror and reprisals upon civilians and things of civilian value, culminating in the senseless bombing of cities like Dresden.

The actual effect of such bombing upon civilian morale and the national will to fight proved to be almost negligible in Germany, as in England, although similar attacks on Japanese cities were apparently more effective in helping to induce surrender. But in both cases civilian bombing signified that an ultimate stage had been reached in the expansion of military power — a stage in which the whole nation had become a direct target of psychological pressure and physical punishment. Before the nuclear age airpower revealed both the possible utility of modern force short of war and its potential uselessness in war.

. . .

THE CHANGING ATTITUDE TOWARD FORCE

In the whole melancholy tale of misadventures accompanying the expansion of force through the period of two world wars, perhaps something as simple yet as imponderable as the prevailing attitude toward force and war affected international order more decisively than the structure and organization of power or the nature of military technology — although, of course, these factors were closely related.

The prevailing attitude toward force did not change as dramatically or as uniformly as military technology; yet there is a tremendous gap between the attitude of the eighteenth century and that of the period following World War I. In the eighteenth century, when the instruments of force were inherently quite limited and power politics was no concern of national publics, war was largely taken for granted as a normal recourse of statecraft. Those who deplored war did so more for its wastefulness, its control by the aristocracy, its cruelty, and its irrationality than for its material destruction of civilian life and its threat to national survival.

The Napoleonic Wars undermined confidence in the orderliness of a supposedly self-regulating balance of power system under the rational direction of enlightened despots and introduced the idea of a concert of power into practical politics. Yet in a decade the wartime concert had given way to the re-establishment of a fluid balance of power system, with the useful addition of customary international consultations.

The Crimean and Franco-Prussian Wars revealed again, in different ways, the fragility of the traditional balance of power system and began another reorientation of attitudes toward force. For one thing, the reaction to these two wars, intensified by the spread of popular education, literature, and the newspaper, greatly strengthened the organized peace movement. Yet this movement had negligible influence on governments until the end of the century. It was dominated on the one hand by advocates (largely confined to the Continent) of improbable schemes of European federation and on the other hand by liberal and pacifist groups (particularly in England) who rested their hopes for peace on popular government, free trade, or the rising voice of workers. Since governments were suspect in the eyes of international reformers, it relied on direct appeals to the public and to parliaments rather than on the more indirect methods of influencing governments.

During the last quarter of the nineteenth century governments became very receptive to an influential group that exalted war, the military virtues, and national expansion. In a kind of reversion to preindustrial attitudes and in reaction to the rising spirit of bourgeois liberal pacifism, this movement extolled international conflict and war as instruments of progress and expressed a strong preference for "total" war and the all-out offensive in contrast to unheroic and inconclusive limited wars. But it is important to note that this glorification of war and the war system still assumed that war was either so quick and decisive as to be moderate in its destructiveness or else so intense as to be increasingly rare. Von der Goltz was typical in basing his identification of total war with progress on the premise that modern wars could be won by destroying only a small portion of armies, since the new intensity of firepower would bring victory by operating on the will of nations; and that, consequently, each new invention that made weapons more destructive would also end wars more rapidly and humanely.

The romanticization of the military ethic reached its ultimate political expression in imperialism, rationalized by the Darwinian doctrine of the survival of the fittest through constant struggle. Yet political Darwinism was really the dying, though vociferous, gasp of laissez faire in international theory. While the militant spirit continued to grow more popular and vocal, the liberal opposition to war and power politics also grew stronger. By the beginning of the twentieth century, the organized peace movement, now appealing directly to governments, had become a powerful voice in political life and diplomacy — witness the two Hague disarmament conferences and the active concern of governments with arbitration treaties. The argument about war's wastefulness and irrationality (by then called "obsolescence") had gained new force with the spectacular advance of industrialism and commerce and the growing interdependence of military preparedness and the civilian economy.

To be sure, on the eve of World War I public spokesmen could still rattle the national sword with an exuberant spirit of military adventure and glory without being considered eccentric or evil. The patriotic thirst for military pageantry and excitement reached its height. Nations could face war with unabashed crusading zeal, exulting in the prospect and then in the reality with a passion more intense than was ever attained in the real Crusades. Yet this was probably the final spasm of massive military enthusiasm in the advanced democratic states. World War I killed the romance in war — except in a tragic or personal sense — and destroyed man's confidence in the beneficence of military laissez faire. The Fascist glorification of war was an evil aberration and seemed so at the time.

One should not depreciate the practical significance of the spreading popular aversion to force and the declining legitimacy of acquisitive war, which has been voiced so conspicuously since World War I, simply because of the continuing discrepancy between the ideal and reality of international politics. The widespread revulsion against the Religious Wars and the Napoleonic Wars probably had more to do with the moderation of war and politics in the eighteenth century and the resolution of crises short of war in the nineteenth than any of the so-called objective factors of international politics. Similarly, the widespread revulsion against war, international laissez faire, and military preparedness after World War I had a decisive impact upon international order. Its impact, unfortunately, was largely negative because it was accompanied by an aversion to the calculated management of force as an instrument of policy.

In the nuclear age preoccupation with the avoidance of war between nuclear powers and their allies has tempered the aversion to war with a novel respect for deterrence and the contrived control of force. It remains to be seen whether it has also created a more stable international order, or only the complacent illusion of self-sustaining order that has eventually proved the nemesis of every other period of equilibrium.

ENDNOTES

1 In perhaps the greatest battle of the Middle Ages, Bouvines (1214), the French had 11,000 calvary and about 20,000 militia infantry, fighting a coalition with 11,000 cavalry and over 70,000 infantry....

2 Sir George Clark, *War and Society in the Seventeenth Century* (Cambridge: Cambridge University Press, 1958), pp. 25ff.

3 ...The greatest organizer of an efficient standing army in the seventeenth century was Sweden's King Gustavus Adolphus, although great advancements in rationalizing military organizations were also made by Richelieu in the army and by Colbert in the navy, under Louis XIV. Whereas Gustavus had about 30,000 men under arms in 1631, Louis XIV is said to have maintained a military establishment of 400,000, with field armies approaching 100,000 — a size not to be duplicated until the French Revolution.

4 ...In size of population, Prussia, with 2½ million, was twelfth among European states in 1740, but largely through conquest this population had doubled by 1786. The Prussian army under Frederick the Great grew to about 200,000, with a field army of about 53,000, at the beginning of the Seven Years' War (as compared to an average size of 47,000 among first-rank field armies in the eighteenth century). Four-fifths of Prussia's revenue went into the army.

5 Among the civilian innovations of the eighteenth-century industrial revolution which transformed military technology in the latter part of the nineteenth were the steam engine, iron metallurgy, the shift from wood to coal for fuel, the rise of industrial chemistry, the establishment of a machine tool industry, and the beginnings of the science of electricity....

6 This is Marshal Foch's pronouncement occasioned by the famous cannonade at Valmy (1792), which marked the end of the Prussian offensive. Foch, *The Principles of War*, trans. Hilaire Belloc (New York: Henry Holt & Co., 1918), p. 29. Much earlier, Goethe and Clausewitz, among others, had interpreted the battle at Valmy as the end of the old warfare and the beginning of the new. Actually, Valmy was tactically insignificant, but it was strategically and politically significant because a citizen army withstood a model eighteenth-century army and permitted the Revolutionary forces to go on to future victories....

7 The conscription system introduced by the Prussian military reformers enabled Prussia to combine a relatively small, highly professional standing army with a large military potential and thereby to join numbers with skill at a tolerable cost. The system entailed compulsory universal service for several years with the regular army and the regular reserve and then with a civilian militia. The military organization of the railways entailed first constructing a railway network, then mobilizing the army, transporting it with weapons and supplies to the right spot at the right time, and finally deploying the forces properly. Prussia made many mistakes in conscription and railway organization in the war with Austria, but the General Staff studied the experience and profited from it. Michael Howard, *The Franco-Prussian War* (New York: Macmillan, 1961), pp. 18-29. Howard's study shows how substantially Prussia's success depended upon superior organization of mobilization and railway utilization.

8 Thus Dobrorolski, in charge of mobilization in Russia, insisted, "The whole plan of mobilization is worked out ahead to its end in all its details. When the moment has been chosen, one only has to press the button, and the whole state begins to function automatically with the precision of a clock's mechanism.... Once the moment has been fixed, everything is settled; there is no going back; it determines mechanically the beginning of war." Quoted in Sidney B. Fay, *The Origins of the World War,* 2d ed. rev. (New York: Macmillan, 1930), p. 481.

9 ...The French, although they developed the

machine gun shortly before the Franco-Prussian War, failed to exploit its potentialities because they used it like artillery instead of like rifles against infantry at close range. Improved models by the Americans Gatling and Browning and the Englishman Maxim were developed in the last half of the century, but the full significance of the machine gun was not demonstrated until World War I.

10 The longbow, which England developed in the thirteenth century and used to great advantage at Crécy (1346), Poitiers (1356), and Agincourt (1415), dominated the battlefield for 100 years and helped mightily to make England a great power. (Only the English mastered it, since only the English trained archers from childhood.) Yet the symbolic power of the British battleship, its peacetime uses, and its linkage with strategy and foreign policy had no counterpart in the longbow.

11 Arthur J. Marder, *The Anatomy of British Sea Power* (New York: Alfred A. Knopf, 1940), p. 9.

12 War games, however, often led to false conclusions. Thus the British Royal Navy's maneuvers of 1892 supported the belief that torpedo boats had little chance of success against fleets at sea. *Ibid.*, p. 166. But the first real example of this new technology in battle, provided by Japan against Russia in the war of 1904-5, contributed much to Japan's astonishing victory when torpedo boats attacked the Russian squadron in Port Arthur and sank a Russian flagship and three other ships in the decisive Battle of Tsushima.

13 The Elder Moltke and Joffre were exceptions in foreseeing a war of attrition, but neither undertook preparations for such a war. Only Lord Kitchener, who became war minister after war was declared, urged preparations for a long war of attrition. England's War Council, however, regarded his views as extravagant whimsy. Sir Philip Magnus, *Kitchener* (New York: E. P. Dutton & Co., 1959). The most detailed and well-reasoned prophecy of a war of attrition was made by Ivan S. Bloch in his six-volume work, *The Future of War in Its Technical, Economic, and Political Relations* (1897-99), which predicted that the increased firepower of guns would force entrenchment and stalemate. However, Bloch shared the consensus that modern war would be economically and socially catastrophic, or "impossible,"...

14 ...According to the official French history of the war, *Les armées françaises dans la grande guerre* (1922-25), French casualties in the month of August alone amounted to about 300,000 out of a field army of 1,600,000.

15 In World War II the mobilization of scientific and engineering talent for military purposes was especially comprehensive and effective in England. The British program grew into a gigantic co-ordinated international effort including Canada and the U.S. A great part of this effort went into the perfection of weapons developed in previous wars; but new inventions — most notably radar, the proximity fuse, and the atomic bomb — played an even more significant role than in World War I.

B: POWER, CAPABILITIES, AND THE USE OF FORCE

From Middle to Foremost Power: Defining a New Place for Canada in the Hierarchy of World Power

James Eayrs

It is the argument of this essay that the term "middle power" no longer does justice to Canada's role in world affairs. Canada has become instead a "foremost power" — foremost in the dictionary definition of "most notable or prominent". I hope to show that this assertion is no chauvinistic trumpery, no Laurier-like extravaganza ("the twenty-first century belongs to Canada"), but rather a realistic assessment of Canadian capabilities in a world where the substance, and hence the distribution, of power have undergone swift and radical change.

"Power" is the master-concept of politics. As life is to biology, space to astronomy, deity to theology, so is power to relations among individuals, groups and nations. Its very centrality in its field has caused theorists to take power for granted, to take power as given. But in politics nothing should be taken for granted, nothing taken as given.

Let us review, therefore, the properties of power, of which three are basic. Power is *perva-* power, of which three are basic. Power is *pervasive;* power is *elusive;* and power is *relative*. (Never dismiss platitudes; they often express essential truths.)

PERVASIVENESS OF POWER

What prose was for M. Jourdain ("Gracious me! For the last 40 years I have been speaking prose without knowing it."), power is for all of us. We may know power as its manipulators, we may know it as its victims, we may, like Jourdain, not know we know. But power is pervasive in our lives. Power is the ecology of politics. To talk of "power politics" is otiose, for there is no other kind.

Resistance to the notion of the pervasiveness of power is as pervasive as power itself. Saints, mystics, gurus of the hour or of the ages are often proclaimed by themselves and their disciples to be beyond the power principle, outside the power nexus.

Gandhi is widely cited as an example of a profoundly significant figure who refused to play the power game. Certainly the "half-naked, seditious fakir" (as Churchill once described him)

Reprinted with the kind permission of the author and publisher from *International Perspectives*, (May/June 1975), pp. 15-24.

appeared to dwell in a kind of power counter-culture — at loggerheads with power, at the antipodes from power. Certainly the saintly figure of the Mahatma in its ascetic's garb seemed even to his fellow Indians on first meeting to be (in Pandit Nehru's words) "very distant and different and unpolitical". How much more so must it have seemed to those worldly British politicians who — their exasperation rising as he remained beyond reach of the sort of argument to which politicians normally respond — tried to negotiate with him about the future of his country!

Gandhi's *satyagraha* — "clinging to truth" — demanded everything that power normally abhors. The shunning of duplicity. The turning of one's cheek. The avoiding of force even in the presence of a weaker adversary. No — the avoiding of force *especially* in the presence of a weaker adversary. And in the presence of a stronger? "I will come out into the open, and let the pilot see I have not a trace of evil against him [*sic*]". Such was Gandhi's bomber-defence system.

The strategy invites at worst derision, at best the comment made by Henry Kissinger about the only kind of pacifist he has the time of day for — "those who bear the consequences of non-violence to the end." "But," Kissinger adds, "even to them I will talk willingly merely to tell them that they will be crushed by the will of those that are strong, and that their pacifism can lead to nothing but horrible suffering."

Such an assessment gravely underrates the power of the Mahatma, which, skilfully deployed, made him the most influential politician — arguably — of our time. To interpret non-violent resistance as the rejection of power is to misunderstand the nature of power. The attraction of *satyagraha*, as of later strategies derived from it (notably Martin Luther King's), is precisely the expectation of potency. Gandhi never doubted it. "Working under this new law of non-violence," he wrote in 1920, "it is possible for a single individual to defy the whole might of an unjust empire." So it proved. Gandhi exaggerated only the novelty of *satyagraha*, which a Judean freedom-fighter had no less skilfully employed against the Romans 2,000 years before him.

PERVASION DENIED

Nations as well as individuals deny that power pervades. Especially newly-independent nations, which are characteristically reluctant to accept the fact that their hard-won freedom is no more than a licence to hunt in the jungle of power. They look on themselves as above the fray, beyond the struggle, reject the cynical aphorisms of the worldly philosophers — Kautilya's definition of an enemy as the state that is on one's border and of a friend as the state that is on the border of one's enemy, Hobbes's depiction of nations "in the state and posture of gladiators". George Washington for the young United States, Leon Trotsky for the young Bolshevik Republic, Raoul Dandurand for the newly-independent Dominion of Canada alike believed that the principles of their respective policies transcended the sordid statecraft of older, debauched societies.

These attitudes are much the same as those that try to claim for a Jesus or a Gandhi an immunity to power, and rest on the same confusion. What distinguishes them is not their exemption from having to play the game of power but rather their style of play. They have not renounced power, which is no more capable of renunciation by statesmen than gravity is capable of renunciation by spacemen. Theirs is not a renunciation at all, but an enunciation of a particular method of pursuing power — the method that strives after power not by the display or resort to bruising force but by the influence that good behaviour may exert upon opinion. It may not work; but that is another matter.

POWER ELUDES

Power pervades: there is no getting away from it. Power also eludes: there is no coming to grips with it. The elusiveness of power is beginning to preoccupy both practitioners and theorists, and about time, too!

> Our territory is large, our people are numerous, our geographical position is good.... It will be intolerable if after several decades we are not the greatest nation on earth.
>
> If we are six feet tall, the Russians are three feet tall, and the Chinese six inches tall.
>
> If one's line is correct, even if one has not a single soldier at first, there will be soldiers, and even if there is no political power, power will be gained.... The crux of the matter is line.
>
> One word of truth outweighs the whole world.

These four quotations — their authors, respectively, are Mao Tse-tung, U.S. Senator William Proxmire, Chou En-lai and Alexander Solzhenitsyn — are all statements about power, assessments of the constituents of power. They cannot all be correct. Those of Chou and Solzhenitsyn come close to saying the same thing, those of Chou and Mao are greatly at variance, while those of Mao and Proxmire are mutually incompatible.

The formulae of Mao and Proxmire do have something in common, however. Both proceed from geopolitical assumptions.

Geopolitical assumptions hold that power is a function of a nation's might, that the might of nations may be calculated more or less precisely, and that in consequence comparisons are possible, nations can be ranked and graded. The American humorist Russell Baker wrote a column — "Let's Hear It for No. 7" — in which he argued, tongue only half-in-cheek, that "countries that are No. 11 or No. 17" (he cites Denmark and Kenya) "don't have to spend all their income to get ready to wipe themselves out" and "as a result are often very pleasant countries". He does not want the United States to drop from No. 1 to No. 17, but sees distinct advantages in seventh place.

BASIS FOR CALCULATION

But how to tell that seventh place — or fourth or fifth or sixth? If might is amenable to calculation, what makes the mighty mighty, what makes them mightier yet?

Geopoliticians' answers differed. Some said mighty populations — the state with the biggest battalions. Others said mighty reserves — the state with the greatest bullion. Some said control of the seas, others control of the land. Some said control of the air, others control of the firmament: "If the Soviets control space, they can control earth" — thus John F. Kennedy in 1960 (making his pitch for the aerospace vote).

The ranking of Japan is a good example of the method, and even better of its limitations. Here power is seen to come not from the barrel of a gun but from the greatest GNP, in anticipation of which (this before the higher cost of a different kind of barrel) Herman Kahn foresaw the emergence of the Japanese super-state by the year 2000. For Edwin O. Reischauer (U.S. Ambassador to Japan during the Kennedy and Johnson Administrations), there is no need to wait so long: "Japan is the No. 2 power in the world."

How does he know? That being too difficult, what makes it so? If the key to Japanese power is export, the key to Japanese export is the qualities of those who make the product high in craftsmanship, low in cost — qualities once epitomized as those of the chrysanthemum and the sword: the sensibility of Japanese design, the zeal of Japanese application to the task at hand, be that overrunning Southeast Asia in the early 1940s or mass-assembling transistor television sets in the early 1970s. A *New York Times* correspondent puts it this way: "American officials and scholars have produced tomes trying to explain why the Japanese have done so well; it may be an oversimplification, but the fundamental reason is that they work like blazes." That does not explain why they work like blazes, but it may be better than no explanation at all.

Elusive as ever, power now seems to reside in the spirit of a people, in their mood and morale — aspects of might about which even neo-geopoliticians do well to hold their peace. "Great things need no firm foundation," the father of Zionism once remarked. "An apple must be placed on a table to keep it from falling. The earth hovers in the air. Thus I can perhaps found a secure Jewish state without a firm anchorage. The secret lies in movement. Hence I believe that somewhere a guidable aircraft will be discovered." (Herzl's metaphor of "a guidable aircraft", evoked some years before the Wright brothers took flight, is almost as remarkable as his forecast, in 1896, of the State of Israel more than a half a century before its birth.) Using a similar metaphor, a commentator accounted in 1905 for the success of British power in India: "The Indian empire is not a miracle in the rhetorician's sense but in the theologian's sense. It is a thing which exists and is alive, but cannot be accounted for by any process of reasoning founded on experience. It is a miracle, as a floating island of granite would be a miracle, or a bird of brass which flew and sung and lived on in mid-air. It is a structure built on nothing, without foundations, without buttresses [compare Herzl's "without a firm anchorage"] held in its place by some force the origin of which is undiscoverable and the nature of which has never been explained."

The modern illustration is surely Yugoslavia. Some wit once dismissed that country as a fifth-rate power. Asked for his impression of Belgrade, he replied: "Imagine a whole city illuminated with a 10-watt bulb." But the power of Yugoslavia is not to be measured by its wattage. "According to all rational calculations," A.J.P. Taylor has written, "Yugoslavia was the country most doomed to disintegrate in the storms of the twentieth century. It has few natural resources: little coal or iron and a territory largely composed of barren mountains.... Historical traditions, though strong, work against unity, not in its favour." Whence, then, derives its power? From defiance — from defying Stalin and succeeding. "Yugoslavia has been living on the strength of this defiance ever since."

The elusiveness of power may be seen not only in its possession by those who, on "rational calculations", have no right to it but also in its lack by those who, on calculations no less rational, have every right to it. Here is the cry of S. John Peskett in *The Times,* who, with the rest of us, has seen the assumptions of geopolitics, like so many sand-castle Gibraltars, washed away by the tide: "All the Queen's horses and all the Queen's men, plus the United States of America, the United Nations, NATO, and all the parachutists and glider troops we so busily train, cannot rescue a couple of hundred hostages and a few million pounds worth of aircraft from a handful of guerrillas half of whom are quarreling with the other."

RELATIVE TO USE

Power is pervasive, power is elusive. Power is also relative — relative not least to purpose. What you have of it depends on what you want to do with it.

The relativity of power is most simply illustrated by the distinction between the power to build and the power to destroy. The power to build — to create, to innovate, to improve — is hard to come by, arduous to exercise. It derives from resourceful diplomacy and nimble statecraft, sustained as these must be by a generous and patient citizenry. Rome was not built in a day; how much longer it takes to build a world free from poverty, ignorance, disease!

The power to destroy — to wreck, to frustrate, to sabotage — is, in contrast easy to come by, effortless to exercise. Little is required to smash some cherished project, to bring things tumbling down — only a rifle with a telescopic sight, an assassin hired by the hour. "I'm as important as the start of World War One," bragged Arthur Bremer to his diary when in Ottawa to try to kill his President. "I just need the little opening and a second of time."

The power exerted by these demolition experts — the Tepermans, so to speak, of the global village — can be very great. But it is the kind of power a blackmailer exerts over a wealthy victim — potent while it lasts, but of short duration and likely to end unpleasantly for both of them. It is the power wielded by a pyromaniac in a fireworks factory. It is the power displayed by the President of Libya, threatening retaliation unless the UN Security Council voted to his liking — "Otherwise we shall see what we shall see. We shall do what Samson did: destroy the temple with everyone inside it, including ourselves. Europe should look out for the catastrophe which is lying in wait for it."

Such are the properties of power. Were they fixed clearly in the minds of those who coined the expression "middle power" to describe Canada's place among the nations? I cannot prove it, but I doubt it.

OBSCURITY PREFERRED

For all that has been written about "Canada's role as a middle power" (and much has been written about it), its meaning remains obscure. Obscurity has, indeed, seemed preferable to clarity, Canadians resisting definition as an earlier generation resisted defining "Dominion status" for fear (as Lloyd George put it) of limiting their constitution "by too many finalities". "It is hard to say now precisely what a middle power is," John Holmes confessed in 1965; but that does not bother him. On the contrary: "I am all for accepting this ambiguity rather than insisting on a logical clarification." And again: "The more one tries to define [middle power], the more difficult and perhaps pretentious it appears to do so at all. Often it seems like describing the obvious. Definition spoils the special quality."

The origins of the term are as obscure as its meaning. If it was not used first in 1943, it was used first in 1944, for by 1945 "middle power" had come into widespread circulation. The year 1943 is when Canadians both in and out of government first gave thought to what their place in the postwar world might and ought to be. From the beginning, the prospect of divergence between that "might" and "ought" was both ominous and real. In 1943 Canada stood in the shadow of the United States and Britain. So long as a war remained to be won, such a position was not intolerable, might be construed as part of the Canadian war effort — unpleasant, but something to be put up with for the duration. But as a permanent stance for the postwar future it was out of the question, and Canadians began to say so.

Articulation of discontent was aroused by the threat of exclusion from the ruling circles of the first of the postwar international organizations. Word that Canada — of all countries — was to be left off the governing body of the United Nations Relief and Rehabilitation Agency sent shocks of anger around the foreign policy community. "We are still trying to run a democracy" (so, with notable asperity, the Government, as quoted in the Pearson memoirs, instructed its agent in Washington charged with arguing his country's case) "and there is some historical evidence to support the thesis that democracies cannot be taxed without representation. We have tried to lead our people in a full-out effort for the war, and we had hoped that we could continue to lead them in such a way as to get their support behind the provision of relief and maintenance for battle-scarred Europe in the postwar years. We will not be able to secure their support for such a programme if it, as well as the economic affairs of the world generally, are to be run as a monopoly by the four Great Powers."

UNITED STATES CRUCIAL

Of the four great powers, the United States was crucial for the Canadian case. If Washington would not offer sympathy and support for the aspirations of its friendly neighbour, who else could? But Washington's response left much to be desired. Our status was but dimly recognized, our stature underrated.

In 1925, an eminent American professor of international politics had placed Canada in the category of "other states of subordinate or doubtful rank". In 1939, President Franklin D. Roosevelt felt bound to telephone the Prime Minister to ascertain whether Canada was bound by a British declaration of war. In 1943, wags in Washington were saying that Canada was in the British Commonwealth Mondays, Tuesdays, Wednesdays, an ally of the United States Thursdays, Fridays, Saturdays, and only on Sundays a sovereign independent state. Canadians were not amused.

On 19 March 1943, the Prime Minister of Canada for the first time since the outbreak of the war was asked in Parliament to set forth his views on foreign policy as it might develop in the postwar world. Here was a subject on which Mackenzie King cared not at all to dilate: "The more [the] public...is diverted to questions about what is going to be the attitude of this country and that country at the peace table and [in] the postwar period, the less the country will be impressed with the fact that this war itself is not yet won." But something needed to be said, and what he chose to say was what he had said in the House of Commons as long ago as May 24, 1938:

> Our foreign and external policy is a policy of peace and friendliness, a policy of trying to look after our own interests and to understand the position of other governments with which we have dealings. It is a policy which takes account of our political connections and traditions, our geographical position, the limited numbers and the racial composition of our people, our stage in economic development, our own internal preoccupations and necessities — in short, a policy based on the Canadian situation. It is not and cannot be under these circumstances a spectacular headline policy; it is simply the sum of countless daily dealings with other countries, the general resultant of an effort to act decently on every issue or incident that arises, and a hope of receiving the same treatment from others.

The authors of the volume in the *Canada in World Affairs* series for 1941-44 in which this passage is quoted allow themselves a restrained but telling comment: "Mr. King did not make any modification of this five-year-old statement to conform with the revolutionary development which had taken place in Canada's war potential and industrial production."

Indeed he did not. That would have been inconsistent with his style — a style which, when he came to enunciate principles of foreign policy, chose (to adapt the lyrics of a song of that era) "to eliminate the positive, latch on to the negative."

Even in 1938 — so it seems to one fair-minded and knowledgeable observer, Nicholas Mansergh — the statement overdrew the difficulties, stressing "the precariousness of Canada's export markets, but not the value of her exports;...regional and cultural tensions within, but not the growing sense of unity;...the conflicting pulls of geography and history to which indeed every 'settled' country is subject, but...not the immense strength of Canada's position in the heart of the English-speaking world." In 1943 the statement greatly underrated the country's power. Canada's uranium alone might have been used to extract from the Anglo-American partners in atomic-energy production virtually any concession on postwar status. But that is not how its leaders chose to play their hand.

Still, it was plain folly to continue to be content with lisping their hope for decent treatment in a world about to gain knowledge of the holocaust and to witness Hiroshima. Such ultra-diffident diplomacy would lose Canada's case by default. Even Mackenzie King was soon compelled to realize as much. July 1943 finds him, for the first time, striving after a postwar status commensurate with wartime stature:

> A number of new international institutions are likely to be set up as a result of the war. In the view of the Government, effective representation on these bodies should neither be restricted to the largest states nor necessarily extended to all states. Representation should be determined on a functional basis which will admit to full membership those countries, large or small, which have the greatest contribution to make to the particular object in question.

Here is the germ of "the Canadian doctrine of the middle powers," for a moment's reflection upon its implications is sufficient to indicate how inadequate the "great power/small power" dichotomy had become. "The simple division of the world between great powers and the rest is unreal and even dangerous," Mackenzie King declared to Parliament in August 1944:

> The great powers are called by that name simply because they possess great power. The other states of the world possess power and, therefore, the capacity to use it for the maintenance of peace — in varying degrees ranging from almost zero in the case of the smallest and weakest states up to a military potential not far below that of the great powers.

Somewhere on this spectrum of power lay Canada.

But where? Policy-makers developed a concern with ranking. "We are moving up in the International League," L.B. Pearson told a Toronto audience in March 1944, "even though we are not yet in the first division." And, in a letter written at that time, Pearson groped closer than anyone had thus far done to the concept of the "middle power":

> Canada is achieving, I think, a very considerable position as a leader, among a group of States which are important enough to be necessary to the Big Four but not important enough to be accepted as one of that quartet. As a matter of fact, the position of a "little Big Power" or "big little Power" is a very difficult one, especially if the "little Big Power" is also a "Big Dominion". The big fellows have power and responsibility, but they also have control. We "in-between States" sometimes get, it seems, the worst of both worlds. We are necessary but not necessary enough. I think this is being felt by countries like the Netherlands and Belgium as well as by ourselves. That is why these countries are not only looking towards the Big Powers, but are looking toward each other for support. There is, I think, an opportunity for Canada, if we desire to take it, to become the leader of this group.

Comparisons may be odious but, as time ran out on Canadian efforts to secure a position on the proposed United Nations Security Council, they became unavoidable. "Just as we are prepared to recognize the great difference in power and responsibility between Canada and the Soviet Union," Mackenzie King told the meeting of Commonwealth prime ministers on May 11, 1944, "[so] we should expect some recognition of the considerable difference between Canada and Panama." Reaffirming, against continued British opposition, its belief that powers other than the great powers should be represented on the Council, the Canadian Government repeated its conviction that their selection "should in some way be related to a dispassionate appraisal of their probable effective contribution to the maintenance of security." "You will, I am sure" — Mackenzie King thought it well to add for Churchill's benefit — "appreciate how difficult it would be for Canada, after enlisting nearly one million persons in her armed forces and trebling her national debt in order to assist in restoring peace, to accept a position of parity in this respect with the Dominican Republic or El Salvador."

Such perceptions were widely shared throughout the country. For some Canadians, indeed, their Government's disclaimer of topmost status — "Canada certainly makes no claim to be regarded as a great power" — seemed to be too bashful, too reserved. "A great world power standing beside Great Britain in the British Empire" was Howard Green's vision of our postwar future. "A country large enough to have world interests," was the assessment of the *Windsor Star*. And a leading Canadian publicist, pondering "A Greater Canada among the Nations", saw our role like this:

> Under the impact of war, Canada has moved up from her old status to a new stature. With her smaller population and lack of colonial possessions, she is not a major or world power like Britain, the United States or Russia. But with her natural wealth and human capacity she is not a minor one like Mexico or Sweden. She stands between as a Britannic Power of medium rank.

In short, a middle power. The term was officially employed for the first time in a despatch from the Department of External Affairs to heads of mission in the five capitals of the countries to which, on January 12, 1945, the Canadian Government made a final (and unavailing) appeal for representation on the Security Council; the exact phrase used was "a so-called middle power". The term was officially defined for the first time in a speech made by R.G. Riddell in 1947: "The Middle Powers are those which by reason of their size, their material resources, their willingness and ability to accept responsibility, their influence and stability are close to being great powers."

PROMOTION SOUGHT

The term "middle power" came into the vocabulary of diplomacy as part of a Canadian campaign to gain promotion from the status of a small power. But that is not the only purpose for which it may be used. It can also be an instrument of demotion. It lends itself not only to aggrandizement but to disparagement as well — as in the expression "merely a middle power."

An instance of how "middle power" may be used for the purpose of demotion and disparagement was reported from Moscow in 1955 on the occasion of Pearson's visit to the Soviet Union. At a reception at the Canadian Embassy for the diplomatic corps, the Canadian and Soviet foreign ministers exchanged some significant banter. "Mr. Molotov and I ought to understand each other," said Pearson joshingly. "We belong to the same trade union but he is a much more important member than I am." "Mr. Pearson is too modest," Molotov responded. "Canada is among the great powers." When Pearson jocularly compared Canada's position between the United States and the Soviet Union to that of the ham in a sandwich, Lazar Kaganovich chimed in to suggest that "a good bridge" was a better comparison. Nor was that the end of it. At a reception some days later, the Canadian Secretary of State for External Affairs found himself (according to one of the reporters present) "in the position of arguing that Canada is a small, rather frail country, while the Russians argued that Canada is a big, important one.... As Mr. Pearson pursued this line that Canada is a small nation, Molotov broke in. He said the Russians do not agree with the foreign minister. In the schools of his country, said Molotov, the children are taught to regard Canada as one of the world's major powers."

Not too much should be made of this exchange (it is not reported in Pearson's memoirs except for a fleeting reference to "flattering toasts to Canada"); it bears, indeed, a close resemblance to what George Kennan recalls as the "slightly disreputable" remarks which passed ritualistically between himself and assorted Latin American presidents some years before ("'You, Mr. Kennan, are an official of the government of a great country; and I am only the President of an obscure little country'; 'Ah, Mr. President, that may be, but we are all aware that there is no connection between the size of a country and the amount of political wisdom it can produce'.") Much more significant is the deliberately depreciating analysis of Canada's place in the world put out from the Prime Minister's office on May 29, 1968, soon after Pierre Trudeau arrived there:

> Canada's position in the world is now very different from that of the postwar years. Then we were probably the largest of the small powers. Our currency was one of the strongest. We were the fourth or fifth trading nation and our economy was much stronger than the European economies. We had one of the very strongest navy [*sic*] and air forces. But now Europe has regained its strength. The Third World has emerged....
>
> These are the broad lines of the international environment in which Canada finds itself today. What are we proposing to do about it? We are going to begin with a thorough and comprehensive review of our foreign policy which embraces defence, economic and aid policies....

Without prejudging the findings of that review, it was nonetheless possible to state in a word what its objective ought to be. The word was "realism":

"Realism — that should be the operative word in our definition of international aim. Realism in how we read the world barometer. Realism in how we see ourselves thriving in the climate it forecasts." And the first requirement of realism was that "we should not exaggerate the extent of our influence upon the course of world events".

In the course of public speaking over the next few months, the Prime Minister returned again and again to this opening theme. On December 18, 1968, asked by an interviewer if Canada should revert to its postwar role as a leader of the middle powers, Mr. Trudeau demurred:

> Personally I tend to discount the weight of our influence in the world....I think we should be modest, much more modest than we were, I think, in the postwar years when we were an important power because of the disruption of Europe and so on. But right now we're back to our normal size as it is and I think we must realize that we have limited energy, limited resources and, as you said earlier, intellectual and [*sic*] manpower. Therefore, we must use modesty....We shouldn't be trying to run the world.

On January 1, 1969:

> ...We're living in a world where the strategy is dominated by two powers. All we can do is talk a little bit about tactics but not much.

And on March 25, 1969 (to the National Press Club in Washington):

> I hope that we Canadians do not have an exaggerated view of our own importance.... We may be excused, I hope, if we fail to take too seriously the suggestions of some of our friends from time to time that our acts, or our failure to act — this or that way — will have profound international consequences or will lead to wide-scale undesirable results.

No one familiar with the role of a prime minister in the formulation of Canadian foreign policy will be surprised to learn that these ideas emerged relatively intact as the basic philosophy of the White Paper embodying the results of the foreign policy review when it appeared in 1970. Much has been written about *Foreign Policy for Canadians* — if the purpose was to spark discussion, it succeeded admirably in that purpose — to which there is no need to add. But one point must be made.

It was the Prime Minister's expectation and intention that the results of the review would endure. He believed that the review would outfit Canadians with a foreign policy that would do them for a couple of decades. "When you make a decision to review your foreign policy," Mr. Trudeau remarked in Calgary on April 12, 1969, "it will last for quite a while.... You only re-examine your foreign policy once in a generation. You can't switch every year, you can't switch after every election."

Here is a major error. You can switch, and you must. To stay put for so long is not just to risk being overtaken by events, it guarantees it.

MAJOR CHANGES

Between 1970 and 1975, three major changes have occurred within the international system that have drastically altered the pattern of power. Each is advantageous — or prospectively advantageous — to Canada.

The first is the emergence of what might be called "le défi OPEC" — that sudden accretion of wealth to the low-cost, oil-bearing countries of the Middle East that is currently netting their treasuries enormous "petrodollar" revenue.

It remains to be seen whether the assorted sheikhdoms and emirates that are the beneficiaries of this windfall can transmute their wealth to power, even whether they will enjoy the prosperity of Croesus or suffer the fate of Midas. (Shah Pahlavi and the late King Faisal show it can go either way.) Two consequences, however, are already clear.

One is that the power of oil-dependent industrial countries — all Western European states that lack access to North Sea sources and Japan — has been drastically reduced. The other is that the power of oil-sufficient industrial countries has been substantially increased — nowhere more so than in Canada, where oil is providentially found in conjunction with other sources of energy (notably coal).

RESOURCE POWER

A second major change of the past five years is the declining capacity of technology to confer power and the growing capacity of resources to confer it. To a world where population continues an exponential rate of climb towards demographic disaster, ultra-modern processes for the transmission and manipulation of data are more and more irrelevant and in less and less demand. Such a world requires computers, photocopiers and satellite communication systems less than it needs raw materials, minerals and — above all — food. Power is shifting from those who control the former to those who control the latter. A recent discussion of *The New Wealth of Nations* by Charles F. Gallagher identifies this trend:

> In a world of finite and dwindling physical assets the balance of market values has shifted, at least temporarily and perhaps for a very long period, from the ability of technology to create and develop new assets to the capacity of existing assets to command considerations that will permit the purchase of technology and the procurement of power. For long technology was joined to capital in a fruitful marriage, a happy coupling that developed material resources and created new assets. Today it is resources which have alienated the affections of capital and created conditions permitting the downgrading of technology to the status of a hand-maiden serving the new connubial union. In short, skills have been reduced to a position in which they are traded at a discount relative to goods. He who has the right materials is better off than he who has the right training....
>
> Because of the revaluation and redistribution of the chips of the game, we have a rearrangement in the classification of nations today.

If this is bad news for the Science Council of Canada, it is good news for the Government of Canada. It means that Canada is exceptionally well endowed to face the worst (short of nuclear war) the future may fling at mankind, exceptionally well equipped for what has been called "the desperate misadventure we are now engaged upon", as well-prepared as any people for those dismal "human prospects" envisaged by melancholiacs who forecast global breakdown. We have what it takes, since we have all it takes.

Canada has almost sinfully bestowed upon it the sources of power, both traditional and new. The technology is there, or waiting. (We need only decide how much technology to develop for ourselves, how much to buy from others.) The manpower is there, or waiting. (We need only decide how many millions more our country needs, then pick amongst the jostling clamourers according to the criteria of our choice.) The resources are there, or waiting, too — animal, vegetable *and* mineral. Hardly a month elapses without the revelation of some new bonanza in our larder. (We need only decide how fast to develop them, how much to charge for them.)

DECLINE OF U.S.

Finally — in part because of these two changes but only just in part — a third change that Peter Wiles has called "the declining self-confidence of the super-powers". These are super-powers now in name only. The decline in self-confidence is most striking in the United States — for reasons that require no elaboration. (The most telling thing about "Watergate" is that it could not have happened in the Soviet Union.) "No nation can pretend to be a super-power," writes C.L. Sulzburger about his country's recent compound fractures, "when its foreign policy suffers such blows as that of the United States in Southeast and Southwest

Asia, when its economy reels, its unemployment zooms, its currency staggers, and when its leadership, symbolized by a Chief Executive who chooses that moment to take time off for golf, faces its crises in paralyzed confusion."

For Canadians to exult in American misfortune for its own sake would be the grossest form of *Schadenfreude*. Not for a moment do I suggest we should. I suggest only that we do so for our own sake.

It has not been good for Canada to have been obliged to exist so long in the shadow of a luminous imperial America, whose achievements in whatever field, measured by whatever standard, have so consistently outclassed our own. On the contrary, this condition has been a prescription for crippling neurosis. America's descent from the dizzy heights of power and responsibility which under successive administrations it has occupied since the era of the Marshall Plan offers Canada a chance to stand with more assurance in the light. Only a masochist could fail to welcome such an opportunity.

The opportunity is there, or waiting. "We live in a century," the Prime Minister of Canada remarked in the presence of the Premier of China, "where, increasingly, national greatness is measured not in terms of martial grandeur or even economic accomplishment but in terms of individual welfare and human dignity. No longer is military might or political hegemony the yardstick of achievement. The true test of a government is found in its ability to provide its people with a sense of worth, of accomplishment, of fulfilment." For the first time since 1945, it has become plausible to argue that Canada's chance of passing such a test is just as good as that of the United States — perhaps even better.

A recent attempt by Peter Dobell to re-rank Canada among the nations in accordance with these new realities promotes us from "middle power" to "minor great power". But such terms as "great power", whether minor or major, have, like "middle power" itself, lost all significance and meaning. I should be content with "foremost power" — if we produce a foreign policy to match.

B: POWER, CAPABILITIES, AND THE USE OF FORCE

To What Ends Military Power?

Robert J. Art

From the end of World War II until now, America's conventional wisdom about the efficacy of military power as an instrument of foreign policy has changed in dramatic fashion twice. Each change in the conventional wisdom was caused by a war, first by the Korean, then by the Vietnamese. The first change occurred almost instantaneously, with the onset of the Korean War. The second took much longer to materialize, coming only after military success repeatedly eluded America in Vietnam. Each change in the conventional wisdom was produced by a marked shift in the thinking about the role that military power could and should play in America's foreign policy. Each change, consequently, altered the balance that had previously been struck among the military, economic, and political tools of statecraft.

From the end of World War II until June of 1950, the foci of America's efforts were Europe and Japan. The prime tools of policy were economic aid and political commitment. Military power, especially in the form of military assistance and of the deterrent effect of her nuclear monopoly, was not irrelevant to America's policy. But military power took third place because fears of internal political subversion, not direct military attack, were what dominated official American thinking. The North Korean attack shattered that assumption. With fear of direct attack now prime, America proceeded to globalize her containment policy, to elevate prior commitment to defend others to a fine art, and to militarize her foreign policy. The hallmarks of the fifties and sixties were large defense budgets, proliferation of alliance and other forms of military commitments, and military interventions. The Vietnam War was both the epitome of that era and its apogee.

The second change — and the third phase — began in the late 1960s. The Nixon Doctrine, which meant that U.S. allies would henceforth have to provide the cannon fodder for future land wars, represented official recognition of the domestic revulsion against the exercise of military power. But two other factors were also at work in devaluing the central role that military power had played. By the early 1970s, America publicly recognized, in the form of the 1972 SALT I Accord, that her strategic nuclear superiority over Russia had ended. Similarly, by unilaterally closing the gold window and in effect devaluing the dollar, America in 1971 publicly testified to the waning of

---

Robert J. Art, "To What Ends Military Power?" *International Security,* Vol. 4 (Spring 1980), pp. 3-35. Reprinted by permission of the MIT Press Journals. Portions of the text have been deleted. Some footnotes have been removed; those remaining have been renumbered.

her economic preeminence. The hallmarks of the 1970s were the touted complexities of economic interdependence, the reluctance of the foreign policy elite to contemplate military interventionism, and a decline in America's overall military position relative to Russia's. The inability, or unwillingness, of America to take military action against OPEC symbolized to most the devaluation of military power as a tool of policy.

...We are clearly in the midst of a third sea-change in the conventional wisdom. Deep concern over Russia's perceived worldwide political and military advances is the underlying factor for change. Frustration with seeming impotence against OPEC and reaction against loss of American prestige are contributory. We may well be on the verge of a prodigious and sustained increase in military spending.

In view of what is likely to be before us, it is vital to think carefully and precisely about the uses and limits of military power. That is the purpose of this essay. It is intended as a backdrop for policy debates, not a prescription of specific policies. It consciously eschews elaborate detail on the requisite military forces for scenarios *a* ... *n* and focuses instead on what military power has and has not done, can and cannot do. Every model of how the world works has policy implications. But not every policy is based on a clear view of how the world works. What, then, are the uses to which military power can be put? How have nuclear weapons affected these uses? And what is the future of force in a world of nuclear parity and increasing economic interdependence?

WHAT ARE THE USES OF FORCE?

The goals that states pursue range widely and vary considerably from case to case. Military power is more useful for realizing some goals than others, though it is generally considered of some use by most states for all of the goals that they hold. If we attempt, however, to be descriptively accurate, to enumerate all of the purposes for which states use force, we shall simply end up with a bewildering list. Descriptive accuracy is not a virtue *per se* for analysis. In fact, descriptive accuracy is generally bought at the cost of analytical utility. (A concept that is descriptively accurate is usually analytically useless.) Therefore, rather than compile an exhaustive list of such purposes, I have selected four categories that themselves analytically exhaust the functions that force can serve: defense, deterrence, compellence, and "swaggering".[1]

Not all four functions are necessarily well or equally served by a given military posture. In fact, usually only the great powers have the wherewithall to develop military forces that can serve more than two functions at once. Even then, this is achieved only vis-à-vis smaller powers, not vis-à-vis the other great ones. The measure of the capabilities of a state's military forces must be made relative to those of another state, not with reference to some absolute scale. A state that can compel another state can also defend against it and usually deter it. A state that can defend against another state cannot thereby automatically deter or compel it. A state can deter another state without having the ability to either defend against or compel it. A state that can swagger vis-à-vis another may or may not be able to perform any of the other three functions relative to it. Where feasible, defense is the goal that all states aim for first. If defense is not possible, deterrence is generally the next priority. Swaggering is the function most difficult to pin down analytically; deterrence, the one whose achievement is the most difficult to demonstrate; compellence, the easiest to demonstrate but among the hardest to achieve. The following discussion develops these points more fully.

The *defensive* use of force is the deployment of military power so as to be able to do two things — to ward off an attack and to minimize damage to oneself if attacked. For defensive purposes, a state will direct its forces against those of a potential or actual attacker, but not against his unarmed population. For defensive purposes, a state can deploy its forces in place prior to an attack, use them after an attack has occurred to repel it, or strike first if it believes that an attack upon it is imminent or inevitable. The defensive use of force can thus involve both peaceful and physical employment and both repellent (second) strikes and offensive (first) strikes.[2] If a state strikes first when it believes an attack upon it is imminent, it is launching a preemptive blow. If it strikes first when it believes an attack is inevitable but not momentary, it is launching a preventive blow. Preemptive and preventive blows are undertaken when a state calculates, first, that others plan to attack it and, second, that to delay in striking offensively is against its interests. A state preempts in order to wrest the advantage of the first strike from an opponent. A state launches a preventive attack because it believes that others will attack it when the balance of forces turns in their favor and therefore attacks while the balance of forces is in its favor. In both cases it is better to strike first than to be struck first. The major distinction between preemption and prevention is the calculation about when an opponent's attack will occur. For preemption, it is a matter of hours, days, or even a few weeks at the most; for prevention, months or even a few years. In the case of preemption, the state has almost no control over the timing of its attack; in the case of prevention, the state can in a more leisurely way contemplate the timing of its attack. For both cases, it is the belief in the certainty of war that governs the offensive, defensive attack. For both cases, the maxim, "the best defense is a good offense," makes good sense.

The *deterrent* use of force is the deployment of military power so as to be able to prevent an adversary from doing something that one does not want him to do and that he might otherwise be tempted to do by threatening him with unacceptable punishment if he does it. Deterrence is thus the threat of retaliation. Its purpose is to prevent something undesirable from happening. The threat of punishment is directed at the adversary's population and/or industrial infrastructure. The effectiveness of the threat depends upon a state's ability to convince a potential adversary that it has both the will and power to punish him severely if he undertakes the undesirable action in question. Deterrence therefore employs force peacefully. It is the threat to resort to force in order to punish that is the essence of deterrence. If the threat has to be carried out, deterrence by definition has failed. A deterrent threat is made precisely with the intent that it will not have to be carried out. Threats are made to prevent actions from being undertaken. If the threat has to be implemented, the action has already been undertaken. Hence deterrence can be judged successful only if the retaliatory threats have not been implemented.

Deterrence and defense are alike in that both are intended to protect the state or its closest allies from physical attacks. The purpose of both is dissuasion — persuading others *not* to undertake actions harmful to oneself. The defensive use of force dissuades by convincing an adversary that he cannot conquer one's military forces. The deterrent use of force dissuades by convincing the adversary that his population and territory will suffer terrible damage if he initiates the undesirable action. Defense dissuades by presenting an unvanquishable military force. Deterrence dissuades by presenting the certainty of retaliatory devastation.

Defense is possible without deterrence, and deterrence is possible without defense. A state can have the military wherewithall to repel an invasion without also being able to threaten devastation to the invader's population or territory. Similarly, a state can have the wherewithall credibly to threaten an adversary with such devastation and yet be unable to repel his invading force. Defense, therefore, does not necessarily buy deterrence, nor deterrence defense. A state that can defend itself from attack, moreover, will have little need to develop the wherewithall to deter. If physical attacks can be repelled or if the damage from them drastically minimized, the incentive to develop a retaliatory capability is low. A state that cannot defend itself, however, will try to develop an effective deterrent if that be possible. No state will leave its population and territory open to attack if it has the means to redress the situation. Whether a given state can defend or deter or do both vis-à-vis another depends upon two factors: 1) the quantitative balance of forces between it and its adversary; and 2) the qualitative balance of forces, that is, whether the extant military technology favors the offense or the defense. These two factors are situation-specific and therefore require careful analysis of the case at hand.

The *compellent* use of force is the deployment of military power so as to be able either to stop an adversary from doing something that he has already undertaken or to get him to do something that he has not yet undertaken. Compellence, in Schelling's words, "involves initiating an action ...that can cease, or become harmless, only if the opponent responds."[3] Compellence can employ force either physically or peacefully. A state can start actually harming another with physical destruction until the latter abides by the former's wishes. Or, a state can take actions against another that do not cause physical harm but that require the latter to pay some type of significant price until it changes its behavior. America's bombing of North Vietnam in early 1965 was an example of physical compellence; Tirpitz's building of a German fleet aimed against England's in the two decades before World War I, an example of peaceful compellence. In the first case, the United States started bombing North Vietnam in order to compel it to stop it from assisting the Vietcong forces in South Vietnam. In the latter case, Germany built a battlefleet that in an engagement threatened to cripple England's in order to compel her to make a general political settlement advantageous to Germany. In both cases, one state initiated some type of action against another precisely so as to be able to stop it, to bargain it away for the appropriate response from the "put upon" state.

The distinction between compellence and deter rence is one between the active and passive use of force. The success of a deterrent threat is measured by its not having to be used. The success of a compellent action is measured by how closely and quickly the adversary conforms to one's stipulated wishes. In the case of successful deterrence, one is trying to demonstrate a negative, to show why something did not happen. It can never be clear whether one's actions were crucial to, or irrelevant to, why another state chose *not* to do something. In the case of successful compellence, the clear sequence of actions and reactions lends a compelling plausibility to the centrality of one's actions.... In successful compellence, state B can claim that its pressure deflected state A from its course of action. In successful deterrence, state B has no change in state A's behavior to point to, but instead must resort to claiming that its threats were responsible for the continuity in A's behavior. State A may have changed its behavior for reasons other than state B's compellent action. State A may have continued with its same behavior for reasons other than state B's deterrent threat. "Proving" the importance of B's influence on A for either case is not easy, but it is more plausible to claim that B influenced A when there is a change in A's behavior than when there is not. Explaining why something did not happen is more difficult than explaining why something did.

Compellence may be easier to demonstrate than deterrence, but it is harder to achieve. Schelling argues that compellent actions tend to be vaguer in their objectives than deterrent threats and for that reason more difficult to attain.[4] If an adversary has a hard time understanding what it is that one wishes him to do, his compliance with one's wishes is made more difficult. There is, however, no inherent reason why a compellent action must be vaguer than a deterrent threat with regard to how clearly the adversary understands what is wanted from him. "Do not attack me" is not any clearer in its ultimate meaning than "stop attacking my friend." A state can be as confused or as clear about what it wishes to prevent as it can be about what it wishes to stop. The clarity, or lack of it, of the objectives of compellent actions and deterrent threats does not vary according to whether the given action is compellent or deterrent in nature, but rather according to a welter of particularities associated with the given action. Some objectives, for example, are inherently clearer and hence easier to perceive than others. Some statesmen communicate more clearly than others. Some states have more power to bring to bear for a given objective than others. It is the specifics of a given situation, not any intrinsic difference between compellence and deterrence, that determines the clarity with which an objective is perceived.

We must, therefore, look elsewhere for the reason as to why compellence is comparatively harder to achieve than deterrence. It lies, not in what one asks another to do, but in *how* one asks. With deterrence, state B asks something of state A in this fashion: "do not take action X; for if you do, I will bash you over the head with this club." With compellence, state B asks something of state A in this fashion: "I am now going to bash you over the head with this club and will continue to do so until you do what I want." In the former case, state A can easily deny with great plausibility any intention of having planned to take action X. In the latter case, state A cannot deny either that it is engaged in a given course of action or that it is being subjected to pressure by state B. If they are to be successful, compellent actions require a state to alter its behavior in a manner quite visible to all in response to an equally visible forceful initiative taken by another state. In contrast to compellent actions, deterrent threats are both easier to appear to have ignored or easier to acquiesce to without great loss of face. In contrast to deterrent threats, compellent actions more directly engage the prestige and the passions of the put upon state. Less prestige is lost in not doing something than in clearly altering behavior due to pressure from another. In the case of compellence, a state has publicly committed its prestige and resources to a given line of conduct that it is now asked to give up. This is not so for deterrence. Thus, compellence is intrinsically harder to attain than deterrence, not because its objectives are vaguer, but because it demands more humiliation from the compelled state.

The fourth purpose to which military power can be put is the most difficult to be precise about. *Swaggering* is in part a residual category, the deployment of military power for purposes other than defense, deterrence, or compellence. Force is not aimed directly at dissuading another state from attacking, at repelling attacks, nor at compelling it to do something specific. The objectives for swaggering are more diffuse, ill-defined, and problematic than that. Swaggering almost always involves only the peaceful use of force and is expressed usually in one of two ways: displaying one's military might at military exercises and national demonstrations and buying or building the era's most prestigious weapons. The swagger use of force is the most egoistic: it aims to enhance the national pride of a people or to satisfy the personal ambitions of its ruler. A state or statesman swaggers in order to look and feel more powerful and important, to be taken seriously by others in the councils of international decision-making, to enhance the nation's image in the eyes of others. If its image is enhanced, the nation's defense, deterrent, and compellent capabilities may also be enhanced; but swaggering is not undertaken solely or even primarily for these specific purposes. Swaggering is pursued because it offers to bring prestige "on the cheap." Swaggering is pursued because of the fundamental yearning of states and statesmen for respect and prestige. Swaggering is more something to be enjoyed for itself than to be employed for a specific, consciously thought-out end.

And yet, the instrumental role of swaggering can not be totally discounted because of the fundamental relation between force and foreign policy that obtains in an anarchic environment. Because there is a connection between the military might that a nation is thought to possess and the success that it achieves in attaining its objectives, the enhancement of a state's stature in the eyes of others can always be justified on *Realpolitik* lines. If swaggering causes other states to take one's interests more seriously into account, then the general interests of the state will benefit. Even in its instrumental role, however, swaggering is undertaken less for any given end than for all ends. The swaggering function of military power is thus at one and the same time the most comprehensive and the most diffuse, the most versatile in its effects and the least focused in its immediate aims, the most instrumental in the long run and the least instrumental in the short run, easy to justify on hard-headed grounds and often undertaken on emotional grounds. Swaggering mixes the rational and irrational more than the other three functions of military power and, for that reason, remains both pervasive in international relations and elusive to describe.

Defense, deterrence, compellence, and swaggering — these are the four general purposes for which force can be employed. Discriminating among them analytically, however, is easier than applying them in practice. This is due to two factors. First, we need to know the motives behind an act in order to judge its purpose; but the problem is that motives cannot be readily inferred from actions because several motives can be served by the same action. But neither can one readily infer the motives of a state from what it publicly or officially proclaims them to be. Such statements should not necessarily be taken at face value because of the role that bluff and dissimulation play in statecraft. Such statements are also often concocted with domestic political, not foreign audiences in mind, or else are deliberate exercises in studied ambiguity. Motives are important in order to interpret actions, but neither actions nor words always clearly delineate motives.

It is, moreover, especially difficult to distinguish defensive from compellent actions and deterrent from swaggering ones unless we know the reasons for which they were undertaken. Peaceful defensive preparations often look largely the same as peaceful compellent ones. Defensive attacks are nearly indistinguishable from compellent ones. Is he who attacks first the defender or the compeller? Deterrence and swaggering both involve the acquisition and display of an era's prestigious weapons. Are such weapons acquired to enhance prestige or to dissuade an attack?

Second, to make matters worse, consider the following example. Germany launched an attack upon France and Russia at the end of July 1914 and thereby began World War I. There are two schools of thought as to why Germany did this. One holds that its motives were aggressive — territorial aggrandizement, economic gain, and elevation to the status of a world empire. Another holds that her motives were preventive and hence defensive. She struck first because she feared encirclement, slow strangulation, and then inevitable attack by her two powerful neighbors, foes whom she felt were daily increasing their military might faster than she was. She struck while she had the chance to win.

It is not simple to decide which school is the more nearly correct because both can marshal evidence to build a powerful case. Assume for the moment, though, that the second is closer to the truth. There are then two possibilities to consider: 1) Germany launched an attack because it *was* the case that her foes were planning to attack her ultimately, and Germany had the evidence to prove it; or 2) Germany felt she had reasonable evidence of her foes' *intent* to attack her eventually, but in fact her evidence was wrong because she misperceived their intent from their actions. If the first was the case, then we must ask this question: how responsible was Germany's diplomacy in the fifteen years before 1914, aggressive and blundering as it was, in breeding hostility in her neighbors? Germany attacked in the knowledge that they would eventually have struck her, but if her fifteen-year diplomatic record was a significant factor in causing them to lay these plans, must we conclude that Germany in 1914 was merely acting defensively? Must we confine our judgment about the defensive or aggressive nature of the act to the month or even the year in which it occurred? If not, how many years back in history do we go in order to make a judgment? If the second was the case, then we must ask this question: if Germany attacked in the belief, mistakenly as it turns out, that she would be attacked, must we conclude that Germany was acting defensively? Must we confine our judgment about the defensive or aggressive nature of the act simply to Germany's beliefs about others' intent, without reference to their actual intent?

It is not easy to answer these questions. Fortunately, we do not have to. Asking them is enough because it illustrates that an assessment of the *legitimacy* of a state's motives in using force is integral to the task of determining what its motives are. One cannot, that is, specify motives without at the same time making judgments about their legitimacy. The root cause of this need lies in the nature of state action. In anarchy every state is a valid judge of the legitimacy of its goals because there is no supranational authority to enforce agreed upon rules. Because of the lack of universal standards, we are forced to examine each case within its given context and to make individual judgments about the meaning of the particulars. When individual judgment is exercised, individuals may well differ. Definitive answers are more likely to be the exception rather than the rule.

Where does all of this leave us? Our four categories tell us what are the four possible purposes for which states can employ military power. The attributes of each alert us to the types of evidence for which to search. But because the context of an action is crucial in order to judge its ultimate purpose, these four categories cannot be applied mindlessly and ahistorically. Each state's purpose in using force in a given instance must fall into one of these four categories. We know *a priori* what the possibilities are. Which one it is, is an exercise in judgment, an exercise that depends as much upon the particulars of the given case as it does upon the general features of the given category.

WHAT HAS BEEN THE IMPACT OF NUCLEAR WEAPONS?

Have nuclear weapons affected either the need that states have for force or the uses to which military power can be put? Stated succinctly, the answer is "no" and "partially."

Nuclear weapons have not obviated the need of states for military power. As we shall see, nuclear weapons have brought some significant changes to international political life, but transformation of the anarchic environment of state action is not one of them. The need for military power derives from the self-help nature of international relations, itself a consequence of anarchy. Nuclear weapons have enabled some states to help themselves better than other states heretofore could, but they have not produced an effective world government and thereby eradicated the necessity for self-help. Because nuclear weapons have left anarchy untouched, military power remains integral to every nation's foreign policy.

Rather, what nuclear weapons have done is to alter the ways in which states that possess such weapons use their military power. For those states, nuclear weapons have downgraded the function of defense, ruled out physical nuclear compellence, enhanced deterrence and nuclear swaggering, and left unclear the utility of peaceful nuclear compellence. To this statement, however, three caveats must be immediately made. First, it would be a mistake to ascribe all the changes in the ways nuclear states have used their military power simply to nuclear weapons. The changes wrought have been due as much to *whom* has had them as it has been to *what* the weapons are physically capable of doing. Second, the changes have manifested themselves primarily in two sets of relations, those between the two superpowers and those between NATO and the Warsaw Pact. Nuclear weapons have not left untouched the relations between each superpower and the nations of Africa, Latin America, the Middle East, and Asia; but the effects on these relations are not readily evident, uniform, or necessarily far-reaching. Third, nuclear weapons have not eliminated the need for nuclear states to deploy non-nuclear forces, nor have they diminished for most non-nuclear states the utility that conventional forces have for attaining their foreign policy goals vis-à-vis one another. In short, nuclear weapons have profoundly affected how some states have used force; but not all states have experienced a radical transformation in the ways that they have employed their military power. One can be impressed equally by the enduring realities of international politics and by the changes nuclear weapons have wrought.

Nuclear weapons can be enormously destructive. They need not be. As the post-World War II era has progressed, scientists have produced "diversified" nuclear weapons. States can now have big ones and small ones, clean ones and dirty ones (those producing a little or a lot of radioactive debris), cheap ones and expensive ones. The destructive power of nuclear weapons today runs the gamut from a few kilotons to many megatons. They can be launched from artillery, aircraft, surface ships, or submarines. They can be targeted on railroad junctions or on a megalopolis. They have permeated the forces of the two superpowers such that today both have nuclear arsenals that when combined total over 25,000 warheads. And yet, in spite of their large number and diversified uses, since their emergence in 1945, nuclear weapons have been physically used only twice, once on August 6 and again on August 9, 1945, by the United States against Japan in order to bring World War II in the Pacific to a close. Why, then, have a few states acquired so many nuclear weapons, and why do so many states want to acquire even a few of them, when not one state professes a desire to use such weapons physically against another?

To ask the question this way is to highlight the effects that nuclear weapons have had on the four functions of force. First, nuclear weapons have helped shift the peacetime planning of the super and great powers away from defense and victory in a general war to prevention of it. This is not to say that no thought or effort at all goes into planning for defense and victory if such a war should occur, only that preventing its occurrence has become the overriding priority of these powers. Why? The answer is that with nuclear weapons, as Schelling puts it, "victory is no longer a prerequisite for hurting the enemy."[5] One can now destroy an enemy without first having vanquished him. Nuclear weapons have separated the power to hurt from the power to defeat. America and Russia each have it within their power to kill the bulk of the population of the other without first having destroyed the other's military forces. America and Russia can each absorb a devastating blow from the other and still retaliate in kind. A general nuclear war between these two offers the reality of mutual annihilation, of simply two losers and no winners. A general nuclear war between the two superpowers does not have to look like that. But it easily could. Therefore, because of what nuclear weapons can do, the avoidance of situations that could lead to such a war between them has the highest priority for each superpower. Because defense against a large scale nuclear attack has been deemed impossible, preventing such an attack by deterring it has become the goal. In a mutual assured destruction (MAD) situation, the peaceful use of force tends to prevail.

Second, nuclear weapons have not been used for physical compellence, save by the United States against Japan in 1945. Such usage has been avoided for three reasons: first is the fear of escalation and loss of control; second is the commitment to preserve the belief that nuclear weapons are different from conventional ones, even when, at low kilotonages, the effects of nuclear weapons are practically indistinguishable from those of conventional weapons; third is the determination of the two superpowers to prevent the spread of nuclear weapons to states other than the six that now unequivocally have them. In their relations with one another, the two superpowers have generally avoided acts of physical compellence of any kind. Such acts carry with them great risks of escalation to a general war. Each superpower, moreover, is too strong and too concerned with its world-wide image to allow itself to be pushed around so blatantly by the other. In their relations with the other's major allies, the two superpowers have also avoided such compellent actions for the same reasons that they have observed restraint in their one-to-one relations. Neither superpower nor the other nuclear states have employed physical nuclear compellence against non-nuclear states because of the far-flung alliances and quasi-commitments of the other superpower and because of the presumed effects that such actions would have on nuclear proliferation. As will be discussed shortly, nuclear weapons bring many advantages to the nuclear states, especially to the two superpowers. In order to retain their monopolistic position, the nuclear states must refrain from actions that increase the incentives of non-nuclear states to join the nuclear club. Using them in acts of war against the nuclear have-nots is not the way to attain this result.

Third, nuclear weapons have much swagger appeal for the great powers of today. Every recent era has had its prestige weapons — dreadnoughts in the 1894-1914 period, bombers and aircraft in the interwar period, nuclear missiles in the postwar period. In each era, those powers that were great, or had the wherewithall to be great, had, or acquired, the period's prestige weapons. For the great powers of the pre-nuclear era, prestige weapons bought prestige because they enhanced the nation's power, autonomy, and security. For the smaller powers that could afford very few of them, such weapons brought greater notice but not greater security or great power status. Today, nuclear weapons have bought prestige for the nuclear great powers, but have not catapulted them into the ranks of the superpowers. Nor is it evident that such weapons have made England, France, India, and even China more secure than they would be without them. Britain and France have argued that their nuclear forces have made them more secure than if they had had to rely solely on the American nuclear guarantee. Both, however, consider themselves dependent ultimately on the United States for their security vis-à-vis Russia. For if they took seriously their own arguments, they would have left the NATO Alliance long ago. India has the interesting virtue of being protected by both superpowers, of having been brought under America's nuclear umbrella in 1965 and of having signed a treaty of friendship and cooperation with Russia in 1971. The greater security that India has acquired by her "peaceful" nuclear explosion of 1974 is not evident. It is not even clear-cut whether China's nuclear forces make her more nearly secure against Russia. America's interest in playing off China against the Soviet Union is probably her best guarantee of security.

It is a mistake, however, to argue that nuclear weapons have no security value at all for these great powers. This is, after all, an uncertain world. Ten hydrogen bombs may be as good as one thousand in order to deter an attack. But the contribution to their security that these weapons make is indefinite enough and the opportunity costs of acquiring strategic nuclear forces, even for these great powers, high enough, to argue that security alone cannot account for the decision to go nuclear. Surely swagger motives loomed heavily in the decision of each. With her nuclear weapons, England for a time was able to buy into the councils of the superpowers, when her other resources no longer justified a position as a preeminent world power. With her *force de frappe*, France was better able to pursue *grandeur* and strike a position more independent of the United States. With her claim to be the leader of the world's nonaligned nations severely tarnished, India's nuclear capability bolstered her sagging prestige. With a rapidly aging conventional army, China's nuclear forces, rudimentary though they are, nevertheless enable her to claim to have at least a foothold into the modern sinews of strength. Some of the same motives that impelled the present great powers to go nuclear are at work today in the great powers of tomorrow, such as Brazil. Because nuclear weapons are one of the prime symbols of today's militarily powerful and politically important state, they enable their possessors to lay claim to be something more than mere regional powers. For the great power nuclear state, even if the capability for a world role is not there, the aspiration and pretension to it are. And, after all, in international politics, aspiration and pretension to greatness are two important ingredients.

Fourth, the political utility of peaceful nuclear compellence is not clear because it is difficult to draw firm conclusions about its efficacy from the few instances in which it has been employed. Peaceful compellence, it will be recalled, involves actions that do not cause physical destruction to a state but that require it (or threaten to require it) to pay a significant price until it changes its behavior. Arms races are the most prevalent form of peaceful compellence. If entered into and intensely pursued, they will result in one adversary altering the behavior of another, or in one adversary countering the actions of the other and producing a stalemate, or in war between the two of them.

The American-Russian nuclear arms race is one instance of peaceful nuclear compellence, but the extent to which each has been able to compel the other is difficult to ascertain. The motives of each superpower in acquiring large, sophisticated nuclear forces have involved goals other than compellence of one another, such as, for example, the preservation of the cohesion of their respective alliances, the retardation of the spread of nuclear weapons, and the courting of domestic political pressure groups. Because the motives of each have been mixed, the measurement of results is complex. An action not designed to compel but that in fact does can hardly be termed successful compellence. Not only the mixture of motives but the incompleteness of evidence makes assessment of this arms race difficult. One can, for example, argue with plausibility that the United States has succeeded in compelling Russia to accept, if not embrace, the logic of mutual assured destruction, and, equally, that it has failed to compel her to do so. In support of the former position, one can point to the severe limitations on ABM systems built into the 1972 Strategic Arms Limitation Accords in order to demonstrate that the Russians have accepted the principle that the nuclear offense should always get through. In support of the latter position, one can point to Russia's current active civil defense program and to the extensive modernization of her offensive, hard-target-kill systems in order to argue that her acceptance of an ABM limitation in 1972 was only a tactical step designed to starve off an American ABM system at a time when the Russians thought the Americans held a lead in defensive technology. The problem is that the evidence supports both positions. As the example makes clear, the mixture of motives and the ambiguity about results make definitive assessment of the compellent aspects of this arms race difficult.

Similar difficulties surround the assessment of the political utility of compellent nuclear threats issued by the superpowers.[6] Was it Khrushchev's threat to use nuclear weapons against England and France, or Eisenhower's firm opposition and threat to cut off American oil supplies, that caused England and France and Israel to withdraw their invasion of Egypt in 1956? Did Khrushchev in fact issue his threats precisely because he knew that the United States was opposed to the Suez invasion? Was it Eisenhower's threat in early 1953 to use nuclear weapons against China, or war weariness, prolonged military stalemate, and especially the re-evaluation of Soviet foreign policy after the death of Stalin in March, that brought the Chinese communists to conclude the Korean armistice on July 27, 1953? Was it Kennedy's implied threat that he would risk nuclear war, or America's local conventional superiority and ability to invade Cuba and humiliate Russia, that caused Khrushchev to remove Russia's offensive missiles from Cuba in 1962? Moreover, how valid a test of the efficacy of peaceful nuclear compellence for the future is the Cuban case, when one superpower had practically a first strike nuclear capability vis-à-vis the other, a condition unlikely to occur again? Was it America's going on a low level, world wide nuclear alert in the midst of the October 1973 Arab-Israeli War, or America's predetermined, calculated strategy of producing a military stalemate (and saving the encircled Egyptian Third Army) as the necessary precursor to negotiations to conclude a real peace, that dissuaded the Russians from sending troops unilaterally into that war? The answers to these questions are not clear cut, and that is precisely the point.

The factors that make judgments about the efficacy of compellent nuclear threats highly tentative also explain the rarity of their occurrence. There are only three possible outcomes to the issuance of a compellent nuclear threat: 1) the threat produces the desired change in the threatened nation's behavior; 2) the threat does not produce the change in behavior and the threatener then implements his threat (uses his nuclear weapons); or 3) the threat does not produce the change in behavior and the threatener chooses not to implement it. The problem with compellent nuclear threats is that the first is not a likely outcome because both the threatener and the threatened are fully cognizant that the second is not a likely outcome either. That leaves the third as the most likely outcome, but then such threats become merely idle ones.

In order for threats to be effective, the persons against whom they are directed must believe that the threats will be carried out if the actions they are designed to produce are not forthcoming. If compellent nuclear threats had to be implemented, they would carry high risk of bringing on a nuclear war, limited or total, because other nuclear nations, especially one or both superpowers, depending on the circumstances, would not be likely to permit the threatener to act with impunity. Each superpower has publicly pledged itself to prevent the use of nuclear weapons and to prevent others from being blackmailed or blasted by them. If either superpower permitted nuclear weapons to be used with impunity, the credibility of its extensive commitments would be weakened and nuclear proliferation further stimulated, two conditions neither superpower wishes to see materialize. But if compellent nuclear threats were issued, were ineffective in producing the desired change in behavior, and were then not carried out, the threatener would suffer a loss of face. Because (or as long as) all nations still desire to preclude the physical use of nuclear weapons, compellent nuclear threats carry little credibility, except in the most pressing, vital, or exceptional circumstances. And in those few instances in which they are issued, because of the great risks potentially involved, they are guarded, ambiguous, or leave sufficient room for backtracking. It is for these reasons that compellent nuclear threats are both rarely made and usually carefully hedged when made.

Are we to assume from the discussion thus far that the changes wrought in international relations by nuclear weapons are merely purported, not real? America and Russia, after all, still deploy extensive conventional forces and still spend the bulk of their defense dollars on them. America's possession of nuclear weapons did not stop the formation of the OPEC cartel nor break it up, did not enable her to win in Vietnam, prevail in Angola, or impose her will in the Middle East. Russia's possession of nuclear weapons has not stopped the slow erosion of her control over Eastern Europe nor enabled her to regain ideological supremacy in the world communist movement. Nuclear weapons are of little utility for overt compellence, have never been tested for their defensive value, and appear suited primarily for deterring attacks on the superpowers' and their allies' homelands and secondarily for swaggering by the great powers. Are we therefore to conclude that nuclear states, particularly the superpowers, are "nuclearly muscle bound," that they cannot use such force politically because all nations believe that it is too destructive to use physically?

Such a conclusion is clearly wrong. Simple analysis will show why. First, the capability that each superpower had to deter attacks on its homeland is not trivial. With its nuclear retaliatory capability, each superpower has achieved a degree of security more comfortable than that which any other great power in the post-feudal era, with the possible exception of England from 1815 to 1900, ever enjoyed. To be secure in a world where others are insecure is a decisive advantage. It means that each superpower has been released from the overweening concentration on physical security that has plagued every other great power of the past. It means that each superpower is freer than other nations to divert its energies and resources to tasks other than buying security. It means that each superpower can use the protection of its nuclear umbrella in order to bargain for and wrest concessions, political, economic, or military, from other nations. It means that each superpower, because it deals from a position of bedrock strength, has the essential prerequisite for conducting an effective diplomacy. One need only compare the post-1968 era with the decade before World War I or that before World War II in order to see how much freer from security worries are the superpowers today than were the great powers yesterday. Such security, finally, can be bought "on the cheap." In order to assure their retaliatory capability, each superpower need spend no more than one-quarter to one-third of its defense budget on strategic nuclear forces. Precisely because security can be bought so cheaply with nuclear weapons is each superpower able to use the bulk of its defense dollars on conventional forces, which can be readily employed and more finely tuned.

To state, therefore, that nuclear weapons have little political utility because they best fulfill only the function of deterrence misses the point. It is precisely because of the high degree of security which nuclear deterrence supplies each superpower that three potentially useful political advantages are created to be exploited diplomatically: 1) a wide margin of safety for diplomatic maneuvering (and error); 2) a capacity to trade its nuclear protection for those things that each superpower values highly and wants from others; 3) a security so efficiently provided that many resources are freed up for other pursuits. Compared to the advantages enjoyed by most nations, these are considerable benefits. Nuclear weapons may be poorly suited for overt compellence, but simply to stop at deterrence in assessing their political utility is wrongheaded. Between simple deterrence and overt compellence lies a large, fertile field for the informal, subtle, behind-the-scenes political employment of nuclear weapons. To focus solely on security, then, blinds one to the political advantages that a nation more nearly secure from attack than others thereby gains. In a world in which security is the prime requisite for successful diplomacy, those who have more of it are better placed to conduct an effective foreign policy than those who have less of it. The superpowers are better placed than the four nuclear great powers, but those four are better placed than the non-nuclear great powers. It is, therefore, the second-order effects of nuclear deterrence that are critical to consider when weighing the political advantages that nuclear weapons bring to their possessors.

Second, it is mistaken to assume that the great destructive potential of nuclear weapons *per se* diminishes their political utility, that somehow great power can lead to utter impotence. There exist two powerful restraints on the physical and political uses of nuclear weapons. One has already been discussed, namely, the intent of the superpowers to avoid those actions that will strengthen the incentives of other nations to acquire nuclear weapons. As the "market leaders," the superpowers understandably do not want the advantages they gain from their forces to be diminished by a gradual erosion of the nuclear oligopoly and of their own special duopolistic position. If the superpowers reap political benefits from their forces without using them physically, if the short term risks in so using them are extraordinarily high, and if such use would stimulate their spread over the medium term, then simple logic dictates avoiding their warlike use and exploiting their peaceful use. But even their peaceful use must be exploited with subtlety; for if the advantages of having them are too clearly demonstrated or too fully and blatantly exploited, the incentives for others to acquire them will be enhanced further. It is, therefore, not the devastation alone that nuclear weapons can wreak, but the desire of the superpowers to preserve their privileged position, that inhibits their physical use and constrains their political use.

Another powerful restraint is presently at work: America's strategic nuclear power is checked by Russia's strategic nuclear power. This has not always been the case. For four years (1945-1949) America held a nuclear monopoly. For the next fifteen years (1950-1965) she had a decisive superiority. For five of those fifteen years (1961-1965) she may even have had a first strike capability vis-à-vis Russia. But even during the years of its strategic nuclear inferiority, the Soviet Union, with its intermediate range missiles and bombers, was able to check America's strategic superiority by holding Western European cities hostage to nuclear threat. And ever since the late 1960s the Soviet Union, with its extensive intercontinental missile capability, has been able to hold American cities hostage too. The simple fact is that for most of the post-1945 era, each superpower has been able to balance the nuclear forces of the other with its own, even when it did not have an intercontinental retaliatory capability.

For the foreseeable future, the strategic nuclear balance between the two superpowers is nearly "indestructible".[7] Each superpower can deter the other. Neither, therefore, can conquer the other. Each can offset any strategically destabilizing actions of the other. Neither, therefore, can hope to achieve a decisive superiority. Each worries about the other's likely reactions to nuclear threats or actions that it might initiate against third parties. Neither, therefore, can be "footloose and free" with its nuclear forces against third parties. Both, moreover, restrain the present nuclear great powers (and will do so for any future entrants) in the uses to which they can put their nuclear forces. The two superpowers are "doomed" to compete without hope of victory. One's nuclear power checks the other's. Nuclear weapons are thus subject to the same laws of international politics as are conventional weapons: it is not absolute but relative power that counts; it is power checking power that restrains the exercise of force. It is because *two* competing superpowers have such large strategic forces, not because each has great nuclear power *per se*, that both are constrained in how they can use it. It takes only "two to balance", and it is the superpower's nuclear *pas de deux* that helps set the parameters for the political utility of these weapons.

Third, in assessing their utility, it is wrong to expect from nuclear weapons that which is beyond the capability of military power in general to achieve. There are inherent limits to what force can accomplish. Military power can be used to conquer the territory of another nation, but not to conquer the minds of its inhabitants. Military power is a necessary ingredient for political power, but is no substitute for political support and political leadership. Military power can create the necessary political preconditions for an economy to prosper, but cannot substitute for the industry of a people or for a sound trading and monetary policy.[8] First and foremost, a state uses its military power to check, deter, or defend against the forces of another nation. With greater difficulty it tries to compel others, but compellence, as we have seen, is difficult to achieve. Force can easily be used to maim and kill, but only with greater difficulty and with great expenditure of effort, to rule and pacify. Nuclear weapons can maim and kill more swiftly and with greater ease than can conventional weapons, but they do not thereby automatically enable one nation to rule or pacify another, nor to bring political harmony to its populace. The effectiveness with which military functions can be discharged does not translate directly into the effectiveness with which political functions can be performed. If that were the case, then military power alone would be sufficient to conduct a successful foreign policy. But that, clearly, is not the case. If one nation possesses a military edge over another, it is in a stronger bargaining position that it would otherwise be. But it still has to bargain, and it is here that diplomatic-political skills and economic resources come into play. In international relations, superior military strength means enhanced resources with which to bargain, but does not guarantee outright control. As Kenneth Waltz has succinctly put it: "Inability to exercise *political* control over others does not indicate *military* weakness."[9]

Even for the greatest of nations, moreover, military power is always in short supply. Great powers have great ambition and, consequently, need to ration their military power among competing goals. Small powers have great needs and little wherewithall to satisfy them and, consequently, must carefully husband their military power for the most pressing needs. For the great and small alike, there are, in addition, always opportunity costs in the exercise of military power. Except in those situations in which a nation is fighting for its very existence, there are always good reasons for limiting the amount of force actually applied to achieve a given goal. Thus, military power is a necessary ingredient for political and economic success in international relations, but not the *sole* ingredient. No matter how militarily powerful a nation is, force cannot achieve those things for which only political skill and economic industry are suited. In an anarchic world, it is better to be militarily strong than weak. But such strength alone, especially when there are other strong powers, is not a panacea. Therefore, to expect from nuclear force that which force in general is poorly suited to achieve is to attribute to the particular type that which is not valid for the class in general.

Nuclear weapons have made a difference to the way that states relate to each other, but they have not radically transformed their relations. These weapons have affected less what states aspire to than how they go about achieving their aspirations. What nuclear weapons have not done is therefore as important to note as what they have done. Nuclear weapons have not made their possessors omnipotent, but neither have they rendered them impotent. Nuclear weapons have not been the great equalizers, automatically catapulting their great power possessors into the ranks of the superpowers; but they have given the nuclear great powers more independence than they might otherwise have had. Nuclear weapons have not obviated the need for most states, even the great nuclear powers, to conclude alliances in order to enhance their security; but these weapons have strengthened the ability of the superpowers to rely less on external alignments (alliances) than internal efforts (second strike retaliatory forces) for their security. Nuclear weapons have not ended war, but so far they have helped to prevent a general war between the superpowers from breaking out.

In the final analysis, it is the last effect that is the most profound. Nuclear weapons have not brought peace to the world, but they have helped to prevent the world wars that plagued the planet in the first half of the twentieth century. By definition, the strongest powers are the most important actors in international politics. What they do vitally affects what happens to the lesser powers. In the past, whenever most or all of the great powers fought amongst themselves, the other nations were inevitably dragged into war. This was the case for the three great power wars of the last two hundred years — the Revolutionary and Napoleonic Wars, World War I, and World War II. Since 1945, the emphasis in the peacetime military planning of America and Russia, this era's great powers, has shifted from defense and victory in a general war to prevention of it. Fears of the consequences of a general nuclear war have helped cause this shift. Nuclear deterrence has been the prime mechanism of prevention. Nuclear deterrence has thereby reinforced the stability in superpower relations (stability defined as a low probability of general war) that is an inherent propensity of a bipolar structure. Nuclear weapons have not ended rivalry between the superpowers, but they have helped to make it stable and predictable. And that stability, the hallmark of post-1945 international relations, has in turn benefited the rest of the world.

WHAT IS THE FUTURE OF FORCE?

If the past be any guide to the future, then military power will remain central to the course of international relations. Those states that do not have the wherewithall to field large forces (for example, Denmark) or those that choose to field forces far smaller than their economies can bear (for example, Japan) will pay the price. Both will find themselves with less control over their own fate than would otherwise be the case. Those states that field powerful military forces will find themselves in greater control, but also that their great military power can produce unintended effects and that such power is not a solution to all their problems. For both the strong and the weak, however, as long as anarchy obtains, force will remain the final arbiter to resolve the disputes that arise among them. As has always been the case, most disputes will be settled short of the physical use of force. But as long as the physical use of force remains a viable option, military power will vitally affect the manner in which all states in peacetime deal with one another.

This is a conclusion not universally nor even widely held today. Three schools of thought challenge it. First are those who argue that nuclear weapons make war, nuclear or conventional, between America and Russia or between the NATO Alliance and the Warsaw Pact unthinkable. Hopefully that is the case. But, as we have argued, one does not measure the utility of force simply by the frequency with which it is used physically. To argue that force is on the wane because war in Europe has not occurred is to confuse effect with cause. The probability of war between America and Russia or between NATO and the Warsaw Pact is practically nil precisely because the military planning and deployments of each, together with the fears of escalation to general nuclear war, keep it that way. The absence of war in the European theater does not thereby signify the irrelevance of military power to East-West relations but rather the opposite. The estimates of relative strength between these two sets of forces, moreover, intimately affect the political and economic relations between Eastern and Western Europe. A stable balance of forces creates a political climate conducive to trade. An unstable balance of forces heightens political tensions that are disruptive to trade. The chances for general war are quite small, but the fact that it nevertheless remains possible vitally shapes the peacetime relations of the European powers to one another and to their superpower protectors.

Second are those who argue that the common problems of mankind, such as pollution, energy and other raw material scarcities, have made war and military power passé. In fact, their argument is stronger: the common problems that all nations now confront make it *imperative* that they cooperate in order to solve them. This argument, however, is less a statement of fact about the present than a fervent hope for the future. Unfortunately, proof of how the future will look is not available in the present. Cooperation among nations today, such as it is, should not make us sanguine about their ability to surmount their conflicts for the good of all. It takes a strong imagination, moreover, to assume that what some nations term common problems are viewed as such by all. One man's overpopulation, for example, is another man's source of strength. China and India are rightly concerned about the deleterious effects of their population growth on their standard of living. But Nigeria, whose source of power and influence within Africa rests partly on a population that is huge by African standards, is not. The elemental rule of international relations is that the circumstances of states differ. Hence so too do their interests and perspectives. Not only do they have different solutions to the same problem, they do not always or often agree on what are the problems. As long as anarchy obtains, therefore, there will be no agency above states powerful enough to create and enforce a consensus. As long as anarchy obtains, therefore, military power deployed by individual states will play a vital role both in defining what are the problems and in hastening or delaying their solutions. Only when world government arrives will the ability of every nation to resort to force cease to be an option. But even then, the importance of force will endure. For every government has need of an army.

Finally, there are those who proclaim that the nations of the world have become so economically intertwined that military power is no longer of use because its use is no longer credible. A nation whose economic interests are deeply entangled with another's cannot use force against it because to do so would be to harm itself in the process. Interests intertwined render force unusable — so believe the "interdependencia theorists." Two of the leading proponents of this view have forcefully argued that when "military force is not used by governments toward other governments within the region," then "complex interdependence" prevails.[10] Under such a condition:

> As military force is devalued, strong states will find it more difficult to use their overall dominance to control outcomes on issues in which they are weak....
>
> The negligible role of force leads us to expect states to rely more on other instruments in order to wield power....
>
> Intense relationships of mutual influence exist among these countries, but in most of them force is irrelevant or unimportant as an instrument of policy.[11]

This condition of complex interdependence now obtains for the United States in its relations with its key allies — Western Europe, Canada, and Japan. And it can be expected to hold for America's relations with other nations where military power is not usable.

This view of the world is odd. How can American military power, which is the cement binding the great powers of the free world together, be "irrelevant or unimportant as a tool of policy?" American military power has created and sustained the political preconditions necessary for the evolutionary intertwining of the American, Canadian, Japanese, and Western European economies. That which the commitment of American power has created and sustained could easily unravel should the commitment be withdrawn. It is therefore strange to argue that force has no utility among states that are closely united when force has been responsible for uniting them. The Japanese, Canadians, and Western Europeans know that they remain dependent for their security on American military power, especially the American nuclear umbrella. It would be odd indeed if this independence were not exploited by the United States on political and economic matters of interest to it. Military preeminence has never ensured political and economic preeminence. But it does put one nation in a stronger bargaining position that, if skillfully exploited, can be fashioned for non-military goals. Force cannot be irrelevant as a tool of policy for America's economic relations with her great power allies: America's military preeminence politically pervades these relations. It is the cement of economic interdependence.

A simple example will clarify the point. In 1945 convinced that competitive devaluations of currencies made the depression of the 1930s deeper and longer than need be, America pushed for fixed exchange rates. Her view prevailed, and the Bretton Woods structure of fixed exchange rates, with small permissible variations monitored by the International Monetary Fund, was set up and lasted until 1971. In that year, because of the huge outflow of dollars over a twenty-five year period, the United States found it to its best interests to close the gold window — that is, to suspend the commitment to pay out gold for dollars that any nation turned in. Under Bretton Woods the relations of the free world's currencies to one another were fixed in the relation of each to the dollar, which in turn was fixed in value by its relation to the standard "one ounce of gold equals thirty-five dollars." By closing the gold window, the United States shattered that standard, caused the price of an ounce of gold in dollars to soar, destroyed the fixed benchmark according to which all currencies were measured, and ushered in the era of floating exchange rates. In sum, America both made and unmade the Bretton Woods system. In 1945 she persuaded her allies. In 1971 she acted unilaterally and against their wishes.

Under both fixed and floating exchange rates, moreover, the United States has confronted her great power allies with an unpleasant choice. Either they could accept and hold onto the dollars flowing out of the United States and thereby add to their inflation at home by increasing their money supplies; or they could refuse the dollars, watch the value of their currencies in relation to the dollar rise, make their exports more expensive (exports upon which all the nations heavily rely), and threaten a decline in exports with the concomitant risk of a recession. America's economic and military strength has enabled her for over twenty years to confront her great power allies with the choice of inflation or recession for their economies. America did not have to use her military power directly to structure the choice this way, nor to make and break the system. Her economic strength, still greater than that of most of her great power allies combined, gave her considerable bargaining power. But without her military preeminence and their military dependence, she could never have acted as she did. America used her military power politically to cope with her dollar valuation problem.[12]

In a similar vein, others argue that the United States can no longer use its military power against key Third World nations to achieve its aims because of its dependence on their raw materials or because of its needs to sell them manufactured goods. In order to assess the validity of this argument, four factors must be kept in mind. First, the efficacy of military power should not be confused with the will to use it. In the mid-and late 1970s, as a consequence of the experience with Vietnam, America's foreign policy elite was reluctant to commit American conventional forces to combat. Its calculation has been that the American public would not tolerate such actions, except for the most compelling and extreme of circumstances. The non-use of American military power in Asia, Africa, and Latin America in the late 1970s stems as much from American domestic political restraints as from anything else.

Second, it is important to recall a point made earlier about the inherent limits of military power to achieve economic objectives. A superior military position can give one state a bargaining edge over another in the conduct of their bilateral economic relations, but bargains must still be struck. And that requires compromise by both parties. Only by conquest, occupation, and rule, or by a credible threat to that effect, can one state guarantee that another will conduct its economic relations on terms most favorable to the (would-be) conqueror. Short of that, the economic relations between two states are settled on the basis of each state's perception of its own economic interests, on differences in the strength, size, and diversity of their economies, on differences in the degree to which each state coordinates the activities of its interest groups and hence centrally manages its economy, and on the differential in their military capabilities. Because military power is only one of the ingredients that determine the economic relations between two states, its role is not always, nor usually, overriding. By itself superiority in arms does not guarantee, nor has it ever guaranteed, superiority in economic leverage. In this sense, although there may be clear limits on what the United States through its military power can achieve in its economic relations with the Third World, much of the constraint stems from the limits that inhere in translating military power into economic ends.

Third, America's economic power relative to others has waned in the 1970s. The 1950s were characterized by a United States whose economic and military power far surpassed that of any other nation. With the emergence of the Soviet Union as a global military power in 1970s, America's freedom to intervene militarily around the world, unimpeded by concerns about the counteractions of another global power, has drastically declined. But America's economic freedom worldwide has also waned. Whether measured by the diminished role of the dollar as the world's reserve currency, by the persistent lack of a favorable trade balance, by a smaller percentage of the world's trade accounted for by American imports and exports, by a decline in the productivity of its labour force, or by a greater dependence on imported raw materials, the United States economy is not as self-sufficient and immune from economic events beyond its borders as it once was. Analysts disagree over the extent to which, and the reasons why, the health of the American economy has become more dependent on the actions of other nations; but they do not disagree on the fact of greater dependence. If the hallmark of the fifties and sixties was America's military and economic preeminence, the hallmark of the seventies has been America's passing the zenith of her power and the consequent waning of this dual preeminence.

A diminishment in the economic power of a state is not easily compensated for by an edge in military capability. When that military edge also wanes, such compensation becomes even more difficult. Although the United States remains the world's strongest economic *and* military power, the gap between her strength in each dimension and that of other nations has narrowed in the seventies from that which was the case in the fifties and sixties. It is therefore wrongheaded to assert that America's diminished ability to get what it wants economically from allies and neutrals is due solely to the devaluation of military power. It is wrongheaded to assert that military power is devalued because it cannot solve economic problems when economic problems have never been readily or totally solved by military measures. It is wrongheaded to blame on military power that which has military and economic causes. The utility of force to a state for compellent purposes does diminish as the relative military power of a state declines. But the utility of force for compellent economic purposes declines even more when a state's economic bargaining power concomitantly wanes.[13]

Fourth, force cannot be efficiently used to achieve goals when ambivalence exists over the goal to be attained. America's increasing dependence on oil imports classically illustrates this problem. Many have taken the decision by the United States not to use military power against OPEC nations in order to get them to lower the price of their oil as a sign of the devaluation of military power in the contemporary world. It would, of course, be absurd to deny the fact that as many of the OPEC nations make strenuous efforts to strengthen themselves militarily, often with American help, the ability of the United States to wield military power against them diminishes. It would be absurd to deny the fact that the potency of the Third World's virulent nationalism has restrained the great powers in their military adventures against those nations. It would be absurd to deny that the 1970s are not different from the 1870s and 1880s, when the European great powers, restrained only by their fears of each other's counteractions, intervened militarily at will in Asia and Africa against poorly armed and politically fragmented "nations." Clearly the political and military conditions for great power military intervention in such areas have drastically changed since then.

It would be equally absurd, however, to ignore the restraint on the use of force imposed by the inherent ambivalence of the United States with regard to the price it should pay for imported oil. In the short term, America's interest is in a stable supply of cheap oil; but if pursued over the long term, such a policy will yield an ever-increasing dependence on foreign oil (as happened by the early 1970s precisely as a consequence of just such a policy), a decline in the replenishment of world oil reserves because of the very cheapness of oil (and especially that of the Middle East), and the lack of a vigorous program to develop alternative energy sources. In the short term, cheap oil reduces America's balance of payments deficit, reduces inflation, and removes a drag on aggregate demand. Over the long term, it promotes greater dependence and rapid depletion of the world's oil reserves. In the short term, expensive oil worsens the nation's balance of payments deficit, increases inflation, and lessens aggregate demand. Over the long term, it promotes conservation, the search for more oil, the development of alternative energy sources, and the likelihood of a decreasing dependence on foreign energy imports.

Faced with such a Hobson's choice, how should America use its military power? It is within her military capability, if she chose to invest the necessary resources, to invade Saudi Arabia, which has a quarter of the world's proven reserves of oil, and secure the oil fields, or better yet, Kuwait, which has smaller though still sizeable reserves, but many fewer people. It would be difficult, but it could be done. *Should* it be done? In the face of the unpleasant choice posed above, and solely on its economic merits, the benefits to the United States of such military intervention are not self-evident. And that is the point. Military power is not useful for solving an economic problem which has no simple or single best solution. Certainly much of America's restraint in her dealings with OPEC, if not her downright ambivalence, stems from an uncertainty over what is in her own best economic interest, or from an unacknowledged but tacit agreement by her foreign policy elite that a rise in the price of imported oil is to America's long-term interest. If it be the latter, then understandably the United States has opted for a stable supply of expensive oil and has used her influence and military power in the Middle East to that end.

American actions aside, the record... simply does not support the assertion that the efficacy of military power is on the wane. Recent Russian successes in Angola, Ethiopia, Southern Yemen, Afghanistan, and Cambodia have all been predicated on the use of Russian military power, sometimes in concert with that of Cuba. Because she continues to pour huge resources into her military machine, Russia evidently does not believe that force has lost its potency. In their relations with one another, conventional military power for the Third World nations remains a vital instrument of foreign policy. Simply recall these events:... The Tanzanian-Ugandan War, the Northern Yemen-Southern Yemen War, the Ethiopian-Somalian War, the Sino-Vietnam War, the Cambodian-Vietnam War, the Libyan-Egyptian border clashes, the Libyan-backed insurgency in Chad, the Angolan-backed insurgency in southern Zaire, the Moroccan takeover of the Spanish Sahara, and the Algerian-backed Polisario War against Morocco. Nuclear weapons continue to entice and lure the non-nuclear power. Brazil and Pakistan in particular are in dogged pursuit of them. China urgently seeks to modernize its obsolete military forces. The NATO Alliance has committed itself to a three percent real increase in its military spending. Above and beyond that, sentiment in the United States is building for a tremendous increase in military spending.

The efficacy of force endures. It must. For in anarchy, force and politics are connected. By itself, military power guarantees neither survival nor prosperity. But it is almost always the essential ingredient for both. Because resort to force is the ultimate card of all states, the seriousness of a state's intentions is conveyed fundamentally by its having a credible military posture. Without it, a state's diplomacy generally lacks effectiveness. Force need not be physically used to be politically useful. Threats need not be overtly made to be communicated. The mere presence of a credible military option is often sufficient to make the point. It is the capability to resort to military force if all else fails that serves as the most effective brake against having to do so. Lurking behind the scenes, unstated but explicit, lies the military muscle that gives meaning to the posturings of the diplomats. Diplomacy is the striking of compromises by parties with differing perspectives and clashing interests. The ultimate ability of each to resort to force disciplines the diplomats. Precisely because each knows that all can come to blows if they do not strike compromises do the diplomats engage in the hard work necessary to construct them. There is truth to the old adage: "The best way to keep the peace is first to prepare for war."

ENDNOTES

1 The term "compellence" was coined by Thomas C. Schelling in his *Arms and Influence* (New Haven: Yale University Press, 1966). Part of my discussion of compellence and deterrence draws upon his as it appears in chapter 2 (pp. 69-86), but, as will be made clear below, I disagree with some of his conclusions.

2 Military power can be used in one of two modes — "physically" and "peacefully." The physical use of force refers to its actual employment against an adversary, usually but not always in a mutual exchange of blows. The peaceful use of force refers either to an explicit threat to resort to force, or to the implicit threat to use it that is communicated

simply by a state's having it available for use. The physical use of force means that one nation is literally engaged in harming, destroying, or crippling those possessions which another nation holds dear, including its military forces. The peaceful use of force is referred to as such because, while force is "used" in the sense that it is employed explicitly or implicitly for the assistance it is thought to render in achieving a given goal, it does not result in any physical destruction to another nation's valued possessions. There is obviously a gray area between these two modes of use — the one in which a nation prepares (that is, gears up or mobilizes or moves about) its military forces for use against another nation but has not yet committed them such that they are inflicting damage.

3 Schelling, *Arms and Influence,* p. 72.

4 Ibid., pp. 72-73.

5 Ibid., p. 22.

6 Recall the distinction between deterrent threats and compellent threats. The former are threats designed to persuade an adversary *not* to change his present behavior. The latter are threats designed to persuade an adversary to *change* his present behavior.

7 The word is Kenneth Waltz's. See his *Theory of International Politics* (Reading, Massachusetts: Addison-Wesley, 1979), chapter 8.

8 For a brilliant sketch of the role that American military power played in creating the political conditions conducive to economic and monetary expansion, see Robert Gilpin, *U.S. Power and the Multinationals* (New York: Basic Books, 1975), chapter 4.

9 Kenneth N. Waltz, "National Force, International Structure and the World Balance of Power," *Journal of International Affairs,* 21 (No. 2, 1967), 227.

10 Robert O. Keohane and Joseph S. Nye, *Power and Interdependence: World Politics in Transition* (Boston: Little, Brown, 1977), p. 25.

11 Ibid., pp. 27, 30, and 32.

12 Even Nye and Keohane admit that "when the direct use of force is barred among a group of countries,... military power can still be used politically" (Ibid., p. 28). Militarily strong states will try to link their military strength to economic and political issues in order to get their way. The fact that they admit to the efficacy of military power politically in a situation of complex interdependence makes it hard for the reader to accept the validity of their prior claim that force is "irrelevant as a tool of policy." Nye and Keohane have confused the issue because they have committed the cardinal error of measuring the political utility of force by the frequency with which it is used physically.

13 Simple though it may sound, this view is at odds with one of the popular current theories, that propounded by Nye and Keohane. For them, "complex interdependence" obtains when military power is devalued as an instrument of foreign policy. I have argued that such a view distorts what has occurred. The world is more complex, if not more interdependent, for the United States, simply because of the waning of her economic and military strength. Nye and Keohane's explanation for what they term complex interdependence is, to my taste, too simple.

C: THE ECONOMY AND IMPERIALISM

Marxism: An Alternative to the Statist Approach to Economic Policymaking

Stephen D. Krasner

Scholars in the Marxist tradition have presented the most extensive analysis of foreign economic policy. Marx himself was primarily concerned with developments within national economies, although he did not entirely ignore international problems. With Lenin's *Imperialism* the international aspects of capitalism assumed a place of first importance for Marxist scholars. The analytic assumptions of this paradigm differ in a number of fundamental ways from the state-centric approach....

Marxist theories can be divided into two basic types: instrumental and structural. Instrumental Marxist theories view governmental behavior as the product of direct societal pressure. In its most primitive form, this kind of argument emphasizes personal ties between leading capitalists and public officials. In its more sophisticated form, instrumental Marxist arguments analyze the general ties between the capitalist sector and public officials. Ralph Miliband is the leading recent exponent of this kind of argument. He maintains that there is a cohesive capitalist class. This class controls the state because public officials are heavily drawn from the middle and upper classes, are in frequent contact with businessmen, and depend on the cooperation of private firms to carry out public policy. In addition, cultural institutions such as the media and churches reflect the dominant conservative ideology. Harold Laski took a very similar position, arguing that "historically, we always find that any system of government is dominated by those who at the time wield economic power; and what they mean by 'good' is, for the most part, the preservation of their own interests."[1] From an instrumental Marxist perspective, the state is the executive committee of the bourgeoisie.[2]

Structural Marxist arguments take a different tack. They do not attempt to trace the behavior of the state to the influence of particular capitalists or the capitalist class. Instead, they see the state playing an independent role within the overall structure of a capitalist system. Its task is to maintain the cohesion of the system as a whole. At particular times this may require adopting policies

---

Stephen D. Krasner, *Defending the National Interest: Raw Material, Investments, and U.S. Foreign Policy.* Copyright © 1978 by Princeton University Press. Excerpts, pp. 20-26, reprinted by permission of Princeton University Press. Retitled. Some footnotes have been removed; those remaining have been renumbered.

opposed by the bourgeoisie, but generally official action and the preferences of leading elements in the capitalist class will coincide.

For structural Marxism, the behavior of the state involves an effort to deal with economic and political contradictions that are inherent in a capitalist system. Economically, capitalism is not seen as a self-sustaining system tending toward equilibrium. Rather, over the long-term profit rates decline because capitalists can only secure profit through the exploitation of labor, but technological innovation reduces the long-term equilibrium ratio of labor to capital. This process also leads to underconsumption: the system produces more goods than its members can consume. It promotes concentration because weaker firms are driven out of the market. Excess capital is accumulated because there is no market for the goods that would be produced by more investment.

Politically, concentration — what Marxists call the increased socialization of the production process — produces tensions. As societies develop, they become more complex and interdependent. However, control is increasingly concentrated in the hands of an ever smaller group of the owners or managers of capital. At the same time, the working class grows and workers come into more intimate and constant contact with each other. The increased socialization of the production process itself and the continued private appropriation of power and profit produce political and social tensions that threaten the stability of the system.

From a structural Marxist perspective, policy analysis can be viewed as a catalogue of state efforts to cope with these tensions. In the area of foreign economic policy the major conclusion is that the state must follow an expansionary, an imperialist, foreign policy. Early Marxist writers elaborated the relationship between colonialism and expanded opportunities for trade and investment. The opening of new areas could help alleviate underconsumption because capitalists could find new markets by eliminating local artisans. Colonies also offered opportunities for surplus capital. This is the major argument presented by Lenin. These contentions have not been sustained by empirical investigations, however. Even in the heyday of empire only a small proportion of goods and capital moved from the mother country to colonial areas.[3] Recent radical analyses have suggested somewhat different motivations for expansion, including protection of the oligopolistic position of large firms, militarism, and the quest for raw materials.

The relationship between advanced capitalist societies, giant firms, and foreign activity has been emphasized by two recent Marxist analysts, Harry Magdoff and James O'Connor. Using arguments from the behavioral theory of the firm, Magdoff suggests that corporations are systems of power. Each firm strives to control its own market. This objective could not be realized during the early stages of capitalism because the level of competition was too high. As concentration increases, however, "the exercise of controlling power becomes not only possible but increasingly essential for the security of the firm and its assets."[4] Businesses seek to maximize control over actual and potential sources of raw materials and over foreign markets. Foreign investment is a particularly effective device for guaranteeing such control, although trading opportunities are not ignored. If control is lost, either to competitors or to socialist regimes, the oligopoly can be destroyed. Since these corporations are the foundation of the American capitalist system, their political power is great, and their collapse would precipitate a deep economic crisis. There are impelling reasons for the United States, the world's leading capitalist nation, to maintain an international economic system with minimum constraints on the operations of giant multinational firms.

James O'Connor has taken an even more classical Marxist position. He maintains that the monopoly sector in modern capitalist systems is the most important source of profits. However, there is an inherent tendency for the productive capacity of the monopoly sector to expand more quickly than demand or employment. This leads to pressure for an aggressive foreign economic policy. Overseas activity can increase sales and profit, and offer opportunities for new investment. The purpose of foreign assistance and more direct military intervention is to keep foreign client states within the capitalist order.

Magdoff, O'Connor, and other structural Marxist analysts have also postulated an intimate relationship between the economic needs of the capitalist system, military expenditure, and imperialism. Military expenditures are a primary source of revenue for some major firms in the monopoly sector. Such expenditures help maintain the stability of the system because they are not subject to the rational calculations of profit and loss that are an inherent part of the capitalist ideology. Finally, militarism is important in a direct sense because the use of force may be necessary to keep foreign areas open to trade and investment.

An argument...which has received new emphasis from Marxists, is that capitalists must have foreign raw materials. This aim was not ignored by classical Marxist writers. Lenin stated that capitalists were driven to control ever increasing amounts of even apparently worthless land because it might contain some unknown material that could lead to economic disaster if it were to fall into the hands of a competitor. Cheap raw materials also contributed to staving off the inevitable tendency toward declining rates of profits: new and rich discoveries could, at least temporarily, provide high profits. Magdoff has maintained that the search for raw materials is part of the general quest of giant corporations for security and oligopolistic profits. Only through vertical integration from mine to final sale can these firms assure themselves of tight market control. Furthermore, the United States and other capitalist states are seen as being vitally dependent on foreign sources for some commodities that are essential for industrial operations and advanced military equipment. One author has argued that all American foreign policy can be explained by the need "to insure that the flow of raw materials from the Third World is never interrupted."[5]

While Marxist writers have dropped some arguments, modified others, and found new ones, there is a central thread that runs through their position. Foreign economic expansion is a necessity. It is not a matter of the preferences of particular enterprises. It is not a policy that has a marginal effect on profits. It is an issue that touches the very core of capitalism's continued viability. Cut off from the rest of the world, the economies of advanced capitalist states would confront problems of great severity. "For Marxism," Tom Kemp avers, "imperialism is not a political or ideological phenomenon but expresses the imperative necessities of advanced capitalism."[6]

For structural Marxists, the state can be treated as having autonomy, not from the needs of the system as a whole, but from direct political pressure from the capitalist class. Indeed, such autonomy is necessary because internal divisions preclude effective bourgeois political organization. To maintain cohesion the state must mitigate the social and political pressures arising from the increasing socialization of the production process coupled with the continuing private appropriation of profits and control. Carrying out this task requires it to pose as a representative of all the people. To appear to follow the explicit preferences of powerful capitalists too slavishly would weaken the stability of the whole system. Compromises, such as the recognition of unions and higher social welfare payments, are essential, even if they are opposed by the capitalist class. Such policies protect the existing structure of economic relationships by disarming and disuniting potential opposition from the oppressed.

The analytic assumptions of Marxist theories, whether of the instrumental or structural variety, differ from the statist approach...in at least three ways. First, the notion of national interest is rejected by Marxists. The aims pursued by the state mirror the preferences of the capitalist class or some of its elements, or the needs of the system as a whole. State behavior does not reflect either autonomous power drives or the general well-being of the society. Second, the behavior of the state is taken by them to be intimately related to economic goals; other objectives are instrumental, not consummatory. In particular, ideological objectives cannot be independent of economic considerations. Ideology is a mask that hides the reality of exploitation and thus helps mislead and mollify those who have no real power. Third, even though structural Marxists may view the state as relatively autonomous, they do not believe that it can really be understood outside of its societal context. The state has peculiar tasks within the structure of a capitalist system, but they are ultimately associated with the interests of a particular class. . . .

ENDNOTES

1 Harold J. Laski, *The Foundations of Sovereignty and Other Essays* (New York: Harcourt, Brace, 1921), p. 289, and *The State in Theory and Practice* (New York: Viking Press, 1935).

2 See Gabriel Kolko, *The Roots of American Foreign Policy* (Boston: Beacon Press, 1969), and Ralph Miliband, *The State in Capitalist Society* (New York: Basic Books, 1969), for applications of instrumental Marxism to the concerns of this study. Recently, Miliband has taken a more structural position.

3 Michael Barratt Brown, "A Critique of Marxist Theories of Imperialism," in Roger Owen and Bob Sutcliffe, eds., *Studies in the Theory of Imperialism* (London: Longman, 1972), p. 44; D.K. Fieldhouse, "Imperialism: An Historiographical Revision," *Economic History Review*, 2nd series, 14 (December 1961); Benjamin J. Cohen, *The Question of Imperialism* (New York: Basic Books, 1973), chapter 2.

4 Harry Magdoff, "Imperialism Without Colonies," in Owen and Sutcliffe, p. 157.

5 Heather Dean, "Scarce Resources: The Dynamic of American Imperialism," in K.T. Fann and Donald C. Hodges, eds., *Readings in U.S. Imperialism* (Boston: Porter Sargent, 1971), p. 149.

6 Tom Kemp, "The Marxist Theory of Imperialism," in Owen and Sutcliffe, p. 17. See also Andrew Mack, "Comparing Theories of Economic Imperialism," in Steven J. Rosen and James R. Kurth, eds., *Testing Theories of Economic Imperialism* (Lexington: D.C. Heath, 1974), p. 40.

C: THE ECONOMY AND IMPERIALISM

Foreign Economic Policymaking in the United States

David H. Blake/Robert S. Walters

The United States is still the leading economic and political power among the center states and within the global economic system. Of course its hegemony is challenged at home and abroad; frequently it is unable to get its own way; and in some regions of the world, other states exercise more economic influence than does the United States. Yet, in terms of the breadth and intensity of its economic and political links throughout most of the world, it is the preeminent state in the global economic system. Developments within the United States as well as specific American policies are likely to have widespread implications for countries throughout the world. Consequently, an analysis of the politics of the global political economy requires an examination of the policymaking process in the United States....

THE RADICAL PERSPECTIVE

The Substance of Foreign Policy. Our purpose is to examine the foreign economic policymaking process within the United States. From the perspective of various radical analysts, however, the assumption must first be made about the substance of U.S. foreign policy. Basically, although with some variation, radical critics feel that the foreign economic and political interests of the United States are synonymous. Therefore, the process by which foreign policy is made is essentially the same, regardless of whether the issue is an economic or a political one. Indeed, for most radicals a distinction between the two is not appropriate.

On this question and on others as well, there is some disagreement among radical analysts.[1] One group, of a Marxist-Leninist orientation, tends to feel that the capitalist system of the United States largely determines its political concerns and that capitalism demands international economic and political involvement to overcome its many domestic shortcomings. According to this view, perhaps represented best by Harry Magdoff, capitalism is a system that inequitably withholds from its workers their fair share of income and wealth. Consequently, the limited purchasing power of the proletariat, coupled with an insatiable appetite for growth by corporations, results in a surplus of manufactured goods and investment capital. The domestic U.S. market cannot absorb enough new production to sustain corporate growth since the proletariat is not earning enough to purchase more

---

David H. Blake and Robert S. Walters, *The Politics Of Global Economic Relations*, 2nd ed. © 1983, pp. 204-218. Reprinted by permission of Prentice-Hall, Inc., Englewood Cliffs, N.J. Some footnotes have been removed; those remaining have been renumbered.

goods. Less new investment capital is needed and less is able to be employed profitably in the United States. Therefore, the capitalist American system needs foreign outlets for its excess goods and investment capital. The foreign political and military policy of the United States is designed to secure and maintain these foreign markets for the benefit of the American economy. As Magdoff states, "the underlying purpose [of imperialism] is nothing less than keeping as much as possible of the world open for trade and investment by the giant multinational corporations."[2]

Magdoff and others go beyond this relationship to point out how dependent the United States is upon a host of critical raw materials found elsewhere in the world. Because these natural resources are necessary for the continued functioning of the highly developed American economy, American foreign policy seeks to safeguard the sources of these materials. This leads quite naturally to an expansionist and adventuresome foreign policy that knows few geographical or political limits. Because of natural resource dependency and the need to have foreign markets absorb goods and capital, the foreign political policy of the United States is designed primarily to serve and advance its economic interests.

Another group of radical critics, especially Michael Hudson, feels that American economic interests and policy are really servants of an expansionary political policy.[3] He observes a self-assertive U.S. government that seeks to dominate other countries or at least to ensure their compatibility with the American system. The expansion of American investments and trade is a conscious policy fostered by a government that is anxious to enhance the overall power of the United States. This outward thrust of state capitalism is based on a different cause-and-effect relationship than that advanced by Magdoff, but in both cases foreign economic policy and foreign political policy are thought to be so highly correlated as to be synonymous.

Richard Barnet combines the two previous radical positions when he ascribes American expansionism to its society and institutions. Like Hudson, he emphasizes the importance of the national security managers (officials in the State Department, Defense Department, National Security Council, CIA, and so forth) who have decision-making authority in foreign policy matters. However, Barnet, like many other radicals, stresses the business background of these officials and the dominance of business interests and attitudes in the government and in the society more generally. The crux of the relationship as he views it is that "the corporations continue to exercise the dominant *influence* in the society, but the *power* keeps passing to the state."[4] The congruence of foreign economic and political interests in American international relations is once more clearly indicated.

Regardless of differences among them, radical critics rarely make a distinction between the American foreign policymaking process regarding political and security matters and the process for economic issues. Since the interests and objectives of business and government regarding both economic and security matters are basically similar, separate policymaking processes do not exist. In other words, decisions on Cuba, arms limitation agreements with the Soviet Union, trade reform, and revision of the international monetary order spring from the same fountainhead of policymaking.

The Formulation of Foreign Policy. Admitting the differences among radical analysts but recognizing their shared conviction that American foreign economic and political interests are similar, several views of how foreign policy is made in the United States can now be examined. It is important to note that discussions of the foreign policymaking process by radical analysts focus frequently on the procedures by which policy is made on political, security, and military issues. Some radical critics like Magdoff discuss the *substance* of American economic policy, but they fail to explore specifically the process by which foreign economic policy is made. Others have addressed this issue more directly. Consequently, an examination of radical analysts' views of the formulation of foreign economic policy in the United States rests upon a combination of direct statements about the policy process and interpretations of their writings on other subjects like political and security issues.

One group of radical thinkers, the instrumentalist school, perceives a U.S. foreign policymaking process that is primarily a reflection of and a response to the interests of the capitalist class and its big corporations. It is a system in which economic and political interests, as defined and advanced by large business enterprises, dominate the substance of political and economic policy as well as the process by which foreign and domestic policies are made.

These radical analysts argue that business dominance is achieved as the result of the congruence between what is good for the United States and what is good for its large business concerns. Radical critics often rely upon statements by policymakers and corporate executives to prove their point. One of the most often-quoted remarks is that of Assistant Secretary of State Dean Acheson in 1944 before a congressional committee concerned about postwar economic planning. Drawing upon the frightening possibility of a new depression after the war, Acheson said, "We have got to see that what the country produces is used and sold under financial arrangements which make its production possible.... You must look to foreign markets."[5] The prospect of limiting production only to what could be consumed in the United States "would completely change our Constitution, our relations to property, human liberty, our very conceptions of law.... Therefore, you find you must look to other markets and those markets are abroad."[6] Thus, he continued, "We cannot have full employment and prosperity in the United States without the foreign markets."[7] Businessman Bernard Baruch was more succinct when he emphasized the "essential one-ness of United States economic political and strategic interests."[8]

Business influence over the foreign policymaking process is ensured by the recruitment of foreign policy officials from the highest ranks of the corporate and financial elite. Consequently, many of the national security managers not only represent business interests but in essence are corporate officials serving the government for a few years in the foreign policy apparatus. In the process, of course, they also further the interests of their corporations and of business in general. G. William Domhoff and Richard J. Barnet present analyses of foreign policy managers in the White House and the departments of State, Defense, and Treasury that reveal that a significant proportion of these officials held top-level positions in corporations, financial institutions, and related corporate law firms prior to their recruitment into government service. Barnet points out, for example, that between 1940 and July 1967, seventy of the ninety-one secretaries and undersecretaries of defense and state, secretaries of the three branches of the armed forces, chairmen of the Atomic Energy Commission, and directors of the Central Intelligence Agency came from large corporations and leading investment houses.[9] Thus, the link between business and foreign policy is forged by a direct sharing of executives by government and business.

More indirectly, but just as critical, is the unrepresentative social and educational background of many of the most important foreign policy officials and their counterparts in business. The similarity in their backgrounds would tend to provide them with basically the same outlook on many economic and political issues. They are likely to move in similar social and intellectual circles. Many of them share the characteristics of significant family wealth, membership in exclusive clubs, listing in *The Social Register*, attendance at select private preparatory schools, and graduation from Ivy League-type colleges. For example, a study by the Brookings Institution revealed that 32 percent of the political appointees to the departments of State, Treasury, Defense, Army, Navy, and Air Force (all of which are important in the making of foreign policy) attended a select list of eighteen private preparatory schools.[10] Political appointees to cabinet departments, regulatory agencies, and other commissions that are less involved in foreign policy matters were much less likely to have attended these prep schools (only 11 percent of them did so).

All this means that this corporate-based power elite will find it quite easy to move between business and government positions, thereby ensuring a foreign policy posture that is compatible with and supportive of big business interests. In the words of a leader in this type of analysis of the elite, "American foreign policy during the postwar era was initiated, planned, and carried out by the richest, most powerful, and most international-minded owners and managers of major corporations and financial institutions."[11] Thus, the unrepresentativeness of foreign policy managers in terms of socioeconomic background and previous positions in and allegiances to corporate America suggest strongly that big business interests help determine the foreign policymaking process.

According to the instrumentalist view, the influence of big corporations on the foreign policymaking process is enhanced further by the activities of a number of important groups that serve to transmit the business point of view to government officials. These transmission belts include a few of the large foundations based on corporate wealth, special blue-ribbon presidential advisory committees, and a small number of research and discussion committees. The Ford Foundation, the Carnegie Corporation, and to a lesser extent the Rockefeller Foundation have been active supporters of programs at universities and of foreign-policy related groups that represent business concerns in the foreign policymaking process. The special presidential committees are blue-ribbon citizens groups selected largely from corporate elites to analyze and to make recommendations regarding specific foreign policy issues. These committees have reported on such things as the nature of American military preparedness and the direction of its foreign aid programs. Seven of the eight most important committees concerned with foreign policy matters were chaired by corporate executives; the eighth chairman was the president of the Massachusetts Institute of Technology. The research and discussion groups referred to are organizations such as the Council on Foreign Relations, the Committee for Economic Development, the Foreign Policy Association, the Trilateral Commission, and RAND, many of whose members and boards of directors come from a big business background.

All these groups act as links between corporations and government officials, and they ostensibly provide expert but nonbiased advice from nongovernmental sectors. In fact, though, the interests, perspectives, and alternatives advantageous to business are conveyed to governmental decision makers through the activities of these groups. These transmission belts sponsor formal face-to-face meetings that allow their largely business membership to exchange ideas and information with American and non-American foreign policy officials. These information and access advantages, combined with good organization and competent staffs, mean that these groups are able to develop thoughtful and comprehensive recommendations about foreign affairs. Indeed, there are almost no other sources outside of the government that can consistently provide such well-informed and coherent analyses of foreign policy issues of direct relevance to foreign policy officials. In other words, these transmission belts enjoy a virtual monopoly of effective interest representation regarding foreign economic and political policy. Moreover, the similar background characteristics of business and government elites ensure the receptivity of the latter to the concerns of the former.

This influence relationship is fostered as a result of the social, intellectual, and value similarities between foreign policy officials and the active membership of these transmission belts. This both follows from and leads to these groups serving as a major source of recruitment for high-level foreign policy officials. As an example of the two-way flow of personnel, prior to becoming secretary of state for President Kennedy, Dean Rusk was president of the Rockefeller Foundation. In the opposite direction, McGeorge Bundy left his position as national security advisor to the White House to become president of the Ford Foundation. There are many more such examples.

Domhoff suggests that the Council on Foreign Relations is probably the most important transmission belt for foreign policy matters. The large foundations and a number of major corporations provide the prime financial support for the council. In addition, top corporate executives are members of boards of directors of the major foundations and are also members of the Council on Foreign Relations. Thus, according to Domhoff, it should not be surprising that the council consciously attempts to increase the interaction between Washington officialdom and its largely corporate membership. These efforts have obviously paid off. For example, John J. McCloy, who has been among many things chairman of the board of Chase Manhattan Bank, high commissioner for Germany, and coordinator of American disarmament activities, once remarked, "Whenever we needed a man [to help direct foreign policy activity during World War II] we thumbed through the roll of Council members and put through a call to New York."[12]

To stimulate this interaction, the council arranges off-the-record speeches and question-and-answer sessions by important foreign policy officials of the United States and other countries. The information learned, the insights gained, and the views exchanged draw together more closely corporate interests and Washington officials. In addition, the council publishes a number of important books and reference works as well as the prestigious journal, *Foreign Affairs*, which frequently contains articles by foreign policy officials.

However, Domhoff feels that the most important activity of the council is the discussion and study groups that examine a specific issue in great detail. Twenty-five business executives, government officials, a few military officials, and a small number of nonradical scholars conduct extensive discussions, often off the record, which eventually result in a book that presents a thorough statement of the problem. Some of the topics considered by these study groups have been instrumental in shaping U.S. policy regarding the nature of the United Nations charter and the development of the Marshall Plan for European recovery and in the early 1970s a full-scale reassessment of American relations with China. In sum, the council, along with the other groups mentioned, serves to encourage business participation in the formulation of foreign policy and to transmit business influence to foreign policy officials in multiple ways. At the very least, such institutions provide an important means of access to and maintenance of contacts with foreign policymakers.

A more recently founded vehicle for implanting corporate views in the councils of governments is the Trilateral Commission. One radical critic referred to it as "the executive committee of transnational finance capital."[13] It is important to note that this organization is comprised of government officials and private persons from the United States, Japan and countries in the European Common Market. This internationalism is an attempt, some would say, to ensure cohesion within the capitalist class across national boundaries and to maintain the dominance of the international capitalist system.

The basic argument of the instrumentalist view is that American foreign policy reflects and represents the interests of big corporations in foreign affairs. Whether governmental political objectives conveyed through state capitalism lead to foreign economic involvement, or vice versa, is not a crucial distinction for our purposes. Either way, the result is a foreign policy that is linked closely and substantively to the interests of corporate America through a foreign policy formulation process that is subject to immense and almost exclusive influence from big business on the executive branch of the government. Congress, the radical analysts feel, is a largely impotent body in foreign policy matters since it often meekly upholds the policies and actions of the executive without acting as an alternate decision-making center. Consequently, corporate efforts to influence foreign policy are logically directed primarily to the executive branch.

A different view, that of the structuralists, rejects the notion that the actions of the state are determined by members of the capitalist class occupying positions of power or influencing those in such positions. Instead, the structure of society and that of the state are the driving forces behind the formulation of state policy. Without examining the complexity of the argument fully, the state structure is dominant because it sets limits for the policy options available and also determines which parts of the state apparatus and society are critical to the policymaking process. Furthermore it ensures the development and survival of those structures that will reinforce the predominance of capitalism in foreign (and domestic) policies.

There are other radical explanations of the foreign policymaking process, but there is substantial agreement that the United States, as the premier power of the world, is largely unconstrained by the interests and concerns of other countries and thus enjoys a correspondingly wide decisional latitude. American political and military policies, in conjunction with foreign economic policies that change economic partners into economic dependents, have enabled the United States to ensure the compliance of most states to its wishes. The radical literature is replete with examples of how the United States has imposed its will on recalcitrant friends and enemies to enrich itself and its corporations and to extend its global dominance at the expense of other countries. Thus, the United States has consciously attempted to structure and use the global economic system in a way that promotes its economic and political hegemony and the subjugation of other states. As a result of this process, American policy is largely unfettered by the wishes and constraints that are imposed by other countries. This gives American business interests free rein to develop and implement the kinds of policies that will advance their interests the most.

A CRITIQUE OF THE INSTRUMENTALIST RADICAL VIEW

Admittedly, this brief sketch of several radical conceptions of the American foreign policymaking process fails to do full justice to both the richness of the arguments and the many significant differences that do exist among radical analysts. Nevertheless, it is appropriate to raise questions about the substance of the instrumentalist view, the methodology used to develop these positions, and the way in which each contributes to an understanding of the foreign economic policymaking process.

Historically, much of the instrumentalist argument has been based on an analysis of American foreign political, security, and military policy. The role of domestic U.S. interests in these policies has been examined extensively, but far fewer attempts have been made to focus on how foreign economic policy has been made. One of the results of concentrating on political and military policy as the outcome of the policymaking process is that frequently there has been much greater unanimity within the United States on these issues because of the perception of serious external threats. Given the Cold War environment as the historical (though not the only) focus of the instrumentalists, the coincidence of national policy and economic interests is not surprising. With large segments of the American population perceiving the existence of the Soviet Union and other communist states as having broad and largely singular implications for all of American society, the concept of bipartisanship or the submerging of different and parochial interests was undertaken for the sake of national unity against a common threat. Business, labor, and government all joined toether to protect the American system from what was perceived to be both a political and economic threat. Thus, the view of business dominance is based largely upon an analysis of political and security issues on which there was wide agreement as to the nature of the situation and American objectives.

A Multiplicity of Business Interests. By focusing on such political, security, and military issues, instrumentalist critics have largely neglected a rich panoply of bureaucratic and political maneuvering that is found in the making of foreign economic policy. Here, the common perception of threat and the unified external posture (with many internal differences and disputes about tactics) dissolve into wrangling associated with the promotion of specific and contradictory objectives by many competing economic and business interests. Thus, the concept of a business interest dominating the foreign policymaking process seems inappropriate for those foreign economic groups that are often at odds with one another. In short, because the instrumentalist view is founded primarily on analyses of overarching political, military, and security issues, some serious problems are created in the transferring of their conclusions to discussions of the formulation of foreign economic policy.

As a result, the analysis fails to define, much less operationalize, the notion of *the business interest*. Instead, it is asserted categorically that a single unified business interest exists. An examination of the policy formulation process on trade or investment issues reveals something quite different. In the first place, different types of industries disagree greatly about the consequences of various foreign economic policy alternatives. For example, imposing tariffs or import quotas to protect the steel, textile, and shoe industries in the United States has been resisted by those industries who can successfully meet foreign competition and who themselves export to other countries. They fear that protectionist moves by the United States will be countered with similar actions by other countries and that their export activities will thereby be harmed. To illustrate these differences, consider this partial list of industries and products that were the subject of congressional testimony by interested unions, trade associations, and companies on the Trade Reform Act of 1973-74:

Agriculture	Musical instruments
Automobiles	Petroleum
Bicycles	Potash
Chemicals	Poultry
Clay	Shears
Dinnerware	Shoes
Eggs	Steel
Flowers	Textiles
Glue	Tools
Leather goods	Vegetables
Marbles	Wine

These specific groups differed greatly on their positions regarding the desirability of raising or lowering tariffs. Moreover, some of them have changed their views since that time, such as the auto industry. A precise and unanimous business interest cannot be observed among these industries, as a brief review of some of the conflicting testimony will indicate.

On certain issues, different firms within the same industry perceive different patterns of gains and losses to result from foreign economic policy. In the coffee industry, giant multinational corporations such as General Foods, Procter & Gamble, and Coca-Cola disagree over the nature of American policy toward the International Coffee Agreement. General Foods was quite concerned about the import of soluable coffee products from abroad, but P&G and Coca-Cola, joined by other smaller firms, did not wish to stem the flow. Quite naturally, each side used political influence in an effort to ensure that its position was advanced or protected by the policy that emerged.

An issue such as tariff reform may also highlight the very real areas of disagreement among different divisions of a multiproduct firm. In their careful study of the politics of tariff policy, Bauer, Pool, and Dexter point out that within the DuPont corporation the division manufacturing paint supported liberalization of trade whereas the rayon yarn division tended to be protectionist. Other parts of the corporation were little interested in the issue.[14] Similar differences can be observed within other corporations that manufacture a variety of products.

In the area of foreign economic policy, at least, American business interests rarely support a single policy position solidly except on the broadest levels, such as enthusiasm for the concept of private enterprise. Instead, the various alternatives available have different implications for different industries, firms, and divisions within specific corporations. As a result, the process by which foreign economic policy is made seems to be subject to the same type of political struggles thought to be characteristic of the domestic policymaking process.

Foreign economic policy has important and varying implications for businesses. Thus, businesses and other economic interests — including unions and a potpourri of various social groups each with their own conceptions of desirable goals — become actively involved in the domestic political process to influence the outcome of policy deliberations. As a result, the formulation of foreign economic policy provokes extensive and at times heated domestic political activity. For example, the hearings before the House Ways and Means Committee on the 1973 Trade Reform Act produced testimony by 96 industry associations and trade groups, 36 companies, 18 union organizations, 17 agricultural groups, 15 public interest groups and 15 individuals. In addition, the committee received written statements from 111 other such groups and individuals. An examination of the hearings emphasizes the lack of consensus among these groups or within each type of group. The positions advanced reflected very specific conceptions of self-interest — not some overall consensus position by business.

Business executives tend to become preoccupied with and most active in specific issues that have definite implications for their business. They are not usually trying to establish and promote a grand design regarding the foreign political and economic posture of the United States. For instance, there is some suggestion that business involvement in organizations such as the Council on Foreign Relations amounts to little more than political dilettantism. Even a leading radical analyst, Domhoff, quotes a study by Bernard C. Cohen that concludes that members of the Foreign Policy Association "seldom seriously discuss political policies at all, let alone alternative policies. They tend to keep discussions apolitical, emphasizing the social, economic, cultural, and historical aspects of foreign affairs."[15] Barnet claims that corporate executives "do not seem to know how to manipulate this great wealth to influence the great decisions of war and peace. Nor do they seem to be particularly interested in doing so."[16]

Differences Within Government. The political, military and security perspective of the radical analysts has led them to understand the governmental process in a way that may not be applicable to the formulation of American foreign economic policy. Just as they assert *a* business interest, so also do they perceive *a* government view of U.S. foreign policy. Such an approach ignores the significance of the different perspectives and interests of various government agencies. Moreover, it neglects the specialized clientele and constituents of each department. Thus, the departments of Labor, Commerce, and Agriculture have different interests and objectives regarding American foreign economic policy as a result of the different sets of pressures they are subjected to by labor, business, and farmers and as a result of different conceptions of the nature of their tasks. Furthermore, within these broad economic sectors and within each of these departments there are disagreements on the consequences of policy alternatives. Thus, it is an oversimplification even to view various departments as passive instruments of their constituencies (labor, business, farmers, and so on) in society, for these groups themselves are not united on all issues.

Another critical assumption at the base of the instrumentalists' view of the American foreign policymaking process involves the nature of the relationship between business and government. As we discussed earlier, they feel that business interests dominate the government. However, there are numerous examples of U.S. policy that contradict this view. The Trading with the Enemy Act prohibits U.S. firms and their subsidiaries from trading with specified enemy countries in a number of defense-related products. In the mid-1970s and early 1980s, this act inhibited some business interaction with the Soviet Union and Cuba, in spite of the requests of American firms to rescind its restrictive provisions. Antitrust concerns of the Department of Justice have also served to retard the growth and success of the foreign subsidiaries of American firms. Moreover, the years of Cold War between the Soviet Union and the United States as well as the many years of American non-recognition of China meant many missed opportunities for doing business with these countries. The inability of American business to change government policy on these matters long after allies and their corporate competitors had opened lucrative business and political contacts is another important instance in which the interests of many corporations were not served by government policy. Despite official U.S. government hostility toward the Marxist regime in Angola, Gulf Oil successfully pursued its oil-drilling operations in that country with excellent relations with the government. Thus, one has to question the degree to which business in fact controls government policy.

Bauer, Pool, and Dexter suggest that in many ways Congress tends to use business lobbyists, rather than vice versa. This study, which examines business and government interactions on the question of tariff reform, indicates that lobbyists are most effective when they aid an already favorably disposed legislator in the attempt to sway colleagues in the House or Senate. Moreover, members of Congress frequently utilize lobbyists to obtain information about an issue so that they can make up their minds on the issue. Although practices obviously vary widely, the basic conclusion of the authors is that Congress is not captive of business lobbyists, or of any lobbyists for that matter.

However, instrumentalist radical critics feel that the legislative branch is relatively impotent in the foreign policymaking process. Thus, much of their argument is based on the extent of business control over the administrative branch. Basically, some radical thinkers *infer* business control from the socioeconomic backgrounds of top-level officials recruited into executive agencies, without offering substantial evidence as to the precise nature of the linkage between background and decision making.

Such critics insist that former corporate employees carry their predispositions and parochial interest directly into their positions in government. Although there is substance to this argument, it is possible that the new experiences and role expectations accompanying their office expand the horizons of former corporate executives beyond their previous views. For example, in assessing the influence of foreign travel on business executives' conceptions of self-interest, Bauer, Pool, and Dexter found that it "made a man see the trade issue in national terms, rather than in the parochial terms of his own industry."[17] One cannot help but wonder whether journeys into government service do not have a similar effect.

The radicals insist that the legislative branch has little to do with the making of foreign policy on political and security issues. (This is the view of many nonradicals as well.) This is probably not the case in regard to international economic issues having important domestic implications. In these instances, different business interests and other economic interests actively urge members of Congress to represent their concerns in the legislative process. The administration's trade bill in 1973 and 1974 stimulated great pressure on Congress from numerous economic groups, and the passage of the bill was delayed by Congress until December, 1974. Congress does fulfill an active and important role in many issues involving foreign economic policy. Yet this role is disregarded by most radical analysts because their frame of reference tends to be focused on military and security issues. It is useful to note, though, that national security policy and executive branch leadership in such matters often overwhelm strong domestic economic interests. The Carter administration's imposition of a grain embargo on the Soviet Union in response to the invasion of Afghanistan is a case in point.

The instrumentalist conception of American foreign policymaking implies or asserts that only high-level political appointees determine the content of foreign policy. Barnet suggests that these national security managers revel in their jobs because of "the sense of playing for high stakes."[18] These foreign policy officials are exhilarated and "intrigued by power, more than money and more than fame."[19] Even if we accept Barnet's characterization, it is hard to imagine these national security managers experiencing much thrill and excitement over attempts to get Japan to reduce automobile exports to the United States or attempts to change the discriminatory trade policies of the European Common Market. Participation in many of these economic issues does not often yield fascinating memoirs testifying to one's diplomatic astuteness and importance.

Instead, many of these economic issues involve exceptionally technical details that are managed more competently by the technical experts in the civil service who inhabit the departments of Treasury, Commerce, and Agriculture. Thus, the important role of the technostructure, on economic issues at least, should not be, but often has been, ignored by some critics who perceive American foreign policy to be the preserve of a small number of political appointees in the State and Defense Departments. It is important to note that there is much more diversity in social backgrounds, educational experience, and career patterns among career civil servants than there is among the top political elites, upon whom some radical critics focus. Moreover, the relationship between the bureaucracy and business interests, especially where regulation is concerned, is often adversarial, reflecting in part the lack of common objectives and career backgrounds.

The point is that business control of government, as proclaimed by followers of the instrumentalist approach, is probably overstated. Radical thinkers fail to specify either what they define as control of foreign policy or the precise nature of the foreign policy decision-making process. They presume that broad conclusions about overall policy outcomes and the backgrounds of certain types of government officials are sufficient evidence to infer the control of business interests over the American foreign policy process. But radical analysts do not tell us what control is and how it can be observed. Their concept of the foreign policy decision-making process is developed from the presumption that a highly unified business interest dictates government policy. No inputs into the foreign policy process other than business interest are examined seriously. The role of Congress and the intense struggles among and within executive agencies, if they receive any attention at all, are considered inconsequential for American foreign economic policy.

Nonetheless, the analyses of the instrumentalist and structuralist critics do provide important insights into the nature of foreign economic policymaking. Whether through the prevalence of common backgrounds or interests among officials or through the structure of the state allowing participation in the process only to those societal institutions that foster the prevailing view, there are wide areas of consensus. In spite of conflicting and vigorous expressions of self-interest about the nature of U.S. foreign economic policy, the fundamental concepts of capitalism and the internationalism of capitalism are widely accepted and rarely debated seriously, much less challenged seriously, in the United States....

ENDNOTES

1 Pat McGowan and Stephen Walker identify five radical approaches to the formulation of foreign economic policy. The general discussion that follows does not explore the diversity of these views or the richness of each. For a more comprehensive treatment, see Pat McGowan and Stephen G. Walker, "Radical and Conventional Models of U.S. Foreign Economic Policy Making," *World Politics*, 33 (April 1981), 347-82.

2 Harry Magdoff, *The Age of Imperialism* (New York: Monthly Review Press, 1969), p. 14. See Vladimir I. Lenin, *Imperialism* (New York: International Publishers, 1939) for the classical Marxist-Leninist view of Imperialism.

3 Michael Hudson, *Super Imperialism: The Economic Strategy of American Empire* (New York: Holt, Rinehart and Winston, 1968).

4 Richard J. Barnet, *The Roots of War* (Baltimore: Penguin Books, 1972), p. 185.

5 Quoted in William Appleman Williams, "The Large Corporations and American Foreign Policy," in David Horowitz, ed., *Corporations and the Cold War* (New York: Monthly Review Press, 1969), p. 95. Parts of this passage have also been quoted in David Horowitz, *Empire and Revolution* (New York: Random House, 1969), pp. 233-34; and Lloyd C. Gardner, *Architects of Illusion* (Chicago: Quadrangle Books, 1970), p. 203.

6 Williams, "The Large Corporations and American Foreign Policy," p. 96.

7 Ibid.

8 Quoted in Benjamin J. Cohen, *The Question of Imperialism: The Political Economy of Dominance and Dependence* (New York: Basic Books, 1973), p. 125.

9 Richard J. Barnet, "The National Security Managers and the National Interest," *Politics and Society* (February 1971), 260.

10 These figures were derived from Table D.9 in David T. Stanley, Dean E. Mann, and James W. Doig, *Men Who Govern* (Washington, D.C.: The Brookings Institution, 1967), pp. 124-25.

11 G. William Domhoff, "Who Made American Foreign Policy 1945-1963?" in Horowitz, ed., *Corporations and the Cold War*, p. 25.

12 Quoted by Joseph Kraft, "School for Statesmen," *Harper's Magazine*, July 1958, p. 67.

13 Jeff Frieden, "The Trilateral Commission: Economics and Politics in the 1970's," *Monthly Review*, 29 (December 1971), 11.

14 Raymond A. Bauer, Ithiel de Sola Pool, and Lewis Anthony Dexter, *American Business and Public Policy* (New York: Atherton, 1963), p. 270.

15 Domhoff, "Who Made American Foreign Policy 1945-1963?" p. 61.

16 Barnet, *The Roots of War*, p. 186.

17 Bauer, Pool, and Dexter, *American Business and Public Policy*, p. 168.

18 Barnet, *The Roots of War*, p. 98.

19 Ibid., p. 97.

C: THE ECONOMY AND IMPERIALISM

Economic Imperialism as a Reductionist Theory

Kenneth Waltz

...The assumptions of the Hobson-Lenin theory [are] economic, not political. Its standing as an explanation of imperialism and of war hinges on (1) whether the economic theory is valid, (2) whether the conditions envisioned by the theory held in most of the imperialist countries, and (3) whether most of the countries in which the conditions held were in fact imperialist. I have specified most, rather than all, countries not in order to weaken the tests that economic theories of imperialism must pass but because exceptions fail to invalidate a theory if their occurrence can be satisfactorily explained. A wind that wafts a falling leaf does not call Newton's theory of universal gravitation into question. So also with Hobson's and Lenin's theories; the assigned causes may operate, yet other causes may deflect or overwhelm them. Hobson's and Lenin's theories may explain imperialism when it occurs, yet not be refuted even if all advanced capitalist countries do not at all times practice imperialism.

Hobson's *Imperialism,* first published in 1902, still merits close study. Indeed, students will save much time and trouble by mastering the sixth chapter of Part I, where they will find all of the elements of later economic explanations of imperialism from Lenin to Baran and Sweezy. "Overproduction," "surplus capital," "maldistribution of consuming power," "recurrent gluts," "consequent depressions": Hobson thickly populates his pages with such concepts, which he develops and combines systematically. In doing so, moreover, he hits upon notions that later authors have taken up — the role of advertising and the importance of trusts, for example, and even the possibility of what is now known as the imperialism of free trade.

Hobson's economic reasoning is impressive. Like Malthus, he anticipates Keynes by questioning the classical economists' belief that if only government would leave the economy alone, effective demand would strongly tend toward sufficiency, that the money demand for goods would clear the market of all that is produced and thus provide suppliers with the incentive to employ the factors of production fully through continued investment. Surpassing Malthus, Hobson was able to explain why effective demand might be deficient and thus to provide reasons for the proposition later established by Keynes: namely, that a free-enterprise economy may come to rest at a point representing less than full employment of the factors of production.

Kenneth N. Waltz, *Theory Of International Politics*, © 1979, Addison Wesley Pub. Co. Inc, Reading, MA. pp. 18-27. Reprinted with permission. Portions of the text have been deleted. Some footnotes have been removed; those remaining have been renumbered.

Because of the concentration of wealth in the hands of the few, Hobson argues, consumption cannot keep pace with increases of productive power; for "the rich will never be so ingenious as to spend enough to prevent overproduction." At a price level that returns a profit, demand will be insufficient to clear the market. There are then, in Hobson's words, "goods which cannot get consumed, or which cannot even get produced because it is evident they cannot get consumed." As for Keynes, the malfunctioning of the economy is caused by a maldistribution of wealth. As for Keynes, the sensible solution is for the government, through its taxing and spending powers, to contrive a more equitable distribution of income in order to bring about an aggregate demand that will sustain the economy in a condition of full employment. As for Keynes, the approach is macroeconomic, examining relations among system-wide aggregates in order to explain the condition of the economy as a whole.[1]

We now have the economic elements of Hobson's theory of imperialism in hand. Faced with a falling rate of profit at home and with underused resources, would-be investors look abroad for better opportunities. Those opportunities are found where they have been least fully exploited — that is, in economically backward countries. Put differently, to say that a country is economically underdeveloped means that it is short of capital. Where capital is scarce, it commands the highest premium. With similar impulses to invest abroad felt by nationals of different capitalist countries, their governments are easily drawn into backing the claims of their citizens for fair treatment by, or for special privileges from, the native rulers in whose countries they are operating. If one government supports its businessmen abroad, can other governments do less? If one government places tariff walls around its colonies, can other governments stand idly by and watch their citizens being discriminated against in more and more of the world's markets? The governments of capitalist states felt the force of the reasoning implied in such rhetorical questions. And so the urge to invest abroad, and the competition among the nationals of different countries responding to that urge, led naturally, it was thought, to waves of imperialist activity. Thus Hobson reached his conclusion: Imperialism "implies the use of the machinery of government by private interests, mainly capitalists, to secure for them economic gains outside their country." Other forces do operate — patriotism, missionary zeal, the spirit of adventure, for example. But the economic factor is the "taproot," the one cause without which the imperialist enterprise withers. Economic forces are the "true determinant in the interpretation of actual policy." Directly or indirectly, moreover, imperialism was thought to account for most, if not all, modern wars.[2] As Harold J. Laski later put it: War's "main causes lie in the economic field. Its chief object is a search for a wealth obtainable by its means that is deemed greater by those who push the state to its making than will be obtained if peace is preserved."[3]

Though imperialism promotes employment through the export of surplus capital and labor, losses suffered by an imperialist nation far exceed gains. Gains are insignificant partly because most of them go to businessmen and investors, a tiny minority of the nation. They reap the profits of imperialism; the nation as a whole bears its considerable expense. In the words Hobson borrowed from James Mill, imperialism is "a vast system of outdoor relief for the upper classes." Redistribution of income would put factors of production to more profitable use. If imperialist activity, moreover, causes all wars and not just the directly imperialist ones, then the costs of the entire "war system," the costs of preparing for wars as well as of fighting them, must be charged to the imperialist enterprise. By such reasoning, costs must vastly exceed gains. In addition to costs counted in pounds, the pursuit of imperialist policies produces unfortunate social and political effects at home. It leads either to the development of militarism in England or to her dependence on native troops; it sets forces in motion that are antagonistic to social and economic reform and that undermine representative government; it sustains and enlarges an effete aristocracy dependent on tribute from Asia and Africa and may ultimately turn most West Europeans into a parasitic people.

That, in Hobson's view, defines one major part of the loss to the imperialist nation. The other major part of the loss comes through the effects of imperialism abroad. The imperialist nation, in exporting its capital goods and its know-how, enables backward countries to develop their resources. Once that is done, there is nothing to prevent, say, China from using foreign capital, and increasingly her own capital, combined with her labor, to produce goods that may supplant "British produce in neutral markets of the world." She may finally "flood" even Western markets with cheap "China goods," reverse the flow of investment, and gain "financial control over her quondam patrons and civilizers."[4] The imperialist country's own actions undermine its position of superiority.

Lenin drew heavily on Hobson and differed from him on only two important points. Hobson believed that the impetus to imperialism could be eliminated by governmental policies designed to redistribute wealth. Lenin believed that the capitalists who control governments would never permit such policies. Imperialism was then inevitably a policy of capitalist states in their monopoly stage. Hobson believed that imperialist contention was the cause of most conflicts among the imperialist countries themselves and the principal reason for their vast expenditures on armaments. Hobson did, however, see the horrible possiblility of capitalist states cooperating in the exploitation of backward peoples. Lenin believed that cooperative arrangements would never endure, given the shifting fortunes of capitalist states and the changing pattern of opportunities for external investment. Capitalism inevitably produces imperialism. That in turn inevitably leads to war among capitalist states, a thought that later supported the belief that socialism could survive in one country.

Using Hobson's analysis, Lenin tried to prove that the effects Hobson thought probable were necessary products of capitalism. Lenin, moreover, liked what Hobson foresaw and deplored: Imperialism is part of the dialectic that brings the demise of the capitalist world by sapping the energies of the advanced states and sharpening the antagonisms within them, on the one hand, and by promoting the economic development of backward areas, on the other. Lenin here fit comfortably into the Marxist mold. In the *Communist Manifesto,* Marx and Engels had sounded a paean to capitalism that would have seemed embarrassingly pretentious had it come from a bourgeois apologist.

> National differences, and antagonisms between peoples [they wrote] are daily more and more vanishing, owing to the development of the bourgeoisie, to freedom of commerce, to the world-market, to uniformity in the mode of production and in the conditions of life corresponding thereto.[5]

Adapting Hobson's explanation of imperialism, Lenin was able to retain both Marx's vision of a benign future and his conviction that capitalist societies contained its seed.

We can now check the economic theory of imperialism against...three questions....First, how good is the economic theory itself? Here we must distinguish between the general merits of Hobson's Keynesian-style theory and its ability to explain the push to export capital that supposedly produces imperialism. Both Hobson and Lenin attribute imperialism to the push that originates in underconsumption at home combined with the pull provided by the lure of higher profits through investment abroad. It is the higher profits that are wanted, however they may be gained, as both Hobson and Lenin would readily say. Hobson's economic theory cannot in itself lead to the conclusion that the building of empires is needed. Capital may flow out of a country in search of higher profits, but whether imperial conquest is required, or is thought to be required, in order to secure them depends on political as well as on economic conditions at home and abroad. Showing how capitalist states may generate surpluses does not determine how those surpluses will be used. Economic reasoning can do no more than explain the appearance of specified surpluses under designated conditions. The question shifts, then, from whether the economic theory explains capital surpluses to whether internal economic condition determines external political behavior. That question cannot be answered by a theory about the working of national economies. Despite this fatal difficulty, one may believe, as I do, that the persuasiveness of the economic reasoning has helped to carry the theory as a whole, despite its failure to pass the second test and its difficulty with the third one.

The second and third tests can be considered together. Recall that for the economic theory of imperialism to be valid, most of the imperialist countries must be both capitalist and surplus-producing and that most of the countries so described must be imperialist. From about 1870 onward, which is the period when the theory is said to apply, all or practically all of the states that could reasonably be called "capitalist" did engage in at least a bit of imperialist activity. Some of the imperialist states, however, exported little capital to their own colonies; and some of them did not produce surpluses of capital at all. A number of imperialist states, moreover, were not capitalist states. The diversity of the internal conditions of the states and of their foreign policies was impressive. Their conformity to the stipulations of the theory was not. England, the premier imperialist state, had about half of its capital invested outside of its colonies at the end of the nineteenth century. That the largest single amount was invested in the United States is at least mildly disconcerting for scrupulous adherents of the theory. France consistently ranked second or third in investments in, and trade with, the territories she owned.[6] Japan in Asia, and Russia in Asia and Eastern Europe, were certainly imperialist, but they were neither capitalist nor surplus-producing. Those few cases illustrate the variety of conditions associated with imperialism, a variety fully sufficient to refute the theory.

These anomalies, from the theory's point of view, awaken further doubts. Imperialism is at least as old as recorded history. Surely it is odd to learn that the cause (capitalism) is much younger than the effect it produces (imperialism). Admittedly, Hobson and Lenin pretend to explain imperialism only in the era of advanced capitalism. But one must then wonder what caused imperialism in bygone periods and why those old causes of imperialism no longer operate, why they have been replaced as causes by capitalism. If there were new things in the world in the late nineteenth century, imperialism was not one of them. Not the phenomenon, but only its cause, was said to be new. It is as though Newton claimed to have discovered the explanation for the free fall of bodies only from 1666 onward, as though he left it to someone else to explain how such objects fell before that date, and as though his newly discovered gravitational effect were something that did not exist or did not operate earlier.

The theory of Hobson and Lenin cannot deal with these problems and did not try very seriously to do so. The acceptance of the theory, which spread and endured marvelously, rested instead on the attractiveness of its economic reasoning and on the blatant truth that the advanced capitalist states of the day were, indeed, among history's most impressive builders of empire. The advanced capitalist states were fiercely imperialist. Then why not identify capitalism and imperialism? The identification was obviously easy to make, for so often one reads of capitalist states forcing their surplus goods and capital on unsuspecting natives, and of the mad scramble of capitalist states for colonies.

If the implied assertions of cause are convincing at all, they are so only until one realizes that in Hobson's day, as in ours, most of the leading states were capitalist. This question is then raised: Are the advanced countries "imperialist" because they are *capitalist* or because they are *advanced*? The growth of industrial economies in the nineteenth century spawned a world-girdling imperialism. Was the hegemony of the few over the many produced by the contradictions of capitalism or by the unlocking of nature's secrets, the transmuting of science into technology, and the organization of the powers of technology on a national scale? Is imperialism the highest stage of capitalism or are capitalism *and* imperialism the highest stage of industrialism? For any theory that attempts to account for imperialism, the answers to these questions are critical.

Some will respond by saying that the burst of imperialist activity in the late nineteenth century can be explained only by economic changes within imperialist countries and that this provides evidence in support of Hobson's and Lenin's theory. The argument misses the point. In rejecting the theory, I am not arguing that capitalism had nothing to do with British and French imperialism. Doing so would be as silly as saying that authoritarian rule had nothing to do with Russian and Japanese imperialism. Particular acts have particular causes, which account for some part of the outcomes that interest us. In dealing with particular causes, however, we are dealing with matters that are more interesting historically than theoretically. To claim that a theory contemplating only the internal condition of states does not sufficiently explain their external behavior is not to claim that external behavior can be explained without reference to internal condition. Capitalist economies were efficient generators of surpluses. Governments of capitalist states therefore had wide ranges of choice and effective means of acting internationally. How they would choose to act, however, cannot be explained by internal conditions alone. External conditions must be part of the explanation since the variety of conditions internal to states is not matched by the variety of their external behaviors.

Through history, the famous three "surpluses" — of people, of goods, and of capital — are associated with imperialist movements. In various versions, they are identified, respectively, as the imperialism of swarming, the imperialism of free trade, and the imperialism of monopoly capitalism. Two points need to be made. First, a country that sustains an imperialist movement must produce one or a combination of such "surpluses" in the specific sense that the imperial country requires a margin of superiority over the people it controls. How else can control be exercised? Second, how the "surplus" is produced, and the nature of the state producing it, appear to be quite unimportant. Republics (Athens and Rome), divine-right monarchies (Bourbon France and Meijian Japan), modern democracies (Britain and America) have all at times been imperialist. Similarly, economies of great variety — pastoral, feudal, mercantilist, capitalist, socialist — have sustained imperialist enterprises. To explain imperialism by capitalism is parochial at best. Rather than refer to capitalist imperialism one might more aptly write of *the imperialism of great power.* Where gross imbalances of power exist, and where the means of transportation permit the export of goods and of the instruments to rule, the more capable people ordinarily exert a considerable influence over those less able to produce surpluses.... Historically, imperialism is a common phenomenon. Where one finds empires, one notices that they are built by those who have organized themselves and exploited their resources most effectively. Thus in its heyday mercantilism was the cause of imperialism in just the same spurious sense that capitalism was later.

If capitalist states, the most advanced states of their day, did not affect others more than others affected them, and at least occasionally engage in outwardly imperialist activity, that would be odd. In this sense, the absence of imperialism in the face of unbalanced power would sorely require explanation. Weakness invites control; strength tempts one to exercise it, even if only for the "good" of other people. The phenomenon is more general as well as older than the theory offered to explain it. The phrase that expresses the root cause that operates across differently organized economies is "the imperialism of great power." The economic organization that will "cause" imperialism (in the sense of enabling a country to pursue imperialist policies) is whatever economic form proves most effective at the given time and within the pertinent area. To complete the comparison suggested above: Newton's gravitational force did work earlier, though it had not been fully identified; the causes of imperialism, present in advanced capitalism, were present earlier, though identification of capitalism with imperialism has obscured this.

After World War I, Lenin and his followers could try out their thesis in its strongest form. Capitalism produces imperialism, and the leading capitalist state will be the fiercest imperialist country. Thus Trotsky foresaw America becoming the world's most imperialist nation and this development as touching off "military collisions" of "unprecedented scale."[7] Not only must the leading capitalist state be the most imperialistic, but also its imperialist policies must be the major cause of war in the world.

In the same period, Joseph Schumpeter wrote his well-known essay, giving an explanation of imperialism contrary to the economic one. "Precapitalist elements, survivals, reminiscences, and power factors" propel states into imperialist ventures. Military classes, once needed for the consolidation and extension of their states, do not disappear upon the completion of their tasks. They live on. They seek continued employment and prestige. They are supported by others who become imbued with their spirit. Such atavistic forces give rise to imperialist tendencies, which are not lacking even in the United States. But, Schumpeter asserts, "we can conjecture that among all countries the United States is likely to exhibit the weakest imperial trend."[8] Like Veblen, and by similar reasoning, Schumpeter assigns the causes of war to the continued vogue of an outmoded militarism and believes that Germany and Japan — countries in which capitalist forces have not fully supplanted feudal elements — will constitute the greatest danger of war.

Does imperialism wither away as capitalism, inherently pacifistic, fully assimilates anachronistic social elements, or is imperialism the last malignant expression of capitalism prior to the advent of socialism? Judged by the accuracy of predictions, Veblen and Schumpeter carry the day. But prediction is an insufficient criterion for accepting a theory's validity, for predictions may be right or wrong for many different and accidental reasons. Veblen and Schumpeter nevertheless posed the problem that latter-day Marxists had to cope with: how to salvage Lenin's theory of imperialism when capitalist states fail to pursue colonial policies — indeed, when none of them any longer clings to its colonies.

The solution is found in the concept of neocolonialism as it developed from the early 1950s onward. Neocolonialism separates the notion of imperialism from the existence of empires. Lenin offers some basis for this separation. He had defined imperialism as an internal condition of certain states rather than as a policy, or a set of actions, or a result produced. Imperialism is simply "the monopoly stage of capitalism." But for Lenin that condition necessarily found political expression. Imperialism originated privately but expressed itself publicly. A policy of imperialism could be pursued only if soldiers and sailors were available to implement it. Empires without colonies, and imperialist policies that require little if any force to back them up, were unimaginable to Lenin.

The first big difference between the old and the new Marxist theses on imperialism is found in the divorce of imperialism from governmental policies and actions. One sees this difference clearly in the quick change of conclusions by Harry Magdoff, one of the leading neocolonial writers. In his 1969 book he emphasizes America's dependence on foreign resources and on profits earned abroad. The nation's economic dependence then requires governmental action to establish a position of dominance that will make the world secure for the operations of American capital. In a 1970 article he joins what is now the neocolonial mainstream. References to America's dependence fade away, and private business supplants government as the engine that drives the imperial machine. The neocolonial thesis contains the ultimate economic explanation of international politics, asserting, as it does, that in capitalist states private economic instruments have become so fully developed that their informal use is sufficient for the effective control and exploitation of other countries' resources.[9] Multinational corporations now operate on such large scales and over such wide areas that they can both develop their own leverage against economically less powerful countries and pursue their own bet-hedging strategies by distributing their operations across countries, some with more and some with less predictably safe and stable governments. The outward thrust of business is so strong, and its ability to take care of itself is so great, that businesses develop their "invisible empires" ordinarily without the support of governmental policies or of national force.

The second big difference between the old and the new Marxist theses on imperialism is found in the estimates of the effects of imperialism on less-developed countries. Older Marxists believed that capitalists dug their own graves in various ways, one of which was by contributing to the economic development of their empires through capitalist investment abroad. An un-Marxist despair has replaced Marx's and Lenin's optimism. Capitalists operating in foreign parts are now said to have the effect either of freezing economic development at relatively low levels or of distorting that development disadvantageously. Backward countries remain the suppliers of raw materials for the more developed countries or are kept at the level of comparatively crude manufacture. In the latter sense, even the relation between the most advanced capitalist country, the United States, and the comparatively less-developed economies of Western Europe are included.

Neocolonial theorists claim to identify and explain yet another "new" imperialism. An examination of neocolonial thought will lead to several important points about international-political theory. They are suggested by the following headings: (1) self-verifying theories, (2) structure without behavior or the disappearance of function, (3) over-explanation and the problem of change.

1. Self-Verifying Theories. Imre Lakatos uses the phase "auxiliary theories" to describe theories that are devised "in the wake of facts" and that lack the power to anticipate other facts.[10] Suppose, for example, that I begin with the conviction that certain types of states are imperialist. Suppose I believe that my theory explains why this is so. Suppose further that I want to maintain my theory substantially intact, even though the activity explained, and those who engage in it, change a good deal over time. To reach that end, I need to do two things: first, redefine the old word to cover the new activity, and second, revise the old theory in order to cover new elements. The evolution of theories about imperialism nicely illustrates both procedures.

According to Hobson and Lenin, if a country builds an empire in order to control the external arena of its economic operations, that is imperialism. According to a later notion, if a country is able to operate abroad economically *without* building an empire, that is also imperialism. The latter definition is embodied in the idea of "the imperialism of free trade," associated most often with the nonMarxist, historically impressive work of Gallagher and Robinson. They emphasize the use of free trade as a technique of British expansion, especially in the middle of the nineteenth century, and they argue that whatever they method used, British interests throughout the century continued to be safeguarded and extended.[11] Now it may well be that Britain's interest in formal empire dwindled in the middle years of the nineteenth century precisely because her dominance of world markets guaranteed that sufficient quantities of her goods would be bought by foreigners whether or not she ruled them. Similarly, one can say that America's foreign economic operations have not required the traditional apparatus of empire and certainly do not now.

The neocolonial school's acknowledgment that American economic operations abroad require little if any backing by military force closely corresponds to reality. Imperialist policies, old style, have languished; empires have nearly disappeared. Now as ever, the superior economic capability of wealthy peoples nevertheless has its impact on those who are poor. Calling the influence of the rich over the poor "imperialism" is the first step toward saving Lenin's theory. Asserting that what capitalists do abroad *is* imperialism — whether or not they do it through empires and by force — helps to turn the theory into a self-verifying one. The theory did not anticipate the facts. It did not lead anyone to expect the decline of visible empires. Instead the definition of what the theory supposedly explained was changed to accommodate what had actually happened. Neocolonialists, in redefining the behavior that capitalist states are expected to display, strikingly show the validity of the point made earlier: namely, how national economies produce surpluses and how surpluses are used are different questions, and the second cannot be answered by a theory about national economies.

2. Structure Without Behavior, or the Disappearance of Function. The new definition of imperialism strongly affects the way in which the traditional economic theory of imperialism has been amended in order to cover recent practices, as can easily be seen by looking at Johan Galtung's "structural" theory of imperialism. By pushing neocolonial theory to its logical end, Galtung unwittingly exposes its absurdity. Imperialism, in Galtung's view, is a relation between more harmonious and richer states, on the one hand, and less harmonious and poorer states, on the other. He makes imperialism into a structural affair, but his structural theory is arrived at partly through reduction. In his definition of international structure he combines a national attribute, degree of harmony, with an international structural characteristic, distribution of capability. The former is an element of national structure, if it is a structural element at all. Because Galtung includes a national attribute in his international structure, his approach becomes reductionist. Structure is a useful concept if it is seen as conditioning behavior and as affecting the way in which functions are performed. Defining international structure partly in terms of national attributes identifies those attributes with the outcomes one is trying to explain. Because Galtung defines structure in that way, behavior and function disappear; a country is called imperialist by virtue of its attributes and aside from the acts it commits. The observation of behavior, its connection with events, and the problem of alternative outcomes — all such complex and difficult matters can be left aside. Thus Galtung can say about Japan in southeast Asia that "there is no doubt as to the economic imperialism, but there is neither political, nor military, nor communication, nor cultural ascendancy." Imperialism, perfected, employs no military force whatsoever, neither direct force nor threat of violence.[12] Rather than being a hard-to-unravel set of activities, imperialism becomes an easily seen condition: the increase of the gap in living conditions between harmonious rich countries and disharmonious poor ones.

Galtung's construction, offered as a theory, merely asserts that the cause of the widening gap in living conditions is the exploitation of the poor by the rich. "Vertical interaction," he claims, is "the major source of the inequality of this world."[13] Why that should be so is not explained but instead is reasserted in various ways. The asymmetry of international trade, the difference of situation between those who make goods and those who merely purvey the products of nature, the different degrees of processing that various nations' exports receive: In unspecified ways such factors supposedly cause the interactions of nations to enrich advanced states while impoverishing backward ones.

To show how, under what circumstances, and to what extent the rich have enriched themselves by impoverishing the poor would require careful analysis, including examination of changes in the terms of trade and of the composition of exports and imports across countries and over time. Such examinations reveal that at times some primary producers do very well. Are they then imperialistically exploiting others? In 1974, exporters of oil and of foodstuffs prospered. Underdeveloped Arab nations and highly developed North American ones fared well in contrast to most other countries. The former are pre-eminently examples of Galtung's exploited countries. They fall into his category of "being" rather than "becoming," of countries selling nature's goods rather than fashioning their own. At the same time, the United States is the world's major exporter of foodstuffs *and* Galtung's very model of an imperialist country. Not only does Galtung's theory offer descriptions rather than explanations, but also his descriptive categories fail to correspond to realities.

Galtung has apparently drawn unwarranted conclusions from a tendency of the terms of trade to move from the early 1950s to the early 1970s against primary products and in favor of manufactured goods. But such trends are not the same for all products nor do they last indefinitely. As variations in the terms of trade occur, some countries gain more from international trade; others gain less. The terms of trade move against countries offering products that are already plentifully supplied by others. Internationally as domestically, the poor are alienated and frustrated because they are so little needed. How can the unemployed be said to be exploited? How can countries offering materials that are in plentiful supply be said to be subsidizing rich nations through low commodity prices? If rich nations stopped buying their products, poor countries would surely be poorer.

Galtung nevertheless believes the rich exploit and impoverish the poor, impede their economic development, and keep them internally and externally disunited as well. His conclusion, first put into his theory and later drawn from it, is that the imperialist relation between the rich and the poor is the major explanation for the well-being of the few and the suffering of the many. One must then ask whether the northern and western parts of the world have indeed impoverished the southern and eastern ones, and whether exploitation of the latter in turn enriched the former. Did imperialism bring economic exploitation, poverty, and strife to people who had not previously suffered those afflictions? Does imperialism now serve to perpetuate those ills? Exploitation and strife are not recent misfortunes, nor is poverty. Those who attribute disunity to imperialism might well recall the earlier condition of most colonial people. Until the middle of the nineteenth century, moreover, nearly everyone everywhere lived at a subsistence level or very close to it. Marx and the earlier Marxists seem to be nearer the truth in believing that without the intervention of dynamic capitalist countries the nonwestern world might have remained in its backward condition forever.

The causes of poverty are many and age-old, and so are the causes of wealth. Those who believe that imperialism is so highly profitable that it accounts for much of the wealth of the wealthy confuse private with national gain, fail to consider the costs of the imperial country including the cost of exporting capital, and forget that for most imperial countries any imperial gain is at best small when measured against its own economy. As markets for goods and as places for investment, moreover, other wealthy nations have been more important to advanced countries, whether or not they were imperialist, than backward countries have been. To say that imperialism has not returned some profits would be wrong. The main point, however, so compelling that it can be said in one sentence, is this: Surely the major reasons for the material well-being of rich state are found within their own borders — in their use of technology and in their ability to organize their economies on a national scale.

Nevertheless, for many of those who explain imperialism economically, the notion that the poor make the rich rich has become a cherished belief. That the rich make the poor poor, and inflict numerous other ills on them, is a belief perhaps as deeply revered. These despairing thoughts, momentary for old-fashioned Marxists because causes embedded in the system were to bring about its destruction, become permanent for today's neocolonialists for reasons that I shall set forth in the next section.

3. Over-Explanation and the Problem of Change. The effort to save Lenin's thesis has led to such a broadening of the definition of imperialism that almost any relation among unequals can be termed "imperialism." The broadening was required to cover the successive refutation by events of key points in Lenin's theory. Marxists used to view foreign investment as a means of breaking through the inevitable stagnation of a laissez-faire economy. But once foreign investment brings capitalist countries a return greater than the amount of their new investment abroad, the "push" principle can no longer be said to operate. Some neocolonialists now point out that the net flow of funds is *to* the United States, and they add that much of the new investment of corporations operating abroad comes from capital borrowed locally.

How then do capitalist states avoid economic stagnation? A simple answer is often given: by spending a lot on defense. Defense budgets are ideal absorbers of surplus capital because defense expenditures are sterile. This explanation, however, ill applies to Japan or to West Germany, the world's second and third ranking capitalist states. Even applied to the United States, the explanation itself admits that any additional objects of large-scale private or public expenditure would do as well, as Baran and Sweezy themselves point out.[14] For our purposes, all that need be noticed is that the foreign investment of states is effectively separated from the Marxist analysis of capitalist economies once foreign investment is no longer seen as a way of compensating for underconsumption internally.

Thus one of the two principal elements of dialectic development is eliminated. The second element has also ceased to operate, for, as explained above, the underdeveloped countries are no longer thought to be uplifted economically through the flow of foreign capital to them. They therefore do not acquire the ability to resist the encroachments of capitalist states in the future. Capitalism does not reproduce itself abroad through its imperialist policies and therefore does not create the conditions from which socialism classically is supposed to emerge.

As the ultimate economic explanation, neocolonialism divorces imperialism from governmental policy. Imperialism, now, resting on an economic imbalance in favor of capitalist states, is a condition that endures so long as that imbalance lasts. Putting it that way reveals the important common quality between Britain's "imperialism of free trade" in the middle of the nineteenth century and America's recent "imperialism of business expansion abroad." Each case is an instance of "the imperialism of great power." When a country produces a third or a quarter of the world's goods, it is bound to affect others more than others affect it. The vehicles of influence — whether they be commodity trade, financial instruments, or multinational corporations — produce their far-reaching effects because of the vast national capabilities that lie behind them.

The only prescription for ending this so-called imperialism is one that tells the poor to become richer and/or the rich to become poorer. And yet the present system is seen as producing, perpetuating, and enlarging the gap between rich nations and poor ones. Those who accept the neocolonial analysis must either end in despair or indulge in fantasy. The fantasy of their prescriptions for undoing imperialism is easily seen. Having defined imperialism as the exploitation of the weak by the strong or of the poor by the rich, Galtung, for example, can see an end to imperialism only through the weak and the poor cooperating and uniting in order to become strong and rich, though the complication of his statements somewhat obscures this prescription. Be strong! Become rich! Advice of that sort is difficult to follow. On occasion, the weak and poor may gain something by combining; but the occasions are few, and the gains are difficult to achieve. The dramatic increase of oil prices promoted by the cartel of oil exporting countries in the middle 1970s suggests that highly special conditions are prerequisites of success. The example mainly shows that those who are well-endowed with a resource in heavy demand prosper at the expense of many others, the more so if some regulation of supply is possible. The example confirms the colloquial saying that "them that's got, git" rather than supporting the hope that poor countries can improve their lots by concerting their efforts. Misery may like company, but when the poor and the weak join hands they gain little if anything in prosperity and strength.

We can now reflect on the theories of imperialism examined above. Hobson, Lenin, and the neocolonialists offer economic explanations of the external behavior of states, with greater differences between the neocolonial school and Lenin than between Lenin and Hobson. Hobson and Lenin saw the expansion and consolidation of empires proceeding along with the development of capitalism. They argued that capitalism caused imperialism, and they concluded that the regulation or elimination of capitalism would abolish imperialism. They made the understandable error of thinking that the solution, even if it were such, of the specific problem of imperialism in the late nineteenth and early twentieth centuries would be a solution to the general and age-old problem of imperialism and also to the problem of war. Latter-day Marxists and other neocolonialists make different and less easily excused errors. They reinterpret the world to make it fit their misinterpretations of an old theory. "Theories" of the neocolonial sort can be rejected as offering not explanations but redefinitions designed less to account for the phenomena than to salvage a theory.

The examination of neocolonial writers alerts us to the common practice of claiming to construct or reconstruct theories while instead engaging in definitional exercises designed to make descriptive categories correspond to changes in observed events. The examination of Hobson and Lenin leads to thoughts about why reductionist approaches may be inadequate for the construction of international-political theory.

Hobson and Lenin concentrated attention on important attributes of some of the major imperialist states of their day. Examining those attributes in the light of Hobson's economic theory does tell us something about changes in national policies and in international politics from the late nineteenth century onward. But what claimed to be a general theory turned out to be only a partial one. As Eugene Staley commandingly demonstrated, although the theory does help to explain some imperialist policies, it is woefully misleading for others.[15] Economic considerations enter into most, if not into all, imperialist ventures, but economic causes are not the only causes operating nor are they always the most important one. All kinds of states have pursued imperialist policies. One who claims that particular types of states cause imperialism would, to be cogent, have to add that at other times and places quite different types of states were also imperialistic. Yet the theories we have examined claim that an imperial relation exists precisely because the imperial state has certain economic attributes. Such theories require one to believe that a condition of international imbalance accords an amount of influence and a degree of control that is usefully described as imperialism only if the more powerful parties possess the prescribed attributes. Thus, according to most of the economic theories, the baleful influence of the strong over the weak is to be found only if the strong states are capitalist. But that is hard to believe. One wonders, for example, if Mao Tse-tung thought of capitalist states as the unique cause of imperialism, and we know that Chou En-lai did not. Conversely, the necessary implication of economic theories is that the strong and the weak can coexist without an imperial connection developing if the strong are properly constituted. If they are, then the autonomy of the weak will be secured by the self-interested wisdom of the strong.

Theories that make such assertions also contain, at least implicitly, the wider assertion that there are no good international-political reasons for the conflict and the warring of states. The reasons for war, as for imperialism, are located within some, or within all, of the states. But if the causes were cured, would the symptoms disappear? One can hardly believe that they would. Though economic theories assign specific causes of war, we know that all sorts of states with every imaginable variation of economic and social institution and of political ideology have fought wars. Internationally, different states have produced similar as well as different outcomes, and similar states have produced different as well as similar outcomes. The same causes sometimes lead to different effects, and the same effects sometimes follow from different causes. We are led to suspect that reductionist explanations of international politics are insufficient and that analytic approaches must give way to systemic ones.

The failure of some reductionist approaches does not, however, prove that other reductionist approaches would not succeed. The defects of economic theories of imperialism and war, though they may suggest general problems met in concentrating explanations of international politics at national or lower levels, cannot be taken to indicate that all reductionist theories of international politics will be defective. Doubts about the adequacy of reductionist approaches would deepen if, one after another, such approaches were tried and found wanting. Even so, we would have no compelling reason to stop hoping that the next try would lead to a viable reductionist theory. We would be more nearly persuaded of reduction's inadequacy by either or both of the following: the construction of a useful nonreductionist, or system's level, theory and/or an explanation of why reductionist theories fail....

ENDNOTES

1 The above three paragraphs are a summary of Part I, Chapter 6, of J.A. Hobson, *Imperialism: A Study* (London: Allen and Unwin, 1902). Keynes gives Hobson full credit for anticipating the major elements of his general theory, though with strictures upon Hobson's lack of a theory of the rate of interest and his consequent excessive emphasis on the oversupply of capital rather than the lack of demand for it. See John Maynard Keynes, *The General Theory of Employment, Interest, and Money* (New York: Harcourt, Brace, n.d.), pp. 364-70.

2 Hobson, *Imperialism,* pp. 94, 96, 126; cf. pp. 106, 356ff.

3 Harold J. Laski, "The Economic Foundations of Peace," in Leonard Woolf, ed., *The Intelligent Man's Way to Prevent War* (London: Victor Gollancz, 1933), p. 501.

4 Hobson, *Imperialism,* pp. 308f., 313.

5 Karl Marx and Frederick Engels, *Communist Manifesto*, trans. unnamed (Chicago: Charles H. Kerr, 1946), p. 39.

6 Herbert Feis, *Europe, the World's Banker, 1870-1914* (New York: August M. Kelly, 1964), p. 23.

7 Leon Trotsky, *Europe and America: Two Speeches on Imperialism* (New York: Pathfinder Press, 1971), p. 29.

8 Joseph A. Schumpeter, "The Sociology of Imperialism," in Joseph Schumpeter, *Imperialism and Social Classes*, trans. by Heinz Norden (New York: Meridian Books, 1955), p. 72.

9 Harry Magdoff, *The Age of Imperialism* (New York: Monthly Review Press, 1969), chapters 1, 5, and "The Logic of Imperialism," *Social Policy*, 1 (September/October 1970), 27.

10 Imre Lakatos, "Falsification and the Methodology of Scientific Research Programs," in Imre Lakatos and Alan Musgrave, eds., *Criticism and the Growth of Knowledge* (Cambridge: Cambridge University Press, 1970), pp. 175-76.

11 John Gallagher and Ronald Robinson, "The Imperialism of Free Trade," *Economic History Review*, 2nd series, 6 (August 1953), 11, 13.

12 Johan Galtung, "A Structural Theory of Imperialism," *Journal of Peace Research*, 8 (No. 2, 1971), 82-84, 101.

13 Ibid., p. 89.

14 Paul A. Baran and Paul M. Sweezy, *Monopoly Capital: An Essay on the American Economic and Social Order* (New York: Monthly Review Press, 1966), pp. 146-53, 223.

15 Eugene Staley, *War and the Private Investor* (Garden City, N.Y.: Doubleday, Doran, 1935).

5

TRANSNATIONAL RELATIONS

Transnational Relations and World Politics

Canadian-United States Corporate Interface and Transnational Relations

The Nation-State and Multinational Enterprise: Erosion or Assertion

Transnational Resource Conflict: The Politics of Whaling

INTRODUCTION

The study of international politics traditionally focuses on states and the range of interactions among them. After examining the impact of state attributes on conflict and its management, we would customarily pass on to the international system in which relations between states are played out. To do so, however, would be to ignore an entire spectrum of intersocietal relations that significantly affect the type and incidence of conflict between states as well as the modes of conflict management.

Raymond Aron, one of the earliest writers to take note of transnational relations, distinguished between an international and a transnational society. A transnational society, he explained, is characterized by "commercial exchange, migration of persons, common beliefs, organizations that cross frontiers and, lastly, ceremonies or competitions open to all these units."[1] Although such a society existed as long ago as ancient Greece, it was only in the nineteenth century that we witnessed a particularly impressive growth in activities that were initiated by private individuals and groups rather than states — the exchange of goods and services, the spread of ideas and knowledge, the movement of peoples and the flow of money — and reached across state boundaries. Transnational processes expanded even further in the twentieth century as technological developments in transportation and communications brought different peoples closer together both in time and space and facilitated the sharing of ideas and the transfer of technology.

Aron thought of transnational society as relatively autonomous from or totally subordinate to the interstate order. In either case, interstate relations remain largely unaffected by transnational relations. It was not until almost a decade later, with the publication in 1971 of a special issue of *International Organization*, that transnational relations became important in the study of world politics. The editors of that special issue, Robert Keohane and Joseph Nye, argue that transnational relations do make a difference: that "contacts, coalitions and interactions across state boundaries that are not controlled by the central foreign policy organs of government"[2] have an impact on interstate relations. We include part of their conclusion in this volume.

Critics allege that such transactions are no more frequent today than they were before 1914, but Keohane and Nye pay attention not simply to their frequency, but to new forms of transnational relationships and their increased political salience. In the first place, the scope of government intervention in the political and economic life of its citizens has grown enormously. Governments not only assume the traditional responsibility of protecting their populations from external aggression, but also accept, as matters of national policy, the obligation to provide full employment, increase national productivity, maintain a stable national currency, preserve a healthy environment and, in general, improve their citizens' welfare. In performing these new functions, governments find they frequently come into conflict with nongovernmental actors as well as with other states over such matters as nontariff barriers, appropriate monetary and fiscal policies, and environmental pollution. Conflicts range over a far broader agenda of issues and the cast of actors embroiled in these conflicts has expanded to include nongovernmental groups as well as governments. The distinguishing feature of transnational relations is that at least one actor in the relationship is not the agent of a government.

Second, there have emerged "powerful and dynamic transnational actors capable of adapting to change and of consciously attempting to shape the world to their interests."[3] Transnational relations have been institutionalized with increasing frequency. Whether they attempt to coordinate and to control intersocietal relations or to promote their own particular interests, transnational organizations act directly in the international arena. While the most prominent of these actors in undoubtedly the multinational enterprise (MNE), others are important as well. We need only think of such transnational organizations as the Roman Catholic Church, the World Council of Churches, international revolutionary networks, Amnesty International, and environmental groups which cut across state boundaries. In his selection in this reader, Robert Mandel describes one such environmental organization, Greenpeace, and its successful interference in international waters to prevent the killing of whales and to focus worldwide attention on their destruction.

But it is the multinational enterprise that is most often cited as the transnational organization *par excellence*. Because of its enormous size and flexibility, and its world wide operations, many considered the MNE the latest in a series of direct threats to the sovereignty of the nation-state — first the dominant class (or power elite), then nuclear technology, and now the MNE. These fears concerning the viability of the nation-state in the face of corporate giants, though justified in some cases, appear for the most part to have been exaggerated. Both because of characteristics of the multinational enterprise itself and the resilience of the nation-state, factors outlined fully in David Leyton-Brown's article, the balance of forces has swung back in favor of the nation-state. But no matter where the pendulum comes to rest, if it ever does, it is quite clear that the MNE has considerable impact on government-to-government relations. Either at the instigation of the home or host government or in pursuit of its own interests, the MNE frequently undertakes actions that conflict with a particular government's policy. In attempting to cope with that challenge to its authority, one government often finds itself drawn into conflict with others. It is this process in which transnational institutions and relations infect or contaminate interstate relations that I.A. Litvak and C.J. Maule describe so well.

Students of international conflict could ignore transnational relations or consign them to the "environment" if their impact were slight or if transnational relations were largely controlled by national governments. But neither condition appears to hold. Indeed, the unprecedented level, scope, intensity, and variety of transnational relations have evoked competing attempts by national governments to regulate these relations. None has been completely successful. The expansion of transnational relations has also precipitated the development of international institutions and international codes of behavior. Consensus among the principal allied powers (excluding the Soviet Union) after World War II facilitated the establishment of intergovernmental institutions and procedures (the International Monetary Fund, the General Agreement on Tariffs and Trade) to foster cooperation and mitigate conflict in the fields of foreign exchange and trade. Unfortunately, as that consensus broke down in the 1970s, conflict among former allies has replaced the earlier cooperation.

The 1970s also witnessed the concerted efforts of the international community to elaborate and adopt internationally accepted rules governing the most important transnational institution, the MNE. Progress has, however, been slow and piecemeal. The Organization for Economic Cooperation and Development (OECD) adopted Guidelines for Multinational Enterprises, and the United Nations has approved a set of Multilaterally Agreed Equitable Principles and Rules for the Control of Restrictive Business Practices. A draft text of the Code of Conduct on Transnational Corporations is now before the United Nations. These agreements are not binding on either businesses or governments, however, and governments continue to disagree on many important aspects of the code. Because of these different attitudes towards the code, the general reluctance of states to cede sovereignty, and competition for the potential benefits that MNEs can offer, international institutions will likely play a supplementary role while national politics continue to dominate the management of the conflict that grows out of transnational relations.[4]

In effect, the political organization of the international system into separate, sovereign states is out of step with a global transnational society. National responses to global problems — trade, monetary, foreign investment — will necessarily result in an intensification of interstate conflict. A focus on transnational relations highlights the wider range of conflicts that states confront today, the limits set on purely national solutions to these conflicts, and the broad range of coalitions of nongovernmental and state actors that engage both in conflict and in attempts at conflict management. Nevertheless, a transnational perspective can only supplement other levels of analysis. As we have already noted, the state has withstood the latest challenge to its continued viability from the MNE. As long as the sovereign nation-state remains the principal actor in world politics, we cannot help but pay attention to the anarchical international system.

ENDNOTES

1 Raymond Aron, *Peace and War: A Theory of International Relations*, trans. Richard Howard and Annette Baker Fox (Garden City, N.Y.: Doubleday & Co., 1966), p. 105.

2 Robert O. Keohane and Joseph S. Nye, Jr., "Transnational Relations and World Politics: An Introduction," *International Organization*, 35 (Summer 1971), 331.

3 Transnational relations do take place also in an unorganized manner, that is without any institution to initiate or sustain them. Transnational forces, such as trade flows, capital flights, and large-scale population movements, do exert an influence on the governments concerned and on their relationships. For a particularly interesting account of this process, involving a large number of Algerian workers in France and their impact on Franco-Algerian relations, see Mark I. Miller, "Reluctant Partnership: Foreign Workers in Franco-Algerian Relations, 1962-1979," *Journal of International Affairs*, 33 (Fall/ Winter 1979), 219-37.

4 A.E. Safarian, "Multinational Policy on Multinational Enterprise," *International Journal*, 34 (Winter 1978-79), 110, 120.

Transnational Relations and World Politics

Joseph S. Nye, Jr. / Robert O. Keohane

World politics is changing, but our conceptual paradigms have not kept pace. The classic state-centric paradigm assumes that states are the only significant actors in world politics and that they act as units. Diverse domestic interests have effects on international politics only through governmental foreign policy channels. Intersocietal interactions are relegated to a category of secondary importance — the "environment" of interstate politics. As Karl Kaiser has pointed out, the reality of international politics has never totally corresponded to this model. Nevertheless, the model was approximated in the eighteenth century when foreign policy decisions were taken by small groups of persons acting within an environment that was less obtrusive and complex than the present one.[1]

Simplification of reality is essential for understanding. A skeptical scholar or diplomat might admit that the state-centric model misses much of the complexity of transnational relations described in this volume, but he might argue that such a simplification is justified because 1) in direct confrontation with transnational actors governments prevail, 2) transnational relations have always existed, and 3) transnational relations do not significantly affect the "high politics" of security, status, or war. We believe that these objections are to a large degree mistaken and that a broader world politics paradigm is necessary if scholars and statesmen are to understand such current problems as the unequal distribution of power and values in the world, the new setting of United States foreign policy, statesmen's feelings of "loss of control," and the new types and tasks of international organization.

I. WHY CHANGE PARADIGMS?

Before elaborating our world politics paradigm and discussing these problems we set forth our reasons for rejecting the major arguments for the adequacy of the state-centric approach.

"Governments Win Direct Confrontations." When transnational relations are discussed, those who wish to preserve the limited state-centric view are likely to stress the point that, in direct confrontations with transnational actors, governments generally prevail.... It is certainly true that national governments are often able to win such confrontations since they have much greater resources of

Joseph S. Nye, Jr. and Robert O. Keohane, "Transnational Relations and World Politics," *International Organization*, Vol. 25, No. 3 (Summer 1971), pp. 721-34. Reprinted by permission of the MIT Press Journals. Portions of the text have been deleted. Most footnotes have been removed; those remaining have been renumbered.

force and popular legitimacy. The Ford Foundation can be expelled from a foreign country or disciplined by the United States Congress. A local Catholic hierarchy can be cut off from Rome. The assets of a multinational business enterprise may be nationalized, and its efforts to impose retaliatory sanctions may come to no avail. IBM and Ford Motor Company may be prevented from investing in the Union of Soviet Socialist Republics. Invading revolutionary guerrillas — or guerrillas operating from a base in an independent state — may be decimated by military force. At a nonorganizational level individuals whose attitudes become too cosmopolitan because of transnational contacts may be deprived of political effectiveness at home.

However, the question "who wins confrontations?" is insufficient. It focuses only on the extreme cases of direct confrontation between a government and a nongovernmental actor. Winning may be costly, even for governments. Transnational relations may help to increase these costs and thus increase the constraints on state autonomy. Expelling a foundation cuts off resources that may be vital to certain important groups.... The Roman Catholic church today is better able than ever before to transfer resources across borders. Even where access is restricted, it remains a signi ficant political factor. Nationalization of the local assets of a multinational business enterprise may prove costly in terms of capital, technology, or markets foregone. Restrictions on American business involvement in Eastern Europe may mean that such dealings are handled through European subsidiaries and thus are more easily isolated from the American political process. It may also mean that the market is left to European rivals.

Because of the rise in the costs to national governments of "winning" in direct confrontations with transnational actors there are more incentives for bargaining. More relevant than "who wins" direct confrontations are the new kinds of bargains, coalitions, and alliances being formed between transnational actors and between these actors and segments of governments and international organizations:...coalitions between the Roman Catholic church and nation-states; new ecumenical alliances between religious groups; coalitions between locally owned companies and governments to gain protection against foreign companies; coalitions between vertically integrated corporations and trade unions to ensure continuity of supplies; coalitions between government and unions to influence or even help overthrow foreign governments; coalitions between scientists to strengthen their position in lobbying for resources at home; coalitions between trade unions to coordinate pressure on multinational business enterprises; coalitions between foreign intellectuals and United States foundations to protect social scientists against their governments; coalitions between revolutionary groups to strengthen their legitimacy in their struggles against governments.

There is considerable variety among the actors involved, the resources available to them, and the outcomes of their coalitions. For example, boycotts of companies and individuals in the entertainment world by Arab governments are coordinated through regional intergovernmental organizations. In one instance (that involving the Norwich Union Fire Insurance Society in the United Kingdom) a boycott proved effective in changing the leadership of a British corporation. In other cases the costs of boycott were too high, and governments did not enforce the agreed-upon sanctions.

...In the 1966 air corridors controversy a transnational actor, the International Air Line Pilots Association, lobbied successfully to prevent an intergovernmental organization, the International Civil Aviation Organization (ICAO), from endorsing the position advocated by the United States government. In general the nongovernmental International Air Transport Association (IATA), run by an oligarchy of airlines, is far stronger than the intergovernmental ICAO in which each state has one vote and minor governments can create obstructions. In some cases airlines have aligned with governments for protection against other airlines or governments.... Pan American World Airways and Trans World Airlines tacitly approved of an Alitalia position in the IATA that thwarted the United States government position on charter airline fares. United States airlines could not have resisted the United States government as well on their own. In its rivalry with Pan American over South Pacific air routes Continental Air Lines is allegedly attempting to enlist the support of an intergovernmental organization — the United Nations Trusteeship Council — to strengthen its position. The complexity of these coalitions in the political struggle to allocate important resources in the field of air transport is not caught by the state-centric paradigm. Nor, we might add, do national governments always prevail.

A sophisticated analysis of contemporary international politics cannot ignore this variety of bargaining situations or the differences in outcomes among issue areas. The state-centric view often fails to forecast outcomes correctly, and state-centric theories are not very good at explaining such outcomes even when the forecasts are correct.

"Transnational Relations Have Always Existed." Raymond Aron was among the first to introduce the concept of "transnational society" into international relations theory. He used the term to describe commercial interchanges, migration of persons, common beliefs, ceremonials, and organizations that cross frontiers. However, he arrived at the skeptical judgment that transnational society as he defined it was relatively unimportant for understanding basic interactions in world politics. In his words: "Before 1914 economic exchanges throughout Europe enjoyed a freedom that the gold standard and monetary convertibility safeguarded even better than legislation. Labor parties were grouped into an International. The Greek tradition of the Olympic Games had been revived ... religious, moral and even political beliefs were fundamentally analogous on either side of the frontiers.... This example, like the similar one of Hellenic society in the fifth century, illustrates the relative autonomy of the interstate order — in peace and in war — in relation to the context of transnational society."[2]

Aron is certainly correct when he points to the existence of transnational relations before 1914.... More generally, as Oran Young has observed, "over the bulk of recorded history man has organized himself for political purpose on bases other than those now subsumed under the concepts 'state' and 'nation-state.'"[3]

Our contention, however, is neither than transnational relations are new nor that they supersede interstate politics but that they affect interstate politics by altering the choices open to statesmen and the costs that must be borne for adopting various courses of action. In short, transnational relations provide different sets of incentives, or payoffs, for states. These altered payoffs were not sufficient to ensure peace in 1914 despite the hopes of men like Norman Angell, who argued in 1910 that "the wealth, prosperity, and well-being of a nation depend in no way upon its political power."[4] Nevertheless, World War I by no means refutes the contention that transnational relations influence interstate politics; it merely warns us against the incautious assumption that transnational relations render war impossible between states linked by extensive transnational ties.

In any case, the analogy between 1914 and 1971 should not be taken too seriously when discussing transnational relations any more than it should be regarded as the key to understanding great-power politics. Transnational relations today take different forms than in 1914, and in our view the contemporary forms have greater political significance than the pre-1914 versions. On the one hand, mutual sensitivity of societies has increased; on the other hand, the growth of transnational social and economic organizations has created powerful and dynamic transnational actors capable of adapting to change and of consciously attempting to shape the world to their interests.

Sensitivity of Societies. The importance of transnational relations depends less on the sheer quantity of such relations than on their political salience and the resulting sensitivity of societies to one another. There are two major reasons for this increased sensitivity. First, improved technology has removed many of the imperfections of communications that once helped separate societies. Second...a given volume of transnational activity may, paradoxically, have greater effects on interdependence when governments are ambitiously attempting to control their economies than in situations of relative laissez faire....In the liberal nineteenth-century world transnational society remained somewhat separate from interstate politics, but today the result of ambitious governmental policies is that transnational relations affect intergovernmental relations and have themselves become politicized. New subjects enter the realm of international relations. As the May 1971 international monetary crisis made clear, governments must often be concerned with the internal economic policies of other governments. This is sometimes referred to as the "domesticization" of international politics. It might better be called the "internationalization" of domestic politics. An important result is that subunits of governments are provided greater opportunities for transnational contacts and coalitions.

By facilitating the flow of ideas modern communications have also increased intersocietal sensitivity. Certainly there have been indirect "contagions" of ideas in earlier periods such as the European revolutions of 1848 or Latin American university reforms in 1917....Today, however, television has created a "window on the West" in the living rooms of the elites of the third world. Widely separated elites, whether functionally similar social groups, students, military officers, or racial minorities, become more rapidly aware of each other's activities. Seymour Martin Lipset has noted that "student culture is a highly communicable one, the mood and mode of it translate readily from one center to another, one country to another."[5] Indeed, although many of the leaders of the student disturbances that shook Europe in the late 1960s were aware of each other's activities, they first came into direct contact when British television producers brought them together after the events.

Not all the political effects of transnational communications are so dramatic. The incremental growth, spread, and change of knowledge, doctrines, and attitudes alter the context within which governments operate and change the payoffs available to them. While these ideas and attitudes are often transmitted by transnational organizations, they are also transmitted by individuals through personal travel and communication....

Transnational Organizations. Not all types of transnational organizations have increased in importance. Those with explicitly political goals seem to have declined in importance. The close links between Communist parties and the international brigades of the 1930s find only the palest of reflections in the Havana-based Tricontinental or the expeditions of radical American students to cut sugar cane in Cuba....Current revolutionary guerrilla groups have a transnational myth to sustain morale and legitimacy rather than a transnational organization to coordinate operations.... A similar trend away from political organization has occurred in labor movements. The international confederations that aggregated labor interests at a very general level and engaged primarily in transnational political struggles have been replaced in prominence by the international trade secretariats which aggregate more specific economic interests and organize to coordinate operations against multinational business enterprises. The greater reliance of the Roman Catholic church in recent years on moral and humanitarian influence, rather than on political alliances with governments, is consistent with this trend away from explicit political activity by transnational organizations.

In contrast to political organizations, however, transnational organizations whose principal goals are social and economic have increased in importance. These organizations, of course, may have very significant political consequences. By far the most important of these organizations is the multinational business enterprise. Multinational enterprises existed at the beginning of this century but on a smaller scale and with much less important effects.[6] Modern communications technology has greatly increased the feasibility of imposing a central strategy on widely scattered subsidiaries and consequently has increased the challenge that enterprises present to state sovereignty. Unlike those of the Hudson's Bay Company, the activities of today's multinational business enterprises often do not coincide with the decision domains of particular states. Their effects on world trade and production can be judged by the fact that the production of overseas subsidiaries of the ten leading capital-exporting states was nearly twice the volume of trade between those countries. Raymond Vernon indicates that overseas subsidiaries may account for approximately 15 percent of world production. Finally, multinational business enterprises have had strong effects on other transnational actors. Trade unions, banks, and public relations firms have all been lured into increased transnational activity by following the lead of the multinational business enterprise.

Arnold Wolfers pointed out over a decade ago that the ability of international nongovernmental organizations "to operate as international or transnational actors may be traced to the fact that men identify themselves and their interests with corporate bodies other than the nation-state."[7] Transnational actors therefore flourish where dual loyalties are regarded as acceptable. In totalitarian societies, and in areas in which one version or another of integral nationalism has taken hold, dual loyalties are regarded as treasonous and transnational forces as potentially corrupting and dangerous. It is hard to imagine a good Soviet citizen avowing loyalty to General Motors Corporation or a contemporary Chilean nationalist identifying himself with Anaconda Company or Kennecott Copper Corporation.

In the modernized Western world and its ancillary areas the acceptability of multiple loyalties is taken for granted. Yet, this toleration seems to be extended more readily when the transnational actor is explicitly economic in purpose than when it is explicitly political. Thus, it seems less incompatible to be loyal to both IBM and France, to FIAT and the United States, or to the Roman Catholic church and Belgium than it does for a loyal citizen of the United Kingdom to pledge allegiance to transnational communism or for Americans to identify with Israel. In the West, therefore, nationalism probably hinders overt political organization across boundaries more than it hinders transnational economic activity. Dual loyalties may be more feasible when the foci of loyalty seem to operate in different areas with different goals. When the competition is directly political, the individual is often forced to choose.

These are mere speculations about the reasons for the mixed trends in transnational organizations, reflecting the rise of economic actors in modernized areas of the world and the decline of transnational political organizations. Whatever the reasons for the trends, however, the increased scale of social and economic organizations and their increased effects on the political sensitivity of societies to each other constitute an important new aspect of world politics.

"Transnational Relations Do Not Affect High Politics." Distinctions between high and low politics are of diminishing value in current world politics. Stanley Hoffmann has described this situation with a useful metaphor: "The competition between states takes place on several chessboards in addition to the traditional military and diplomatic ones: for instance, the chessboards of world trade, of world finance, of aid and technical assistance, of space research and exploration, of military technology, and the chessboard of what has been called 'informal penetration.' These chessboards do not entail the resort to force."[8] Hoffmann observes that each "chessboard" has rules of its own but is linked as well to others by "complicated and subtle relations." High and low politics become difficult to distinguish. Thus, during the international monetary crisis of May 1971 it became clear that an implicit bargain had been struck between American and West German statesmen and central bankers by which the willingness of West German authorities to hold United States dollars was a condition for a large United States army in Europe.

...On a number of Hoffmann's "chessboards," or issue areas, transnational relations are extremely important. As sensitivity to other societies increases, new subjects are brought into the realm of world politics. Issue areas that were formerly quite distinct from political calculation have become politically relevant, particularly insofar as governments have attempted to extend their control over domestic economic activity without sacrificing the benefits of transnational intercourse. Since these issue areas are often of great significance to governments, they cannot be merely dismissed as "low politics," allegedly subordinate to a "high politics" of status, security, or war. Butter comes before guns in New Zealand's diplomacy.

In these issue areas, furthermore, force may be neither appropriate nor effective. Insofar as force is devalued for a particular area of interaction, transnational interactions and the activities of transnational relations are likely to be important — even for France, the United Kingdom, and the United States.

We find ourselves in a world that reminds us more of the extensive and curious chessboard in Lewis Carroll's *Through the Looking Glass* than of more conventional versions of that ancient game. The players are not always what they seem, and the terrain of the chessboards may suddenly change from garden to shop to castle. Thus, in contemporary world politics not all players on important chessboards are states, and the varying terrains of the chessboards constrain state behavior. Some are more suited to the use of force, others almost totally unsuited to it. Different chessboards favor different states. For example, relations between Norway and the United States are quite different on shipping questions than on questions involving strategic arms. When international oil prices are negotiated, Iran is more important than it is on world trade issues in general. High and low politics have become tightly intertwined.

II. THE WORLD POLITICS PARADIGM

Although we use the word "paradigm" somewhat loosely, we wish to make it clear that we seek to challenge basic assumptions that underlie the analysis of international relations, not merely to compile a list of transnational interactions and organizations. Nor are our concerns merely academic. "Practical men, who believe themselves to be quite exempt from any intellectual influences," are usually, as John Maynard Keynes once pointed out, unconscious captives of paradigms created by "some academic scribbler of a few years back."[9]

...We define world politics as political interactions between any "significant actors" whose characteristics include autonomy, the control of substantial resources relevant to a given issue area, and participation in political relationships across state lines. Since we define politics in terms of the conscious employment of resources, "both material and symbolic, including the threat or exercise of punishment, to induce other actors to behave differently than they would otherwise behave," it is clear that we are positing a conception of world politics in which the central phenomenon is bargaining between a variety of autonomous or semiautonomous actors.

The difference between our world politics paradigm and the state-centric paradigm can be clarified most easily by focusing on the nature of the actors. The world politics paradigm attempts to transcend the "level-of-analysis problem" both by broadening the conception of actors to include transnational actors and by conceptually breaking down the "hard shell" of the nation-state.

This can be illustrated by a diagram that compares the range of actors included within our world politics paradigm with that included in the state-centric model. Figure I displays the characteristics of actors in world politics on two dimensions: 1) the degree to which they are governmental or nongovernmental in position and 2) the extent to which they consist of coherent and centrally controlled organizations rather than subunits of governments or of transnational organizations.

	Position		
	Governmental	Intergovernmental	Nongovernmental
Maximal central control	A States as units	C International organizations as units	E Transnational organizations as units
Minimal central control	B Governmental subunits	D Subunits of international organizations	F Subunits of transnational organizations; also certain individuals

A + C = Actors in the state-centric paradigm
B + D = Actors in transgovernmental interactions
E + F = Actors in transnational interactions

FIGURE I. ACTORS IN WORLD POLITICS

The first dimension distinguishes actors according to formal position — governmental, intergovernmental, or nongovernmental....however, there is another dimension of world politics that the classic state-centric paradigm with its assumption of states as unitary actors fails to take into account. This second dimension, centralization of control, involves the realization that subunits of governments may also have distinct foreign policies which are not all filtered through the top leadership and which do not fit into a unitary actor model. Thus, scholars have recently developed a "bureaucratic politics approach" to foreign policy analysis, explaining decisions of governments in these terms.

Bureaucratic politics is not limited to governments but can be applied to nongovernmental actors as well. Multinational business enterprises are frequently unable to act as unitary actors, and we have seen that the Roman Catholic church, the Ford Foundation, guerrilla movements, and organizations of scientists are hardly monolithic. Furthermore, just as American military officers may negotiate with their Spanish counterparts and Congressman Wilbur Mills with Japanese textile companies, so may local divisions of a multinational business enterprise or of the Roman Catholic church strike bargains and form coalitions with national governments or subunits thereof.

The combination of these two dimensions in figure 1 portrays a complex model of world politics in which the state-centric paradigm focuses on only two of the six cells. Another way of illustrating this point is shown by figure 2. The state-centric paradigm covers only four of the 36 possible types of politically important interactions across state boundaries that are identified by the world politics paradigm. This gives us an idea of the richness of possible transnational coalitions that determine outcomes in world politics and that are now largely relegated to the subsidiary and largely undifferentiated category of "environment."

Adding the second dimension, centralization of control, allows us to specify a paradigm of world politics that brings together traditional international politics, the bureaucratic politics approach to foreign policy analysis, and transnational actors as defined in the introduction. Yet, it also poses certain conceptual problems....Transnational interactions could be easily identified by the involvement of nongovernmental actors. Thus, definition on the basis of formal position —

Actor	A States as units	B Governmental subunits	C International organizations as units	D Subunits of International organizations	E Transnational organizations as units	F Subunits of transnational organizations; also certain individuals
A States as units	IS	TG	IS	TG	TN	TN
B Governmental subunits	TG	TG	TG	TG	TN	TN
C International organizations as units	IS	TG	IS	TG	TN	TN
D Subunits of international organizations	TG	TG	TG	TG	TN	TN
E Transnational organizations as units	TN	TN	TN	TN	TN	TN
F Subunits of transnational organizations; also certain individuals	TN	TN	TN	TN	TN	TN

IS * Interstate interactions
TG * Transgovernmental interactions
TN * Transnational interactions
TG + TN = Transnational relations
TG + TN + IS = World politics interactions

FIGURE 2. BILATERAL INTERACTIONS IN WORLD POLITICS

governmental or nongovernmental — led to a clear delineation between transnational and interstate interactions. This narrowed the issues and omitted problems of central control, but it did achieve an initially useful simplification and clarification. Unlike that of formal position, however, the concept of centralization of control is a continuum — there can be more or less central control, and lines that are drawn will necessarily be somewhat arbitrary. How, then, do we distinguish various types of behavior along this dimension?

Our first step is to introduce a new type of interaction in addition to "transnational interactions" and "interstate interactions".... Transnational interactions necessarily involve nongovernmental actors, whereas interstate interactions take place exclusively between states acting as units. Transgovernmental interactions, however, are defined as interactions between governmental subunits across state boundaries. The broad term transnational relations includes both trans*national* and trans*governmental* interactions — all of world politics that is not taken into account by the state-centric paradigm.

As we have defined world politics, any unit of action that attempts to exercise influence across state boundaries and possesses significant resources in a given issue area is an actor in world politics. Thus, this concept of transnational relations calls attention to the activities of subunits of governments or intergovernmental organizations as well as to the behavior of individuals and nongovernmental organizations. Yet, we still need to specify when an actor is behaving "as a unit" and when its subunits possess significant autonomy.

On an abstract level we distinguish transgovernmental from interstate interactions by the extent to which actors are behaving in conformity to roles specified or reasonably implied by the formal foreign policy structure of the state. The problem of discovering deviations from formally prescribed roles is difficult and sometimes impossible because of the ambiguous specification of role at high levels of authority.... At lower levels of authority the transgovernmental behavior of those in formal governmental positions is much easier to identify, for example, the coalition of United States and Canadian weather bureaus to overcome a Department of State decision on control of international meteorological research. The difficulties of delineation in this murky area of control are admittedly great, but it would hardly be sensible to promulgate a supposedly "new" paradigm for world politics without including reference to transgovernmental politics.

To explain this more complex world the study of world politics must proceed by the analysis of particular issue areas and the relations between them. It must take into account the differences in the way the game of world politics is played on Hoffmann's different chessboards or, to escape from bipolar imagery, poker tables. Who are the players? What are their resources? What are the rules? How do the players, resources, and rules differ from game to game? Most important, how are the different games related to each other? Are winnings and resources transferable, and, if they are, at what discount?...

ENDNOTES

1 Karl Kaiser, "Transnationale Politik: Zu einer Theorie der multinationalen Politik," *Politische Vierteljahresschrift*, 1969 (Special Issue No. 1), pp. 80-109. An English translation of this important essay appears in *International Organization*, 25 (Autumn 1971).

2 Raymond Aron, *Peace and War: A Theory of International Relations*, trans. Richard Howard and Annette Baker Fox (Garden City, N.Y.: Doubleday & Co., 1966), p. 105.

3 Oran R. Young, "The Actors in World Politics," in *The Analysis of International Politics*, ed. James N. Rosenau, B. Vincent Davis, and Maurice A. East (Glencoe, Ill: Free Press, 1972); see also Adda B. Bozeman, *Politics and Culture in International History* (Princeton, N.J.: Princeton University Press, 1960).

4 Norman Angell, *The Great Illusion: A Study of the Relation of Military Power in Nations to Their Economic and Social Advantage* (3rd rev. and enl. ed.; New York: G. P. Putnam's Sons, 1911), p. 34.

5 Seymour Martin Lipset, "The Possible Political Effects of Student Activism," *Social Science Information*, 20 (April 1969), 12.

6 See Mira Wilkins, *The Emergence of Multinational Enterprise: American Business Abroad from the Colonial Era to 1914* (Cambridge, Mass: Harvard University Press, 1970).

7 Arnold Wolfers, *Discord and Collaboration: Essays on International Politics* (Baltimore, Md: Johns Hopkins Press, 1962).

8 Stanley Hoffmann, "International Organization and the International System," *International Organization*, 24 (Summer 1970), 401.

9 John Maynard Keynes, *The General Theory of Employment, Interest and Money* (London: Macmillan & Co., 1957), p. 383.

Canadian-United States Corporate Interface and Transnational Relations

Isaiah A. Litvak/Christopher J. Maule

Transnational relations involving parent companies of United States multinational enterprises with subsidiaries in Canada have begun to interest not only the social scientist but also the politician and businessman. What is the effect of such transnational relations on the economic resources and performance of each country? What political means are used to influence corporate behaviour? What is the effect of the constitutional system on such transnational relations? What are the ways in which the countries reacted to resolve certain related interstate conflicts?

Each of these issues arises from the emergence of the multinational enterprise. Contemporary business transactions often have no single geopolitical base, and these interactions accentuate the costs and the benefits that flow across national borders in complex patterns involving concerns and interests of several nations. The complexity of these patterns is heightened by the form and behaviour of the multinational enterprise....

Isaiah A. Litvak and Christopher J. Maule, "Canadian-United States Corporate Interface and Transnational Relations," *International Organization*, Vol. 28, No. 4 (Autumn 1974), 713-31. Reprinted by permission of the MIT Press Journals. Portions of the text have been deleted. Most footnotes have been removed; those remaining have been renumbered.

A basic model for analysing Canadian-United States conflicts identifies four actors — the United States and Canadian federal governments, the parent company in the United States, and its subsidiary company in Canada — and the relationships between them (see figure 1). This model can be made more complex in a number of ways, such as through the addition of provincial or state and local governments and of trade unions. Reference to these additional actors is made in the subsequent analysis.

Six components in the system of relationships can be identified, five of which involve transnational processes, in that at least one of the actors is not a government. Relationships 1, 4, and 5 are clearly transnational. Numbers 2 and 3 refer to government-company relationships in their respective countries and have transnational implications in that they can be used to channel effects into the other country through the parent-subsidiary relationship. Number 6 is an interstate, government-to-government relationship and is of relevance in that it is used to handle some of the issues that arise due to the other five interactions. The content and significance of these interactions are now examined in terms of the conflicts that arise between corporate decisions and governmental decisions or policies.

Four ways in which conflict originates are as follows: from essentially corporate-initiated policies, from US government-initiated policies that are transmitted through the parent to the subsidiary in Canada, from Canadian government initiatives and transmission through the subsidiary to the US, and from joint initiatives by the two governments that affect the relationship between parent and subsidiary. None of these conflicts are necessarily independent of each other. For example, in the case of corporate-initiated policies, they all take place within a legal framework established by government.

CORPORATE-INITIATED POLICIES

The parent company makes decisions as to the organization of production within the corporate system, establishing where each item will be produced, where research will be undertaken, where financing will be done, where the subsidiary will be allowed to export, where the entrepreneurial drive will originate, what transfer prices and final product prices will be set, where cutbacks in production will occur in times of recession, and what information will be disclosed by the subsidiary. In sum, the whole range of functional areas within the corporate system are subject to numerous decisions emanating from the parent company. These decisions have to be made, and assuming that they are made in the best interests of the corporation, they will at times come into conflict with Canadian national objectives established by the federal government, and thus give rise to

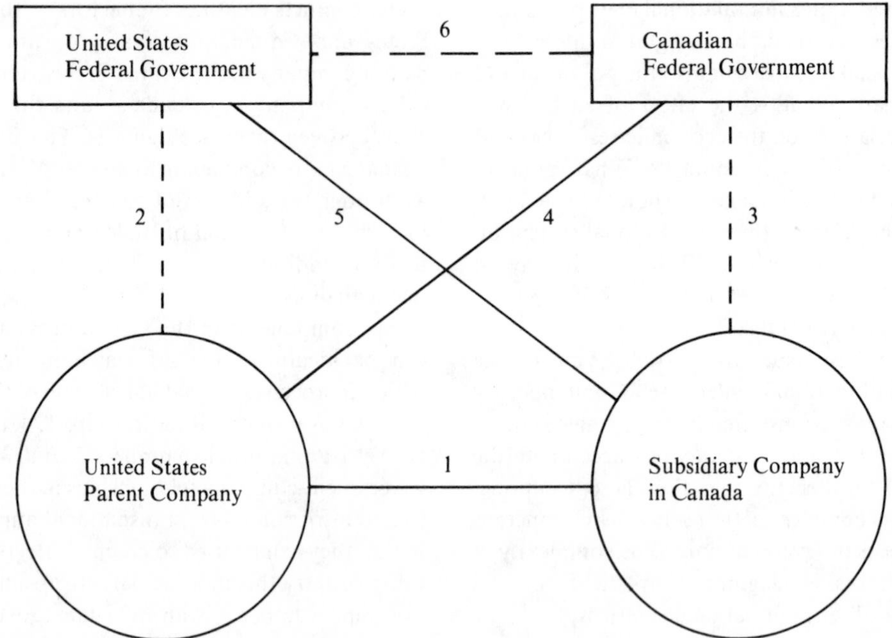
United States
Federal Government
6
Canadian
Federal Government
2
5
4
3
United States
Parent Company
1
Subsidiary Company
in Canada
Numbers 1, 4, and 5 (indicated by a straight line) are transnational relations.
Number 6 (indicated by a broken line) is interstate relations.
Numbers 2 and 3 (indicated by a dotted line) are intrastate relations with transnational implications.

FIGURE 1. PRINCIPAL COMPONENTS OF THE TRANSNATIONAL SYSTEM INVOLVING GOVERNMENTS AND CORPORATIONS IN CANADA AND THE UNITED STATES

conflicts that are identified as being of United States origin. From an economic point of view, the decisions may reflect the approximate underlying conditions of comparative advantage, but this is no answer to the student of international relations. If interests in Canada perceive these conflicts to exist and to have a U.S. dimension, then there exists a problem for relationships between the two countries.

Our earlier case studies provide examples of some of these issues.[1] The lack of research activity in the subsidiary operations conflicts with the Canadian government's objective of promoting a research and development capability in Canada as espoused by the Canadian Department of Industry, Trade and Commerce. It has further important implications in the area of educational policy. The aims of postsecondary education include the production of a distribution of skills in the labour force with emphasis on highly skilled and qualified manpower. To the extent that these skills are not in demand because of the ownership characteristics of the manufacturing sector of the economy, then a problem exists or is perceived to exist. This problem might be inconsequential if it were not for the fact that a high proportion of Canadian industry is U.S. owned and controlled, and this is particularly the case for growth and research-intensive industries such as automobiles, aircraft, chemicals, and electronics. Issues of research capability and educational opportunities have become politicized in Canada as a result of the investigations and reports of the Senate Special Committee on Science Policy, entitled *Science Policy For Canada.*[2]

Lack of research in the subsidiary is often reflected in a lack of entrepreneurship in the subsidiary. This tends to vary with the organization of production. In the case of the *miniature replica effect*, the output of the parent company is duplicated by the subsidiary, which at the extreme becomes a mere assembly operation for parts imported from the parent in the United States. The opportunities for the exercise of entrepreneurial drive by the Canadian management of the subsidiary are minimal in this instance. Where the subsidiary is in a vertically integrated relationship with the parent company, buying components from the parent, making other components, and reselling the output to another subsidiary or elsewhere, then some exercise of entrepreneurship may be undertaken with respect to the manufacture of components. This occurs with Garrett Manufacturing, Limited (Canada), which builds aircraft components for sale to other parts of the Garrett Corporation in the United States and to third parties. Finally, there is the specialization of production format, which is a variation of the foregoing, whereby the subsidiary is detailed to produce a particular item in the corporation's product range for sale worldwide, with responsibility for the product from research through to marketing resting with the subsidiary. Imperial Oil Limited experiences this with certain products and is notable for a degree of entrepreneurial autonomy in some areas.

The specialization format may seem to apply to the automobile industry, since the Canadian-U.S. automotive agreement has led to certain plants in Canada being allocated the production of certain types of cars. However, this does not lead to any entrepreneurial autonomy in the Canadian plants for two reasons. First, although the Canadian plants often specialize in the production of a certain model, the same model is usually produced in one or more plants in the United States; so the Canadian plant is not unique. Second, the technology of automobile production is such that it can be concentrated in one place, which is almost always near the parent company, and is then modified and transmitted to different plants that produce different models in the product range.

The way in which foreign investment has undermined the entrepreneurial drive of Canadians has been highlighted by Professor Kari Levitt, who points to past Canadian tariff policies leading to foreign investment in Canada. She suggests that the problem with the tariff was that it did not result in a Canadian bourgeoisie becoming entrepreneurs and stimulating growth of Canadian industries but created a bourgeoisie satisfied with managing a branch-plant economy.[3] It is now recognized that this deficiency, which is often attributed to past Canadian policies, is one that needs to be overcome if Canadian-owned and controlled enterprises are to be born and are to flourish. This position is reflected in the objectives of the Canada Development Corporation, in the Program for the Advancement of Industrial Technology of the Department of Industry, Trade and Commerce, and in its policies to promote Canadian firms.

These examples of the commercial behaviour of the parent giving rise to concern and response by the Canadian government have not led to major political incidents comparable to that involving the Mercantile Bank and the First National City Bank of New York, but they are examples of forces described by Professor H. G. Johnson as the *new mercantilism.*[4] Governments are seeking ways to protect or promote their industrial capability, and in the absence of tariff barriers, they are resorting to programs of special support and subsidy for their native industry at the expense of imports or in order to promote exports. An example of this in Canada, although not involving a United States company, was the U.S. reaction to the subsidies given to the Michelin Tire Company to locate in Nova Scotia. On 10 February 1973 the United States government applied a 6.6 percent surcharge on Michelin tire imports in reaction to a $50 million loan from the Province of Nova Scotia and a large grant from the federal Department of Regional Economic Expansion to Michelin to locate in Nova Scotia. (Most of its tires were to be exported to the American market.) The United States government claimed that the countervailing duty was to offset a "bounty or grant" to the exports which could be interpreted as unfair competition under General Agreement on Tariffs and Trade (GATT) rules. A further example of the new mercantilism is the continuing discussion by the Canadian government of an industrial strategy for Canada. The point is that corporate policies lead to government reaction which in turn leads to further corporate and government reaction in other countries. The era of the new mercantilism may only be in its infancy, but if allowed to flourish, its ramifications for international relations, including Canadian-United States relations, will be considerable.

Other types of corporate-initiated policies that have brought forth a Canadian response are the constraints imposed on many subsidiaries preventing them from exporting to third countries. This is especially true of companies that have a regional form of organization. The Canadian government response can be found in its establishment of a screening agency for foreign takeovers, one criterion for which would be the extent to which the subsidiary would promote exports from Canada.

Considerable concern has been expressed in Canada over the way in which the parent company cuts back production in time of recession. The claim is often made that where an option exists, and this depends on the organization of production, the subsidiary's output is reduced and labour laid off first in the Canadian subsidiary and only later in related plants in the United States. This becomes an extremely sensitive domestic political issue concerning unemployment among Canadian workers which is traced to U.S. corporate sources. An example of this behaviour can be found in the plant shutdowns in the automobile industry in the Windsor, Ontario, area in 1972. Not only does this issue involve the two governments but also relations between the locals of the unions involved, which view themselves as playing a zero-sum game. Current discussions concerning the need for multinational collective bargaining are in part a response to this concern about employment.

The issue of transfer pricing usually results from the parent company's attempt to minimize its tax payments to the governmental authorities. In such instances, negotiations may take place between the Canadian Department of National Revenue and the U.S. Internal Revenue Service, illustrating the role of lower-level central government bureaucracies, both of which are faced with transfer-pricing problems.

Switching funds between parent and subsidiary is another corporate activity that creates problems for the functioning of Canadian monetary and exchange rate policy. Under a system of flexible exchange rates, the immediacy of the effects on exchange reserves is less important; but even with flexible exchange rates, the central government will intervene in the market to prevent violent fluctuations that may undermine trade, and thus corporate activity cannot be ignored. The foreign exchange crisis of January 1968, when Canada had a fixed exchange rate, involved the speculative activity of U.S. companies with Canadian subsidiaries, and was only ameliorated after negotiations had taken place between representatives of the United States and Canadian governments at both political and bureaucratic levels. An interesting aspect of this crisis was that it resulted from the corporate system's response to U.S. government policies which in turn led to a Canadian reaction at the governmental level.

Corporate pricing policies have given rise to charges of price discrimination by firms against Canadian purchasers of farm machinery. In 1967, it was noted that Ford tractors manufactured in the United Kingdom were being sold in Canada at substantially higher prices than in the U.K. The differential could not be explained away in terms of transportation and distribution costs but was due to higher profits earned on the tractors sold in Canada. The ability to sustain this differential was due to an artificial separation of the British and Canadian markets; the Ford Motor Company made its U.K. dealers sign an agreement not to sell their products for export from the UK.

This example is slightly more involved as it brings in Ford's British subsidiary as well. Ultimately, however, the situation is similar to those examined earlier. The parent company of Ford in the United States initiates a policy of price discrimination that is transmitted through its U.K. subsidiary to its dealerships in Canada. Canadian combines (antitrust) authorities attempted to deal with this situation but appear to have received little assistance from either U.S. or U.K. authorities, who felt they experienced few ill effects from the incident. The United Kingdom has no legislation dealing with pricing behaviour that discriminates between domestic and export prices, although concern may be expressed about lost export earnings. U.S. affiliates, even if they wanted to act, argue that the pricing behaviour originates in another national jurisdiction, and the Canadian government finds itself impotent to affect behaviour in the U.K. It is probable that government cooperation on such issues is not likely to take place until a number of countries find themselves subjected to similar problems concerning multinational enterprises on which general agreement can be reached or issues traded.[5]

U.S. GOVERNMENT-INITIATED POLICIES

Relationship number 2 in figure 1 refers to policies initiated by the U.S. government that apply to the parent company, but with the intent of influencing its subsidiary's operations by getting the parent to implement certain commercial policies in the subsidiary. A number of actions fall into this category, including antitrust policy, balance-of-payments policy, freedom-to-export rules, and Domestic International Sales Corporation (DISC) legislation.

In the antitrust field, United States policies have led to cases where a U.S. company was prevented from acquiring a Canadian company, e.g., the proposed take-over of Labatt Breweries by the Jos. Schlitz Brewing Company. In other U.S. court decisions, the ownership composition of Canadian corporations has been altered, as in the case of Alcan Aluminum Limited and Canadian Industries Limited. This action led to joint Canadian-U.S. ministerial statements and to notification agreements in the event of future extraterritorial application of United States laws to firms in Canada. The introduction of amendments to the Canadian Combines Investigation Act in November 1973, which block the application of foreign court judgments to firms in Canada, indicates that the

Canadian government feels that something stronger than a notification agreement is needed in this area.

A more sensitive political issue has arisen where United States laws and policies have prevented the export of goods from subsidiary operations in Canada, because of the U.S. Trading With The Enemy Act and related export control regulations that apply to United States companies. Similar sensitivity has been shown when U.S. balance-of-payments policies have influenced the flow of funds between parent and subsidiary, either by restricting the outflow of funds to the subsidiary or by encouraging the repatriation of earnings or the repayment of loans from the subsidiary to the parent.

In these three instances there is an obvious potential conflict with Canadian national objectives. Freedom-to-export and balance-of-payments policies may conflict with Canadian policies, and U.S. antitrust policies may conflict with the structure of industry desired by the Canadian government. The actual effects of the antitrust and freedom-to-export policies have probably been minimal to date, although there may be an iceberg effect in that the parent and subsidiary may refrain from exporting because of the known attitude of U.S. authorities. In these circumstances, it is not the known cases that count but rather the general restraint exercised because of the existence of the policies.

All these activities have become sensitive political issues in Canada because of the obvious linkage of subsidiary commercial behaviour with government policies in the United States. Official Canadian government reports, by commenting on them, have also served to focus attention on this issue of extraterritoriality. The other side of the coin is seldom stressed, namely that certain extraterritorial U.S. policies may redound to the benefit of Canada. For example, the United States has tended to provide leadership in the promotion of automobile safety standards, drug testing, and environmental protection. The standards that have been applied to U.S. manufacturers have often been applied to their subsidiaries in Canada even when Canadian laws do not require them.

An evolving area of concern is that posed by U.S. legislation on pollution. It may well be that its effect will be to encourage the location abroad of certain activities that present a high environmental hazard and a low labour content, such as oil refining. Refineries have already been located in the Canadian Atlantic provinces, attracted there, it is true, by provincial authorities. As with many of the other issues mentioned above, the Canadian authorities are free to prevent this locational pattern. However, Canadian constitutional arrangements present certain difficulties. Provincial governments in the depressed regions of Canada are loath to turn away any industrial activity because of the economic stimulus it provides. The formulation of any federal policy toward foreign investment in Canada has been severely constrained by the attitudes, largely favourable to foreign investment, of the individual provinces, which have the right to attract industrial activity. In fact, competition between provinces for foreign investment often results in substantial benefits from the investment being lost to the country as the result of the provincial governments offering tax concessions to the foreign investors.

The new mercantilism of government support for industry has its strong supporters in the United States as well as in Canada and elsewhere. Manifestations of it can be found in the DISC policy of the U.S. government, which offers tax incentives for export development located in the U.S. The implementation of DISC may not substantially affect Canadian industry, but its existence serves to increase the tension between the two countries.

CANADIAN GOVERNMENT-INITIATED POLICIES

Relationship number 3 in figure 1 refers to attempts by the Canadian government to influence the subsidiary operations in Canada. These attempts are positive as well as negative and include trying to induce existing U.S. subsidiaries in Canada to expand their operations, to increase their technological and innovative capability, and to locate in certain areas of the country with the assistance of regional economic incentives. As noted above, provincial governments provide incentives as well through such measures as tax relief and subsidies.

The restraining influence of the Canadian government is exercised most obviously through its establishment of a foreign take-over screening agency, which can be viewed as a way of restricting or controlling the opportunities for United States and other foreign companies to acquire subsidiary operations, to establish new operations, or to expand existing operations into unrelated fields in Canada. The criteria for assessing a potential foreign take-over reflect some of the issues concerning U.S. direct investment about which Canadians are sensitive. However, the Foreign Investment Review Act (Bill C-132) is only the most recent in a series of policies produced largely on an ad hoc basis over time.

Canadian foreign investment policies have been discussed in detail elsewhere and can only be summarized here.[6] Essentially, they identify certain sectors of the Canadian economy as key sectors that should remain Canadian by some means, such as a limitation of foreign ownership, Canadian content requirements in the mass media, the assurance of some Canadian presence in certain industries, and special assistance to Canadian-owned firms. In addition, the Income Tax Act contains special provisions relating to Canadian-owned and foreign-owned firms; the new Canada Corporations Act requires a majority of Canadians on the boards of directors of federally incorporated companies; the Department of Industry, Trade and Commerce issues voluntary guidelines for good corporate behaviour by Canadian subsidiaries of foreign companies; and the Canada Development Corporation has been established with the objective of helping to "develop and maintain strong Canadian-controlled and Canadian-managed corporations in the private sector."

The purpose of these policies initiated by the Canadian government is to influence the performance of foreign subsidiaries either by regulating performance directly or by establishing ownership conditions in order to influence performance. The provisions of the Income Tax Act and the Canada Development Corporation have less direct impact on subsidiary operations but are intended to be complementary policies by promoting the development of Canadian-owned industry.

Relationship number 3 (figure 1) aims at influencing the subsidiary in Canada but has transnational implications in that what happens to the subsidiary is likely to affect its relationship with the parent company in the United States. Outstanding examples of these policies that led to political issues between the two governments occurred in the Mercantile Bank affair and with respect to *Time* and *Reader's Digest*. One reason these cases became highly politicized was the influence that certain American business interests could muster within the U.S. government, combined with the willingness of that government to act on behalf of such firms. In addition, there was strong American objection to the introduction of retroactive legislation that would adversely affect the two periodicals. The United States government often appears to act resolutely in instances that if carried out by the Canadian government could provide examples for other countries to follow, i.e., may lead to a domino effect which would result in retroactive action against U.S. companies elsewhere. In the case of *Time* and *Reader's Digest*, Canadian sensitivity was increased because of the sociocultural and political dimensions of the issues involved.

JOINTLY INITIATED POLICIES

The U.S.-Canadian automotive agreement and the defense production sharing agreement are examples of two agreements made at the interstate level (relationship number 6 in figure 1) but that affect the parent-subsidiary relationship (number 1). The outcome and implications of these agreements for two companies, Ford Motor Company of Canada,

Limited, and Garrett Manufacturing, Limited, have been examined elsewhere. For the purposes of the present essay, the main observation to make is that the performance of the companies under the agreements has been such that one government or the other has wanted to renegotiate the arrangement because the outcome has not been as anticipated or has been felt to be harmful.

The foregoing relationships, numbers 1, 2, and 3, are fairly familiar, although when aggregated they present a formidable array of transnational actions undertaken by governments or firms. The other two relationships, numbers 4 and 5, are less obvious, and number 5 probably has little if any content. That is to say, it is unlikely that the United States government, except perhaps through its officials in Canada, will interact with the subsidiary company. It has no need to because of relationship number 2, interaction with parent company, and number 6, interstate politics. Even the example of U.S. courts requiring the surrender of documents from a subsidiary, which is banned by law in Ontario and Quebec, is primarily a case of approaching the parent company to recover documents from its subsidiary.

Relationship number 4 is more pervasive and is of growing importance. It refers to contacts made between the Canadian government and the parent company in the United States. This takes place in a number of different ways. The Trade Commissioner Service of the Department of Industry, Trade and Commerce provides one level of contact with U.S. companies which may or may not be parent companies at the time of contact. More relevant examples are the discussions held by federal and provincial bureaucrats with United States companies in order to induce them to invest in Canada, to expand, or do something new in the case of firms with existing subsidiaries in Canada. This activity may be undertaken in conjunction with relationship number 3, where the Canadian government provides incentives through its regional policies or research and development policies to encourage firms to invest in Canada. Examples of these activities include the negotiations leading up to the location of International Business Machines (IBM) Corporation in Quebec, the expansion of Control Data Corporation in Ontario, and the location of Lockheed Petroleum Services in British Columbia. IBM, Control Data Corporation, and Lockheed Petroleum Services all received financial assistance from the Canadian government.[7]

The defense area is illustrative of another procedure, namely the offset agreement or bargained reciprocity. In instances where the Canadian government purchases large items of military equipment from United States firms, such as aircraft, offset agreements are negotiated between Canadian government officials and United States firms to ensure that a certain amount of production is located in Canada. A similar example can be found in the civil aviation field when Air Canada purchases U.S. aircraft. In this case, Air Canada, being a crown corporation, has to clear the offset agreement with the Canadian government before closing the deal.

A further example of this linkage is the 30 percent equity interest in Texas Gulf Sulphur, a United States company with operations in Canada, acquired by the Canada Development Corporation which is financed by the Canadian government. This action represents a form of Canadian nationalization of a U.S. company, both the parent company in the United States and its subsidiary in Canada.

In sum, relationship number 4 is illustrative of some of the ways in which the Canadian government attempts to implement an industrial policy using the public purse and its bargaining strength. The significance of this relationship is that it promotes bilateral trade resulting from reciprocal negotiations rather than open market transactions, and it encourages countries to establish nontariff barriers to trade.

The basic model used to analyze the six relationships discussed above can be modified in a number of ways. More explicit recognition can be given to the role of provincial and state governments and to the inclusion of trade union activities, and the case of Canadian parent companies with subsidiaries in the United States can be introduced together with the case of U.S. subsidiaries in Canada that in turn have subsidiaries in third countries.

Taking the case of Canadian parent companies, in 1969 Canadian direct investment abroad totaled $5,040,000,000, of which 54.8 percent was located in the U.S.. However, 30 percent of the total was investment made by US-controlled corporations in Canada. The oft quoted remark that Canadians per capita invest more heavily in the United States than Americans do in Canada has to be modified by details of the real origin of the investment.

Take the following instance of Canadian investment in the United States. Maclean-Hunter in Canada has in recent years expanded its American operations, which may explain the change in this company's attitude toward the activities of *Time* and *Reader's Digest* in Canada. During the hearings before the Royal Commission on Publications, Maclean-Hunter argued against the two American periodicals being given special tax treatment in Canada. However, Maclean-Hunter reversed this position in its submission to the Special Senate Committee on the Mass Media in 1970. Fear of retaliation against its operations in the United States may have led to this change of heart. Or consider the state of New York's advertising campaign, "It pays to locate in New York State," and the state's offer of financial incentives to attract Canadian firms (especially from Ontario) to locate there. State officials have published a brochure listing the Canadian firms that have responded to their campaign. Across the border in Ontario, the issue of financial subsidies to firms to locate in that province has given rise to a political issue because a number of large US companies have been the recipients of these subsidies. Thus at the provincial or state level, the public purse has been used to persuade foreign enterprises to locate abroad.

A more complex example of Canadian foreign investment is that of the Ford Motor Company of Canada, which itself has subsidiaries in South Africa, Australia, New Zealand, and Singapore (and Rhodesia from 1960 to 1967). This organizational setup reflects the system of imperial tariff preferences that gave an advantage to firms operating within the British Empire. However, since 1965 the group director of the Canadian Overseas Group has been responsible to an executive vice-president of Ford-U.S. in charge of overseas operations. The relationship of the Canadian Overseas Group to Ford-Canada has merely been as a financial pass-through. However, the relationship is sufficient to involve the Canadian government in cases where the United States applies its foreign trade regulations through such subsidiaries in third countries.

The fourth example is still more complex. In 1971 the government of Guyana nationalized the Demerara Bauxite Company, a wholly owned subsidiary of Alcan. While Alcan is about 50 percent Canadian owned and has its head office in Montreal, it had American antecedents and not until the 1950s did a U.S. antitrust court decision separate the ownership of Alcan from that of Alcoa (Aluminum Company of America). Moreover, it is well known that Alcoa used Alcan prior to 1940 to gain proxy membership in the international aluminum cartel based in Europe. It is not surprising, therefore, that the Guyanese government perceived Alcan as one of the North American multinational corporations in the aluminum industry, and felt that Alcan was being subjected to pressure by corporations such as Alcoa, Reynolds, and Kaiser not to give in to the demands of the Guyanese. These companies were concerned that nationalization would provide a demonstration effect in the Caribbean where they had interests, such as in Surinam and Jamaica, as well as in other parts of the world.

The Guyanese believed the United States government to have a direct interest in the outcome of the negotiations for nationalization since the U.S. companies were insured by the federal government under the Overseas Private Investment Corporation (OPIC). Moreover, the involvement of Mr. Arthur Goldberg, counsel for

Reynolds Aluminum, in the compensation negotiations was seen as involving an emissary from the U.S. government because of his earlier official positions. In fact, the Guyanese saw the U.S. government as being more involved in the negotiations than was the Canadian government, which at the time was trying to develop its own policy toward foreign investment in Canada. Prime Minister Burnham described the role of the Canadian government during the negotiations as "impeccable," a comment reflecting the hands-off attitude taken. The significance of this example is that in the aluminum industry, certain companies are identified by bauxite-producing countries as North American companies with little or no recognition given to the Canadian aspects of Alcan. The U.S. government is known to be active on behalf of its corporations with overseas investments and it is assumed that they act on behalf of Alcan as well. The absence of a stated policy by the Canadian government toward outward investment serves to substantiate this view and is likely to lead to future issues in Canadian-U.S. relations.

CONFLICT RESOLUTION

The resolution of conflicts arising from the parent-subsidiary relationship shown in figure 1 has taken a number of different forms, including unilateral action by each government and bilateral governmental action involving interstate negotiations. Those policies of the Canadian and United States governments identified as the new mercantilism are examples of unilateral actions. Bilateral negotiations have taken place over balance-of-payments, freedom-to-export, and antitrust issues, at times leading to concessions or early-warning agreements, over special arrangements for industry sectors such as the automobile industry, and over special concessions granted to firms such as the Michelin Tire Company.

Conflicts are also resolved within the corporation between the management of the parent and that of the subsidiary. As with transfer-pricing procedures, the form and nature of such conflict resolution is difficult to determine. However, it is clear from discussions with the management of Canadian subsidiaries that at times they will argue against parent company directives that are viewed as not being in the best interests of Canada. Sometimes this reaction may be due to a concern for Canada and sometimes to a belief that the image of the subsidiary and its associated commercial performance will be harmed by the action required by the parent company. Where Canadians manage the subsidiary they frequently display a personality whose loyalty is split between the U.S.-controlled corporate system and Canada.[8]

In the context of Canadian-U.S. interstate relations, the multinational enterprise has increased the importance of politico-economic bargaining across multiple issue areas involving governmental and nongovernmental actors. Professor Stanley Hoffmann took note that "the competition between states takes place on several chessboards in addition to the traditional military and diplomatic ones: for instance, the chessboards of world trade, of world finance, of aid and technical assistance, of space research and exploration, of military technology, and the chessboard of what has been called 'informal penetration.'"[9] It is our belief that the preeminent presence of the U.S. multinational enterprise in Canada has increased the subtle and complex linkages between these chessboards for both players. For example, although the U.S. government is host to the headquarters organization of the multinational enterprise, and has the legal authority and power to affect certain commercial activities of U.S. multinational enterprises, it may choose not to do so for political and/or economic reasons because of its relations with Canada. This has been evident in the concessions by the United States in the areas of freedom-to-export, antitrust, balance-of-payments, automotive, and defense-sharing agreements. Implicit in any bilateral consultative agreement is the giving up of some freedom of action by both parties.

Our case studies have shown that the presence of the multinational enterprise promotes the interdependence of political and economic issue areas between Canada and the United States. Offset agreements are becoming an important consideration in the negotiations between the two governments, limiting their scope in some areas, while expanding it in others. It appears obvious that the U.S. multinational enterprise has increased the potential costs of applying certain actions by one nation against another if both are constituents of the same corporate system. This phenomenon will make the multinational enterprise an increasingly important ally or opponent in interstate politics — depending on whether the national interests of the governments involved coincide or conflict with those of the corporation. Consideration of cases involving Canadian companies with subsidiaries in the United States and elsewhere reinforces this view. Thus, the multinational enterprise may be seen as a constraint on a nation's autonomy, which applies to both parent and host governments. In short, the multinational enterprise as a transnational actor presents nations with a revised set of payoffs in their interactions with one another.

ENDNOTES

1 Isaiah A. Litvak, Christopher J. Maule, and R. D. Robinson, *Dual Loyalty: Canadian-U.S. Business Arrangements* (Toronto: McGraw-Hill, 1971).

2 Canada Senate, Special Committee on Science Policy, *Science Policy for Canada*, vol. 1 (1970), vol. 2 (1972), vol. 3 (1973).

3 See Kari Levitt, *Silent Surrender: The Multinational Corporation in Canada* (Toronto: Macmillan of Canada, 1970).

4 "Mercantilism: Past, Present and Future," paper presented at the Canterbury Annual Meeting of the British Association for the Advancement of Science, 20 August 1973.

5 The conflict between the Swiss-based company, Hoffmann-LaRoche, and the U.K. government concerning the pricing of Librium and Valium is a further example of one government requiring the assistance of another. See U.K. Monopolies Commission, *A Report on the Supply of Chlordiazepoxide and Diazepam* (London: Her Majesty's Stationery Office, 11 April 1973).

6 See Department of Industry, Trade and Commerce, Foreign Investment Division, Office of Economics, *Selected Readings in Laws and Regulations Affecting Foreign Investment in Canada*, March 1972, plus amendments nos. 1, 2, 3. A discussion of these policies can be found in *Dual Loyalty*, pp. 36-47.

7 Among the numerous examples of provincial governments seeking U.S. investment are speeches made to the business community in New York by Premier Bourassa of Quebec and ex-premier Smallwood of Newfoundland extolling the advantages of locating industry in these provinces. In addition, the Province of Saskatchewan negotiated with the state of New Mexico to support its potash industry.

8 The ability to resolve conflicts within Canada is also constrained by federal-provincial relationships where provincial governments are anxious to promote industrial activity at almost any price. In the case of Quebec, little distinction is made between English-Canadian capital and that from the United States. In fact, at times there seems to be a preference for the U.S. variety.

9 Stanley Hoffmann, "International Organization and the International System," *International Organization*, 24 (Summer 1970), 401.

The Nation-State and Multinational Enterprise: Erosion or Assertion

David Leyton-Brown

A decade ago, many observers of the world economy argued that the sovereignty of the nation-state was "at bay,"[1] being eroded by the increase of economic interdependence among states and the rise of an economic and political actor whose decision horizon exceeded that of any national government — that is, the multinational enterprise (MNE). Joseph Nye and Robert Keohane suggested that the expanding agenda of government objectives in an increasingly interdependent world populated by transnational actors would result in a growing gap between a government's aspirations to control its environment and its capabilities to do so.[2] Charles Kindleberger said "the nation-state is just about through as an economic unit,"[3] and concluded that "at the moment...the multinational corporation is evolving into the international one faster than national governments are girding themselves to produce adequate policies to meet it."[4] More recently, it has become evident that any trend toward the erosion of national sovereignty has been halted, if not reversed. Because of certain inescapable characteristics of multinationals themselves, and changes in the objectives, policies, and circumstances of governments, we are now seeing the widespread reassertion of authority of the nation-state vis-à-vis the multinational enterprise.

SOVEREIGNTY AT BAY?

Those who saw the nation-state in decline commonly based their case on three arguments: the desire of governments to exercise economic control within their borders was countered by the ability of multinationals to evade government power; foreign subsidiaries of a multinational were used as tools of the policies of the parent government; the global corporate interest of a multinational led to decisions and actions indifferent to or in conflict with governmental policy.

That the attainment of economic objectives was not wholly under the control of governments was due in part to the interdependence of the world economy and in part to the activities of multinationals. Governments are judged and held responsible by their electorates for their handling of economic affairs in many areas in which the growth of multinationals has hampered their ability to determine the outcome: a continuous improvement in the standard of living, low unemployment, stability in the value of money, quality of social services, and the organization of industry and the economy. Traditional economic policy measures have proven inadequate to achieve national economic objectives when multinationals are significantly involved. Taxation for purposes of raising revenue or redistributing income could be frustrated by the artificial transfer pricing of a multinational which can take its profits in countries where taxes are low and minimize profits where taxes are high. Monetary policy may be

---

Reprinted from *Behind the Headlines*, Vol. 40, No. 1 (1982) by permission of the Canadian Institute of International Affairs. Some footnotes have been removed; those remaining have been renumbered.

irrelevant if the inter-affiliate purchasing practices of multinationals are unaffected by currency devaluation as was alleged to have occurred when inter-affiliate imports by United States-owned subsidiaries rose following the devaluation of the Canadian dollar in 1962. The guidelines of national economic planning can be avoided if the subsidiary of a multinational can draw on autonomous corporate resources rather than the national capital market or government incentives.

The responsiveness of multinational enterprise to commands of the parent government further threatened the effective sovereignty of the host government. The extraterritorial outreach of parent government policy is often interpreted as an intrusion into the domestic affairs of a host country. The United States government, parent to a majority of the world's multinationals, has sought to influence the behaviour of foreign subsidiaries of American multinationals in three main ways.[5] Under the Trading with the Enemy Act and the Export Administration Act, the United States government has sought to prohibit certain dealings by foreign subsidiaries which might have been legal or even encouraged under host government policy. American antitrust policy has sought to force disclosure of information by foreign subsidiaries, and has prevented mergers or acquisitions abroad by American companies and compelled United States parents to divest themselves of their foreign affiliates, even though such action might not be approved by the host government. In its voluntary and mandatory balance-of-payments guidelines in the 1960s, the United States government sought to increase net capital inflow to the United States by influencing the investment, procurement, and profit repatriation policies of American multinationals. MNEs of other states such as Japan and France work much more closely with their parent governments that do those of the United States, and their compliance with parent government policy, though less visible, is no doubt more extensive. The activities of multinationals in less developed countries were considered by some observers to support hegemonial policies of the advanced industrial parent state, and to reinforce an international economic structure of dominance and dependence.

The major argument of those who envisaged the progressive erosion of the nation-state was the challenge to governments posed by external decision-making. Interference in the domestic affairs of the host state by the parent government has already been discussed. But host and parent governments alike are bound to enter into conflict with multinationals that think in larger than national terms. As George Ball put it: "How can the government make an economic plan with any confidence if a board of directors meeting 5,000 miles away can make a decision that will have a major impact on country C's economic life for reasons that are thoroughly sound for the world economy, but irrelevant to the economy of country C?... [The multinational corporation's] capacity to operate in the world economy without regard to national boundaries will have a long-term effect in bringing about the gradual erosion of the national state as an economic unit."[6] The flexibility of multinationals, able to draw on the resources of more than one country in pursuit of global efficiency and profit, can contradict and erode the thrust of government policy. What is in the global corporate interest of a multinational firm, in terms of location of operations, product lines, investment, profit repatriation, prices, sales and distribution networks, procurement patterns, and the like, may well not conform to the interests and policies of the government of any one of the nation-states in which the multinational operates, simply because their decision horizons and decision criteria are different.

The mobility of multinational enterprise promised it great leverage in dealing with governments. It allowed the firm to play off governments against each other to exact the most favourable terms of entry, and to threaten governments with removal of its operations if it became displeased. The vertical integration of production stages within the structure of a single multinational enterprise was seen as an additional constraint on the bargaining position of an individual government. Even the ultimate governmental recourse of expropriation would be profitless if the subsidiary in question produced only some intermediate component, the only market for which was another affiliate of the multinational.

A vertically integrated production and marketing structure makes it even more likely that a multinational will subordinate local national economic goals to global corporate interests. Chrysler quickly settled a strike at its Rootes plant in the United Kingdom in 1971 for a 20-per-cent wage increase, rather than holding to the 10-per-cent wage guideline urged by the British government, because a production stoppage in Britain halted the entire production and marketing system of Chrysler International. These concerns were felt in parent countries as well as in hosts. The Burke-Hartke bill in the United States was prompted by the move of American multinationals to locate production in lower cost offshore areas in pursuit of corporate efficiency.

Faced with these multi-dimensional challenges, the nation-state was indeed seen to be at bay. Efforts by separate national governments to re-establish control were expected to be fruitless at best, and injurious to global welfare at worst. It was commonly considered that the only productive recourse would be international action, to make multinationals accountable to some form of public authority coterminous in geographical reach with the companies themselves.

MULTINATIONAL ENTERPRISE AT BAY?

Recent developments on a number of fronts have called into question the conclusion that the nation-state is at bay in its relations with multinationals. Inherent characteristics of multinational enterprise have rendered companies more subject to governmental influence than was anticipated, and certain presumed advantages of multinationals have been turned against them by governments. While some multinationals appear over-extended and increasingly vulnerable to government pressure, governments have strengthened their efforts to maximize benefits and minimize costs in their dealings with MNEs. Systemic change has resulted in a stronger bargaining position for governments, and an ordering of national objectives has clarified just what those governments will bargain for. Several new or more fully developed policies have led to satisfying results for governments. Indeed, the future may find multinationals not dictating to increasingly subservient governments, but responding to conflicting demands of assertive nation-states.

Formerly the size of multinationals was considered an advantage in dealings with governments, and tables comparing company sales, asset or value-added figures with gross national products suggested that many multinationals possessed considerable economic power. It is increasingly recognized that such size and geographic spread entails diseconomies as well as economies of scale. Co-ordination costs and inevitable bureaucratic delays subvert the purported global efficiency of the MNE. Commercial organizations are as prone to the misdirected enactment of standard operating procedures as are governmental organizations. Executives in subsidiaries often develop parochial outlooks, seeking to enhance the profitability of the subsidiary operation, and hence their own career prospects, rather than subordinating local interests to global efficiency. The inefficiencies of size are compounded in the effort to integrate international operations, particularly when this involves changes in culture and lifestyle, or established patterns of labour relations. A United States subsidiary in Italy sought to raise productivity by eliminating the two-hour lunchtime at home for its workers, but was unable to persuade its employees to accept the change. The attempt by the Ford Motor Company to transform its collective agreement with its British workers into a legally binding contract on the American model led to costly strikes and repudiation in the British courts.

Not only are multinationals less efficiently

integrated and operated than the myth describes, but some of their presumed advantages can be shown to work both ways. The vertical integration of production and marketing which initially appeared to subordinate national economic goals to global or regional corporate economic interests also exposes the multinational simultaneously to several national jurisdictions. "...any government in a position to seize some sensitive part of the anatomy of a multinational network has the potential for influencing the rest of the network as well: when Mexico demands that its foreign-owned automobile subsidiaries export their components to other markets, Sao Paolo and Detroit are bound to suffer."[7] Each of several governments has the power to break or disrupt one step in the production and marketing chain of a vertically integrated multinational, thus grinding the entire mechanism to a halt. The company's defensive response of multiple siting of each production stage contradicts the goal of efficiency. The size of a subsidiary in a host country can also be turned against the parent company. Where a large operation in a host country was typically considered to threaten economic domination, the value attached by the multinational to its fixed assets can be used as a lever to influence its future behaviour. Subsidiaries are hostages to good behaviour as well as outposts of influence. Multinationals will be reluctant to jeopardize the profitability of existing operations, and so will be more amenable to host government wishes if those operations are threatened. Despite the rhetoric of mobility of the multinational, fixed assets are not easily or profitably transferred from one country to another. The very growth and development of the MNE has made it more exposed to pressures from the governments of the states in which it operates.

The logical development of the nature of the MNE is only one of the factors which have improved the bargaining position of national governments vis-à-vis the multinational. There have been systemic changes in four main areas which have benefited governments, and tipped the balance more in favour of the nation-state: markets, resources, alternatives, and politics.

The importance of host countries and regions as markets for the MNE is growing as economic development proceeds in many less developed countries and as regional economic groupings spring up to encourage local production. The profitable rate of return in these large and growing areas and the oligopolistic drive to safeguard global market share impel multinationals to enter such markets if they have not already done so. Trade barriers are a stimulus to investment, and thus are an incentive to supply those markets from a local subsidiary rather than through imports. Multinationals want market access and need not be persuaded to enter.

Even more than markets, a number of other resources needed by multinationals are found within the jurisdiction of national governments. Some host countries can provide raw materials (for example, oil) on which multinationals and developed countries are dependent. Some can provide productive low cost labour and thus are seen as "export platforms" from which world markets can be suppled more competitively. The greatest bargaining asset governments possess is control of access to their territory, and they are learning how to use it.

Multinationals may increasingly need what the nation-state has to offer, but national governments are less reliant on what any individual multinational can provide. Where formerly capital, technology, management, and market access could most efficiently be obtained as a package from a monopolistic multinational, such factors are now offered by rival firms, thus diluting the unique strengths of any single enterprise, or are "unbundled," with capital obtained on private markets, technology acquired under licence, and management or distributors hired directly.

Government personnel even in less developed countries are more informed, better educated, and more able to understand and respond to the phenomenon of multinational enterprise. Particularly in many less developed countries the forces of modernization and public mobilization have led to a change in public and élite attitudes toward foreign investment and economic and political independence. Though in some less developed countries local élites identify themselves with the interests of foreign investors, and serve as a "comprador" class perpetuating domestic and international inequalities, in an increasing number of cases local élites are coming to see multinationals as a potential resource for serving their own local interests. Nation-states, and groups of nation-states, are more politically cohesive and determined in their dealings with multinationals.

In the troubled world economy of the late 1970s and early 1980s, government objectives vis-à-vis multinational enterprise have crystallized around the issue of jobs. Host (and parent) governments are seeking to reduce unemployment directly rather than assuming it will result automatically from economic growth. Traditional mercantilism was a trade policy of reducing imports, stimulating home production, and promoting exports, in order to achieve a balance-of-trade surplus with a resulting increase in the stock of wealth — gold. Neomercantilism, practised to a greater or lesser extent by most countries today, involves a policy of government intervention in the economy to reduce imports, stimulate home production, and promote exports, mainly in order to achieve an increase in the stock of jobs. It is neomercantilist sentiment that lies behind the Burke-Hartke bill and the protest against the loss of jobs to low cost offshore production. It is neomercantilist sentiment that lies behind the theory of unequal exchange and much of the rhetoric of the new international economic order. It is neomercantilist sentiment that presents multinational enterprise with a priority demand from governments worldwide — increase employment. Though the benefits sought by governments from the operations of MNEs are many, the underlying ordering of objectives makes the conduct of government policy more pointed and effective.

Government policy toward multinational enterprise has become more imaginative and self-assured, as states have seized the initiative and seen the results. They have exploited their control over access to their territory more systematically and purposefully. They have entered more directly into economic activity through public enterprise and in support of local private enterprise. Finally, they have demonstrated that, difficult though it may be, governments can affect the continuing operations of established multinationals to their benefit, without recourse to the ultimate weapon of nationalization.

Most host countries have a screening mechanism with which to judge the benefits of proposed investments and bargain for future undertakings. Through such a process, access can be denied or restricted in certain sectors, or granted in exchange for specified commitments involving employment levels, capital inflow, export performance, technology transfer, local production and procurement, and so on. The foreign investment policy of the nations of the Andean Pact indicates the systematic way in which market access can be exchanged for explicit restrictions on corporate behaviour. In addition to restricting investment in certain sectors, the pact commits foreign investors to a divestiture of majority ownership to local investors within a specified number of years, a ceiling on annual profit repatriation, and restrictions on licensing agreements, assigned export markets, and other drains on subsidiary profits. Canada recently demonstrated another way in which control of market access can be used to stimulate domestic production when it informed potential suppliers of the $2.34 billion of new fighter aircraft to be purchased for the Canadian Armed Forces that one of the major criteria to be used in determining the winning bid would be the amount of offset production and economic benefit provided to Canada.

It has commonly been argued that developed countries have used their control over access by exacting favourable commitments from foreign multinationals through their screening process, while less developed countries have followed the strategy of the obsolescing bargain. Host governments initially follow permissive policies with high incentives to attract investment when their bargaining position is weak. Then, when the investment has proven profitable, new requirements are imposed which the multinational is likely to accede to, in order to continue making its profit. Progressive rounds of renegotiation typically involve, first, laws of general application such as tax, land use, or labour practices, second, improved linkages between the foreign investor and the local economy, such as increased purchase from local suppliers, and, third, participation of the government in ownership or management decisions.

In a variety of ways governments have supported domestic enterprise, both public and private, as an alternative to the MNE. Tax concessions, research subsidies, and the like have encouraged the growth and ultimately the multinationalization of local enterprises. It has been argued that recently governments have attempted to regain autonomy in an interdependent world by intervening directly in the economy in the role of entrepreneur, merchant banker, and trader.[8] The Canada Development Corporation, the Industrial Reorganization Corporation in Britain, and France's Institut de développement industriel are government bodies designed to support mergers and promote industrial reorganization and competitiveness in the private sector, but they have at times been involved in bringing private enterprises under public ownership or control. It is striking that the CDC acquired a 30-per-cent equity in Texasgulf, the parent company of one of Canada's largest mineral producers, and not in its Canadian subsidiary. Similarly, when the British government approved the acquisition of Rootes Motors by Chrysler, among the undertakings it required of Chrysler were a 15-per-cent shareholding in Rootes for the IRC, the right to nominate a member of the Rootes Board of Directors, and the nomination of a British Rootes Director to the Board of Chrysler International. Governments have sought access to decision-making centres of MNEs, as well as control over their local economies.

The Canadianization provisions of Canada's National Energy Programme mark something of a shift from this pattern. The emphasis has been on control or participation in decision-making of national firms and subsidiaries, rather than of parent multinationals. Indeed a repeated tactic has been the acquisition of a minority shareholding in the parent company, and then its exchange for control or total ownership of the Canadian subsidiary. This may be a narrowing of view to the national scale through the "window on the industry," or it may result in the growth of international-scale Canadian firms.

Even after the moment of entry, governments have sought to influence the continued operations of foreign-owned subsidiaries. Some have issued guidelines of good corporate behaviour, and while these have to date been unenforceable and largely ineffectual, they may indicate the thrust of future developments. Countervailing legislation has been produced in many countries to shield the local economy from interference by the parent government. Conflicting legal requirements in the area of antitrust or export controls can again leave the multinational in a "no win" situation, uncomfortably exposed to national jurisdictions simultaneously threatening legal penalties for failure to comply with mutually exclusive demands.

Several governments of raw material exporting, less developed countries have used their control over the subsidiaries of foreign multinationals to push up the price of those exports. Producers' cartels such as The Organization of Petroleum Exporting Countries (OPEC) are not so much aimed at making gains at the expense of the multinational as they are at increasing the returns realized from consumers to be shared between producing states and the multinationals. The fact that the multinationals have been largely able to pass on the effects of producers' cartels to the consumer should not blind us to the fact that host governments rather than the multinationals operating in their territory are making decisions concerning pricing and the amount of production.

The ultimate recourse of a government displeased with the conduct of a multinational in its territory is expropriation, with full, partial, or no compensation. But expropriation is not only a weapon of retaliation. As discussed above, the final stage in the obsolescing bargain involves government equity ownership and/or decision-making control of the enterprise. This may well become an increasing trend, in developed as well as less developed countries. The resistance of multinationals to expropriation, even with "prompt, adequate, and effective" compensation, or to the progressive phasing out of their operations, is understandable and perhaps even inevitable. But it would be wrong to conclude that every such governmental action would be met with vigorous economic and political retaliation by the MNE. The behaviour of International Telephone and Telegraph (ITT) in Chile must be seen in contrast to the behaviour of the oil companies in Venezuela, which adjusted comfortably and profitably to management and service contracts without equity ownership.

Host governments have many measures short of expropriation at their disposal to influence the continuing operations of multinationals. The Andean Pact, for instance, requires the establishment of majority local ownership and control of all enterprises within fifteen to twenty years. The Canada Development Corporation purchased a controlling interest in Texasgulf, an American multinational, through a public stock offer and in so doing assured itself of participation in management decision-making. Prior to the speedup of the timetable for nationalization of the Venezuelan oil industry, President Caldera set minimum production levels for the industry and established fines for insufficient production. New statutory requirements for better housing and the settlement of labour disputes prompted the Cerro de Pasco Corporation to offer to sell its copper operations to the Peruvian government in 1972, but an acceptable price could not be worked out. Informal persuasion can range from moral suasion, through the harassment of tax audits and public health inspections, to a kind of protection racket in which the government of an unstable country might be "unable" to guarantee the security of employees and property of a multinational. Such informal pressure is less likely to occur in developed countries than less developed ones, but on occasion it may be contemplated there too, as illustrated by the leader of the opposition, Joe Clark, in 1979 when he suggested the multinational oil companies could be compelled to comply with government objectives through the selective application of Canada's environmental and public health laws. Informal hostile acts by governments would be bound to stimulate informal retaliation, but it is important to recognize that governments can act along a spectrum of policy measures. Through new legal requirements and informal persuasion, many governments are able to assert their interests with increasing effectiveness in dealing with multinationals.

Even when appearing to be manipulated by multinationals, governments, if they have the will, have the ability to improve the terms in a negotiation seemingly structured against them. The financial assistance provided to the foundering Chrysler Corporation is instructive in this regard. A cynic may be of the opinion that Chrysler held the governments of Canada and the United States to ransom and extracted hundreds of millions of dollars worth of assistance to overcome the problems caused by its own short-sighted management. A more careful investigation reveals that while the governments would have found it politically impossible not to provide massive assistance to save Chrysler, the Canadian government provided substantially less than it was asked for, and in return obtained commitments from Chrysler for substantial economic benefits in the areas of investment, product lines, employment, and research and development.

Throughout the winter of 1979-80, Chrysler appealed for aid from the governments of the United States and Canada to stave off its financial collapse and allow for modernization of its equipment and restructuring of its organization. In return it offered major investments over the coming five to ten years. In December 1979, the

United States government enacted loan guarantees of $1.5 billion contingent upon Chrysler raising $1.43 billion from other sources and Chrysler appealed to Ottawa for $750 million in guarantees and grants. The United States Chrysler Loan Guarantee Board deferred its decision on the $1.5 billion loan support programme until the completion of Chrysler's negotiations in Canada, which gave the Canadian government increased leverage. Ottawa was concerned that the level of aid should be proportionate to the relative share of Chrysler's North American investment proposed for Canada, and demanded a number of commitments in return for the aid. In line with the international emphasis on employment discussed earlier, and in an environment where in the last six months Chrysler had laid off 5,000 of its 14,500 employees in Ontario, Ottawa made job guarantees a central concern. The final deal announced on 10 May 1980 provided for $200 million in loan guarantees beginning in 1982 (by which time Chrysler would be through the worst of its immediate financial crisis) in return for Chrysler's pledge of $1 billion investment in Canada by 1985, including $400 million for the conversion and expansion of Chrysler's van plant in Windsor for the exclusive production of a new small fuel-efficient van-wagon for the world market, and $600 million for modifications to existing plants, including the possible production of a small fuel-efficient car in Canada to ease the reliance on big car production. Chrysler also agreed that none of Chrysler's Canadian facilities would be permanently closed without ministerial approval, accepted the Canadian government's right to name a director to Chrysler Canada's board, and gave the following assurances: transfer pricing between parent and subsidiary would not be used to Canada's detriment, Chrysler would make its best effort to increase sourcing of parts in Canada, and Chrysler Canada would become autonomous with regard to purchasing, marketing, and production. Chrysler could not deviate from its investment, financing, facilities, product, or employment plans without government approval or it might lose the loan guarantees. On the crucial issue of job guarantees, initial negotiations had focussed on a minimum job level of 15,900 by 1984. However, Chrysler later argued that it could not guarantee to meet an absolute job level in the event of a general downturn in the North American automobile industry. The final agreement took the form of guaranteeing Chrysler's Canadian employment at a minimum level of 9 per cent of its total United States employment in 1980-1, and a minimum level of 11 per cent (the traditional level) in 1982-6. The government of Ontario rescinded its earlier offer of an addition $50 million in loan guarantees when more stringent job guarantees were not obtained. It did, however, provide a $10 million grant toward the establishment in Ontario of a $20 million research and development facility related to the use of aluminium and plastics, which would revert to government ownership if Chrysler collapsed.

The ability of government to extract concessions from a multinational even when bailing it out of difficulty is also evident in the next round of the Chrysler crisis, when the Canadian government countered Chrysler's attempts to improve the bargain. In January 1981, in the face of further financial difficulties, Chrysler appealed for another $400 million in loan guarantees from the United States government, and asked the Canadian government to maintain its promised level of support though the company itself proposed to cut back its planned investment in Canada from $1 billion to $600 million, and in so doing to eliminate the plan to locate some small car production in Canada. Rather than bow to this pressure, the Canadian government threatened the termination of all loan guarantees if Chrysler altered its commitments, and after renewed negotiations a new deal was struck in February. Again, in an effort to spread the burden, United States government assistance was made contingent upon the successful completion of negotiations with Canada. The Canadian government accepted a reduction in planned investment from $1 billion to $681 million, but in turn reduced its loan guarantees from $200 million to $150 million and specified that the guarantees would not be available until 1983 (one year later than previously agreed). An additional $50 million in loan guarantees would be available if Chrysler invested in significant additional projects in Canada. In exchange for this amended agreement, Canada exacted some new commitments from Chrysler. In addition to maintaining the commitment to a minimum level of employment in Canada at 11 per cent of the United States total, Chrysler guaranteed an absolute minimum of 12,300 Canadian jobs. Chrysler also gave a firm commitment to begin production of the K car in Canada in 1984, and the new van-wagon in 1983.

Host governments have also been able to use foreign-owned multinationals as instruments of their policy vis-à-vis the parent government. The Canadian government achieved significant economic and political gains vis-à-vis the United States government through its pressures on American multinationals.[9] By threatening unilateral changes in the Canadian tariff structure, it succeeded in enlisting the United States automobile companies in its drive to rationalize the continental automobile industry through the 1965 Canada-United States Automotive Agreement, which provided employment and production benefits to Canada. At the time of the voyages of the *Manhattan* through the Northwest Passage, and American government objections to Canada's 100-mile pollution-free zone in the Arctic, Canada successfully persuaded Humble Oil to sign formal letters of compliance accepting Canadian pollution regulations. The simultaneous location of the multinational within multiple national jurisdictions makes possible the exercise of national influence in both directions, and exposes the multinational to the possibility of conflicting demands from states.

The problems of multiple jurisdiction continue to grow,[10] as multinationals find that business behaviour which is acceptable or even required in any one country may run counter to public policy or group interests elsewhere. The veil of legal secrecy drawn over the uranium cartel of the 1970s does not obscure the fact that the governments of Canada and the United States expected very different behaviour from the branches of multinational uranium companies operating within their jurisdictions. Multinationals may be trapped like "monkeys in the middle" in conflicts not of their own making between clashing actors in different nation-states.[11] MNEs generally respond to such a situation by trying to satisfy the concerns of both or all the governments involved by orchestrating some mutually acceptable middle-ground solution. Where such an outcome is not feasible, however, the multinational is forced uncomfortably to make a clear choice — to co-operate with one government and frustrate the interests of another. Even where the most extreme and damaging taking of sides can be avoided, a recent study found that "Most of the companies had perceived a loss of relative power before the conflict was fully resolved — in trying to remain *competitive* they were forced to soften their positions by making partial concessions to the governments involved, vis-à-vis compromise behaviour."[12]

The case of the Arab boycott of Coca-Cola is an instructive illustration of the exposed position of a multinational enterprise caught between competing pressures. The Tempo Bottling Company of Tel Aviv applied for a Coca-Cola bottling franchise in December 1964, and was rejected a month later. Tempo complained of prejudicial treatment to the Anti-Defamation League of B'nai B'rith in the United States, which issued a report in April 1966 charging Coca-Cola with submitting to the Arab boycott of Israel. Coca-Cola denied the charges, and offered counter-explanations, but the American Jewish community threatened a consumer boycott of Coke. A week later, Coca-Cola awarded an Israeli bottling franchise to a prominent Jewish-American businessman, thus averting the threat to its United States domestic market share. The commissioner general of the Arab League Boycott Committee warned Coca-Cola that its plants in Arab countries would be closed if it commenced business with Israel. At the November 1966 Annual Boycott Conference,

Coca-Cola was formally banned by the Arab League, and nine months later, its plants in all Arab countries except Morocco, Tunisia, and Algeria were closed. Coca-Cola preserved its domestic market share and gained the Israeli market, but it lost virtually all of the Arab market, which is one of the world's highest per capita consumers of soft drinks. Because of the mutually exclusive nature of the demands placed upon it by governmental and non-governmental groups, Coca-Cola could not satisfy all parties and, because of the highly reproducible nature of its product and its vulnerability to consumer retaliation, it had little leverage to encourage one of the parties to compromise its position. Coke could not win and it did not win.

Multinationals can be subjected to conflicting demands even within a single nation-state. McDonnell Douglas, the ultimately successful bidder for Canada's $2.34 billion new fighter aircraft contract (for the F-18A Hornet), made substantial last minute changes in its promised package of industrial offsets and economic benefits to locate much more of them in Quebec to satisfy regional demands. The Quebec government, Liberal members of parliament from Quebec, and General Dynamics, the manufacturer of the competing aircraft, the F-16, mounted a last-ditch effort to have the McDonnell Douglas bid rejected because it offered insufficient benefits to the Quebec aircraft industry. Canada did not gain more from McDonnell Douglas as a result of this political pressure, but Quebec did.

Fred Bergsten suggests that the "trend is toward collaboration between the multinational firms and their hosts, and greater distance between the firms and their home governments."[13] The analysis above suggests that that may well be the case if a single host government brings pressure to bear on the part of a multinational under its jurisdiction, but that a quite different picture will emerge if the firm is subjected to conflicting demands by equally assertive states that cannot be satisfied simultaneously. Vernon suggests that this latter situation would project the multinational into the role of informal arbiter of the conflicting demands of sovereign states. He suggests the model of the oil companies which rationed the world's oil during the oil crisis of 1973 and 1974 and subsequently doled out limited markets among producing states seeking increased sales.[14] I am less inclined to foresee multinationals as informal arbiters of state demands than to see them whipsawed between contradictory and inescapable pressures.

CONCLUSIONS

Pendulums swing, and it should come as no surprise that the initial incursions of multinational enterprise have been responded to with a reassertion of state prerogatives. Richard Rosecrance and his associates have observed the cyclical and uneven interdependence since 1945 and have suggested that increasing interdependence leads governments to act to reduce its actual or potential impact upon domestic policies, and to safeguard or insulate domestic economies from international forces.[15] The challenge to state sovereignty associated with the growth of multinationals and the loss of control over domestic affairs led governments to strive to assert that control.

But just as the erosion of the nation-state did not proceed in linear fashion, neither should we expect the nation-state to be everywhere in the ascendancy and multinationals in disarray. Governments do not, and will not, always prevail. More importantly, neither are they, nor will they be, increasingly victimized by multinational enterprise.

At the moment of entry, the multinational enterprise has a strong bargaining position if there is competition among governments to attract the investment, if there are no non-political resources (such as raw materials, labour) to incline the multinational to one state over alternative locations, if the investment is of high risk or uncertainty, and if the state's need for investment is highly inelastic. The national government has a strong bargaining position if alternative sources of capital, technology, management skills, and market access exist, if such factors can be unbundled and obtained separately, and if the desire of the multinational to gain access to particular markets or resources is highly inelastic. The geographically extended and vertically integrated structure of a multinational and its potential or actual threat to withdraw its operations from a country give it great leverage in continuing interactions with governments if its operations are marginally profitable, if its assets are portable in the short run, if the nature of the technology involved is changeable with the local economy dependent on continual up-grading by the multinational, if there is strong product differentiation and brand-name loyalty in marketing, and if its products, capital, technology, and market structure are not readily reproducible. National governments can bring effective leverage to bear on multinationals (for example, the obsolescing bargain) if the fixed assets of the firm are large and immobile, if the technology is stable and mature, if the operations of the firm within the state are profitable, if the firm has a continuing need for access to the particular resources of the state, and if the costs of adjustment can readily be passed on to the consumer.

Multinational enterprise stands exposed to a multiplicity of national jurisdictions and interests. The likelihood is that increased assertiveness by larger numbers of nation-states in their dealings with multinationals will trap the enterprise in the conflicting aims of governments. If this degenerates into a beggar-my-neighbour competition among governments for immediate advantages, it would not lead to the erosion of the nation-state, but it could lead to an erosion of general welfare. The consequences of the assertion of the nation-state vis-à-vis the multinational enterprise will be one of the crucial questions of the next decade.

ENDNOTES

1 The phrase was drawn from the title of Raymond Vernon's book, *Sovereignty at Bay: The Multinational Spread of U.S. Enterprises* (New York: Basic Books, 1971), though Vernon himself never subscribed to the often simplistic views associated with the approach. A good survey of those supporting the approach labelled a "sovereignty at bay model" can be found in Robert Gilpin, *U.S. Power and the Multinational Corporation: The Political Economy of Foreign Direct Investment* (New York: Basic Books, 1975), p. 220.

2 Robert O. Keohane and Joseph S. Nye, Jr., ed., *Transnational Relations and World Politics* (Cambridge, Mass.: Harvard University Press, 1972), pp. xxii-xxiii.

3 Charles P. Kindleberger, *American Business Abroad: Six Lectures on Direct Investment* (New Haven, Conn.: Yale University Press, 1969), p. 207.

4 Ibid., p. 210.

5 See David Leyton-Brown, "Extraterritoriality in Canadian-American Relations," *International Journal*, 36 (Winter 1980-81).

6 George Ball, "Multinational Corporations and Nation States," *Atlantic Community Quarterly*, 5 (Summer 1967), 248-9.

7 Raymond Vernon, *Storm over the Multinationals: The Real Issues* (Cambridge, Mass.: Harvard University Press, 1977), p. 212.

8 Jeanne K. Laux, "Global Interdependence and State Intervention" in Brian Tomlin, ed., *Canada's Foreign Policy: Analysis and Trends* (Toronto: Methuen, 1978).

9 David Leyton-Brown, "The Multinational Enterprise and Conflict in Canadian-American Relations," *International Organization*, 28 (Autumn 1974).

10 Raymond Vernon "Sovereignty at Bay Ten Years After," *International Organization*, 35 (Summer 1981), 525.

11 Thomas N. Gladwin and Ingo Walter, *Multinationals Under Fire: Lessons in the Management of Conflict* (New York: Wiley, 1980), ch.7

12 Ibid., p. 257.

13 C. Fred Bergsten, "Coming Investment Wars?" *Foreign Affairs*, 53 (October 1974), p. 143.

14 Vernon, *Storm over the Multinationals*, p. 181.

15 Richard Rosecrance, *et al.*, "Whither Interdependence?" *International Organization*, 31 (Summer 1977).

Transnational Resource Conflict: The Politics of Whaling

Robert Mandel

Global resource scarcity has recently led to a proliferation of nonviolent resource conflicts on the international level. This study examines one environmental issue — the politics of whaling — in order to highlight some of the precipitants and patterns of this new type of resource conflict and to gauge the effectiveness of confrontation as a means of attaining conservationist goals. The specific focus is on the transnational conflict, involving direct physical confrontation on the high seas, between the conservationist organization Greenpeace and the foreign whaling ships. The hypothesis of this article is that in an era of global resource scarcity, transnational resource conflict initiated by private lobbying groups may under certain conditions be more effective in achieving conservationist objectives than the more traditional government-to-government negotiations on environmental issues. The discussion examines the possibilities and limits of generalizing findings on the whaling issue to other resource areas.

Reprinted with permission of the author and the International Studies Association from the *International Studies Quarterly*, Vol. 24 (March 1980), pp. 99-104, 108-27. Portions of the text have been deleted. Some footnotes have been removed; those remaining have been renumbered.

THE NATURE OF GLOBAL RESOURCE CONFLICT

In the past quarter of a century, international conflict has undergone some dramatic changes. One major trend has been an increase in economic conflicts, usually consisting of nonviolent clashes of interest waged with economic instruments to maintain or increase national economic security. This trend seems to derive primarily from the obsolescence of territorial conquest as a viable means of achieving national objectives, the increased flexibility (in comparison to traditional military conflict) offered by economic instruments in a dispute, the reduced costs and risks — especially in terms of human life — of such economic instruments, and the reduced potential for entry or threat of nuclear weapons in an economic conflict. Many of these economic conflicts are, in essence, resource conflicts, because the clashes are over acquisition of or access to raw materials. Of course, in a broad sense, all conflicts — including traditional military ones — involve an attempt to gain or consolidate control of a resource: For example, wars concerning territory and spheres of influence involve fighting for the resource of land, and some classify even the Vietnam war as a resource conflict in which the United States tried to protect its access to tin, rubber, and rice. But in recent years, primarily because of some changing conditions in the global environment, a new and distinctive form of resource conflict is emerging.

Several special precipitants have instigated this new resource conflict:

1 a decreasing and inelastic supply of resources on a global rather than a local or national level.
2 an increasing (or constant) inelastic demand for these resources on a global rather than a local or national level.
3 a change from a preceding period of abundance in which unrestricted access to these resources by many nations did not provide a sustained and equitable distribution of benefits.[1]
4 an increasing importance of collective or jointly controlled resources — "common pool" resources — rather than private or nationally monopolized resources.
5 an increase in spillover effects of one nation's resource management policy on other nations.
6 an increase in international interdependence — mutual dependence that need not be symmetrical — in extracting, processing, and distributing these resources.
7 an increased impact of transnational forces — nongovernmental actors — in determining the use of these resources.

These precipitants of the new resource conflict explain the current difficulties of states trying to cope with global resource scarcity. In general, these precipitants indicate that resource conflict is likely to arise because of the lack of national control over the central issue of exploitation and distribution: Which of a growing number of national aspirants gets a piece of the shrinking resource pie and determines its rate of shrinkage?

The last precipitant, the increasing involvement of transnational forces in resource issues, is particularly important in making government-to-government bargaining inadequate to resolve disagreements. For example, the activities of the multinational corporations in the Arab oil embargo of 1973-1974 show the importance of nongovernmental actors in global disputes. While many Western nations have tightened the reins on the actions of multinational corporations for this reason, many other private groups in these states — including private lobbying groups — still enjoy great freedom from governmental direction and control.

A number of major patterns of global resource conflict emerge from these precipitants. One pattern indicates that powerful industrial states initiate conflict to achieve growth in resource consumption in order to satisfy their citizens' insatiable resource appetites.[2] As the developed states' population and technology grow, so do their resource demands, because most advanced technology requires more and wider ranges of resources; these states then turn outward because domestic sources cannot readily satisfy these demands. A system composed of such states almost inevitably produces clashes of interest. A second pattern has weaker states banding together and initiating conflict in order to achieve a redistribution of existing resources away from the few strong states monopolizing the scarce materials.[3] Many developing nations have the potential power to withhold supplies or to use special pricing or supply policies, especially when no substitutes are available on short notice and when the developing countries involved have large foreign exchange reserves. But when Third World states undertake these policies in an attempt to emulate the consumption patterns of the industrialized world, they may be pursuing an impossible dream due to global resource scarcity. A third pattern of resource conflict is more transnational in character and has multinational corporations engaging in conflict with nations — primarily in the Third World — in order to maximize corporate profits through gaining or maintaining access to or control of resources in these states.[4] The bargaining power of the developing nations with respect to multinational corporations has risen dramatically in recent years owing to cooperation among Third World states, their increased access to relevant information and expertise, and the scarcity of resources; but the inertia of the neocolonial relationships of the multinational corporations to the developing countries, and the intensity of the demand for resources located almost exclusively in the Third World, perpetuates the conflict. All three of these conflict patterns point to heightened tension between the developed and developing nations.

One pattern of global resource conflict that has not attracted much notice is the growing clash between private lobbying groups oriented toward conservation and foreign governments violating these groups' environmental guidelines. This type of transnational resource conflict is based neither on a desire by the private group to achieve growth in resource consumption, nor on a desire to achieve a redistribution of existing resources, nor on a desire to maximize profits, but rather on a desire to preserve the environment and thereby maintain the ecological quality of life.

The high level of activity of conservationist groups, the direct involvement of several major powers, and the ease of isolating the small-scale operations of the industry account for this study's selection of whaling as the context of transnational resource conflict. While international relations analysts normally assume that private lobbying groups have few direct effects on the global level and are more effective at the local and national levels, special circumstances — which do occur in some other resource areas — seem to permit an international impact in this case. Although the whaling issue is clearly not the most pressing global resource controversy in the world today, this issue provides many of the clues to the more general nature of the new transnational resource conflict.

The selection of whaling as the case study will provide insights that directly connect with the existing body of thought on collective goods. Collective goods (which environmentalists generally label common pool resources) are those with no possibility of excluding consumers from utilizing them and with no additional marginal costs resulting from an increase in the number of consumers. On the international level, collective goods are usually not subject to a common authority with enforcement powers, and therefore they open up complicated, extrajurisdictional legal issues with few workable precedents for determining control and usage guidelines acceptable to contending states. The primary root of this lack of voluntary agreement on usage guidelines is the "free rider" problem in which each user of a resource acts "irresponsibly" in trying to ride on the contributions of others. As will be discussed in depth in a later section, the common pool nature of whaling creates some special difficulties in attempting to achieve conservationist goals.

• • •

THE CONSERVATIONIST-WHALING NATION RESOURCE CONFLICT

In the decade of the 1970s, conservationist groups concerned with whaling began a battle against the whaling nations — particularly Japan and the Soviet Union — that remained quite separate from the regulation efforts of the antiwhaling governments. Two main actions emerged from this private lobbying group effect — a boycott against all products of Japan and the Soviet Union initiated in 1973 and the direct physical interference with whaling ships in international waters initiated in 1975. This study focuses on the second of the two approaches, primarily because of its greater effectiveness, but the first provides a useful basis of comparison and exposes some unique features of the second. Both actions are somewhat more extreme than most international actions by conservationist groups in other resource areas.

The Animal Welfare Institute (AWI) in the United States initiated the boycott of Soviet and Japanese products, and by 1974 the effort had the support of 21 conservationist groups with a total of almost 5 million members.[5] Thousands of Americans have sent letters and signed statements supporting the boycott, and the president of the Datsun Motor Division in the United States reported that his company alone received hundreds of letters from people who refused to buy Datsuns or any other Japanese product until Japan stops killing whales. The Japanese government has subsequently voiced tremendous concern over these foreign reactions to its whaling and has hired an American public relations firm to defend the Japanese position. The boycott has centered on Japan, because the Soviet Union is less vulnerable since it sells fewer consumer goods in the United States.

The Greenpeace Foundation, a conservationist group founded in 1970 in Vancouver, British Columbia, has used ocean voyages by its small fleet of ships to prevent the killing of whales. These annual voyages cost up to $100,000 a summer, are funded by private contributions, and have the Soviet whaling ships as their primary target because these ships operate much closer to the United States than do the Japanese vessels.

In June 1975, Greenpeace sent into the Pacific the *Phyllis Cormack*, an 85-foot fishing vessel manned by an international crew composed mostly of Canadians, and it encountered a Russian whaling fleet 60 miles west of Eureka, California. Upon approaching the Russians, the conservationists placed themselves right between the harpoon guns and the whales in inflatable rubber boats. One Soviet harpoon vessel fired a 250-pound explosive harpoon right over one of the boats to kill a whale. The captain of the Greenpeace vessel told the Russian factory ship *Dalniy Vostok* "to stop killing whales at once" or else the Greenpeace boats would do "everything" possible to save the whales. The crew of the *Phyllis Cormack* then filmed as much as they could of the Soviet whaling operation, gathering documentary evidence that the Russians had taken illegally undersized whales; later in September 1975, Greenpeace presented this evidence to the International Whaling Commission (IWC). In the end, Greenpeace reported they did actually save a few whales — 8 out of a pod of sperms.[6]

The subsequent Greenpeace voyages proceeded in similar fashion except they were more successful because of greater experience and superior equipment. In June 1976, Greenpeace sent out the *James Bay*, a 153-foot converted minesweeper that was fast enough to keep up with the whaling fleets and had the aid of up to 14 aircraft in locating whaling ships. The vessel chased a Soviet fleet from the California coast all the way across the Pacific, and then went farther north to search out the Japanese whaling fleet. In June 1977, Greenpeace launched the *James Bay* and the *Ohana Kai*, a 175-foot converted submarine chaser whose maximum speed of 26 knots was faster than the whaling ships. The conservationists confronted both Soviet whaling fleets in the North Pacific, and in addition to speaking to the Russian crews, they even boarded a Soviet harpoon boat. In May 1978, the Greenpeace office in London launched the *Rainbow Warrior*, a former ocean-going trawler, to trail the Icelandic whaling fleet in the North Atlantic; in July 1978, their vessel *Peacock*, another converted minesweeper, shadowed the Soviet factory ship *Vladivostok* in the North Pacific. In this latter mission Greenpeace reported that for the first time the Soviets did not confront the Greenpeace boats and did not attempt to kill a single whale while Greenpeace was tailing them.

The Greenpeace voyages take place in order to prevent physically the killing of whales and to focus public attention on the whale slaughter. These conservationists assume that "the presence of humans blocking the path of fire would deter the harpooner from pulling the trigger."[7] Overall, Greenpeace has been quite successful in saving whales: It estimates that it has directly prevented the killing of about 100 whales and has indirectly prevented (through detaining and sidetracking whaling ships) the slaughter of up to 1400 whales. Although Greenpeace's own estimates of the number of whales saved by these voyages may involve some exaggeration, this type of interference clearly makes whaling much more costly in both time and money, especially in light of the increasing difficulty of finding any whales to kill in the first place. The actual number of whales saved may on the surface appear insignificant in light of the total number of whales killed each year, but conservationists try to achieve their objectives in a symbolic or psychological manner (much like terrorists) — through small-scale moves rather than more quantitatively impressive action. In other words, preventing the slaughter of whales is not only an end in itself but also, through the dramatic form in which it takes place, a means of raising the environmental consciousness of both the resource consumers and the world at large.

In comparing the physical confrontation of the whaling ships by Greenpeace to the economic boycott of Japanese and Soviet products by the AWI, the Greenpeace operation appears to have a greater impact on conserving the whale resource. Because of the attractiveness of Japanese products in industries like electronics and automobiles, it seems unlikely that large groups of consumers would switch away from purchasing them; even if foreign sales of these items declined, some critical ambiguity would exist for Japan's government and corporations in interpreting the causes of the decline — it could just as well result from the rising prices of Japanese goods on the American market as from concern about whales. An evaluation by the Sierra Club's Whale Task Force in the summer of 1976 confirmed that the boycott had not reduced the Japanese export sales in the United States (which continued to grow in volume and value) and had actually hurt U.S.-Japanese cooperation on some more critical issues. So in summer 1977, most of the major conservationist groups withdrew from the boycott. Such a boycott would clearly be more effective if undertaken by the American government rather than by private lobbying groups because of the magnitude of the economic impact, but the previously mentioned restraints on the United States completely prevent it from taking such action. In contrast, the Greenpeace action is unambiguous and directly helps to achieve the goal of saving whales without any difficulty of interpretation by the whaling nations. This strategy also does not significantly affect other spheres of the economic relationship — such as trade — with the whaling nations.

There appears to exist little precedent for this type of unilateral, militant intervention by one nation's private lobbying group in the affairs of other nations in environmental issues or elsewhere. Greenpeace consulted no governmental authorities to gain permission for its action, and thus it lacks a certain type of legitimacy for its direct, physical interference with activities that are nationally and internationally sanctioned. Neither the American nor the Canadian government has criticized Greenpeace's efforts because of the huge public support for these missions, although Greenpeace is currently having difficulty obtaining tax-exempt status because of its "interference in the legal business" of other states. Similarly, the government of the Soviet Union (and of Japan) has remained silent, apparently because it does not wish to draw attention to the confrontation.

Initially, it may seem that this transnational resource conflict between the conservationists and the whaling nations may entail significantly higher risks than the more traditional government-to-government negotiations on environmental issues. The Greenpeace expeditions clearly contain a possibility of dramatic escalation, even bloodshed: For example, the whalers may accidentally injure one of the interfering conservationists, as a number of close calls have already occurred. This possibility appears even more likely when one realizes that the responses of the whaling ships generally depend on the individual judgment of their captains and not on directives from the relevant governments. Some conclude that the actions of private lobbying groups may severely damage American relations with Japan or the Soviet Union, and consequently that Americans should instead rely on their government to pressure other nations to stop whaling. But, in assessing these risks, it is interesting to note that Japan reacted far more angrily to the boycott — a seemingly less provocative action — than the Soviet Union has to the Greenpeace interference. Furthermore, the absence of major crises in four years of Greenpeace's disruptions of Soviet whaling casts doubt on the riskiness of at least this particular transnational approach. Perhaps the knowledge by the Soviets that Greenpeace is firmly opposed to violence and the use of force, combined with their awareness of the strong public support for the

Greenpeace action, inhibits Russian belligerence in response to the conservationists. In any case, of course, international norms strongly work against one nation's intentionally injuring the private citizens of another during peacetime.

Although implausible at first glance, the current state of the whaling industry seems to provide an extraordinary opportunity for a small, well-organized private effort to influence significantly and cumulatively the activities of foreign powers primarily because of (1) the small scale of Soviet and Japanese whaling operations, permitting a few encounters virtually to immobilize the entire industry and (2) the strong support from world public opinion. With a weaker antiwhaling stand from the United States, or a more diffuse and large-scale whaling operation by Japan and the Soviet Union, the Greenpeace voyages would be much less effective in gaining even their most primitive objective of publicity for the whaling issue.

Underlying these two principal factors needed for the success of this private lobbying group action is the absence of a large number (globally) of producers and consumers that consider the whaling resource absolutely essential. Most resources are considered necessary not so much for some intrinsic reason but rather for the specific societal functions they serve. Whale products today are used in cosmetics, clothing, human and pet foods, illumination, and lubrication and cleaning, and in all these areas there appear to be not only substitutes available, but substitutes that would involve fairly low transition costs. For some other types of resources — like fossil fuels — substitutes may also be available, but transition costs seem high because of the massive technological investment required by current patterns of resource use. In these cases, people tend to perceive the resources as essential, and support for conservationist-sponsored restrictions on consumption remains low. Perceiving a resource as essential often creates a paramount concern about distributional issues — who gets how much — rather than growth issues — how rapidly the resource is depleted. Environmental groups like Greenpeace seem to have much more potential for slowing the depletion rate of a resource than for equalizing its distribution, owing to their lack of a well-developed political infrastructure. Thus, there seems to be an inverse relationship between the perceived necessity of a resource and the effectiveness (and, in fact, political legitimacy) of transnational conservationist group action. But conservationists can often break through this logic by attempting to change popular images of how essential a resource is at any point in time; even in whaling, with its low transition costs, this is part of the Greenpeace strategy.

In the context of the growing effectiveness of other transnational groups confronting strong opponents — such as transnational labor groups in their battles against multinational corporations — the success of Greenpeace may not seem that surprising; it is the physical confrontation involved in the Greenpeace expeditions that makes them so unusual, for in many other circumstances such missions might be interpreted as direct instigations to violence. Of course, private lobbying groups have frequently used such physical confrontations on the national and local levels — such as in strikes or sit-ins — but, prior to Greenpeace, rarely with much effectiveness on the international level.

UNDERPINNINGS OF THE CONSERVATIONIST-WHALING NATION DISPUTE

Several major differences exist in the assumptions of the whaling nations and the conservationists about the whaling resource. These disagreements are typical of the contending positions of resource-consuming and resource-conserving factions in many other environmental issues.

First, the whaling nations view their own need for the resource as high with few possibilities for substitution, while conservationists view that need as low with many substitution possibilities. The Soviet Union claims its Siberian population needs whale meat for protein, and Japan compares the place of whale in the Japanese diet to hamburger in the American diet. Conservationists retort by stressing the availability of cheap substitutes — like soybean cakes and the oil of the jojoba plant — for whale products.

Second, the whaling nations view their own use of the resource — and their consequent responsibility for its scarcity — as low, while the conservationists view that use and responsibility as high. The Soviet Union and Japan assert that their whaling operations are now quite small and unprofitable and that the blame for the scarcity of whales lies with the indiscriminate whaling prior to 1945 by the United States, the United Kingdom, the Netherlands, and Norway. Conservationists place this blame on the Russians and Japanese because of these nations' preponderant role in the current whaling industry.

Third, the whaling nations view the size of the existing resource stock — and the consequent viability of continued exploitation of the resource — as high, while the conservationists view that stock and viability as low. Japan and the Soviet Union contend that there are still enough whales to warrant continued whaling and that they desire to preserve the species. Conservationists respond that whales are "near the abyss of biological extinction" and that the whaling nations are deliberately "whaling themselves out of business" by killing as many whales as possible until they become extinct.

Finally, the whaling nations view their own conformity to international regulations on the resource as high, while conservationists view that conformity as low. This last difference is especially important because it underscores the weakness of an intergovernmental solution to resource conservation. Japan states that it will "abide by, without any reservation, the conclusions reached by IWC," and this nation frequently mentions its strict monitoring of its whaling ships and its support for the international observer scheme. Similarly, the Soviet Union asserts that it observes IWC regulations so faithfully that "Soviet legislation envisages various measures of punishment for violators of the rules, including the institution of criminal proceedings." This state contends that "the international observation system should involve all regions and types of whaling" in order to eliminate "the unwholesome atmosphere of distrust" among concerned nations. But the actions of these nations seem more in line with the skeptical view of the conservationists. In September 1973, the Japanese decided to disregard the IWC's quotas and set their own in accordance with "Japanese interests" because they claimed the IWC action had no scientific basis, and the Soviets quickly followed suit. A number of conservationists have reported that Japanese whalers kill and process whales well under the internationally agreed legal size, and Greenpeace has found the Soviet whalers do the same. There are indications that the Soviets have resisted international observers because they feared the infiltration of spies, that their fleets sailed early while an agreement was being ratified so that observers could not get aboard. And even the Japan Whaling Association admits that Japan obtains 17% of its whale imports from nonIWC nations, despite the recent IWC prohibition on this action.[8] Although this disregard for international regulations is typical of other resource issues, the impact is particularly great in whaling because of the small size of existing stocks.

These disagreements show the applicability of the general framework presented earlier of the precipitants of the new resource conflict. The whaling nations' opinion that they really need the resource and that there are few substitutes increases these nations' inelasticity of demand for the resource; their idea that they are not responsible for its scarcity and that it is possible to continue whaling increases their unwillingness to treat whales as a common pool resource, to realize the change from a past period of abundance to a present period of scarcity, or to recognize the spillover effects of their policies and their interdependence with other consuming nations. On the other hand, the conservationists' assumption that the resource is extremely scarce — that its supply is inelastic — makes them exceedingly sensitive to the spillover effects and the interdependence of every national resource policy and to the common pool nature of the resource; their assignment of blame to the current whaling nations for the resource scarcity — through violating IWC regulations and taking unnecessarily large catches — increases the transnational involvement of these environmental groups in opposition to the whaling nations. Under such conditions, resource conflict becomes highly likely.

THE CONTEXT OF GENERAL DEBATES ABOUT RESOURCE SCARCITY

The whaling controversy raises issues that relate directly to the two principal dimensions of the more general debate about global resource scarcity. The first dimension, which is "temporal," focuses on the choice between "steady-state" versus growth in global resource consumption. Widely known as the "limits-to-growth" debate,[9] this issue revolves around the underlying question of whether man will accept resource limitations and try to adapt to them or, alternatively, whether he will attempt to manipulate resource limitations so as to surmount them.[10] The second dimension, which is "spatial," emphasizes the choice between "equitable" and stratified global resource distribution. Recognized in many circles as the "tragedy-of-the-commons" debate,[11] this issue rests on the underlying question of whether a decentralized, pluralistic, laissez-faire system can provide a sufficiently equitable distribution of resources to ensure the survival of all mankind during global scarcity.[12] Thus, the first dimension depends more on technology and the second more on politics, though they clearly interact with each other.

Placing the whaling issue in the context of the "limits-to-growth" debate increases understanding of the disagreement between the conservationists and the whaling nations. The conservationists assume that a natural limitation has emerged because of overexploitation of whales and consequently suggest reducing consumption — specifically through a moratorium on killing whales —in order to achieve a steady-state whale population. On the other hand, the whaling nations deny that a natural limit has been reached in whaling and contend that current consumption patterns must continue. These nations attempt to compensate for and overcome the scarcity of whales by accelerating the technology of whale-killing and catching younger and smaller whales. Even if the whaling nations were intentionally "whaling themselves out of business," this policy makes some economic sense because managing a common pool resource "irresponsibly" — depleting a renewable resource like whales — can create a short-run higher rate of profit and a greater overall return on investment than "responsible" resource management.

The authors of *The Limits to Growth* perhaps best explain this disagreement:

> The story of the whaling industry demonstrates, for one small system, the ultimate result of the attempts to grow forever in a limited environment. Whalers have systematically reached one limit after another and have attempted to overcome each by increases in power and technology. As a result, they have wiped out one species after another. The outcome of this particular grow-forever policy can only be the final extinction of both whales and whalers. The alternative policy is the imposition of a *man-determined limit* on the number of whales taken each year, set so that the whale population is maintained at a steady-state level.... The basic choice that faces the whaling industry is the same one that faces any society trying to overcome a natural limit with a new technology. *Is it better to try to live within that limit by accepting a self-imposed restriction on growth? Or is it preferable to go on growing until some other natural limit arises in the hope that at that time another technological leap will allow growth to continue still longer?*[13]

Although the increasing scarcity of whales has effectively eliminated growth in the whaling industry, there appears to be little prospect of a self-imposed limit on consumption of whales beneath the maximum the whaling nations can physically attain at any point in time.

The "tragedy-of-the-commons" debate indicates that continued whaling will almost inevitably lead to a grossly inequitable distribution of the whale resource, given the lack of effective regulation by the IWC. The logic of the commons causes each whaling nation to maximize its catch of whales in order to get as large a share as possible of the scarce resource. Thus, in the short run the ruthless nations that ignore whale quotas get most of the resource, while the quota-abiding nations lose out. The idea of enlightened self-restraint, which those repulsed by this logic claim might permit a laissez-faire system to provide an even-handed distribution of resources, appears unrealistic for the whaling industry. The idea fails because of the absence of reliable whale data, which would be conducive to such enlightenment, and to the inflexible demand for whale products within many of the whaling nations. The common pool nature of the whale resource inhibits the possibility of "intrinsic responsibility," where the group making a decision directly bears its consequences, in the management of whaling. The notion that "mutual coercion, mutually agreed upon" can work for common pool resources on the international level seems flawed, especially for whaling, because of the differing value systems and the difficulty of having effective coercion with a multiplicity of types of actors and of instruments of force. One expects the pattern of "competitive overexploitation" to characterize a nonrenewable resource like petroleum, which generally fosters a zero-sum relationship among its consumers; but what is noteworthy is that the same pattern occurs when dealing with a renewable resource like whales, where a non-zero-sum relationship among consumers could exist owing to the sustainable yield deriving from cooperative and controlled exploitation.

Because all ecological resources are in a very broad sense common pool resources, this situation is symptomatic of the distributional difficulties in most environmental issues characterized by scarcity. Once again, one questions continuation of freedom in consumption patterns if that freedom causes a dangerously stratified distribution of resources. The tradeoff between freedom and equality under conditions of resource scarcity almost invariably necessitates some kind of social control. But it is quite difficult to devise an effective and realistic form of social control that will lead to the establishment of an equitable — or steady-state — pattern of resource consumption. Because few resources — including whales — are by themselves absolutely necessary for human survival, on the global level the temporal question of whether nations are depleting resources too quickly often takes precedence over the spatial question of whether the existing distribution of these resources among the nations is a fair one.

CONCLUSIONS AND PRESCRIPTIONS FOR THE FUTURE

In dealing with most issues of global resource scarcity, the norm is to suggest that only grand schemes work to achieve significant improvements in resource conservation because of the holistic nature of the field. Some suggest the adoption of a new set of world values stressing communalism and frugalism,[14] while others advise the creation of a world government run by a new egalitarian elite.[15] Regarding the whale resource, suggestions range from a new United Nations whaling convention representing the interests of all nations and having a research program funded by nations which received the largest past benefit from whales, to a global agency empowered to sell hunting licenses to nations for killing whales, with license fees paying for education, research, and enforcement of agency policy. The common thread among most of these suggestions is that they stress the need for some form of global harmonization through an international authority, having legitimacy in the eyes of national governments or having coercive powers over them, in order to deal with global environmental problems.

The transnational resource conflict between Greenpeace and the whaling nations indicates a potentially more effective strategy of preventing resource waste and overexploitation on the international level. This approach bypasses completely the diplomatic table and goes quickly and directly to the physical protection of the scarce resource. Because there is no need for explicit government approval, this action is not hampered by its relationship and possible inconsistency with other aspects of a nation's foreign policy. Because there is no need for global coordination, this action is not delayed by having to wait for acceptance by other nations, not watered down by the negotiations inherent in such coordination, and not distorted by the possible unrepresentativeness of the parties to the negotiation. And because participation in the Greenpeace voyages is completely voluntary by the organization's members, this action need not concern itself as much with an effective organizational structure or enforcement powers — both of which prove elusive in environmental issues. The action is both unambiguous and isolated in its effects, and it apparently has a low risk of escalating beyond desired limits. Finally, because this action both prevents depletion of the scarce resource and raises environmental consciousness on the resource issue, it can work simultaneously as part of a short-term stopgap strategy to save the resource and a long-term transition strategy to attain a new eco-value system.

But how generalizable is the usefulness of this type of transnational resource conflict? From the preceding analysis, this conflict initiated by private lobbying groups against foreign nations seems most effective in achieving conservationist goals under these conditions:

1 A few nations dominate the "wasteful" consumption of the scarce resource.
2 This resource is found in a limited geographical area outside of any state's jurisdiction.
3 The bulk of relevant world opinion opposes these nations' patterns of resource consumption.
4 These nations do not seriously perceive that their very survival is predicated on consumption of this resource.
5 Even these nations perceive a critical scarcity in this resource.
6 Preventing the consumption of the resource is relatively easy to monitor and execute.

All of these conditions need not be fulfilled for transnational resource conflict to be effective — indeed there are few cases where all six are present — but each contributes to the probability of the strategy's success. The first and third conditions appear to be the only ones absolutely necessary for private conservationist groups to have a sizable impact on global resource issues: The key appears to be intense and pervasive international antagonism toward a small group of resource consumers. An example of how this global private lobbying effort can work even within state boundaries — when world public opinion is sufficiently strong — is the increasingly prominent environmentalist action restricting nuclear energy development since the negative sentiment generated by the Three Mile Island nuclear accident. The international application of this conservationist group strategy does not appear to be in any way restricted to resource questions that revolve around endangered species questions like whales (as opposed to other types of questions like energy development), although the sentimental issues invariably associated with endangered species seem more likely (all else being equal) to unify world public opinion.

Thus, several other areas of resource conservation seem ripe for the application of Greenpeace-like strategy. In the realm of ocean resources, there appear to be excellent opportunities for preventing the overexploitation of certain minerals, fossil fuels, and food resources located in limited areas and used by a small number of nations. Outside of the fishing industry, the most promising areas seem to be conservation of offshore oil and gas located beyond the continental margins and of hard minerals like manganese nodules located in the deep seabed. Regarding offshore oil and gas, the national habit of unilaterally grabbing offshore petroleum deposits — begun by the United States in 1945 — has recently been complicated by the discovery of significant deposits of hydrocarbons in extra-jurisdictional areas out in the ocean. Already disputes over this resource have occurred between Greece and Turkey and between China and Vietnam, for there is no international agreement on how to allocate petroleum deposits that span national jurisdictions. Regarding manganese nodules, the discovery of large concentrations of this renewable but scarce resource on the ocean floor after World War II created the potential for competitive overexploitation. The principal current dispute over this resource has the technologically advanced nations, with the capability to mine the nodules, wanting to maximize their profits from such mining and the developing nations, which export minerals, wanting to prevent such mining from lowering the prices of the minerals in this resource. Current international regulations on exploitation of manganese nodules are full of loopholes.

A direct physical confrontation by conservationist groups of the sea-based mining operations of the nations extracting these resources appears feasible and desirable because of the failure of intergovernmental negotiation and the escalating exploitation. This configuration could take the form, for example, of conservationists directly interfering with deep-sea mining operations through blocking the movement of equipment, supplies, and the extracted oil or nodules. Thus, the environmentalists could increase the costs of these operations, slow down the rate of exploitation, and at the same time publicize the resource consumption and generate global opposition. Even these two cases do not perfectly fit the six conditions: Deep-sea oil is viewed as essential by many states, and manganese nodules are not located in a narrow geographical area. But owing to the small number of nations with access to the technology for extraction, global resentment has resulted and could translate into widespread support for intervention by transnational conservationist groups. This environmentalist action seems especially useful here, because of the lack of widespread awareness of deep-sea mining's far-reaching political and environmental consequences, which are particularly important if the extraction is done improperly.

Conservationist groups in the United States seeking to emulate the Greenpeace strategy for achieving environmental objectives in other resource areas need to realize, however, that proliferation of such approaches could easily backfire in this country — which is, after all, the dominant and most wasteful consumer of a number of scarce resources. And these groups would be vulnerable to criticism that their action is tantamount to a new form of cultural imperialism, involving a subnational intervention in another state's traditional way of life that is perilously close to terrorism in terms of the complete disregard for questions of political legitimacy. A drastic increase in the violation of international and national laws by these conservationists could ultimately be a disruptive and destabilizing force in the international arena. But the imminence of the imperatives of global resource scarcity, often obscured by the short-term invisibility of much ecological deterioration, makes the new approach provided by transnational resource conflict an essential addition to the arsenal of the environmental activist.

ENDNOTES

1 In this article, the scarcity of a given resource for a given nation at a given point in time is considered a function of (1) physical depletion of the resource from the earth, (2) existing technology of extracting and processing the resource, and (3) political and social constraints on accessing the resource.

2 N. Choucri & R.C. North, *Nations in Conflict: National Growth and International Violence* (San

Francisco: Freeman, 1975); D.W. Orr, "Modernization and conflict: the second image implications of scarcity," *International Studies Quarterly*, 21 (December 1977).

3 C.F. Bergsten, "The threat from the third world," *Foreign Policy*, No. 11 (Summer 1973); R.L. Heilbroner, *An Inquiry into the Human Prospect* (New York: Norton, 1975).

4 R.J. Barnet and R.E. Muller, *Global Reach: The Power of the Multinational Corporations* (New York: Simon & Schuster, 1974).

5 The main conservationist groups originally supporting the boycott were the National Audubon Society, National Wildlife Federation, Sierra Club, Friends of the Earth, Fund for Animals, and Environmental Defense Fund.

6 M.Herron, "A not-altogether quixotic face-off with Soviet whale killers in the Pacific," *Smithsonian*, 7 (August 1976), 26, 28.

7 P. Watson, "Greenpeace VII: 1976 Send-off," *Greenpeace Chronicles*, 2 (Spring 1976), p. 3.

8 In 1978, the Japanese government issued an "administrative guidance" to Japanese companies requesting that they cease importing whaling products from nonIWC nations, but it is still too early to evaluate this action.

9 Harold and Margaret Sprout, *The Ecological Perspective on Human Affairs with Special Reference to International Politics* (Princeton, N.J.: Princeton University Press, 1965), chapters iii-iv.

10 For the antigrowth position, see Donella H. Meadows, *et al., The Limits to Growth* (New York: Universe Books, 1972). For a critique of this approach, see H.S.D. Cole, *et al., Models of Doom* (New York: Universe Books, 1973).

11 For views supporting the tragedy of the commons, see G. Hardin and J. Baden, *Managing the Commons* (San Francisco: Freeman, 1977). For a critique of this approach, see M.S. Soroos, "The commons and lifeboat as guides for international ecological policy," *International Studies Quarterly*, 21 (December 1977).

12 W. Ophuls, *Ecology and the Politics of Scarcity* (San Francisco: Freeman, 1977).

13 Meadows *et al., Limits to Growth,* pp. 157-58.

14 Ophuls, *Ecology and the Politics of Scarcity*, chapter viii.

15 R.A. Falk, *This Endangered Planet* (New York: Random House, 1972), chapters vii-x.

THE SYSTEM 6

STRUCTURE AND CONCEPT A

SYSTEM EVOLUTION B

MECHANISMS OF REGULATION C

INTRODUCTION

While states are not the only international actors, they remain the principal units of analysis in the study of international conflict and its management. Not only their attributes, however, but also the relationships among states and their interaction affect the frequency and intensity of conflict. We begin this section with an analysis of the concept of system and its application to international relations, then proceed to trace the historical evolution of international political systems, and finally examine the mechanisms of conflict regulation within systems.

All systems have boundaries, structures, units, and regular patterns of interaction among these units. K.J. Holsti defines an international system as "any collection of independent political entities... that interact with considerable frequency and according to regularized processes."[1] International systems commonly have identifiable geographic, cultural, or issue boundaries and hierarchical structures which, according to Glenn Snyder and Paul Diesing, are defined by the number of major actors and the distribution of capabilities among them. We analyze systems by looking at the most common forms of interaction among the principal units: patterns of diplomatic contact, trade, rivalries, and organized violence or warfare.[2] In most systems, these characteristic interactions and processes are governed by explicit or implicit rules and customs. If these rules or moral values are violated, the system very likely will be transformed. Morton Kaplan explores these "essential" and "transformation" rules to discover the various kinds of international systems that develop under different circumstances and why these systems remain stable or change.[3]

Since systems do vary over time and in different regions, historians and political scientists pay particular attention to the evolution of international systems, our second focus of attention. Most analysts have identified two basic structures in history: the multipolar in which rivalry occurs among several units of nearly equal capabilities, and the bipolar system where two members outclass the rest. Variations of these two types have been identified historically in the systems of ancient India, ancient China, ancient Greece, and medieval Italy.

The characteristic pattern of conflict in multipolar and bipolar systems differs. Multipolar systems, because they have a large number of principal actors, generate a greater incidence of international conflict, though each dispute has less significance. In bipolar systems, as Raymond Aron observes, and the histories of Athens and Sparta as well as Rome and Carthage attest, the two strong states are almost always enemies. Consequently, while the number of disputes may be less in this kind of system, their intensity is invariably greater as actions are interpreted in the context of the two-power rivalry.[4] Leaders tend to evaluate changes in the status quo as gains or losses and generally exclude the possibility of mutual gain; consequently, conflict assumes a "zero-sum" quality. In this section, we focus our analysis first on the multipolar system generally known as the "balance of power" and then on the bipolar system that developed after 1945.[5]

The concept "balance of power" is one of the most ambiguous in international relations.[6] We use it here to describe the multipolar system of approximately five major powers that prevailed after the Treaty of Westphalia in 1648 until the end of World War II. Although the identities of the principal European members varied over time, all were relatively equal in military capabilities, so that alliance partners were interchangeable. All states were acceptable alliance partners not only because of their rough equality in military capabilities, but also because of the similarity of their political institutions: they were all monarchies that functioned within the shared political culture of Christendom. States formed temporary alliances, with England — a naval power — playing the role of balancer by joining the weaker side to prevent the domination of Europe by any single state.[7]

The basic aim of the balance of power system, as Gulick observes, was to ensure the survival of independent states; but, as members ensured their survival and independence, they simultaneously preserved the system. Some analysts treat the balancing process as automatic, similar to Adam Smith's "invisible hand," while others emphasize its manipulation by statesmen. A.J.P. Taylor envisions the balancing mechanism as "self-operating": according to the laws of political physics, states naturally reacted to prevent hegemony.[8] Henry Kissinger, however, attributes the success of the balancing process to the motivation and skills of the diplomats of the time.[9]

Crucial to the operation of the balancing mechanism were the limited goals of members of the system. These limits were a function of the constraints of technology and the absence of intense ideological conflict, as well as the realization that restraint was a prerequisite to mutual self-preservation. Wars for territorial objectives could be fought outside the boundaries of the system in the colonies, but major states were careful not to seize important provinces from their European rivals without compensation. To do so, as Germany did when it annexed the French provinces of Alsace and Lorraine at the end of the Franco-Prussian War, was to compromise the flexibility of alliance partners and polarize the system.

When we turn our attention to the bipolar system which emerged after World War II, we can identify important structural changes from the decentralized balance of power system. Foremost is the concentration of power in the two superpowers who dominate the system. Continental states formerly at the periphery of international relations, the two superpowers are now in a class by themselves.[10] The rivalry between them, as John Herz demonstrates, is a product both of the nuclear revolution and their antithetical ideologies.[11] Because of their capabilities and their competitive ideologies, their goals are far less limited than those of the major powers in the balance of power system. But, as Hedley Bull points out in the reading we have included, the ambitions of the United States and the Soviet Union are tempered by the constraints of mutual deterrence. Implicitly, Bull suggests that the nuclear balance of terror is a two actor version of the old balance of power. But the danger of mutual nuclear destruction, John Lewis Gaddis argues, creates common interests as well as rivalry in the Soviet-American relationship. This mixture of shared constraints as well as competing interests generates agreements on arms control as well as conflict and brinkmanship.

The heavy concentration of power within two blocs in the early postwar years has become somewhat more diffuse in the contemporary bipolar system. Polycentrism within the blocs and, even more to the point, the importance of states outside the blocs who control scarce and valuable resources, have given new significance to members other than the two superpowers in the contemporary system. Unlike the balance of power system, which contained roughly five major units of relatively equal capabilities, the system today includes some 160 states with widely different capabilities and numerous transnational and international actors. This exponential increase in the number of units, however, can be misleading. As Stanley Hoffmann argues, although power is more diffuse than it was thirty years ago, we have not returned to a balance of power system.[12] The second-strike capabilities of the two superpowers assure that no other state can militarily challenge the two giants, much less play the role of "balancer" as Britain did in the balance of power system.

How then do we define today's world in systemic terms? Analysts debate that question vigorously and some even insist that the contemporary system is evolving too rapidly for categorization.[13] Perhaps the best description is that of Kissinger, who refers to the contemporary system as "bipolar militarily" and "multipolar politically."[14] Even then, as Joseph Nye observes in the reading that follows, increasingly the nonnuclear states are challenging the claim of the Soviet Union and the United States to be the nuclear trustees of mankind. While nuclear proliferation will not challenge Soviet and American military dominance in the foreseeable future, the consequences of the spread of nuclear weapons are ominous for the long-term stability of the system. The proliferation of nuclear weapons, as well as the growing conflict between the rich and the poor in the contemporary system, underscore the urgency of regulating international conflict.

Throughout history, students and practitioners of international politics have searched for effective strategies to manage conflict. Traditionally, they have turned to moral norms, international law, collective security, and diplomacy and negotiation. We look at each of these in turn.

Moral norms broadly constrain and channel interests. As Max Weber pointed out, they serve as the tracks along which interests run.[15] Each international system has been governed by a set of moral norms or rules which help to limit conflict. In the balance of power system, member states recognized these norms as the basis of their relationships with each other. As Gordon Craig and Alexander George put it, "Despite the wars that pitted European states against each other, there was a general assumption that they were members of a comity of states that were bound together by common ties of family relationship, religion and historical tradition."[16]

Given the diversity of state interests in today's international system, agreement on the rules of the game cannot be as precise as it was in the past. Our contemporary global society resembles a "primitive political system," with little agreement on the meaning of such concepts as "justice," "liberty," and "democracy."[17] As Hoffmann argues, because each state remains ultimately responsible for its own security, so too is it the interpreter of the legitimate use of force. Despite efforts at regional integration and the creation of a multitude of international organizations in the postwar period, movement toward disparate rather than shared norms has intensified.[18] Disagreement on basic rules will likely continue to grow in the face of enduring ideological bipolarity, growing regionalism, and the proliferation of new states.

Law, or the codification of moral norms, also constrains conflict by channeling it into manageable boundaries, as Richard Falk makes clear in his essay. The international law which was formulated during the balance of power system was designed to regulate conflict among states that shared similar norms. Since international law has often been more successful in producing an ordered rather than a just system, the existing corpus is under attack from many of the new states in today's international system. Because they did not participate in its development, many of the new states consider that international law represents the interests of the rich established members. Consequently, they treat existing law as illegitimate and demand its fundamental revision — we need think only of the long and arduous negotiations over the law of the sea or a new international economic order. If conflict in the bipolar system is to be regulated, new institutions will have to be created to accommodate these challenges. Historically, leaders have looked beyond law to international institutions to manage conflict.

We can trace the attempt to create an international institution capable of regulating conflict among states to the post-Napoleonic era, in the balance of power system. After the French Revolution, the principal states of Europe acted collectively to legitimate change without endangering the system. Richard Elrod notes that the great powers acted in concert as a "collective conscience," restraining each other's intemperate ambitions through multilateral diplomacy. To be effective, the Concert of Europe required the subordination of national to European interests, a difficult challenge in the age of nationalism. Although it worked effectively to regulate conflict for a time, eventually it was undermined by the widening divergence in norms between autocratic Russia and parliamentary Britain. The Crimean War signaled that the Concert had not prevented war in Europe, but only postponed its occurrence.

After the devastation of World War I, Woodrow Wilson hoped to regulate conflict among states by creating an international organization to administer collective sanctions against an aggressor.But the experience of the League of Nations and its successor, the United Nations, demonstrates that the expectation that all states will collectively punish aggression irrespective of their own interests is unrealistic.[19] The Finkelsteins make clear that an effective collective security system is dependent upon agreement among the great powers, an historically unlikely occurrence made even less probable by the ideological divisions of the bipolar system. International organizations have tended to reflect rather than ameliorate great power divisions. For many years, on many issues, the Security Council of the United Nations has been stalemated by the rivalry between the two superpowers.

In part because of the stalemate, members of the United Nations looked beyond the formal arrangements for peaceful settlement of disputes and collective security. In an original and creative contribution to the regulation of international conflict, Canada, during the 1956 Suez crisis, pioneered the concept of peacekeeping, or the use of voluntarily contributed international forces to separate belligerents.[20] Over the last two decades, the United Nations has frequently sent peacekeeping forces into the field to contain a conflict that threatened to escalate. More recently, however, peacekeeping has been undertaken outside the framework of international organizations by states that enjoy the confidence of the parties to the dispute.[21]

Given the failure of international organizations to regulate conflict and the inability of states to guarantee their own security in the contemporary nuclear system, states continue to seek security from aggression through alliances, just as they did in the balance of power system. Yet alliances today are strikingly different from those that operated in the balance of power system. First, ideological divisions make the flexibility of alliance partners unlikely. States like Yugoslavia that leave one bloc cannot enter the other, but tend instead to join the growing ranks of the nonaligned. Second, since potential allies can add very little to the military capabilities of the superpowers, alliances now resemble treaties of guarantee more than reciprocal commitments. Third, as Robert Osgood argues, the American alliance system has long failed to meet the criteria of shared interests and recognition of a common threat.[22] Fourth, the shift of concern within the alliance from military to economic issues, which Immanuel Wallerstein describes, has further accelerated the deterioration of the American alliance network. America's military partners are now its economic competitors. Moreover, Europe's economic ties with members of the Soviet bloc have further undermined alliance solidarity. Despite these multiple changes, as Gaddis argues, the United States continues to rely on containment, a strategy developed in the 1940s, to manage its conflict with the Soviet Union in the 1980s.

Because informal norms, formal law, international institutions, and even alliances have not been wholly effective in managing international conflict, diplomacy remains a crucial regulatory instrument. Indeed, historically it has been the function of diplomacy, through the process of negotiation, to identify common interests in a relationship of conflict. Yet, diplomacy, like international law, faces new challenges in the contemporary international system. First, the aristocratic, professional diplomatic service of the balance of power system has been transformed by developments in communications and transportation as well as by modern democratic politics. Easily transmitted messages and quickly dispatched personnel have centralized the management of conflict and undermined the independence and importance of the expert in the field. Second, political leaders often seek the accompanying benefits of publicity through the international media as well as substantive foreign policy agreements. Third, as Gilbert Winham argues, diplomacy is far more complicated today both because of the larger number of states that must be reconciled in the international system and the proliferation of interests that must be satisfied in the domestic political system. As he points out, a modern diplomat may well spend more time negotiating with his own rather than with foreign governments. Finally, the subject matter of modern negotiations is increasingly technical and complex. Negotiation over such policy issues as the limitations of highly sophisticated weapons systems, pollution of the international environment, and the redistribution of credit in international institutions requires the skills of experts in specific technical fields as well as the wisdom of the generalist in international relations. Indeed, some analysts suspect that conflict over resource scarcities, food shortages, inflation, and overpopulation may be beyond "the reach of conventional diplomacy to even address, let alone remedy."[23] This is so, as the Harvard Nuclear Study Group makes clear in its analysis of the negotiation of arms control agreements, because progress is tied not only to technical competence but to a broader political consensus on shared constraints and common dangers. It is strikingly apparent that the regulatory capacity of the contemporary international system lags dangerously behind the challenges humanity confronts in these revolutionary times and is likely to face in the future.

ENDNOTES

1 K.J. Holsti, *International Politics: A Framework for Analysis*, 4th ed., rev. (Englewood Cliffs, N.J.: Prentice-Hall, 1983), p. 27.

2 Ibid., p. 28.

3 Morton A. Kaplan, *Systems and Process in International Politics* (New York: John Wiley & Sons, Inc., 1957), and "Balance of Power, Bipolarity and Other Models of International Systems," *American Political Science Review*, 51 (September 1957), 684-95.

4 Raymond Aron, *Peace and War: A Theory of International Relations*, trans. Richard Howard and Annette Baker Fox (New York: Frederick A. Praeger, 1966), ch. 5, and Richard Rosecrance, "Bipolarity, Multipolarity and the Future," *Journal of Conflict Resolution*, 10 (September 1966), 314-27.

5 On the historical evolution of the international system, see Gordon A. Craig and Alexander L. George, *Force and Statecraft* (New York: Oxford University Press, 1983).

6 On this point see Inis L. Claude, Jr., *Power and International Relations* (New York: Random House, 1962); Martin Wight, "The Balance of Power," in Herbert Butterfield and Martin Wight, eds., *Diplomatic Investigations* (Cambridge, Mass.: Harvard University Press, 1968), pp. 149-75; and Ernest B. Haas, "The Balance of Power: Prescription, Concept, or Propaganda," *World Politics*, 5 (July 1953), 446-77.

7 See "Memorandum by Sir Eyre Crowe on the Present State of British Relations with France and Germany, January 1, 1907," reprinted in G.P. Gooch and Harold Temperley, eds., *British Documents on the Origins of the War, 1898-1914* (London: His Majesty's Stationery Office, 1928) and Winston S. Churchill, *The Second World War*, Vol. I: *The Gathering Storm* (Boston: Houghton Mifflin, 1948), pp. 207-08.

8 A.J.P. Taylor, *The Struggle for Mastery in Europe, 1848-1918* (Oxford: Clarendon Press, 1954), p. xx.

9 Henry A. Kissinger, *A World Restored* (Boston: Houghton Mifflin, 1957).

10 William T.R. Fox, *The Super-Powers* (New York: Harcourt Brace, 1944) and "The Super-Powers Then and Now," *International Journal*, 35 (Summer 1980), 417-36.

11 John Herz, *International Politics in the Atomic Age* (New York: Columbia University Press, 1959).

12 Stanley Hoffmann, "In a World of Five Major Units," *New York Times*, March 6, 1972, p. 33.

13 Morton A. Kaplan and Nicholas de B. Katzenbach, *The Political Foundations of International Law* (New York: John Wiley & Sons, Inc., 1961), maintain that by the time its rules have been codified, the system has been transformed.

14 Henry A. Kissinger, *American Foreign Policy*, 2d ed., rev. (New York: W.W. Norton & Co., 1974), Part Two.

15 H.H. Gerth and C. Wright Mills, *From Max Weber: Essays in Sociology* (New York: Oxford University Press, 1946), p. 63, cited by Werner Levi, "The Relative Irrelevance of Moral Norms in International Politics," *Social Forces*, 44 (December 1956), 228.

16 Craig and George, *Force and Statecraft*, p. 21.

17 Roger Masters, "World Politics as a Primitive Political System," *World Politics*, 16 (July 1964), 595-615.

18 See Joseph S.Nye, Jr., *Peace in Parts* (Boston: Little, Brown, 1971).

19 Leland M. Goodrich, "Peace Enforcement in Perspective," *International Journal*, 24 (Autumn 1969), 657-72.

20 See John Holmes, *The Better Part of Valour* (Toronto: McClelland and Stewart, 1970).

21 Multinational forces outside the auspices of the United Nations are performing peacekeeping functions in the Sinai peninsula and in and around Beirut.

22 See also Arnold Wolfers, *Alliance Policy in the Cold War* (Baltimore: The Johns Hopkins University Press, 1959).

23 Roger Morris, "Diplomacy: On the Road to Anachronism," *New York Times*, February 23, 1975, p. E13.

A: STRUCTURE AND CONCEPT

Political Structures

Kenneth N. Waltz

I define domestic political structures first by the principle according to which they are organized or ordered, second by the differentiation of units and the specification of their functions, and third by the distribution of capabilities across units. Let us see how the three terms of the definition apply to international politics.

1. ORDERING PRINCIPLES

Structural questions are questions about the arrangement of the parts of a system. The parts of domestic political systems stand in relations of super-and subordination. Some are entitled to command; others are required to obey. Domestic systems are centralized and hierarchic. The parts of international-political systems stand in relations of coordination. Formally, each is the equal of all the others. None is entitled to command, none is required to obey. International systems are decentralized and anarchic. The ordering principles of the two structures are distinctly different, indeed, contrary to each other. Domestic political structures have governmental institutions and offices as their concrete counterparts. International politics, in contrast, has been called "politics in the absence of government."[1] International organizations do exist, and in ever-growing numbers. Supranational agents able to act effectively, however, either themselves acquire some of the attributes and capabilities of states, as did the medieval papacy in the era of Innocent III, or they soon reveal their inability to act in important ways except with the support, or at least the acquiescence, of the principal states concerned with the matters at hand. Whatever elements of authority emerge internationally are barely once removed from the capability that provides the foundation for the appearance of those elements. Authority quickly reduces to a particular expression of capability. In the absence of agents with system-wide authority, formal relations of super- and subordination fail to develop.

The first term of a structural definition states the principle by which the system is ordered. Structure is an organizational concept. The prominent characteristic of international politics, however, seems to be the lack of order and of organization. How can one think of international politics as being any kind of an order at all? The anarchy of politics internationally is often referred to. If structure is an organizational concept, the terms "structure" and "anarchy" seem to be in contradiction. If international politics is "politics in the absence of government," what are we in the presence of? In looking for international structure, one is brought face to face with the invisible, an uncomfortable position to be in.

Kenneth N. Waltz, *Theory Of International Politics*, © 1979 Addison Wesley Pub. Co. Inc, Reading, MA. p.p. 88-99. Reprinted with permission. Portions of the text have been deleted. Some footnotes have been removed; those remaining have been renumbered.

The problem is this: how to conceive of an order without an orderer and of organizational effects where formal organization is lacking. Because these are difficult questions, I shall answer them through analogy with microeconomic theory. Reasoning by analogy is helpful where one can move from a domain for which theory is well developed to one where it is not. Reasoning by analogy is permissible where different domains are structurally similar.

Classical economic theory, developed by Adam Smith and his followers, is microtheory. Political scientists tend to think that microtheory is theory about small-scale matters, a usage that ill accords with its established meaning. The term "micro" in economic theory indicates the way in which the theory is constructed rather than the scope of the matters it pertains to. Microeconomic theory describes how an order is spontaneously formed from the self-interested acts and interactions of individual units — in this case, persons and firms. The theory then turns upon the two central concepts of the economic units and of the market. Economic units and economic markets are concepts, not descriptive realities or concrete entities. This must be emphasized since from the early eighteenth century to the present, from the sociologist Auguste Comte to the psychologist George Katona, economic theory has been faulted because its assumptions fail to correspond with realities. Unrealistically, economic theorists conceive of an economy operating in isolation from its society and polity. Unrealistically, economists assume that the economic world is the whole of the world. Unrealistically, economists think of the acting unit, the famous "economic man," as a single-minded profit maximizer. They single out one aspect of man and leave aside the wondrous variety of human life. As any moderately sensible economist knows, "economic man" does not exist. Anyone who asks businessmen how they make their decisions will find that the assumption that men are economic maximizers grossly distorts their characters. The assumption that men behave as economic men, which is know to be false as a descriptive statement, turns out to be useful in the construction of theory.

Markets are the second major concept invented by microeconomic theorists. Two general questions must be asked about markets: How are they formed? How do they work? The answer to the first question is this: The market of a decentralized economy is individualist in origin, spontaneously generated, and unintended. The market arises out of the activities of separate units — persons and firms — whose aims and efforts are directed not toward creating an order but rather toward fulfilling their own internally defined interests by whatever means they can muster. The individual unit acts for itself. From the coaction of like units emerges a structure that affects and constrains all of them. Once formed, a market becomes a force in itself, and a force that the constitutive units acting singly or in small numbers cannot control. Instead, in lesser or greater degree as market conditions vary, the creators become the creatures of the market that their activity gave rise to. Adam Smith's great achievement was to show how self-interested, greed-driven actions may produce good social outcomes if only political and social conditions permit free competition. If a laissez-faire economy is harmonious, it is so because the intentions of actors do *not* correspond with the outcomes their actions produce. What intervenes between the actors and the objects of their action in order to thwart their purposes? To account for the unexpectedly favorable outcomes of selfish acts, the concept of a market is brought into play. Each unit seeks its own good; the result of a number of units simultaneously doing so transcends the motives and the aims of the separate units. Each would like to work less hard and price his product higher. Taken together, all have to work harder and price their products lower. Each firm seeks to increase his profit; the result of many firms doing so drives the profit rate downward. Each man seeks his own end, and, in doing so, produces a result that was no part of his intention. Out of the mean ambition of its members, the greater good of society is produced.

The market is a cause interposed between the economic actors and the results they produce. It conditions their calculations, their behaviors, and their interactions. It is not an agent in the sense of *A* being the agent that produces outcome *X*. Rather it is a structural cause. A market constrains the units that comprise it from taking certain actions and disposes them toward taking others. The market, created by self-directed interacting economic units, selects behaviors according to their consequences. The market rewards some with high profits and assigns others to bankruptcy. Since a market is not an institution or an agent in any concrete or palpable sense, such statements become impressive only if they can be reliably inferred from a theory as part of a set of more elaborate expectations. They can be. Microeconomic theory explains how an economy operates and why certain effects are to be expected. It generates numerous "if-then" statements that can more or less easily be checked. Consider, for example, the following simple but important propositions. If the money demand for a commodity rises, then so will its price. If price rises, then so will profits. If profits rise, then capital will be attracted and production will increase. If production increases, then price will fall to the level that returns profits to the producers of the commodity at the prevailing rate. This sequence of statements could be extended and refined, but to do so would not serve my purpose. I want to point out that although the stated expectations are now commonplace, they could not be arrived at by economists working in a pre-theoretic era. All of the statements are, of course, made at an appropriate level of generality. They require an "other things being equal" stipulation. They apply, as do statements inferred from any theory, only to the extent that the conditions contemplated by the theory obtain. They are idealizations, and so they are never fully borne out in practice. Many things — social customs, political interventions — will in fact interfere with the theoretically predicted outcomes. Though interferences have to be allowed for, it is nevertheless extraordinarily useful to know what to expect in general.

International-political systems, like economic markets, are formed by the coaction of self-regarding units. International structures are defined in terms of the primary political units of an era, be they city states, empires, or nations. Structures emerge from the coexistence of states. No state intends to participate in the formation of a structure by which it and others will be constrained. International-political systems, like economic markets, are individualist in origin, spontaneously generated, and unintended. In both systems, structures are formed by the coaction of their units. Whether those units live, prosper, or die depends on their own efforts. Both systems are formed and maintained on a principle of self-help that applies to the units. To say that the two realms are structurally similar is not to proclaim their identity. Economically, the self-help principle applies within governmentally contrived limits. Market economies are hedged about in ways that channel energies constructively. One may think of pure food-and-drug standards, antitrust laws, securities and exchange regulations, laws against shooting a competitor, and rules forbidding false claims in advertising. International politics is more nearly a realm in which anything goes. International politics is structurally similar to a market economy insofar as the self-help principle is allowed to operate in the latter.

In a microtheory, whether of international politics or of economics, the motivation of the actors is assumed rather than realistically described. I assume that states seek to ensure their survival. The assumption is a radical simplification made for the sake of constructing a theory. The question to ask of the assumption, as ever, is not whether it is true but whether it is the most sensible and useful one that can be made. Whether it is a useful assumption depends on whether a theory based on the assumption can be contrived, a theory from which important consequences not otherwise obvious can be inferred. Whether it is a sensible assumption can be directly discussed.

Beyond the survival motive, the aims of states

may be endlessly varied; they may range from the ambition to conquer the world to the desire merely to be left alone. Survival is a prerequisite to achieving any goals that states may have, other than the goal of promoting their own disappearance as political entities. The survival motive is taken as the ground of action in a world where the security of states is not assured, rather than as a realistic description of the impulse that lies behind every act of state. The assumption allows for the fact that no state always acts exclusively to ensure its survival. It allows for the fact that some states may persistently seek goals that they value more highly than survival; they may, for example, prefer amalgamation with other states to their own survival in form. It allows for the fact that in pursuit of its security no state will act with perfect knowledge and wisdom — if indeed we could know what those terms might mean. Some systems have high requirements for their functioning. Traffic will not flow if most, but not all, people drive on the proper side of the road. If necessary, strong measures have to be taken to ensure that everyone does so. Other systems have medium requirements. Elevators in skyscrapers are planned so that they can handle the passenger load if most people take express elevators for the longer runs and locals only for the shorter ones. But if some people choose locals for long runs because the speed of the express makes them dizzy, the system will not break down. To keep it going, most, but not all, people have to act as expected. Some systems, market economies and international politics among them, make still lower demands. Traffic systems are designed on the knowledge that the system's requirements will be enforced. Elevators are planned with extra capacity to allow for human vagaries. Competitive economic and international-political systems work differently. Out of the interactions of their parts they develop structures that reward or punish behavior that conforms more or less nearly to what is required of one who wishes to succeed in the system.... Why should a would-be Prime Minister not strike out on a bold course of his own? Why not behave in ways markedly different from those of typical British political leaders? Anyone can, of course, and some who aspire to become Prime Ministers do so. They rarely come to the top. Except in deepest crisis, the system selects others to hold the highest office. One may behave as one likes to. Patterns of behavior nevertheless emerge, and they derive from the structural constraints of the system.

Actors may perceive the structure that constrains them and understand how it serves to reward some kinds of behavior and to penalize others. But then again they either may not see it or, seeing it, may for any of many reasons fail to conform their actions to the patterns that are most often rewarded and least often punished. To say that "the structure selects" means simply that those who conform to accepted and successful practices more often rise to the top and are likelier to stay there. The game one has to win is defined by the structure that determines the kind of player who is likely to prosper.

Where selection according to behavior occurs, no enforced standard of behavior is required for the system to operate, although either system may work better if some standards are enforced or accepted. Internationally, the environment of states' action, or the structure of their system, is set by the fact that some states prefer survival over other ends obtainable in the short run and act with relative efficiency to achieve that end. States may alter their behavior because of the structure they form through interaction with other states. But in what ways and why? To answer these questions we must complete the definition of international structure.

2. THE CHARACTER OF THE UNITS

The second term in the definition of domestic political structure specifies the functions performed by differentiated units. Hierarchy entails relations of super- and subordination among a system's parts, and that implies their differentiation. In defining domestic political structure the second term, like the first and third, is needed because each term points to a possible source of structural variation. The states that are the units of international-political systems are not formally differentiated by the functions they perform. Anarchy entails relations of coordination among a system's units, and that implies their sameness. The second term is not needed in defining international-political structure, because so long as anarchy endures, states remain like units. International structures vary only through a change of organizing principle or, failing that, through variations in the capabilities of units. Nevertheless I shall discuss these like units here, because it is by their interactions that international-political structures are generated.

Two questions arise: Why would states be taken as the units of the system? Given a wide variety of states, how can one call them "like units"? Questioning the choice of states as the primary units of international-political systems became popular in the 1960s and '70s as it was at the turn of the century. Once one understands what is logically involved, the issue is easily resolved. Those who question the state-centric view do so for two main reasons. First, states are not the only actors of importance on the international scene. Second, states are declining in importance, and other actors are gaining, or so it is said. Neither reason is cogent, as the following discussion shows.

States are not and never have been the only international actors. But then structures are defined not by all of the actors that flourish within them but by the major ones. In defining a system's structure one chooses one or some of the infinitely many objects comprising the system and defines its structure in terms of them. For international-political systems, as for any system, one must first decide which units to take as being the parts of the system. Here the economic analogy will help again. The structure of a market is defined by the number of firms competing. If many roughly equal firms contend, a condition of perfect competition is approximated. If a few firms dominate the market, competition is said to be oligopolistic even though many smaller firms may also be in the field. But we are told that definitions of this sort cannot be applied to international politics because of the interpenetration of states, because of their inability to control the environment of their action, and because rising multinational corporations and other nonstate actors are difficult to regulate and may rival some states in influence. The importance of nonstate actors and the extent of transnational activities are obvious. The conclusion that the state-centric conception of international politics is made obsolete by them does not follow. That economists and economically minded political scientists have thought that it does is ironic. The irony lies in the fact that all of the reasons given for scrappping the state-centric concept can be restated more strongly and applied to firms. Firms competing with numerous others have no hope of controlling their market, and oligopolistic firms constantly struggle with imperfect success to do so. Firms interpenetrate, merge, and buy each other up at a merry pace. Moreover, firms are constantly threatened and regulated by, shall we say, "nonfirm" actors. Some governments encourage concentration; others work to prevent it. The market structure of parts of an economy may move from a wider to a narrower competition or may move in the opposite direction, but whatever the extent and the frequency of change, market structures, generated by the interaction of firms, are defined in terms of them.

Just as economists define markets in terms of firms, so I define international-political structures in terms of states. If Charles P. Kindleberger were right in saying that "the nation-state is just about through as an economic unit,"[2] then the structure of international politics would have to be redefined. That would be necessary because economic capabilities cannot be separated from the other capabilities of states. The distinction frequently drawn between matters of high and low politics is misplaced. States use economic means for military and political ends; and military and political means for the achievement of economic interests.

An amended version of Kindleberger's statement may hold: Some states may be nearly washed up as economic entities, and others not. That poses no problem for international-political theory since international politics is mostly about inequalities anyway. So long as the major states are the major actors, the structure of international politics is defined in terms of them. That theoretical statement is of course borne out in practice. States set the scene in which they, along with nonstate actors, stage their dramas or carry on their humdrum affairs. Though they may choose to interfere little in the affairs of nonstate actors for long periods of time, states nevertheless set the terms of the intercourse, whether by passively permitting informal rules to develop or by actively intervening to change rules that no longer suit them. When the crunch comes, states remake the rules by which other actors operate. Indeed, one may be struck by the ability of weak states to impede the operation of strong international corporations and by the attention the latter pay to the wishes of the former.

It is important to consider the nature of transnational movements, the extent of their penetration, and the conditions that make it harder or easier for states to control them. But the adequate study of these matters, like others, requires finding or developing an adequate approach to the study of international politics. Two points should be made about latter-day transnational studies. First, students of transnational phenomena have developed no distinct theory of their subject matter or of international politics in general. They have drawn on existing theories, whether economic or political. Second, that they have developed no distinct theory is quite proper, for a theory that denies the central role of states will be needed only if nonstate actors develop to the point of rivaling or surpassing the great powers, not just a few of the minor ones. They show no sign of doing that.

The study of transnational movements deals with important factual questions, which theories can help one to cope with. But the help will not be gained if it is thought that nonstate actors call the state-centric view of the world into question. To say that major states maintain their central importance is not to say that other actors of some importance do not exist. The "state-centric" phrase suggests something about the system's structure. Transnational movements are among the processes that go on within it. That the state-centric view is so often questioned merely reflects the difficulty political scientists have in keeping the distinction between structures and processes clearly and constantly in mind.

States are the units whose interactions form the structure of international-political systems. They will long remain so. The death rate among states is remarkably low. Few states die; many firms do. Who is likely to be around 100 years from now — the United States, the Soviet Union, France, Egypt, Thailand, and Uganda? Or Ford, IBM, Shell, Unilever, and Massey-Ferguson? I would bet on the states, perhaps even on Uganda. But what does it mean to refer to the 150 odd states of today's world, which certainly form a motley collection, as being "like units"? Many students of international politics are bothered by the description. To call states "like units" is to say that each state is like all other states in being an autonomous political unit. It is another way of saying that states are sovereign. But sovereignty is also a bothersome concept. Many believe, as the anthropologist M.G. Smith has said, that "in a system of sovereign states no state is sovereign."[3] The error lies in identifying the sovereignty of states with their ability to do as they wish. To say that states are sovereign is not to say that they can do as they please, that they are free of others' influence, that they are able to get what they want. Sovereign states may be hardpressed all around, constrained to act in ways they would like to avoid, and able to do hardly anything just as they would like to. The sovereignty of states has never entailed their insulation from the effects of other states' actions. To be sovereign and to be dependent are not contradictory conditions. Sovereign states have seldom led free and easy lives. What then is sovereignty? To say that a state is sovereign means that it decides for itself how it will cope with its internal and external problems, including whether or not to seek assistance from others and in doing so to limit its freedom by making commitments to them. States develop their own strategies, chart their own courses, make their own decisions about how to meet whatever needs they experience and whatever desires they develop. It is no more contradictory to say that sovereign states are always constrained and often tightly so than it is to say that free individuals often make decisions under the heavy pressure of events.

Each state, like every other state, is a sovereign political entity. And yet the differences across states, from Costa Rica to the Soviet Union, from Gambia to the United States, are immense. States are alike, and they are also different. So are corporations, apples, universities, and people. Whenever we put two or more objects in the same category, we are saying that they are alike not in all respects, but in some. No two objects in this world are identical, yet they can often be usefully compared and combined. "You can't add apples and oranges" is an old saying that seems to be especially popular among salesmen who do not want you to compare their wares with others. But we all know that the trick of adding dissimilar objects is to express the result in terms of a category that comprises them. Three apples plus four oranges equals seven pieces of fruit. The only interesting question is whether the category that classifies objects according to their common qualities is useful. One can add up a large number of widely varied objects and say that one has eight million things, but seldom need one do that.

States vary widely in size, wealth, power, and form. And yet variations in these and in other respects are variations among like units. In what way are they like units? How can they be placed in a single category? States are alike in the tasks that they face, though not in their abilities to perform them. The differences are of capability, not of function. States perform or try to perform tasks, most of which are common to all of them; the ends they aspire to are similar. Each state duplicates the activities of other states at least to a considerable extent. Each state has its agencies for making, executing, and interpreting laws and regulations, for raising revenues, and for defending itself. Each state supplies out of its own resources and by its own means most of the food, clothing, housing, transportation, and amenities consumed and used by its citizens. All states, except the smallest ones, do much more of their business at home than abroad. One has to be impressed with the functional similarity of states and, now more than ever before, with the similar lines their development follows. From the rich to the poor states, from the old to the new ones, nearly all of them take a larger hand in matters of economic regulation, of education, health, and housing, of culture and the arts, and so on almost endlessly. The increase of the activities of states is a strong and striking uniform international trend. The functions of states are similar, and distinctions among them arise principally from their varied capabilities. National politics consists of differentiated units performing specified functions. International politics consists of like units duplicating one another's activities.

3. THE DISTRIBUTION OF CAPABILITIES

The parts of a hierarchic system are related to one another in ways that are determined both by their functional differentiation and by the extent of their capabilities. The units of an anarchic system are functionally undifferentiated. The units of such an order are then distinguished primarily by their greater or lesser capabilities for performing similar tasks. This states formally what students of international politics have long noticed. The great powers of an era have always been marked off from others by practitioners and theorists alike. Students of national government make such distinctions as that between parliamentary and presidential systems; governmental systems differ in form. Students of international politics make distinctions between international-political systems only according to the number of their great powers. The structure of a system changes with changes in the distribution of capabilities across the system's units. And changes in structure change expectations about how the units of the system will behave and about the outcomes their interactions will produce. Domestically, the differentiated parts of a system may perform similar tasks. We know from observing the American government that executives sometimes legislate and legislatures sometimes execute. Internationally, like units sometimes perform different tasks. Why they do so, and ... the likelihood of their doing so varies with their capabilities.... Meanwhile, two problems should be considered.

The first problem is this: Capability tells us something about units. Defining structure partly in terms of the distribution of capabilities seems to violate my instruction to keep unit attributes out of structural definitions. As I remarked earlier, structure is a highly but not entirely abstract concept. The maximum of abstraction allows a minimum of content, and that minimum is what is needed to enable one to say how the units stand in relation to one another. States are differently placed by their power. And yet one may wonder why only *capability* is included in the third part of the definition, and not such characteristics as ideology, form of government, peacefulness, bellicosity, or whatever. The answer is this: Power is estimated by comparing the capabilities of a number of units. Although capabilities are attributes of units, the distribution of capabilities across units is not. The distribution of capabilities is not a unit attribute, but rather a system-wide concept. Again, the parallel with market theory is exact. Both firms and states are like units. Through all of their variations in form, firms share certain qualities: They are self-regarding units that, within governmentally imposed limits, decide for themselves how to cope with their environment and just how to work for their ends. Variation of structure is introduced, not through differences in the character and function of units, but only through distinctions made among them according to their capabilities.

The second problem is this: Though relations defined in terms of interactions must be excluded from structural definitions, relations defined in terms of groupings of states do seem to tell us something about how states are placed in the system. Why not specify how states stand in relation to one another by considering the alliances they form? Would doing so not be comparable to defining national political structures partly in terms of how presidents and prime ministers are related to other political agents? It would not be. Nationally as internationally, structural definitions deal with the relation of agents and agencies in terms of the organization of realms and not in terms of the accommodations and conflicts that may occur within them or the groupings that may now and then form. Parts of a government may draw together or pull apart, may oppose each other or cooperate in greater or lesser degree. These are the relations that form and dissolve within a system rather than structural alterations that mark a change from one system to another. This is made clear by an example that runs nicely parallel to the case of alliances. Distinguishing systems of political parties according to their number is common. A multiparty system changes if, say, eight parties become two, but not if two groupings of the eight form merely for the occasion of fighting an election. By the same logic, an international-political system in which three or more great powers have split into two alliances remains a multipolar system — structurally distinct from a bipolar system, a system in which no third power is able to challenge the top two. In defining market structure, information about the particular quality of firms is not called for, nor is information about their interactions, short of the point at which the formal merger of firms significantly reduces their number. In the definition of market structure, firms are not identified and their interactions are not described. To take the qualities of firms and the nature of their interactions as being parts of market structure would be to say that whether a sector of an economy is oligopolistic or not depends on how the firms are organized internally and how they deal with one another, rather than simply on how many major firms coexist. Market structure is defined by counting firms; international-political structure, by counting states. In the counting, distinctions are made only according to capabilities.

In defining international-political structures we take states with whatever traditions, habits, objectives, desires, and forms of government they may have. We do not ask whether states are revolutionary or legitimate, authoritarian or democratic, ideological or pragmatic. We abstract from every attribute of state except their capabilities. Nor in thinking about structure do we ask about the relations of states — their feelings of friendship and hostility, their diplomatic exchanges, the alliances they form, and the extent of the contacts and exchanges among them. We ask what range of expectations arises merely from looking at the type of order that prevails among them and at the distribution of capabilities within that order. We abstract from any particular qualities of states and from all of their concrete connections. What emerges is a positional picture, a general description of the ordered overall arrangement of a society written in terms of the placement of units rather than in terms of their qualities....

ENDNOTES

1 William T.R. Fox, "The uses of international relations theory," in Fox, ed., *Theoretical Aspects of International Relations* (Notre Dame: University of Notre Dame Press, 1959), p. 35.

2 Charles P. Kindleberger, *American Business Abroad* (New Haven: Yale University Press, 1969), p. 207.

3 Smith should know better. Translated into terms that he has himself so effectively used, to say that states are sovereign is to say that they are segments of a plural society. M.G. Smith, "A structural approach to comparative politics," in David Easton, ed., *Varieties of Political Theories* (Englewood Cliffs, N.J.: Prentice-Hall, 1966), p. 122.

A. STRUCTURE AND CONCEPT

System Structures

Glenn Snyder/Paul Diesing

While the international system may be described in terms of many variables, two are of paramount importance...(1) the "structure" of the system, i.e., the number of major actors and the gross distribution of military power among them, and (2) the nature of military technology. Our historical research has encompassed two distinct international systems in terms of these variables. The system in the latter part of the nineteenth century and up to 1945 was multipolar in structure, and non-nuclear (conventional) in technology. Since 1945 it has been bipolar and nuclear. The international system at present seems to be in a transitional period leading to a new form of multipolarity and perhaps eventually to a proliferation of nuclear weapons....

The "structure" of an international system is defined by the *number* of major actors in the system and the *distribution of military power* and potential among them. In a multipolar system there are several (more than two) "Great Powers" whose military power is roughly equal, and whose rivalry and cooperation dominate politics in the system. In addition there are, of course, a number of smaller states who do not play significant roles except as they serve as objects of the Great Power competition or create disturbances among themselves that engage the Great Powers. A bipolar system is one with only two Great Powers and a number of smaller states. These are definitions of ideal types, from which real international systems will deviate, more or less. The multipolar systems of 1870-1914 and 1918-1939 approximate the ideal type quite closely; the bipolar system since 1945 somewhat less so. In the latter, some of the "smaller states" were considerably more powerful than others and played roles more significant than mere objects of superpower competition. However, this "deviation" is much less important than the power inequality between the "superpowers" and all others.

Of course, the power structure among the actors is not the only important dimension of an international system. The total system comprises its structure, the pattern of relations among the state-actors, their specific interactions, and their internal attributes....

We emphasize that the "poles" in our two structural types are *states*, not alliances or "blocs" of states. Alliances and blocs are types of *relations* between states in the system that are influenced by the prevailing structure but do not constitute that structure. Thus the rough equality between the two alliances prior to 1914 did not make the system

---

Glenn H. Snyder and Paul Diesing, *Conflict Among Nations: Bargaining, Decision Making, and System Structure in International Crisis.* Excerpts, pp. 419-29. Portions of the text have been deleted. Some footnotes have been removed; those remaining have been renumbered.

bipolar, nor did the loosening of the U.S. and Soviet blocs during the 1960s and early 1970s make that system multipolar.

The most fundamental relational phenomenon affected by structure is the identification of friends and enemies, potential or actual. For the superpowers in a bipolar system, the identity of the opponent is fully determined by structure; for the lesser powers, considerably so. The United States and the Soviet Union could not help but perceive each other as rivals after World War II, since for each one, the other was the only state in the system that posed a serious military threat to its own security or to smaller states whose independence or affiliation was deemed essential to that security. Ideological conflict had little to do with this basic identification although it did exacerbate the resulting antagonism. Specific conflicts of interest and hostile acts reflected more than they created the antagonism. Thus, while the *degree* of tension and hostility in the Cold War was undoubtedly increased by incompatible ideologies and specific hostile behavior that tended to confirm initial perceptions of threat, the initial perceptions themselves were a function of the preponderance of these two powers over all others. In short, the rivalry was structurally ordained.[1] This rivalry does not necessarily mean unremitting hostility. While always regarding each other as the principal opponent, the Big Two have found it possible and mutually advantageous at times to cooperate, to some degree and for particular purposes, as in...détente. But détente can never develop into entente or alliance, as it may in a multipolar system, because there is no third party powerful enough to provide a sufficient incentive for alliance.

The alignment of the lesser states in a bipolar system is determined by some combination of structural forces and specific historical, geographic, or ideological circumstances. It might be argued that their alignment is not affected by the logic of system structure at all. If left to their own devices, they will align with the superpower that appears least threatening to their own security or that is most congenial ideologically. If there is no threat, or no strong ideological affinity or repulsion, they will not align at all.

However, they will not be left to their own devices. The structural compulsions on the superpowers themselves will indirectly affect the alignment of the lesser states. Each of the giants, fearful of the other, will seek hegemony over, or alliance with, some of the states in the space between them, out of their own security concerns. When one of them starts this process, the other will perceive it as threatening, as will the rest of the small states, and these will then join in a counteralliance. This is essentially what happened in Europe after World War II. The Soviet Union asserted dominance over the Eastern European countries when it had the chance as the result of its liberation of these countries from German control. It probably did so primarily for security reasons, security against a possibly resurgent Germany backed by the immense power of the United States. The Western European countries and the United States perceived this as threatening to their security and formed NATO in response. It may be plausibly contended that something like this would have occurred in any case, whatever the detailed factual circumstances that attended the birth of the bipolar system. The superpowers, facing a power vacuum in the space intervening between them, would have each sought to fill it, or part of it, in order to preempt the intolerable security threat that would have resulted from the rival having filled all of it.

Of course the logic of structure does not fully determine which state will be in which camp, only that alignments will form. Membership in each alignment will depend on empirical circumstances, in this case primarily geography and the limits of Soviet power. Among the states that remained outside the Soviet embrace, some (e.g., Sweden, Switzerland) did not join NATO, but they were nevertheless beneficiaries of a tacit U.S. security guarantee. The membership of some states on the periphery of the blocs may be problematical (e.g., Yugoslavia), and the superpowers may offer their protective mantle to some states for non-security reasons (e.g., the United States' tacit commitment to Israel).

Once the alignments are formed, dealignment or realignment of the lesser powers is unlikely, either because they have no incentive to realign or because, if they try, their superpower protector will prevent it. But here again, the unlikelihood of realignment results from some combination of structural necessity and specific factual circumstances. The lack of incentive to realign, for example, is largely a function of the ideology of regimes; the inability to realign, for Warsaw Pact members at least, can be traced largely to structural necessity as it determines the security interests of the superpower.

The Sino-Soviet split and the United States-China rapprochement do not violate this logic, since this realignment involved a state outside the central arena, with enough independent power to escape the embrace of its former protector. Also, China represents a potential third "pole" in a system evolving toward multipolarity. The current fluidity in world politics partly reflects this developing structural change, which is still some decades away from completion. Hence, the contemporary transitional system exhibits some of the characteristics we here ascribe to bipolarity, and some which we will attribute to multipolarity; we may speculate that the latter will grow more prominent as the system evolves.

In a multipolar system such as that of the nineteenth century, enmity and amity are not determined by structure per se. To be sure, if one state grows dangerously powerful and/or reveals generally aggressive intentions, thereby threatening a structural transformation, it will attract the antagonism of at least some others, who will typically unite against it in the familiar pattern of the balance of power. Short of this, from the structural standpoint alone, each major actor perceives all others to be equally eligible as potential allies or potential opponents. Hence the vaunted "flexibility" of a multipolar system. Some degree of determinacy is introduced, however, by *particular* conflicts of interest, ideological attractions and repulsions, geographical configuration, and traditional, ethnic or sentimental ties. Hence, the conflict of interest between Russia and Austria in the Balkans in the latter part of the nineteenth century predisposed those two states to enmity and inhibited alliance between them, as did the Alsace-Lorraine conflict between Germany and France. Various specific conflicts between Russia and England seemed to make them "natural" opponents, and alliance between France and England was likewise inhibited by imperial conflicts. Ideological similarity among the three eastern regimes exerted some attraction between them and some repulsion toward Britain and France, themselves mutually attracted by their democratic institutions. Ethnic ties predisposed Germany and Austria to friendship and exerted a weaker pull between these two and England. The upshot of these criss-crossing forces was, first, the German-Austrian alliance of 1879, which, in Bismarck's calculations, brought along England as a "sleeping partner" and produced in reaction the Franco-Russian alliance, which, notably however, was delayed 15 years, largely because of mutual ideological distaste, but also because of Bismarck's diplomatic skill in keeping Russia tied to Germany.

Such particular interests, conflicts, and affinities are more influential in determining alignment in multipolarity than they are in bipolarity. Because of them, a multipolar system is less flexible than its glorifiers have sometimes claimed. However, the "logic of particular interests" is hardly ever completely determining. It competes with, and interacts with, another logic, the "logic of flexibility," which is inherent in the structure of the system and independent of the particular interests of its members. Given that all other major states are powerful enough to be a potential threat to one's own, there is always some degree of compulsion to coalesce with some others, any others. Some states are likely to prefer the certainty of some definite allies and some definite enemies to the uncertainty of "each against each" and the disastrous possibility of "all against one." Fear of aggression or aggressive alliances by others need not be well-substantiated to trigger the first combination, and, once the first is formed, a countercoalition is likely to form in response. Particular interests and conflicts may affect the *choice* of allies, but the compulsion to align or counteralign exists apart from them, and may override them. Thus, Bismarck chose to ally with Austria, but the principal reason why he made any alliance at all was his fear that Austria might combine with France, tacitly bringing England along via her common interests with Austria in opposing Russia in the eastern Mediterranean. In a five-member system, Bismarck preferred to be in a party of three rather than two, so he simply preempted the party of three. The fact that he preempted *from France* reflected a particular conflict, but that he felt compelled to preempt at all reflected the logic of the system, as did, subsequently, the counteralliance between France and Russia that overrode the particular conflict (of ideology) between these two countries....

Typically, the alliances are never absolutely firm and may be quite tenuous or tacit; consequently the dangers and opportunities of realignment are ever-present. The possible combinations and variants inherent in such flexibility are many. The main point is that although there is not in multipolarity, as there is in bipolarity, much clear guidance as to what one "must" do in any specific sense, this very indeterminacy amid a plethora of dangers and opportunities exerts a powerful compulsion toward a certain kind of behavior that is governed by the rule: "Avoid isolation or being caught in a minority coalition, but get the most you can from your partners, at minimum cost and risk."

The "logic of flexibility" produces a category of *general* interests for the participants that should be carefully distinguished from the *particular* interests mentioned above. Particular interests may be "strategic" interests vis-à-vis specific other states, or they may be "intrinsic" interests — interests valued for reasons other than their strategic — i.e., power — significance. General interests are interests with respect to the general configuration of power in the system. Typical general interests are "be in a majority coalition," "resist the disturber," "preserve the balance of power," etc. States face the problem, in any situation, of predicting whether the particular or general interests of other states will be dominant, and of determining which category should guide their own behavior. Those who guess or choose wrongly may come to grief. For example, when, around the turn of this century, England made an alliance bid to Germany, the Germans asked a very high price, thinking that England's theoretical alternative of alignment with France and Russia was absolutely foreclosed because of particular imperial conflicts. But England's general interest in ending her isolation was greater than the sacrifices necessary to resolve these conflicts. The result was the ententes of 1904 and 1907 and, it might also be argued, the defeat of Germany in World War I.

There are both particular and general interests in bipolarity as well. What is distinctive about bipolarity is the *clarity* of the general interest. The dominant general interest is the preservation of the balance of power against the other superpower — concretely, to deter and prevent the latter's expansion — or alternatively, to gain a power advantage for one's own "pole." As Kenneth Waltz has pointed out, each superpower will resist the other's attempted expansion at every point, and the other can confidently predict such resistance.[2] Waltz argues that this clarity about "who will oppose whom" is an important factor making for "stability" in a bipolar system, as compared to multipolarity where ambiguity about possible opposition may tempt an aggressor to gamble. There are several reasons for such ambiguity in multipolar systems. First, a state may think of the expanding state as a potential ally against another; hence an increase in its power should logically be encouraged rather than resisted. Second, a potential resister, while visualizing the expanding state as a threat, may face a greater threat from another quarter and be reluctant to subtract power deployed against the latter for use against the aggressor. Third, the state in question may consider both the aggressor and his target as threats to itself and prefer to stand aside and let the two weaken each other. Fourth, there is the broad consideration that the potential resister may prefer not to act until the power configuration in the system obviously represents a direct threat to itself; pending that time it will look only to its particular interests. All such uncertainties provide plenty of material for wishful thinking and possibly miscalculation in a state bent on aggrandizement.

In bipolarity there is little scope for such miscalculation because of the certainty that a power gain for one superpower means a power loss for the other. Loosely speaking, they are in a two-person zero-sum game in power terms, as compared to the more complex and more ambiguous *N*-person non-zero-sum game of multipolarity. Constant vigilance and resistance to the opponent's every forward move, no matter how minor, is therefore the guiding rule of behavior. Partially opposed to this clarity of interest, however, as Waltz also points out, is a relatively low *intensity* of interest. The power of the superpowers themselves is so great in relation to the power resources of the rest of the system that no particular new acquisition by one or the other, by conquest or realignment, can change the fundamental balance of power between them. Waltz considers this to be a complementary source of stability in the system: while clarity of interests inhibits attempts to change by force, low intensity of interest (in power terms) makes the changes that occur easy to absorb.[3]

In a multipolar system, while the *definition* of general power interests is often unclear, their intensity is likely to be high. That is, the expansion, defeat, or realignment of any major actor will significantly change the power distribution in the system, but the other actors may be uncertain whether the change is to their advantage or detriment. One might hypothesize that when the system is most fluid and the identity of friends and foes most ambiguous, this lack of clarity in power interests will tend to inhibit responses to change and tempt potential aggressors. Conversely, when alignments are clear and firm, the strength of the interest in preventing the defeat of an ally or an opponent's increase in power will encourage resistance and favor deterrence of aggression. The most dangerous condition is that in which alliance commitments *seem* questionable to outsiders but are in reality quite firm.

Another important difference is in the function of alliances relative to "interests." In bipolarity, alliances usually merely *register* the general interests of the members, interests already inherent in the power structure of the system. During the Cold War period, the United States had a clear interest in defending against Soviet expansion all countries outside the Soviet orbit, as the Soviet Union had likewise in its sphere, whether alliances were made or not, and the lesser states on each side had a clear interest in being protected. The formation of NATO, the Warsaw Pact, and other alliances did not create any new interests for the parties, although they did clarify and perhaps add somewhat to the strength of the existing interests, and they also served important functions in facilitating military and political collaboration and in educating public opinion.

In a multipolar system, on the other hand, alliances and alignments often actually *create* interests that did not previously exist. Alliances in multipolarity reflect the fact that no state controls enough power under its own sovereignty to meet all the threats that may arise. There is therefore an incentive to pool power, and the pooling has two major effects: first, by *identifying* friends and foes, perhaps somewhat arbitrarily, it makes clear *whose* expansion is to be regarded as threatening, and whose is to be considered advantageous. In a very real sense, the compulsion to pool power as a general systemic necessity actually creates relations of enmity and amity; it does not just reflect prior relations, although in most cases, what actually occurs is some mixture of "creation" and "reflection." This creation of opponents and friends obviously also creates interests in resisting the one and defending the other, interests that did not exist before, at least not so strongly. For example, when England made her entente with France in 1904, Germany, previously only a vague source of concern, became identified as an enemy and France as a partner, and these identifications were not merely clarified but also strengthened as the entente developed from a mere colonial agreement to something approaching an alliance. In fact, the gradual strengthening of the ties and sense of common interest with France, and the intensification of rivalry with Germany, reciprocally acted and reacted upon each other in a kind of vicious circle. In deciding to pool her power with France to escape isolation, England had to pay the inevitable price of "creating," for Germany, the role of opponent, a role that was previously only latent or weakly defined and might not otherwise have materialized. As for France, her conflict of particular interest with Germany over Alsace-Lorraine, which had previously inhibited but not absolutely foreclosed alliance with Germany, now became subsumed in a more general power competition with Germany as the irreconcilable foe.

The second reason why multipolar alignments "create" interests is that the pooling of power entails the obligation to defend at least some of the ally's particular interests, which may be quite different from one's own. These interests, to a degree, become one's own interests as a derivative of the interest in maintaining the alliance. Unlike bipolarity, where alliances involving the superpowers are actually unilateral guarantees by the latter to their dependent allies involving no reciprocal expectation that the clients will come to the aid of their protectors (whatever the wording of the alliance document), in multipolarity they are bilateral or multilateral exchanges of commitment. The fulfillment of, or the intention to fulfill, the commitments is a condition of obtaining the benefits and, in fact, for the continuing viability of the alliance itself. However, since the contingencies that might activate the commitments cannot be fully and exactly stated in alliance contracts, and since many alignments are no more than tacit understandings that may mean something different to each partner in concrete situations, alliances and alignments never overcome completely the basic ambiguity of interest in multipolarity. And since alignments are temporary and constantly subject to change, the interests created by them are also changeable.

Finally, as Robert E. Osgood has pointed out, the general power interests of allies tend to be *homogeneous* in bipolarity and *heterogeneous* in multipolarity.[5] In the central arena of a bipolar system, the dominant concern of all the partners is to deter and resist expansion by the opposing superpower or its wards, although in peripheral subsystems (e.g., the Middle East) the local threat from opponents in that subsystem may loom larger for the ward than the superpower threat, and vice versa for the superpower ally. By and large, there is little or no disagreement between allies as to *which* threat is to be resisted, since one threat dominates all others. Differences tend to center instead on *how* the threat is to be met, on the mix of resistance and accommodation to be employed in dealing with the opponent, the kind of military strategy to be adopted, the allocation of defense costs among the allies, etc. In a multipolar system, by contrast, allies are likely to have somewhat different interests, to feel threatened in different degree from different quarters. These differences are largely due to factors of geographical location and particular conflicts with different opponents. Thus in the latter part of the nineteenth century, Austria had a strong interest in resisting Russian influence in the Balkans, while for Germany, as Bismarck put it, the Balkans were not "worth the bones of a Pomeranian grenadier." Austria, conversely, cared little for Germany's interest in containing and isolating France. The mirror image of this heterogeneity occurred in the Franco-Russian alliance. The divisive effects of such differences are reduced by the common interest in preserving the alliance. Nevertheless, heterogeneity of interests is a source of conflict and strain within multipolar alliances that, in a crisis, may appear as a reluctance of the ally not directly concerned to stand firm against the opponent's demands. Typically, the supporting ally will face a hard choice between somewhat incompatible interests: preserving the alliance vs. avoiding war over the ally's special interests, which are only partly shared if at all.

The homogeneity of interest in bipolarity is qualified by its regional character. Thus, while the United States and its NATO allies share interests to a high degree in Europe, the allies have not been enthusiastic supporters of the United States in non-European crises, nor has the United States shared European interests in *their* adventures outside Europe. Obvious examples are Quemoy 1958 and Suez 1956. An extreme case was the Yom Kippur war of 1973 when the Europeans actively obstructed U.S. efforts to re-supply Israel. However, the interest involved in these cases was not primarily the *general* one of resisting the opposite superpower but rather the *particular* interests of the United States or its allies.

To summarize, in bipolarity, the identity of friends and foes and the definition of interests is largely a consequence of the structure of the system; alliances register but do not create interests; interests are clear and relatively unchanging, and are shared in high degree among allies. In multipolarity, enmity and amity are not determined by structure but by conflicts of particular interests and a systemically induced compulsion to align with others to escape the dangers of isolation; alignments create interests to some degree; interests are often ambiguous but are potentially or actually intense; interests tend to be changeable, reflecting changing alignments, and are imperfectly shared among allies....

ENDNOTES

1 That the imperatives of system structure were the primary cause of the Cold War is the leading theme of Louis Halle's *The Cold War as History* (New York: Harper and Row, 1967). These imperatives are overlooked by revisionist writers, who see the Cold War as caused by the nature of the U.S. capitalist system, and also by traditional writers who find its cause in "Soviet imperialism." For analyses of the revisionists' blind spot on this point, see especially Robert W. Tucker, *The Radical Left and American Foreign Policy*, Studies in International Affairs, No. 15, The Washington Center for Foreign Policy Research, 1971, pp. 89-90; also James Richardson, "Cold-War Revisionism: A Critique," *World Politics*, 24 (July 1972), 579-613.

2 Kenneth Waltz, "The Stability of a Bipolar World," *Daedalus*, 93 (Summer 1964), 882-883.

3 Ibid., p. 886.

4 Robert E. Osgood and Robert W. Tucker, *Force, Order and Justice* (Baltimore: The Johns Hopkins University Press, 1967), p. 172.

B: SYSTEM EVOLUTION

The Aims of Europe's Classical Balance of Power

Edward Vose Gulick

No one who has watched a boat being built would regard a barnacle as essential to its structure. In similar fashion, once the edifice of aims of the balance of power is exposed, the observer, seeing what its main elements are, can easily distinguish what is germane from what is incidental.

PRESERVE INDEPENDENCE AND SECURE SURVIVAL

The basic aim of the balance of power was to insure the survival of independent states. This may be taken as fundamental to the classical balance-of-power system and should be distinguished from those goals, such as "peace" and (to a lesser degree) the "status quo," which were incidental to it.

Writers on the balance of power expressed their recognition of this basic aim in various ways. Brougham, for example, held that "the whole object of the [balance of power] system is to maintain unimpaired the independence of nations."[1] Heeren spoke of the balance of power as the "mutual preservation of freedom and independence, by guarding against the preponderance and usurpation of an individual."[2] Vattel, in elucidating the "general Principles of the Duties of a Nation to Itself," summarized them with the dictum: "To preserve and perfect one's existence is the sum of all duties to self."[3] We find in all three a repeated emphasis on the primacy of the survival of independent states. Similarly, where the old British Mutiny Act provided for the levy of troops, it was associating an instrument of war (the levy) with the two ideas of "the Safety of the United Kingdom... and the Preservation of the Balance of Power in Europe," and was by implication asserting that survival took precedence over peace as an aim of the balance of power.[4]

PRESERVE THE STATE SYSTEM

Taking the survival of the independent state as his base, the equilibrist erected his aims by piling two more blocks on top of the first. The second block consisted of the argument that the best way to preserve the individual state was to preserve the system of which it was a part. Self-interest, according to this line of reasoning, could best be pursued by attention to group interest. By preserving the state system you would preserve the parts

---

thereof. For a superb illustration of this second block, carefully aligned and cemented by the master mason himself, we look at a famous passage in the *Mémoires* of Prince Metternich, creator and preserver of intricately balanced structures:

> *Politics* is the science of the vital interests of States in its widest meaning. Since, however, an isolated state no longer exists, and is found only in the annals of the heathen world... we must always view the *society* of states as the essential condition of the modern world.... The great axioms of political science proceed from the knowledge of the true political interests of *all states*; it is upon these general interests that rests the guarantee of their existence.... What characterizes the modern world and distinguishes it from the ancient is the tendency of states to draw near each other and to form a kind of social body based on the same principle as human society.... In the ancient world isolation and the practice of the most absolute selfishness without other restraint than that of prudence was the sum of politics.... Modern society on the other hand exhibits the application of the principle of solidarity and of the balance of power between states.... The establishing of international relations, on the basis of reciprocity under the guarantee of respect for acquired rights,... constitutes in our time the essence of politics.[5]

The same concern for the state system was mirrored in the first secret article of the treaty of April 11, 1805, between Russia and Great Britain, which spoke of "the establishment in Europe of a federative system to ensure the independence of the weaker states by erecting a formidable barrier against the ambition of the more powerful."[6] Gentz also had it in mind when he wrote:

> The fate of Europe depends upon the fortunes and political relations of the powers which preponderate in the general system. If the balance be preserved among these; if their political existence and *international organization* be safely established; if, by their mutual action and reaction, they protect and secure the independence of the smaller states...; if there is no dangerous preponderance to be perceived, which threatens to oppress the rest, or to involve them in endless war; [then] we may rest satisfied with the *federal constitution* which fulfills these most essential points, notwithstanding many errors and defects. And such was the federal constitution of Europe before the French revolution.[7]

This quotation fairly radiates concern for the *group* of states comprised in the state system.

These selections indicate the structure built by the supporters of balance-of-power policy. It will be observed, however, that their reasoning was not derived by a strict logic but had a certain admixture of faith, the cement between the first two blocks being two parts logic and one part faith, in spite of what the masons might protest to the contrary. Where a writer found balance of power to be an obvious maxim of self-interest, a careful scrutiny of his statement will reveal it to be merely a plausible half-truth. There are, to be sure, circumstances in which equilibrist policies would be obvious self-interest, especially those times when the balance of power was in danger of being upset to the disadvantage of the state. There are, however, numerous occasions when a violation of the principles of the balance of power would undeniably be self-interest: for example, when an opportunity for safe conquest and annexation appeared. Under such circumstances, balance-of-power theory demanded restraint, abnegation, and the denial of immediate self-interest.

NO ONE STATE SHALL PREPONDERATE

Once the second block was in place, there was no choice about the third. If one granted that the survival of independent states was the primary aim and added that the best chance of achieving it resided in preserving the state system, a relentless logic led to the obvious axiom of preventing the preponderance of any one member of the state system. "Nations [should] unite, or... prepare for their defense, as soon as they perceive anyone becoming dangerously powerful."[8] Failure to do so was "an inexcusable breach of duty."[9] Similar formulations have often been made by writers, typical of whom again was Friedrich Gentz in his assertion "That if the states system of Europe is to exist and be maintained by common exertions, no one of its members must ever become so powerful as to be able to coerce all the rest put together."[10]

There has never been any divergence of opinion among equilibrist writers on this third general proposition. Their statements vary a bit in phraseology and tone, but they convey the same substance. The position is well stated by Gaspard de Réal de Curban, writer on government in the middle of the eighteenth century:

> For several centuries Europe has been worrying about the smallest manifestation of ambition which it perceived in a Power. Each nation, while it tries to rise above the others, is occupied with maintaining a certain balance, which bestows upon the smallest states the force of a large section of Europe, and preserves them in spite of the weakness of their armies and the defects of their governments. This equilibrium of power is based on the incontestable principle that the greatness of one Prince is, properly speaking, only the ruin or the diminution of the greatness of his neighbor, and that his might is but another's weakness.[11]

Peace. We may say that survival, a degree of cooperation, and the prevention of a hostile predominance were all germane to the balance-of-power theory, as indicated. We may also say that peace was not germane. However desirable it may have been, however passionately the theorist may have longed for it, however devotedly he may have consecrated his life to its realization, peace was no more essential to equilibrist theory than the barnacle to the boat.

An appreciable amount of confusion has arisen on this point as the result of mistaken analysis of balance-of-power theory. Indeed, peace has occasionally been urged as the pre-eminent aim of balance-of-power policies: "A balance of power aims primarily to preserve peace and the *status quo*."[12] The same idea is often found in treaties when the balance of power is mentioned; witness one of the treaties of Utrecht, that between Great Britain and Spain (July 2/13, 1713), which contains the following phrase: "in order to secure and stabilize the peace and tranquility of the Christian world by a just equilibrium of power (which is the best and most solid basis of mutual friendship and durable harmony)."[13] Although many who have written on the balance of power have adopted this point of view, there are reasons why their position is untenable.

Consider, for example, the striking content of the diplomatic history of the last five hundred years in Europe, from the Italian Renaissance to the present, which has literally brimmed with parallel evidence of both balance of power and war, during the very period when the balance of power was at its height. Accepting such a finding, it is possible to deal with this coincidence in two ways: one may say that the balance of power aimed at peace but perennially failed, or that balance-of-power theory aimed at the survival of the state system and regarded war as a means of preventing the breakdown of that system. With regard to the first of these propositions, we cannot help asking if the balance-of-power system was, in the period of its most consistent practice, as ineffectual as the proposition suggests. It is tempting to say yes and drive another nail into the balance-of-power coffin, but the answer surely lies in the direction of the second proposition, and for several reasons.

It is noticeable that wars were fought in the name of balance of power against Charles V, Louis XIV, and Napoleon, to mention only the most outstanding and to ignore myriad examples of lesser importance. One also notices that the clearest-headed theorists of equilibrium have not only *not* claimed peace as the principal aim, but have actually envisaged war as an instrument for balancing power: Vattel, Gentz, Brougham, Christian Wolff, in company with such practical statesmen as Talleyrand, Metternich, and Castlereagh, all thought of war as an instrument to preserve or restore a balance of power. One observes also the almost placid acceptance by Rousseau and Kant of the hideous nature of competition within the state system and their obvious belief in a successful balancing system in spite of it. The argument of these advocates conforms to theory and fact by showing that the incidence of war was not evidence of the ineffectiveness or absence of balance-of-power policies but that such incidence indicated widespread practice (often malpractice, to be sure) of the balance of power, of which war was an instrument. Their contention explains where the first proposition obscures, and, by explaining, effectively cuts the ground from under the "peace" point of view.

We would be correct in listing peace as one of the incidental by-products of equilibrist policy, or as one of its secondary aims. There is no doubt that peace has often been temporarily preserved as a result of balance strategy; but we may also be sure that a system of independent, armed, and often mutually hostile states is inherently incapable of remaining at peace over a considerable period of time merely by the manipulation of balance techniques.

Status Quo. Returning to the assertion that a balance-of-power system "aims primarily to preserve peace and the *status quo*," we must still examine the *status quo* as an admissible, primary aim of balancing theory. In this case we may not say that one finds merely a casual connection between the two, as in the case of "peace" and the balance of power. We are not dealing with a barnacle on the hull of the theory; rather, the design of the ship itself is at stake, for here we find separate groups of writers arguing separate interpretations of the relationship between balance of power and *status quo*. Some assert and some deny the need to preserve the *status quo*, their disagreement being most vividly illustrated in their different attitudes toward the partitions of Poland in the eighteenth century, when Poland was, by 1795, extinguished as an independent state. There were writers who found this act a hideous breach of balance-of-power precepts, which were designed to preserve, rather than dissolve, the independence of states. Others argued that Poland was weak, a prey to outside interference, and an area doomed to ultimate absorption; consequently, a series of partitions which distributed Polish areas among three neighboring powers was a desirable and even outstanding achievement of balance-of-power policy; war was avoided and a political vacuum was eliminated from eastern Europe. Thus some writers abhorred the political extinction of an independent state, others even applauded it. The latter writers obviously regarded the *status quo* as untenable or unrealistic.

The matter may be clarified by a return to first principles. The first aim of balancing theory called for the survival of independent states. Without such states, there could be no state system; and without the system, there could be no balance of power. Although so much may be said without cavil, the aim is quite general and invites interpretation. What, for example, was meant by the "survival of independent states?" Did this phrase mean all states in the system? Or did it mean merely some? Could a theorist legitimately, according to balance-of-power theory, insist on the survival of key states only, or did he have to preserve each and every member of the state system? It was at this crossroads that writers marched off in different directions. If a theorist argued for the preservation of all states, he was arguing for the *status quo*; if he argued for the survival of some only, he was disregarding the *status quo*. The arguments in favor of each position demand scrutiny before judgment may be passed on their relative value.

In support of the *status quo* as the proper interpretation of the primary aim of balance-of-power theory, one may argue both from the theoretical position and from the historical record. In theory, if the *status quo* of the Europe of 1648 or 1713, when Europe was dissected into many states, could have been preserved indefinitely, it would have assured forever that there could be no preponderant power. Neither France nor Austria, both of them prominent at those dates, was sufficiently powerful to dominate the continent. Moreover, England, Prussia, Spain, Sweden, and others were not negligible in the equilibrium. A freezing of such a divided Europe for all time would have meant the perpetuation of a state system and the avoidance of preponderance. Under those circumstances, "the survival of independent states" (meaning all states) would have involved the fighting of wars to maintain or restore the territorial framework which existed before the war. The logic of this interpretation is satisfactory, if somewhat superficial; furthermore, the historical record has some encouraging words to add. For example, in the period from 1648 to 1792, there were, generally speaking, no great territorial changes in continental Europe, except for the first partition of Poland. We note some minor changes: the "corrections" of European territory by Louis XIV, the Spanish Netherlands becoming the Austrian Netherlands, Gibraltar and Minorca being taken by Britain, Silesia seized and secured by Prussia, and certain Ottoman areas going to Russia. But it would be no mistake to disregard these as outstanding changes in general European territories. The major impression which the observer receives from the state system of 1648-1792 is one of relative stability, although Poland offers contrary evidence, because the first partition of that unhappy land witnessed the loss of about one-third of her territory, together with the loss of considerable prestige, the important grain areas of Galicia, and her access to the Baltic. Nevertheless, one may treat that partition as an unfortunate exception to general practice in the period before 1792. The record is, indeed, a remarkable one for preservation of the *status quo*. Wars, an all-too-familiar disfigurement of the seventeenth and eighteenth centuries, repeatedly ended in restoration of either the *status quo* or a close approximation of it. More dramatic changes were a characteristic of the overseas phases of the wars to a much greater degree than of the continental theater itself. Indeed, the trifling changes in Europe, where Frederick the Great fought two wars within twenty-three years to secure for Prussia at great risk no more than the province of Silesia, were in dramatic juxtaposition to the Gargantuan slabs of territory which changed hands overseas. In the peace treaty at the end of the Seven Years' War, Great Britain swept France from the great subcontinent of India and gutted the French empire in North America, only to lose the American colonies herself within another twenty years. The apogee of the theory of balance of power, or at least an important part of it, was indeed contemporary to a notable retention of the general outlines of the *status quo* in Europe over a period of many years. So much may be accepted. There remain, however, powerful arguments against acceptance of the *status quo* interpretation as the only legitimate one.

The second interpretation, that is, the one which rejects slavish attention to the *status quo*, focuses attention on the unavoidable movement of history (as opposed to the possible freezing of a state system into a given *status quo*) and tends to emphasize the preservation of key members of the system at the expense, if necessary, of smaller or weaker powers. According to this point of view, one must take into account the dynamism of history, the flow of power and wealth from one area to another, the decadence of once-great powers in the general equilibrium, and the emergence of new, dynamic powers. The Greeks had a word for it — flux. Indeed, one of the great justifications of studying history is the insights which one gets into the process covered by this word. One of the few things that we can be sure of in all history is that everything changes. In the long run, flux will upset the best-laid plans of an earlier epoch. What once balanced nicely will for another generation hang as awkwardly as a wet toga. There is, then, a theoretical justification, and a strong one, for the reading of the phrase "survival of independent states" as some states, or key states, and not all states. With regard to the historical record, this school of thought can point an accusing finger at the opposition for its selection of 1792 as a terminal date for evidence. The use of evidence chosen only from the period before 1792 is arbitrary in the extreme, because such selectivity avoids the necessity of dealing with the awkward facts of 1793-1814, when Europe went through the most violent phase of the French Revolution, as well as two partitions of Poland, the excesses of Napoleonic imperialism, the violence of coalition warfare, a great modern broadening of warfare itself, the consolidation of German states, and the creation (coupled with the later destruction) of a great continental empire under Napoleon.

When the time came for peacemakers to discuss the restoration of the European state system, the unresolved controversy over the *status quo* bubbled at once to the surface. Some voices were raised for the restoration of the frontiers of 1789, 1790, or 1792, but there was vigorous rejection of such reasoning by many others. Times had changed, it was asserted by the latter, and the reconstruction of outworn boundaries would not serve the purposes of a new Europe which had been deeply modified and invigorated by the French dynamism of the 1790's and the Napoleonic period. We see here the typical cleavage in interpreting the phrase "survival of independent states" — the supporters of the *status quo* against those of flux. The latter could show with cogency how a restoration of the old state system of the period before 1792 was impossible under the circumstances. For one thing, it was impossible to prevent further Russian gains in what had been Poland — Russia was one of the victorious powers; Russian policy was adamant in seeking to place a new small Poland under the Russian tsar; and, most persuasive of all, Russian troops effectively occupied Polish soil.

One may show that, although both had their weaknesses, the flux doctrine was better adapted to the harsh realities of history than the *status quo* position, particularly in the era of pronounced and fundamental changes from 1792 on. The supporters of the *status quo* represented a kind of idealistic conservatism, at once more artificial, more legalistic, and more anachronistic than its tougher cousin. The theorists who rejected the *status quo* in favor of a more fluid equilibrium represented a point of view which was more tenable as a long-term adjustment to the flow of history, tougher and more workable in the harsh world of statecraft by diplomacy. The former was more a short-term policy and a typical small-power attitude; the latter, a safer long-term one and more an expression of a big-power point of view.

Balance of Power and Machiavellianism. Balance-of-power policies have often eventuated in singularly sordid diplomatic acts and practices. No one denies this, but such an unsavory history has given rise to further confusion, this time with regard to the "Machiavellian" aims of the balance of power. In the twentieth century one lives, as far as equilibrist theory is concerned, in the shadow of an able and violent denunciation of balance-of-power policies by nineteenth- and twentieth-century liberals. Richard Cobden, for example, reeled off one of the most pungent bits of invective when he shouted in print: "The balance of power is a chimera! It is not a fallacy, a mistake, an imposture — it is an undescribed, indescribable, incomprehensible nothing; mere words, conveying to the mind not ideas, but sound."[14] Woodrow Wilson, an intellectual descendant of Cobden in his attitude toward the balance of power, helped greatly to consolidate its bad reputation in utterances like the following characterization of the balance as "a thing in which the balance was determined by the sword which was thrown in on one side or the other; a balance which was determined by the unstable equilibrium of competitive interests; a balance which was maintained by jealous watchfulness and an antagonism of interests."[15] The criticism of these and other men was so thundering that it succeeded in identifying balance of power with "Machiavellianism," both of which terms have now long been used and abused as derogatory. There is an appreciable gulf between the two as theoretical systems, and the matter is best settled at once. Attention is called to their respective aims, which are signally different.

Balance-of-power aims begin with the survival of the independent state and go on to group concern and the thwarting of preponderance of any one state. Where balance-of-power theory asserts that self-interest is best served by group interest, we have shown the argument to be partly a matter of faith. No such faith is apparent in Machiavelli, who accepts proposition number one (the survival of the independent state) and rejects propositions number two (group concern) and number three (preventing the preponderance of any single state). He may be said to argue, not that self-interest is best served by group interest, but that self-interest is best served by more and better attention to self-interest. His distillation of political advice in *The Prince* is a good illustration of this point.

There is, first of all, no direct concern with the state system in *The Prince*. The author, having lived in a time of troubles, when thrones were quickly won and lost, was primarily concerned with two things — how a prince could get and keep his crown and how he could get on in the world. *The Prince* thereby becomes a document for the individual state or the individual ruler, and not for the state system. The balance of power is neither discussed nor referred to in any important passage, although Machiavelli does urge something closely akin to it under certain circumstances:

> Again, the prince who holds a country differing in the above respects [language, customs, or laws] ought to make himself the head and defender of his less powerful neighbours, and to weaken the more powerful amongst them, taking care that no foreigner as powerful as himself shall, by any accident, get a footing there; for it will always happen that such a one will be introduced by those who are discontented.[16]

Here again, however, the concern of the author is not with the preservation of a system, but merely with the prince, who must maintain himself in adversity that he may be ready when opportunity should knock. An opportunity to conquer the world, a wholesale heresy to the equilibrist, would have been acceptable to Machiavelli, whose advice was directed toward possible aggrandizement, with no element of self-discipline which the balance theory would impose. The fact that *The Prince* was avidly read and greatly admired by Bonaparte is an accurate index to its essential incompatibility with the principles of balance of power, just as the disdain of Vattel — the careful and rational equilibrist — for Machiavelli is a similar indication of the same antithesis between the latter's ideas and equilibrist principles.

Moreover, *The Prince* is overwhelmingly concerned with domestic policy, typical examples of the author's advice being:

> It is necessary for a prince wishing to hold his own to know how to do wrong, and to make use of it or not according to necessity.[17]
>
> Injuries ought to be done all at one time, so that, being tasted less, they offend less; benefits ought to be given little by little, so that the flavour of them may last longer.[18]
>
> The chief foundations of all states, new as well as old or composite, are good laws and good arms; and as there cannot be good laws where the state is not well armed, it follows that where they are well armed they have good laws.[19]
>
> Those who solely by good fortune become princes from being private citizens have little trouble in rising, but much in keeping atop.[20]

The Prince, then, is not a balance-of-power document. It assumes the desirability of greatness for the individual state, whatever the cost to the system, and urges the unmitigated self-interest of the state. The balance-of-power theory, on the other hand, can be shown to be, at best, a theory of the general good, a theory of self-discipline, a theory of survival for the group and a theory of moderation; witness, for example, the following illuminating quotation from Koch, an early nineteenth-century writer on the balance of power:

> This system [balance of power] has for its object the preservation of the public tranquillity, the protection of the weak against the oppression of the strong, the blocking of the ambitious projects

of conquerors, and the prevention of discord, which in turn leads to the calamities of war. Uniting [the powers]...by one interest, it compels them to sacrifice their personal views to the general welfare, and it makes them...a single family.[21]

None of these benevolent characteristics may properly be claimed for the policies urged by Machiavelli. Compared to the nakedly "realistic" Machiavelli, the theorists of the balance of power appear as pure as an angel's intention — in theory, let us remember. It is perhaps possible that *The Prince* might have been substantially different, possibly even a balance-of-power handbook, if it had been written thirty years earlier, when the Italian peninsula still enjoyed a balance-of-power framework sufficient unto itself. Its author might even have made notable contributions to the theory. The peninsula framework was dealt its deathblow in the 1490's, however, and Machiavelli, writing in 1513, seems to have absorbed the pessimism of those later circumstances. He accepted the contemporary international anarchy as a situation incapable of mitigation, whereas the inchoate theory of balance of power was to move one step in the direction of order and organization and assert that a mitigation of existing international disorder was possible. Its remedies may have been far from perfect, but they did represent a step toward an ordered and stable Europe....

ENDNOTES

1 Lord Henry Brougham, *Works* (London and Glasgow, 1855-61), VIII, 80.

2 A.H.L. Heeren, *History of the Political System of Europe and Its Colonies* (Northampton, Mass., 1829), I, 12-13.

3 Emmerich de Vattel, *The Law of Nations* (Washington, 1916), III, 13, no. 14.

4 Cited by T.J. Lawrence, *Principles of International Law* (Boston, 1910), 130. Text may be found in George K. Rickards (ed.), *The Statutes of the United Kingdom of Great Britain and Ireland* (London, 1804-69), XXVIII, pt. I, 34.

5 Prince Metternich, *Mémoires, documents et écrits divers* (Paris, 1880-84), I, 30; cited by H. du Coudray, *Metternich* (New Haven: Yale University Press, 1936), 167-168.

6 French text in J. Holland Rose (ed.), *Select Despatches...relating to the Third Coalition against France, 1804-05* (London, 1904), App., 273; quoted by W. Alison Phillips, *The Confederation of Europe* (2d ed., New York, 1920), 40-41.

7 Friedrich von Gentz, *The State of Europe before and after the French Revolution* (pamphlet, London, 1801; trans. from *Von dem politischen Zustand von Europa vor und nach der französischen Revolution*, Berlin, 1801), 93; quoted by Theodore H. Von Laue, "History of the Balance of Power, 1494-1914," (unpubl. ms), p. 3.

8 Brougham, *Works*, VIII, 73.

9 Ibid. 72.

10 Friedrich von Gentz, *Fragments on the Balance of Power* (London, 1806), pp. 61-62.

11 *La science du gouvernement* (Paris, 1765), VI, 442; hereafter cited as Réal, *Science du gouvernement*. Quoted in Von Laue, "History of the Balance of Power," pp. 37-38.

12 Sidney B. Fay, "Balance of Power," *Encyclopaedia of the Social Sciences* (New York, 1937), I, 397.

13 J. Dumont, *Corps universel diplomatique du droit des gens* (Amsterdam, 1731), VIII, 391, col. 7.

14 Richard Cobden, *Political Writings* (London: 1867), I, 258.

15 Wilson in his response to an address at the Guildhall, London, Dec. 28, 1918, in Ray Stannard Baker and William E. Dodd, eds., *The Public Papers of Woodrow Wilson: War and Peace* (New York and London, 1927), I, 342.

16 *The Prince* (trans. by W.K. Marriott, London and New York, 1908), p. 20; for a passage which virtually trespasses upon the balance of power see ibid., pp. 178-179.

17 Ibid., p. 122.

18 Ibid., p. 73.

19 Ibid., p. 97.

20 Ibid., p. 53.

21 C.G. Koch, *Histoire abrégé des traités de paix, entre les puissances de l'Europe, depuis la paix de Westphalie* (re-ed. by F. Schoell, Paris, 1817-18), I, 3; quoted by Von Laue, "History of the Balance of Power," p. 62.

B: SYSTEM EVOLUTION

The Great Irresponsibles? The United States, the Soviet Union, and World Order

Hedley Bull

The behaviour of the United States and the Soviet Union in the late 1970s and 1980s suggests that they may be forfeiting the claims they had begun to build up in the 1960s and early 1970s to be regarded by others as responsible managers of the affairs of international society as a whole. These claims were never very strong, and the acceptance of them by other states was never more than partial and tentative, but the ability of the two superpowers to sustain this role was one of the slender sources of order in a basically disorderly world, and their apparent inability to sustain it any longer is one of many signs that these sources are drying up.

The concept of a great power has always had normative as well as positive connotations. To say that a state is a great power is to say not merely that it is a member of the club of powers that are in the front rank in terms of military strength, but also that it regards itself, and is regarded by other members of the society of states, as having special rights and duties.[1] The rights that a great power has include that of being entitled to a voice in the settlement of international issues beyond those that are of immediate concern to it, as for example the United Nations Charter recognizes when it accords special rights to permanent members of the Security Council over matters of peace and security. The duties that are expected of a great power include that of taking account of the interests and the views of other states in formulating their own policies, and the responsibility of defining its interests widely enough to encompass the preservation of an international system in which the bulk of member states regard themselves as having a stake.

Great powers are in a position to make a special contribution to the maintenance of international order. In the first place, they may do so by managing their relations with each other in an orderly way. The general peace and security of the international system is primarily a matter of relations among the great powers, and the steps they may take (but often fail to take) to preserve a general balance of power in the system, to avoid or control crises, and to limit or contain wars contribute to order in the sense of the maintenance of

Reprinted from the *International Journal*, Volume 25 (Summer 1980), pp. 437-47 by permission of the Canadian Institute of International Affairs.

elementary conditions of social life. In the second place, great powers may contribute to order by imposing it in areas where they are locally preponderant, by concluding understandings about spheres of influence that confirm one another's local preponderance and avoid friction, and sometimes by co-operating with one another to impose their joint will.

It is, of course, inherent in the position of great powers that their claim to special rights and duties should be constantly subject to challenge, even when they are in fact seeking to promote order and in this sense acting "responsibly". The order they are maintaining — not only in asserting local hegemony over weaker neighbours, agreeing upon spheres of influence, and uniting to impose their will on others, but also in co-operating to preserve peace among themselves — is their preferred order, and there are always forces abroad in the international system that will seek to replace this order with one that will embody some different set of values. The idea of the special rights and duties of great powers, moreover, embodies a principle of hierarchy that is at loggerheads with the principle of the equal sovereignty of states. Shifts in the distribution of power, furthermore, from time to time undermine the claims of the states to great power status and breed ambitions for it in others: at present, for example, it is not clear that Britain and France "deserve" the status conferred upon them by their permanent membership of the Security Council, while such ascendant states as West Germany, Japan, India, and Brazil either "deserve" a greater status that they have, or believe that they do.

Nevertheless, great powers are often able to make their special privileges acceptable to others for long periods. The desire for some minimum of order in the international system is so powerful and universal that there is a certain disposition to accept an order that embodies the values of the existing great powers in preference to a breakdown of order. Great powers are sometimes able to pursue policies that serve to make their special rights acceptable to others. It helps, for example, if they are meticulous in accepting the duties of great powerhood along with the rights, if they do not insist on spelling out their special rights explicitly, if they refrain from overtly disorderly acts themselves, if they show that they can be responsive to demands for change, and if they are able to co-opt secondary powers as collaborators or partners.

At the end of the Second World War only the United States and the Soviet Union were capable of playing the traditional role of a great power in world politics. The use of the term superpower to describe them (it was introduced in 1944 by W.T.R. Fox, who also applied it to Great Britain, then still at least in form one of the Big Three in the coalition against the Axis and the centre of a vast Empire-Commonwealth) recognized the gap which existed between these states of continental dimension, whose resources for military power had now been mobilized, and the older European great powers: just as, with the emergence of European states such as Austria, Spain, and France, Italian city-states could no longer aspire to be great powers, so European states in turn had been eclipsed. The term superpower does not add anything to the concept of a great power and is of only transitory importance. The significance of the perception that after the Second World War the United States and the Soviet Union were in a class of their own as superpowers was that it led to the recognition that in terms of power only these two states were fully capable of playing the role of great powers.

Neither superpower, however, was well suited to fulfil the normative requirements of great powerhood. The United States, it is true, had a vision of an international order based on economic liberalism and institutionalized co-operation to which many governments could be rallied. It possessed unprecedented wealth and was prepared to use it to restore societies and economies that had been shattered by the war and to influence them to accept its values and leadership. The openness of government in the United States made it uniquely accessible and intelligible to outsiders, and this too helped to make it acceptable as a world leader. Its role as the guarantor of the international monetary system was generally recognized, at least throughout the non-communist world, to be one which no other state could play. But apart from its involvement in Pacific affairs, it had no continuous tradition of involvement as a great power manager in co-operation with other great powers: in Europe its record was one of oscillation between isolationism and messianic interventionism, and in Latin America one of participation only on the basis of unchallenged primacy, if not of domination. Its power, at least in the first two decades after 1945, was overwhelming: indeed, if in this period there was any "threat" to the general balance of power, in the sense of a distribution of power throughout the system such that no one state was preponderant, it was from the United States rather than from the Soviet Union that this came. Flushed with victory and supremely confident of its own values, it sought, sometimes unilaterally and sometimes through the medium of the United Nations and a host of associated international organizations in which at the time it had a commanding position, to promote its own preferred vision of international order.

The Soviet Union was heir to the tradition of Russian great power diplomacy, but had repudiated this tradition and under Stalin as later under Khrushchev and Brezhnev continued to proclaim itself the centre of the world revolution. The vision of solidarity of the peoples of the world represented by communist parties enabled it to build up a network of states and movements loyal to its leadership, but it was a vision which antagonized the capitalist majority of the governments of the world. The Soviet Union, moreover, was not able to distinguish between the interests of the world communist movement and its own state interests and, beginning with the conflict between Stalin and Tito, drove its own communist allies into one form or another of rebellion and secession from the Soviet bloc, or of sullen acquiescence in a Soviet leadership based on coercion. The Soviet Union gained a certain credit in other areas of the world as a consequence of the role it played in checking the power of the United States: although in no sense the equal of the United States in economic or even in military power before the end of the 1960s, it nevertheless represented the second most important concentration of power in the world and the chief obstacle to American preponderance. The Soviet Union's power was thus the condition of other states' freedom of manoeuvre, and especially in the Third World a virtual alliance, if only for limited purposes, grew up between Moscow and those states and political movements whose main objective was to escape domination by the United States and its allies: in particular, the struggle of Third World states and movements against colonial rule, white supremacism in Africa, and economic dependence on the West was much facilitated by Soviet support. But Soviet power was also used to impose Moscow's own forms of domination, and as it grew those exposed to it in Eastern and Western Europe, in China and Japan, in the Middle East, and more recently in Africa and southwest Asia came to fear Soviet power itself more than they valued its contribution to global equilibrium.

Neither in the United States (despite its attachment to a theory of 'checks and balances' in domestic politics) nor in the Soviet Union is there even today any instinctive understanding of the principle that the overweening power of a state, even if it has been accumulated by innocent processes of domestic economic and social progress, provides other states and peoples with grounds for legitimate concern. In both there is rather an instinctive belief that the menace to others of superior power is cancelled out by virtuous purposes — the good intentions of a democratic society with a unique vocation for human betterment, or the progressive historical mission of a communist party and state dedicated to the liberation of oppressed peoples and menacing only to reactionary governments. The United States and the Soviet Union, moreover, are both societies (the former more than the latter) that are self-absorbed and inattentive to values and perspectives other than their own, in a way that only very large societies can be (China and India also have this characteristic). In addition, the United States and the Soviet Union, when they assumed the status of superpowers, were in a position of relative economic self-sufficiency and lack of dependence upon the international economy which, even though it has since declined, still leaves them (as Kenneth Waltz has recently pointed out) much less dependent that the traditional European great powers were.[2]

Given these beginnings, it is scarcely surprising that the United States and the Soviet Union, having created in the United Nations Security Council a more highly formalized instrument for great power co-operation in managing the international system than any which had existed previously, quickly discarded it and became embroiled in a struggle as to which of their respective visions of the future would prevail. Yet between 1963 and 1974 — from the Partial Test-Ban Treaty to the Vladivostok Accords — the superpowers nevertheless managed to create a structure of co-operation which, rudimentary although it was, was widely recognized throughout international society as a whole to embody hopes, if not for the building of peace in any positive sense then at least for the avoidance of general nuclear war. This structure of co-operation did not originate in the traditional outlooks or foreign policy doctrines of the United States and the Soviet Union, nor was it the consequence of any tendency to convergence as between the one and the other, such as was sometimes proclaimed to be taking place. It was improvised in response to new and unexpected dangers that gave them a sense of a common interest in survival. This sense of a common interest in avoiding a ruinous nuclear war, which had developed during the height of the Cold War in the 1950s, came in the course of the 1960s and early 1970s to be translated into at first inchoate rules or guidelines for the avoidance and control of crises and into understandings about arms control, which later in some cases were institutionalized in formal agreements, the most important of which were, of course, the strategic arms limitation and related agreements of May 1972.

It is important not to exaggerate the significance of the agreements of this period. The sense of common interests that underlay them was limited to the avoidance of nuclear war. Projects for a more comprehensive détente — a general relaxation of the Soviet-American struggle, leading to progress from coexistence to positive co-operation, as distinct from a mere understanding that the struggle would be conducted within certain limits — did not come to fruition. It is true that the sense of common interest in avoiding nuclear war was sometimes accompanied by a sense of common interest in resisting challenges to superpower predominance, as from nuclear proliferation in France, China, and (as a theoretical possibility, but one with which the Soviet Union in its approach to the Non-Proliferation Treaty displayed an obsessive concern) West Germany. It is true that the agreements about arms control and crisis avoidance were in fact followed up by the series of agreements normalizing relations and legitimizing boundaries in Europe, initiated by West German Ostpolitik but embracing the superpowers and others through the 1971 Berlin agreement and the 1975 Helsinki Final Act. It is true that the Nixon-Kissinger program for an "era of negotiation," a "structure of peace" embracing many-sided co-operation between the superpowers, aroused in the American public hopes of a comprehensive relaxation of tension and "end of the Cold War," the bitter disappointment of which underlies the present American reaction against both the Soviet Union and Western détente policies. But these hopes were never justified, and it is unlikely that any such relaxation was ever contemplated on the Soviet side.

Nor did the agreements concluded in the field of arms control (most notably the Partial Test-Ban Treaty, the Outer Space Treaty, the Seabed Treaty, the Non-Proliferation Treaty, and ABM Treaty, and the interim agreement on strategic offensive missile launchers) do more than enable the superpowers to take a few faltering steps towards the objectives which arms control theory prescribed. Apart from the ABM Treaty (whose effects on stability are ambiguous and which now seems in danger of being dismantled) nothing was accomplished by formal agreement to increase the stability of the strategic nuclear balance: most importantly, the threat to stability posed by the improving counterforce capacity of strategic offensive forces was left uncontrolled, and from the time of the United States Senate's ratification of the 1972 SALT I agreements, the Strategic Arms Limitation Talks (SALT) came to centre upon a quest for strategic "parity" which was essentially irrelevant to the goal of strategic stability. Still less did arms control agreements achieve such goals as the curbing of the strategic "arms race" or the reduction of the level of strategic arms. The most that was achieved by arms control was that the superpowers were shown to be capable of reaching serious agreements in this field; that a body of experience about the negotiation of agreements and their implementation and verification was accumulated; and that certain areas of arms competition of secondary importance to the superpowers were placed out of court for the time being (atmospheric nuclear testing, stationing of weapons of mass destruction in outer space and on the seabed, biological weapons, dissemination of nuclear weapons).

It should also be remembered that the coming together of the superpowers in the 1960s and early 1970s was by no means universally acclaimed by the rest of the world: there was concern, in some cases legitimate concern, that bargains were being struck at the expense of others. The Soviet Union's drawing closer to the United States took place *pari passu* with an open rupture of its relationship with China, and in response China developed a thesis of the threat from "superpower hegemonism" that gained a good deal of support within the Third World. France, which like China sought to develop itself as a nuclear weapon power, boycotted the Soviet-American-led arms control process and sought to downgrade its significance. India and other "threshold nuclear powers" that felt that the Non-Proliferation Treaty would constrict them developed a thesis of the need to balance "horizontal proliferation" with "vertical proliferation," a thesis designed to show to how little an extent the accumulation of nuclear arms by the superpowers had been affected by arms control discussions. In both Eastern and Western Europe fears grew that a Soviet-American conflict might be fought out in Europe while the territories of the superpowers themselves were spared. There were fears in Western Europe, expressed in the de Gaulle-Adenauer axis in the 1960s, that the United States, in entering into the "adverse partnership" with the Soviet Union, would sacrifice European interests; and in Western Europe there was concern, partly vindicated when the United States failed to respond to the Soviet invasion of Czechoslovakia in 1968, that superpower understanding meant that the Soviet Union now had a free hand within its own sphere of influence.

We have also to remember that collaboration between the superpowers, even if it had gone much further than the short distance it went between 1963 and 1974, was in any case a very insufficient basis for international order: the ability of the superpowers, even when united, to control international events appeared to be declining in this period. At the beginning of the era of détente, the feeling was sometimes expressed (by John Strachey among others) that the United States and the Soviet Union could combine to impose some form of condominium on the world, at least in respect of possession of nuclear weapons.[3] But the recovery of Western Europe and Japan during the 1960s, China's emergence at the end of that decade from the Cultural Revolution, and in the early 1970s the demonstration of oil power by a group of Third World countries and the defeat of the United States in Vietnam demonstrated the limits of superpower control. Kissinger, while in office, sought to respond to this with his vision of a wider concert of powers, but this remains no more than a vision. In the 1980s few would argue that a combination of the superpowers, even if it were available, would offer a viable route to world order.

Nevertheless, the United States and the Soviet

Union, by drawing together in these years, did give the impression that they were creating at least the foundation of a more secure international order. Having stepped back from the brink at which they stood in the 1962 Cuban missile crisis, they set about creating some rules and guidelines, such that when they faced one another in crisis situations again, as in the 1967 and 1973 Middle East wars, their behavior seemed more predictable. The world came to sense that some of the tension had lessened in the relationship between the superpowers, that the danger of nuclear war was less immediate, that the perils of the nuclear age might after all be surmounted, at least in the short run. As against the picture of nuclear powers rushing madly towards one another on a collision course, drawn, for example, by Bertrand Russell during the Cuban missile crisis, the United States and the Soviet Union had begun to make credible their claims to be acting responsibly. There was never any doubt that for all the fears, the genuine fears expressed by third parties of bargains struck at their expense, the avoidance of a superpower nuclear war was a vital interest not only of the United States and the Soviet Union but of all the states and peoples of the world.

Great powers cannot expect to be conceded special rights if they do not perform special duties. What we have been witnessing since the mid-1970s is the abandonment by the superpowers of their postures as responsible managers. The work of erecting a structure of co-operation has been abandoned, and what had been put in place is beginning to decay. The comprehensive détente which Kissinger sought to bring about has wholly disappeared, and the policy of working for it is so deeply rejected by the American public that Kissinger himself has virtually erased it from his own record of the period.[4] The SALT negotiations have been all but abandoned, and even if they were to be resumed, it is unlikely that the momentum that was originally behind them could be built up again. The answer which the superpowers were once able to give non-nuclear weapon signatory states of the Non-Proliferation Treaty, that they were negotiating seriously towards a reduction of nuclear armaments, cannot now command a shred of credibility. Both superpowers are now engaged in massive increases of arms and arms expenditure and are displaying an increasing resolve to threaten and use force.

I am not concerned here to judge the question which superpower is responsible for the collapse of détente — to weigh the American charge that the Soviet Union in its strategic nuclear build-up, its pursuit of theatre superiority in Europe, and its new military interventionism in the Third World has broken the rules of détente, against the Soviet Union's charge that it is being encircled by a coalition of the United States, Western Europe, Japan, and China and that the rules of détente never required a cessation of the ideological struggle. I do not even make the assumption that the collapse of détente could have been avoided at all: it may be that we shall come to recognize that two such rivals could never in any case have cohabited on this basis for more than a fleeting moment, that projects for a solid and enduring partnership were from the beginning illusory.

We do have to recognize, however, that this change has come about. The United States and the Soviet Union today have little claim to be regarded as nuclear trustees for mankind; as in the 1950s they are mobilizing against themselves one of the most powerful emotions in the world today, the fear of war. The Soviet Union, through its military action in Afghanistan and its indirect interventions in Africa, is creating in the Third World the same antagonism towards itself that has long been felt for the countries of the West and which, because of the accident of its lack of historical involvement in most parts of the Third World, it had previously been able to avoid. The United States, through its belligerent statements and preparations for renewed military intervention, its policies evidently fashioned to express moods rather than to achieve results, its inability to withstand domestic forces of chauvinism and greed, has done much to undermine its own position as the leader of the West and to accentuate the ugliness of the face it turns towards the Third World. The disintegration of the international order at the present time has other sources besides the recent behaviour of the superpowers, and there is no more shallow diagnosis of our present discontents than that which attributes them solely to what has been done or not done by the United States and the Soviet Union, but it is difficult to find evidence in any part of the world that they are still viewed as the "great responsibles".

ENDNOTES

1 This is spelt out at length in my *The Anarchical Society* (London: Macmillan, 1977), chapter 9.

2 Kenneth Waltz, *Theory of International Politics* (Reading, Mass: Addison-Wesley, 1979).

3 See John Strachey, *On the Prevention of War* (London: Macmillan, 1962). The concept of condominium is explored by Carsten Holbraad in *Superpowers and International Conflict* (New York: St. Martin's Press, 1979).

4 Henry A. Kissinger, *The White House Years* (Boston: Little, Brown, 1979).

B: SYSTEM EVOLUTION

The U.S. and Soviet Stakes in Nuclear Nonproliferation

Joseph S. Nye

In the aftermath of the invasion of Afghanistan and the advent of the Reagan administration, cooperation between the U.S. and the Soviet Union seems to have diminished, particularly in the area of arms control. Nuclear nonproliferation is the oldest area of Soviet-American cooperation in arms control, dating back to the establishment of the International Atomic Energy Agency (IAEA) in the 1950s. But the fact that the two countries have a common interest does not mean that there is necessarily an equal interest or that it can survive the current tension.

Some analysts argue that the Soviet Union has more at risk from proliferation than does the United States. For example, many of the potential new entrants to nuclear weapons status — India, Pakistan, Korea, Taiwan, Iraq — are countries geographically close to the Soviet Union and distant from the United States. Thus, it could be argued that the Soviet Union has more to fear than we do, and from the zero-sum perspective of the U.S.-Soviet hostility, further proliferation may hurt the Soviet Union more than the United States. To judge whether this is a sensible basis for policy, or whether cooperative action is a better basis, requires a closer look at the skeptical arguments.

Joseph S. Nye, "The U.S. and Soviet Stakes in Nuclear Nonproliferation," *PS*, Vol. 15 (Winter 1982), pp. 32-39. Reprinted with the permission of the American Political Science Association and the author. Portions of the text have been deleted. Some footnotes have been removed; those remaining have been renumbered.

DOES PROLIFERATION MATTER MUCH?

A basic skepticism argues that proliferation of nuclear weapons does not matter and might even have a beneficial stabilizing effect on world politics.[1] Just as nuclear weapons have produced prudence in the U.S.-Soviet balance of power over the last 35 years, so may they also stabilize regional balances of power. From this point of view, there is little American interest in halting proliferation. But the transferability of prudence assumes stable governments, stable command and control systems, the absence of serious civil war and strife, the absence of strong destabilizing motivations such as irredentist passion, and discipline over temptation for preemptive strikes during the early stages when new nuclear weapons capabilities are soft and vulnerable. Clearly, such assumptions are unrealistic in many parts of the world. On the contrary, rather than enhancing its security, the first effects of acquiring new nuclear capability in many circumstances may be to increase a state's vulnerability and insecurity. The question of preemptive strike which has been treated as a purely hypothetical situation up to now has been given a new sense of reality by the Israeli raid upon Iraq's research reactor in June 1981.

The destablizing aspects of proliferation are further complicated if one thinks of possible roles of nonstate actors. Whatever the prospect of successful acquisition of a nuclear device by a terrorist group, even threats of such action may create severe civil difficulties. Moreover, the possible theft of weapons-usable materials and black market sale to maverick states means that the problems posed by nonstate actors do not depend solely on their technological capabilities.

DOES PROLIFERATION MATTER TO THE SUPERPOWERS?

A second and more limited version of the skeptic's argument is that proliferation may be dangerous for the particular countries that become involved in a regional nuclear arms race, but that such an arms race would have little effect on the rest of the world. In particular, the skeptics argue, it would not affect the global balance of power since the nuclear superpowers could always technically outrace the new entrants. From this point of view, it is not worthwhile for the two superpowers to invest much political capital in preventing the erosion of the nonproliferation regime.

But this argument is also flawed. While there may be some areas in which proliferation might lead to a degree of disengagement by the United States, there are many regions where the United States as a global power cannot be uninvolved. In such situations, the presence of insecure nuclear weapons makes the projection of our power (especially the safety of our troops) more dangerous. The same can be said for the Soviet Union.

In addition, it is not true that local proliferation would have no effect upon the central strategic balance. One of the most striking features about the current balance of power is the continued bipolarity at the nuclear level — an outcome of World War II that both the United States and the Soviet Union share an interest in maintaining.

Since 1945, the two great powers of the pre-war period, Germany and Japan, have been reintegrated into world coalitions and politics as the third and fourth most powerful states in economic terms without their feeling it necessary to develop equivalent nuclear military power. This makes the central strategic balance more calculable and contributes to stability in Europe and Asia. While theoretical arguments have been made about the stability of multi-balances compared to bipolar balances, these have all involved pre-nuclear periods in history, and one cannot generalize to the nuclear era.

If there were widespread nuclear proliferation it might call into question the basic decisions hitherto maintained by Germany and Japan and thus have a quite powerful effect upon the strategic balance which even the most sanguine superpower strategists could not ignore. On the other hand, if countries are able to achieve their goals of security, status and economic well-being without the necessity of developing military nuclear power, the prospects improve for the evolution of new forms of effective power, coalitions, and institutions.

It is worth noting that the rate of the spread of nuclear weapons makes a big difference. If the rate of spread is slow, it is easier to manage the destablizing effects. A rapid rate of proliferation, on the other hand, may lead to a tipping point or scramble in which the destablizing effects are difficult to manage diplomatically, and the prospects increase that nuclear weapons might be used. And even a local use of nuclear weaponry would be a serious breach of a 35-year global taboo.

Finally, the spread of nuclear weapons increases the prospects that nonstate groups and terrorists will gain access to materials. It is unlikely that the superpowers would necessarily remain isolated from the effects. Indeed, given the openness of Western society and the closed nature of Soviet society, this dimension might be worse for the West than for the Soviet Union.

Given our limited experience, there are no

decisive answers in the debate over the effects of proliferation. Particular outcomes may differ in different regions. Some cases may start a disastrous chain of events; others may turn out to have benign effects. Nonetheless, the United States as a superpower, particularly one that plays a critical role in maintaining an international regime of norms and rules that discourage proliferation, must take a prudent and cautious approach to the assessment of possible effects of proliferation. The consequences of guessing wrong about effects are not the same in both directions. A stable outcome may be a happy regional surprise, but an unstable outcome that triggers a chain of proliferation events could have severe consequences for our global interests.

DOES PROLIFERATION HURT THE SOVIETS MORE THAN THE U.S.?

A third argument made by the skeptics is that while proliferation may be bad for local countries involved and bad for superpowers in general terms, it is sufficiently worse for the Soviet Union than for the United States and that there is a silver lining in terms of American interests. Paul Zinner, for example, argues that proliferation would threaten Soviet security, diminish its ability to project power through military means, and reduce its stature as a global power. Proliferation would constitute "still another roadblock in the tortuous Soviet march toward hegemony and might thus change the style and method of Soviet foreign policy to make it less abrasive and less confrontationally oriented." In sum, Zinner says, "under the impact of the nuclear proliferation the Soviet Union would become a more sensible member of the global community and play a more constructive role in it."[2]

This argument is not very convincing. While proliferation might interfere with Soviet capabilities to project power at low levels of risk, it would also interfere with similar American capabilities. There are other ways of increasing the risks for the Soviets in projecting power at a lower level of cost to the United States' global interest than by encouragement of nuclear proliferation. Zinner argues that the possession of nuclear weapons by both Iran and Pakistan would tend to interdict the introduction of significant military force into Afghanistan for fear of precipitating a regional crisis that could get out of hand. This was written before the invasion of Afghanistan and the revolution in Iran, but it is hard to see how a weak, vulnerable nuclear capability in Iran, Pakistan, or Afghanistan would have significantly altered the outcome of events in that area in the late 1970s. If anything, the experience of being targeted by weak, unstable regimes might have increased Soviet willingness to take risks rather than diminished it.

Zinner also argues that a nuclear-capable South Africa could effectively prevent the supply of significant amounts of conventional armaments to various insurgency and national liberation movements which threaten its safety and security. This would reduce Soviet opportunities. But it is hard to follow this reasoning. How credible and effective would a South African nuclear capability be against guerilla forces or as a threat against neighboring countries' acquiescence or support for the activity of guerilla forces? Economic or conventional military instruments are more effective, and even they have not prevented the dynamics of the racial issues of southern Africa from unfolding.

At a more general level, Zinner argues that further proliferation would diminish the applicability of military power as an effective instrument of foreign policy and thus enhance the utility of political and economic tools, particularly in the Third World. This, he argues, would benefit the United States compared to the Soviet Union. In this sense,

> proliferation would tend to put the existing relationship between the two superpowers in its true perspective. The Soviet Union has achieved parity with the United States in the military area only.... By curtailing the application of military power, nuclear proliferation would substantially contribute to

> dispelling this illusion. Under the circumstances the Soviet Union could not offset the superior ability of the United States to increase its influence through political and economic means.[3]

This argument rests upon a view of nuclear weapons as a great equalizer. But nuclear weapons are not such an equalizer. There is more difference between having a few crude explosives which cannot be mated to a modern delivery system and having an advanced nuclear arsenal than there is between apples and oranges. It is more the difference between having one or two apples and having a productive orchard. In short, this argument rests upon an over simplified view of the political and military effects of nuclear weapons.

A policy of encouraging proliferation as a way to redress U.S. strategic weakness is like using amputation to cure a sprained ankle. A far better policy instrument is to improve our own defense posture. We would have far more control and there would be fewer collateral political costs from that type of response. In short, the three skeptical arguments remind us not to be doctrinaire about our support for nonproliferation. But an analysis of their arguments and a council of prudence leads us back to the main lines that have formed our policy and Soviet policy over the last two decades.

PAST AND PRESENT U.S.-SOVIET COOPERATION

When we look at the past record of Soviet and American cooperation on nonproliferation, we find that it is imperfect but, compared to the overall relationship, relatively impressive. On the other hand, just as in overall relations, there is always a tension between the zero-sum and nonzero-sum aspects of the relationship.

In the 1950s, during the establishment of IAEA, the Soviets attempted to curry favor with India but eventually came around to a stricter view of international safeguards.[4] Similarly, in the 1960s during the discussions of the Non-Proliferation Treaty (NPT), the Soviets tried to use the proliferation issue to divide Germany and the United States. And even in the 1970s, in the meetings of the Nuclear Suppliers Group, there were still echoes of the Soviet anti-German campaign.

Nonetheless, the core of cooperation in the late 1970s (before Afghanistan) was relatively impressive. The Soviets cooperated in the formation of the Nuclear Suppliers Group in 1975 and agreed to compromises which allowed the Nuclear Suppliers guidelines to be promulgated in January 1978. They cooperated by insisting that India attach safeguards to all facilities in which Soviet heavy water might be used rather than the looser standard of safeguards which India preferred. They shared information with the United States regarding the possibility of a nuclear test site in the Kalahari area in South Africa in 1977, and later acceded to American requests for behaviour in the United Nations that would not prevent negotiation aimed at extending the presence of international safeguards over South African facilities. In the late 1970s, there was no reason to complain that the Soviets accentuated the zero-sum over the common interests aspects of the proliferation relationship any more than the United States did.

Indeed, ... the United States has not always informed the Soviet Union of its actions in the nonproliferation area as fully as it had promised to do. While this reduced contact and consultation reflects the overall state of U.S.-Soviet relations, it is the United States which is the immediate source of the reduction.

Current U.S. policy on nonproliferation remains quite similar to that of previous administrations. There is a considerable contrast between the seven-point program announced by the Reagan administration in July 1981 and some of the earlier press reports of the intention to change proliferation policy early in the new administration.[5] To some extent, this reflects the tendency of all new administrations to accentuate the political difference of their approach from that of their predecessors during the highly politicized early days and their gradual adjustment to the realities of the international security situation as time goes on. The Israeli raid in June also speeded up the process. In any case, American policy is not radically changed, and there are not major differences between Soviet and American general policies toward nonproliferation and nuclear exports.

Soviet policy on nuclear exports has always been quite stringent.[6] In the past, the Soviets have required not only IAEA safeguards but return of spent fuel from the reactors they have exported to Eastern Europe and Finland. This means that the spent fuel cannot be reprocessed locally to recover the plutonium-a weapons-usable materials. The Soviets strongly supported the concept of full-scope safeguards in the Nuclear Suppliers Group meetings.

The United States has some current concern, however, about Soviet plans to export nuclear materials and reactors to two countries outside of Eastern Europe: Libya and Cuba. A Soviet-built research reactor in Libya is not a matter of great concern since its small size and use of highly enriched uranium does not make it suitable for clandestine weapons material production. However, the Soviets have also contracted to build a 440 megawatt power reactor in Libya. While it will probably be a decade before this project comes to fruition (if ever), the United States has expressed concern about nuclear exports to Libya in general and about return of any spent fuel in particular.

Similarly, it will probably be a decade before the two 440 megawatt power reactors that the Soviet Union has planned to build in Cuba will come on stream. The United States has again expressed concern that the Soviet Union should require the return of the spent fuel. The Soviets, on the other hand, have argued that logistical problems make this difficult for exports at such a great distance.

More such problems might arise in the future. There is reason to believe that the Soviet capability to produce nuclear reactors once their large Atomash plant goes fully into production will exceed their ability to find domestic locations for the plants, and that the Soviet Union will wish to become a larger factor in the world export market. On the other hand, this domestic capability is well behind schedule; world demand is slack, and the problem may not arise for some time. In any case, both in general and in specific cases mentioned above, there are grounds for the United States to wish to reinforce Soviet stringency on nuclear export policy.

AREAS OF POSSIBLE FUTURE COOPERATION

Looking ahead, one could imagine a number of possible areas for cooperation between the United States and the Soviet Union in nonproliferation. They can even be ranked in rough order of their difficulty of achievement in terms of the overall political climate between the countries. I will discuss these possibilities in ascending level of difficulty.

1. Increase Low Level but Regular Consultations. During the first half of the Carter administration, there were regular consultations between the United States and the Soviet Union on nonproliferation policy issues both in the context of the Nuclear Suppliers Group meetings and the regular meetings of the IAEA as well as diplomatic approaches relating to specific problem cases. The frequency of such conversations has diminished, now being limited primarily to the IAEA Board meetings. Such consultations can be quite useful in terms of information and coordination of policy on relatively noncontroversial issues such as full-scope safeguards, attitudes toward international plutonium storage and so forth. With low political visibility, they can be relatively decoupled from the problems of the overall U.S./Soviet political relationship.

2. Joint Demarches on the NPT. There is some value to having the superpowers indicate that, despite their differences, the Nonproliferation Treaty is a matter of importance to both. Joint demarches asking states to adhere to the Nonproliferation Treaty can be useful in their symbolism, as well as in their direct effect. In the past, the Soviet Union has suggested such joint demarches and the United States has agreed to coordinate. But in the recent past, this coordination has fallen into abeyance.

3. Completing the Treaty of Tlatelolco. The Treaty of Tlatelolco, signed in 1967, establishes a nuclear free zone in Latin America.[7] Unless a signatory waives the condition, it is not fully binding until all signatories have completed ratification. Argentina and Cuba have not completed ratification. While the treaty is not a perfect instrument, it nonetheless serves as another layer of normative constraint on potential proliferators in the Latin American area. If Argentina fulfills its promise given to the U.S. in 1977 to ratify the treaty, only Cuba will remain as a non-ratifying state in the region. The Soviets could be helpful in pressing the Cubans toward ratification.

4. Spent Fuel Return. As mentioned above, the United States is concerned about the return of spent fuel from Libya and Cuba. In the recently signed nuclear cooperation agreement between the U.S. and Egypt, there is an important provision allowing the United States to require the return of the spent fuel. Generalization of the Egyptian-type provisions to areas of tension, such as the Middle East or areas of concern such as Eastern Europe or the Caribbean, could be a useful layer of protection against diversion of spent fuel for weapons purposes. This might be further related to multilateral efforts in the IAEA to develop international spent fuel and plutonium storage depots.[8] In any case, the standard of additional stringency toward spent fuel in the areas of tension would a be a useful step for the superpowers to endorse.

5. A Middle Eastern Zone. Eugene Rostow... has expressed an interest in developing a nuclear-free zone in the Middle East. Given the hostility among the parties in the area and their refusal to talk directly with each other, the obstacles are enormous. On the other hand, the idea of developing an additional level of restraint in the Middle East makes sense. One way to do this would be to try to generalize the existing Israeli statement that they will not be the first to introduce nuclear weapons in the Middle East.

In the absence of agreement to negotiate among the states in the area, this might be done by having the two superpowers offer a guarantee of no nuclear attack against any state which agrees with the superpowers not to be the first to introduce nuclear weapons in the Middle East (and verified by a no explosion pledge). In other words, the agreement would be between the separate parties in the Middle East and the two superpowers, and the *quid pro quo* would be the superpower non-attack guarantee. While this would take a considerable degree of superpower coordination, it is one way of approaching a Middle East nuclear weapons free zone in a situation where the local parties are unable or unwilling to talk to each other.

6. Sanctions against Proliferators. From time to time it has been argued that if there is a violation of IAEA safeguards or if there is another explosion of a nuclear device, the reaction of the superpowers will be critical in terms of the effect of the particular event upon further proliferators. The IAEA safeguard system is a set of legal undertakings not to divert nuclear materials from peaceful to military uses and to allow international inspectors to verify that fact. The system need not be perfect to deter diversion. It requires a reasonable probability of detection and a reasonably strong response. Basically, it is like a a burglar alarm. If the alarm works but the police do not react, it will have little effect as a deterrent in the future.

On the other hand, this is the kind of situation where each superpower is tempted to seek separate political advantage by limiting the degree of its reaction against the new proliferator. The mildness of the American and Soviet reactions to the Indian explosion in 1974 is a case in point. While this may be the most difficult area to achieve any cooperation in a time of superpower hostility — witness the geopolitical conjunction of Pakistan and Afghanistan — its importance nonetheless remains.

CONCLUSIONS

Nonproliferation remains an area of joint interest to the superpowers. As the largest states in the system, they have a particularly important role in maintaining the regime of norms, institutions and procedures which has placed the burden of proof upon the proliferator. This normative presumption against proliferation is a rare outcome in a world of sovereign states. Moreover, as superpowers unable to separate their interests from those of all regions, they have an interest in avoiding the prospect of local instability taking on a nuclear dimension.

Despite these common interests, U.S.-Soviet cooperation will be limited by their hostility and their competitive relationship. To the extent that they focus upon the zero-sum dimensions of the two-party game of U.S.-Soviet relations, there will be temptations to sell short the common interest in proliferation in order to score points against each other. But each is involved in other games as well. And for these other games, proliferation would not be beneficial. In that sense, the tensions in the cooperation over proliferation are unavoidable. But so also are the joint gains. We hurt our national security if we neglect them.

ENDNOTES

1 See, for example, Kenneth Waltz, "What Will the Spread of Nuclear Weapons Do to the World," in John Kerry King, ed., *International Political Effects of the Spread of Nuclear Weapons* (Washington: G.P.O., 1979); also, *The Spread of Nuclear Weapons: More May Be Better* (London: International Institute for Strategic Studies, 1981).

2 Paul E. Zinner, "The Soviet Union in a Proliferated World," in J. King, ed., *International Political Effects* p. 122.

3 Ibid., p. 113.

4 See Lawrence Scheinman, "The International Atomic Energy Agency," in Robert Cox and Harold Jacobson, eds., *The Anatomy of Influence* (New Haven: Yale Univ. Press, 1973).

5 President Reagan, "Nuclear Non-Proliferation," July 16, 1981 (Washington: Department of State, Current Policy No. 303).

6 See Gloria Duffy, "Soviet Nuclear Exports," *International Security*, 3 (Summer 1978), 83-111.

7 See Alfonso Garcia Robles, *The Latin American Nuclear Weapon Free Zone* (muscatine, Stanley Foundation Occasional Paper 19, 1979).

8 For elaboration, see J.S. Nye, "Maintaining a Non-Proliferation Regime," in George Quester, ed., *Nuclear Proliferation* (Madison: Univ. of Wisconsin Press, 1981).

C: MECHANISMS OF REGULATION

The Use of Force and Moral Norms

Stanley Hoffmann

TAMING THE UNTAMABLE

The problem of the use of force is central to the subject of ethics and foreign policy. In the first place, the use of force in international affairs is obviously the greatest obstacle to moral behavior; the belief so well expressed by General Sherman that "war is hell," and that therefore there is nothing one should or can do to "refine" it, is a manifestation of this. As long as states use force against one another, citizens will be torn between their duties as citizens and their consciousness as reasonable and moral beings whose thoughts and feelings transcend borders. Also, wars provide the greatest opportunities for national self-righteousness and for the denial of the humanity and the rights of others. Finally, it is in war that the greatest opportunity exists for statesmen, and for military commanders, to plead necessity, to argue that they really have no choice, that what they do is literally imposed upon them by military imperatives. And yet the use of force remains the essence of the international milieu despite all of the efforts of lawyers and statesmen to do away with it, despite the League of Nations and the Briand-Kellogg pact and despite the U.N. Charter.

The contradiction between attempts at moralizing international politics and the actors' free resort to force accounts for the ideological and historical diversity of the ways of dealing with this subject. Ideologically, at any given moment we find a range of attitudes which go at one end from absolute pacifists, adepts of non-violence who reject any use of force at all, to the glorification of war at the other end — as a historical necessity and a moral good, as a force which, as Hegel saw it, makes people transcend the selfishness, mediocrity, and inevitable corruption of civil society and tests the virtue of citizens and states. Historically, the attempts at introducing ethical considerations into this subject have gone through three very different phases. Many centuries were dominated by the "just war" theory, which was a doctrine of restraints on the causes and on the conduct of war before the sovereign territorial state became the prevalent structure of the international system. Then, during a second phase, which lasted two and a half or three centuries, the age of sovereignty, war was treated essentially as a morally neutral fact and therefore could be indulged in by states whenever they had a reason for it; the only

---

Stanley Hoffmann, *Duties Beyond Borders: On the Limits and Possibilities of Ethical International Politics* (Syracuse, N.Y.: Syracuse University Press, 1981), pp. 45-55. Some footnotes have been deleted; those remaining have been renumbered.

rules which tried to deal with war were rules on how to fight, but not on why to fight: rules on the conduct of war. Finally, for the last half century or so, an extraordinary discrepancy has grown between the collapse, for ideological and technological reasons, of all the restraints which had been more or less carefully worked out in the past, and the frantic search for new, more drastic restraints on the other. So that the literature which now deals with the problem of ethics and the use of force can be seen as an attempt at building up a new "just war" theory, for an age in which the territorial sovereign state is still very much with us — indeed, it keeps proliferating — but war has gone completely out of hand and threatens to destroy sovereignty itself.

This literature has been growing rapidly in the recent past. One most important addition is Michael Walzer's *Just and Unjust Wars.*[1] Since I share his moral theory and agree with many of his precepts, much of this essay will read like a gloss on his work. I will again begin with a look at the dilemmas and then suggest some answers.

It is useful to start with an examination of the old "just war" theory which remains the only coherent doctrine that has ever lasted on this subject for no less than a dozen centuries.[2] Looking at what would happen to it if it were applied in the twentieth century tells us a great deal about the ethical dilemmas in the realm of force. The most obvious point is the inadequacy of traditional "just war" theory to the world in which we are, and the roots of the trouble are fairly clear. There is an old root and there is a new one. The old one dates from the beginning of the age of the territorial state. In a fragmented world of territorial states without a sovereign over them, in a world in which each actor resorts to self-preservation and self-help, how can one assure that moral imperatives dealing with force will be neither so loose as to permit practically everything in the competition of states, or so strict as to be absolutely inapplicable given that competition? The new root of trouble which has been added by the twentieth century is also very obvious — how can any system of restraints be respected in the new technological circumstances of this age? In other words, even if one could overcome the fundamental contradiction between restraints and sovereign states, which is not very easy, could one still corset war, given the technology which is now in use? "Technology cannot make men bad, but it may surely give rise to circumstances in which it is increasingly difficult to be good."[3]

The old doctrine was an attempt at dealing with the problem of force not by a ban but by a harness. The Catholic writers from Saint Augustine on realized that violence was part of human life and could not be suppressed or denied in the earthly city; the problem became one of using it for the good of people rather than for evil. The result of this attempt at harnessing force was a series of restraints both on ends and on means. War would be just only if fought with the right intention by the prince — peace and justice, not revenge — and waged for a just cause which could be either self-defense *or* a cause of sufficient concern to the community of mankind — redressing a serious injury to one's people or one's possessions. As for the means, they were to be restricted by a series of objective and subjective restraints. The objective restrictions were quite numerous — one was allowed to use only means which had a reasonable chance of success, only means which were proportional to the stakes, and there was the most important objective prescription of noncombatant immunity. As for the subjective restraints, the most famous is the formidable double effect rule, which said that an act of war that was likely to have an evil effect, such as killing noncombatants, would be morally tolerable only under two conditions: first of all, that the direct intended effect be morally acceptable (and of course, given the rule of proportionality, superior to the evil effect) and second, that the evil effects be unintended, and not a means toward the end. The whole theory was a remarkable blend of different elements; it took the two perfectly contradictory Christian impulses, one toward pacifism and the other toward crusades, and partly blended them, partly restrained them both. It was a mix of formal rules, like noncombatant immunity, and utilitarian precepts, like the calculation of consequences; it was both an ethics of intentions and an ethics of actions.

The reason it cannot be followed purely and simply and expected to work in the contemporary world is that it was based on assumptions derived from a totally different political and technological universe — and also because it encounters all the difficulties of utilitarianism. If one took those criteria seriously today, their application could produce one of two things, which happen to be exactly opposite, and both bad. If one applied them in one way, one could easily get disaster by excessive permissiveness. Take the notion that a just war can be a war for self-defense. If it is left as vague as this, it could easily lead to generalization of preventive or preemptive war (should one argue that under modern technological conditions survival requires one to strike before one is attacked), and in fact to a generalization of war altogether, because it does not tell you against what self-defense is just — against an armed attack? A seizure of hostages? An expropriation of enterprises? The mistreatment of one's nationals? For instance, under the old doctrine could not the British and French have validly argued, as they did in 1956, that Nasser's closing of the Suez Canal, which was not done by force, justified a reply by force; and could not the United States have argued, as it did with a great deal of tortuous skill, that the placing of Soviet missiles in Cuba, which were pointed but not shot at the United States, would have justified a reply by force, an attack on those bases? Similarly, the notion that a nondefensive war can be just if it is fought for a cause that is objectively serious enough to be of general concern could be an extraordinary source of conflict generalization. Both the Brezhnev doctrine and what was sometimes called a Johnson doctrine about our right to save from communism countries such as the Dominican Republic could be used with reference to the old theory.

On the other hand, if one applied it in a more strict and rigorous way, the conclusion would be that all modern large-scale war is unjust. Take the fairly careful blend of ends and means which the old doctrine entails; even good ends like a valid cause or self-defense, if fought with the modern means, stop being attempts at vindicating the social order. In just war doctrine the ends to which just wars are fought amount to a protection, through the use of force, of the international social order which has been violated by an attack on certain fundamental rights; but with the modern means of war the pursuit of even good ends can become a factor of destruction of the whole fabric of mankind.

The doctrine was elaborated for three sets of circumstances which are no longer with us; first of all, for a world in which the Princes were sufficiently Christian to have the "right intention" required, or in which the Church was sufficiently strong in authority and power to define and interpret morality — not for a world in which the right intention becomes a matter of self-righteous and self-serving self-interpretation.

Secondly, it was elaborated for wars that were very different from the present Frankenstein monsters which we call total wars — whether they are "total" in the sense of all-out wars with modern technologies of destruction, or "total" because they are political wars for control of a population, fought by rival factions in a civil strife or by guerrillas. The just war doctrine states that it is fair to use means which have a chance of success; on the other hand, they must be proportional to the stakes. If one argues that it is fair to use whatever has a reasonable chance of success, sometimes the only means which have such a chance will happen to be totally disproportionate to the stakes; think of what is sometimes necessary to win an anti-guerrilla war — think of Vietnam, or of the Soviets in Afghanistan. Moreover, the whole notion of proportionality of means to the stakes becomes meaningless as a restraint in modern war for a very simple reason. Both World War I and World War II produced an escalation of stakes. When people throw millions of men into the battlefield and suffer enormous losses and have to give themselves reasons for the horror, the stakes escalate; if you apply the principle that means are just as long as they are proportional to the stakes, once the stakes become defined as nothing less than the salvation of mankind, or the victory of a sacred cause, the proportionality of means becomes a rather sinister joke. The best example is the dropping of the atomic bomb on Japan. If one thinks that unconditional surrender and the total destruction of the forces of evil are indeed the right stakes of a just war, then abbreviating it by dropping the bomb becomes perfectly arguable. Modern wars also play havoc with the double effect rule. It says essentially that there should be no direct intentional killing of civilians; if one takes that literally it would eliminate — which would be very good indeed — all obliteration bombing clearly aimed at the civilians; but it would still allow enormous "incidental" killings. The United States in North Vietnam did not intentionally bomb civilian targets, but the military targets it selected allowed for fairly large "incidental" massacres — unless one accepts Robert W. Tucker's distinction that these kinds of massacres, while they are not desired, are nevertheless intended, in which case one comes back to the moral outlawing of all the means of modern war.[4] But if one outlaws the means of modern war, then even a just war of self-defense could become impossible to wage in certain circumstances — the "moral" power would be at the mercy of its foe. (I am thinking of the argument sometimes made on behalf of Britain's resort to city bombing in November 1940, when such bombing was practically the only means available to Britain.) Modern war, given its technology, provokes enormous inevitable killings of civilians which may be indeed "incidental," unintended, but which are perfectly well known and accepted.

Thirdly, the doctrine was elaborated for circumstances in which there was a fairly clear distinction between peace and war; and yet we now live in an age in which peace and war have become blurred, not only because wars are seldom declared, and because especially the big powers want to fight (often through proxies) *and* keep talking, but above all because war often takes the form of powers intervening violently in the violent domestic affairs of other states without respecting the traditional rules of international law which assimilated civil war to interstate war once it had reached a certain level; and also because what dominates our lives is deterrence, an extraordinary condition in which one lives in peace while preparing for war, in which one accumulates all the means of war while saying that they are aimed at peace. Nothing is more disturbing or instructive than reading theologians, twisting, wriggling, and squirming when they face the problem of deterrence. After all, one can argue that the United States, the Soviet Union, and the other nations which accumulate the means of nuclear deterrence, have the right intention, which is to maintain peace, and a good cause, the avoidance of war. However, deterrence consists of threatening to do evil, and the effectiveness, the credibility of deterrence, depends on making oneself able to get the adversary to believe that one is indeed capable of carrying out the threat of mass murder. Even if you think that what really matters is the right intention and a good cause, you have to remember that in order to make the threat credible, in other words in order to maintain peace, since many factors make the balance of terror delicate, statesmen must escalate the arms race, and cease relying exclusively on increasingly less credible threats of instant annihilation; and even though more limited options are supposed to make war less destructive should deterrence fail, the likelihood remains that if deterrence fails these restraints might collapse, and destruction would be colossal.

Such is the plight of the just war theory; and the reactions to it by those who have tried to remain within its inspiration and intellectual orbit have been rather unsatisfactory. For instance, the pronouncements of the Vatican II Council on the subject of war do not take us very far. The Church explicitly recognized the right of lawful self-defense if all peace efforts have failed, but it never explained what self-defense meant — against, what kinds of crimes or violations it was legitimate — and it never pronounced on whether anticipatory self-defense, preemptive strikes, like the Israeli *Blitz* in 1967, were legitimate or not. Vatican II condemned genocide, total war, the arms race, and the "indiscriminate destruction" of cities and whole areas. This fudged the issues raised by the rule of double effect: what about the "discriminate" destruction of cities, what about unintended, indirect, and nevertheless perfectly effective obliteration? Not a word was said about the morality of deterrence, except for a cryptic sentence stating that "many people" deem it the most effective way of maintaining "some sort of peace" at present.

As a result, theologians have scattered all over the field; some, mainly Catholics, have retreated into nuclear pacifism, which is a simple position, but not one backed by the Council. Others, mainly Protestants, have resorted to the kind of casuistry which atheists in the past liked to call Jesuitic. Many of them have been looking for a way in which, in the world of total war, one could somehow go back to just wars by waging limited wars; that the moral problem of war could be solved, if only the qualitative factor introduced by nuclear weapons could somehow be removed. But there are two difficulties with this attempt. First, what kinds of limitations can one advocate that are really convincing in this day and age? Should they be limitations on ends? Self-interpretation would soon breed distortions.[5] Should they be restraints on means? Let us assume that states agree to limit their armaments efforts on one front; this may encourage unlimited efforts on the others — we have seen this even in the so-called SALT process, where it has been called the sausage effect: you constrain the sausage in one or two points and it bulges everywhere else, you limit one kind of weapon, and you compensate by building huge amounts of those that are not banned, so that in between arms control agreements, the nuclear forces of the two superpowers have increased as never before. Similarly, let us suppose that the nuclear states manage to agree on something which many experts and theologians like, a statement by each one of the nuclear powers that it would not use nuclear weapons first. This sounds like a perfectly moral and fine "categorical imperative" attempt to limit war; however, one has to reintroduce the consideration of consequences. It might encourage nuclear proliferation — by those states which had felt protected by a superpower as long as that superpower was willing to threaten or hint that it might use nuclear weapons first if the ally is attacked. Another try at finding morally tolerable limits reminiscent of the old tradition is the notion, expertly upheld by Paul Ramsey, that limited counterforce nuclear war would be morally right, by contrast with large-scale countercity war, which would be the result if deterrence by threats of mutual assured destruction failed...clearly there are formidable obstacles. A limited, clean, surgical counterforce war requires perfect command and control and fortunately nobody has ever had any experience of such a war. Also, this suggestion assumes that it is easy to distinguish countercity war from counterforce war; that may be possible when one buries one's missiles in desert areas, as the superpowers in part have done; but the distinction makes absolutely no sense when one thinks of Europe, where all of the military objectives, which would be the targets of counterforce warfare, happen to be situated a few kilometers from major cities because of high population density.

The attempt at "saving" the morality of limited war encounters a second difficulty as well: what if the successful quest for limits makes war look less horrible, and makes it thereby more likely? One has to weigh, against the "attractiveness" of limited war (as opposed to nuclear holocaust), not only the possibly lesser deterrent value of the prospect, but also the chance that the "limited" war might not remain limited. This is another drawback of counterforce objectives, and of the no-first-use proposal, which might make more likely conventional wars that risk not remaining conventional if the loser, feeling trapped by necessity, resorts to his nuclear weapons after all. And even if the "limited" war stays limited, but only in the sense of not being nuclear, does anyone deem a conventional World War III moral? Those who ask: What if nuclear deterrence fails, and suggest measures to keep war limited in that case, should be asked in return: What if a repetition of World War II worked?

These are the dilemmas one faces when one tries to rescue the just war theory. However, there is no need to abdicate moral judgment yet. We must try to find some guidelines that address themselves to the moral issues of modern war, and thus go beyond either strategic engineering or legal exegesis....

ENDNOTES

1 Michael Walzer, *Just and Unjust Wars* (New York: Basic Books, 1977).

2 The most exhaustive (and exhausting) analysis is to be found in E.B.F. Midgley, *The Natural Law Tradition and the Theory of International Relations* (New York: Barnes and Noble, 1975). See also Frederick O. Bonkovsky, *International Norms and National Policy* (Grand Rapids, Mich.: Eedmans, 1980).

3 Robert W. Tucker, *The Just War* (Baltimore: The Johns Hopkins University Press, 1960), p. 199.

4 Robert E. Osgood and Robert W. Tucker, *Force, Order and Justice* (Baltimore: The Johns Hopkins University Press, 1967), pp. 311-13.

5 In his enormous book, *The Just War* (New York: Scribners, 1968), Paul Ramsey, who seeks to make just war possible, does not address himself to the problem of ends.

C: MECHANISMS OF REGULATION

The Regulation of International Conflict by Law

Richard Falk

There are three perspectives from which it is useful to think about the actual and potential contribution of law to the regulation of international conflict. First, there is the conflict-restraining role played by legal rules and processes in the existing system of international relations. Law helps international actors to confine conflict within manageable boundaries. Second, there is the conflict-restraining role that might be played by law in an international system in which a limited world government has emerged; that is, substantial disarmament has taken place simultaneously with the buildup of international institutions and welfare activities. Third, there is the conflict-restraining role of law as a transformative agent in the movement from the existing decentralized order to a more centralized system. This third perspective is the least familiar. It can be identified with the contribution that law is able to make to the solution of the transition problem. If an objective of foreign policy is to construct a stable peace system, does this fact influence the role of law in the contemporary world? For example, does this pursuit encourage a self-denying respect for legal rules by powerful states that is intended to raise the confidence of nations in the reliability of the international system? One way to envision the system-changing perspective is in terms of transfers of sovereign prerogative to the organs of the United Nations, transfers that are themselves designed to accelerate the global acceptance of a phased process of general and complete disarmament. Sensitivity to this focus on transition highlights such political preconditions of limited world government as the need to make elites and publics sympathetic to a world community orientation as an emerging substitute for the predominantly national orientations and loyalties that continue to dominate political attitudes relevant to the conduct of international affairs.

Scholarly emphasis upon a world community orientation is itself a political and normative act, affirming certain supranationalizing tendencies in the existing legal order and looking forward to a world in which the nation as a social unit occupies a greatly diminished status. A consequence of national control over the major instruments of force is that significant recourses to violence, whether of an offensive or defensive character, are largely determined on the national level even if these decisions are subject to a formal right of

---

review by the United Nations or a regional security organization. At the same time, it is possible to apprehend the growing importance of supranational, infranational, and transitional actors in world politics. These actors generate norms, procedures, and institutions that fall within the enterprise of international law. International law is an umbrella conception despite its literal reference to inter-nation transactions that expresses the totality of legal phenomena germane to the control of international conflict. The following subcategories suggest the major components of the world law concept. First, there is the traditional system of international law concerned with the development of rules and processes that pertain to direct relationships among sovereign states. Second, there is United Nations Law that grows out of the claims and activities of the various organs and agencies that comprise the Organization. A conception of United Nations Law is needed to govern the peacemaking operations of the Organization. Such a legal order also serves to establish a constitutional structure of "United Nations." This structure is needed to legitimate claims by the United Nations to use its authority to prevent or moderate violence that threatens international peace. Thus the role of the United Nations in Seuz in 1956, in Lebanon during 1958, or in the Congo after 1960 generates standards and precedents about the allocation of authority between the host state government and the Organization. Third, there is the network of legal rights and duties that results from the activities of regional organizations. The Organization of American States makes claims to act as a collective unit that possesses a different legal status than if made either by a single state or by the United Nations. The various efforts by the United States to get OAS support for its undertakings against Castro's Cuba can be understood in part as an effort to legitimate national policy by placing it within a regional setting.

Fourth, there is a consistent, if vague, trend toward the effective realization of a universalistic legal consciousness. The regulatory basis is the unity of the human community and the object is the promotion of the human dignity of the individual person. This trend has been identified by one author as "the common law of mankind,"[1] a phrase placing stress upon the directness of the contact between the legal claim and the human conduct, and disregarding the interposition of national governments. The Charter, by providing for the promotion of human rights, gives the United Nations some authority, as yet undeveloped, to apply the rules of the common law of mankind regardless of objections made by the government of the nation within whose territory the activity takes place. Civil strife and human rights are the principal areas where the connection between human conflict and this new basis of claim is most evident. These matters would, by traditional notions, be considered to fall within the domestic jurisdiction of a sovereign state, the constituent acts being performed mainly by nationals subject to the paramount authority of their territorial government. A universal legal order denies the "domesticness" of the activity by claiming the competence to prevent human abuse and political violence wherever it takes place and regardless of the character and status of the combatants.

And fifth, there is the complex set of rules and procedures that concern the interaction among regions, blocs, nations, international organizations, and individuals in their relations with one another, identified here, with some reluctance, as supranational law. The relations between the Congo and the United Nations, between Cuba and the Organization of American States, between a corporation and a foreign government that are parties to a concession agreement, between the Warsaw Pact and NATO illustrate this complex legal network.

The heritage of the past deepens one's understanding of the growth and deficiencies of law in world affairs. The Catholic Church in medieval Europe provided an institutional and normative center for the resolution of conflict among the leading international actors, all purporting to be obedient to the will of Rome. On several occasions the Church performed peacekeeping roles; for example, the papal bull *Inter coetesa* served as the basis for allocating colonizing claims between Spain and Portugal in the treaties of Tordesillas (1494) and Saragossa (1529). With the Reformation, the secularizing spirit of the Renaissance, and the rise of strong nation-states, a heroic attempt was made to combine the Roman Law heritage of Europe with the natural law tradition to form a common normative framework for international activities. This law tried to regulate national recourse to violence by positing a doctrine of just war. Such a doctrine specified standards of justice that were assumed to be acceptable to every reasoning man and to every Christian sovereign, standards which, if adhered to, would preclude war. But the absence of an authoritative decision-maker allowed each sovereign to claim the presence of a just cause whenever *raison d'état* dictated war. Normative authority proved insufficient to restrain an ambitious nation possessing the capability for and will toward aggression. Legal doctrine was invoked to rationalize national policy rather than to constrain it. The maintenance of peace, so far as maintained, depended on alliances that confronted the potential aggressor with the prospect of defeat if he made the costly recourse to forcible forms of conflict. Law did not contribute to this process. Sovereignty counted far more than did universal norms embodied in the natural law tradition.

This led international jurists in the eighteenth and nineteenth centuries to identify law with the manifestations of sovereign *consent*. Thus treaties (express consent) and custom (implied consent) replaced *reason* as the foundation of authority in international affairs. State governments would not agree, however, to qualify their discretion to use force to promote national ends. From a legal point of view recourse to warfare was treated as legal as a proper matter for sovereign discretion. A peace treaty legitimated the fruits of conquest. Law did help restrict the *scope* of violent conflict be defining the rights and duties of neutrals and belligerents toward one another, thereby compromising the interest of nonparticipants in maintaining normal commercial intercourse despite the war with the interest of the belligerent in achieving a maximum negative impact upon its enemy. Rights of blockade, notions of contraband, rules for the visit and search of merchant ships on the high seas were designed, in elaborate detail, to allow the war to go on without drawing neutrals into the fray. As well, law tried to provide rules designed to eliminate *unnecessary suffering* from the belligerent experience. Rules concerning the treatment of prisoners, the care of the sick and wounded, the obligations of belligerent occupation were aspects of this effort to humanize war. These efforts culminated in the conferences at The Hague prior to World War I and were partly renovated in the Geneva Conventions of 1949 after World War II. This compatibility of war with law during the early centuries of the state system was partly a consequence of the limited objectives pursued by major states in warfare between themselves. There was a general recognition that international stability depended upon the continuing existence of the major national actors.

World War I signified the end of the aloofness of law from national determinations to use force. The hardening of alliance patterns in the pre-1914 period led to a struggle for dominance that typically takes place whenever two adverse power centers aspire to increase their power, prestige, and wealth at each other's expense. This polarity encouraged one side to work toward attaining a superior military capability to eliminate the only other competitor for world dominance, as well as to avoid being eliminated. Moreover, military technology (submarine, aircraft, mass armies) and the absoluteness of belligerent objectives (unconditional surrender) undercut the restraining limits developed through several centuries by the earlier variety of international law. Almost all trade became contraband, submarines and aircraft could not visit and search neutral ships, and the reliance on the distinction between civilian and soldier and between military and nonmilitary targets was seriously challenged by bombing expeditions and strategies designed to weaken the enemy's industrial base and will to defend. The higher stakes of war — national impotence or ascendancy — and the greater destructiveness of the new technology led nations after World War I to plan for the elimination of war from international life. The League of Nations might be considered as a search for a new balancing mechanism that would confront a potential aggressor with overwhelming force — that is, the unified capability of the League membership brought to bear to frustrate the objectives of the warmaker — just as the possibilities for realignment in nineteenth century Europe had been used to discourage aggression by redressing the power relationships in favor of the defense. Legal technique and institutions were expected to implement this attempt to achieve a new kind of security: organized collective security. This new reliance on the collective strength of the overall world community, a return to the expectation of the early natural law theory that nations would aggregate their own strength to defeat an unjust user of force, was reinforced by the Kellogg-Briand Peace Pact of 1928 prohibiting national recourse to force in international affairs except for purposes of self-defense. Despite the formal assertion of these radical legal claims to control conflict, the primacy of national sovereignty over collective restraint produced a new polarization of political power that exploded in the form of World War II. The trends toward belligerent absolutism present in World War I were carried much further by the acceptance of the concept of total war, by the development of modern air power and radar, and by the use of rockets and atomic bombs. The role of law in restraining the nature of belligerent confrontation seemed trivial indeed. Traditional limiting notions were subordinated to belligerent strategy, including the sustained bombardment of cities without even a consistent restriction to military or industrial objectives.

Post-World War II gave rise to the United Nations, an increased effort to prohibit recourse by states to violence by proposing to deal collectively with the state that violated the peace. The will of the community was formalized by the unanimous endorsement of the General Assembly of the Principles of the Nuremberg Judgment, chief principle among which was the conclusion that planning and preparing for or engaging in an aggressive war is the most serious of all crimes against mankind. Whereas the League failed to thwart Italy's flagrant aggression against Ethiopia, the United Nations has succeeded in mobilizing sufficient defensive forces to frustrate aggressors in Korea and Suez, the two major instances of overt recourse to force across a boundary. However, the basic decentralization of power and authority persists, baffling every realistic prospect for effective long-term control. Once more a destabilizing repolarization of power has taken place in international society, this time augmented by nuclear technology and rigidified by ideological fervor....

The reality of conflict is pervasive and multifaceted. However, in world affairs, the urgency of concern about the prevention of war encourages a concentration upon the relevance of conflict to the control of political violence in interstate relations. This orientation conditions thought about law. It leads law to be conceived frequently, albeit simplistically, as the one alternative to force in the resolution of international disputes; this dichotomy is much too sharp as it overlooks the dependence of law upon force and fails to appreciate the moderating effects that law can have even when violence has been introduced into social relations by threat or use. Nevertheless, this chapter accepts the premise that the regulation of violence is the proper focus for a study of the relevance of law to international conflict, an acceptance predicated upon the paramount importance of maintaining nuclear peace.

There has been a tendency on the part of those who view law and force as mutually exclusive alternatives to devote their attention to the description of existing, and the invention of new, procedures and institutions for the pacific settlement of disputes. Pacific settlement provides a significant series of opportunities for international actors locked in conflict to resolve their differences in a nondestructive manner. As such, these procedures and institutions are important, especially as either anticipations or ingredients of a more ordered world; but a present emphasis on methods of pacific settlement distracts one from an appreciation of the role that law can presently play in world affairs. Although the renunciation of force must be accompanied eventually by reliable substitutes, there is not yet in sight a significant disposition on the part of nations to entrust vital disputes to legal tribunals and procedures for third-party settlement.... Diplomacy, rather than law — although the divorce is not a separation (law affects the course of diplomatic negotiation) — is the realm for fruitful pacific settlement.

A major criticism of the approach taken by specialists in international relations to the contribution law makes to the control of international conflict arises from their tendency to overstress formal apparatus: the World Court and treaty-making procedure. If this apparatus is extolled as even potentially adequate to guard the peace, it encourages a naïvely optimistic outlook. If law is categorically dismissed because the apparatus is unable to regulate reliably the more fundamental aspirations of states for power, wealth, and security, then an equally naïve cynicism emerges that is quite misleading. Legal process and order have contributed, and continue to contribute significantly to the avoidance of destructive conflict and to the reduction of its destructiveness, but *not* by providing the kind of institutional structure or law-making procedure that has led us to rely so heavily upon the judiciary and legislature in our domestic life. The character of law in world affairs is shaped by the decentralized distribution of power....

ENDNOTES

1 C. Wilfred Jenks, *The Common Law of Mankind* (London: Stevens and Sons, 1958), pp. 62-172.

C: MECHANISMS OF REGULATION

The Concert of Europe: A Fresh Look at an International System

Richard B. Elrod

Relations between states differ from all other forms of social interaction. As Raymond Aron reminds us, interstate relations "involve, in essence, the alternatives of peace and war."[1] Moreover, the sources of international dissension and discord generally seem to over-balance the forces for harmony. The study of international politics must proceed from certain inescapable assumptions: the inevitable clash of national interests and prestige; the perceptions and misperceptions of statesmen and would-be statesmen; the operation of impersonal technological and social forces that imprison both leaders and led; the irrepressible friction between change and inertia. All these factors — and others — constitute the dynamics of interstate relations that make peace a precious, precarious matter.

History reveals, however, that statesmen were more successful in some periods in the past than during others in managing and controlling these unavoidable tensions. Certain constraining and moderating forces operated that compelled or induced sovereign states to refrain from adventurous and aggressive foreign policies. From 1815 to 1854, European interstate relations clearly conformed to that pattern. No wars occurred between the great powers; a large measure of security and stability characterized the international system. Statesmen exercised self-restraint and cooperated in regulating several diplomatic crises that could easily have degenerated into catastrophe. The explanation for this uncommon willingness on the part of great powers to act with patience and self-abnegation is not simple. Some scholars credit the diplomats of that era with extraordinary skill and perception. In the aftermath of the long and costly wars against revolutionary France, European leaders were understandably appreciative of the need for peace, and they displayed impressive versatility in its preservation. Adherents of the now fashionable premise of the primacy of domestic politics tend to seek the answer in the relative quiescence of internal affairs in the postwar period. Most observers, perhaps, continue to attribute

---

Richard B. Elrod, "The Concert of Europe: A Fresh Look at an International System," *World Politics*, Vol. 28, No. 2 (January 1976). Portions of the text have been deleted. Some footnotes have been removed; those remaining have been renumbered.

peace to the restoration and operation of the European balance of power.[2]

These explanations are plausible and no doubt partially correct; peace, no less than war, issues from a multiplicity of causes. Yet one important element is often overlooked: the Concert of Europe, the international system within which European governments formulated and conducted policy. The Concert seldom receives much credit for the long period of peace after 1815; some would dispute its peace-keeping function entirely, others would deny its very existence.[3] In this essay, I will consider the Concert of Europe as a conscious and generally effective attempt by European statesmen to maintain peaceful relations between sovereign states. I will also offer some general reflections and tentative conclusions about the meaning, the nature, and the operation of concert diplomacy. For the European Concert — the machinery it developed, the rationale that lay behind it, the rules and procedures it engendered — constituted an essential ingredient of European peace and stability between the Congress of Vienna and the Crimean War. It was a functioning and promising system of international relations, one that differed quite radically from the balance-of-power politics of the eighteenth century and the total wars of the first half of the twentieth. It is worthy of a brief re-examination.

ORIGINS OF THE CONCERT

The concept of concert diplomacy hardly emerged fully defined or completely thought-out. Certain assumptions and procedures became customary and prescriptive through application. In the first instance, the Concert derived from the common realization of European statesmen of the Napoleonic era that something new and different must be devised to mitigate the increasingly chaotic and warlike balance-of-power system of the previous century. Both critics and defenders of the balance-of-power idea, even during its apogee, recognized that it was unsatisfactory. By the end of the eighteenth century the satirical observation of Alexander Pope, issued as early as 1711, had become ominously prophetic:

> Now Europe's balanc'd, neither Side prevails,
> For Nothing's left in either of the Scales.[4]

Balance-of-power politics — the politics of confrontation — generated intolerable international tensions, produced increasingly serious armed conflicts, and inspired progressively extravagant plans of aggression. It neither maintained peace nor preserved the independence of sovereign states; by the time of the French Revolution, the international system had broken down altogether.

Friedrich von Gentz, writing in 1818, applauded the progress made by European statesmen in transcending the balance-of-power idea, "the principle which has governed, and has also too often troubled and bloodied Europe for three centuries."[5] John Capodistrias, the advisor of Alexander I of Russia, similarly deplored a return to "the terrible empire of anarchy and revolutionary despotism with all the horrors of the *divide et impera* of the old diplomacy."[6] This common determination to surmount the malignant system of the past represented, as one writer remarks, " a revolution in diplomatic history."[7] The Concert of Europe was born, and with it a genuine sense of solidarity and responsibility for Europe, a spirit of "national self-restraint, respect for the public law as defined in treaties, and willingness to enforce its observance by concerted action. . . ."[8]

The Concert connoted, first of all, a new method of diplomacy — diplomacy by congress or conference (or, as Gentz once called it, "the diplomacy of the highway"). In this connection the Concert may be defined as the great powers meeting together at times of international crisis to maintain peace and to develop European solutions to European problems. Statesmen who had finally recognized the necessity of cooperation in the last coalition against Napoleon continued to believe in the advantages of collaboration to maintain the postwar settlement. Lord Castlereagh of Great Britain, who frequently called the congresses "reunions," especially emphasized this function: "I am quite convinced that past habits, common glory and those occasional meetings, displays and repledges are among the best securities Europe now has for a durable peace."[9]

But the Concert of Europe was more than an innovation in diplomatic technique. It cannot be confined simply to the era of the great European congresses between 1815 and 1823. The essential precepts of concert diplomacy survived the congress era and assisted materially in the maintenance of peace until 1854. For the European Concert was also a conceptual norm among the great powers of the proper and permissible aims and methods of international politics. It gradually came to embody a code of conduct for international behavior, one that transcended the ideological division between the three conservative Eastern powers and the more liberal Western states. Each side naturally aspired to use concert diplomacy as an instrument of its own political creed and was sometimes tempted to seek alternative methods to the Concert. Yet for over three decades European statesmen generally shared the assumptions which predicated concert diplomacy, and in most cases were willing to abide by its rules.

RULES OF CONCERT DIPLOMACY

What, then, were the underlying assumptions and the unwritten rules of concert diplomacy? First of all, the Concert of Europe meant great-power tutelage over the rest of Europe. It consisted only of the great powers; lesser states were occasionally consulted when their interests were involved, but they possessed few rights and certainly not that of equality. In the context of the post-Napoleonic period this development was natural and probably necessary. On the surface, moreover, it hardly represented a significant deviation from actual practice in the past. But the idea of the great powers acting in unity was in itself somewhat novel and clearly rested upon a fresh postulate. The recognition of a European community of interests, and commitment to its defense, required of the great European states a new posture and a special accountability. Great-power tutelage was obligatory, for only the great powers possessed the resources, the prestige, and the vision to contend with the transcendent concerns of peace or war, of stability or disorder. As Castlereagh observed in 1818, "the Great Powers feel that they have not only a common interest, but a common duty to attend to."[10] Gentz concluded in the same year that "the five powers at the head of the federation are the only ones who could destroy the general system by changing their policies. Squabbles and changes among the others could never have that effect."[11] Implicit in this judgment was the cynical but accurate assessment that so long as the great powers were in agreement, the lesser states could cause little trouble.

The smaller states were thus shunted aside because the great powers had the responsibility of preserving the peace of Europe and of protecting a European society menaced by revolutionary principles. Equally important was that the emphasis upon great-power unity constituted a barrier against unilateral action by any state; it served to constrain even the great powers. No one power could attempt to settle a European question by an independent and self-regulated initiative. European problems must receive European answers; the policies of each were subject to the scrutiny and sanction of all. Prince Metternich verbalized this concept in 1820 when he remarked that the most essential basis of European repose was "the most absolute solidarity...in all questions of a general interest" and the assurance that none of the great powers would ever "proceed alone on such matters."[12] This explains the natural and virtually imperative tendency in concert diplomacy to internationalize diplomatic questions, to replace individual claims and prerogatives by European ones. Aversion to unilateral action or aggrandizement gave birth to the first of the unwritten rules of concert diplomacy: that the proper way of dealing with international crises was through conference diplomacy. Acceptance of this precept was general throughout the first half of the nineteenth century. Admittedly, statesmen sometimes explored other possibilities first and often became exasperated with the cumbersome and time-consuming procedure of diplomacy by conference. Great-power conferences, furthermore, could not resolve all the problems that they considered. Even so, realistic diplomats had to acknowledge the basic efficacy of joint consultation and action. The conference method clearly tended to moderate more extreme positions and to reinforce the conception of the European great powers as a special group, with special responsibilities as well as special privileges.

A second and closely related rule followed logically: that territorial changes in Europe were subject to the sanction of the great powers. Though sometimes an imperfect and unharmonious method of acknowledging necessary alterations, this procedure was the only means of legitimizing new arrangements. The great powers acting in concert determined the acceptable and appropriate limits of change. They revised settlements considered too drastic, and substituted European action and guarantees for unilateral claims. The insistence of the great powers upon reviewing modifications in the international order represented another significant deterrence against immoderate international conduct. By the simple process of submitting questions to "collective deliberation" the actions of revisionist powers were circumscribed.[13]

The two rules of diplomacy by conference and of great-power sanction of change enjoyed a remarkable longevity in European diplomatic practice. They were appealed to, and many times utilized, throughout the nineteenth century. These first two canons, however, pertained only to the general objectives and machinery of concert diplomacy. Among the other ingredients that accounted for the willingness of the great powers to participate in the Concert and to accept its decisions there are two additional prescriptions which were crucial to the successful operation of concert diplomacy. The third dictum was that essential members of the states system must be protected and defended. Obviously this pertained first to the five great powers. But certain areas in which the great powers were in contention could be just as important to the system as the great powers themselves. Excessive weakness as well as superabundant strength of an essential member posed a serious menace to the system. The Ottoman Empire, for example, was necessary to the European system simply because its demise would raise problems so dangerous that general European war and upheaval could not be avoided. European cabinets thus relied upon concert diplomacy to sustain the Turkish Sultan — to replace unilateral pretensions by a European guardianship, to avoid as long as possible the inevitable scramble over the spoils, and to insure that no one power acquired exclusive preponderance in an area affecting the interests of all.

The final rule of concert diplomacy was that great powers must not be humiliated. They must not be challenged either in their vital interests or or in their prestige and honor. Concert diplomacy assigned itself the delicate task of restraining revisionist or aggressive states as well as of regulating European difficulties by peaceful means — replacing the confrontation and inherent brinkmanship of balance-of-power politics. Perhaps the oldest and thorniest problem of international systems again challenged diplomatists: how to reach decisions, and how to enforce them, when the disputants were great powers. Inevitably, concert diplomacy proved most vulnerable to the criticism that the Concert functioned well in handling trivial matters concerning the small and weak states, but performed miserably when really important questions were at stake. This charge is both untrue and unfair. Responsible statesmen must approach international affairs, in the apt phrase of George Kennan, as "gardeners and not mechanics."[14] The purpose of concert diplomacy was to maintain peace among the great powers, to prevent unavoidable conflicts of interest from degenerating into actual hostilities. Concert diplomatists realized that no surer method of provoking conflicts existed than openly to confront a great power —

to menace its vital concerns or to impugn its honor and prestige. So long as the European Concert functioned, the five great powers had the assurance that both their legitimate rights and their self-esteem would be respected.

That consideration accounts for the evolution of a rather elaborate cumulation of semi-formal procedural safeguards against offending the sensitivities of the great powers. Inattention even to the slightest detail in such matters could seriously debilitate or preclude the operation of the Concert entirely. Consequently, concert diplomacy actively cultivated the conception of the great powers as a unique and special peer group. While lesser states might possibly attend an international gathering, they did not break the magic circle of the elite and powerful. The great powers retained the exclusive prerogative of decision making. Under no circumstances did one invite, in any capacity, a state of the second or third rank which was an enemy of a great power. Furthermore, since decisions had to be voluntary, unanimity rather than majority rule prevailed in European meetings. A legitimate settlement of any question was impossible if even one of the great powers declined to accept it. Such considerations predetermined the agenda of conferences. Questions that entailed a possible challenge to the interests or an affront to the prestige of a great power could not be feasibly discussed or resolved; issues that were embarrassing to any participant had to be excluded. As a result, many important and urgent problems did not receive treatment — simply because concert statesmen preferred to avoid questions that might produce confrontation and possibly war. Concert diplomacy manifestly sought not the best, but the least objectionable, solutions.

THE CONCERT IN OPERATION

The protections against great-power humiliation were necessary and they help greatly to explain the success of conference diplomacy in this period. For one thing, while the conferences met on an *ad hoc* basis, they were definitely not meetings summoned on the spur of the moment, or in which anyone expected mere personal contact between responsible statesmen to surmount all disputes and conflicts of interest. Diplomacy by conference required elaborate and often lengthy preparations. Some delay was necessary to allow passions to cool, to give diplomats time to consult their colleagues and to work out their positions, and above all, to discover what would and what would not be palatable to the other powers in conference. The requisite order included extensive *pourparlers,* perhaps a conference, and then a congress. This procedure insured that only those issues that were amenable to diplomatic treatment were introduced, and constituted a necessary precondition for successful summit diplomacy.

The procedure of concert diplomacy reveals also its primary technique of restraining and moderating intemperate policies on the part of the great powers. In the language of the time, the purpose was "to group" the offending state. Instead of direct military confrontation, the principal means was moral suasion — an appeal to the collective responsibility of the great powers for European peace and stability, to the norm of what the other powers considered appropriate and legitimate behavior. In a sense, the Concert idea became the collective conscience of the European great powers, reminding each of its responsibilities and obligations in international politics. As Metternich observed in 1837 during a conversation on the Eastern Question with the British Ambassador, "Europe is now advanced to the rank of a spectator and a judge and that is what precludes a continuation of the system under which the encroachments of Russia were heretofore conducted."[15] The Tsar, aware that he was now under the observation of his peers, would modify his policy according to their standards. On the whole, concert diplomacy proved remarkably efficacious in rekindling and reinforcing the spirit of self-restraint among the great European powers. Nineteenth-century diplomatic history furnishes several examples of states forgoing gains which they could probably have gotten, mainly because they would otherwise have placed themselves outside the European community and damaged their moral position. Few similar instances can be cited either in the eighteenth or the twentieth centuries. The Concert perhaps never achieved its potential, but neither were its accomplishments insignificant or purely transitory.

Assuredly, nostalgia should not blind us to the obvious imperfections of concert diplomacy. The European Concert was always an unwieldy and often an ineffectual instrument. It depended perhaps too much upon the "good will" of its members, upon the personal dispositions of individual leaders. It did nothing, in short, to challenge directly the doctrine of the ultimate sovereignty of states. Invariably the Concert dealt with the symptoms rather than the causes of international conflict; it was always a negative concept, called into operation by events. Even so, to admit these shortcomings does not vitiate the achievements or refute the promise of concert diplomacy. It was, after all, primarily a vehicle (and a fairly successful one) for the peaceful management of great-power rivalries. Above all, the Concert idea was realistic in the best sense of the word — attuned to, but not narrowly bound by reality. At its worst, the Concert was an impotent assembly, merely adhering to the formalities, unable to resolve important and pressing issues. At its best, it represented a reasonably satisfactory solution to the most difficult problem of international systems: how to accommodate the forces of change and yet preserve peace and stability. Concert diplomacy allowed the great powers to sanction necessary alterations of the existing order; it provided the means of legitimizing change without endangering the general system.

One more thing is clear. European relations during the era of concert diplomacy were characterized by a sense of security, a respect for the public law of Europe, a recognition of a commonly accepted standard of conduct, and a willingness to keep one's own conduct within those limits, that was unknown both to earlier and to later periods. An effective system of restraints existed against unilateral action in concerns that affected the interests of more than one power; so too did a method and a rationale for averting or moderating conflicts between the great powers. Through concert diplomacy the great powers were reminded of what constituted responsible international conduct. The Concert possessed a surprising capability to persuade sovereign states to observe those limits.

THE CONCERT AS AN INTERNATIONAL SYSTEM

A number of provisional conclusions about concert diplomacy may be advanced. One is that certain practices, procedures, and beliefs can, with time and usage, become fairly well-established rules of international behavior. Perhaps the central emphasis placed upon international organizations is misdirected. Concert diplomacy suggests that something practicable is possible between the extremes of an absolute consensus upon right and wrong in international relations (which makes institutional structures for adjudication and enforcement unnecessary), and of elaborate international governmental and judicial organs (which are rendered sterile by the lack of an agreed-upon charter for interpretation and administration). To repeat, the Concert was realistic in trying to manage rather than to eradicate international dissension. Yet it simultaneously advanced a standard for responsible statesmanship and developed an instrumentality that periodically reminded even the most powerful nations of their obligation to conform to that standard.

A second point implied by concert diplomacy, and an important one for operative international systems in general, is that some distribution and equalization of both responsibilities and opportunities is essential among the states considered necessary to the system. No state should be asked to take the lead in maintaining the system, and to bear all the necessary burdens, while another reaps all the benefits. The recognition of some collective responsibility for order demands more than lip service, though historically some states have enjoyed the luxury of being able sporadically to ignore the general international system of which they are a part. States are thus separate, individual, and identifiably different actors; they cannot merely be labeled *A*, *B*, and *C*, and their posture and probable behavior within a system mathematically calculated. Because of disparities in resources, geographic position, composition, history, and a plethora of other factors, the European states of the nineteenth century had different domestic and foreign situations with which to contend, and different roles to play in the European community. Furthermore, the nature and structure of the international system itself affected each state differently. As long as member states accepted the existing system, they had to recognize these differences and structure their policy accordingly. Nineteenth-century diplomatic history indicates that when a power, or a group of powers, is demonstrably bearing the essential burden of maintaining the order, it should be supported and not be taken advantage of by other states simply because the special position and circumstances of the latter allow them to do so.

Finally, the history of concert diplomacy implies something about the role of ideology in international systems. In the years immediately after the defeat of Napoleon, there was a conservative, antirevolutionary consensus among the great powers (Alexander of Russia was for a time the most liberal member). Moreover, the subsequent division of Europe into two competing ideological camps has been exaggerated. The controversies over both the Holy Alliance and the principle of nonintervention were, at bottom, false issues. Neither had much impact upon actual diplomatic practice. Undeniably, an ideological rift did develop between East and West from the 1820's onward, and the Holy Alliance and nonintervention became convenient symbols and slogans in the resulting debate. Yet concert diplomacy continued to function. It did so because a great-power consensus persisted that transcended political ideology. Efforts to base the Concert upon ideology served only to enfeeble it and to limit its functions. Despite ideological divergences, the European powers still agreed upon the necessity of peace among themselves and accepted concert diplomacy as the means to manage crises that might jeopardize that peace.

But the temptation to play fast and loose with the rules of the game became more and more irresistible. The revolutions of 1848 further eroded the presuppositions of concert diplomacy and produced new leaders and new expectations. The culmination came in the Crimean War, another international crisis over the Eastern Question and one that was, in fact, no more serious that others previously managed successfully by the Concert. It was, moreover, the type of crisis in which concert diplomacy had always been at its best: the avoidance of great-power confrontations over matters of prestige. This time, however, statesmen in key positions failed to exercise self-restraint and refused to honor the rules of the Concert. The sea powers, in particular, were determined to inflict a humiliating defeat upon Russia and to conduct the war as a liberal crusade against autocracy. The Concert of Europe was the victim. To be sure, remnants of the techniques and assumptions of concert diplomacy endured, but the Concert system itself had been destroyed. Nothing emerged to replace it until the 1870's; and then stability was achieved on another, less cooperative and conciliatory basis. To this degree, then, the destruction of the European Concert was willful, if rather lighthearted and frivolous. The other side of the argument is that the forces of change and progress simply bypassed the concept of concert diplomacy. Perhaps so; no one would deny that the European Concert was the product of a specific political, social, and intellectual milieu. Industrialization with all its social and political ramifications surely helped to undermine the essential foundations of concert diplomacy. A variety of developments increased the enticement to use foreign policy to divert domestic disharmony. Perhaps the Concert could not accommodate the age of national states. Most simply, however, concert diplomacy broke down because statesmen refused to abide by its rules — and did not give much thought to what rules of international politics they would prefer as a substitute. They knew only that they had grown weary of its restrictions. The destruction of the European Concert was thus at least in part a generational problem. The remark of Theodore Fontaine, in reference to the 1848 revolutions, applies equally well to the demise of the Concert: "One was tired of the old approach to things. Not that one had suffered particularly under it; no, it was not that. It was rather, that one was ashamed of it."[16]

European statesmen, however, had made more progress than they realized. The Concert of Europe was certainly not the only factor making for peace in the first half of the century; nor could it contend successfully with all the political, social, and economic developments that these decades produced. It could only abate and not remove the causes of interstate rivalry. But in the real world of international relations it performed amazingly well. In a certain sense the evolution of concert diplomacy displays some rather striking parallels to "the growth of political stability" in domestic politics.[17] The European system in the era of the Concert approached the fulfillment of the three conditions posited by Stanley Hoffmann — of "security, satisfaction, and flexibility" — to which all political orders must aspire.[18].

ENDNOTES

1 *Raymond Aron, Peace and War: A Theory of International Relations,* trans. by Richard Howard and Annette Baker Fox (Garden City, N.Y.: Anchor Books, 1973), p. 6.

2 See, for example, A.J.P. Taylor, *The Struggle for Mastery in Europe, 1848-1918* (Oxford: Oxford University Press, 1954), pp. xix-xx.

3 W.N. Medlicott concludes that "it was the peace which maintained the Concert and not the Concert that maintained peace." *Bismarck, Gladstone, and the Concert of Europe* (London: Athlone Press, 1956), p. 18. Another common view is that the Concert was just the old balance-of-power system perpetuated in another guise: Edward V. Gulick, *Europe's Classical Balance of Power* (New York: Norton, 1955), pp. 88n., 156-59. Concert diplomacy admittedly accepted and incorporated the principle of the balance of power. But I believe that a distinction must be drawn (and in fact was drawn) between the balance of power, seen simply as a distribution of power among essential members of the states system, and balance-of-power politics, which featured confrontation as the first premise, and which had a natural tendency to seek preponderance rather than balance. See Richard Rosecrance, *Action and Reaction in World Politics* (Boston: Little, Brown, 1963), for some perceptive comments on this subject.

4 *Minor Poems,* Norman Ault and John Butt, eds., Twickenham edn., 6 (London: Methuen, 1954), 82.

5 *Dépêches inédites du Chevalier de Gentz aux Hospodars de Valachie,* ed. Anton von Prokesch-Osten (Paris: Plon, 1876-1877), I, 344-.45. An English translation of this essay ("Considerations on the Political System Now Existing in Europe") is available in Mack Walker, ed., *Metternich's Europe, 1813-1848* (New York: Harper, 1968), pp. 71-83.

6 Patricia K. Grimsted, *The Foreign Ministers of Alexander I* (Berkeley: University of California Press, 1970), p. 239.

7 H.G. Schenk, *The Aftermath of the Napoleonic Wars: The Concert of Europe — An Experiment* (New York: Oxford University Press, 1947), p. 27.

8 Gordon A. Craig, "The System of Alliances and the Balance of Power," in the *New Cambridge Modern History,* 10 (Cambridge: Cambridge University Press, 1960), 267.

9 Charles K. Webster, *The Foreign Policy of Castlereagh: Britain and the European Alliance, 1815-1822,* 2d ed. (London: G. Bell, 1934), p. 144.

10 Ibid., p. 160.

11 Gentz, *Dépêches*, p. 477; Walker, ed., *Metternich's Europe*, p. 73. Castlereagh wrote in September 1815

that "There is not a Power, however feeble, that borders France from the Channel to the Mediterranean that is not pushing some acquisition under the pleas of security and rectification of frontier. They...are foolish enough to suppose that the Great Powers of Europe are to be in readiness to protect them in the enjoyment of these petty spoils. In truth, their whole conception is so unstatesmanlike that they look not beyond their own sop; compared with this, the keeping together of a European force has little importance in their eyes." W. Alison Phillips, *The Confederation of Europe*, 2d ed. (London: Longmans, Green, 1920), p. 138.

12 G. Bertier de Sauvigny, "Sainte-Alliance et Alliance dans les conceptions de Metternich," *Revue Historique*, 223 (April-June 1960), 263.

13 Phillip E. Mosely, *Russian Diplomacy and the Opening of the Straits Question in 1838 and 1839* (Cambridge: Harvard University Press, 1934), p. 73.

14 George Kennan, *Realities of American Foreign Policy* (Princeton: Princeton University Press 1954).

15 Charles K. Webster, *The Foreign Policy of Palmerston, 1830-1841* (2 vols., London: G. Bell, 1951), I, 505.

16 Joachim Remak, *The Gentle Critic: Theodore Fontaine and German Politics* (Syracuse: Syracuse University Press, 1964), p.13.

17 J.H. Plumb, *The Growth of Political Stability in England, 1625-1725* (London: Macmillan, 1967).

18 Stanley Hoffmann, *The State of War: Essays on the Theory and Practice of International Relations* (New York: Praeger, 1965), p. 20.

C: MECHANISMS OF REGULATION

The Nature of Alliances

Robert E. Osgood

1. WHY ALLIANCES?

Alliances are an integral part of international politics. They are one of the primary means by which states seek the co-operation of other states in order to enhance their power to protect and advance their interests. This instrument of co-operation is so pervasive that every state must have an alliance policy, even if its purpose is only to avoid alliances.

The subject of this analysis, however, is broader than alliances. Alliances are only one kind of commitment by which states enhance their power. Moreover, there are many kinds of alliances, and alliances serve a variety of purposes. One cannot properly assess the value and the prospects of alliances without examining the alternatives to alliances and distinguishing between the various kinds of alliances.

In this study an alliance is defined as a formal agreement that pledges states to co-operate in using their military resources against a specific state or states and usually obligates one or more of the signatories to use force, or to consider (unilaterally or in consultation with allies) the use of force, in specified circumstances. It differs in principle from a "collective security" agreement. Strictly speaking, such an agreement obligates its members to abstain from recourse to violence against one another and to participate collectively in suppressing the unlawful use of force by any member. It may also obligate its members to resist aggression by a non-member against any of them, but what distinguishes it from a mere collective defense agreement is that it presupposes a general interest on the part of all its members in opposing aggression by any of them and entails procedures for the peaceful settlement of disputes among the members.

A defensive alliance presupposes only a common interest in opposing threats from specific states or groups outside the alliance and does not necessarily or usually entail provisions for settling disputes among its members. An offensive alliance aims at forcibly changing the international status quo, territorially or otherwise, to increase the assets of its members.

A defensive alliance may also be a local or regional collective security agreement. The OAS [Organization of American States] for example, is both. Alliances, although ostensibly or actually directed against an external threat, may additionally

---

Robert E. Osgood, *Alliances and American Foreign Policy* (Baltimore: The Johns Hopkins University Press, 1968), pp. 17-31. Reprinted by permission of The Johns Hopkins University Press. Portions of the text have been deleted, and some footnotes removed.

or even primarily be intended to restrain a member, limit its options, support its government against an internal threat, or control its foreign policy is some fashion. In this respect, many alliances have actually been as much concerned as a collective security agreement would be with organizing relations between allies, although national sensitivities may have counseled against making such concern explicit or public. The internal concern of alliances tends to increase with their duration and with the diminished perception of an external threat.

Alliances commonly reflect more than a single, explicit, and identical interest between members. Allies may wish to support a variety of interests that include merely complementary or parallel interests and even divergent ones. Some of these interests may be specified in the agreement, but some are more prudently left unspecified, whether they are mutual or not. In any case, the full substance and significance of an alliance is seldom revealed in the formal contract or treaty for military co-operation, any more than the essence of marriage is revealed in the marriage certificate. The contract is simply an attempt to make more precise and binding a particular obligation or relationship between states, which is part of a continually changing network of interests and sentiments. An alliance, therefore, reflects a latent war community, based on general co-operation that goes beyond formal provisions and that the signatories must continually cultivate in order to preserve mutual confidence in each other's fidelity to specified obligations.

As a formal contract for military co-operation, however, an alliance may be difficult to distinguish from other kinds of military contracts such as military subsidies, military assistance agreements, or military base agreements. Most alliances specify (if only in a general phrase) the contingencies under which force will or will not be used by the members and against whom it will be used, but they may be worded so broadly that these particulars can only be inferred. Conversely, others kinds of military contracts may contain explicit political provisions concerning the use of weapons and facilities. In any case, like alliances, they are based on definite understandings and expectations (whether shared by both partners or not) about the purposes and circumstances of the specified military co-operation.

Even in the absence of formal contracts for military co-operation, unilateral declarations of intentions can go far to commit states to the use of force in behalf of other states. Such declarations are particularly important now that the communication of military intentions for the sake of deterrence plays such a prominent role in international politics. Their importance is indicated by their extensive use to reinforce and refine formal reciprocal commitments.

But military commitments need not depend even on unilateral declarations. They are often established and conveyed indirectly by countless official and unofficial words and actions, creating understandings and expectations that are no less significant for being implicit. These understandings and expectations are the substance of alignments of power and interest, and alliances and other explicit commitments would be useless without them.

Why, then, do states make alliances? Generally, because alliances are the most binding obligations they can make to stabilize the configurations of power that affect their vital interests. Alliances add precision and specificity to informal or tacit alignments.

More than that, the fact that alliances are *reciprocal* and *formal* agreements increases the obligations of signatories to carry out specified commitments and co-operation. The ceremony and solemnity accompanying the formation of an alliance signify that sovereign states have surrendered important aspects of their freedom of action and obligated themselves to an interdependent relationship.

Moreover, the obligation of alliance relates directly to the response of signatories to contingencies that call for a possible resort to war. Alliances impinge more fundamentally upon the vital interests of nations and more broadly upon the whole range of their foreign policies than agreements designed merely to provide for the use of goods and facilities. For this reason alliances are also more likely to provoke rivals and adversaries and lead to countervailing combinations, which may further limit the political options and enhance the interdependence of allies.

The political significance of alliances is all the greater in this era of popular (including undemocratic) governments because alliances generally presuppose national or ideological affinities that go beyond the matter-of-fact expediencies involved in more restricted contracts.

Thus, whatever its benefits, an alliance tends to cost more than other kinds of military commitments because it limits a member's political options and freedom of action more. For this reason the signatories of an alliance feel entitled to continual assurance of each other's fidelity and their own net benefit. Consequently, an alliance of some duration encourages further claims upon its members and tends to require repeated regeneration through adjustments of their liabilities and assets. Lacking recourse to supranational instrumentalities to enforce an obligation that could involve their very survival as nations, states must rely on diplomatic co-operation against an adversary and on other manifestations of good faith and common interest. These by-products of alliance may entangle states in each other's affairs to an extent that is not always easy to anticipate when an alliance is formed.

As an investment in future returns of national security and welfare, an alliance is apt to be more open-ended and consequential than other kinds of military contracts. Therefore, although alliances are a pervasive element of international politics, the capacity and incentive for states to engage in alliance are far from universal. Relatively few states have the resources, the internal cohesion, or the coherence of national interest to become effective allies. Some states that will freely seek and accept military assistance or base agreements may regard even the most limited alliance as an unwise political entanglement.

2. THE FUNCTIONS OF ALLIANCES

There are four principal functions of alliances, and they are not necessarily mutually exclusive: accretion of external power, internal security, restraint of allies, and international order.

The accretion of power entails increasing the military power of allies by combining resources and eliciting positive co-operation. This has been the basic and the most common function of alliances. The ultimate purpose of accretion is to enhance the relative power of one or more allies against another state or states for defensive or offensive ends (although some states, especially the smaller ones, may want power largely in the form of status).

Internal security is sometimes a more important function of alliance for a weak state than accretion of its external power. In recognition of the international significance of internal threats and developments, which are often supported covertly from outside, alliances may be intended principally to enhance the security or stability of an ally's government or regime, often by legitimizing material assistance or military intervention against internal opposition. This purpose is usually not made explicit, however, since intervention in the domestic affairs of another state, even at that state's invitation, has acquired a stigma in the age of popular national governments.

Next to accretion, the most prominent function of alliances has been to restrain and control allies, particularly in order to safeguard one ally against actions of another that might endanger its security or otherwise jeopardize its interests. This function may be accomplished directly by pledges of non-intervention or by other reassurances that one ally will not contravene the interests of another, or it may be the by-product of commitments that limit an ally's freedom of action and provide its partner with access to, and influence upon, its government.

International order is the broadest and the least attainable function of an alliance. An alliance may aim to preserve harmony among its members and establish an international order — that is, a stable, predictable, and safe pattern of international politics — within an area of common concern. In its ultimate form, this function of an alliance becomes collective security. In different ways, the Quadruple Alliance after the Napoleonic Wars and the OAS have exercised this function of maintaining order. Before the onset of the cold war, the United States expected the Big Three, as the core of the United Nations, to be guarantors of a new world order. Some people believe that NATO [North Atlantic Treaty Organization] has served indirectly as a framework for a new Western European order or even an Atlantic Community.

3. THE DETERMINANTS OF ALLIANCES

Among the numerous factors that may affect the creation, continution, or decline of alliances in various parts of the world, several "determinants" (in the nondeterministic sense) seem particularly important. These determinants also affect the characteristics of alliances and the nature of their functions, but they are principally relevant to the elementary questions of the existence or nonexistence, utility or disutility, and vitality or impotence of alliances. They are:

The Pattern of Conflicting and Converging Interests. If states have no interests that they need to support by military power against other states, they lack sufficient incentives to form alliances. If two or more states feel no need for each other's assistance in improving their military capacity to protect or advance their interests against other states, an alliance is not likely to be created, and an existing alliance is likely to erode.

Even if mutual military needs exist, the creation or maintenance of an alliance often requires a convergence of interest that goes beyond a common interest in security. Most notably, there must be sufficient affinity and harmony of policies. The importance of this convergence is directly proportionate to the comprehensiveness and mutuality of the alliance's obligations and to the duration of the alliance; it is inversely proportionate to the intensity of the security threat.

In the case of existing or prospective alliances in which interallied control or order is an important function, the urgency of a commonly felt threat to security may be less determinative, but then the pattern of conflicting as well as converging interests among allies becomes crucial.

The Distribution of Military Power. The formation and preservation of an alliance depends on the military capacity of states as well as their political incentive to co-operate militarily (even though one state may only provide bases and facilities or promise to remain neutral). The capacity of states to help each other depends on the relationship of their concerted power to the power of potential adversaries.

The interaction of this distribution of power with the pattern of interests among states affects not only the desirability and feasibility of alliances but also the characteristics of alliances and the nature of alliance policies. For example, it establishes the polarity of power, or, more specifically, the number of states that are engaged in a dominant international political conflict, are projecting decisive military power, and are undertaking independent military commitments. Whether there are two, or many, "poles of power" has many implications for alliances....

The changing distribution of power between an alliance and its opponents may affect the cohesion of an alliance. For example, adverse changes in the external distribution of power may create dissatisfaction with the distribution within an alliance. Such dissatisfaction and the effort to overcome it may change alliance policies and even alliance functions.

Alliance Capability. Even if the preceding determinants should support the creation or maintenance of an alliance, the states that are concerned may lack certain minimum military and political prerequisites of alliance. Most important among these prerequisites are: (a) enough internal stability, executive authority, and economic strength, along with a sufficiently coherent and predicatable foreign policy, to enable a state to be a reliable collaborator and (b) adequate capacity of a state to dispose its military power effectively for the benefit of an ally. (Again, the capacity of one state may be confined to a relatively passive role.)

Alliance-Mindedness. Related to the preceding determinant, and also of special significance for the future of alliances among the small and newer states in the Third World, is the subjective attitude of governments toward alliances. For example, some small, recently independent states are averse to alliances with the chief protagonists of the cold war. The subjective inclination or disinclination to enter alliances may be closely related to considerations of expediency; yet it goes beyond sheer reasoned calculation of security requirements and reflects hopes, suspicions, and ideals that are deeply rooted in the national culture and experience. In America's period of physical invulnerability and political insulation, its high-principled denigration of alliances was as important as its glorification of them in the cold war.

These determinants should be considered as a whole because they reinforce, qualify, or offset each other. None of them is sufficient by itself to account for the past, present, or future of alliances. The first two determinants, however, are particularly important.

4. THE EVOLUTION OF ALLIANCES

All the functions and determinants of alliances that I have cited apply to contemporary alliances, but the context and methods of application have changed throughout modern history as basic changes occurred in the military and political environment. One way of comprehending these changes is to note the shifts of emphasis among several contrasting types of alliances: between offensive (or revisionist) and defensive (or status quo), wartime and peacetime, bilateral and multilateral, guarantee and mutual assistance, institutionalized and noninstitutionalized alliances. The distinctions among them should be apparent in the brief description of the evolution of alliances that follows.

In the eighteenth century, alliances were the primary means by which states tried to improve their military positions, since the strength of their armed forces was relatively fixed. The typical alliance was a bilateral agreement, or several interlocking bilateral agreements, made during a war or in anticipation of war, after which it was terminated or became inoperative. It usually involved one or several of the following kinds of commitments: a subsidy to support another state's troops; a guarantee to fight on the side of another state (often with a specific number of troops) under stated circumstances; a pledge of nonintervention or mutual abstention from war in the event that one or both of the signatories should become engaged in war with other states; or a division of the territorial and other spoils of war.

Before the last part of the nineteenth century, alliances entailed no extensive military preparations or co-ordination. The undeveloped state of technology, the limited economic capacity of states to carry on war, and the small scale of warfare made such arrangements infeasible and unnecessary. Moreover, states had few of the inhibitions against going to war that arose later when modern war revealed its awesome potential for civil destruction, and they lacked the need and the capacity to sustain alliances as peacetime instruments of military deterrence. War was not yet so terrifying as to create this need and capacity. It was a more or less normal recourse.

Consequently, although there were a few multilateral defensive alliances of long duration, there were scores of offensive alliances — chiefly bilateral — that were intended to acquire territory by means of war. Both offensive and defensive alliances aimed as often at restraining an ally by limiting his political options and deflecting him from an opposing alliance as they did at aggregating military power. The ideal was to keep alliances flexible and commitments limited. Toward this end secret alliances and secret clauses in published alliances were commonly arranged, not only to conceal aggressive designs, but also to increase diplomatic options by making deals with other states without giving offense to allies.

The eighteenth and the first half of the nineteenth centuries were notable for the large number of alliances that were formed and unformed; but a more significant feature of alliances at that time was their limited and flexible nature, which enabled them to adjust readily to shifting interests with little regard for the later constraints of sentiment and ideology or the imperatives of aggregating power in peacetime. The flexibility and secrecy of alliances created a good deal of diplomatic turmoil, but, because there was a fairly equal division of power among the several major states of Europe, these qualities helped to sustain a working equilibrium that restrained and moderated ambitions and acquisitions and kept any single state or coalition of states from dominating the others. The politics of alliances were punctuated by frequent wars, but the limited scale and destructiveness of warfare made it a tolerable instrument for maintaining an equilibrium.

The Napoleonic Wars revealed the new scope, intensity, and dynamism that war could attain when based on the mobilization of manpower and popular enthusiasm. This revelation compelled the European states to combine in a grand coalition to defeat Napoleon's bid for hegemony, just as they had combined against Louis XIV and earlier aspirants to hegemony. This time, however, a wartime alliance became a novel peacetime coalition. In 1815 the victors formed the Concert of Europe, which combined the eighteenth century conception of equilibrium (insofar as the territorial-political settlements and the Quadruple Alliance were aimed at checking France) with the new conception of a multilateral combination of states pledged to concert their power and to consult among themselves in order to preserve the international order against further liberal and nationalist revolutions as well as against divisions among themselves. Therefore the Concert might be called the first modern experiment to form an organization for international order — a forerunner of the League of Nations and the United Nations.

The Concert of Europe was undermined by differing national interests, especially by Britain's refusal to join in suppressing revolutions. After 1822, when the British left the Quandruple Alliance, nothing remained of the Concert except the habit of consultation during crises. International politics returned to flexible, limited, and mostly offensive alliances in a multipolar international system. Taking advantage of the fragmented structure of power, Bismarck acquired territory at the expense of Denmark and Austria, and he rounded out Germany's boundaries with a quick victory over France in 1871. He shored up his accomplishments with a complicated network of bilateral and trilateral alliances designed to keep power fragmented and to prevent combinations that could revise the status quo by setting up balanced antagonisms. Primarily his alliances were intended to limit the options of allies while keeping Germany's commitments to them equally limited.

Yet Bismarck actually helped to undermine his own system of alliances and to set the stage for a different kind of alliance system. The suddenness and decisiveness of Prussia's victories demonstrated the efficacy of its continuing peacetime military preparations, particularly the conscription system, the use of railroads, and the professional planning and direction of war under a general staff. To withstand such an assault, a state would have to be as well-prepared during peacetime as during wartime. Furthermore, military preparedness would require advance arrangements for the co-operation of other states and the co-ordination of military plans and operations. (The French defeat was partly due to France's mistaken calculation that she could acquire allies after war broke out.) The dramatic development in the last quarter of the nineteenth century of the technological and economic capacity of major states to advance their military positions by quantitative and qualitative arms increases indicated that the internal development of military capacity might replace shifting alliances as the dynamic element of power.

In these circumstances Bismarck's alliance system led to counteralliances that, under the growing pressure of military preparedness through arms races, tended to polarize international conflict between two opposing coalitions, the Triple Alliance and the Triple Entente. These two alliances were far from being tightly knit diplomatically, and they were only partially co-ordinated militarily by military conventions and staff conversations. Nevertheless, they provided the political frameworks within which military commitments were consolidated; and the consolidation of military commitments in turn tightened the alliances. Thus alliances evolved from a means of fragmenting military power to a means of aggregating it.

The consolidation of defensive alliances before World War I, combined with the build-up of military power, made states more susceptible to being triggered into war by an ally (as Austria's war against Serbia entangled Germany). This consolidation encouraged a chain reaction of involvement, once war began, and practically guaranteed that any war involving one ally would become a general war. Nevertheless, if states had been primarily concerned with military deterrence rather than simply with preparing to fight, and if they had not permitted military plans (especially those for total mobilization) to take precedence over diplomatic opportunities to accommodate disputes short of war, the polarization of alliances need not have been incompatible with the peace and security of all. In fact these were not primarily deterrent alliances but rather alliances formed in anticipation of war. Unfortunately, statesmen deferred to their general staffs, who were absorbed in preparing maximum offensive striking power for a war that they expected to be as short and decisive as the Franco-Prussian War.

Contrary to prevailing expectations, World War I turned out to be a devastating war of attrition, and modern firepower chewed up the manpower and resources of Europe. This grim surprise led to a widespread reaction in the victorious countries against alliances, which were regarded as one of the principal causes of the war. Woodrow Wilson caught the popular imagination by proposing an "association" of power, in opposition to the discredited balance of power system. According to his conception of the League of Nations, all states would be organized against aggression from any quarter. He expected the chief deterrent to aggression to be the power of world opinion rather than the threat of force. Other American proponents of the League idea thought the United States should concert its power with that of Britain and France to preserve a new postwar order. However, it is doubtful that the nation as a whole was prepared to participate in power politics to the extent required of a major ally, for Americans still retained the sense of physical security that underlay their isolationist tradition. Until they became convinced by America's involvement in World War II and the onset of the cold war that aggression abroad impinged directly upon American security, they would not enter a peacetime alliance.

The ascent of Hilter's Germany showed that a peacetime deterrent coalition, whatever its effects in other circumstances might be, was essential to peace and order in the face of the most dangerous bid for hegemony since Napoleon. Unfortunately, the major democratic countries failed to form such a coalition. Although Wilsonian collective security would have been unworkable as a universal supranational order, even if the United States had joined the League, this ideal served as an excuse for avoiding an alliance, especially for Britain, which turned down France's bid for a defensive alliance against Germany. Yet World War II led the major democratic states to draw a lesson from this interwar experience that became the psychological foundation of America's postwar system of deterrent alliances. This system came to dominate the postwar history of alliances.

In the cold war, alliances have been as important in international politics as in any other period of history. But among the advanced states several developments have reduced their flexibility (but, by the same token, enhanced their stability). Their primarily deterrent function, the inhibitions against major states going to war in the nuclear age, the increased importance of peacetime military forces, the sensitivity of governments to public sentiment and ideological positions, the persistence of a dominant international conflict and structure of power that have been essentially bipolar — all these developments have tended to restrict the number of alliances and the frequency of shifts of alliance among major states. At the same time, the emergence of many new states in previously colonial and politically inactive areas has meant that the great majority of states lack the basic external and internal prerequisites for engaging in alliances. One consequence of these new constraints on alliances is that other forms of military commitments have come to play a proportionately greater role in international politics. Another is that intra-alliance functions have assumed greater importance....

C: MECHANISMS OF REGULATION

Friends as Foes

Immanuel Wallerstein

The year 1980 marked the midpoint in a global process: the steady erosion of the hegemonic position of the United States in the world-economy. The political keystone of this hegemony has been a strong alliance with Western Europe and Japan. Until 1967 the United States dominated the world military arena and political economy — including the markets of other industrialized countries — and Western Europe and Japan followed U.S. leadership willingly and completely. By 1990 the former allies will have parted company with the United States.

This process is not fortuitous, mysterious, or reversible. Roughly comparable declines in the capitalist world-economy have taken place twice before: Great Britain from 1873 to 1896; and, although this is less well-known, the United Provinces (the modern-day Netherlands) from 1650 to 1672. In each case, a nation of unquestioned supremacy fell to the lesser status of a very powerful state defending very central economic interests in the world-economy, but nonetheless one state amid several. And, in each case, in the decades following the loss of hegemony, the former predominant power continued to decline as a center of political-military strength and of high-profit enterprise, to the advantage of other states within the world-economy.

Such cyclical patterns — the rise and decline of hegemonic powers and the more frequent expansion and stagnation of the world-economy — exist within the framework of long-term secular trends that have been leading to a systemic crisis that transcends the immediate difficulties of the moment. These trends, characteristic of a capitalist world-economy, may be seen in the constant development of the division of labor in the world-economy as a whole and in the continued development of the interstate system.

For 400 years the development of the division of labor has involved a steady increase in the degree to which production has been mechanized, land and labor made into commodities purchasable on the market, and social relations regulated by contracts rather than by customary rules. This secular division of labor has proceeded in a step-like fashion that alternates 20-30 year periods of expansion with similar periods of contraction (sometimes called Kondratieff cycles, or A-phases and B-phases). Each A-phase of expansion has culminated in a major blockage of the world accumulation process, resulting in stagnation. And each B-phase of stagnation has been overcome by the further concentration of capital, the launching of new product cycles, the expansion of outer boundaries of the world-economy, and the expansion of effective demand — in short, by the spreading and deepening of the capitalist world-economy and the

---

Immanuel Wallerstein, "Friends as Foes". Reprinted with permission of *Foreign Policy*, 40 (Fall 1980).

further polarization of distribution as measured globally and not within individual states.

The development of the interstate system has involved the elaboration and institutionalization of power in each of the member states, within the constraints of interstate rules that have become increasingly explicit. As the roles of the state machineries have become more prominent, the state has become even more the focus of antisystemic forces — social movements opposed to the basic mode of operation of the world-system — that have sought power in the name of socialist and nationalist ideologies. The strengthening of capitalist forces and the development of the world-economy itself have bred these antisystemic forces, whose own strength has increased significantly in the twentieth century.

A MATURE LIBERALISM

This is the context within which the United States became the political center of global economic forces between 1945 and 1967. During that great postwar boom, despite the paranoia of American leaders and the constant clamor about national danger, there was no serious opposition in the world to U.S. hegemony. In the late 1950s, it was the communist world (with de-Stalinization) and not the West that was undergoing political crisis. The Soviet Union was easily contained; indeed, it was struggling to hold its own politically and economically, while it sought to rebuild militarily. Western Europe and Japan, the main beneficiaries of a massive creation of global effective demand via U.S. economic aid and military support, operated as virtual client states during the 1950s. Decolonization in Asia and Africa went smoothly, largely to the political advantage of the United States. And at home, the anticommunist political repression of the 1940s and 1950s (from President Truman's loyalty oaths to McCarthyism) seemed to stifle the dangerous social tensions of earlier periods.

The one major exception to complete U.S. hegemony was China, where the accession to power of the Communist party represented an effective overthrow of foreign domination and a radical alteration of China's position in the world-system.

For the most part, a generalized self-congratulatory contentment pervaded the United States during the Kennedy administration, evincing the liberalism of a mature hegemonic power and encouraging the growth of its offshoots — the Peace Corps, civil rights, and détente.

This liberal self-confidence explains the tremendous psychological shock experienced by U.S. political and business leaders in response to the events of 1967-1968: the currency and gold crises that marked the fall of the U.S. dollar from its pedestal; the Tet offensive against South Vietnam that revealed that a small Third World people could hold U.S. military power in check; the student-worker rebellions — such as those at Columbia University and in France — that showed that internal struggles within Western states were once again on the agenda.

In retrospect, the sudden explosions of 1967-1968 should not have been so surprising. The economic reconstruction of Western Europe and Japan created centers of competition with U.S.-based firms and contributed to the global over-expansion of world production. By concentrating on the military sphere, the Soviet Union had increased its military strength relative to that of the United States. At the same time, direct U.S. military intervention had severe financial and economic consequences for the United States. The steady decolonization of the world could not possibly remain a controlled and formal process; it would inevitably become more radical and spread to the Western industrialized, or core, countries themselves (to the "Third World within"). And the liberalism of the mature hegemonic power would retreat once its largess was rejected by oppressed groups asserting demands on their own terms.

All of a sudden, in 1967 the United States found itself in a B-period, a period of decelerated growth. In the world-economy, the most significant result of this period of relative economic stagnation has been a striking decline in the competitiveness of U.S.-based production organizations compared with those located in Japan and Western Europe, excluding Great Britain. This relative decline is evident upon comparing growth rates, standards of living, capital investments as a percentage of gross national product, growth in productivity, capital-labor ratios, share in the world market, and research and development expenditures. The decline is also reflected in the relative strengths of currencies and in the rates of inflation and unemployment.

A second striking result of this B-phase has been the relocation of industry. On a world scale, this relocation involved the rise of the newly industrializing countries and the opening of free trade zones — the creation of the so-called new international division of labor. In general, the bargaining power of large semiperipheral countries such as Brazil and countries with key commodities such as the Organization of Petroleum Exporting Countries (OPEC) bloc has been greatly strengthened.

ACQUIESCENCE OR COLLUSION

With respect to the changing world-economy, it is the OPEC price rises that have caught everyone's attention and that politicians and the press have transformed from consequence into cause. Two things should be noted about the oil price rises. First, they began in 1973, not in 1963 or 1953. The oil-producing countries did not suddenly become avaricious. Rather, in 1973 oil price rises became, for the first time, economically and politically possible, in large part because the global rise of industrial production entailed a vast increase in demand for current energy production. This overproduction in turn promoted competition among the core powers, thereby limiting their economic and military bargaining power. OPEC simply capitalized on this situation.

Second, the oil price rises met little opposition from the core states. This cannot be written off to political lassitude resulting from economic stagnation. There probably also existed U.S. acquiescence, even collusion. It is hard otherwise to account for the crucial support in 1973 for this policy by the Saudi and Iranian governments, without which there would have been no OPEC price rise. James Akins, former U.S. ambassador to Saudi Arabia, reported that the Saudis went along with the price rise only when they could not persuade the United States to put pressure on Iranian price demands.

The United States could have seen two short-run advantages in the 1973 oil price rise: a competitive boost relative to Western Europe and Japan because of their greater dependence in 1973 on imported oil: and the creation of financial bases for the shah and to a lesser extent the Saudis so they could serve as proconsuls for the United States, relieving in part the U.S. political and financial burden.

There are also long-run advantages for the core powers collectively in the oil price rises — advantages that probably outweigh any disruptive effects. In a situation of global stagnation, one key problem concerns possibilities for new industrial complexes of high-profit growth. One such complex could involve new energy sources and energy-saving devices. The first advantage, then, is that the higher cost of petroleum created a major incentive for this kind of complex. Former Secretary of State Henry Kissinger after all did talk of a floor for petroleum prices and not of a ceiling.

The second major advantage is that inflation itself can in fact lead to a considerable decline in the real wage bill of the core countries, redistributing surplus to owners in a form that is far more manageable than the bread lines of 1933.

German Chancellor Helmut Schmidt has spoken of the struggle for the world product, emphasizing only interstate allocations. This might better be called the world class struggle in which reallocations are being made within as well as between states. For example, if the oil-producing states have gained considerably in the last decade, it is scarcely the large oil multinationals that have lost. It is, rather, the middle and lower strata in both core and peripheral countries.

The decline of U.S. hegemony has had major effects on the interstate system as well. Alliances that emerged after World War II are collapsing. The Sino-Soviet split, begun in the 1950s but consecrated in the 1960s, did not necessarily serve the interests of the United States as a global power. The split made it impossible to consolidate stability through a political deal with the USSR and muddied irremediably ideological waters. And when the United States came to terms with China, Western Europe and Japan could not simply maintain their old alliance with the United States, but were forced to reconsider all the options.

The Sino-Soviet split was liberating for national movements in the Third World. The split closed the books on the Communist International and forced liberation groups to move where they were under pressure to move anyway — to action that was autonomous of the world alliance system. Despite U.S.-Soviet détente, a de facto U.S.-Chinese alliance, and socialist wars in Southeast Asia, the 1970s saw a steady acceleration of revolutionary movements (southern Africa, Central America and the Caribbean, and the Middle East) rather than the reverse.

THE WEST-WEST CONFLICT

The most difficult issues, however, that confront U.S. policy makers in the coming decades are neither East-West issues (notwithstanding Afghanistan) nor North-South issues (notwithstanding Iran). Rather they are West-West issues that are based on the great economic and therefore political threat of the two significant U.S. rivals, Western Europe and Japan. President Carter's handling of the crises in Afghanistan and Iran as well as his decision to develop the MX missile could be viewed as attempts to maintain U.S. political leadership in the West and regain economic supremacy via ideological pressure on U.S. allies. Indeed, the effort to constrain U.S. allies bids fair to become the priority concern of U.S. foreign policy.

What are the real problems facing the United States in this growing West-West conflict? There is the immediate problem of fending off the worst aspects of the economic decline of the 1980s. There is the more important, long-run concern of trying to profit maximally from the probable renewed economic expansion of the 1990s.

Because there will have to be major contraction in some centers of world production, the basic issue for the 1980s is who will export unemployment to whom. Thus far inflation has masked this issue, at least politically; but should a dramatic fall in world prices occur, minimizing the resultant economic damage will become a matter of survival for regimes throughout the West.

In the short run, the United States has two major mechanisms at its disposal. It can prop up technologically doomed industries (the Chrysler handout), which reduces unemployment in one sector at the expense of others and also diminishes the capital available for investment in industries that will make America competitive in the 1990s. In addition, it can increase military expenditures, also at the expense of long-run development.

For the 1990s the basic policy issue is who will gain the competitive edge in the new technologies of microelectronics, biotechnology, and energy resources. Success will be determined by an interlocking triplet of research and development innovations; reduction of real costs of production; and increased access to markets for the older sectors of production — formerly high-profit sectors, now medium-profit sectors — such as electronics, automobiles, and even computers.

What is happening today in industries such as steel, automobiles, and electronics is a double process. First, West European and Japanese firms are undercutting U.S.-based firms, even in the U.S. home market. Second, production processes are being broken up. Large parts of production chains are being moved to semiperipheral countries, including socialist countries, and the chains themselves are more likely to end in Western Europe and Japan rather than in the United States.

The structural causes of this massive shift in production centers outside the United States — a shift that is likely to accelerate sharply in the 1980s — are twofold. On the one hand, given larger and older U.S. industrial hardware, there are the higher costs of amortization of the overall plant. On the other, there is the higher U.S. wage bill. The real difference between U.S. costs of production and those of Western Europe and Japan does not lie in the wages paid a skilled mechanic. The political bargaining strength of workers is basically the same in all parts of the West. The real difference in costs — paid in part directly by companies, in part indirectly through government expenditures — lies in the salaries of the well-to-do middle stratum (i.e., professionals and executives).

It is not that the individual incomes of U.S. executives or professionals exceed those of their allied counterparts. In many cases, the opposite is true. Rather, it is that in the United States the well-to-do middle stratum is a significantly larger percentage of the total population. Hence, the social bill of the U.S. middle class is dramatically higher, and it is impossible for either the government or the large corporations to do anything about it.

An attack on these expenditures of a magnitude sufficient enough to make U.S.-based industry cost competitive again would entail higher political costs than anyone dares pay, especially because American political structures are heavily dominated by precisely those people whose incomes would have to be cut. It is therefore far easier for a multinational corporation to consider shifting its sites of production and research and eventually even its headquarters than to try to reduce costs directly. This has already begun to occur.

The process of disinvestment in the old industries will affect the research and development expenditures on the new ones by reducing both the U.S. tax and profit bases of U.S.-based companies. The markets for the new industries will be located primarily in the core countries themselves, but the markets for the older industries will be more world-wide. It will be important for producers to find fresh markets — zones whose expansion depends upon the products of these older industries. Such zones encompass the semiperipheral countries that are industrializing and that, even if they have their own plants and production sites, will need advanced machinery and hardware. The European Economic Community countries are up front in this effort in terms of their economic partnership with developing countries covered by the Lomé Convention. The largest likely market of the 1980s and, to an even greater extent, of the 1990s will comprise the socialist countries. Behind the Sino-Soviet controversy lies a struggle to be this market in the most advantageous way possible. This is called catching up or modernizing.

EUROPEAN-SOVIET COOPERATION

Within this economic reality — this B-phase of stagnation — lie the bases for the realignment of alliances in the interstate system. In a sense, China jumped the gun by its dramatic and successful attempt to make an arrangement with the United States. It is no accident that this diplomatic turnabout was done with Richard Nixon, who represented those U.S. forces whose deep anticommunist ideology was not tightly linked to a commitment to a North Atlantic Treaty Organization alliance structure.

Japan, no doubt miffed by its exclusion from the very first diplomatic steps, quickly allowed its true interests to prevail in the Sino-Japanese reconciliation. Because of the strong, complementary economic interests of the two countries and the fundamental link of civilization (still a major factor in policy making), the reconciliation is even more important than the joint U.S.-Chinese Shanghai communiqué.

If the United States has moved in the direction of China, it is because such movement makes geopolitical, strategic sense. And given that during the 1970s the economic fruits of détente with the Soviet Union were clearly being garnered by Western Europe rather than by the United States, these strategic considerations seemed worth the risk.

In terms of the political economy of the world-system, Western Europe and the USSR have much to offer each other, both positively and negatively. Were the two sides to move slowly toward a de facto structure of cooperation that need not involve anything affirmative in the sphere of military alliances, the USSR could obtain the capital equipment it needs to improve its long-term relative position in the world-economy, thus meeting the most pressing demand of its own cadres. Of course, the Soviet Union would also thereby obtain security against any dangers (real or imagined) implied by the U.S.-Chinese structure of cooperation.

In conjunction with Western Europe — and probably not without it — the Soviet Union could also effectuate a significant breakthrough in economic links with the Middle East. This presumes that the USSR and Western Europe would be able to complete the Camp David process by an arrangement between Israel and the Palestine Liberation Organization. In addition, a Middle East agreement might partially defuse the Soviet Union's greatest internal danger point, the potentially higher consciousness of the central Asian Moslem peoples.

Moreover, an arrangement of this sort between the Soviet Union and Western Europe — in which the German Social Democratic Party would have to play a large part — could also discourage the revolt of Eastern Europe against the USSR. The uprisings in Prague during spring 1968 threatened the USSR in two ways. The idea of liberalization might spread eastward, particularly to the Ukraine. And Czechoslovakia might move out of the Soviet orbit, especially in economic terms, and into that of West Germany. In the context of West European-Soviet cooperation, the latter fear would become less relevant.

Such an arrangement could look equally attractive to Western Europe. The Soviet market would be opened in some meaningful sense to Western Europe-based industries. The resources of the Soviet Union would become available, at least over a crucial 20-30 year period. And the USSR and East European countries could serve as geographically convenient and politically constrained reservoirs of relatively cheap labor for participation in Western Europe's claims of production.

Furthermore, a solution to the East European question from the Soviet perspective is also a solution from the viewpoint of Western Europe. Cooperation would permit the reintegration of Europe — culturally, economically, and eventually politically — a development that has up to now been barred by Soviet military strength. In particular, cooperation would permit, at a minimum, the two Germanies to move closer together.

An amicable, working relationship with the Soviet Union would even have political advantages for Western Europe. Just as the USSR might not gain a breakthrough in the Middle East without Western Europe, so might the reverse be true. In addition, by guaranteeing a relatively strong position to West European firms during the difficult years of the 1980s, a structure of cooperation would insure the continuance of the high degree of social peace that Western Europe is currently enjoying. On the ideological front, it would also contain in part the USSR.

A NEW HEGEMONY?

Needless to say, the ideological sentiments on both sides remain very strong — but not unswerving. In the case of West Germany, ideological commitments have not changed, but their role has: In the 1950s and 1960s, West Germany's economic interests were served by emphasizing ideological commitments, whereas in the 1970s and the 1980s, these same economic interests are being advanced by playing down political beliefs.

Should this kind of realignment come about, the most indecisive power will be Great Britain, which faces difficulty no matter which way it turns. But in any West-West split, Britain will probably have to stay with the United States, if only because in the very important geopolitical struggle over southern Africa, British and American interests are closely linked. And in a world in which British markets are declining everywhere, southern Africa might be one of the last secure trading partners.

In this picture of potential realignments, what happens to the North-South struggle? At one level, a realignment of the Northern powers along the lines suggested would create incredible ideological confusion in the South. At another level, it might lead to an ideological clarification. The process of disintegration of the world system, brought about by the cumulative strength of the world's antisystemic forces, cannot be controlled by the United States or the Soviet Union. Revolutions in, say, Honduras, Tunisia, Kenya, or Thailand are not primarily a function of geopolitical arrangements among the great powers. What realignments may bring about is a greater disillusionment among these revolutionary movements regarding the efficacy of achieving power via the control of individual state structures. After a century of detour, the emphasis may return to the importance of creating real worldwide inter-movement links —ones that would cut across North-South and East-West boundaries. This is what is meant by ideological clarification.

And this is why even if the world-economy takes a major upturn in the 1990s and even if Western Europe begins to play the role of a new ascending hegemonic power, the world is not entering merely another cyclical moment of the present system. It is in this sense that the underlying, long-run systemic crisis of world capitalism may be more meaningful over the next 50 years. In the middle run, world capitalism will seem to recuperate; in the long run, it will be transformed fundamentally.

In the short run, however, the biggest traumas will be felt by the United States. Americans have spent the past 30 years getting used to the benefits of a hegemonic position, and they will have to spend the next 30 getting used to life without them. For the majority of the world, it may not make that big a difference. For that majority, the real question is not which nation is hegemonic in the present world-system, but whether and how that world-system will be transformed.

C: MECHANISMS OF REGULATION

Containment: Its Past and Future

John Lewis Gaddis

Nations, like individuals, tend to be prisoners of their pasts. Rarely has this been more true than in the thirty-five years of Soviet-American competition we know as the Cold War. That phenomenon, one of the longest-running in modern times, has appeared, more than once,to be on the verge of passing from the scene, but it never really has. Something always seems to happen to revive it — Korea, Hungary, the U-2, Vietnam, Czechoslovakia, Angola, the Carter human rights campaign, Afghanistan — just as pundits are about to consign the Cold War to those scavengers of dead issues and defunct controversies, the historians.

Why this extraordinary durability? How is it that a rivalry that arose three and a half decades ago — over issues few leaders on either side today would be capable of recalling, much less discussing intelligently — can still preoccupy us today, in a world that could hardly be more different from that of 1945? And how is it that this rivalry, which would long ago have produced war in any other age, has not in fact done so — even though by anyone's standards there has been ample provocation? What are the prospects that this standoff between competition and caution will continue? What politics should the United States adopt in the 1980s to insure that it does?

THE INTERNAL AND EXTERNAL DIMENSIONS OF THE COLD WAR

The Cold War began as a direct result of the way World War II ended: Victorious powers on opposite sides of the globe were separated, both in Europe and Northeast Asia, by power vacuums. It was probably inevitable that the uneasy coalition Hitler had given rise to would break up, once the force that had brought it together ceased to exist. The controversies that ensued over Eastern Europe, Germany and Berlin, the Balkans, Turkey, Iran, Japan, and Korea were all part of the process of post-war adjustment among the superpowers. These controversies grew out of the probes and counter-probes by which great states demarcate spheres of influence, organize blocs, establish tacit "rules of the game," and in general settle down to the condition of wary co-existence.

The ideological competition between communism and capitalism had been present, of course, since the days of the Bolshevik Revolution, but it was not a primary cause of the Cold War. Both

---

John Lewis Gaddis, "Containment: Its Past and Future," *International Security*, Vol. 5 (Spring 1981), pp. 74-102. Reprinted by permission of the MIT Press Journals. Some footnotes have been removed; those remaining have been renumbered.

Russians and Americans tended to view ideology more as a justification for action than as a guide to action; both, as they showed during World War II, were capable of subordinating ideological differences to pursue common interests where those existed. Once those interests disappeared, though, ideology did become the chief means by which each side differentiated friend from foe. The Soviet Union moved, somewhat belatedly, to consolidate its sphere of influence in Eastern Europe by imposing communist regimes there; the United States, also somewhat belatedly, came to see in the ideological orientation of states and movements reliable evidence of where it stood in the global competition for power. Admittedly, the pattern was not always perfect. The Soviet Union did not insist on imposing communist governments everywhere within its sphere of influence — Finland was the notable exception. Nor did the United States, as the case of Yugoslavia showed, consign to the outer darkness all communist states. In general, though, and with increasing frequency as time went on, ideology did become the mechanism by which alingments were drawn in the Cold War — even to the point that the United States neglected, for many years, the possibility of cooperating with the People's Republic of China in a task in which both had a strong interest, namely containing the Russians.

Once it was underway, the Cold War took on yet a third dimension — that of an arms race. Here, appearances were more important than reality. We now know that throughout the first two and a half decades of the Cold War, the Soviet Union was inferior to the United States in all major categories of weapons except manpower. But until the deployment of satellite reconnaissance capabilities in the early 1960s, Washington had no reliable means of verifying that fact, nor were the Russians cooperative in providing such means. As a consequence, the arms race appeared to be closer than it actually was: the United Staters until 1961 perceived itself as operating from a position of strategic inferiority, or something very near to it; after 1961, when Washington convinced itself that it was in fact ahead of the Russians, it was actually in the process of losing that advantage, thanks to the Kremlin's decision to switch its emphasis from rhetorical weapons to real ones in the wake of the Cuban missile crisis.

A fourth dimension the Cold War took on was that of a competition for influence in the so-called "third" or "non-aligned" world. This, again, was an aspect of the struggle that did not surface immediately: Stalin's interest in supporting national liberation movements beyond his control was notoriously tepid. With Khrushchev, though, the arena of competition did shift to Asia, Africa, and Latin America, greatly aided by the grievances that inhabitants of those regions had against the industrialized West.

There is yet a fifth dimension of the Cold War that is more difficult to characterize than the others, but no less important: this is the Cold War as the product of internal influences within the two major countries involved. George F. Kennan had argued as early as 1946 that the Soviet leadership required the existence of a hostile outside world to justify its own repressive rule; there was nothing the West could do to allay Moscow's paranoia, he seemed to be saying, because the regime needed external threats to provide internal legitimacy.[1] Similarly, revisionist critics of American foreign policy have more recently made the argument that the requirements of capitalism force the United States into an imperial posture: they maintain that the Americans, not the Russians, find it necessary regularly to disrupt the international order.[2] Whether one accepts that argument or not, it is not too difficult to suggest groups or interests within the United States who might benefit from a continuation of the Cold War: defense contractors eager for arms sales; ethnic groups who for one reason or another nurse grudges against the Russians; career bureaucrats and military personnel whose budgets and promotion opportunities are tied to high levels of defense spending; and, perhaps most important, politicians attempting to win favor with the voters by the time-honored tactic of running against Moscow.

Presumably parallel, though not precisely equivalent, impulses operate within the Soviet Union as well.

There have been, then, not one but several Cold Wars, and it is this multidimensional character that helps to explain the conflict's remarkable durability. It has had the capacity to shift from one arena of competition to another, so that as settlements are reached in one area, rivalries break out elsewhere. It is as if a virus had the capacity to evolve into new and more resistant strains as each new antigen is developed against them. Although the last three dimensions of the Cold War — the arms race, the struggle for influence in the third world, and external hostility as the product of internal interests — are the most virulent today, there is no reason to think that this process of shifting has ended, or is likely to any time soon. It may be some time, then, before we can safely regard the Cold War, in its entirety, as history.

COLD WAR: MOTIVES AND RESPONSIBILITY

Before examining current aspects of the Cold War, some attempt should be made to address the tangled question of responsibility for it. Students of international affairs generally shy away from issues of responsibility: it is more important, they argue, to find out *what* happened rather than why it happened; to get into arguments over "why" is to slide into the slippery realm of metaphysics.[3] That attitude may be appropriate enough for purely scholarly purposes, but when it comes to the policy implications of scholarly analysis, it will not do. To avoid judgments on responsibility for past events is to weaken standards necessary for guidance in the future. We need careful thought about this question of responsibility if we are to avoid both the smug complacency of imagined moral superiority and the self-destructive effects of blaming everything that happens in this less-than-perfect world on ourselves.

In a sense, both superpowers have perceived themselves as acting primarily for defensive reasons during most of the Cold War. Both the Soviet Union and the United States have explained their projection of influence over much of the rest of the world as necessary to protect themselves against the other. We will not get very far, then, by attempting to evaluate responsibility on the basis of whether defensive motivations existed or not. Great powers often do offensive things for defensive reasons. The more productive approach is to ask which great power was more capable of meeting its security requirements within the context of the existing international order, and which required fundamental changes in that order to be secure. It is from this perspective that we can best shed light on the issue of responsibility.

Over the years, Americans have had the reputation of wanting to change the international order. One thinks of Woodrow Wilson's Fourteen Points, Cordell Hull's schemes for reforming the world trade system, the Atlantic Charter, the original campaign for the United Nations. But not one of those initiatives was ever considered vital to the security of the United States: they were put forward sincerely and with good intentions, but without the implacable determination — the unwillingness to compromise — that occurs when one's vital interests are at stake. Those of the United States never really were at stake in this somewhat utopian, irregularly pursued effort to remake the world; as far as fundamental security interests were concerned, Americans were as content with the existing international system as the most cynical — and, in this country, most criticized — of their old world allies.

Not so the Soviet Union. It is true that Stalin often spoke in traditional balance-of-power terms: all would be well, he implied, if the Soviet Union could only be granted its legitimate security interests. The problem was that he never made clear how far those interests extended. The West was reluctantly prepared to grant Stalin the boundary concessions and subservient governments he wanted in Eastern Europe, and it did not balk at meeting his initial territorial demands in the Far East, despite the Soviet Union's minimal role in the war against Japan.[4] But Stalin wanted more: the northern provinces of Iran, for example, or control of the Turkish Straits, or a unified but subservient Germany, or the right to occupy Hokkaido. Stalin also quite clearly refused to abide by promises he had made to hold free elections in the areas he occupied, notably Poland and North Korea, and he used (though cautiously) communist parties elsewhere to promote the objectives of the Soviet Union. It was not that Stalin had global ambitions or any fixed timetable for achieving them. It was just that he could not resist exploiting opportunities, and he had the patience to wait for them to arise.

Thus, there was a fundamental difference in the way Soviet and American influence expanded in the post-war years. Soviet expansion reflected discontent with the world as it was, together with a determination to change it in such a way as to accommodate Moscow. American expansion took place, not so much out of dissatisfaction with the world as it was, as with the world as it would be if the Russians had their way. Soviet expansion took place for the most part against the wishes of the third parties involved; American expansion took place almost entirely at the fervent invitation of those worried about the Russians.[5]

This is not to say that both nations, once they acquired empires, did not behave in an imperial manner. Both fell into the habit of looking at the world in terms of a zero-sum game, in which gains for one invariably meant losses for the other. Both tended to lose sight, as a consequence, of the distinction between vital and peripheral interests. Both responded, at various times, by overcommitting themselves; Americans, who tended to do their own fighting, allowed this to happen more often than did the Russians, who relied more heavily on proxies.

These similarities in behavior, however, should not obscure the superpowers' very real differences in motivation. Throughout the history of the Cold War, the United States has, on the whole, been reconciled to living with the world as it is; the Soviet Union, more for historical and institutional reasons than ideological ones, has seen its security as dependent on changing it. In this sense (though not in the classic Marxist-Leninist sense), the United States has been the *status quo* power and the Soviet Union has been the revolutionary power — a fact that should not be overlooked in assessing responsibility for the Cold War.

SYMMETRICAL AND ASYMMETRICAL RESPONSE AND THE PERCEPTION OF MEANS

If we can establish that the dominant pattern in the Cold War has been one of Soviet action and American reaction — for this is what is suggested by the conclusion that the Soviet Union finds it more difficult to live with the existing world order than does the United States — then the question arises: how has the United States handled this problem over the years? How, and with what results, has it responded to Moscow's efforts to restructure the international system to its advantage?

The answer, of course, is containment, but it is immediately necessary to differentiate the various approaches to that strategy that have been tried over the years. All post-war administrations have seen American security as tied up with the maintenance of a global balance of power. All have seen the Soviet Union as the major threat to that balance, though they have differed over the extent to which Moscow is capable of drawing other communist nations into that enterprise. All have sought to harness American resources, along with those of allies, in an effort to restrict the further growth of Soviet influence in the world, in order to maintain the diversity upon which our system depends.[6]

Nevertheless, there have been two distinct styles of containment in the post-war era: symmetrical and asymmetrical response. Symmetrical response simply means reacting to threats to the balance of power at the same location, time, and level of the original provocation. It implies the idea of calibration: one tailors response to offense, doing no more but also no less than is necessary to counter the threat in question, without running the risk of escalation or suffering the humiliation of surrender. Asymmetrical response involves shifting the location or nature of one's reaction onto terrain better suited to the application of one's strengths against adversary weaknesses. In the process, however, one may run the risk of escalation or, by not countering the original provocation where it occurred, humiliation.

Both approaches have been tried at various times during the post-war period. George Kennan's original containment strategy was an example of asymmetrical response: it sought to counter the fear brought about by the Soviet military presence in Europe and Northeast Asia not by building up countervailing military force, but by relying on United States economic aid to rehabilitate war-shattered economies in Western Europe and Japan, thereby creating the self-confidence that would allow those countries to resist the Russians on their own. Containment would be achieved, Kennan argued, if the four vital centers of industrial-military power not then in Soviet hands — the United States, the United Kingdom, the Rhine valley, and Japan — could be prevented from becoming so.[7]

By 1950, though, arising from a sense of vulnerability as a result of not matching perceived Soviet military capabilities (and especially after the unexpectedly early first test of a Soviet atomic bomb), Washington shifted, with NSC 68, to symmetrical response. The United States had to be prepared, the argument ran, to counter whatever aggression the Russians threw at us, but without resorting to nuclear weapons, in which we no longer possessed a monopoly, and without capitulating — an action which could lead to an erosion of credibility everywhere.[8] The way in which the United States fought the Korean War was an excellent example of symmetrical response: American forces countered an enemy provocation at the location, time, and in the manner of its original occurrence, without surrendering, but also without setting off a wider war. The effort proved costly, though, and the American people grew impatient with it. Those frustrations contributed to the victory at the polls in 1952 of General Eisenhower and the Republicans. Their objective was to maintain American interests throughout the world against what was seen as a monolith controlled from Moscow, but to do it at less cost than the symmetrical response strategy of NSC 68 had entailed. Accordingly, they went back to the concept of asymmetrical response, but this time with reliance on the threat to use nuclear weapons as the primary deterrent. The idea was to create uncertainty in the minds of potential adversaries as to what the United States might do if aggression took place, thereby making the risks appear to outweigh the benefits.[9] We would respond to aggression, as Dulles liked to say, "at times and in places of our own choosing."

Unfortunately, though, the Eisenhower-Dulles strategy of asymmetrical response had two major liabilities: it seemed to risk nuclear war over minor matters (Quemoy and Matsu were conspicuous examples), and it seemed incapable of preventing communist victories under the guise of national liberation movements in the third world. It was in part by capitalizing on these deficiencies that John F. Kennedy and the Democrats gained the White House in 1961. There was nothing very original about their strategy, though, as they took the country quickly back to the symmetrical response approach of NSC 68. Like the authors of that earlier document, Kennedy and his advisers regarded American interests in the world as indivisible, but they also saw means as expandable; therefore, they argued, the United States could afford to counter aggression wherever it occurred, without either the dangers of nuclear war or of humiliation.

The chief result, of course, was the war in Vietnam, the most egregious American example of offensive actions taken for what were perceived to be defensive reasons — a war that was consistent with prevailing national strategy but also in the end discredited it. The debacle in Vietnam paved the way for the Nixon victory in 1968 and for a return once again to asymmetrical response.

The Nixon-Kissinger strategy reflected this emphasis in several respects. Through the Nixon Doctrine, it called for cutting back American commitments in the world: allies, it implied, would bear a greater share of the burden of their defense, with the United States helping out where needed by furnishing technology but not manpower.[10] It called for countering Soviet challenges to the balance of power through a combination of pressures and inducements designed to get Moscow to accept certain "rules of the game" — to persuade the Russians that it was in their own best interests to accept the world as it was, rather than to try to change it. This process was intended to work through the application of linkage — in itself an asymmetrical concept, implying the withholding of concessions in some areas until others were granted elsewhere. The goal was a multipolar world operating on balance-of-power principles — an idea not too different from what Kennan had sought some twenty-five years before.[11]

This emphasis on asymmetry continued through the end of the Ford Administration, but not without coming under sharp attack from symmetrically-minded critics who charged that détente had produced an erosion in American strategic and conventional capabilities relative to those of the Soviet Union.[12] Despite ample provocation from the Russians, the Carter Administration did not accept that argument, less out of respect for the strategic legacy of Henry Kissinger, one gathers, than from the fact that no one has yet demonstrated how the nation can afford a return to symmetrical response in an era of energy dependency and double-digit inflation.

What is striking about this oscillation between symmetry and asymmetry is how little most of it had to do with what the Russians were up to at any given point. Without exception, shifts in strategies of containment since 1947 have coincided less with new Kremlin initiatives than with shifts in perceptions of means in Washington. Perceptions of means have played a larger role than perceptions of threats in shaping U.S. policy toward the Soviet Union. The implications are not encouraging for those who seek a consistent, coherent foreign policy insulated from domestic considerations.

DÉTENTE AND LINKAGE: ASYMMETRICAL WEAPONS OF THE COLD WAR

There have been several attempts at détente in post-war Soviet-American relations: the "thaw" following Stalin's death in 1953; Eisenhower's attempts, in 1959 and 1960, to establish a dialogue with Khrushchev; Kennedy's comparable efforts, partly successful after the Cuban missile crisis; Johnson's continuation of that approach, frustrated by the change of leadership in Moscow and American escalation in Vietnam. Not until 1969, though, did the same interest in a relaxation of tensions exist in roughly the same proportion on both sides. The decade that followed saw a sustained attempt on the part of both Moscow and Washington to move beyond Cold War rigidities which must now, in light of Afghanistan, be regarded as having failed.

The reason, it would seem, is that both sides were prisoners of Cold War thinking to a greater extent than they realized at the time. Americans and Russians embraced détente with differing expectations of what it would produce — expectations colored, to a considerable degree, by legacies of the past.

Nixon and Kissinger, for example, thought of détente as an updated form of containment.[13] Their idea was to achieve nothing less than a modification of Soviet behavior by rewarding actions showing a disposition to accept the world as it was and by discouraging, through the application of pressures and constraints, those that did not. It was a bit like trying to train a rat or a pigeon in a psychology laboratory to perform certain tricks in response to a carefully crafted and precisely measured series of rewards and punishments.[14]

The Russians, on the other hand, saw détente as a means of rendering safer the process of changing the international order. It was, they clearly said, a means of controlling competition in dangerous areas like nuclear weapons, while continuing it in others. The idea, in short, was compartmentalization.[15] True, the Soviet Union could benefit from certain concessions from the West, especially in the form of trading privileges. But it would not pay all that much to get them; in fact, Kremlin leaders probably believed they would not have to pay anything at all, given the venality of Western capitalists eager to find buyers, even if communist, for their products.

For a time, it seemed possible to patch over the differences. The Russians at Moscow in 1972 signed a statement of "Basic Principles" that appeared to rule out efforts to exploit third world crises at the expense of the United States.[16] Summit meetings proceeded on a more or less annual basis during the early 1970s, with declarations of friendship covering up the fact that fewer and fewer meaningful agreements were being made. By the middle of the decade, cracks in the facade were becoming too noticeable to ignore.

One was Moscow's alleged failure to prevent the 1973 Egyptian attack on Israel and the 1975 North Vietnamese offensive against South Vietnam, acts of omission that seemed inconsistent with injunctions against profiting from the discomfiture of others so solemnly invoked at the first Moscow summit. Another sign of strain came over the issue of human rights, with first Congress and then the Carter Administration making changes in the Soviet treatment of Jews and dissidents a prerequisite for progress on economic and other issues. A third problem arose from the projection of Soviet power and influence into Africa, chiefly through the use of Cuban proxies, in what seemed to be a clear attempt to exploit remaining anti-colonial sentiment there to the disadvantage of the West. Still another nail in the coffin of détente was the Soviet Union's continuing build-up in the strategic missile capabilities. Although it did not directly contravene the SALT I agreements, this trend at least seemed ill-matched to the spirit of mutual restraint that most Americans believed those accords had implied. Afghanistan, of course, was the final blow.

In retrospect, it is not difficult to pick out the deficiencies in the American approach to détente during this period. The Nixon Administration probably pushed linkage too vigorously, demanding that the Russians act to restrain countries over which they had limited leverage in the first place. It is not at all clear that the Russians could have stopped the Egyptians in 1973 or the North Vietnamese in 1975, even if they had wanted to. Then, too, linkage implied tight control — knowing just when to apply rewards and punishments, without going overboard on either. But the Nixon Administration lost control of the linkage process almost at once, with the introduction in the fall of 1972 of the Jackson-Vanik amendment. In the years that followed, Kissinger alternately yielded to and resisted Congressional pressures to link détente to the Soviet performance on human rights, although legislators showed no clear notion of what precisely should be demanded or what should be granted in return. The Carter Administration compounded the confusion by first elevating the question of human rights to the level of universal principle and then abandoning the idea of linkage, which seemed to offer the best hope of securing Soviet cooperation in that area in the first place.[17]

Similarly, on the issue of strategic arms, the administrations of Nixon, Ford, and Carter all tried, from the unfavorable position of diminishing American military power relative to the USSR, to negotiate arms control treaties that would limit further Soviet gains without imposing dangerous restrictions on the United States. To a remarkable degree, they succeeded: critics have yet to demonstrate convincingly how the SALT I agreements or their unratified SALT II counterparts left the United States inferior to the Russians in the overall calculus of strength that goes to make up deterrence. But the agreements did require tolerating asymmetries, and that idea was difficult to sell to an uneasy public (and Congress) which saw quantitative indices of strategic power declining but failed to see the justification for freezing that disproportion permanently.

The United States also erred in not taking Brezhnev and his colleagues at their word when they said that détente would not preclude efforts to aid "liberation" movements in the third world. Angola, Somalia, Ethiopia, and Yemen were perceived as symbols of Soviet bad faith, but in fact the Russians were only honoring their own public promises. The most ridiculous manifestation of aggrieved American innocence came in the summer of 1979, when the Carter Administration, hoping at once to defuse critics and avoid leaks, made public through Senator Frank Church the "unacceptable" presence of a Soviet combat brigade in Cuba — only to have to find it "acceptable" after all when it developed that the unit had been there for years, and that Washington had no practical means of getting it out. Calling public attention to one's own impotence is, even in the best of circumstances, an unlikely way to enhance one's credibility.

Before carrying these criticisms too far, though, it is worth noting that things have not always worked out well for the Soviet Union either. The effect of the 1973 Middle East war, despite the ensuing oil embargo, was to boost the reputation of Americans, not Russians, in the Arab world. The 1975 Helsinki agreement, proposed initially by Moscow as a means of legitimizing its control over Eastern Europe, is now remembered more for the attention it shed on human rights violations there and in the Soviet Union than for the purposes for which the Kremlin wanted it. Soviet incursions into Africa may have won Moscow temporary control in certain countries, but they are hardly all reliable allies today. Moreover, Africans are coming to see Russians rather than Americans as inheritors of the imperialist tradition there: as one observer has put it, "U.S. policy in fact lost a country [Angola] and gained a continent."[18] Moscow's clumsy handling of its relations with Japan produced similar results: for the sake of a few barren islands in the Sea of Okhotsk, the Russians have managed to drive the two major powers in the Far East, Japan and China, into an "anti-hegemonal" alignment directed, however discreetly, against Russia. Finally, the Soviet military build-up has now set off corresponding trends in the West; just as the Russians may have reached the stage, for economic reasons, of needing to taper off.[19]

Afghanistan is, of course, a wholly new order of provocation. For the first time since World War II, the Soviet Union has used its own troops, not proxies, in an area that has not been generally regarded as lying within its immediate sphere of influence. It is startling to realize that the Red Army has suffered far more combat casualties in the past year and a half than in the previous thirty-five. The West can no longer rely, as it has in recent years, on the cautious nonadventurism of the Kremlin gerontocracy. The old men did bestir themselves to act, this time in an adventurous and unpredictable way.

Taking the longer view, though, Afghanistan is likely to be regarded as a strategic error of the first order on Moscow's part, akin to the decision to blockade Berlin in 1948, or to authorize the North Korean invasion of South Korea in 1950, or to place missiles in Cuba in 1962. It is difficult to see how whatever gains the Russians have won in that inhospitable country outweigh their losses: 1) within the Islamic world, which, before Afghanistan, had reason to be hostile to the United States because of the Palestinian impasse and events in Iran; 2) in Western Europe, where NATO's sense of common danger has counterbalanced the potentially decisive effects of disproportionate deficiencies; 3) in American domestic politics, where the result has been to boost the fortunes of candidates the Russians would no doubt prefer to have been defeated; 4) in the non-aligned world, where the painfully acquired leadership of a Soviet satellite, Cuba, has been abruptly discredited; and 5) in Eastern Europe and the Soviet Union itself, where the leadership has encountered as a consequence not only nuisances in the form of an American grain embargo and restrictions on technology transfers, but also unaccustomed problems of public relations with respect to the Olympic boycott, the task of explaining what its troops are doing in Afghanistan, and more significantly, the dilemma of how to deal with what must certainly seem a more dangerous situation in Poland at a time when it finds its forces bogged down in an apparently interminable war several thousand miles away.

One should not be too hasty then, in deciding who gained the most from détente. All that can be said at the moment is that both sides went into it with differing expectations; that both, in varying degrees, have had their expectations disappointed; and that we are now entering a new and unpredictable stage in that long and complex phenomenon we call the Cold War.

THE NEW CONTAINMENT

Containment therefore will very likely remain the goal of U.S. strategy toward the Soviet Union during the 1980s. Before suggesting what new forms it might take, it would be well to consider what American interests are likely to be in the decade to come, and what is most likely to threaten them.

United States officials have been surprisingly consistent in defining the American nation's vital interests. John F. Kennedy was only saying explicitly what his predecessors and successors have believed when he proclaimed, two months before his death, that "the interest of the United States of America is best served by preserving and protecting a world of diversity in which no one power or combination of powers can threaten the security of the United States."[20] It has been in the *balancing* of power, rather than in its unilateral or imperial exercise, that U.S. security has most often been seen to rest. That there have been occasional departures from this pattern only demonstrates the untidiness of generalizations in history, not their overall invalidity.

What is it, then, that is most likely to threaten the existing distribution of power in the world in the 1980s? Despite Afghanistan, it is not the Russians, at least not in any immediate sense: knowing the virtues of patience, they are unlikely to undertake overt and large-scale challenges to the balance of power. It is certainly not communism, not in an age when the most strident calls for Western unity and strength regularly emanate from the proletarian mandarins in Peking. It is, rather, a small and poorly understood group of states — primitive, by most standards, in their economic development; medieval in their subordination of state and even multi-state interests to the dictates of religion; unsophisticated in their knowledge of the outside world and for the most part heedless of the effects of their actions upon it; and yet in a position, thanks to accidents of geology and the insatiable appetite for fossil fuels of the industrialized West, to bring it grinding to a halt at any moment, whether on the whim of militant students, greedy sheikhs, or fanatical ayatollahs.

The Russians, it is important to note, did not create this situation — the West did that itself. But the Soviet Union is in an excellent position to exploit it, whether by gaining control of the oil-producing regions, or by interdicting lines of supply, or by simply intimidating the shaky regimes of that area to such an extent that they dole out their principal commodity not according to the laws of economics or the needs of the West but by a rationing plan devised in Moscow.

Coupled with this is the less immediate but no less worrisome danger posed by the Soviet Union's attainment of parity, and in certain areas, superiority, in the arms race. That achievement stems from no recent decision on the part of Kremlin leaders; the military build-up has been steady since Brezhnev and Kosygin took office in 1964, greatly aided by the American involvement in Vietnam, which diverted U.S. resources away from measures needed to keep up with the Russians and then, by debauching the currency, made it difficult if not impossible to afford to catch up. A condition of actual, as opposed to imagined, Western military inferiority is a new element in the history of the Cold War, the effects of which can be foreseen as not very reassuring.

What we face, then, is the task of defending our vital interest — the diversity that comes from having an international order in which no one power is dominant — from a position of approaching military inferiority and already present resource dependency. It is not the most favorable position upon which to make a stand. Within this general context, if not with reference to the immediate crisis in Afghanistan that gave rise to it, President Carter had some justification for making the statement that the West now confronts "the greatest threat to peace since the Second World War."[21]

A REVISED STRATEGY OF LINKAGE

There are no quick solutions to this double problem of energy dependency and declining military strength. Both can be dealt with, but it will take years before substantial progress will be seen. What we need now are short-term measures to tide us over this crisis period, without at the same time disrupting the long-term initiatives necessary to eliminate it altogether.

Because we will be operating from a position of stringency, if not outright weakness, during this period, one thing is clear at the outset: symmetrical response will not do. The United States and its allies cannot afford to meet future challenges to the balance of power on terrain and in circumstances selected by their adversaries. The West is going to have to persuade the Russians to play by *its* rules rather than their own.

Moscow for years has seen détente as "compartmentalized competition" — one agrees not to compete in dangerous areas, but to do so in others. But this approach gives special advantages to the power that, by its own admission, is not content with the world as it is. It allows the Russians the luxury, in setting out to change the world, of picking how and where they will do it, with the knowledge that the United States, if it follows the rules of compartmentalized competition, will not be able to shift the theater of action onto more favorable terrain. It obliges the U.S. to contest the Russians on their terms, not its own, to respond to Soviet challenges where they occur while carrying on business as usual elsewhere.

The Russian view of détente also poses problems for the West because of its fragmented structure of political authority. Compartmentalized competition requires not only an abundance of means, but also tight coordination and control; where that is lacking, as it is to a considerable extent in the United States, the NATO countries, and Japan, the way is left open for divide-and-conquer tactics. The Russians can make advantageous offers to allies or to special interest groups within the United States — farmers, businessmen, ethnic groups, even athletes — with the expectation that self-interest can usually be counted upon to overshadow the national interest, as officially defined in Washington.

Soviet "rules of the game," not surprisingly, thus offer greater benefits to the Russians than to the United States. The alternative, of course, is linkage — the idea developed by Henry Kissinger that all elements in the Soviet-American relationship are interconnected, and that concessions in one area must be compensated for by roughly equivalent concessions in others.

There are, to be sure, problems with linkage, not the least of which is that the Russians have never really accepted it. It implies leverage where none may in fact exist. It can easily be overloaded, as Congress has more than once demonstrated. It runs the risk of escalation — of introducing areas, issues, or weapons previously unrelated to the question at hand for the purpose of gaining points of pressure. However, given the disadvantages of compartmentalized competition, linkage seems the preferable alternative.

How do we do it? What do we link? One of the lessons of the Kissinger years is that linkage should not be a tit-for-tat arrangement: progress on SALT, for example, in return for restraint in Africa. The problem with such bargaining is that it creates artificial confrontations over questions of common interest (like SALT); it assumes Moscow's willingness to attach the same value that

Washington does to the various stakes in the game; it relies on the administration's ability to insulate the linkage process from outside pressures. What we need, instead, are linkages that do not require precise calculation but will nonetheless allow the West to apply its own strengths against Soviet weaknesses, to retain the initiative while minimizing costs.

One way to do this might be to incorporate into the idea of linkage a concept not unfamiliar to the Russians — the "correlation of forces," the overall direction of movement in world affairs which, Kremlin ideologists believe, is progressing inexorably toward the triumph of socialism as a matter of historical imperative. It is to the West's advantage to do this because world trends are not in fact proceeding in that direction, if by "socialism" one means, as the Russians do, a world congenial to their own domestic institutions. The world may be moving in a confused variety of directions at once — toward triumphs of nationalism, religion, ethnicity, irrationality, even anarchy — but there is no evidence of spontaneous movement toward the kind of world Kremlin leaders would choose, if they could.

A major if unremarked phenomenon of the 1960s and 1970s was the declining appeal of Soviet institutions as models elsewhere. Whatever gains the Russians may have made in Angola, Vietnam, Ethiopia, Yemen, or Afghanistan, they can hardly compensate for their loss of influence in China, Indonesia, Egypt, Iraq, and among the communist parties of Western Europe. The Soviet Union is bucking the trend toward diversity that characterizes the contemporary world, and that is the West's great advantage. Whether one is dealing with wind, water, or world politics, survival is largely a matter of accommodating oneself to irresistible forces, not fighting them. And the West (using the term loosely to include Japan) is in a far better position to do that than the Soviet Union.

The objective of containment in this context should be to bring home to Soviet leaders something Americans and many of their allies discovered long ago: that the "correlation of forces" in the world favors the hegemonial aspirations of no one, and that the superpower that can bring itself to accommodate diversity now will be the one most likely to maintain its status and position over the long haul. It is in this sense, relating irreversible trends to immediate situations, that a revised strategy of linkage can be made to work.

But what, specifically, will be necessary to accomplish this?

CONSISTENCY AND THE NEW CONTAINMENT

First, the United States must achieve a much larger degree of consistency and coordination in its foreign policy than has been evident in recent years. Indecisiveness in individuals may be irritating, quaint, or even charming, but in great nations it is without exception unsettling. It is painful, but probably accurate, to acknowledge that instability in world affairs during the past half-decade has arisen as much from Washington's failure to define a strategy as from Moscow's single-minded determination to pursue one.

It is worth inquiring into the sources of Washington's present vacillations:

— The beginnings of the problem can be located fairly precisely in 1972, when Senator Henry Jackson prevailed upon his Capitol Hill colleagues to take a direct role in the negotiation of trade and arms control agreements with the Soviet Union. The result was that talks with the Russians had to be conducted with a view to what Jackson would tolerate as well as what the Kremlin would accept. That requirement significantly complicated the task of aligning pressures and inducements to produce desired effects.

— Domestic politics compounded the problem, as the election of 1976 vividly demonstrated. In no recent campaign has there been such a complete subordination of international priorities to internal political concerns. The sight of an incumbent President embracing a party platform that repudiated his own foreign policy was disconcerting, at best. And many of the initial blunders of the Carter Administration — the letter to Sakharov, the Vance mission to Moscow on SALT, the public commitment to pull troops out of South Korea, the abandonment of linkage — reflected hasty, ill-conceived promises made during the campaign as the challenger's means of putting distance between himself and what he perceived to be the weaknesses of the Ford-Kissinger policies.

— Still another source of instability has been the peculiar operating style of Carter himself. As if in deliberate reaction against the centralized decision-making style of Henry Kissinger, the new chief executive encouraged openness, flexibility, and divided authority, to the point, some would say, of cultivating inconsistency as a Positive Good. As a consequence, his administration failed to work out and articulate a coherent set of assumptions upon which to base policy, a distinction that makes it unique in the post-war era.

Now it could conceivably be argued that inconsistency is a good thing: it keeps one receptive to new situations and ideas; it avoids the rigidities associated with more structured systems of thought; it certainly keeps enemies guessing. But if one is interested in building a more stable relationship with the Soviet Union, the kind of inconsistency the United States has manifested over the past few years is not likely to work. It undermines the linkages necessary to impress upon the Kremlin the fact that the global "correlation of forces" is not in its favor. It upsets allies: it is disconcerting to make difficult and unpopular decisions in the interests of coordinating policy with Washington, and then have Washington adopt a new policy the following week. And, most important, it is the procedure least likely to establish any kind of acceptable basis for dealing with the Russians. Whether at home or abroad, there is nothing the Kremlin abhors more than unpredictability. It is odd that a self-proclaimed revolutionary power should take that position; certainly it does not always exhibit predictability in its relations with others. But that is what the Soviet Union has been brought to, partly by its ideology, which does not allow for the abrupt, the idiosyncratic, the accidental, partly by its aging leadership — old men may, from time to time, inflict surprises on others, but they do not like to have them inflicted upon themselves.

During recent years the United States has startled the Russians more than once (and the rest of the world as well): it is here that action needs to be taken first if a new strategy of containment is to succeed. There can be no real improvement in Soviet-American relations — indeed, in the United States' position in the world generally — until the administration in power in Washington "gets its act together."

FRICTION: LETTING THE ADVERSARY CONTAIN ITSELF

A second requirement for the success of any new approach to containment should be to take advantage of what Clausewitz a century and a half ago called "friction." The resistance an army encounters as it moves across a battlefield, he pointed out, is only partly that provided by the enemy. It arises as well from the combination of inertia, incompetence, and accident that attends any complex enterprise. Horses get tired, columns get lost, it rains, roads turn to mud, bridges wash out, ink on maps runs, boots leak, guns rust, reinforcements and supplies fail to arrive on time; after a while, the whole offensive can break down without encountering a single enemy soldier.[22] "Friction," in short, was Clausewitz's anticipation of Murphy's Law: "What can go wrong will go wrong."

In strategy, this means that an offensive movement has several strikes against it from the beginning. It must overcome powerful and at times unforeseen forces of resistance even before confronting an adversary. The effect, Clausewitz believed, was to give the advantage to the defense, all else being equal. All else has not, of course, always been equal: asymmetries in technology, resources, or training have favored offense over defense from time to time, as demonstrated by Europe's colonization of much of the rest of the world in the late nineteenth century or the Nazi blitzkrieg in the first years of World War II or the Allied victories that ended that conflict. The more frequent occurrence, and surely the one most likely today, in a world whose dominant ideology is nationalism and whose technology and resources are widely diffused, is resistance rather than acquiescence to efforts to achieve what the Chinese call "hegemony."

This is where the great hidden advantage of "friction" comes in. It is always more costly and ultimately more discouraging to try to change the world than to accommodate oneself to it. Since we, and not the Russians, seem best suited to make that accommodation, it is they who face the uphill battle.

This raises the possibility of enlisting Clausewitzian "friction" in the task of containment, an accomplishment that could make the task of limiting Soviet expansion seem far less daunting and less expensive than it does today. But what, specifically, can be done to facilitate that process?

The answer is to know when to leave well enough alone. There are situations (Afghanistan may be one) in which the natural forces of resistance are strong enough to tie down an offensive power without significant external help, or with relatively little help compared to the effort required to mount the offensive in the first place. Frenetic efforts on our part to organize formal alliances or overbearing aid programs might well transfer local forces of resistance in such cases from the Russians to ourselves, as happened with the ill-conceived Eisenhower Doctrine in 1957.

A second thing we can do is to get away from the unfortunate habit of defining our adversaries by their ideological orientation. George Kennan made the argument in the 1940s that communism was a divisive, not a unifying, force in world affairs. Sooner or later, he argued, the communist world would break up, if for no other reason than from arguments over who was to say, at any given point, what the true faith was. This has in fact happened; we have come to realize that the real threat to diversity in the world is not communism but the Soviet Union, and that communists elsewhere can at times be enlisted in defense of that goal. Still, the temptation to revert to indiscriminate anti-communism strikes deep chords in the American body politic, especially at quadrennial intervals, and it should be guarded against. For example, nothing could better create friction for ourselves, and conversely minimize it for the Russians, than to treat the freely elected Marxist government of Zimbabwe in the same casually myopic way that we dealt with the freely elected Marxist government of Chile a decade ago.

A third thing the United States can do to avoid friction is to deny the Russians tempting opportunities. These can arise from commitments to allies that outlast their ability to command popular support, as in Nicaragua and Iran, or from such exaggerated deference to allies that it creates openings for adversaries, as in our long-standing tendency to let Israel dictate our Palestinian policy. The most tempting opportunity of all, though, is our energy dependency. That we have survived this far without disaster is no guarantee for the future, as the war between Iran and Iraq has recently shown. When a turkey obligingly places its neck on a chopping block, it is too much to expect that someone will not take advantage of the opportunity sooner or later and chop it off.

Friction, though, will not always defeat a determined adversary. There may well be times when the United States and its allies will have to act themselves, whether directly against the Soviet Union or (much more likely) against Moscow's proxies and accomplices. Our strategy for undertaking such operations should be to seek maximum effect at minimum cost. Here we could well learn something from Mao Tse-Tung and Ho Chi Minh, whose strategies achieved just this coordination of carefully selected military action with those natural forces of resistance that can cause an adversary, by his own weight, mass, and clumsiness, to defeat himself.

Friction could be a considerable asset, then, in

bringing the Russians to the realization that the "correlation of forces" is not in their favor — and we would do well to make the most of it.

THE MILITARY COMPONENT OF CONTAINMENT

The question of how and in what circumstances the West might need to use force to maintain the balance of power brings up the role of the military in any new strategy of containment. What strikes one immediately in looking at this question is the often remarked disparity between the amount of hardware great powers can command and their ability to project influence in the world. There seems to be no very obvious correlation between military strength and political (or economic) influence. To see the problem, one need only look at the capacity of small powers — at times, even factions — to manipulate larger ones, as in the taking of hostages in Iran and the resistance which a small, disorganized band of rebels has maintained against the Russians in Afghanistan.

It might be argued that the sophistication of nations can be measured by the extent to which they recognize the multi-dimensional nature of power — that is, the extent to which nations realize that influence in international relations does not grow solely out of the barrel of a gun but is also the product of political, economic, ideological, psychological, and even religious considerations. The United States, through painful experience, has gained some appreciation of this fact in recent years. But just as it began, as a consequence, to broaden its means of projecting influence in the world — and certainly the Carter human rights policy, whatever its other shortcomings, has had that effect — the Soviet Union has been concentrating more and more on the military instruments of power.[23] That nation, which once sought to extend influence through a broad range of ideological, social, economic, political, as well as military means, now seems to rely primarily on the latter to shape external events to its liking.

It is as if Moscow had been following Washington's lead in this respect, but from a time lag of roughly two decades. Thus, the Russians built a big missile system after the United States did, they built a big navy after we did, they seem now to be in the "imperial" phase we went through in the 1950s and 1960s, and they now, in Afghanistan, even have their own Vietnam. This might suggest that we should encourage their further expansion in this direction on the grounds that if our own experience is any guide, they will sooner or later overextend, exhaust,and ultimately contain themselves.

The argument has some validity, but it should not be carried too far. Experience also suggests that power balances rarely sustain themselves automatically. Even short-term disproportions of power can be destabilizing, whether by tempting the temporarily dominant side into adventurism or by wrecking self-confidence on the side that is, for the moment, behind. Since Soviet military power relative to that of the West has increased steadily in recent years,[24] the United States would be well-advised to inquire into the state of its own defenses, lest it incur either of those risks.

United States military forces are likely to serve two main functions in the 1980s: 1) deterring the Russians from taking or authorizing others to take actions that could in some significant way upset the balance of power, and 2) deterring others from actions that could have the same effect, especially by exploiting the vulnerable sources and supply lines upon which the West's appetite for imported oil has now made it dependent. The first task is in some ways the simpler one, since there is only a single center of authority upon which we must make an impression.

At the strategic level, it would appear that existing or planned forces will be adequate to do that. NATO's recent decision to deploy Pershing II and cruise missiles will counterbalance Soviet SS-20s targeted against Western Europe. The approaching vulnerability of United States land-based missiles will be remedied by the development of the MX, the Trident submarine, the air-launched cruise missile, and possibly (provided they can be reconciled with the SALT I Treaty and prove feasible) new developments in anti-ballistic missile technology.[25] Western strategic forces may be able to make deterrence work in the 1980s not by matching the Russians missile for missile, but simply by creating sufficient uncertainty regarding the consequences of an attack to discourage its being attempted in the first place.

The more serious problem lies in the area of conventional forces. The Russians long have had superiority in ground capabilities; they are well on the way to achieving at least approximate parity at sea and in the air as well. These are areas that require careful but urgent remedial action. Particularly worrisome is the possibility of a Soviet conventional attack, say in Europe or the Middle East, that would leave the West with no means to respond other than through the use of nuclear weapons. The resulting dilemma would be a cruel one, for the informal ban on the military use of such weapons that has grown up since Hiroshima and Nagasaki has probably done more than anything else in the post-war period to limit escalation in crises. Maintenance of the nuclear-conventional weapon "firebreak" is a vital if too often unacknowledged interest, not to be sacrificed lightly. And yet our inferiority in ground forces together with the approaching stand-off at sea and in the air might require the use of nuclear weapons to preserve the balance of power — surely an example of resorting to means likely to destroy what one is trying to save.

It is obviously a difficult problem though not a new one. What *is* new is the possibility of solving it, at least in part, by exploiting revolutions in guidance and reconnaissance that have taken place in conventional weaponry in recent years. Future military historians may well regard the combination of precision-guided munitions and sophisticated reconnaissance capabilities as a revolution in the fighting of wars, approaching in importance the nuclear weapons revolution of 1945. The ability to locate and destroy targets with unprecedented precision by non-nuclear means should at the least reinforce Clausewitz's dictum about the superiority of the defense over the offense and should, as a consequence, be fully exploited by the West.

The question of precision-guided munitions raises the second major military problem the West will face in the 1980s: preventing attacks on objects or areas of vital interest by smaller nations or even terrorist groups. This, in some ways, is a more difficult problem than deterring the Russians, since one is frequently at a loss to know how, where, or against whom to respond. One scenario will suffice to illustrate the problem: how would the United States and its allies react if terrorists should demonstrate a capacity, using mobile but highly accurate surface-to-surface missiles launched from hidden shore positions, to knock out selected supertankers transitting the Straits of Hormuz or Malacca? It would not have to happen more than once for the rise in insurance rates alone to accomplish the desired effect, yet retaliation, or the threat of it, would be no easy matter to make credible.

The long-term solution to this problem, as to so many, is to end the West's energy dependency, but that is not going to happen any time soon. In the meantime, we may have to revive some ideas little heard from since the days of mercantilism: that a nation's power is measured in large part by the degree of self-sufficiency it is able to muster; that a major function of a nation's armed forces is to protect its commerce on the high seas; that the main threat to that commerce may come not from the rival states one has armed oneself against but from autonomous and largely uncontrollable raiders, marauders, and pirates.

The military components of containment in the 1980s, therefore, will be neither easily developed nor implemented, although creation of a Rapid Deployment Force — small, highly mobile elite units capable of acting anywhere on short notice — may help. Demands of both prudence and economy will dictate some compartmentalizing of our own in dealing with this problem. One of our main concerns must be to avoid confusing the two kinds of threat we face — the Russians and *n*th powers — and in particular to not take action against one which could have the effect of bringing it into alignment with the other. Non-proliferation is an admirable objective, whether one is dealing with nuclear weapons or with adversaries who might provide occasions to use such weapons.

DÉTENTE AND CONTAINMENT RECONCILED

It is worth remembering, though, that containment is and should always be regarded as a means to an end, not as an end in itself. From the beginning, that strategy has been viewed as a preliminary to negotiating with the Russians, although there have been differences from administration to administration as to when those negotiations could safely take place and what is negotiable. The diplomatic component of containment complements the military and should be considered as well in any discussion of where United States policy toward the Soviet Union should go in the 1980s.

One point should be made at the outset. It is not now and has never been a vital interest of the United States to make progress toward reducing world tensions contingent upon changes in the internal nature of the Soviet state. Kremlin leaders resent outside interference as much as do leaders of any sovereign nation and are likely to forgo other benefits to avoid "meddling" which seems to strike at the foundations of their authority. Even if externally inspired changes in the Soviet system were feasible, there is no guarantee that they would contribute anything more to the goal of maintaining a global balance of power than does the existing one. But the main reason why we should not set out to change the internal nature of foreign governments is a deeper one: the strength of the West lies in its ability to tolerate and co-exist with states of differing social systems. To try to change other systems as a matter of deliberate national policy strikes at the very advantage the West has over the Russians: its ability to deal self-confidently with a diverse world.

This raises the question, then, of the extent to which concern over human rights should play a role in American policy toward the USSR. There is no question that the espousal of human rights is important to the United States. It is the closest thing we have to an ideology, and that is not to be taken lightly; nations must stand for something. It is probably the case that the Carter human rights policy has won more friends for the United States than it has lost.

But no nation should take its ideology so seriously that it neglects vital interests. Certainly the Soviet Union does not do this: the most consistent element in its diplomacy over the years has been the subordination of ideological to national priorities. The United States has not always reciprocated. For a time during the early Carter Administration, our official determination to make a point about human rights was allowed, whether deliberately or not, to overshadow our interest in pursuing détente, with unfortunate results for SALT and other issues of mutual concern. A better approach might have been to take advantage of the fragmented nature of the American body politic in dealing with this issue — to have had the government remain aloof from anything other than general expressions of concern regarding the plight of dissidents inside the Soviet Union, and then rely on the very considerable capacities of private organizations to keep specific cases, as they should be kept, in the public eye.

One of the illusions under which the United States operated during the 1970s was that as relations with the West improved, Kremlin leaders would become more tolerant of dissent within their borders. That did not happen — indeed, the condition of the dissidents probably worsened under détente, as American concern for them fed Moscow's paranoia. Nor should Americans be under any illusions that the majority of Russians sympathize with the efforts we make on behalf of the dissidents; the incentives and genuine rewards offered to those who work "within the system" are far too strong.

The United States faces the simple fact that concern for human rights as a matter of principle is not a universally shared aspiration, nor is the promotion of human rights a vital American interest. Like communism in the Soviet Union, it is an aspiration to be respected and striven for where feasible, but is not one upon which the stability of the international order or the security of the United States crucially depends.

Apart from the issue of human rights, however, negotiations should play a major role in any new approach to containment. Though they have been competitors over the past 35 years, the United States and the Soviet Union nonetheless share a surprising number of common interests. Negotiations aimed at enhancing these can provide the inducements that complement pressures in making containment work. America should not allow the Russians' misadventures in Afghanistan to blind it to the fact that opportunities for mutually advantageous negotiations still exist. The world is not likely soon to revert to a condition in which all gains for one side automatically mean losses for the other.

Possible areas for negotiation include:

The Avoidance of Nuclear War an interest so obvious that it scarcely requires mentioning and, related to it, a less apparent but hardly less important interest: seeing to it that the three and a half decade ban on the use of such weapons is maintained.

Arms Control both at the strategic and conventional level. The costs of arms are a crushing burden for both superpowers, probably more so for the Russians than for the United States. It is obviously in our interests, where safe, to lower those costs, but as SALT II has shown, it is difficult to do so when technology keeps outrunning verification capabilities. Still, there are advantages simply in regularizing the procedure of verification, even if reductions in expenditures and weapons systems do not materialize. Reliable knowledge of what the other side has and can do constitutes a form of arms control in itself.

Economic Relations. The Soviet Union will be for some time to come a food- and technology-importing country, items the United States and its allies are in a position to export. We cannot and should not do this in a political vacuum: where one has leverage, one ought to use it. Nor should we fall for the fallacious argument that economic interdependence alone will insure harmony; the experiences of Germany and Russia in 1914 or Japan and the United States in 1941, not to mention the recent history of détente, should be sufficient to dispel that notion. When conducted without illusions, though, trade can meet complementary needs and to that extent offers opportunities for negotiations.

Energy. Here there is a major potential for conflict, since the West is and the Soviet Union is becoming energy-deficient. The single most important issue between Washington and Moscow in the 1980s may well be whether the search for foreign oil that both will need to undertake will assume competitive or cooperative forms. At the moment, competition seems more likely, but since the commodity in question is volatile in more ways than one and hence capable of being lost in the rush to acquire it, there may be more interest than is now apparent in an alternative approach. At any rate, the possibilities should be explored; that is what negotiations are for.

It might appear at first glance that "détente" and "containment" are contradictory terms. The first would seem to imply a harmonious relationship; the second, an antagonistic one. But there is less incongruity here than meets the eye, if one remembers the importance of sequence: containment is a means of bringing about the condition of mutual restraint that must precede a relaxation of tensions, if it is to last. Containment must also be coupled with opportunities for negotiation if one is to avoid reinforcing the sense of insecurity in adversaries that made the strategy necessary in the first place. In the absence of incentives for restraint, negotiations alone are unlikely to produce détente. With incentives provided by an updated version of containment, however, it might be possible to reconstitute the relatively amicable relationship of the early 1970s — but this time on a basis more firmly grounded in the selfish, though not necessarily mutually exclusive, interests of both sides.

CONCLUSION

To write of the future of containment is to risk dispensing bromides: there is a fine line, in these matters, between the profound and the platitudinous. There is a curious fascination with how policy is formulated at the expense of what it should contain; with process over substance. To an extent, this is unavoidable in a country where diverse centers of power contend vigorously for the privilege of saying what policy should be (and where academics compete with equal vigor to chronicle the process). But the world will not tolerate domestically derived irresolution indefinitely, at however sophisticated a level, without exacting a price. The time will come when we will need to return to simple thoughts about interests, threats, and feasible responses in world affairs. When that happens, the bromides of containment, sufficiently revised to reflect contemporary realities, are likely to provide the most appropriate mechanism.

ENDNOTES

1 See Kennan's telegrams from Moscow of February 22 and March 20, 1946, in U.S. Department of State, *Foreign Relations of the United States: 1946,* VI, 696-709, 721-723.

2 Robert W. Tucker, *The Radical Left and American Foreign Policy* (Baltimore: Johns Hopkins University Press, 1971), pp. 28-39, provides a succinct summary of the revisionist argument.

3 See, for example, Daniel Yergin, *Shattered Peace: The Origins of the Cold War and the National Security State* (Boston: Houghton Mifflin Company, 1977), p. 7; also, from a methodological perspective, David Hackett Fischer, *Historians' Fallacies: Toward a Logic of Historical Thought* (New York: Harper & Row, 1970), pp. 14-15, 182-83; and Robert Stover, "Responsibility for the Cold War — A Case Study in Historical Responsibility," *History and Theory*, 11 (1972), 145-178.

4 Further details can be found in John Lewis Gaddis, *The United States and the Origins of the Cold War 1941-1947* (New York: Columbia University Press, 1972), pp. 77-79, 133-173.

5 For a recent confirmation of this thesis, see Bruce R. Kuniholm, *The Origins of the Cold War in the Near East: Great Power Conflict and Diplomacy in Iran, Turkey, and Greece* (Princeton N.J.: Princeton University Press, 1980), pp. 345, 381-382.

6 Seyom Brown, *The Faces of Power: Constancy and Change in United States Foreign Policy from Truman to Johnson* (New York: Columbia University Press, 1968), pp. 7-14.

7 George F. Kennan, *Memoirs: 1925-1950* (Boston: Little, Brown and Company, 1967), p. 359. See also John Lewis Gaddis, "Containment: A Reassessment," *Foreign Affairs*, 55 (July 1977), 873-87.

8 NSC 68, "United States Objectives and Programs for National Security," April 14, 1950, *Foreign Relations of the United States: 1950*, I, 237-292. For a recent reassessment, see Samuel F. Wells, Jr., "Sounding the Tocsin: NSC 68 and the Soviet Threat," *International Security*, 4 (Fall 1979), 116-158, and commentaries on that article by Paul Nitze and the present author, *Ibid.*, Vol. 4 (Spring 1980), 164-176.

9 The best analysis is Glenn H. Snyder, "The 'New Look' of 1953," in Warner R. Schilling, Paul Y. Hammond, and Glenn H. Snyder, *Strategy, Politics, and Defense Budgets* (New York: Columbia University Press, 1962), pp. 379-524.

10 The clearest formulation of the Nixon Doctrine is in Nixon's first annual foreign policy report, February 18, 1970, *Public Papers of the Presidents: Richard M. Nixon: 1970* (Washington, D.C.: 1971), pp. 905-906.

11 See especially, in this connection, Nixon's speech at Kansas City, July 6, 1971, *Public Papers of the Presidents: Richard M. Nixon: 1971* (Washington D.C.: 1972), p. 806; and the interview with him in *Time*, XCIX (January 3, 1972), p. 15.

12 Alan Tonelson, "Nitze's World," *Foreign Policy*, Number 35 (Summer 1979), pp. 74-90.

13 Coral Bell, *The Diplomacy of Détente: The Kissinger Era* (New York: St. Martin's Press, 1977), pp. 1-3.

14 The analogy is Stanley Hoffmann's in *Primacy or World Order: American Foreign Policy Since the Cold War* (New York: McGraw-Hill, 1978), p. 46.

15 A succinct statement of the Soviet view of détente can be found in Leonid Brezhnev, *On the Policy of the Soviet Union and the International Situation* (Garden City, New York: Doubleday, 1973), pp. 230-231.

16 *Department of State Bulletin*, 66 (June 26, 1972), 898-899.

17 See, on this point, Strobe Talbott, *Endgame: The Inside Story of SALT II* (New York: Harper & Row, 1979), pp. 48-49, 146-147.

18 Peter Jay, "Regionalism or Geopolitics," *Foreign Affairs*, 58 ("America and the World: 1979"), 500.

19 Andrew Marshall, "Sources of Soviet Power: The Military Potential in the 1980's," in "Prospects of Soviet Power in the 1980's, Part II," *Adelphi Papers*, #152 (London: IISS, 1979), p. 11.

20 Speech at Salt Lake City, September 26, 1963; *Public Papers of the Presidents: John F. Kennedy: 1963* (Washington, D.C.: 1964), p. 736.

21 Remarks at White House briefing for members of Congress, January 8, 1980, *Weekly Compilation of Presidential Documents*, 16 (January 14, 1980), 40.

22 Carl von Clausewitz, *On War*, edited and translated by Michael Howard and Peter Paret (Princeton: Princeton University Press), 1976, pp. 104, 119-121.

23 Helmut Sonnenfeldt and William G. Hyland, "Soviet Perspectives on Security," *Adelphi Papers*, #150 (London: IISS, 1979), pp. 15, 19-20.

24 The most complete discussion is John M. Collins, *American and Soviet Military Trends Since the Cuban Missile Crisis* (Washington, D.C.: Center for Strategic and International Affairs, Georgetown University, 1978).

25 *Aviation Week and Space Technology*, 62 (June 16, 1980), 213-221, reviews the new ABM technology.

C: MECHANISMS OF REGULATION

The Future and Collective Security

Marina S. Finkelstein / Lawrence S. Finkelstein

Collective security is like a mirage. It beckons on the horizon. It seems full of promise. But it remains unattainable. It remains unattainable because the basic requirement of collective security — that nations subordinate their conflicting purposes and interests to collective action for the suppression of prohibited acts no matter how or where they may occur — has remained an illusion. Since the will to act collectively in specific instances in support of this very general purpose is the essence of collective security, it has simply remained unrealized.

Experience has shown that collective security is dependent, at the very least, on a firm nucleus of great power agreement. The United Nations Charter came close to an accurate reflection of the irreducible, the essential "collective will," in its requirement for great power unanimity as the condition for Security Council decisions on all but procedural matters. In spite of the storm of criticism at San Francisco of the "concurring votes" provision of Article 27, there was also recognition that collective security would be impossible without great power unanimity. Of course the smaller powers resented the privileged voting position of the five permanent members of the Security Council. At the same time, however, they recognized that when the "Big Five" were able to agree on what they wanted, it was in the interest of the smaller states to accept that agreement. In 1945, besides, to oppose the great powers meant to risk not having any Charter at all. In addition, it was recognized that the Charter represented an advance over the Covenant in that it substituted "for the rule of complete unanimity of the League Council a system of qualified majority voting in the Security Council."[1]

However, the hoped-for great power unanimity failed to materialize in the face of bitter ideological and political schism and military confrontation between the Soviet Union and the non-Communist permanent members of the Security Council. The United Nations, in spite of its many significant activities in the field of security, has not been an instrument of collective security.

The United Nations has, however, been put to the service of collective defense. In the Korean case, for example, the fact of North Korean aggression was clearly authenticated by a United

---

Nations agency, and the United Nations majority which resisted the aggression was thus able to enjoy the legal umbrella of United Nations authority. What took place was war, with the special moral and legal cachet that derives from the ability to command "legitimization" by the international organization. In the words of a recent paper, the United Nations has certain "obvious advantages for playing the role of custodian of the seals of international approval and disapproval. While the voice of the United Nations may not be the authentic voice of mankind, it is clearly the best available facsimile thereof...."[2]

At a different level, regional agencies have given legitimacy, of a somewhat different sort, to collective defense measures or arrangements. For example, the Organization of American States gave its blessing to the actions of the United States in the Cuban missiles crisis of 1962. The potentialities for competitive legitimization of military collective defense measures by the NATO and Warsaw Pact organizations in mutual conflict have, fortunately, not been put to the test.

It is sometimes argued that collective security may have a better chance in the regional organizations, because to a significant degree each such organization may represent a common cultural or religious heritage or a common historical experience of its members. However, such bonds of themselves do not ensure a common view on foreign affairs. Thus, the Arab League and the Organization of African Unity are, in different degrees, riven by disputes over ideological and political influence, over boundaries, questions of leadership, and various points of concrete foreign policy. The Organization of American States, which is the only regional organization to include formal collective security obligations in its constitutional documents, and which has on occasion been able to carry out collective security policies, is also subject to pulls in different directions. Fear of intervention by the northern "colossus" vies thus with the concept of collective security, with the outcome in any given instance unpredictable.

PEACE-KEEPING AS AN ALTERNATIVE TO COLLECTIVE SECURITY

In the United Nations, the frustration of the early hopes has produced various efforts to improvise effective means of dealing with the threats to peace posed in the decades since 1945. On the whole, the United Nations has proved remarkably resilient and surprisingly able to devise new responses to evolving needs, within the limits imposed by the fact that, through much of this period, the world was polarized around two great power centers in conflict.

In this history, Korea marked a turning point. In the early years of the United Nations, until the Korean War, the organization was able to perform two important peace and security functions. The first was to act as a forum for mobilizing resistance to Communist expansion, with a consequent legitimizing of the contingent threat that United States power would be applied in any given instance. One example was the Security Council's role in the issue posed by the continued presence of Soviet troops in Iranian Azerbaijan. Another was the Greek case, in which it was possible to set up partially effective means of observation and border patrols, intended to cut off the illicit flow of arms into Greece for the use of Communist-supported guerrillas. In Korea, as has already been pointed out, the presence of the United Nations Commission on the spot was fortuitously decisive in the determination of aggression when it occurred in 1950.

Experience until 1950 even led to the belief, expressed in the "Uniting for Peace" Resolution of November, 1950, that the United Nations might be developed into an effective instrument of collective defense. After all, in spite of all the difficulties and conflicts, the United Nations had been able to perform some collective defense functions. The Soviet Union had at least tolerated this use of the organization, most markedly when it did not withdraw from the United Nations despite its role in blocking achievement of Soviet goals in Korea.

All this inspired the belief that the veto could be evaded by relying on the General Assembly's powers to recommend actions to members. It was of course recognized that the General Assembly, unlike the Security Council, could not require members to act.

Throughout this early period the United Nations had also been playing another role, that of dealing, and with some success, with threats to the peace that did not directly involve the two hostile blocs. There had, in other words, proved to be enough consensus, even if sometimes of a tacit nature, to enable the United Nations to intervene effectively in a number of instances.

Thus in 1947 the United Nations began its intervention in the Palestine problem. In 1948 the dispute between Pakistan and India as to the future status of Kashmir came before the Security Council. Although no agreement on the future of the area proved possible, a United Nations military presence was interposed and is still stationed at the disputed border to supervise the carrying out of truce arrangements. In the Indonesian case the United Nations had a more positive success, the international organization being able through its good offices to help the Dutch colony achieve independent status (1947-1949).

However, even in this period, it was clear that the United Nations could be relevant to the central sphere of great power conflict only in a marginal way. This does not mean that matters concerning the peace settlements and the future of Europe did not appear on the agenda. They did. Various aspects of the German problem, Trieste, the Corfu Channel case, peace treaty violations by the East European satellites, all these did find their place before United Nations bodies. Indeed, the United Nations even provided the venue for the opening of negotiations leading to the settlement of the intense crisis over Berlin (1948-1949). However, this experience only underlined the fact that lack of agreement, coupled with the importance of the issues to the two blocs, made it impossible for the United Nations to have a determining role in these issues. The main response of the West to the need for a mobilization of collective defense took place not in the United Nations but in the Brussels Pact of 1948 and in the North Atlantic Treaty of 1949.

As has already been mentioned, Korea marked a turning point in a number of ways. From this time on, the United Nations' role as a forum to mobilize against Communist expansion declined while its role as a peace-keeper in "third world" conflicts became more prominent. There were a number of reasons which help to explain why the attention of the organization shifted in this way. First of all, the Soviet atomic explosion of 1949 had introduced a new element into the international power equation, one which seemed to many to offset United States predominance and thus to make its "lead" less compelling. Second, the emergence of Communist China as an important actor of considerable power on the international scene injected an increasing element of caution into the policies of a number of nations.

The results flowing from these changes were reinforced by later developments. First of all, Stalin's death in 1953 and the consequent evolution of Soviet foreign policies seemed to decrease the likelihood of dangerous threats from the Soviet Union and, by reducing fear of such Soviet initiatives, reduced willingness to engage in political controversy within the United Nations. Europe seemed to be entering a period of increased political stability. In 1955, in a surprising turnabout, the Soviet government agreed to sign the Austrian Peace Treaty. Even the ruthless Soviet suppression of the Hungarian Revolution in 1956, though it served as a jolt for many, did not reverse this trend. Bolstering this reluctance to react forcefully was a second factor: the development of a concept of nonalignment, first among Asian members and then among the rapidly growing group of African members. This introduced an almost professional "middle man" role, first significantly exhibited in the Indian mediation during the Korean crisis.

To sum up: a lessening of the United States predominance in some eyes, a seeming "softening" of Soviet policy, and the development of nonalignment — all these contributed to make it increasingly difficult, and perhaps also less necessary, to mobilize majorities for a vigorous United Nations role in bloc conflicts.

What was possible became therefore more limited. It also became more significant, as the movement of colonial areas into independence added a new dimension to the problems of the "third world." In this setting, the United Nations combined old and new devices to produce somewhat different patterns for preventing the breakdown of order under certain special circumstances. The process began with the Suez crisis of 1956-1957. What has emerged has been labeled "peace-keeping."

The purpose of peace-keeping is to prevent the breakdown of international order, or to mitigate it, should it already have taken place. Taken this far and no further, peace-keeping may seem identical with collective security. In actuality, however, the two are very different. Collective security is intended to apply against any threat to international peace, no matter where or by whom posed; it calls for universal participation; and its aim is to strike down the aggressor, the lawbreaker, and to enforce the decision of the international community. Peace-keeping, on the other hand, is limited in application, posits no "enemy," and is essentially voluntary.

Thus, peace-keeping is not intended to operate against threats to the peace anywhere in the world and without regard to the states involved. It is intended to operate in areas which do not fall within the spheres of great power interest, and especially where there is a risk that the great powers might be drawn into a mutual confrontation in such areas. Where such a situation is shaping up, the United Nations may be called on by its members to intervene with the consent of the parties, in a number of different ways: to prevent bloodshed, to supervise truces or cease-fire arrangements, to investigate, to perform pacifying missions of observation or patrol, or to give a new government a chance to survive and establish itself.[3] To achieve these ends, United Nations forces have been mobilized from national units voluntarily contributed through individual national decision. The permanent members of the Security Council do not normally contribute men to such United Nations forces. However, in practical terms, their role in the formation of the guiding United Nations resolutions, and their role, or the role of some of them, in terms of money, supplies, and equipment may be of crucial importance to the success of any peace-keeping operation. Nevertheless, it is possible to say that in a sense, instead of supplying security as the Charter envisioned, the great powers now consume it. Finally it should be pointed out that in peace-keeping operations, a special guiding responsibility has fallen to the Secretary-General, in the context of the members' interests and policies.

As was stated earlier, peace-keeping operates under rather special conditions. It involves functions and powers which were not specifically contemplated in the Charter. In purpose and character, such functions and powers seem more closely related to the Security Council's role with respect to the pacific settlement of disputes or situations which might lead to international friction or give rise to disputes, than to its powers of enforcement after it has determined "the existence of any threat to the peace, breach of the peace or act of aggression." In other words, peace-keeping seems more closely related to Chapter VI of the Charter than to Chapter VII.

A number of consequences flow from this constitutional interpretation. Because peace-keeping is based on Chapter VI and not on Chapter VII, it assumes no "enemy" as such and seeks to "defeat" no one. As Ralph Bunche, United Nations Under-Secretary, put it in discussing the operation of the United Nations Force (UNF) in the Congo,

> The United Nations in the Congo has neither sought to replace the Congo Government nor to make it a captive. The UNF is in the Congo as a friend and partner, not as an army of occupation.[4]

On this basis, United Nations forces as a rule are instructed not to use armed force except in self-defense, and many of their functions can be likened more to policing functions than to traditional military ones.

Since peace-keeping is based on the United Nations' enforcement powers under Chapter VI, it follows that peace-keeping must be voluntary. Therefore, it cannot start without the consent of the parties or without the permission of the government or governments on whose territory it is to take place. Nor can the decision to engage in a peace-keeping operation create any obligations on United Nations members to contribute forces or supplies or give permission for the use of any facilities. Impressed by the difficulties which arise from the ad hoc nature of peace-keeping as it has developed so far, some nations have decided to "earmark" units of their own forces for future peace-keeping service but these have been national, voluntary decisions and the actual use of such units is subject to national decision each time.

The argument which has developed in the United Nations as to the proper way to finance such operations centers on whether the financing of voluntary operations should also be voluntary or whether it should be governed by the provisions of Article 17, which give the General Assembly the power to "consider and approve" the budget and which state further that "the expenses of the Organization shall be borne by the Members as apportioned by the General Assembly." The argument arises out of a Charter ambiguity, the fact that Article 17 gives the General Assembly a power of compulsory assessment while the only other compulsory power is assigned to the Security Council under Chapter VII. The Soviet Union and France lead those who argue that financing of peace-keeping should not be compulsory; the United States leads those who advocate the principle of collective responsibility, which was supported by the International Court of Justice in an advisory opinion in 1962. As things developed in 1964 and 1965, it would seem that the principle of collective financial responsibility does not enjoy the support of a large enough majority to make it stick. Underlying this issue is the fact that national policies may differ — as in the Congo — concerning the objectives to be pursued and the sharing of control to reflect national influence in peace-keeping operations. The Soviet Union, for example, has been insisting that only the Security Council can undertake operations involving the deployment of military force for any purpose, obviously because of interest in strengthening Russian influence over peace-keeping decisions through its "veto" in the Security Council.

At the same time, even though the principle of collective financial responsibility does not seem to have wide support, the principle of peace-keeping does have large majority support. Therefore, while it may not now be possible to agree on the general principle of peace-keeping financing or on general guidelines for future peace-keeping decisions, it does seem likely that future "third world" crises which are not dealt with satisfactorily in other ways will precipitate enough agreement to make United Nations ad hoc intervention possible. Even so, this may depend on whether the great powers, the United States and the Soviet Union in particular, will be able to agree, at least tacitly, that prevention of crisis escalation to avoid the risk of a mutual encounter (or of Chinese gain) is more important than the independent pursuit of competitive interests.

Just what the decision would be in such instances is not at all clear. Independent Soviet action in the Congo, the appearance of Soviet weapons on Cyprus, United States insistence on the right to support governments which request its help as in Vietnam, intervention in the Dominican Republic in 1965, great power inability to agree on the financing of peace-keeping operations or on the general guidelines for the initiation of such operations in the future — all these suggest that the great powers may have conflicts in the "third world" which may make it difficult for them to agree on impartial peace-keeping measures when crises arise. It is at least probable, however, that in individual situations the interest of the majority in avoiding the deterioration of a tense situation will press the great powers toward the minimal agreement necessary to achieve the limited goal of insulating the crisis. In this connection it may be worthwhile to recall that it is possible for a permanent member of the Security Council to abstain from casting a yes or no vote. Since the Iranian case in 1946, it has been considered that a permanent member's abstention does not count as a veto. The Security Council may thus act without the concurrence of a great power, provided that it shows acquiescence by abstaining.

In this connection it may also be worth mentioning the Soviet complaint that "Socialist" members of the United Nations have been excluded from both direction of and participation in peace-keeping efforts. This may be important. In the future it may become necessary to find some accommodation in this matter if peace-keeping operations are to continue on the basis of adequate great power consensus. If the development of polycentric tendencies in Eastern Europe continues, it may become less undesirable to do so. Also significant has been the Soviet emphasis during the spring of 1965 on the possibility of revitalizing the Military Staff Committee, perhaps with an enlarged membership, as a means of strengthening the Security Council's capacity to control peace-keeping operations.

In short, the future development of the peace-keeping function may come to depend on a mutual effort to find a consensus through some degree of mutual accommodation. Progress toward such consensus might be eased if the United Nations majority were to press for a limitation on the use of the veto in order to reduce the temptation for great powers, especially the Soviet Union, to hamstring the Security Council capriciously. In particular, limiting the use of the veto to issues specifically stated by a permanent member to be a matter of "vital importance, taking into account the interests of the United Nations as a whole,"[5] might be a useful approach, consistent with the expectations in 1945 as to the purposes for which the veto might be employed. In May, 1965, the permanent representative of Pakistan to the United Nations advocated a similar standard when he suggested that:

> ...the Security Council would be restored to its full authority if the permanent members under took to refrain from using the veto in the case of disputes in which they are not directly involved or on which the General Assembly had made recommendations under Article 10 of the Charter....[6]

Whether it will be possible to arrive at necessary accommodation will depend, of course, on great power willingness to forgo competitive advantage in "third world" crises and to arrive at "ground rules" limiting national intervention in such crises to make impartial intervention both possible and necessary. It may then become possible to make the Security Council work as originally intended. If this is not possible, there will have to be at least enough consensus to enable the General Assembly to perform the peace-keeping function without causing the breakup of the organization.

The development of peace-keeping was unplanned and unexpected. It is a promising development. However, it does not amount to collective security since it involves interposition with the consent of all concerned and not the imposition of a collective will on a recalcitrant state.

PROSPECTS OF DEVELOPING COLLECTIVE SECURITY UNDER THE UNITED NATIONS

The next question to ask is obviously whether there might develop a consensus which could support collective security activities as well as peace-keeping. The answer is by no means self-evident.

It may be quite reasonable to assume that, if the United States and the Soviet Union should find enough consensus to lead them to support a peace-keeping operation, that consensus may stretch to support collective security enforcement measures if they should become necessary. As Paul H. Nitze, later to become Secretary of the Navy, put it in 1957,

> As the destructive power of the weapons systems possessed by the major powers approaches the absolute, these systems cannot be invoked except in support of absolute and unlimited objectives. Any involvement of the forces of the major powers, even limited forces in support of limited objectives, may involve an intolerable risk that the objectives and means employed will spread as a result of the military and political interaction of a war situation. The risks involved are of vital concern not just to the major powers but to the world as a whole. A growing realization of this situation among the politically effective masses of mankind can in the long run lay the foundation on which the necessary political consensus which is the pre-condition for a functioning United Nations force can be expected to arise.[7]

In other words, the argument here runs that the nuclear "balance of terror," in however uncertain a fashion, deters both major powers from taking intolerable risks and that this situation may be laying the basis for the development, however haltingly, of that political consensus which is the prerequisite for functioning international forces of an undefined character. Though not denying the very real possibility that the Soviet Union may elect to sow dissension, to ship its arms to tense areas for the use of one side or the other, and otherwise to create chaos, it is assumed in the following pages that such consensus should be helped to grow, at least in situations in which the so-called "vital and direct" interests of the powers are not immediately involved. If this point is correctly taken, then it should be a guideline of United States policy to seek to impress on all its desire to move toward a situation in which the enforcement provisions of the United Nations Charter in this area can be carried out as they were intended and to show how existing peace-keeping procedures might best be developed to their fullest usefulness in this area.

There is an obvious inconsistency in the proposition stated in the preceding paragraph. The inconsistency lies in the effort to pursue simultaneously the goal of seeking to establish enough great power consensus to enable the Security Council to work and pressing for Security Council intervention in individual cases, when to do so may obviously appear to be directed against the interests of a reluctant great power, especially the Soviet Union. There is no solution to this dilemma. However, a great deal might depend on the selection of issues to be pressed in the Security Council. Obviously, for the very reasons that make a veto power necessary, caution should be shown with respect to issues that directly affect what may be legitimately considered vital interests of a great power. Thus, to put it in more specific though hypothetical terms, the United States should not press for enforcement measures in the Warsaw Pact area and should resist proposals for United Nations enforcement measures in the NATO or OAS areas but should be willing to press for such intervention in Africa, the Middle East, and South and Southeast Asia.

From the above it is clear that collective security is not likely to operate in areas in which the great powers are directly or vitally concerned. This conclusion implies a certain risk of disagreement between the great powers and the rest of the members, already foreshadowed in the remarks of the Mauritanian delegate on the final day of the abortive nineteenth session of the General Assembly:

> We do not want to entrust to five great Powers or to two great Powers the task of deciding...what our common destiny will be....[8]

However, this is not a new argument but an old one, already hotly contested at San Francisco in 1945. Although the marked change in United Nations membership since that time makes it difficult to predict exactly how a discussion over relations in the organization between greater and lesser powers would come out now, a different conclusion seems unlikely. When the great powers agree that intervention is needed to prevent a breakdown of the peace, it is still probable that the other United Nations members will find it in their interest to agree or at least to acquiesce.

Recent events even evoke a question which has hitherto been unthinkable. As has been pointed out, United Nations history underscores the obvious conclusion that whatever role the United Nations may develop, that role is unlikely to be relevant to zones of most direct great power interest — Eastern Europe, the North Atlantic, and Latin America. Now, however, one can begin to speculate about a question which is no doubt remote but nevertheless of interest, namely, whether we can begin to detect any signs that the weakening of alliance ties and of leadership from Washington and Moscow may not point, however tentatively, to a day when United Nations intervention may become possible even in some parts of these sanctuaries. Thus it might be pointed out that in the Cuban missile crisis and in the Dominican crisis of 1965 the United Nations accepted responsibilities in relation to a problem of peace and security in Latin America.

Obviously enough, one cannot predict that United Nations collective security or even a peace-keeping function will become possible in these areas. But for the first time since the Potsdam Conference of 1945 it becomes possible to speculate as to whether such a role might become possible. In Eastern Europe and in Latin America new stresses and strains may create uncertainties regarding the roles of the great powers. It may be that relations within the areas and with interested great powers may be worked out with relative calm and without outside intervention. On the other hand, it is perhaps more likely that changes within the areas may bring serious hazards to world peace, which may lead to threatening great power confrontations or to new needs for intervention to stabilize difficult situations. These might involve roles for the United Nations.

Whether such roles will actually be possible is unclear. One possibility is that the great powers will extend to these areas any consensus they may develop in other parts of the world to permit impartial intervention as an alternative to their direct intervention. Or, on the other hand, the great powers might pose such severe threats to each other over these especially important areas that they and the rest of the world might welcome rescue by the world organization. In such circumstances, there might be a limited and transitory agreement to avoid a severe threat of catastrophe.

One should pause briefly at the question of the role of China in this context. While it is not impossible to conceive of peace-keeping operations and in some instances even of collective security operations in areas close to the periphery of China without strong opposition from Peking, it is very difficult to believe that Peking would readily acquiesce in such measures. Moreover, China's influence in other parts of the world may grow. It is clear that a "consensus" which does not include that country is a limited consensus. Nations within the reach of Chinese influence may not be anxious to become involved in international operations close to that country against its opposition. It is likely that Chinese influence will grow rather than decrease, barring some drastic change. Therefore, it is essential to keep in mind that any discussion of collective security or peace-keeping actions on the periphery of China, in areas in which that country has expressed an interest, would start out under a strong inhibition. The consensus of which we talk here thus remains limited, though if it were to come about, it would be significant.

COLLECTIVE SECURITY AND DISARMAMENT

Thus far, this analysis of collective security possibilities has been concerned with a world slowly evolving from today's baseline, a world heavily armed, organized in competing major coalitions and with a large neutral or nonaligned floating vote. Beset by new uncertainties, this world also confronts new opportunities arising out of the loosening of the binding cement in the major alliance systems.

However, one should also ask what would be the implications for collective security of a quantum jump, in the nature of major progress in disarmament. That there is a close connection has been well established. Secretary of State Herter, for example, in February, 1960, defined the United States task as the double one of trying to "create a more stable military environment" and of subsequently trying

> to cut national armed forces and armaments further and to build up international peacekeeping machinery, to the point where aggression will be deterred by international rather than national forces.[9]

The point crops up also in varying forms in the proposals of both the United States and the Soviet Union for general and complete disarmament.

In the first place, it is important to recognize that there is a point of demarcation, hard to identify and perhaps never precisely measurable, between a projection of *today's world* in which the main contemporary assumptions still apply even though national armaments have been reduced and a *new world* in which the reduction of armaments has proceeded so far that new measures for policing world order may be necessary. It seems reasonable to speculate that in a world of thermonuclear weapons, the transition point is more likely to be encountered late in the disarmament scale rather than early.

It is only when the great powers' nuclear capacity to deter each other and to dominate other powers has been brought into question that a thoroughly new situation will have been created. That point will probably not have been reached before disarmament has progressed well into the third of the three stages of the United States Draft Outline of 1962. While the Draft Outline calls for United Nations peace-keeping capabilities to be built up prior to that stage and, in fact, makes transition to the third stage contingent on prior success in this regard, it is clear that United Nations peace forces can only be subsidiary to great power strength and dependent upon great power collaboration, as is true today, until reduction of arms has destroyed great power dominance. Put this way, the argument is virtually tautological.

The contrary argument, that United Nations capabilities can be built up so that they dominate great power strength, even while the great powers remain very strong, or at least provide a new balancing force, postulates a degree of great power consensus as to the goals, methods, and control of a United Nations force which it is virtually impossible to conceive of. Such vague generalizing as the Soviet Union and the United States have been willing to indulge in so far on this subject indicates that they are poles apart in their conceptions of what United nations forces in the context of a disarming world might be like. And China has not yet joined the dialogue, such as it is. It is difficult, nay virtually impossible, to conceive of the powers bridging their differences, short of such a complete resolution of all their differences as would make complete or near-complete disarmament possible.

There is, however, a school of thought which urges that the thing to do is to divorce both disarmament and world policing from ideological, political, economic, or social questions. The notion that a regime in which ultimate power is vested in some peace-keeping authority can be based on a common interest in controlling the risks of national armaments and the hazards of war is an attractive one. As one author put the argument,

> *It may well be that many governments now regard disarmament not as a way of establishing world order acceptable to all nations, but as a way of changing the means of independently pursuing the national interest....* In other words, the interest in disarmament may have arisen from a growing acceptance of "the hypertrophy of war" as a *means*, rather than from a growing acceptance of world order as an *end*.[10]

Attractive this argument is. But it is also totally unreal. In a world in which important differences persist and the risk of international conflict continues so that a world peace authority is thought necessary, how likely is it that states with vital interests at stake will entrust decisive power to a mechanism which must in these circumstances itself be an important object of competition? The point is really quite simple. Defense of important interests in such circumstances would depend on ability to control the world peace authority. How can such a world peace authority be set up by nations which do not have substantial ideological and political consensus? Without such consensus, how can they agree on arrangements to control the authority? And if they cannot agree on such arrangements, can they really be expected to agree in the first place on the disarmament which would make the authority necessary? The argument, it will be urged, is circular. The charge is correct because the problem is circular. Disarmament, collective security, and political consensus, like love and marriage in the popular song, are inseparable: "You can't have one without the other."

Another approach to the problem leads to the same conclusion. One of the central dilemmas confronted by those who have been concerned with schemes for maintaining world peace and security has been the relationship of arrangements to keep the peace to the nature of the peace that is to be kept. To say that a peace and security system can maintain peaceful procedures in a world in which important states or many states and their populations are not satisfied by the existing distribution of the world's territory, assets, or justice, and by the procedures on which agreement can be reached to alter that distribution is like saying that the lid can be kept on a kettle full of boiling water. Security and justice are intimately related. Where there is strong dissatisfaction, the maintenance of peace depends on the existence of agreed procedures to change the state of affairs. A complete system of peace and security must, therefore, include arrangements for what has been called "peaceful change." Perhaps it might have to come to include a so-called "legislative power." It is clear that any agreement on such procedures would require a high degree of consensus to start with.

In sum, disarmament, world policing, and peaceful change are not separable phenomena but part of one tightly knit package. All of them depend on the existence of a willingness among nations to subordinate their individual interests to agreed procedures for resolving their differences. That is a large order. It involves more consensus by a good deal than exists in today's world.

CONCLUSIONS

It is striking that, however the question of collective security is approached, the lesson appears to be the same. Change, whether in the short-term task of peace-keeping, in the longer-term development of collective security under the United Nations, or in movement toward the ultimate vision of a world peace authority, depends on the development of consensus. There is no short cut here.

Our recent experiences with the Soviet Union are instructive. There appears to be a minimum though not too certain consensus today. In part it has developed by chance. The death of Stalin marked an important turning point. President Kennedy's appearance on the national scene in the United States had a good deal to do with it also. In part, it may be a response to the deterioration of Sino-Soviet relations, and it may be debatable whether the world is in balance better off as a result of the developments in Chinese doctrine which played an important part in that split. But in considerable measure the United States-Soviet consensus is undoubtedly the result of confrontation and tension over a long period. Through this experience the two countries have learned to fear and respect each other as adversaries. Their disproportionate strength puts limits on their desire to fight each other. Out of this amalgam of circumstance, context, and constraint has come a degree of agreement which offers some hope of a better future relationship.

Fortunately, the United Nations exists as a forum in which to strive to reach broader accommodations, both with the Soviet Union and other nations. All powers which seek disarmament and world order as their ultimate goals should seek to engage in the United Nations in a process of accommodating their differences through dialogue and tension. Out of the crucible may emerge an evolving consensus which will enable the world to move by stages to a higher degree of collective policing capability on the part of the organized international community.

ENDNOTES

1 *Report to the President on the Results of the San Francisco Conference*, by the Chairman of the United States Delegation, the Secretary of State, June 26, 1945, Department of State Publication 2349, Conference Series 71 (Washington, D.C.: Government Printing Office, 1945), p. 75.

2 Inis L. Claude, Jr., "Collective Legitimization as a Political Function of the U.N.," Study Group on International Organization, European Centre of the Carnegie Endowment for International Peace, Geneva, 1965, mimeo., OI 12.65, p. 9.

3 Since 1956 such operations have taken place in the Middle East to patrol the lines between Israel and its neighbors (1956-); in Lebanon (1958); in the Congo (1960-1964), as well as in West Irian (1962-1963), Yemen (1963), and on Cyprus (1964-).

4 *Security Council Official Records*, Fifteenth Year, Supplement for July, August, September, 1960, Doc. S/4451 (August 21, 1960), pp. 114-115.

5 General Assembly Resolution 267 (III), April 14, 1949.

6 Ambassador Amjad Ali, Special Committee on Peace-Keeping, Prov. SR of 6th Mtg., May 6, 1965, A/AC.121/SR.6, May 11, 1965, pp. 4-5.

7 Paul H. Nitze, "When and Under What Circumstances Might a United Nations Police Force Be Useful in the Future," in William R. Frye, *A United Nations Peace Force* (New York: Oceana, 1957), pp. 119-121, at p. 121.

8 UN Document A/PV.1330, p. 47.

9 February 18, 1960, Address at National Press Club, *Department of State Bulletin*, March 7, 1960, pp. 354-358.

10 Arthur I. Waskow, *Quis Custodiet? Controlling the Police in a Disarmed World*, A Peace Research Institute Report Submitted under ACDA Grant ACDA/IR-8 (Washington, D.C.: Peace Research Institute, Inc., 1963), pp. 6-7.

C: MECHANISMS OF REGULATION

Negotiation as a Management Process

Gilbert R. Winham

I. INTRODUCTION

Negotiation is an enduring art form. Its essence is artifice, the creation of expedients through the application of human ingenuity. The synonyms of the word "art" are qualities we have long since come to admire in the ablest of negotiators: skill, cunning, and craft. We expect negotiators to be accomplished manipulators of other people, and we applaud this aspect of their art when we observe it in uncommon degree. Negotiation is considered to be the management of people through guile, and we recognize guile as the trademark of the profession.

Our appreciation of guile goes back a long way. In Greek mythology, the god Hermes was chosen by his colleagues for diplomatic missions, representing as he did the qualities of charm, trickery, and cunning. A more recent expression of the value of craftiness can be found in the writing of an ambassador from the court of Louis XIV. In a book that Sir Harold Nicolson has described as "the best manual of diplomatic method ever written," François de Callières in 1716 recorded the following observation about the diplomatic practices of a predecessor:

> Before his elevation to the cardinalate, Cardinal Mazarin was sent on an important mission to the Duke of Feria, Governor of Milan. He was charged to discover the true feelings of the Duke on a certain matter, and he had the cunning to inflame the Duke's anger and thus to discover what he would never have known if the Duke himself had maintained a wise hold over his feelings. The Cardinal indeed had made himself absolute master of all the outward effects which passion usually produces, so much so that neither in his speech nor by the least change in his countenance could one discover his real thought; and this quality which he possessed in so high a degree contributed largely to make him one of the greatest negotiators of his time.[1]

In contemporary times we continue to acknowledge cunning. In a recent article on the Vietnam cease-fire agreement, Tad Szulc recorded with obvious enthusiasm the performance of Henry Kissinger in achieving a negotiated settlement to the war.[2] As Szulc's account makes clear, Kissinger

---

Gilbert R. Winham, "Negotiation as a Management Process," *World Politics*, Vol. 30, No. 1 (October 1977). Portions of the text have been deleted. Some footnotes have been removed; those remaining have been renumbered.

certainly demonstrated on this occasion that the hoary tactics of manipulation and concealment were important tools in the contemporary management of international relations. However, lest we overstrcss the importance of these tools, it is well to ask ourselves why brilliant performances in diplomacy seem so few and far between, and why there are apparently so few diplomats today who enjoy the equivalent of Kissinger's reputation. Perhaps it is because negotiation, like leadership, is a skill applied in a situation, and there are relatively few situations in international relations today that call forth the skills Kissinger so ably demonstrated. Times are changing, and the world is a less suitable stage for the diplomat's machinations in the 1970's than it was in the time of Monsieur de Callières.

The typical negotiation situation today bears little resemblance to those that obtained in the service of Louis XIV. Most diplomacy is conducted less discreetly and more under the surveillance of domestic interests than was the case previously. Negotiations are often more multilateral than bilateral; even when relationships are pursued on a bilateral basis, "reality is not bilateral," as Neustadt has observed. Both the operations of domestic groups and the incidence of multilateral negotiation enormously complicate the task of the diplomat. But more complicating yet are the changes in the subject matter of contemporary negotiations. The preoccupations of traditional diplomacy were war, sovereignty, territory, and the personal ambitions of rulers; although these could be painful subjects, they at least were comprehensible through the application of political acumen and common sense. Negotiators today spend more time discussing technology than did their predecessors, because technology — whether it takes the form of information systems, industrial processes, or nuclear weapons — has a proportionately greater impact on human existence now that it did in the past. And technology is in a state of rapid change, often at an exponential rate; it creates an enormous problem of comprehension and adaptation for contemporary society.

Unquestionably, modern negotiation continues to be a contest of will and wit, but the emphasis has shifted. The principal problem for most contemporary negotiators is not to outwit their adversaries, but rather to create a structure out of a large mass of information wherein it is possible to apply human wit. The classical diplomat's technique of the management of people through guile has given way to the management of people through the creation of system and structure. The process is not as glamorous and individualized, but it requires no less the application of human intelligence than did the trickery of the classical diplomat.

Modern international negotiation represents a meshing of great systems. It is commonplace today to observe that the world is becoming more interdependent — and one symptom of this interdependence is the fact that complex political and economic problems are increasingly handled at the level of international negotiation rather than exclusively at the domestic level. Today, negotiators function as an extension of national policy-making processes rather than as a formal diplomatic representation between two sovereigns. The number of people involved in international negotiation has increased sharply, with consequent depersonalization of the process. It is unlikely that the "true feelings" of leaders or diplomats are as important as they once were, but it is erroneous to assume that personalities are irrelevant — particularly as they combine in various decision-making settings. In past eras it was fashionable to describe negotiation as art, and art it continues to be, but it is now more akin to the art of management as practiced in large bureaucracies than to the art of guile and concealment as practiced by Cardinal Mazarin.

The aim of this essay is to explore the nature of modern negotiation, especially multilateral negotiation, and to contrast it with previous styles of international negotiation. The contention is that rapid changes have been occurring in the negotiation process, and that these changes should be reflected more than they now are in thinking about international relations. It will be argued that the changes affect the nature of negotiation, and that an understanding of this fact is important in evaluating the usefulness of conducting negotiations. The changes also affect certain theories about the practice of negotiation, and they affect especially the importance of concessions and convergence in the negotiation process. Most important, the changes reflect different tactics which are employed by negotiators and which should be understood in order to propose improvements in the process.

II. THE NATURE OF MODERN INTERNATIONAL NEGOTIATION

Politicization. Since 1945, international negotiation has been under pressure from two sides. External pressure has occurred from significant changes in the international system — principally from the increased number of nation-states and the consequent trend toward multilateral diplomacy in the United Nations system. Internal pressure has occurred from the increasing impact of citizen input and bureaucratic politicking on the negotiating process. International negotiation is a more politicized affair than previously, and as a consequence the distinctions between foreign affairs and domestic affairs are blurring.

Some aspects of the external pressure on negotiations are well known. Some time ago, Sir Harold Nicolson called attention to the increasing trend toward conducting negotiation by public conference, and observed that the process violated the rule that sound negotiations must be confidential and continuous.[3] More recently, certain developments have occurred that Nicolson did not foresee. The increased number of nation-states since 1945 has ensured that national positions are more varied and more difficult to reconcile than ever before. New states tend to raise issues that more established ones consider as settled; as a consequence the negotiation process can rely less on precedent to create a common referent for bargaining. This problem was illuminated in a study of the Law of the Sea negotiation in 1958, where some of the newer states objected to the concepts of international law and the administrative-legalistic style of negotiation with which Western countries had long been familiar.[4] A similar example occurred at the U.N. Environmental Conference in Stockholm, where less developed countries were successful in forcing the issues of human poverty and underdevelopment into the definition of environment, and hence onto the agenda of the conference.

Internal pressures have also affected the negotiation process. In de Callières's day, the process of representing a sovereign abroad was simpler than it is now. Monsieur de Callières viewed negotiation neither as troubled by bureaucratic constraints nor as a bureaucratic process in itself. The contrast between this image and that of modern negotiation could not be more striking. Most modern negotiations are carried on between teams that represent bureaucracies, and in large negotiations the teams themselves approach the status of small bureaucracies. That this system would increase the scope of bureaucratic politics in negotiation is self-evident, and there are many examples. John Newhouse, writing on the Strategic Arms Limitation Talks, observed that the U.S. SALT delegation replicated the SALT bureaucracy in Washington, and that "most importantly, SALT [was] an internal negotiation."[5] A similar sentiment was expressed by an experienced U.S. negotiator: "I would say about nine-tenths of my time of negotiation was done with my own side."[6] In the Kennedy Round, the leaders of major delegations had to exercise considerable skill in managing internal problems, and one such leader described his role in terms of mobilizing effectively the resources of the team, of reconciling different interests, and of bringing in the right people at the right time to handle the tasks that confronted the delegation.[7]

The bureaucratic dissensus that negotiators must contend with is often a reflection of the demands of pressure groups at home. In any major negotiation the interests of large groups must be accounted for, and this creates a problem of organization, distillation, and representation for the negotiating team. The problem was accurately, if perhaps unjoyously, portrayed by a U.S. official in connection with the American position at the current trade negotiations in Geneva: "The U.S. negotiating team is particularly restrained by having to respond to 45 private-sector committees composed of 900 knowledgeable people who are well aware of their own interests.... The E.C. confronts the same problem."[8] Nor is this problem appreciably lessened in a smaller system. In connection with the same trade negotiation, the Canadian Government received a request from the Province of Manitoba to include representatives from the Province during the final stages of the negotiation. Since the positions of the Federal and Provincial Governments on trade and tariff matters are not congruent, the outcome of Manitoba's request will probably complicate the work of the Canadian delegation no matter how the issue is resolved.

Technological Change. The increased complexity in negotiation due to human factors is matched by an equivalent impact from non-human factors. Technological change is occurring in all countries, and with increasing intensity. The rate of change poses two principal problems that frequently create difficulties at the negotiating table. One is the scale, or variety, of relationships. International relationships today encompass an enormous variety of interaction which gives rise to an equivalent variety of items in the negotiation process. Consider one example. In the Kennedy Round, the negotiators dealt with levels of protection on tens of thousands of products traded by 82 states, and in addition considered questions such as problems of dumping and assistance to less developed countries. Most states were therefore burdened by a portfolio of staggering complexity, which would be unknowable in any sense in which we might apply the term. Nor was this problem a special product of economic relations, trade negotiations, or the Kennedy Round in particular. A similar situation obtained in the SALT talks and in the current Law of the Sea negotiation. Indeed, it seems that when one looks at the areas where major negotiations have been held, the complexity of the sort described in the Kennedy Round is the rule rather than the exception.

A further problem is uncertainty. If technological progress creates variety, it also creates uncertainty, for in many areas we are simply unaware of the implications of modern technology on human life. Moreover, we are uncertain about the means for managing such technologies. These observations apply to defense, to off-shore mineral exploitation, and to food distribution (all areas in which there have been international negotiations), but they pertain especially to problems of the international economy. Economists are simply uncertain about some of the most important questions regarding the international economy, and this uncertainty is reflected at the bargaining table when governments negotiate on various problems. In trade negotiations, for example, there are no satisfactory ways to measure the effect of tariff reductions on trade, and hence this creates the difficulty of not having any ultimate guidelines by which to evaluate the results of the negotiation. The same is true of weapons negotiations, where there are no clear and unambiguous ways to assess the relation between numbers of nuclear weapons and the national security. The conclusion, then, is that the environment within which states must conduct their relationships is becoming increasingly complex, both because of the operation of technological progress and because of certain changes that have occurred in the structure of domestic and international politics.

Response to Complexity. The political response to the increasing complexity in domestic societies has been to enlarge the scope of the governmental bureaucracy. Bureaucracy helps to structure the political process by providing rules and standardized procedures within which that process can operate. Furthermore, bureaucracy provides a means for coping with the variety and uncertainty inherent in an increasingly complex environment:

it provides variety in governmental operations to match the variety in the environment, and it provides guidelines for action in situations that are too uncertain for rational (or synoptic) analysis. In short, the function of bureaucracy in domestic governments has been to increase human control over changes in the society, thereby reducing the uncertainty and increasing the stability of human life. In international politics, however, there is no organizational structure to accomplish the function that bureaucracy serves in domestic society. Certainly there has been an increase in international bureaucracy, but there is insufficient consensus in international politics to permit a "bureaucratic-rational" solution to many problems. Instead, governments turn to the negotiating process — a method that has gained acceptance in the history of nation-states — to achieve the same purpose that bureaucracy achieves in domestic society.

The main thesis of this paper is that much international negotiation, especially multilateral negotiation occurs as an attempt by the parties to manage some aspect of their environment. Negotiations often do not occur simply to resolve specific points of dispute between the parties, although disputes are certain to be embedded in the fabric of any negotiation. An important purpose of negotiation is to reduce complexity; the technique is to achieve, through negotiated agreement, a structure that will limit the free play of certain variables in the future.[9] This can be seen quite clearly in the case of the Kennedy Round. The immediate objective of the Kennedy Round negotiators was to reduce barriers to international trade, especially tariff barriers. However, an underlying and more important concern was to secure a regulated level of tariff support that would preclude the destablizing forces of competitive protectionism. Once tariffs are regulated by international agreements, the nations participating in these agreements are locked into a pattern of mutual obligation. That is true even where tariffs are not reduced, as in the case where governments agree not to raise low tariffs (i.e., bind). Observance of these obligations effectively reduces unilateral control, and therefore reduces the uncertainty about tariff levels with which exporting countries must contend.[10]

A similar concern occurs in other negotiations as well; the SALT negotiation affords an excellent example. The impetus behind SALT, as Newhouse's excellent analysis has made clear, was not a desire to reduce arms, but rather a need to stabilize defense relations between the United States and the Soviet Union. The main threats to stability were a competitive arms race, uncertainty about future force levels, and the consequent need to assume the worst in projecting defense needs in the future. SALT did not reduce arms appreciably, but it did permit Soviet and American planners to exercise greater control over the environment in which they project defense needs. As in the case of the Kennedy Round, an underlying purpose of SALT was control of uncertainty, as was made clear by the U.S. chief delegate to SALT, Gerard C. Smith:

> A major driving force behind the strategic arms competition — at least from the American standpoint — has been uncertainty as to what future Soviet force levels would be. If the Vladivostok accords evolve into a formal limitation agreement, the U.S. will be assured of the maximum number of Soviet launchers during the next decade. Even though the number is high, it will be known.... Assurance about the future maximum size of the forces...should encourage stability in the American-Soviet strategic relationship.[11]

The attempt to reduce variety and uncertainty through negotiation, and consequently to increase international stability, is not a new feature of international diplomacy. Indeed, as Nicolson has noted, the chief aim of diplomacy is international stability, and governments have long tried to reduce their uncertainty about the intentions or capabilities of their adversaries through negotiated agreements. What is different is that the complexities of the present age are greater, due largely to technical change, and as a result environmental control is a more urgent task than before. National leaders are uncertain about the future, and, as Newhouse reminds us "it is the unknown, not the known, that fosters instability."[12] Many statesmen today feel under pressure to create values or structures in international politics that will replace the uncertainties of unilateral action with the certainty of negotiated agreements. Secretary of State Henry Kissinger expressed such a sentiment when he said of the U.N. Conference on the Law of the Sea (L.O.S.): "Unilateral legislation would be a last resort.... It [the Conference] must succeed. The United States is resolved to help conclude the Conference in 1976 — before the pressure of events and contentions places international consensus irretrievably beyond our grasp."[13]

. . .

Implications. To view international negotiations as a process for reducing uncertainty involves important implications for our understanding of the negotiation process. One implication is that negotiation is no longer viewed principally as a dispute-settlement or distributive procedure. This distinction was apparently appreciated by Dr. Kissinger when he described the L.O.S. negotiation in the following terms: "We are at one of those rare moments when mankind has come together to devise means of preventing future conflict and shaping its destiny, rather than to resolve a crisis that has occurred or to deal with the aftermath of a war."[14] Dispute settlement, or crisis resolution, is the common model we usually adopt for understanding most international negotiation. This model usually entails the tabling of an opening position, and the movement (or convergence) toward a compromise position through step-by-step concessions. The burden on the negotiator is to maintain as much of his position as possible while moving toward an outcome that will be mutually acceptable. This process emphasizes concealment, competitive strategies, and the ability to persuade.

The model of dispute settlement continues to be appropriate in international politics, and certain elements of it can operate in negotiations where dispute settlement is not the main purpose of the negotiation. At the Kennedy Round negotiators certainly engaged in haggling and compromise; they exchanged concessions; and they vigorously tried to persuade other parties of the justice and merit of the positions they had staked out. However, the basic structure of the negotiation, viewed in its entirety, was quite different. A more appropriate model for negotiation in a complex situation is one that replaces strategy with search for information, and is concerned with process as opposed to outcome. Negotiators tend not to estimate acceptable outcomes, because outcomes are distant and unknowable. They focus instead on the process of negotiation and what they want the process to achieve, such as exchange of information about both parties' principal concerns, decision-making procedures, or the like. The process of negotiation involves a search for acceptable solutions, where strategy is more a matter of forestalling the consideration of certain unattractive solutions than a matter of extracting a change of position from an adversary. This process is akin to the tactics of integrative bargaining as described by Walton and McKersie, or the procedures of "debate" as described by Rapoport.[15] The process will be further explored in the next section of this paper.

The second implication of viewing negotiation as a process for reducing uncertainty is that the development of common perceptions becomes more important to the negotiating process than the exchange of concessions. In complex situations, negotiators tend to negotiate over the "definition of the situation," and theories of how people develop common perceptions of complex information are more likely to be useful than theories of how people outwit others in bargaining contests. When negotiators deal with each other over complex subjects, they often represent societies that have evolved entirely different methods of accomplishing certain social tasks, and as a result the first problem is to establish a definitional basis from which to proceed. Newhouse has appreciated this aspect about the SALT negotiations; he concludes a description of the first negotiating session with the statement: "The two sides parted as they met, still speaking a different strategic vocabulary." He further quotes an interviewee: "We were so absorbed in our own definitional problems we made no serious effort to anticipate theirs."[16] In Zartman's words: "The whole process of the Strategic Arms Limitation negotiation is a search for referent principles and then for the implementing details."[17]

The process described above normally requires some agreement on the negotiating rules, or some similar formula for standardizing the approach of different parties. In the Kennedy Round, the problem of negotiating rules was dealt with explicitly, but it may be more common for negotiators to establish referents or formulas implicitly as part of the discussion of a problem. Also, establishing such formulas can be an ongoing procedure during a negotiation, and will be part of the process that occurs naturally when parties take up new issues. An analogous procedure to the use of negotiation formulas is the creation of a bargaining language to assist negotiators to exchange proposals. A bargaining language essentially consists of cognitive structures that facilitate communication between negotiators. These structures can be very general, such as the notions of "parity" in weapons negotiations, or "reciprocity" in trade negotiation, or they can be common definitions or evaluation procedures that enable negotiators to evaluate their progress in the negotiation. In complex negotiations, a bargaining language can serve as a mechanism for simplifying the information that negotiators must handle in the course of moving toward an agreement. It is a means of developing common perceptions about the bargaining environment, and its use in itself constitutes some measure of agreement between the parties.

III. THE PRACTICE OF MODERN INTERNATIONAL NEGOTIATION

If the purpose of international negotiation has changed since de Callières's time, so also has the practice. Negotiation today is an extension of the policy process from the domestic to the international arena, and negotiators behave in a manner more akin to that of national bureaucrats than of classical diplomats. The distinction between negotiation and management is blurring. The most useful concepts for understanding the practice of modern negotiation come from the literature of decision making, business management, and organization theory, and not necessarily from studies of negotiation or bargaining theory. Of special importance are the concepts for understanding decision making in complex situations — most notably the principles of cybernetic decision making.[18]

The practice of negotiation in complex situations is heavily influenced by a desire to maintain control over the situation and to avoid uncertainty. The principal activity is a process of creating one's own position while adapting to the demands and offers of others. This activity is a bureaucratized activity (e.g., negotiation by working groups), dealing with a subject matter that has been decomposed into compatible subgroups (e.g., product sectors in trade negotiations). Large-scale negotiations like the Kennedy Round evolve over considerable time. Negotiators proceed toward agreement by initially tabling a position that is exploratory at best. At this stage, negotiating teams rarely have a concept of what a final, acceptable agreement might look like, for two reasons. The first is lack of attention by governments; serious thinking about what is acceptable is often done only after serious negotiation has begun. The second reason is that what is acceptable is a function of what is available, and that is only demonstrated in the act of negotiation. The result is that negotiators proceed with more understanding of and attention to the process of negotiation than of where the process will lead.

The negotiating process is a programmed set of operations that has evolved from considerable experience. It consists of tabling a position, decomposing and aggregating the relevant information wherever possible, and then setting about point by point to reconcile the different positions of the parties. Negotiators incrementally explore the interface between the bargaining positions of states much as army ants explore the interface of their colony and the environment. Over time, the negotiation accumulates a settlement from the bottom up, a phenomenon which the participants refer to as "building a package." In this process, negotiators monitor certain feedback variables, such as domestic support for the negotiation, which indicate the willingness of their government and others to cooperate in a negotiated settlement. Inherent in the programmed nature of the negotiation is the risk that negotiating procedures will not be sufficiently flexible to take advantage of unusual or unorthodox opportunities. For example, in the Kennedy Round agricultural products were not included in the general agreement. Agricultural restrictions are generally not amenable to the same negotiating procedures as industrial tariffs, and in the opinion of several interviewees, opportunities to liberalize agricultural trade were missed because this area was outside the "ground rules" of the negotiation.

The negotiation process described above contains several elements that deserve further attention. One such element is the concept of problem-solving search, and particularly search as a means for establishing communication and structure between the parties. A second element is programmed operations, which bring about most of the reconciliation of the conflicting positions of the parties. Finally, a third element is the conclusion of a negotiation and the codification of the process that has been occurring. Special problems arise at the conclusion of a negotiation that set it apart from the rest of the process.

Problem-solving Search. A common way to portray international negotiation is a continuum. The positions of the parties are juxtaposed at opposite ends of the continuum, and if an agreement is to be reached, it is through a process of compromise and convergence. In this conception, negotiators think of their position in terms of what they desire and what they will settle for, and they try to generate realistic expectations about the "probable outcome" of the bargaining and the "minimum disposition" of their adversary. Concessions are a crucial step in this process, and the strategy of concession making has been a major focus of studies of negotiation and bargaining. The concern over concession making is understandable, for if one portrays negotiation as a process of convergence, one can almost define negotiation itself as a process of exchanging concessions.

However useful the concepts of continuum and convergence may be for describing certain aspects of modern negotiations, they do not serve as an adequate picture for the overall process, and consequently are not a good guide for negotiating behavior. The notion of continuum loses force in the complex situations that characterize many international negotiations. The imposition of a continuum on negotiation represents a considerable degree of structure. However, international negotiations are often characterized by structural uncertainty—that is, where the nature of the possible outcomes and not just the probability associated with different outcomes is unknown. In many situations, negotiators negotiate precisely to find out what the issues are; hence, it is beyond the scope of their analytical abilities to project probable outcomes. Furthermore, in keeping with an unstructured situation, negotiators do not have a conscious strategy on concessions worked out in advance, not do they appear to evolve one during the negotiation. In sum, the concepts of continuum and convergence assume more structure than is usually present in large negotiations. A better way to conceptualize large negotiations is as trial-and-error search, which is a basic concept in cybernetic decision making.

Cybernetic decision making occurs in environments that are too complex to permit analysis; hence, decision makers define their environment through their actions, and not through analysis. Decision makers take actions, assess their outcomes, and then recalculate the actions that led to the outcomes obtained. Analysis is a matter of comparing a past action with an outcome, deciding whether it was a good outcome, and then choosing another action. Negotiators proceed very much in the same way. Negotiation in complex situations is largely a matter of trying out new combinations of ideas in an effort to "move the negotiation along." Where the ideas are accepted, they create a structure along which the negotiation will proceed; continued success will enable the negotiators to "build a package." Where ideas are not accepted, they are scrapped, and something else is tried. If too many ideas are scrapped, the negotiation runs the risk of becoming "bogged down" or running into a "dead end." In such cases the negotiation will continue, if at all, after the occurrence of a "breakthrough" at which major concessions may have been granted; more likely, there will have been a redefinition of the problem, moving the negotiation onto a different plane. The entire process is more akin to fitting the pieces into a puzzle than to convergence along a continuum.

There are two types of creative acts that often occur in the process just described. One is to establish structure through the use of a formula or referent principle (or "negotiating rules") to guide the negotiation. This practice is fairly well understood and is overtly pursued by negotiators. In the Kennedy Round, two formulas were instrumental in moving the negotiation along: one established the principle of linear cuts, where states negotiated tariff reductions over large numbers of products rather than on an item-by-item basis; a second one ("decoupage") helped to break an impasse that developed late in the negotiation in the crucial chemical sector. In the SALT negotiations, a more implicit referent principle served as a point of departure through the entire negotiation. This was the analysis, originally presented by Robert McNamara to the Soviets at the Glassboro meetings in 1967, that the development of an ABM system was an inherently destablizing factor in the nuclear balance between the superpowers. Throughout the ensuing negotiation, this referent principle appeared to be major motivating factor in the negotiating strategy of both sides.

A second procedure by which negotiators establish structure in complex situations is to create hierarchies in the negotiating situation. This procedure is often used implicitly, although it is less well understood in an analytical sense. The principle behind the use of hierarchy to establish structure has been explored in a philosophical essay by Herbert A. Simon: "Hierarchy, I shall argue, is one of the central structural schemes that the architect of complexity uses."[19] For Simon, hierarchy has at least two meanings. One is the common notion of formal organization, which is a system composed of subordinate subsystems. This form is commonly encountered in society; business firms, governments (and negotiating teams) exhibit this kind of parts-within-parts structure. A second notion of hierarchy is perceptual, and amounts to an ordering that can be imposed on an environment. The second notion is dependent on the property of "decomposability," or the extent to which systems can be reduced to subsystems that are approximately independent of each other. The capacity of decision makers to perceive (or, presumably, to create) decomposability in a complex environment is related to the capacity to understand and take action in that environment. As Simon says, "The fact, then, that many complex systems have a nearly decomposable, hierarchic structure is a major facilitating factor enabling us to understand, to describe, and even to 'see' such systems and their parts."[20]

In complex situations like trade negotiations, negotiators use hierarchy and relational thinking to understand and to create structure in their environment. Some hierarchies are easily established and follow naturally from the data in the environment. For example, products can be grouped and negotiated in sectors, and sectors can be further categorized in turn. Formal organization (such as working groups) can be created to jibe with structure implicit in the subject of the negotiation. Also, less orthodox hierarchies can be established and the material dealt with, depending on what serves the purpose of the negotiation. For example, products or sectors can be ranged in terms of the percentage of world trade each accounts for, or by the nature of trade barriers applied; or a ranking might be established depending on the extent of disparity (and hence, presumably, the extent of negotiating difficulty) between the tariff structures of various negotiating partners.

The more creative hierarchies are less obvious. One important hierarchy that must be established is a ranking of priorities in relation to the negotiating process. In the course of the negotiation, negotiators must establish what they principally want; without this, the negotiation cannot generate the major trade-offs that are the structure around which agreements are built. Achieving a ranking of priorities is a difficult process; experience from the Kennedy Round and the simulations of the Kennedy Round suggest it can be done effectively only as part of the negotiating process, and not simply as an internal process prior to participating in the negotiation. A time schedule is another hierarchy. The time dimension is of crucial importance to a negotiation because of the sequential and compartmentalized nature of the process. A time schedule forces negotiators to think hierarchically over time — that is, to think of the completion of parts within parts of an overall agreement, and hence to build up the components of a general settlement. An obvious deadline is likely to be advantageous to the negotiation process. Without such a deadline, the time schedule imposes proportionately less structure on the negotiation, and thus less pressure for resolution of the issues.

Programmed Operations. The reality of negotiation is not a rapid exchange of creative ideas, even though creative ideas are part of the process. The reality of negotiation is tedium. There are good reasons why this is so. First, the barriers to agreement are political, not intellectual, and it takes time and patience for governments to persuade themselves to accept change. Second, the search for agreement is a combination of trial and error plus insight, and it takes time for the process to be played through. Negotiations reflect the cutting edge of change in the international system, and the process of accepting change is a discontinuous and drawn-out affair.

Most actual negotiation is a form of programmed operations that follows from general principles established by the parties. As one Kennedy Round interviewee put it, "The orchestration of negotiation is almost mechanical." Problem areas are broken down into their constituent parts, and are taken up by small working groups of negotiators. Working groups have agendas, and these agendas call for a sequential treatment of the topics scheduled for discussion. Topics are usually discussed rather than haggled over (admittedly, this is a fine distinction), particularly through the early and middle stages of the negotiation. Bargaining is exploratory and communication is relatively free.

There are several principles that govern the programmed operations in a large negotiation. One is the quasi-resolution of conflict. Issues are brought up sequentially and the positions of the parties are explored. Where disagreement exists, various suggestions are pursued to resolve the disagreement. Trade-offs are discussed, and alternative compromises are attempted. In some cases, the conflict will be resolved through concession, compromise, and convergence. Where conflict is resolved, the issue is put aside and is usually not raised again. As the area of agreement widens, the parties develop a greater stake in the negotiation, and this creates a positive momentum toward a final, overall agreement. If in this process parties are unable to agree, they will drop the issue and hence postpone the conflict. The issue in question will be moved up for consideration at a higher level in the negotiating bureaucracy. The same procedure will be used; hence, the most difficult and conflictual issues will be put off until the end of the negotiation.

A second principle is that negotiators do not try to deal with all the material that comes under their cognizance in a complex negotiation. They solve the problem of too much variety in the situation by ignoring much of that variety, concentrating instead on simple operational feedback variables. These variables tend to be internal, relating to the organizational work of the negotiating team or relations with the home government, rather than external. The reason is that negotiators are more concerned with presenting their own position than with relating to their adversary. That point has been made in both classical and modern literature, and has also been observed in the runs of the trade negotiation simulation.

There are several feedback variables that negotiators focus on especially in complex negotiations. One is their organization and control over their own negotiating position. Problems of control over the negotiating position stem from bureaucratic politics on the negotiating team, from the constant need to obtain new information to defend the position and its changes, and from the inherent difficulties of maintaining consistency when a large body of data is in constant change. It is especially important that negotiators be able to project an image of being in control of their portfolio; failure to do this provides ammunition for whatever opposition may exist at home. Another key feedback variable is the extent to which negotiators can maintain domestic consensus for the negotiation. Objectively this variable is always important, but it has a profound subjective impact on negotiators because of the difficulty of communicating structural problems to the adversary. In the Kennedy Round, American negotiators worried about Congress, and their anxiety was increased by E.E.C. negotiators who apparently did not appreciate the need to maintain support for the negotiation in Congress. Conversely, E.E.C. negotiators worried about the uncertainties of decision making in the E.E.C. and the fragility of support for the Kennedy Round, and *their* anxiety was increased by apparent American insensitivity to Brussels.

Another feedback variable that is monitored, and one that relates primarily to the adversary, is "the will to negotiate." Governments enter a negotiation to achieve certain principles, and they monitor the behavior of their adversaries to ensure that it does not represent a pulling back from the principles of the negotiation. Individual concessions are not a major concern — they are a fairly structured and hence unimportant phenomenon — but the failure to resolve certain problems, or the failure to "move in a certain direction" can become a major stumbling block in the negotiation. In such cases, disputes crop up, often on fairly trivial matters. A case in point was the bitter dispute in the Kennedy Round between the Common Market and the United States over the matter of the American Selling Price (A.S.P.) in chemicals. This issue, as the American negotiators correctly pointed out, was of little direct consequence to trade, but the form of the restriction gave the American Government the unilateral right to decide the issue, either in applying the restriction or in dropping it (which required congressional confirmation). The Common Market found the A.S.P. repugnant because, by maintaining a unilateral freedom of movement for the Americans, it created uncertainties for the Common Market countries and hence was contrary to one of the fundamental purposes of the Kennedy Round negotiation. From the perspective of the E.E.C., the A.S.P. was a matter of principle because it raised the question of the United States' "will to negotiate" reductions in trade restrictions.

A third principle inherent in the programmed operations of negotiation is organizational learning, a concept which has been analyzed in the literature of organization theory. Negotiating teams are usually assembled from governmental bureaucracies on an *ad hoc* basis, and are disassembled at the conclusion of their task. These teams confront problems that are often novel in substance, and are certainly novel in terms of procedures and personalities. In the succession of encounters that constitute day-to-day negotiation, the teams achieve various kinds of organizational learning: they gather and store information, they develop procedures for communication, and they adapt organizational goals to fit the possibilities in the situation. Above all, negotiating teams learn how other countries perceive the problems that are up for negotiation, and what priorities these countries place on different issues.

Over time, negotiating teams learn to develop procedures that facilitate negotiation. Negotiators are required to develop concepts, or to create relationships in the bargaining situation that are not obvious to internal decision makers, but that may be necessary to facilitate bargained exchanges between states. Negotiators accomplish this partly through the creation of a bargaining language, which, like other bureaucratic languages, is a collection of task-oriented symbols or concepts that facilitate the work of the organization. There were several examples of bargaining language in the Kennedy Round; the concept of "reciprocity" has already been mentioned in this context. The notion of reciprocity was itself refined into more specific concepts, such as measures (e.g., weighted average reductions) for making quantitative assessments of reciprocity. By common agreement, such measures were not accurate in an economic sense, but they did give negotiators a language for communicating and for exchanging tariff reductions. These measures allowed negotiators to build an agreement, but they had inherent limitations from the standpoint of reaching a final settlement. In order to reach a final settlement, negotiators had to develop the flexibility to move beyond the structures and the bargaining language that had been successful throughout most of the negotiation.

Final Agreement. Most negotiations have a deadline for the completion of the work. Occasionally such deadlines are beyond the immediate influence of negotiators. However, even when deadlines can be manipulated, they create a pressure to conclude the negotiation, since senior members of governments cannot be detained indefinitely in an exercise that appears to be going nowhere. The expectation that negotiation must soon be concluded not only increases the tempo of the exercise, it also changes the nature of the task. Concluding a negotiation puts more emphasis on decision making than occurs in the early phases, and proportionately less emphasis on bargaining and communication.

The situation as complex negotiations like the Kennedy Round or SALT negotiations conclude is that many outstanding issues must be woven together into a package deal. In different areas of the negotiation, issues which have proven troublesome have been postponed. Conflicts have only been partially resolved. The negotiators must bring the unresolved problems together in the concluding period of the negotiation in a way that the various governments can accept. Usually, difficult issues cannot be resolved by dropping them: they have become interlocked in a complex negotiation, and to drop any major issue late in the game leads to an unravelling of other agreements that are contingent on its solution. Negotiators are thus put in a position where they must find a formula to resolve the principal issues or acknowledge that the negotiation has failed to produce the agreements that had been envisioned.

The elements in the conclusion of a negotiation inescapably increase the pressure on the negotiators. There will usually be considerable political momentum behind a negotiation, especially where the negotiation is publicized, visible to internal politics, and where it is obvious that much effort has been put in. The negotiation normally will represent a considerable sunk cost in terms of government decision-making time, and there will be a major personal and professional investment for the negotiators concerned. Furthermore, there will be an increasing awareness of the political values that will be lost if the negotiation fails, especially the value of extending greater control over the international environment through international agreement. All these factors will militate toward compromise and settlement of the outstanding issues. On the other hand, as the conclusion nears, negotiators will be under increasing pressure not to give way on issues of concern to home governments and domestic interests. Those issues are outstanding precisely because they are areas where change is least easily accepted. The conclusion of a negotiation tends to expose these areas, and the government and domestic interests involved counter by bringing pressure not to reach settlement in the negotiation. One Kennedy Round negotiator summed it up simply: "The pressure comes from everywhere."

The conclusion of a negotiation increases the complexity and uncertainty that have faced the negotiators throughout the exercise. The sequential handling of issues gives way to a situation that demands that many issues be handled at once. Negotiators find it more difficult to resolve problems within established categories (e.g., the category of industrial products in trade negotiations); they are required instead to seek relationships between dissimilar categories (e.g, agricultural versus industrial sectors). This means that the programmed operations that have evolved for achieving balances thus far in the negotiation are less helpful as a guide to negotiators in the last stages of the negotiation. Striking a final overall balance is less a bargaining process with the other side than a political process of convincing capitals to accept what negotiators are prepared to deliver. New methods must be evolved to deal with what have become old problems in the negotiation.

The task of concluding a negotiation necessarily falls to senior negotiators, and Kennedy Round interviewees agree that it is more political than administrative in nature. The bureaucratized procedures, programmed operations, and technical notions of balance that delegations may have relied on previously have become less relevant. There is a need for negotiating teams to change "set"; that is, to shift from procedures that facilitate interdelegation bargaining (e.g., procedures for calculating reciprocity in trade negotiations) to procedures that permit general overarching restatements of the problem. A clear example of this need was observed in the trade negotiation simulations. As in the real negotiation, simulation subjects used various quantitative measures to calculate reciprocity. However, subjects were unable to use these methods profitably at the end of the negotiation because there was insufficient time to make the needed calculations and because the methods produced results that were too precise for the needs of the moment. In fact, subjects who persisted in such calculations lost their grip on the overall developments in the negotiation, usually to their own disadvantage. The simulations support the contention that the conclusion of a negotiation requires the same kind of general, formula-oriented solutions as does the start of a negotiation. It is primarily an exercise in creative problem solving, where educated political guesswork is more important than shrewd calculation of advantages.

There is ample evidence that the last-minute decisions in a large-scale negotiation are taken amid great confusion. Interviewees from the Kennedy Round admitted as much, and in an interesting way. Senior political members of negotiating teams asserted that much of the competence to understand the accords rested with the technical people, while the technical people maintained that much of the Kennedy Round was "political" and hence outside the scope of their competence. In short, each group professed a lack of competence to understand the overall process, albeit for different reasons. Others as well have remarked on the confusion and uncertainty that obtains at the conclusion of a large negotiation. One of the most perceptive journalists covering the Kennedy Round started his story about the completion of the negotiation with the following paragraphs:

> Deep and very widely shared satisfaction over settling the major Kennedy Round controversies is alternating here with genuine ignorance as to what the settlements may mean in detail. At this stage even senior officials in the various delegations have not yet broached the task of analyzing the precise contents of the agreements reached.
>
> It is not just a matter of detailed information remaining unpublished until the accord has been formally signed a few weeks hence. The hasty deals reached by top negotiators in the frantic final hours often have not yet been translated into actual texts, nor sometimes

even communicated to those on the next steps of the hierarchy.[21]

Lest this observation be thought confined to trade negotiations, one can cite a similar observation by Newhouse about the conclusion of the SALT negotiation in Vladivostok: "As confusing as all this may seem, it was only slightly less so to the experts themselves. After the White House party returned to Washington, several meetings of the verification panel were spent largely in trying to establish exactly what had been agreed to on SLBM's and what precisely it all meant."[22]

The fact that the negotiation becomes increasingly difficult to comprehend does not mean that negotiators are incapacitated by complexity, or without a strategy for concluding the process. For one thing, negotiators tend to focus on aspects that are relatively certain, such as the positions that governments take on the issues, and pay less attention to those that are less understandable, such as the significance or value of those positions. Thus, the conflict that is inherent in any negotiation helps to clarify and structure that situation, and it is taken advantage of by negotiators. Second, negotiators try to structure the way they handle conflict. For example, a Kennedy Round interviewee indicated that on conflictual issues, negotiators at different levels tended to argue their position "to a point of incompetence," after which (as we have seen) the issue would be taken up in the next higher level in the negotiating bureaucracy. This procedure brings new faces and new ideas to difficult problems. Also implied in this procedure is a stratagem that was followed by some delegations in the Kennedy Round, namely that of keeping senior people at home and away from the negotiation until late in the game. This stratagem helps to avoid delegations from becoming psychologically committed to single interpretations of difficult problems, and it creates the flexibility and freedom to make decisions on the solution of issues.

IV. CONCLUSION

In this essay it has been argued that the nature and practice of international negotiation have changed; namely, the kinds of issues that are raised on the agenda of international relations have changed, which changed the diplomatic processes whereby governments handle those issues. In brief, these diplomatic processes have become more bureaucratic and more characteristic of decision making as it is practised in big government and big business. Given this development, one can reflect on the nature of the negotiation process itself. Why do states negotiate international issues? Are they likely to continue to use negotiation (and bargaining) as principal methods of conducting diplomacy? And, are they likely to turn to formal international bureaucracy instead of international negotiation, to accomplish in form what — as has been argued in this paper — already exists in practice?

The reasons why states (or any organization) negotiate an issue is because they share a mixture of agreement and disagreement with other states on that issue. Negotiation is a mixed-mode relationship — a mixture of cooperation and conflict; if either mode is absent, the relationship between the parties will change. Pure conflict brings hostilities, or if governments pursue conflict passively, it brings boycotts or other measures whereby states studiously ignore one another. Pure cooperation brings rules, normally in the form of administration or bureaucracy, whereby governments agree in advance how to handle the issues and leave the process to formal mechanisms. A mixture of conflict and cooperation brings negotiation, where there are few rules, but where cooperation is sought because states seek ends they cannot achieve unilaterally. The area in international relations where mixed-mode relationships are appropriate is growing. Today, governments need more control over forces in the international environment than they can manage independently; conflictual acts like military hostilities, imperial relationships, or alliance building cannot establish the control they once might have. On the other hand, there is not sufficient consensus in world politics to turn over the most pressing of the world's problems to international organizations. We are entering an era in which international negotiation appears to be the predominant mode of relations between states, and conditions in the international system are likely to maintain this mode for some time to come.

ENDNOTES

1 François de Callières, *On the Manner of Negotiating with Princes,* trans. by A.F.Whyte (Notre Dame, Ind.: University of Notre Dame Press 1963). Sir Harold Nicolson's tribute is in *The Evolution of Diplomacy* (New York: Collier 1954), p. 85.

2 Tad Szulc, "How Kissinger Did It: Behind the Vietnam Cease-Fire Agreement," *Foreign Policy,* No. 15 (Summer 1974), 21-69, esp. 23-24.

3 Nicolson, *The Evolution of Diplomacy*, chap. IV.

4 Robert L. Friedheim, "The 'Satisfied' and 'Dissatisfied' States Negotiate International Law: A Case Study," *World Politics,* 18 (October 1965), 20-41.

5 John Newhouse, *Cold Dawn: The Story of SALT* (New York: Holt, Rinehart & Winston, 1973), p. 43.

6 Robert W. Barnett, in *Observations on International Negotiations* (Transcript of an Informal Conference, Greenwich, Conn., June 1971, Academy for Educational Development, Inc., 1971), p. 112.

7 Personal interview.

8 S. Bruce Wilson, Office of the Special Representative for Trade Negotiations, Washington, D.C. (personal communication, April 1, 1976).

9 Clearly there are many negotiations in which control of complexity is a lesser problem, such as disputes over fishing quotas or beef imports. However, negotiations on specific issues (for instance, Canadian-Egyptian negotiations on cotton textile imports) often occur within the context of a more general negotiated framework. Thus, the Cotton Textile Agreement of 1964, established to regulate international textile trade, sought the purpose of reducing uncertainty as outlined here.

10 Negotiations are employed to reduce not only uncertainty, but also variety in the international environment. An example is the attempt at the current multilateral trade negotiation to identify and codify various types of non-tariff restrictions to trade.

11 Gerard Smith, "SALT after Vladivostok," *Journal of International Affairs,* 29 (Spring 1975), 7-18; quote from 8.

12 Newhouse, *Cold Dawn*, p. 77.

13 Address by Secretary of State Kissinger, "International Law, World Order, and Human Progress," delivered before the American Bar Association at Montreal, Canada, on August 11, 1975. *Department of State Bulletin,* 73 (September 8, 1975), 335-62; quote from 359.

14 Ibid., p.359.

15 Richard E. Walton and Robert B. McKersie, *A Behavioral Theory of Labor Negotiations* (New York: McGraw-Hill, 1965); Anatol Rapoport, *Fights, Games and Debates* (Ann Arbor: University of Michigan Press, 1960). See also Sawyer and Guetzkow: "The process of devising more favorable alternatives and outcomes may be characterized as one of 'creative problem-solving' since it involves innovation rather than mere selection among given possibilities. As with creative processes more generally, however, relatively little is understood of its operation." Jack Sawyer and Harold Guetzkow, "Bargaining and Negotiation in International Relations," in Herbert C. Kelman, ed., *International Behavior* (New York: Holt, Rinehart & Winston 1966), pp. 466-520; quote from p. 485.

16 Newhouse, *Cold Dawn*, p. 176.

17 I. William Zartman, "Negotiations: Theory and Reality," *Journal of International Affairs,* 29 (Spring 1975), 73.

18 See John D. Steinbruner, *The Cybernetic Theory of Decision: New Dimensions of Political Analysis* (Princeton: Princeton University Press, 1974).

19 Herbert A. Simon, "The Architecture of Complexity," in *The Science of the Artificial* (Cambridge: MIT Press, 1969), p. 87.

20 Ibid., p. 108. A senior GATT official expressed a similar sentiment when he said one of the most important abilities of a negotiator was to "grasp relationships."

21 H. Peter Dreyer, "Tariff Talks Package Gets Mixed Reaction," *New York Journal of Commerce* (May 1967), 1.

22 Newhouse, *Cold Dawn*, p. 254.

C: MECHANISMS OF REGULATION

The Realities of Arms Control

The Harvard Nuclear Study Group

Albert Carnesale, Paul Doty, Stanley Hoffmann, Samuel P. Huntington, Joseph S. Nye, Jr., Scott D. Sagan

In an imperfect world, few people have been willing to adopt pure pacifism, which means the refusal to defend one's self, family, country, or allies from any kind of attack. Those who are not pacifists must wrestle with many difficult choices about weapons, their existence, and their potential use. This has always been true. Warfare is as old as human history, and disarmament as a prescription for avoiding it dates back at least to biblical times. Though the implementation of disarmament has been rare, its basic premise — that war is not possible without weapons — is both simple and appealing.

Regrettably, the premise is flawed. The supply of weapons is not the sole or even the prime cause of war. Disarmament may remove the most destructive weapons, but others will be found.

One reason successful disarmament efforts are rare is that they require a degree of political accommodation that is difficult to achieve. Unless some political trust exists, efforts to disarm prove fruitless. But political accommodation and trust are built slowly, so complete disarmament — as contrasted with limited arms control — is a long-term rather than an immediate prospect.

Complete disarmament would require some form of world government that would deter actions of one nation against another. In a disarmed world, without such a government armed with sufficient force to prevent conflict between nations, differences in beliefs and interests might easily lead to renewed conflict and the threat of war. But any world government capable of preventing world conflict could also become a world dictatorship. Given the differences in ideology, wealth, and nationalism that now exist in the world, most states are not likely to accept a centralized government unless they feel sure of controlling it or minimizing its intrusiveness. A weak central machinery would be ineffective. And even a strong one — assuming that governments would agree to set it up — could still be faced with breakdown. If breakdown occurred, individual nations would re-arm, and those who were able would race to make nuclear arms.

Complete disarmament would be a leap into the unknown; each state would accept disarmament only if the dangers it feared could be ended or if it thought that the danger of nuclear

---

Excerpted by permission of the publishers from *Living With Nuclear Weapons* by the Harvard Nuclear Study Group, Cambridge, Mass.: Harvard University Press, First published in *The Atlantic Monthly*, June, 1983.

holocaust outweighed the risks involved in nuclear disarmament. Despite the present costs of national military forces and arms competition, despite the limited gains that the threat to use weapons now brings, and despite the enormous risks such uses may entail, nations with nuclear weapons still see a clear national advantage in keeping them. They are thought to provide the possibility of deterring aggression and of projecting political influence. Disarmament would not necessarily ensure a state's position in the international contest between states. It would not necessarily ensure a state's security. Nor would it guarantee that the funds saved from weapons would necessarily be devoted to raising the living standards of poor peoples. For these reasons, governments have preferred a combination of arms, self-restraint, and arms control to complete disarmament.

While complete disarmament may be a worthy long-term goal, trying to achieve it before the requisite political conditions exist could increase the prospects of war. If the political pre-conditions of trust and consensus are missing, complete disarmament is inherently unstable. In a disarmed world, the first nation to acquire a few arms would be able to influence events to a much greater extent than it could in a heavily armed world. Nuclear weapons greatly magnify this danger. Moreover, nuclear weapons can be easily hidden or quickly reinvented. When many nuclear weapons exist, a few hidden bombs do not matter. But in a disarmed world, if political mistrust persists, rumors of hidden bombs or fears of their reinvention by any number of nations could lead to the worst kind of nuclear-arms race — a crash program, in which weapons would be built without the safety features of existing weapons.

Nuclear-arms races do not guarantee peace and security either, of course. Instead, they can guarantee enormous destruction if war occurs either by design or, more likely, through accident, miscalculation, or misunderstanding. With no safe port in complete nuclear disarmament or in unrestricted competition, mankind has been compelled to seek safety by using arms control to lower the risks that nuclear weapons impose on peace and security.

"Arms control" has to a large extent replaced "disarmament" in the specialist's vocabulary since about 1960, but as long as disarmament is not taken to mean complete disarmament, the terms overlap. Arms control includes a wider range of actions than the removal of arms. It includes steps that improve stability and help avoid accidents. Some arms-control agreements reduce armaments, but not all do.

A common criticism of arms-control advocates is that they mistake the symptoms for the disease: since the origins of conflict are not in the existence of weapons, the cure should not be sought in their restraint. But the easy recourse to weapons in times of stress or panic does increase the likelihood of their use. Arms control alone, then, is not enough. It is also important to attack the sources of conflicts. The ultimate hope for peace clearly lies with improving international relations to the point at which conflict does not threaten to erupt into war, and reconciliation replaces aggression. Whether the world eventually reaches this goal or not may depend on the combination of arms control with effective deterrence over the next decades.

During the past three decades, the military establishments of the United States and the Soviet Union have become the most powerful and most expensive institutions ever created. Such enormous bureaucracies naturally resist the changes that arms-control initiatives attempt to introduce. On the American side, the annual budget for the Arms Control and Disarmament Agency is lower than the cost of two F-16 fighter aircraft. Ideally, arms control and security policy go hand in hand. But many arms-control initiatives do not survive the raised eyebrows of the defense community, and defense decisions may be made without regard for their arms-control implications.

This bureaucratic imbalance would ordinarily suppress most arms-control initiatives were it not for heads of governments, who have been chiefly responsible for any arms-control initiatives. Arms control, then, is precarious, and vulnerable to the changing views of successive administrations;

nevertheless, at least in democracies, polls show a continual public support for efforts at arms control. Presidents ignore these efforts at their own political peril.

Another difficulty encountered by those who advocate arms control is the unusual U.S. constitutional clause on the ratification of treaties. The United States alone among industrialized Western countries requires a two-thirds majority in the Senate to ratify treaties. This means that a minority, one that often represents much less than one third of U.S. voters and is motivated by diverse interests, can block ratification. The role of arms control would have been much greater in the past decade if ratification required only a majority vote.

On the Soviet side, arms-control negotiations have been a constant ingredient of relations with America for a quarter of a century. Not only do they make for diminished risks and greater effectiveness in both sides' military planning, they have helped establish the Soviet Union's claim to coequal status with the United States. As might be expected in a country that has steadily increased its military spending for two decades and whose defense programs are insulated from fluctuating public attitudes, Soviet arms-control policy has been tightly integrated with Soviet military policy.

Until about 1960, the Soviet Union was in such an inferior position strategically that it resisted Western arms-control initiatives for the understandable reason that agreements would have frozen it in perpetual inferiority. However, it camouflaged this position by campaigns for general and complete disarmament and offers to ban weapons first and work out verification later. Nevertheless, from 1959 through the 1960s, a number of limited agreements were negotiated that prohibited nuclear deployments in Antarctica, space, and the seabed; banned nuclear tests in the atmosphere; and created the Non-Proliferation Treaty. With the approach to parity in the 1970s, it became possible to open up negotiations in the domain of central strategic forces.

The approach of the Soviet Union was limited by its concept of deterrence, which emphasizes that whoever can deliver the greatest blow first is more likely to remain dominant. This explains the Soviet preoccupation with land-based, highly controlled, large ICBMs — inter-continental ballistic missiles. A main Soviet arms-control objective has been to retain ICBM forces and to ensure their modernization. The Soviets have resisted American efforts to use arms control to encourage greater Soviet reliance on their submarines, which they have regarded as an area of American advantage. At the same time, they have accepted a number of measures that do not reduce their own central forces, such as a series of bans and limitations on new weapons or weapons in the planning stage. The successful treaty limiting anti-ballistic-missile defenses was one of this sort.

Another preoccupation of the Soviets has been with what they call "equal security," which, they have argued, requires more than an equal number of weapons. They use the term to justify claims of compensation necessary for geographical handicaps, for American nuclear weapons assigned to NATO, and for British, French, and Chinese nuclear weapons. They are not receptive to U.S. claims that they have an advantage because of their proximity to Europe. Their demand for equal security has complicated efforts to negotiate reductions that maintain rough parity.

The Soviets, like the Americans, often use arms-control proposals as propaganda — but much more easily than Americans can, because there is no effective public opinion in the Soviet Union. The extent to which the Soviet Union publicizes its role in negotiations seems to tell something about the seriousness with which it wants a compromise agreement. The negotiations of SALT I and SALT II were generally carried out with considerable privacy until the late stages. The same pattern apparently is being followed in START (Strategic Arms Reduction Talks) as well. However, the INF (intermediate nuclear force) negotiations have been carried out in public view almost from the beginning. One of the Soviet objectives in these negotiations is to split Western Europe from the United States and thereby halt or limit the deployment of intermediate-range forces. If this tactic fails, an INF agreement may be possible.

The START proposals of the Reagan Administration would cut deeply into Soviet land-based forces, which have been sacrosanct in the past. The "deep cuts" approach runs counter to the Soviet penchant and tradition for small increments of change. In a period of political transition, Soviet leaders often find it especially hard to move in radical directions. The new Soviet leader, Yuri Andropov, is a product of this system and is beholden to military support in attaining his office. Not surprisingly, the Soviets have offered proposals only for modest reductions and restrictions on new systems of interest to the U.S.

Andropov came into office last November [1982] at the age of sixty-eight. With only a few years to leave his mark, he may wish to move faster in arms-control negotiations. More important, he faces serious political and economic problems: a decreasing Soviet work force; minority pressures for larger roles; a chronically incompetent agricultural system; inadequate consumer-goods production; unrest in Eastern Europe; and, most of all, a shrinking economic growth rate that does not provide the base it once did for the Soviet military machine. Together, these pressures may induce a more active search for maintaining the military competition with the West at lower levels of risk and expenditure.

Given the distrust between East and West, only arms-control agreements that are verifiable are likely to be negotiated and ratified. In the 1950s, the West routinely proposed, and the Soviet Union routinely rejected, measures to monitor arms-control and disarmament agreements that involved on-site inspection — that is, provision for the physical inspection of a country's weapons and facilities by foreign experts. During the next twenty years, however, both sides developed complex verification technology — most important, photo-reconnaissance satellites.

It was the revolution in verification technology in the 1960s that made possible the more ambitious efforts of SALT. Of necessity, the SALT process reflected the limitations of verification technology. Only delivery vehicles that were large enough to be seen from space (for example, ICBM launchers) or that, if mobile, could operate only from relatively few, known bases (heavy bombers and strategic submarines) could be verified. It was possible, however, to set limits on warheads and bombs, which were too small to be verified directly, by agreeing to somewhat arbitrary counting rules. Each type of missile, for example, was counted as having the maximum number of warheads ever tested on it, rather than the actual number deployed, which might be much less.

While the Soviets have elaborate surveillance equipment, they have less interest in verification than the United States, because of the very different nature of the two societies. The high level of reporting about American defense plans — from congressional hearings, media coverage, and leaks from officials — makes it likely that any American violation of an agreement will be publicized. This makes verification much easier for the Soviet Union. Exacting verification procedures are seen by the Soviets as something they "give" to the United States, for which they often want something in return. At the same time, the Soviets are extremely secretive about military matters, a tradition with deep roots in the history of their country, which has been invaded frequently. Many of the verification measures proposed by the U.S. look like espionage measures to the Soviets. Over the years, negotiations have helped convince the Soviets that such procedures are not a cover for espionage but an essential requirement for ratifiable arms-control measures. Yet in each instance, procedures must be justified in minute detail and negotiated in ways that minimize intrusiveness.

It should be remembered that the vast system of monitoring and intelligence collection that the United States must use for verification is needed whether arms-control agreements exist or not. Arms-control agreements, especially SALT II, have greatly increased our knowledge of the Soviet nuclear arsenal; both sides have promised not to interfere with each other's surveillance devices, and both have agreed that certain activities will not be concealed but will remain open to monitoring. The verification in future agreements will thus have a broader foundation on which to build. Moreover, improvements in verification technology continue, and it is reasonable to expect that capabilities that were not possible in the past will exist in the future.

When matters of national security are at stake, both the government and the public wish to know for certain whether agreements are being kept. But in daily life, we know that we must live with some uncertainty. Verification of arms-control agreements is no different; some risks are inevitable. But an unrestrained arms race also creates risks. Risks must be balanced and judgments made about the adequacy of verification, which must enable us to detect any Soviet violation large enough to threaten our security in time for us to be able to make a sufficient response. If there were deep reductions in numbers, minor violations might be more dangerous than is the case with current high levels of weaponry.

Much of the U.S. internal debate during the SALT II negotiations and ratification hearings focused on such problems. Although the verification of some treaty provisions was seen to be less adequate than that of others, the trade-offs made between uncertainty and the importance of the item to be limited were generally agreed to be prudent.

The new weaponry scheduled for deployment in this decade raises new problems. Cruise missiles will present a special challenge to verification. They are small and can be easily changed from conventional to nuclear warheads. The focus may have to be on restricting the ships and planes that carry cruise missiles and the regions of their deployment. Close monitoring of both sides' production plants may also help. Two difficult judgments will have to be made: what kinds of violations have significant adverse consequences on American security, and what is the probability that such violations could be detected? If one insists on absolute certainty in verification, then very little can be verified and arms cannot be controlled. On the other hand, if verification procedures are absent or lax, cheating may occur and confidence in the other side's compliance will be lost. The task is to find the right middle ground.

Verification procedures in future agreements will be subject to even greater scrutiny, for two reasons. First, the Soviet Union refused to cooperate with American efforts to discover whether an outbreak of anthrax in a Soviet city was a violation of the Biological Weapons Convention of 1972. Second, there is increasing evidence of the use of poison gas by the Soviet forces in Afghanistan and the use of toxins by the military forces they support in Cambodia. Neither the Geneva Protocol of 1925 nor the 1972 convention has the elaborate verification provisions and procedures that the SALT treaties have. These presumed Soviet actions have reinforced the importance of having such provisions in any future arms-control agreements.

Despite all of these difficulties, however, over the past twenty-five years there has been a gradual improvement in Soviet willingness to provide information, to negotiate details of on-site inspections — for example, in the 1974 Threshold Test-Ban Treaty — and to engage in the discussion of verification requirements. It has been a slow process, but it should not go unnoticed.

Although no arms-control treaties of significance have been ratified during the past decade, the numerical growth of nuclear forces has been somewhat restrained compared with what it might have been, because of limits in the SALT II agreement (even though it was not ratified) and the retirement of aging weapons. From 1978 to 1982, the number of strategic launchers actually decreased by about one percent for the Soviet Union and about 9 percent for the U.S. The total number of warheads and bombs deployed by the U.S. remained essentially constant during that period. The Soviet Union, completing its MIRV (multiple independently targeted re-entry vehicles) programs, did, however, increase its strategic warhead total by 60 percent, reducing the U.S. lead in that category.

The arms race in recent years has been not in numbers of weapons but in technological improvements. Both sides, for example, have greatly improved the accuracy of their forces. More improvements are to come. If new arms-control restraints are not negotiated, the next few years will see new weaponry incorporating even more remarkable technological changes: the building and testing of new bombers, new ICBMs, and new SLBMs (sea-launched ballistic missiles); the deployment of new cruise missiles on bombers, trucks, ships, and submarines; the attainment of absolute accuracy; and the development of anti-satellite weapons. Although many of these are planned replacements, there could be an increase of about 25 percent in numbers of weapons by 1990 if no agreements are reached.

Arms control proposals can be judged by whether they contribute to three dimensions of stability. The first is deterrence stability — assuring that our forces are capable and credible enough to deter the Soviet Union from political adventures that could lead to war through miscalculation. The second is arms-race stability — controlling the weapons buildup in the two countries so that the military relationship is more predictable and resources can be used for purposes other than weaponry. The third is crisis stability — creating forces of a type that provide no incentive for either side to launch a first strike in a time of crisis. In addition to these central criteria, arms-control proposals can be judged in terms of negotiability and possible verification.

People frequently think of arms control simply as formal treaties for reducing existing weapons. But bargaining and agreements can be informal as well as formal, and agreements can affect future types of forces even if they do not reduce existing forces. Some arms-control measures may be designed to build confidence or stability through improved communications rather than changes in forces. The range of possibilities for arms control can be usefully grouped under four headings, and some components from different approaches can be combined in interesting and complex proposals. At the risk of oversimplification, the four main categories are reductions, freezes, force restructuring, and stabilizing measures.

Reductions in the number of existing weapons are probably the most common measure by which the public judges arms control. They address the view, shared by many experts, that the nuclear arsenals of both sides have grown irresponsibly large, and that a much smaller nuclear force would be adequate and cheaper. An abundance of weapons, some argue, encourages further planning for nuclear war-fighting, which leads to demands for even more weapons.

Reductions are, however, not as simple as they first look. The wrong kind of reductions could increase, not lessen, instability. For example, if single-warhead missiles were reduced instead of MIRVed missiles — which may happen, because MIRVed missiles are newer and more powerful than single-warhead missiles — fears of pre-emption would increase. That is so because each of the many warheads on a MIRVed missile threatens an entire missile on the other side. Imagine that each side had only 100 missiles, all of them MIRVed. An aggressor might be tempted to strike first because it could reasonably hope to knock out many of the other side's missiles with just a few of its own, secure in the knowledge that it would still have a large retaliatory force. But if each side had only 100 *single*-warhead missiles, an aggressor would have to fire all of its missiles to hope to knock out the other side's force; and it would know that anything less than complete (and unlikely) success would leave it open to unanswerable retaliation. This example is entirely theoretical, of course, because it leaves out nuclear submarines and bombers, but it does illustrate why MIRVed missiles are though to be destabilizing.

Certain types of proportional cuts, such as cutting all existing categories by 50 percent, could also be destabilizing. It might be dangerous, for example, to cut in half the number of strategic submarines. Because we keep half of our nuclear submarines in port, fewer than ten submarines would then have to be tracked and destroyed for a successful surprise attack against what is now the most invulnerable part of our force.

Another problem arises because the forces on the two sides differ so much that each side prefers reductions in different areas. Each side urges reduction schemes that remove the weapons it most fears on the other side but that permit retention of its own preferred weapons. Disagreements over what is to be reduced take up much negotiation time. Treated wisely, however, asymmetries can become the means of agreeing on important trade-offs that have to be made if negotiations are to succeed.

Another problem with the deep-reductions approach is focus: if all efforts were concentrated on such reductions, would other aspects of arms control be neglected? The danger is that the search for the perfect becomes the enemy of the good. All arms control might be stalled or discredited.

This problem can be seen in both the Soviet and the U.S. opening position at the START negotiations. There are clear benefits in the reductions described in both proposals. The U.S. proposals attempt to alter the balance within the Soviet forces of land-based and sea-based missiles. These proposals are made in the interest of improved stability, but they require changes the Soviet Union is unlikely to make unless it is compensated by substantial gains elsewhere in the treaty. The U.S. proposal to postpone restrictions on bombers and cruise missiles, where much of the U.S. growth will take place, is also unlikely to be attractive to the Soviets, who propose severe restrictions only on areas of American advantage: cruise-missile deployments, new bombers, and new submarines. An agreement will not be easy. Still, there may be enough common interests to make a compromise possible.

Two new features are coming into prominence in negotiating reductions in missiles: rapid reload and mobility. Launchers for some new-generation missiles can be used more than once, and can be reloaded and refired if more missiles are available in nearby storage. Arms-control agreements would have to be worked out that would ban storage of extra missiles near the launcher. This was done for ICBMs in SALT II. The principal problem with mobile missiles is verification. The U.S. has taken the position that the side that proposes such deployments is obligated to devise an accompanying verification system satisfactory to the other side.

Finally, it should be noted that little progress has been made in working out verification procedures for aircraft other than the heavy bombers treated in SALT II. The smaller and more numerous the aircraft, the more difficult it is to monitor them. The very large numbers of aircraft whose sizes lie between medium-bomber and short-range tactical aircraft can deliver both nuclear and conventional weapons; so can cruise missiles. Some easily recognized external feature on the missile or the carrier that distinguishes between conventional and nuclear weapons may solve the verification problem in principle, but negotiations will still be difficult.

Freezes present much the same verification problems as reduction schemes. SALT II was primarily a partial-freeze agreement, and the most time-consuming part of its negotiation concerned verification. In the current discussion of freezes, the importance of reaching an agreement in a relatively short time has stimulated some to propose that what is initially frozen be simply the items discussed in previous negotiations. This would include the strategic launchers of SALT II, atmospheric nuclear tests, and possibly anti-satellite weapons.

Another approach lies in taking the SALT II agreement as the starting point and modifying it to prohibit the deployment of the one new ballistic missile it allowed to each side, to carry out reductions over a number of years until 50 percent reductions have been achieved, and to halt the deployment of all cruise and Pershing II missiles in return for the elimination of the Soviet SS-4s, SS-5s, and SS-20s. This is about half a freeze and half a reduction scheme.

The real challenge comes in finding ways to

meet the demanding requirements of those proposals that have produced such large public followings: to freeze the production, testing, and deployment of all nuclear-weapons systems on the two sides in a verifiable manner, and to negotiate this quickly enough to stop the arms race. Consider what this involves. It means devising and then negotiating verification procedures for the development, testing, production, and deployment of nearly a hundred kinds of weapons and delivery systems that make up the offensive and defensive forces at the strategic, intermediate, and battlefield levels of both sides. If stability is to be maintained in the long run, one must freeze countermeasures to these weapons, such as anti-submarine-warfare capabilities and air defenses. And one must decide what kind of maintenance and modernization is to be allowed for each weapons system. Are replacements to be allowed? If so, can they be improved versions of the same weapons systems? What if the original factories and components no longer exist? How much improvement is to be allowed?

A comprehensive freeze or comprehensive reductions would require extensive and elaborate negotiations. It seems unimaginable that such negotiations would not require several years, unless the arms-control budgets of the superpowers were raised a hundredfold or more, and many teams negotiated simultaneously and were convinced that both nations wanted a comprehensive agreement. This is the challenge presented by those who advocate a negotiated comprehensive freeze or comprehensive reductions.

It may be too easy, however, to undercut the freeze idea by driving it to its maximum interpretation. Much of the public would be satisfied with far less than a total freeze. The verification problems for less-than-total freezes might be less difficult. Total bans of some new weapons systems may be simpler to verify than limits, because only one sighting would be sufficient to prove a violation. However, in the end there would undoubtedly remain some systems that would require special verification measures inside the other country; such requirements would have to be met if the freeze were to be truly comprehensive.

It might be possible to freeze the most destabilizing weapons first, followed by less dangerous weapons. Here there is a conflict, however, between two strongly held points of view. Many want a freeze that will stop all technology and development as completely as possible. Others see danger in disassembling the whole nuclear-weapons research-and-development and production establishment. These groups see virtue in allowing certain developments to proceed in order to allow less vulnerable and more stable weapons to replace existing systems. For example, a freeze in 1959 would have stopped deployment of our invulnerable Polaris submarine-based missiles, which would have made the 1960s *less* safe. On the other hand, a freeze in 1969 would have avoided the instability that was caused by the introduction of MIRVs on missiles in the 1970s.

It is an open question whether a freeze today would enhance crisis stability or not. Some threatening systems would be stopped. But a freeze could also prevent such developments as the new small single-warhead land-based missile that many experts, including the Presidential Commission on Strategic Forces, believe is the best way to remedy the problems created by MIRVs.

Clearly, there is a strong case for pursuing discriminating restraints on weapons technology rather than a total freeze. One such limited freeze is a cap on the number of nuclear warheads — each side has roughly 11,000 warheads on weapons with ranges of over 1,000 miles — requiring that any warheads added to either arsenal be compensated for by at least an equal number withdrawn. This would be consistent with the simplicity that is the great virtue of the freeze idea. It leads to a quick agreement on what is to be frozen (strategic warheads); it might be negotiated soon; and it would be verifiable by the already negotiated SALT rules and procedures being observed by both sides, coupled with negotiated procedures to verify warheads on cruise missiles and intermediate-range missiles. The cap on warheads would avoid the potentially dangerous approach of freezing the modernization of certain forces while letting their countermeasures run free. Moreover, it would lead quickly to more complex arms-control negotiations without reducing Soviet incentives to bargain.

Force restructuring is an approach that seeks simple agreements to change only certain weapons on each side. If other negotiations fail or proceed too slowly, it can still be tried. The proposed change could be one of several kinds: elimination, reduction, freeze, or replacement with new weapons less threatening to the other side. For example, the U.S. might propose, as it did several years ago, not to deploy the MX missile if the Soviet Union eliminated some proportion of its MIRVed ICBM force. Or, as the Soviet Union has already proposed, the construction and deployment of large ballistic-missile submarines could be stopped on both sides. If several such trades could be made in separate agreements, the effect would equal that of most proposed negotiations of a more comprehensive sort.

The most ambitious proposal of this kind seeks to solve one of the most debated problems confronting the two sides: the vulnerability of land-based missiles. This proposal would provide a schedule by which current land-based missiles would be replaced by much smaller mobile missiles. The schedule of replacements would be coordinated so that neither side could reap a temporary advantage. The key feature of the proposal is that the smaller missiles can carry only one warhead, and not a very large one. The consequence would be that over a period of ten to fifteen years, all the MIRVed land-based missiles on both sides would be replaced with single-warhead missiles, which are less useful in a first strike. This trade-off may appear to be unattractive to the Soviet Union, because of its investment in and commitment to large land-based missiles. It may be necessary to allow two or even three new missiles for each MIRVed land-based missile destroyed. In any event, the result would be not only a dramatic reduction in the numbers of warheads but a vast decrease in the vulnerability of the land-based forces of both sides, a feature that may become increasingly attractive to the Soviet government.

Stabilizing measures aim not so much to diminish or restructure nuclear forces as to introduce ways to make their use less likely. They try to reduce the chance of accidents that might lead to war, to bolster crisis stability, to ban certain weapons and tests, and to build confidence in the East-West strategic relationship by introducing a much higher level of communication. A few examples will illustrate this approach.

An agreement for both sides to abandon the development of weapons in space, either for satellite destruction or for ballistic-missile defense, would profoundly improve all three kinds of stability — deterrence, arms-race, and crisis — over the next few decades. Satellites have become increasingly central to early warning and to the command and control of nuclear forces. An attack on them would so threaten to blind the other side that it would be considered an act of war requiring immediate retaliation. Stopping work toward the capability to attack them would be mutually reassuring, as would stopping work on space stations from which ballistic missiles might be destroyed shortly after being launched. The costs of space stations might make them politically impossible, and their vulnerability would make them militarily unreliable; still, unless agreement is reached to prohibit them, development is likely to proceed on each side.

Stability would also be promoted by an agreement to prohibit the close approach of submarines to Soviet and American coasts, which puts bomber bases at special risk because it reduces warning time of an attack below that required for bombers to become airborne. Such an agreement would also reduce the risk of a "decapitation" strike, by giving more time for political leaders to evacuate in time of war. Another stabilizing measure would be an agreement defining ocean sanctuaries for submarines carrying nuclear missiles, reducing the likelihood of accident or misunderstanding in a crisis.

Another measure, already proposed at START, would be to agree to extensive notification of planned missile tests so that there would be no ambiguity when launches were observed. Bans or limits on flight tests (or nuclear tests) could help to reassure both sides that the pace of modernization of weapons was limited, and could reduce the confidence of any government considering striking first in a crisis.

Stabilizing measures and force-restructuring suggestions might best be handled by separately organized and continuing talks involving, for example, staffs of the Joint Chiefs and their Soviet counterparts as well as representatives from the other parts of government usually involved. Such a continuing forum could also try to resolve other important matters that might become conflicts, such as naval incidents, the meaning of ambiguous intelligence reports, misunderstandings that might arise from changes in force deployments in places such as Poland and the Caribbean, and technological developments that may be of benefit to both sides.

The establishment of a joint crisis-management center, suggested by Senators Sam Nunn and Henry Jackson, deserves serious examination. They have each proposed that the currently existing hot line be supplemented by a jointly manned information center, where all facts relevant to a developing crisis would be examined and discussed within permitted limits. Even more radical developments might be possible, such as establishing linked teleconferencing centers in both capitals, again jointly manned, which would be ready for use by high-level government officials whenever needed.

A number of initiatives to build further confidence could also be tested and perhaps brought into operation through the technique of reciprocal restraint. For example, one side could announce that it would hold its nuclear submarines back a certain distance from the other's shores if the other side reciprocated, or that it would restrain its development of certain weapons if the other side did so. In short, even if formal and comprehensive arms control fails or proceeds slowly, there is much else that can be done outside such proceedings by means of separate steps. There is nothing to prevent such outside measures from being explored while formal negotiations are proceeding.

When a country is faced with a military threat, there is a strong impetus to match that threat. But an equally valid response is to try to constrain the threat. Arms control is an effort to constrain the Soviet military threat. If pursued wisely, it can save money as well as enhance our security. It should be seen as a part of a national-security policy that is as important as the defense budget. The two are not alternatives. They are partners in the pursuit of stability and security.

Although reductions and freezes have captured the most attention, partial agreements, informal approaches, and stabilizing measures can be of equal importance in averting nuclear war. If properly applied, these various approaches can be complementary rather than competitive with each other.

Viewed this way, arms control has accomplished more in the past two decades than is sometimes realized by those who point to the absence of deep reductions. Certain areas and technologies (for example, anti-ballistic-missile systems) have been "fenced off" from competition. A system has been set up to slow the spread of nuclear weapons to additional countries. Limits on existing arsenals may have helped to keep weapons and expenditures below what they otherwise might have been. Most important, the beginnings of a process of communication and cooperation have been established between the two major nuclear adversaries, and the process has weathered very difficult times.

Unfortunately, there are limits to what arms control can accomplish. It cannot be totally separated from the political problems in U.S.-Soviet relations. Even if both sides avoid the tactical temptation of linking progress on arms control to behavior in other political and economic matters, complete separation is impossible, particularly in democratic politics. Thus arms control will to some extent be limited by the overall condition of

American relations with the Soviet Union. In the long run, arms control must be accompanied by some improvement in U.S.-Soviet relations if humanity is to cope with its nuclear predicament.

7 THE FUTURE INTERNATIONAL SYSTEM

Whither Interdependence?
Change and War in the Contemporary World
Alternatives to the Contemporary States System
Death in the Nuclear Age

INTRODUCTION

Predicting the future has become a fashionable intellectual exercise. It is, however, one fraught with danger. Some forecasters, for instance, are so captivated with change that they fail to recognize important continuities with the past. Michael Sullivan disputes the widely accepted thesis of the transformation of world politics which results from the appearance of new actors and new issues, the increase in interdependence, and the decline in the utility of force. His empirical study suggests that world affairs are better characterized by continuity than by change.[1]

Even if the scope of change is considerable, prediction of the future, based on the projection of present trends in the contemporary international system, takes little account of the capacity of major actors to control and channel change. Robert W. Cox illustrates how extrapolation from observed trends led to a prediction in the early 1970s that the wave of the future lay with the multinational enterprise rather than the nation-state.[2] These forecasts failed to consider, as David Leyton-Brown points out in an essay included in this collection, the concerted efforts by both home and host governments to reassert control over their national economies. Similarly, in their article, Richard Rosecrance and his colleagues note how "a gradual and progressive detachment of individual national policies from the general trend toward interdependence" casts serious doubt upon predictions of a continuing linear increase in interdependence in the period since 1945. They conclude that the future of interdependence is indeterminate.

The opposite tendency is equally dangerous. Just as it is possible to exaggerate the extent of change, so too it is possible to minimize its scope. Some observers are so mesmerized by the present, so imprisoned by the concepts and principles of the contemporary international system, that they ignore important new trends in world politics. In calling for a new perspective on world society, Donald Puchala and Stuart Fagan emphasize the limitations of the old paradigm of security politics.[3] Still others enage in wishful thinking and predict their preferred international outcome, most frequently a form of world government. They do so arguing that the intolerable present makes change unavoidable. Here, prediction and prescription are blurred. Such wishful thinking is, for example, characteristic of much of the writing on environmental policy and disarmament.

Hedley Bull, however, is an exception. In the essay that follows, he examines various alternatives to the international system of sovereign states without succumbing to this temptation. Indeed, he quite deliberately refrains from proposing solutions to the problem of maintaining order in world politics. His comprehensive treatment does underline, however, that conflict and the ensuing dilemmas of conflict management will persist in almost any conceivable form of international system. Even if world government were to be established, conflict would not disappear, but change in form from interstate disputes to conflict within world society. For those who draw a parallel between world society and the kind of political organization that existed in western Christendom in the Middle Ages, Bull's conclusion is no less disconcerting: in the past, universal society contained "more ubiquitous and continuous violence and insecurity than does the modern state system."

While we recognize the risks inherent in futurology, we nonetheless believe that students and practitioners of world affairs must have at least a broad notion of how, where, and why the world is moving. Policy-makers plan and initiate action premised on assumptions about the future. "It is therefore prudent," as Robert Gilpin warns us, "...to seek an understanding of the dynamics of world politics for guidance. It is important to appreciate the real dangers as well as the possible unappreciated opportunities of the present moment." What we need in an era of rapid change is a careful analysis of the present, both to help us anticipate the kinds of conflict we may confront in the future, and to devise effective strategies of conflict management.

The four readings that follow adopt very different approaches to the study of conflict in the future. Rosecrance applies a precise definition of interdependence to the analysis of relations among six industrial countries from 1890 to 1975. Drawing tentative conclusions from these data, he speculates about the future of interdependence. Gilpin starts from the proposition that U.S. preponderance is declining and examines whether an era of "eroding hegemony" is likely to be as unsettling for the future international system as the decline of British influence was in the interwar period. Bull systematically lays out all imaginable future worlds and examines the likely prospect of each. Finally, in a timeless article, Hans Morgenthau investigates the human failure to grasp fully the implications of the nuclear revolution and its unsettling implications for the future.

Despite their differences, these four authors all recognize that conflict will be as much a part of our future as it is of our present. They also share an overriding concern to devise effective procedures to manage international conflict. The failure to meet this challenge may, as Morgenthau reminds us, spell the doom of our civilization.

ENDNOTES

1 Michael Sullivan, "Transnationalism, Power Politics, and the Realities of the Present System," in Ray Maghroori and Bennett Ramberg, eds., *Globalism Versus Realism: International Relations' Third Debate* (Boulder, Colorado: Westview Press, 1982), pp. 195-221.

2 Robert W. Cox, "On Thinking About World Order," *World Politics,* 28 (January 1976), 175-96.

3 Donald Puchala and Stuart Fagan, "International Politics in the 1970s: The Search for a Perspective," *International Organization,* 28 (Spring 1974), 247-66.

Whither Interdependence?

R. Rosecrance / A. Alexandroff / W. Koehler / J. Kroll / S. Laqueur / J. Stocker

It is a commonplace that the structure of world economic interdependence has changed in the past decade. One can no longer argue that sovereignty is universally at bay, or that the nation-state is just about through as an economic unit.[1] Those who, in the late 1960s, prophesied that economic power, trade, and influence would become more important than military power and its surrogates are now baffled by events. Those who believed that world interdependence was accelerating have to admit that nation-states have gone to considerable lengths to reshape the economic, technological, and ecological forces acting upon them, seeking to reduce interdependence. It is no longer clear what kind of international economic order obtains, and where it is moving. The essay which follows is an attempt to narrow the range of these uncertainties (though not finally to resolve them), by offering a new and more properly economic concept of interdependence and new data on interdependent relations among six industrial countries, [the United Kingdom, France, Germany, Japan, the United States, and Canada] 1890-1975.

R. Rosecrance, A. Alexandroff, W. Koehler, J. Kroll, S. Laqueur, and J. Stocker, "Whither Interdependence?" *International Organization*, Vol. 31, No. 3 (Summer 1977), pp. 425-444. Reprinted by permission of the MIT Press Journals. Portions of the text have been deleted. Most footnotes have been removed; those remaining have been renumbered.

INTRODUCTION

The term "interdependence" has so many and varied meanings that it is no longer fully clear what investigators intend to signify when they use the term. In a very loose and general sense, one can say that interdependence is a state of affairs where what one nation does impinges directly upon other nations.[2] In this most general use, higher foreign trade, the ability to threaten atomic war, the development of worldwide inflation or recession all mean higher interdependence among states. The more one nation has to take into account what other states might do in charting its own international and domestic policy, the higher the interdependence. This use of the term, however, is quite unsatisfactory for analytic purposes. On this definition, knowing that there is high interdependence tells one very little about the actual state of relations between nations. The highest interdependence, one surmises, would actually be attained by opponents in war. Then any improvement in one state's position would directly and adversely affect the other. Their fates would be completely joined. Fully conflictual, as well as fully cooperative relations among states would be characterized by high interdependence.

Most students, of course, have wished to use interdependence in a positive sense to see higher interdependence as a fundamental force for better relations among nations.[3] If interdependent relations are to be interpreted in this positive way, the loose and general notion of interdependence must yield to more precisely and narrowly defined concepts. In this paper, by "interdependence" we mean the direct and positive linkage of the interests of states such that when the position of one state changes, the position of others is affected, *and in the same direction.*[4] Interdependence, then, suggests a system in which states tend to go up or down the ladder of international position (economic strength, power, welfare, access to information and/or technology) together. Of course, some relationships, which would be deemed "interdependent" on previous notions, would no longer be "interdependent" on the revised definition. But this more specific, narrower definition is more useful in understanding world politics for it means that wherever interdependence is high, there should be high cooperation.

The measures of interdependence have made definitions even less clear by blurring such distinctions. Up to now economic interdependence among industrial countries has largely been gauged by horizontal flows: transactions, trade, and other financial movements.[5] The greater the magnitude of trade, investment, or other transactions (absolutely or in comparison to the domestic sector) the greater the presumed interdependence. But, as we have seen above, a greater "connectedness" in international politics does not necessarily mean higher interdependence. Whether it does or not depends upon how nations react to the increasing international sector. Some states may develop common policies while others fashion opposed policies. Some nations may try to reduce the domestic impact of international economic forces; others may shape policies to conform with their impact. Such horizontal transactions, even if very large, tell us little about the responses of particular nations. It is possible, fortunately, to follow this pattern of action and reaction by examining factor prices of the two economies. In formal economic terms two economies can be considered integrated (very highly interdependent) when there is an equalization of factor prices between them. Under such conditions any increase of consumer price, interest rate, or factor cost would be expected to stimulate flows of the more highly valued commodity, capital, or labor from one market to the other, producing a re-equalization of factor prices. An increase of such prices in Country A would bring a new supply of goods, capital, and labor from Country B, having the effect of raising prices in B and lowering them in A. Just as an increase in A will lead to an increase in B, a decrease in A will lead to a decrease in B and vice versa. Even within a single economy, of course, factor prices are not always equalized across all regions. There are limits to the mobility of factors of production, and wage labor is particularly immobile. Between two separate national economies, then, one should not expect a complete equalization of factor prices. It should be anticipated, however, that between highly interdependent economies factor prices would move in the same direction. The greater the simultaneity and similarity in their movements, the more the economies are identically responding to the movement of factors between them, and the higher the interdependence. At least two measures of such "vertical" (as opposed to horizontal) interdependence are obvious: (1) a correlation of the movement of factor price indices between the two societies; and (2) a correlation of the changes in such movements. The first gives the central tendency or trend, the second the fluctuation around it.[6]

These measures, charting the actual economic responses of one society to another, are considerably more sensitive indicators of interdependence than the size of the international sector. If governments allow international economic forces to impinge on their economies without compensatory action, these policies will be clear in factor price trends. If, on the other hand, governments seek to influence or reshape these forces, through high interest rates, contractionist fiscal policies and other measures, different national policies will show up in different price trends. These responses reveal interdependence much more directly than notions of "vulnerability" or "invulnerability." If governments are relatively invulnerable to interdependent effects but take no action to insulate themselves from foreign price movements, they are behaving as if they were vulnerable and interdependent. If governments are relatively vulnerable, but make major efforts in political and economic policy to reduce their vulnerability and to reshape the impact of external forces, they are to that degree less interdependent and less vulnerable. What is important in international politics is what nations perceive and what they do; not what they might do if they perceived things differently.

TWO CONCEPTS OF INTERDEPENDENCE

There are thus two different concepts and two sets of measures of interdependence. The size of the transactions between two societies is *horizontal* interdependence. It charts the flow of money, men, goods, and so on. (But even here, of course, horizontal interdependence is only interdependence in the *first* sense, defined above; it implies only "connectedness.") *Vertical* interdependence, in contrast, shows the economic response of one economy to another, in terms of changes in factor prices. It is possible to imagine conditions where there might be high horizontal interdependence (a large international sector, growing amounts of trade either absolutely or in relation to GNP) and yet low vertical interdependence. Nations might respond differently to the commercial intercourse between them; factor prices might proceed in different directions; government policy might be inflationary in one case and deflationary in another. In the net there is an amalgam of influences: high horizontal flows tending to produce an equalization of prices; different governmental policies producing divergent prices. Thus, high horizontal interdependence could be consistent with either high or low vertical interdependence. On the other hand high horizontal interdependence is the necessary (but not sufficient) condition of high vertical interdependence. High factor price correlations without a substantial flow of goods, services, capital, and other factors of production between societies could hardly be taken to indicate true interdependence. In the absence of such horizontal flows, parallel changes in factor prices might simply be the result of worldwide economic forces impinging upon economies in similar fashion or of parallel, but independent, policies. Where horizontal flows are high, however, this cannot be the case. The flows themselves are both cause and result of factor price changes.

APPROACHES TO INTERDEPENDENCE

There are at least four different orientations ("schools" is too strong a word) toward contemporary economic interdependence. One, initiated by Deutsch and Eckstein, sees interdependence secularly declining with industrialization.[7] From this standpoint interdependence may have been at a peak in 1913, but has certainly decreased since. A second view, which relates interdependence to the absolute size of the foreign sector, sees interdependence among developed societies increasing more or less continuously since 1945. This view has also been associated with the idea that political modernization forces national governments to recognize and take due account of international economic forces as they impinge upon the domestic electorate. Even if the size of the foreign sector was not continually increasing, there would still be high interdependence because the political significance of world economic trends would be high or growing. Thirdly, there is the view that interdependence is fundamentally a product of an existing political-military regime in world politics. Economic interdependence tends to be high under the aegis of a *Pax Britannica* or *Pax Americana* but to decline when these regimes are challenged or overthrown. Thus, in this view, interdependence among industrial countries was high until shortly before World War I, and was briefly high again after 1945. After some point in the 1960s, however, it has declined with the erosion of the American dominance of world politics.[8]

A potential fourth approach to such relationships

would see interdependence increasing with the size of the foreign sector until a point is reached where governments act to reduce its actual or potential impact upon domestic politics. This would represent a second stage in the politicization of economic activity. In most countries, such politicization occurred after World War I and was further increased by the impact of the Depression and World War II. Full employment acts, Beveridge plans, and commitments to domestic growth and welfare abounded after 1945. This did not mean, however, that in any given choice between maintenance of domestic expansion and the preservation of international trade the first would always win out. Bretton Woods, reflecting on the disastrous "beggar thy neighbor" system of the 1930s, instituted new measures of domestic restraint and discipline designed to protect and nourish the international economy. Nations were not supposed to devalue their currencies except in cases of "fundamental disequilibrium." Exchange controls were to be gradually dismantled. Under GATT [General Agreement on Tariffs and Trade] qualitative and quantitative restrictions on trade were discouraged. The typical means of overcoming a short-term payments crisis was through provision of liquidity. The general assumption of the post-World War II economic era was that nations would continue to exercise the domestic discipline necessary to keep their international positions in equilibrium. Certainly it was not assumed that a nation would simply tailor its international economic policies to protect a domestic "hothouse" environment.

A second stage in the politicization of international interdependence would be reached, then, if nations decided to seek actively to reduce their dependence upon each other or to limit the impact of international forces in order to safeguard or insulate their domestic economies. Even more precisely, a new stage would be attained if nations found means of gradually detaching their domestic economies from foreign pressures without great and obvious harm to the international economic system. Such a change might come if governments decided not to impose cuts in wages or employment in order to meet international obligations. This fourth approach to interdependence would not depend upon a particular pattern of political-military relationships in world politics, but would result from a keener awareness of the limitations placed by domestic economic and political forces upon a nation's participation in an interdependent world.

Each of these approaches has much to commend it in historical and theoretical terms. Nonetheless, since the contentions are partly contradictory, they cannot all be true. According to the first, one would expect to find high vertical and horizontal interdependence before 1913, but a major decline thereafter. The second approach would see a marked increase of interdependence since 1945, proceeding more or less linearly to the present. The third would see high interdependence in the 1890s when the British had hegemony in world politics, and high interdependence again between 1945-1960 when America was dominant. The other periods, however, should be characterized by low or declining interdependence. The fourth approach, largely focused on the contemporary era, would see increases from 1945 to 1960 and a stabilization or decline since.

THE VALIDATION OF POSITIVE INTERDEPENDENCE: THE UNITED STATES CASE

Is there such a thing as positive interdependence among separate economic and social units? Or do economic societies advance at the expense of one another, with constant or zero-sum relationships among contending participants? Traditional theories of international trade, beginning with Adam Smith and David Ricardo, have contended that all nations can benefit from trade and exchange. If positive interdependence exists, it should first be discerned among the constituent markets of a major nation-state. Since no one would question that the level of integration and interdependence is very high in such a case, the measures of positive interdependence should surely underscore the point. A brief excursion into economic links between separate regional markets in the United States affords a test case for the measures of positive interdependence. If there is no relationship among factor prices in the American case, they can have no validity for relations among nations. If both measures of vertical interdependence are extremely high and stable, on the other hand, a standard of positive interdependence is set to which cases involving individual nation-states can be compared. A brief study of the United States example is more relevant in that, unlike the economy of Luxembourg or Belgium, there is more than one market and more than one major city. Indeed, the very geographic extent and climatological variation in the United States might be expected to produce some of the same differences among regional markets that are attained between national markets on the continent. The American data, therefore, take on unusual importance.

Interestingly, but not surprisingly, the results... indicate that both relative and absolute measures of vertical interdependence capture the underlying interdependence and integration of US markets. This is especially true of consumer prices where price indices and also changes in such indices are highly correlated. If any result stands out, it is that American markets have become even more integrally related since 1941. Wage and manufacturing data are less related, but even here most relationships are strong. Traditionally, of course, one would expect wages to be less interdependent than say, prices or interest rates, because of labor immobility. The somewhat lower correlations of manufacturing prices may be due to inclusion of different commodities in the bundle of manufactured goods in different markets.

A number of features of the US data should be underscored. First, vertical measures of interdependence appear clearly to have captured the high integration of US regional markets. Both correlation of price indices and correlation of changes in such indices are high. The massive flows of goods, persons, capital, and other factors of production between regional markets does in fact produce significant and positive relationships between factor prices. If such correlations could be observed among national markets at the international level, one could justly claim that they were highly interdependent. Second, the high correlation of factor prices is not found only among indices, but also among change in such indices. This suggests that not only are the general trends moving in the same direction, but also that individual and detailed changes in factor price in one market will bring similar changes in another. Finally, the high economic integration of US regional markets has great political significance. There could be no major economic change in different sections of the country without important political repercussions. This means that interdependence and politicization can occur simultaneously, at least where there is a single decision-making center.

INTERDEPENDENCE BEFORE WORLD WAR I

An intriguing question is whether the high interdependence of markets attained domestically in the United States can ever be approximated internationally. Prima facie one might assume that the coherence of the US national economy depends upon the centralization that is achieved only within the nation-state; between states, therefore, interdependence must perforce be much lower. But any such conclusion is clearly premature. The pre-World War I system demonstrated high interdependence among separate national markets even though these were not held together by a political bond. Many studies have attested to the high horizontal flows of capital and goods between countries. International trade was in general a higher proportion of national income than it is today. Direct and indirect investment was a much larger fraction of Gross National Product than is now the case. The City of London was dominant in the international market, producing a greater financial integration among nations than has been achieved since. Most of the six countries did large shares of their trade with each other, an amount ranging from 30 percent in the case of Germany to 90 percent in the Canadian case. Further, since 1913, only the United States and Germany have re-attained the percentile levels of trade reached before World War I with their industrial partners. Wholesale price indicators evince high correlations of both absolute trends and changes in such trends. Consumer prices display a weaker association and are available only for four countries. French prices react differently from the other three, and the strongest relationship appears to be that between the United States and the United Kingdom....

Interest rates indicate a strong interdependence of the European members of our set of six industrial countries. Data gathered include not only a measure of association among indices (the Pearson *r*) but also a convergence measure used by Hawkins in his study of interest rates within the EEC.[9] The latter is the absolute value of the sum of the differences in rates between two countries, divided by the total number of dyads for the period. The lower the convergence statistic, the greater the degree of equalization among rates. Such high convergence is amply demonstrated in the scores for France, Germany, and Britain; even more precisely, one finds high convergences of French and German rates with British. The Canadian financial market is very closely tied to Britain's and thus is also associated with trends in the other European countries. Correlation measures point to similar interdependencies. The intra-European relationship is very strong, although the US connection with Britain is also marked. It appears, not surprisingly, that London is the link between continental and North American markets.... To test for changes in interdependence within the period we have also divided the data into two parts: 1890-1900 and 1901-13. The results...show no obvious decline in interdependence as World War I approaches. The correlations of absolute indices increase as one moves toward 1913; but the correlations of changes decline.

The pre-World War I international system was highly interdependent in a number of respects. Horizontal flows among states were large; one economy responded very quickly to price changes in another. Wholesale price levels are closely associated. Not only are absolute correlations high; there also is a strong relationship among price changes. In 1913 the United States was being drawn into an association with European countries, and a core of European financial strength was in process of consolidation. The percentage of significant correlations among factor prices and price changes does not approach the very high figures attained in the domestic American case, and one does not want to claim that the same form of structural interdependence has been attained. Strictly speaking, if full interdependence with all states moving in the same direction is achieved, that relationship should become permanent and stable. No state should have an incentive to better its position in respect to any other state. In the real world this ideal interdependence has not yet been approximated. While short of this standard, it remains noteworthy that in 1890-1914 wholesale price relationships among the European three and between the three and the United States are both strong and significant.

There was only limited politicization of economic ties among nations, however, and economic interdependence did not constrain nations from going to war in 1914. The political significance and relevance of economic relationships was not yet fully established. The data from 1890-1914 accord broadly with the Deutsch-Eckstein approach to interdependence, apparently supporting the notion that interdependence would reach a peak relatively early in the process of economic development and fall as nations were able to replace imports with products of their own manufacture. A problem with this approach, however, is that interdependence remains very high as late as 1913, well after the first phase of industrialization in Britain and France. Interdependence also remains high at a stage when British power has declined in relation to Germany and the United States. The *Pax Britannica* is over; yet the halcyon afterglow continues.

INTERDEPENDENCE IN THE INTERWAR PERIOD

The relatively high interdependence attained in 1913 was shattered by the Great War. In order to finance arms programs, economic ministries sold their foreign assets, indulged in wholesale borrowing and in the printing of money. The ensuing inflation caused a dramatic depreciation of currencies against gold. While the international financial mechanism was partly reestablished after the war, Britain no longer had the resources and reserves to be lender to the system. The United States might have filled the gap, but was disinclined to do so. In part this was because the United States wanted its war debts repaid, and did not extend credit to the degree necessary. Ultimately, no single international financial center emerged, and nations held their reserves in Paris and New York as well as London.

The financial rivalry between Paris and London was reinforced by different policies toward Germany. The French, determined that Berlin should pay for the war, demanded immediate fulfillment of reparations obligations. The British and to some degree the Americans recognized that Germany could not pay without being able to borrow and lent considerable sums. But the central core of the international economy — the links between Britain, France, and Germany — was broken by the war. The magnetic power of the continent, drawing the United States and Japan into an essentially Europe-centered system, greatly lessened. America became a mighty financial and trading power in its own right and moved to an independent position.

A second major consequence of the war was the politicization of economic activity. No longer could governments stand aside as international economic forces determined domestic economic welfare. This change had two effects: first, it greatly raised the significance of the external economic sector; secondly, it spurred finance ministries to find new means of controlling that sector. The first greatly furthered international interdependence by increasing the political saliency and relevance of economic relationships. The second, however, represented a net reduction of interdependence because it meant reshaping international relationships according to national criteria.

Three different phases of the interwar period must be distinguished. In the first, from 1920-29, the German inflation stemming from the war and from the French occupation of the Ruhr, cut the ties with other European economies. Exchange rate manipulations began. Trade fell off both absolutely and relatively. Insecure governments sought to protect themselves against foreign financial and trading competition. France and Germany engaged in economoc warfare, while neither power moved in step with its erstwhile British and American colleagues. Both wholesale and consumer price indicators fluctuated irregularly, often in opposed directions.... Interest rates moved apart, with France closer to the American than to the British market....

In the second period, 1930-32, the financial crisis and the onset of the Depression produced a momentary galvanic response that sent all economies in the same direction. The correlations of wholesale and consumer prices returned briefly to high levels, though the relationship of the European three to the United States was stronger than their relationship to each other. The US-Canadian tie was still the primary interdependent bond in world politics.... Despite the Franco-German divergence, interest rates began to move in tandem. These short-term links did not inaugurate a new era of economic harmony; they were but the prelude to autarky and conflict. After 1932 governments sought to insulate their economies from the impact of worldwide Depression, and the resulting patchwork of national policies undermined the structure of homogeneity and interdependence. Between 1933-39 the spurious unanimity of the 1930-32 economic crisis gradually dissolved. The number of significant price correlations fell from 80 percent in the crisis period to 36 percent by 1939. The same change occurred in interest rates. In 1930-32, 30 percent of the correlations were significant. By 1939 the figure had fallen to 14 percent....

As vertical interdependence (as measured by the relationship of factor prices) declined, so also did the horizontal flows and investment. Between 1921 and 1938 total world investment decreased by 168 percent. In the decade before 1938 world trade fell by 55 percent. This absolute decrease paralleled a decline in the proportion of its trade that each one of the six countries did with the others.... Seeking new trading partners each country did about 10 percent less of its trade with the five others in 1938 than it did in 1913. Perhaps most significant was the breakdown in intra-European trade. By 1938 France, Britain, and Germany were doing about half the percentage trade with each other that they had done in 1913.

The interwar system of international relations thus marks the breakup of the core of interdependence: the European relationship. There is a high politicization of economic activity, but this does not forward interdependence. Horizontal flows of factors of production have greatly declined. The correlation of factor prices has diminished and that of factor price changes is virtually nonexistent. The only period of prima facie interdependence, between 1930-32, is in fact the result of the immediate impact of the financial crisis and Depression. As states fashion individual policies to cope with the economic downturn, they move further and further apart. By 1939 the patterns of economic interdependence mirror the political conflicts that are about to cause World War II.

The decline of interdependence between 1913 and 1939 accords broadly with the Deutsch-Eckstein thesis that the external sector becomes less significant as nations industrialize, though the special circumstances of worldwide depression may offer a spurious confirmation of their findings. One caveat in this conclusion, however, is that if the decline should be greatest immediately after the completion of the first phase of industrialization, one should expect the largest decreases in interdependent relationships to be found in the cases of Germany and Japan. No special circumstances of this sort, however, appear to obtain. The second approach which sees interdependence growing or decreasing with the size of the international sector would of course anticipate a marked decline in interdependence during the thirties; and it certainly occurs. The third argument also holds in this period: there is no political hegemony in world politics, and economic relationships begin to fall apart.

INTERDEPENDENCE AFTER THE SECOND WORLD WAR

The received wisdom of many students and practitioners is that 1945 ushered in a new era of world interdependence.[10] Even if relations with the Soviet bloc and the developing countries were not immediately transformed, the inexorable processes of economic development and transnational communications fashioned a world in which the major democratic and Western industrial nations were clearly interdependent. The size of the international sector grew enormously: trade, investment, and technological advance altogether outstripped their prewar equivalents. Domestic economies became more "sensitive" to international forces. In a number of areas of production, national economies became more dependent upon products from a few suppliers and hence more vulnerable to any interruption in their supply. If anything, the political centrality of economic policy increased and domestic electorates were taught that their economic welfare was partly dependent upon decisions taken in other states. For perhaps the first time, investment of Western developed states seemed to concentrate in each other, increasing their mutual stake in trade and domestic growth.[11]

Trade charted a similar course. While foreign trade as a whole increased by a factor of five since 1945, the percentage trade of the six countries with each other also rose. The most significant increase, somewhat surprisingly, was that for the United States. The US did 33 percent of its trade with the five other countries in 1950, but by 1972 this figure rose to 56.4 percent, exceeding the percentage in 1913. In the cases of Britain, France, and Germany marked increases also occurred....

But the question has remained: if worldwide trade and investment flows are increasing, if national economies are more sensitive to one another, and if governments cannot insulate their populations from the impact of the external sector — do these features alone assure high vertical interdependence? The answer to this question is not yet entirely clear, but preliminary data indicate that economies have not uniformly responded to these flows in a fully interdependent manner over the thirty-year period. Indeed, it is impossible to talk of the magnitude or type of interdependence without distinguishing between at least four time periods: 1950-58; 1959-72; 1973-74 (the energy crisis); and 1975 (the post-crisis period).

1. 1950-58. The first period, 1950-58, is marked by a general restoration of international trade under the leadership of the United States. Factor prices and factor price changes mark a new stability in relationships among economies. These do not quite attain the strength of the patterns before 1914, but they are still very significant. The percentage of significant correlations among wholesale prices and price changes rises to 73.3 and 46.6 respectively. The figures for consumer prices are 80 and 26.6 percent. The homogeneity and stability of interdependence can be seen in the almost complete absence of negative signs.... Trade and factor prices, however, seem to attain normal relationships before interest rates. Partly because of convertibility and other problems, the international financial system remains somewhat disconnected in this period. The relatively strong financial interdependence of the United States, the United Kingdom, and France does not extend to Japan and Germany. Japanese rates in particular seem to be following an independent path. Wage rate correlations clearly show that the French labor market is distinct from that of other industrial countries....

2. 1959-72. The period of the 'sixties is decisive for many theories of interdependence. Those who argue that interdependence is increasing secularly with the size of the international sector and industrial and political modernization see the 1960s as a period in which the force of economic interdependence tends to overwhelm parochial nationalism. The 'sixties display the maximum thrust of American foreign investment, and represent the heyday of the multinational corporation. On the other hand, those who believe that high interdependence is linked to a given pattern of political dominance in world politics would expect to see interdependence diminish at the end of the 'sixties as the American influence declines. Those who are convinced that interdependence declines with industrialization and economic development would also expect a marked decrease in the 1959 - 72 period. They might have expected that the 'fifties could show an increase of interdependence as the artificial restraints and blockages occasioned by the Depression and World War II were overcome. But the 'sixties should, from this point of view at least, demonstrate a renewed decline in interdependence.

The 'sixties are also critical to the fourth approach to international interdependence. This approach, stressing a renewed politicization of international economic forces, would expect to see a loosening of interdependent ties among nations. This argument would stress the beginning in the early 'sixties of a greater national willingness to use inflation as a means of escaping the domestic discipline otherwise required to maintain equilibrium in the balance of payments. Instead of taking the domestic contractionist measures to produce a balance of imports and exports, nations regain a formal equilibrium by either exporting their currencies (in the case of the United States) or engaging in devaluation (Britain, France, and other countries). In the US case the demand that nations hold excess dollars in payment for US obligations contributed to the informal dollar glut which eventually forced a formal devaluation in 1971 - 73. In the case of most other countries, the lack of wage restraint and the political need to maintain full employment eventually required devaluation. But devaluation in its turn brought inflation, and an increase of export prices which could only be remedied by further devaluation. The alternative course — price and wage restraint — appeared to be politically impossible. In the United States, these tendencies were obvious as early as the Kennedy Administration. In Britain they attained dominance between 1964 - 67, and in France at least by 1968.

We therefore have conflicting theoretical expectations for the 'sixties: some posit new peaks of interdependence; others a slackening or decline of interdependence. Viewed from these standpoints the data on factor price relationships are remarkably tantalizing, for what we find... is a very substantial increase in the relationship among consumer price indices, and a very considerable fall in the relationship among changes in wholesale prices. The consumer price correlations are 100 percent significant. The wholesale price correlations are stronger, if no more significant than those of the previous period. These tendencies would seem to indicate greater interdependence. Economies now seem to be moving generally in the same direction.

As we look at the changes in prices, however, the precise association of the 1950 - 58 period disappears. The significance of the correlation of price changes either remains the same or falls precipitously. Whereas 46.6 percent of wholesale price change correlations were significant in 1950 - 58, *none* is significant in the period 1959 - 72. At the very minimum this would appear to suggest that while in terms of general economic trends the six industrial countries are moving in the same direction, the specific economic policies employed to reach the general goal have become different for different countries. One begins to see the intervention of domestic economic authorities in the international process. The automaticity of the international economic mechanism declines and even partly disappears.

The range or amplitude of international economic change has greatly increased. The pattern of the 'sixties seems to indicate that price trends can go in one direction, while price changes can go in another. Individual responses to interdependence become less predictable. These ambivalences occur at a time when there is a short period of harmony in international financial markets.... During 1959 - 72 Germany responded to capital flows in much the same way as other members of the international financial system. Only Japan followed an individual course.... However, Japan eventually rejoined the system. By 1965 her financial policies corresponded closely with those of other industrial states. The same period finds the reconsolidation of the European labor market, with very high correlations among wage rates and changes among the European three.... Canada and the United States seem closely associated with this pattern. Again, only Japan followed a different path.

The 'sixties therefore can be all things to all men. Individual tendencies both confirm and deny the existence of greater interdependence. The detachment or partial decoupling of individual factor price reactions from general factor price trends, however, would appear to give greatest support to those who see a gradual shift in favor of individual national policies within a context of broad interdependence. This conclusion would seem most congenial to those who underscore the gradual loosening of the American hegemonic grip or who believe that domestic imperatives are gradually gaining ascendancy over international imperatives in the formulation of national economic policy.

3. 1973 - 74. The ambivalence of the 1959 - 72 data makes a study of subsequent periods even more important. Perhaps some of the ambiguities of the 'sixties can be resolved by later information. But the next period, 1973 - 74, also coincides with the oil crisis. On the basis of the data on 1930 - 32, one would expect that a major shock to the system would find economies reacting almost in unison. Thus 1973 - 74 should produce high correlations of factor prices and price changes, temporarily obliterating the effects of separate national policies. This is precisely what happens.... Consumer prices remain almost perfectly correlated, and (in contrast to 1959 - 72) the correlation of wholesale prices and wholesale price changes rises very significantly. The percentage of significant correlations equals or exceeds even that of 1950 - 58. If the oil crisis effects were permanent, one might be tempted to say that a stage of new and higher economic interdependence had been attained among industrial countries.

Unfortunately, however, its effects do not last. Even the interest rate data show how rapidly separate national economic policies can assert themselves. While initially all countries raise their rates, Germany (the strongest nation financially) can afford to reduce them rapidly. Thus for most of the period German rates appear inversely correlated with those of other industrial countries.... One anticipates, moreover, that these financial divergencies will later manifest themselves in equally contradictory price trends.

4. 1975. This expectation is amply borne out for 1975. While consumer price and price change correlations are even more uniformly significant, the association among wholesale prices is almost completely shattered. Only 20 percent of wholesale price relationships attain significance, the lowest level since 1929.... Not only Germany but also France have embarked on divergent economic policies. In finance Canada and Britain are unique in stressing high or increasing rates, manifesting trends contrary to those of the other members of the system.... Relationships among European nations are less close than they were, and the United States no longer cements the system together. The US-Canadian tie in wholesale price relationships is still very strong, with the United Kingdom drawn in via the American market. The system, however, is very mixed with Japan associating with the US, Britain, and Canada in price relationships and with Germany and France in interest rates. But no pattern obtains throughout the data. The harmony of the Franco-German financial market is marred by entirely different wholesale price structures and movements. Most noticeable of all, perhaps, is the decline in the central role of the American capital market. In all previous periods the United States leads other countries in the number of high and positive correlations with other markets. In 1975, however, Germany, Japan, and France produce the strong relationships, and the US is relegated to a peripheral role.

The ambivalence of 1975 is if anything greater than that of 1959 - 72. The difference between consumer and wholesale price patterns is more marked. In the former period wholesale and consumer price trends were closely linked; the divergence occurred in price changes. In 1975 the price trends themselves diverge. This pattern, of course, cannot continue indefinitely. Wholesale price changes eventually reflect temselves in retail or consumer prices, though with a lag. It seems likely that subsequent data will show a similar change in consumer price trends. If so, it would represent a gradual attenuation of factor price links between industrial countries, and to that degree a decline in economic interdependence. The temporary peaks in association of 1950 - 58 and (briefly) 1973 -74 would then have given way to independent national policies.

CONCLUSIONS AND IMPLICATIONS

A number of conclusions seem warranted from this investigation of interdependence among developed nations. First, factor price relationships do appear to be a sensitive indicator of the degree of interdependence among markets as defined for the purpose of this article. This is evidenced clearly in extremely strong relationships between regional markets in the United States. But it is also shown by the high but less uniform correlations attained before 1914, and the collapse of those relationships by 1939. If the conventional wisdom is correct in concluding that interdependence was high in the 1950s, our measures appear to be valid in pointing to similar conclusions. It thus seems important to claim that such vertical data must accompany horizontal data if we are to ascertain the presence of "positive" interdependence (as opposed to mere "connectedness") among nations.

Second, the pattern of contemporary interdependence is much more mixed than many have believed. The amplitude of economic change has increased, and the response of one economy to another has become more unpredictable. Relationships no longer appear to be stable across time. Interdependence may be becoming unstable.

Third, the four theories of interdependence do not fare equally well in the period 1890 - 1975. Least supported by our data are those which prescribe either secular increases or declines in interdependence. There is little evidence that interdependence has decreased steadily since 1890 - 1913. Interdependence in 1950 - 58 is far higher than that in the 'twenties or 'thirties, rivaling even the pre-World War I era. On the other hand, the steady increases in interdependence predicted for the post-1945 period also have not emerged. The 1950s represented a temporary plateau of interdependence, but the experience since has been very uneven. The theory that links interdependence with patterns of hegemony in world politics is partly confirmed by our data in that the highest points of interdependence are reached prior to 1914 and again in the 1950s. The first can be roughly identified with British preeminence, the second with American primacy. In neither case, however, is the relationship exact. Interdependence does not fall off between 1900 - 14 despite the relative decline in British power. The interdependence of factor price indices (as opposed to factor price changes) remains high in the 1960s even though American influence is declining. The fourth theory, involving a re-politicization of international economic policies after 1960, seems to receive the greatest support from factor price data.

Fourth, data from recent years indicate a gradual and progressive detachment of individual national policies from the general trend toward interdependence. This detachment, if very recent data are to be credited, may even have an effect in altering that trend, reducing the positive and direct relationship among industrial economies. Over time this might or might not reduce general world interdependence. We have seen numerous cases in international relations where consciousness of declining solidarity has been a stimulus to new measures of political and institutional cooperation and interdependence. Setbacks in European integration sometimes bring a *relancement*. It is also possible that the decline in the relationship among industrial countries may reflect a more intimate relationship of these economies with outside states — the oil producers, the developing world, or the Communist nations. In this case a decline in specifically industrial interdependence might assist a broader world interdependence. At the moment, however, one of the unique characteristics of the post-World War II era, the increasing dependence of industrial countries upon each other, seems to have been overborne.

At the very least this casts doubt upon theories of continuing linear increases in interdependence in the post-World War II period. Interdependence appears to have cycled up and down, and to have varied in qualitative aspects. Economic changes have been abrupt and discontinuous, and international relationships have been subject to sudden reversals. Such transformations have occurred when the American hand was weakening on the tiller of world politics, but it is difficult to explain them entirely on this basis. In certain respects the result is due not only to American weakness, but to the weakness of several industrial countries under pressure from the domestic electorate. Even the movement to flexible exchange rates internationally conforms with this trend: it makes it easier for governments to avoid domestic economic discipline. Balance of payments equilibrium can be found through exchange rate adjustments without a major effort to control prices or wages.

The net result, of course, is international inflation. There is a continuing debate about the seriousness of the problem: whether employment and growth can be stimulated without concern for inflation; or whether inflation (if unchecked) must inevitably set limits upon growth. If a boom with inflation ultimately forces monetary authorities to intervene or causes consumers to stop buying it may be that sustained growth depends upon some control of increases in prices and wages. But this in turn requires political authorities to undertake the unpleasant tasks that they have sought to avoid in the past ten years. If inflation could be restrained in industrial societies, interdependence would almost certainly rise. For what we have seen in the past decade has been differential responses to inflation in one country after another, leading to separate domestic and international economic policies.

It is much too early to say whether such control is possible. Political factors will affect the outcome as much as economic ones. Indeed, political patterns of intervention in the economic process have had a crucial effect on interdependence over the years. One of the reasons for high interdependence among economies before 1914 was the general disinclination to intervene in the relatively free play of the international financial system. Tariffs existed of course. But within very general limits, the flow of goods, persons, and capital was permitted to influence a nation's domestic price levels and employment. Interdependence before 1914 was the interdependence of states largely open to international economic influences. After 1950, in contrast, interdependence occurred partly because national economic planners reacted more or less in unison to international economic forces. Concerted political action under American leadership kept developed economies in line and in touch with one another. Since 1960, however, there has been no automatic and uniform registration of the effects of international flows. The advantages deriving from nineteenth century openness no longer obtain. At the same time, the advantages that might be gained from international coordination and central regulation have not been seized upon. There seems to have been a loosening of the linkage between domestic and international economic policy since the 1950s. The episodic attempts at a re-integration have largely failed. Kingston and the various economic summits have merely transformed the de facto into the de jure. One legitimizes what is already occurring rather than planning a new, cooperative system. Above all, one avoids centralized authority.

The future of interdependence among industrial countries, then, lies open. It is likely to be determined by the structure of political cooperation among states. At the moment, political responses to declining economic interdependence seem inadequate to provide the greater coordination that is manifestly needed. But there is nothing inevitable about this. Nations, facing great problems, have concerted solutions before, and they can do it again.

ENDNOTES

1 The original contentions were those of Raymond Vernon and Charles Kindleberger. For a revised view see C. Fred Bergsten, "Economic Tensions: America v. The Third World" in R. Rosecrance, ed., *America as an Ordinary Country: U.S. Foreign Policy and the Future* (Ithaca, N.Y.: Cornell University Press, 1976) and the same author, "Let's Avoid a Trade War," *Foreign Policy,* No. 23 (Summer 1976).

2 See the definition offered by Edward Morse in "Transnational Economic Processes" in R. Keohane and J. Nye, Jr., eds., *Transnational Relations and World Politics* (Cambridge, Mass.: Harvard University Press, 1972).

3 This is not true of Kenneth Waltz. See his "The Myth of Interdependence" in C. Kindleberger, ed., *International Corporation: A Symposium* (Cambridge, Mass.: MIT Press, 1970).

4 It is striking that the literature has made little or no mention of the difference between situations in which interdependence means movement in the same direction and when it means movement in opposed directions. If complete interdependence in the former sense were achieved, nations would

have no incentive to seek advantage at the expense of each other.

5 For a summary of argument and current horizontal data see Peter Katzenstein, "International Interdependence: Some Long-Term Trends and Recent Changes," *International Organization*, 29 (Autumn 1975), 1024-34.

6 The former defines the long-term or secular trend in vertical data while the latter affords a measure of the cyclical or short-term variation. High interdependence should be reflected in high correlations on both measures.

7 The key work here is K. Deutsch and A. Eckstein, "National Industrialization and the Declining Share of the International Economic Sector: 1850-1959," *World Politics*, 13 (January 1961), 267-99.

8 This thesis was offered particularly by Robert Gilpin in "The Politics of Transnational Economic Relations" in Keohane and Nye, eds., *Transnational Relations*. It has been subjected to partial test in S. Krasner, "State Power and the Structure of International Trade," *World Politics*, 28 (April 1976), 314-47.

9 See Robert G. Hawkins, "Intra-EEC Capital Movements and Domestic Financial Markets," in Fritz Machlup, *et al.*, eds., *International Mobility and Movement of Capital* (New York: National Bureau of Economic Research, 1972), pp. 51-77.

10 See *inter alia*, Oran Young, "Interdependencies in World Politics," *International Journal*, 24 (Autumn 1969); E. Morse, "The Politics of Interdependence," *International Organization*, 23 (Spring 1969); and Richard N. Cooper, *The Economics of Interdependence* (New York: McGraw-Hill, 1968).

11 Recent investment in Europe is one example. While Europe, Oceana, and Africa constituted only about 1.8 percent of long-term direct investment made by Japan between 1951-59, Europe alone comprised 20.1 percent of the Japanese total in 1973. The European share of US direct investment was 14.7 percent in 1950, but had risen to 32.6 percent by 1972. In 1958 only 8 percent of British earnings on direct investment came from Europe, but by 1971 the total was 17.7 percent. France and Germany were even more strongly committed to Europe. France had 16.8 percent of its long-term investments in the EEC in 1962; ten years later the total had grown to nearly 25 percent. In 1961 Germany invested 38.6 percent of its long-term funds in Europe; by 1970 the total was nearly 57 percent.

Change and War in the Contemporary World

Robert Gilpin

At the end of the last hegemonic struggle in 1945, the United States stood at the apex of the international hierarchy of power and prestige. American economic and military power was supreme, and it provided the basis for an American-centered world economic and political order. By the 1980s this Pax Americana was in a state of disarray because of the differential growth of power among states over the previous few decades. The proliferation of nuclear weapons, the rise or reemergence of other centers of economic power, and especially the massive growth in Soviet military strength had weakened the political foundations of the international system established at the end of World War II. Events in Iran, Afghanistan, and elsewhere signaled that world politics were entering on a new and uncertain phase.

Sensing the ominous portents of this changed situation, numerous commentators and statesmen have reflected and written on its meaning. Parallels have been drawn between our own age and the periods preceding other great wars, particularly World War I. Contrasting unhappily with the seemingly halcyon days of the early 1960s, an uneasiness has settled over world affairs. The Middle East in 1980 has been compared to the pre-1914 Balkans, and a former secretary of state, Henry Kissinger, spoke of a period of maximum danger ahead when Soviet military power reaches its zenith. A book entitled *The Third World War — August 1985*[1] became a best seller, and evidence mounted that the general public had begun to take seriously the possibility of a war between the superpowers.

[Our] purpose... is to assess the world situation at the beginning of the decade of the 1980s... and to consider whether or not events and the fundamental forces at work suggest a world once again out of control and on the verge of another global hegemonic struggle. Although no one can predict the future, the fact is that both statesmen and the public act on assessments of the trend of events, and prognostications frequently become self-fulfilling prophecies. It is therefore prudent to turn to the past and to seek an understanding of the dynamics of world politics for guidance. It is important to appreciate the real dangers as well as the possible unappreciated opportunities of the present moment. Dispassionate analysis in an era of rapid change is needed to help avoid cataclysmic war.

Using the terminology of... international political change... we may say that a disequilibrium has developed between the existing governance of the international system and the underlying distribution of power in the system. Although the United States continues to be the dominant and most prestigious state in the system, it no longer has the power to "govern" the system as it did in the past.

It is decreasingly able to maintain the existing distribution of territory, the spheres of influence, and the rules of the world economy. The redistribution of economic and military power in the system to the disadvantage of the United States has meant that the costs to the United States of governing the system have increased relative to the economic capacity of the United States to support the international status quo. The classic symptoms of a declining power characterize the United States in the early 1980s: rampant inflation, chronic balance-of-payments difficulties, and high taxation.

Responding to this disequilibrium and a severe fiscal crisis, the United States has employed the traditional techniques for reestablishing equilibrium between the costs and the benefits of the existing international system. The United States has retrenched its forces and withdrawn from exposed positions in Southeast Asia, the Far East, Latin America, and the Middle East, frequently leaving a vacuum for the Soviet Union or other powers to occupy. It has formally recognized the Soviet sphere of influence in eastern Europe and negotiated a rapprochement with China, and it is reluctantly acceding to the wishes and ambitions of growing regional powers: India, Brazil, Nigeria, etc. It has accepted strategic nuclear parity with the Soviet Union, as well as loss of control over the world petroleum industry, and it finds itself unable to prevent the continued proliferation of nuclear weapons. It no longer unilaterally sets the rules regarding international trade, money, and investment. In brief, the United States, through political and military retrenchment, has sought to reduce its international commitments much as Great Britain did in the decades immediately preceding the outbreak of World War I.

At the same time, the United States also has attempted to generate new resources to support its reduced but still-dominant international position. It has urged its European and Japanese allies to increase their contributions to the common defense. It has increased its own defense expenditures and has moved toward a quasi-alliance with China to resist Soviet "hegemonism." Perhaps most significant of all, the United States, on August 15, 1971, announced a new foreign economic policy and forced changes in the rules governing international trading and monetary affairs that would benefit the American economy, especially to improve America's declining trade position. In addition, decreasing the public-sector consumption and increasing domestic investment in order to increase productivity and the reindustrialization of the American economy have become major preoccupations of political and economic leadership. President Ronald Reagan, in his inaugural address, called for "a national renewal." Finally, the United States has told "client" states around the globe that they will have to increase their contributions to their own defense (Nixon doctrine). Thus, through traditional techniques the United States is also attempting to increase its resources in order to maintain its dominant international position.

It is obviously too early to determine if the United States can or will retrench to a more modest but secure position, if it can generate additional resources to maintain its global hegemony, and if, through some combination of both responses, it can restore a favorable equilibrium between its power and commitments. This will depend not only on specific policy initiatives of the United States but also on those of other governments in the years ahead. The thrust of political, economic, and technological forces creates challenges and opportunities; domestic politics and political leadership create the responses of states to these challenges and opportunities. The course of history is indeterminant; only in retrospect does it appear otherwise.

In the meantime, the contemporary era has been aptly described as one of "eroding hegemony."[2] Such a condition in world politics has, of course, existed in the past. The interregnum between British dominance and American dominance of international economics and politics, what E.H. Carr called the "twenty years' crisis" (1919-39), was such a period; the former hegemonic power could no longer set the rules, and the rising hegemonic power had neither the will nor the power to assume this responsibility.[3] In the absence of rejuvenation by the old hegemony or the triumph of its successor or the establishment of some other basis of governance, the pressing issues of world order (rules governing trade, the future of the international monetary system, a new regime for the oceans, etc.) remain unresolved. Progress toward the formulation of new rules and regimes for an international system to follow the Pax Americana has been slow or nonexistent.

Yet, on the basis of the analysis of political change advanced in this study, there are reasons for believing that the present disequilibrium in the international system can be resolved without resort to hegemonic war. Although the danger of hegemonic war is very real, what is known about such wars provides grounds for guarded optimism. Whereas the contemporary world displays some of the preconditions for hegemonic conflict, other preconditions appear to be totally or partially lacking. An evaluation of the current international situation reinforces the hope that a gradual process of peaceful change, rather than war, may characterize the present era of world politics.

An extremely important reason for guarded optimism is the relative stability of the existing bipolar structure. As Waltz argued, the present bipolar system appears to be relatively stable.[4] Historically, however, as this study has shown, five types of developments tend to destabilize bipolar systems and trigger hegemonic conflict. Fortunately, none of these destabilizing developments appears imminent in the contemporary world (1980), at least for the immediate future.

The first potentially destabilizing factor is the danger that one of the pair (like Sparta prior to the outbreak of the Peloponnesian War) will fail to play its balancing role. Through neglect, it permits a dangerous shift in the balance of power to take place. As long as the United States and the Soviet Union maintain a system of mutual nuclear deterrence, this is unlikely to happen. Although many Americans and others fear that the United States has permitted a dangerous shift in the military balance to take place in favor of the Soviet Union, the strategic nuclear relationship continues to be one based firmly on the presumption of "mutually assured destruction" in the event of hegemonic war: each superpower has the capability to devastate the other. Yet, it must be added that a continuing deterioration in the American military position could remove this constraint on the system of mutual deterrence; at the least it could encourage Soviet leadership to exploit politically the belief that the Soviet Union has become the reigning hegemon.

The second potentially destabilizing factor is the danger of the rise of a third party to upset the bipolar balance. Although students of international relations disagree on the relative stability of bipolar systems versus multipolar systems, almost all agree that a tripolar system is the most unstable configuration. As long as western Europe lacks political unity, Japan remains weak militarily, and China continues in a backward state, this danger is minimized, though by no means eliminated. Certainly the Soviet Union has a genuine fear of an encircling alliance composed of these neighboring powers and the United States. The United States, for its part, would regard the loss of one of these powers or the loss of the oil fields of the Middle East as a major setback. Thus, although the contemporary bipolar distribution of power is basically stable, it does contain the potential for dangerous tripolar structures of power.

The third potentially destabilizing factor is the danger of polarization of the international system as a whole into two hostile camps. In such a situation, international relations become a zero-sum game in which a gain to one camp or bloc is a loss to the other. This was the case prior to the outbreak of World War I, when minor tensions in the Balkans flared up into a major conflagration. Such a polarization has not yet developed (1980). To repeat an earlier metaphor, political space is not closing in. On the contrary, the world is becoming more pluralistic, with the emergence of a number of regional actors and issues. The outcomes of political conflicts in Asia, Africa, and elsewhere do not necessarily advantage one or another of the two superpowers so as to force the other to take decisive counteraction. Yet the emergence of frequently unstable new powers in the so-called Third World, the proliferation of nuclear weapons to these states, and the conflicts among them could involve the superpowers in highly volatile situations.

The fourth potentially destabilizing factor is the danger of entanglement of the major powers in the ambitions and difficulties of minor allies. It was the ambitions of Sparta's ally, Corinth, and its provocations of Athens that precipitated the great war between the Peloponnesian and Delian leagues. The difficulties of Germany's ally, Austria, beset with a decaying multiethnic empire, escalated into World War I. In neither of these cases could the major power tolerate the defeat or disintegration of its minor ally. Fortunately, these dangers do not appear imminent today. Even though particular allies of both superpowers have unfulfilled ambitions and/or serious political problems of their own, it is unlikely that they could or would set in motion a series of untoward events that would precipitate conflict among the two superpowers; this is because these allies are insufficiently independent and the superpowers are sufficiently self-reliant. Again, however, one must not too quickly dismiss this potential danger. A Sino-Soviet confrontation, workers' revolts in eastern Europe, or political instability among America's allies in western Europe and the Middle East could pose dangers for the international system.

The fifth potentially destabilizing factor is the danger of loss of control over economic, political, and social developments. Eras of rapid and revolutionary change within and among nations create dangerous uncertainties and anxieties that lead political elites in great powers to miscalculate. Hegemonic wars signal not merely changes in political relations among states but frequently social and economic upheavals as well; World War I, as Halévy showed[5], represented a collapse of the decaying European social and economic order. The crisis of world capitalism in the 1980s (high rate of inflation, rising level of unemployment, and low rate of economic growth) and the equally severe crisis of world communism (as represented by the workers' revolt in Poland) signal major strains in both systems.

Although the decades following World War II frequently have been called an age of political turbulence, the international system in that period has actually been characterized by remarkable resilience. It has accommodated a number of major developments: an unprecedented process of decolonization, rapid technological changes, the emergence of new powers (India, Brazil, China), sociopolitical revolutions in developing countries, massive shocks to the world economy, and the resurgence of non-Western civilizations. Yet the basic framework of an international system composed of two central blocs and a large nonaligned periphery has remained essentially intact.

This relative stability of the system has been strengthened by the domestic stability of the two dominant powers themselves. In contrast to the situations prevailing before World Wars I and II, neither power has been torn by powerful class or national conflicts. Although racial strife in the United States and ethnic problems in Russia are causing tensions in both societies, these internal difficulties pale in comparison with the nationalistic struggles of the Austro-Hungarian Empire in 1914 and the intense class conflicts of the European powers in the 1930s. The basic domestic stability of the United States and the Soviet Union today helps to ensure that revolutionary upheavals in these societies will not disrupt the international system.

Yet it would be foolish to be complacent regarding the underlying social stability of the system. A prolonged period of restricted economic growth could erode the political stability of the United States and the Soviet Union. A more probable threat to world stability would be untoward developments in important peripheral areas, in particular eastern Europe and the Middle

East. The dependence of Soviet security on the subservient eastern European bloc and the dependence of the West on Middle Eastern petroleum constitute worrisome factors in contemporary world politics. The maintenance of stable conditions in these areas over the long term is a formidable challenge. Another continuing danger is that one or both of the superpowers might engage in foreign adventures in order to dampen internal dissent and promote political unity.

Another reason for guarded optimism regarding the avoidance of hegemonic war is that in the closing decades of the twentieth century, economic, political, and ideological cleavages are not coalescing but instead are running counter to one another. In the past, a precondition for hegemonic war in many cases has been the coalescence of political, economic, and ideological issues. In periods prior to the outbreak of hegemonic war, conflict has intensified because the contending parties have been at odds with one another on all fronts and have had few interests in common to moderate the antagonism. In such situations, compromise in one issue area becomes increasingly difficult because of its linkage to other issue areas. As a consequence, disputes in one area easily spill over into other areas, and the joining of issues leads to escalation of the conflict. The great wars of world history have tended to be at once political, economic, and ideological struggles.

In the 1980s, however, although the United States and the Soviet Union find themselves in political and ideological conflict, they share a powerful interest in avoiding nuclear war and stopping the proliferation of nuclear weapons. Moreover, they also share certain economic interests, and both countries have numerous economic conflicts with their political and economic allies. This intermingling of interests and conflicts is thus a source of stability. Ironically, a less autarkic Soviet Union challenging the United States in world markets and competing for scarce resources would be, and might very well become, a destabilizing factor. A decline in Soviet production of petroleum or Soviet entry into world markets may change this situation and increase the level of economic tensions.

The contemporary situation is somewhat anomalous in the multiple nature of the challenge to the dominant power in the system. On the one hand, the position of the United States is challenged economically by Japan, western Europe, and the members of OPEC. On the other hand, the military and political challenge comes principally from the Soviet Union. Although there are those writers who believe that the economic confrontation between the United States and its allies is threatening to world peace,[6]... the worst danger to international stability is the Soviet-American confrontation. From this perspective, the primary consequence of the economic competition between the United States and its allies has been to undermine the capacity of the United States to meet the Soviet challenge; however, if Japan and West Germany were to convert their military potential into actual capability, then the balance of military and political power could be changed dramatically, probably with important unforeseen consequences. At best, therefore, one can say that the long-term significance of contemporary developments for the future of the system is ambiguous.

Finally, and most important of all, hegemonic wars are preceded by an important psychological change in the temporal outlook of peoples. The outbreaks of hegemonic struggles have most frequently been triggered by the fear of ultimate decline and the perceived erosion of power. The desire to preserve what one has while the advantage is still on one's side has caused insecure and declining powers to precipitate great wars. The purpose of such war frequently has been to minimize potential losses rather than to maximize any particular set of gains.

Here, perhaps, is the greatest cause for anxiety in the years immediately ahead. What would be the reaction of the United States if the balance of power is seen to be shifting irrevocably to the Soviet advantage? What would be the Soviet response to a perceived threat of encirclement by a resurgent United States, an industrialized China, a dynamic Japan, a hostile Islam, an unstable eastern Europe, and a modernized NATO? How might one or another of these powers (the United States today, Russia tomorrow) respond to the continuing redistribution of world power?

A generally unappreciated factor in the preservation of world peace over the past few decades has involved the ideological perspectives of the United States and the Soviet Union. Each rival power subscribes to an ideology that promises inevitable victory to its own system of values and assures it that history is on its side. For the United States, freedom, democracy, and national independence are the most powerful forces in the world; for the Soviet Union, communism is the "wave of the future." These rival belief systems have been sources of conflict but also of reassurance for both nations. Despite their clashes and struggles, neither side has experienced the panic that has preceded the great wars of history, a panic that arises from fear that time has begun to run against one. Neither nation has felt the need to risk everything in the present in order to prevent inevitable defeat in the future. Fortunately for world peace, both the United States and the Soviet Union have believed the logic of historical development to be working for them. Each power has believed the twentieth century to be its century. But the foundations of both of these faiths are experiencing strain.

At the end of World War II, the United States held a position of unparalleled preeminence in the international system. During the first decades of the postwar period, its power and influence expanded until it was finally checked in the jungles of Southeast Asia and by more fundamental changes in the international distribution of economic and military power. The administration of Richard Nixon constituted a watershed in that it was the first to deal with the challenge posed by the increasing disequilibrium between America's international position and America's capacity to finance it. The United States has worked to meet this challenge through political retrenchment, efforts toward detente with the Soviet Union, rapprochement with China, and the generation of additional resources through changes in its domestic and foreign economic policies.

The fundamental task of the United States in the realm of foreign affairs has become one of responding to its changed position in the world as new powers arise on the world scene. It must bring its power and commitments into balance, either through increasing the former or reducing the latter or by some combination of both strategies. Although this is a serious challenge, it need not be a source of alarm. Other great powers have succeeded in this task and have survived, maintaining their vital interests and values intact. There is danger, however, that the military challenge of the Soviet Union and the changing economic fortunes of the United States might generate severe anxiety in the American public. Although there is certainly cause for concern in these matters, exaggerated rhetoric over the relative decline of American power and wealth can itself give rise to panic and irrational actions.

Despite its relative decline, the American economy remains the most powerful in the world and dwarfs that of the Soviet Union. However, American society has placed on its economy consumption demands (both public and private) and protection demands beyond its capabilities at the same time that productive investment and economic productivity have slackened. Although the Reagan Administration can greatly increase defense expenditures to meet the Soviet challenge in an era of restricted economic growth, it could do so only at high cost to consumption or investment or both. The inherent danger in a massive expansion of defense expenditures is that it will be inflationary and will further undermine the productivity of the economy. The long-term well-being and security of the United States necessitate judicious allocation of national resources among the areas of consumption, protection, and investment.

The Soviet Union is, of course, the rising challenger, and it appears to be the one power that in the years to come could supplant the American dominance over the inter-national system.

Although the growth and expansion of Russian power have deep historical roots, the acceleration in the development of Soviet industrial and military might in recent decades has been formidable. The Soviet Union has fashioned a powerful military machine from a state that was near defeat and collapse during World War II. Further, it occupies a central position on the Eurasian land mass and enjoys conventional military superiority over the United States in important areas. A major question for the future is whether or not the Soviets can translate and are willing to translate these expanding military capabilities into decisive political gains in Europe, Asia, and elsewhere in the world.

Meanwhile, the relative decline in American power and the continuing restraint on the use of military force has given rise to an era of uneasy coexistence between the superpowers. The erratic process of detente, if ultimately successful, may turn out to be an unprecedented example of peaceful change.[7] What it could well signify is a change from an America-centered global system to a more nearly equal bipolar system, and, perhaps eventually, a multipolar global system. The apparent settlement of the German and central European questions has stabilized, at least for the moment, the outstanding territorial issue dividing the two superpowers. The fundamental issue in the strategic-arms-limitation talks has been the stabilization of the nuclear arms race on the basis of strategic parity. Both powers favor steps to discourage further proliferation of nuclear weapons. There remain, however, many other issues about which the two superpowers continue to have antagonistic interests that could destabilize their relations. The Soviet aggression in Afghanistan is a case in point, and, of course, the rise of other powers could undermine this emergent bipolar structure over the longer term.

At the present juncture, it is the United States whose position is threatened by the rise of Soviet power. In the decades ahead, however, the Soviet Union also must adjust to the differential growth of power among states. For the Soviet Union, the burden of adjusting to the transformation of the international system from a bipolar system to a tripolar or even multipolar system could be even more severe than it would prove to be for the United States. In the wake of the collapse of Communist ideological unity and the rise of a rival ideological center in Peking, the Soviet Union finds itself surrounded by potentially threatening and growing centers of industrial power. Although it possesses unprecedented military strength, it could lose the reassurance of its ideology, and it is sluggish with respect to economic growth and technological development. If its neighboring powers (Japan, western Europe, and China) continue to grow in economic power and military potential, Russia's logistical advantage of occupying a central position on the Eurasian continent is also a political liability. On all sides, centrifugal forces could pull at this last of the great multiethnic empires as neighbors make demands for revision of the territorial status quo and as subordinate non-Russian peoples seek greater equality and autonomy. Such external and internal challenges could give rise to powerful defensive reactions on the part of the Soviet governing elite.

Several years ago, Ernest Mandel, a leading European Marxist, ascribed the changing fortunes of the United States to the law of uneven development: "After having benefited from the law of unequal development for a century, the United States is now becoming its victim"[8] Similarly, one may make the same observation regarding the future of the Soviet Union; this law plays no favorites between capitalists and communists. Observing the growing challenge of a unified and developing Communist China, an Indian political scientist writes that the uneven development of socialism is creating contradictions in the system today. Chatterjee put it best: "In the long run, the law of uneven socialist development may pose a greater threat to the Soviet Union than does the law of uneven capitalist development to the United States. In the years ahead, both nations may need to adjust to a world in which power is diffusing at an unprecedented rate to a plurality of powers."[9]

We conclude this epilogue on a cautiously optimistic note. Although there are powerful forces that could lead to hegemonic war between the superpowers, the historic conditions for such a war are only partially present. The redistribution of military power in favor of Russia as the rising state in the international system and the possibility of further redistributions of power to other states pose serious threats to the stability of the system; in response the superpowers might precipitate a course of events over which they could lose control. However, these potentially destabilizing developments are balanced by the restraint imposed by the existence of nuclear weapons, the plurality of the system, and the mutual benefits of economic cooperation. The supreme task for statesmen in the final decades of the twentieth century is to build on the positive forces of our age in the creation of a new and more stable international order.

ENDNOTES

1 John Hackett, *et al., The Third World War — August 1985* (New York: Macmillan, 1978).

2 Robert O. Keohane & Joseph S. Nye, Jr., *Power and Interdependence: World Politics in Transition* (Boston: Little, Brown, 1977).

3 Edward Hallett Carr, *The Twenty Years' Crisis. An Introduction to the Study of International Relations* (London: Macmillan, 1951).

4 Kenneth N. Waltz, *Theory of International Politics* (Reading, Mass.: Addison-Wesley, 1979).

5 Elie Halévy, *The Era of Tyrannies* (New York: Doubleday, 1965), p.212.

6 This is the thesis of Mary Kaldor, *The Disintegrating West* (New York: Hill and Wang, 1978).

7 It must be acknowledged that the Soviet Union and the United States have quite different conceptions of the meaning of detente. For the Soviets, detente does not mean an end to the class struggle or the historic movement toward the victory of communism. For the United States, detente is indivisible; the Soviet Union must not use detente to advance its political control over other nations.

8 Ernest Mandel, *Europe vs America — Contradictions of Imperialism* (New York: Monthly Review Press, 1970).

9 Partha Chatterjee, *Arms, Alliances and Stability: The Development of the Structure of International Politics* (New York: Halsted Press, 1975), p.8.

Alternatives to the Contemporary States System

Hedley Bull

We must begin our inquiry into alternative paths to world order with the question: what forms of universal political organisation, alternative to the present states system, are there? The number of alternatives that can be conceived is, of course, boundless. Here I confine my attention to a few that may be judged significant.

Before we can answer the question…we must remind ourselves what the essential attributes of the states system are — or we shall be in danger of mistaking for an alternative to the states system what would be merely a change from one particular phase or form of the states system to another. The essential attributes of the states system, as they have been defined here, are first a plurality of sovereign states; second, a degree of interaction among them, in respect of which they form a system; and third, a degree of acceptance of common rules and institutions, in respect of which they form a society.

ALTERNATIVE FORMS OF STATES SYSTEM

A number of changes in the present political structure of the world may be conceived that would be quite basic, yet nevertheless would represent simply a transition from one phase of the states system to another, not the supersession of the states system itself.

A Disarmed World. One such change would be the advent of a "disarmed world", the realisation of the vision of "general and complete disarmament" contained in the American and Soviet disarmament plans and ritually endorsed by successive disarmament conferences. In both plans it is envisaged that in the final stage of a process of phased disarmament, sovereign states would cease to possess armaments and armed forces, except for purposes of internal security. In the American plan it is envisaged also that as states are progressively deprived of armed force, there will be a simultaneous process of the strengthening of a world authority, in whose hands armed force might ultimately be concentrated.

The realisation of the idea of "general and complete disarmament" would imply so radical a transformation of the present structure of international politics as to require us to think out the whole basis of relations among states afresh if we were to render it intelligible. It would not, however, represent the demise of the states system, for it does not in itself involve an end to the existence of sovereign states, to systematic interaction among them or to their forming together an international society. If — as the American plan allows

---

Hedley Bull, *The Anarchical Society* (London and Basingstoke: Macmillan, 1977), pp. 233-256. Reprinted by permission of the Macmillan Press Ltd. and Columbia University Press. Portions of the text have been deleted. Some footnotes have been deleted; those remaining have been renumbered.

— the achievement of this state of affairs was accompanied by the development of a world authority commanding force and political loyalty sufficient to undermine the supremacy of states in their own dominions and over their own populations, this would imply the demise of the first of the three essential attributes. But this is not a logically necessary consequence of a disarmed world. It is possible to visualise such a world as one in which — as in the final stage of the Soviet plan — the central authority that exists does not command armed force in its own right, and is still subject to the veto of the great powers.

The argument in favour of a world in which disarmament is general, in the sense that it involves all powers, and complete, in the sense that it embraces all categories of armaments and armed forces, sometimes takes what may be called the "strong" form — that total disarmament would make war physically impossible, because states would not be able to make war even when they wanted to; and it sometimes takes the "weak" form, that the maximum possible disarmament would make war less likely.

When Litvinov first advanced the idea of total disarmament in the context of the League of Nations disarmament discussions it was the strong form of the argument that he put forward. His contention was that total disarmament was qualitatively different from any lesser form of disarmament. On the one hand, it promised more than any lesser kind of disarmament; for if arms and armed forces were completely abolished, war would be simply unavailable as an instrument of policy even to those states which sought to resort to it. On the other hand, it was easier to achieve than any lesser form of disarmament, such as "the reduction of national armaments to the lowest point consistent with national safety and the enforcement by common action of international obligations" (the formula propounded in Article VIII of the Covenant of the League of Nations, to the realisation of which the disarmament discussions of that time were directed). This was because, Litvinov contended, if nations agreed to disarm totally they could bypass "the thorny questions" that inhibited attempts to agree on what arms and armed forces would be retained.

The objection to "total disarmament" in Litvinov's sense is that there can be, in principle, nothing of the kind; the physical capacity for organised violence is inherent in human society, and cannot be abolished by treaty. It is not merely that all actual proposals for so-called "total disarmament" envisage the retention of internal security forces, and sometimes also of forces that could be made available to a world authority for the maintenance of order. Even a disarmament system which made no provision for the retention of any such forces would leave states with the capacity to wage war on a primitive level; and, moreover, with the capacity to raise this level — to re-establish what has been disestablished, to remember or to re-invent what has been put aside. All that a disarmament treaty can do is prohibit certain kinds of arms and armed forces that are specified, and the effect of this is to augment the strategic significance of whatever is left outside the scope of the treaty. What is called "total disarmament" is not in fact qualitatively different from lesser forms of disarmament.

Thus there is no force in Litvinov's contention that "total disarmament" would make war physically impossible in some sense in which lesser forms of disarmament would not. Moreover, even the most drastic disarmament system must leave some states with greater capacity for war than others; a nation's war potential does not reside simply in its "armaments", but in the whole complex of its economic, technological and demographic resources, strategic position, political leadership, military experience and ingenuity, morale, and so on. Thus it will be a consequence of "total disarmament", just as much as of any lesser form of disarmament, that it leads to a ratio of military power within the "disarmed world". It follows from this that there is equally no force in Litvinov's other argument, that the simplicity of "total disarmament" enables it to bypass the difficulties of negotiation.

The weak form of the argument for general and complete disarmament is not open to objections of this kind. It is not logically impossible or contrary to the nature of human society that armaments and armed forces should be few in number and primitive in quality; nor is it impossible that there should exist habits, institutions, codes or taboos which might help preserve this state of affairs. There is a strong *prima facie* case for holding that a world in which sophisticated armaments and advanced forms of military organisation and technique had been abolished would provide more security against war than a world in which states are armed as they are now. In particular, it may be argued that, other things being equal, in such a world wars would be less likely to break out, because large military establishments would not exist as a factor making for war, because there would be less strategic mobility and thus fewer other states within military striking distance of any one state, and because there would not exist weapons-systems capable of generating the fear of surprise attack. It might also be argued that, other things being equal, such a world war, if it did break out, would be less catastrophic, because it would be more slow-moving, less costly and would involve less physical destruction and economic dislocation.

Whether or not the realisation of the vision of a disarmed world is in any sense practically attainable, the common instinct is soundly based that leads us to see in this vision a superior kind of world order to that which is provided in the contemporary form of the states system. We have also to recognise, however, that merely to have imagined a world in which states have disarmed to low quantitative and qualitative levels is not to have given an account of how order in such a world would be maintained. The vision of a disarmed world is at best an incomplete one, if it is not accompanied by an explanation...of the rules and institutions by which the elementary goals of social life can be attained.

There is first of all the question of how the states of the world, having disarmed to low levels, are to be kept disarmed. This must lead us to a consideration of a system of verification that will detect violations of the disarmament agreement, and of a system of sanctions or reprisals that will deter such violations, or provide for the security of innocent parties in the event that they occur. There are strong reasons for holding that in a system of drastic disarmament that included the complete abolition of nuclear weapons and other weapons of mass destruction, successful violation of the system would place the violator in a position of military preponderance in relation to other states. In order to deter violations of this kind, or to assure the security of innocent parties in the event that they take place, it would seem essential to presuppose a world authority with a preponderance of military power, including nuclear weapons.

More serious, however, than the question of how the system of drastic disarmament is to be preserved, is the question of how order in general is to be provided for. A disarmed world, as we have seen, is still a world in which the capacity for organised violence exists and must play its part in human affairs. It is still a world divided into sovereign states and subject to the political conflicts by which such a world has always been characterised. Internal or domestic order would still have, as one of its requirements, the existence of preponderant armed force in the hands of governments. International order would still depend on the operation of rules and institutions to control or contain the use of military power — whether by preserving a balance of power, allowing for its use in law enforcement, limiting the means by which it is conducted, facilitating the settlement of political conflicts that might involve the use of force, or exploiting the preponderance of the great powers in concert.

The idea of a disarmed world, in addition to raising these familiar questions concerning the maintenance of order, also raises questions about the achievement of just change. If a disarmed world were to prove more peaceful and secure than a heavily armed world such as exists now, this might also mean that it was a world less amenable to just change brought about by force, and more dependent on the availability of institutions of peaceful change. Whether a lightly armed world is less capable of providing for just change, or more capable, the point is that merely to have imagined drastic disarmament is not to have shown how this function can be fulfilled.

In other words, the same range of issues that arise concerning the maintenance of order in the present, heavily armed world could also be expected to arise in a lightly armed world. This does not mean that the former is preferable to the latter, but it does mean that the vision of a disarmed world does not by itself indicate an alternative path to world order.

The Solidarity of States. Another possible political structure of the world would be one in which the United Nations, or some comparable body founded upon the co-operation of sovereign states on a global basis, had become the predominant force in world politics. Such a state of affairs we might describe as one in which the United Nations Charter is observed by member states in the way in which it was hoped that they would do so by the more visionary founders of the organisation. It would represent the fulfilment of the Grotian or solidarist doctrine of international order, which envisages that states, while setting themselves against the establishment of a world government, nevertheless seek, by close collaboration among themselves and by close adherence to constitutional principles of international order to which they have given their assent, to provide a substitute for world government.[1] Its central assumption is that of the solidarity, or potential solidarity, of most states in the world in upholding the collective will of the society of states against challenges to it. Again, such a condition of world politics would be radically different from what exists now, but would represent a new phase of the states system, not its replacement by something different.

The Grotian or solidarist doctrine seeks to achieve a more orderly world by restricting or abolishing resort to war by individual states for political ends, and promoting the idea that force can legitimately be used only to promote the purposes of the international community. It thus seeks to reproduce in international society one of the central features of domestic society. The system of rules which Grotius devised was intended to assist the triumph in any war of the party or parties whose cause was just, and who therefore were acting on behalf of the community as a whole.

In the twentieth century,... neo-Grotian ideas have been reflected in the Covenant of the League of Nations, which prohibited member states from going to war in disregard of certain procedures which it laid down — the Paris Pact of 1929, which prohibits resort to war as an instrument of national policy, and the United Nations Charter, which prohibits the use or threat of force against the territorial integrity or political independence of any state — or in any other manner inconsistent with the purposes of the United Nations. The Covenant and the Charter, while imposing these restrictions on resort to force by states, at the same time provide for the use and threat of force by states acting in the name of the international organisation to uphold a system of collective security. The principle of collective security implies that international order should rest not on a balance of power, but on a preponderance of power wielded by a combination of states acting as the agents of international society as a whole that will deter challenges to the system or deal with them if they occur.

The solidarist formula promises a superior form of maintaining order because it seeks to make force solely or chiefly the instrument of international society as a whole. It is, however, crucially dependent on the actual existence among states of a sufficient degree of solidarity in recognising common objectives and acting to promote them. In the actual circumstances of the twentieth century this solidarity has not been present. The attempt to apply the Grotian or solidarist formula has had the consequence not merely that the attempt to construct a superior world order is unsuccessful, but also that...classical devices for the maintenance of order are weakened or undermined. The action taken by the League of Nations against Italy in 1935 over the invasion of Abyssinia, and against the Soviet Union in 1939 over the invasion of Finland, not only failed to vindicate the principle of collective security, but also endangered the objective of preventing Germany's overthrow of the balance of power. The action taken by the United Nations General Assembly in 1950 to endorse the role of the United States and its allies in Korea as a collective-security operation not only served to weaken rather than enhance the role of the organisation in world politics, but, by presenting the issue as one in which the law-enforcing powers confronted the delinquents, impeded the processes of great power diplomacy.

If in the twentieth century the attempt to apply the solidarist formula has proved premature, this does not mean that the conditions will never obtain in which it could be made to work. The whole history of relations among states could be adduced in support of the view that sovereign states are inherently incapable of achieving solidarity in subordinating the use of force to common purposes. But to conclude that this is so would be to go beyond the evidence.

A World of Many Nuclear Powers. Another basic change in the character of the contemporary states system, which would still fall short of the replacement of the states system by something different, would be the emergence of a world of many nuclear powers. This alternative to the contemporary form of the states system attracts attention more because it is widely held that the process of nuclear proliferation may eventually bring it about than because it is thought that it embodies a more effective means of achieving world order, although advocates of nuclear proliferation sometimes take that view.

A world of many nuclear powers would be most dramatically different from the present one if the conditions were present for what Morton Kaplan has called "the unit veto system" and Arthur Burns "the deterrent system".[2] This would require that nuclear weapons were available not merely to many but to all states, or to all groups or blocs of states. (It is in fact easier to visualise a world in which every state enjoyed the protection of some group or bloc "nuclear umbrella", than to imagine that all of the 140 or so states in the world possessed nuclear forces of their own.) It would also require that there existed relationships of mutual nuclear deterrence among all of these states or blocs. We have to assume, in other words, not merely that every state or bloc possesses nuclear weapons, but also that it can inflict "unacceptable damage" upon every other state or bloc, but cannot prevent their inflicting such damage upon itself.

The central characteristic of the "unit veto" system is thus the ability of each state or bloc to veto the deliberate and "rational" resort to unlimited nuclear war by each of the others, in the same way that the United States and the Soviet Union possess a veto of this kind in relation to each other at the present time. It is important to note that this is in itself a very incomplete description of what the behaviour of states in a "unit veto system" would be, from which only limited inferences can be drawn. It is only by making assumptions extraneous to his model that Kaplan can argue that "the unit veto system" would be a Hobbesian state of nature in which the interests of all are opposed; that actors within the system can exist only at one level; that coalitions and the shifting or balancing of alignments in such a system would be eliminated; that no role in it could be played by universal actors such as the United Nations; that the system would perpetuate the existing state of affairs; and that it would be non-integrated and non-solidary to a high degree, and would be characterised by extreme tension.[3]

If we were to make the assumption that strategic nuclear weapons are the only instruments available to actors in the "unit veto system" for promoting their objectives, then the possession by every actor of a veto over the use of this instrument by every other actor would lead to consequences of this kind. This, however, would be a very odd assumption to make. If "the unit veto system" were to embody on a universal scale the characteristics of what may be called the present, Soviet-American mutual veto system, then each actor, while being able to neutralise the use of strategic nuclear weapons by the others, would also be able to bring into play other instruments of power and influence — military, political and economic — through which diplomatic conflict and collaboration would continue. It should not be assumed, therefore, that gradations of power and influence among the various actors would not continue to exist, that coalitions and the shifting of alignments would not continue to play a role, or that changes could not be effected in the *status quo*; nor does it follow that the system must be a Hobbesian state of nature, or that it must be marked by extreme tension or that universal actors such as the United Nations could play no role in it. It is not inconceivable that the actors in such a system, while neutralizing their strategic nuclear instruments, at the same time might contain if not resolve their political disputes. It might even be imagined that an international system existing for generations under the discipline of fear might eventually discover that the order it had achieved could exist independently of that discipline, that the apparatus of universal nuclear deterrence had become superfluous and could be discarded like an empty shell. These are, of course, mere speculations; my point is that behaviour of this kind is just as consistent with the assumption of a "unit veto system" as are the deductions made by Kaplan.

Are there any grounds for considering that a world of many nuclear powers is a form of the states system more conducive than the present one to world order? There is a familiar argument that the more states that possess nuclear weapons, the more able the international system will be to achieve the objectives of peace and security, since this will generalise the factor of mutual nuclear deterrence that has helped to preserve peace in the relationship between the United States and the Soviet Union. This argument exaggerates the stability of the Soviet-American relationship of mutual nuclear deterrence, which can be overthrow by political or technical change, and which even while it lasts does not make nuclear war impossible but simply renders it "irrational".... Moreover, it wrongly assumes that the spread of nuclear weapons will necessarily result in the duplication in other relationships of international conflict of the relationship of mutual nuclear deterrence that exists between the super powers; it assumes, in other words, that the spread of nuclar weapons is bound to lead to a "unit veto system", which of course it is not.

There is a stronger argument, which is that whether or not the spread of nuclear weapons would lead to increased security, it would, if it made these weapons available to all states or blocs, advance the cause of international justice. International justice in the sense of equality with regard to the possession of nuclear weapons can be met fully only by complete nuclear disarmament, or by a system in which these weapons are available to all states or blocs. Any regime which draws a distinction between nuclear-weapon states and non-nuclear-weapon states is open to objection on this score. It is important to note that in the argument between those powers which support and those which oppose the 1968 Nuclear Non-Proliferation Treaty, or more generally between nuclear "have" and "have-not" powers, the issue is not whether or not a line should be drawn between nuclear-weapon states and non-nuclear-weapon states, but rather where this line should be drawn, which states should be within the club and which left outside. The principal "recalcitrant" states — China, France and India — while they have sometimes justified proliferation with arguments that apply to others as well as themselves, have at no stage argued in favour of general and complete nuclear proliferation, and have been principally concerned to remove obstacles to their own inclusion in the nuclear-weapon club. This is one area in which goals of international order and of international justice or equal treatment are in conflict with one another.

Whether a world of many nuclear powers is

taken to represent a desirable alternative to the present form of the international system or not, it must be reckoned an alternative that has a fair prospect of being realised. Like the vision of a disarmed world, the vision of a world of many nuclear powers is by itself incomplete. The prospects of order and of justice in an alternative form of states system characterised by many nuclear powers would depend on other factors besides the prevailing military technology and the number of states with access to it.

Ideological Homogeneity. Another alternative form of states system is one marked by ideological homogeneity, as distinct from the ideological heterogeneity that prevails in the states system at present. The exponents of political ideologies frequently maintain that the triumph of their doctrines throughout the states system as a whole would, in addition to conferring other benefits, eliminate or reduce the sources of war and conflict, and lead to a more orderly world. Theorists of the Reformation and the Counter-Reformation, of the Revolution and the Counter-Revolution, and in our own times the apologists of Communism and of Anti-Communism, alike maintain, even as they are calling for war, that their own cause is the cause of peace.

These ideological revolutionaries and counter-revolutionaries, as has been noted, sometimes embrace the goal of a universal society that would replace the states system.... But they also sometimes adhere to the vision of a world that is still organised as a system of states, but in which all states embrace the true ideology and can in consequence maintain harmonious relations with one another. It is this vision that concerns us here.

Kant's espousal of the ideology of the French Revolution led him to the idea that peace should be founded upon a world republic or *civitas gentium*, but in *Perpetual Peace* he despairs of this and turns to the "negative surrogate" of a league of "republican" or constitutionalist states, which averts war and seeks to spread itself over the globe. The Legitimist ideologists of the post-Napoleonic era saw the prospects of international peace and domestic tranquillity as lying in a Holy Alliance of sovereign states held together by bonds of piety and dynastic right. Mazzini saw the prospects of peace as lying in the universal triumph of nationalism, which would be assisted by a Holy Alliance of the Peoples among whom no conflicts of interest existed. In their different ways President Wilson in the United States, the members of the Union for Democratic Control in Britain and the Bolsheviks in Russia all held that control of foreign policy by democratic or popular forces was a source of peace and concord among states.

Marx saw the prospects of peace as bound up with the abolition of capitalism and class struggle. He held that the state was simply an instrument of class struggle, and also (although the point is less clear) appears to have thought of the nation as a transitory phenomenon; hence his theory may be taken to imply that with universal proletarian revolution the state, and hence the states system, will disappear. On the other hand, Marx and Engels sometimes spoke as if separate units would still exist after the revolution. Marxists-Leninists since 1917 have had to settle for the "negative surrogate" of a league of socialist states or Socialist Commonwealth. They live in a world in which proletarian revolution has taken place only in a limited number of countries, and in which even in these countries the state survives as an instrument of the dictatorship of the proletariat. In the thinking of Marxist-Leninists today the vision I have in mind is exemplified by the doctrine that relations among socialist states, while they are governed by the principles of "socialist internationalism", are to be distinguished on the one hand from the relations among capitalist states, which are governed by the principles of "imperialism", and on the other hand from the relations between socialist and capitalist states, which are subject to the principles of "peaceful coexistence".

The vision of a states system that achieves order or harmony through the triumph in all countries of the true ideology is different from the Grotian or solidarist vision, for the latter assumes that conflicts of interest will continue to exist among states, and seeks to curb them through the overwhelming power of the collectivity, whereas the former maintains that when the true ideology is universally enthroned, conflicts of interest will not exist or will only be of slight importance. The two visions, however, are sometimes uneasily combined in the thinking of the same person or persons; President Wilson, for example, placed his hopes on the solidarist idea of the League of Nations, but he was also drawn to the idea that this should be a league of democracies; and the architects of the United Nations, who were also primarily committed to a solidarist vision, nevertheless made a bow to the notion that true ideology is the source of peace in their requirement that the member states of the organisation should be "peace-loving".

We should distinguish the idea that an ideologically homogenous states system would be more orderly because it would rest on a single ideology, and would not give rise to conflicts of ideology, from the idea that it would be more orderly because the particular ideology it would rest upon would reduce or eliminate conflicts of interest among states. The latter idea is open to some powerful objections, whatever the ideology in question.

In the era when foreign policy was shaped by monarchs and their ministers, and wars were occasioned by dynastic conflicts and fought by standing armies led by landed aristocrats, liberal or bourgeois ideologists were able to make plausible the thesis that international conflicts were artificially manufactured by the prevailing political groups, and that domestic political change on a universal scale would reveal a natural harmony of interests among peoples. This was the perspective that led Paine to the view that the cause of war lay in monarchial sovereignty, Cobden to hold that commerce was the grand panacea, and Comte to proclaim a general incompatibility between war and industrial society.

But as domestic changes took place that led to a decline in monarchial and aristocratic control of foreign policy and increased the role of the middle classes, this thesis became less plausible; German and French burghers and Manchester manufacturers were less moved by dynastic quarrels and rivalries, but this did not mean that they were without motives of their own for international conflict. Reasons of state came to be given content in terms of national interest, rather than dynastic interest, and royal pride or passion, as a cause of conflict and war, was replaced by the public pride or passion of nationalism. Early in the twentieth century Lenin, with some help from Hobson, was able to make plausible the thesis that it was precisely the struggle of finance capitalists and industrialists that led to international tension and war, and that the prospects of peace lay in another domestic political change that would bring the proletariat to power.

But just as bourgeois governments, while free of some of the motives that led the feudal classes to war, had motives of their own that led to war, so governments which reflect the interests of the proletariat, as defined by the Communist Party, have motives of their own that lead to international conflict, even if they are free of some of the motives that bourgeois or capitalist governments have had. The experience of the Soviet Union, the People's Republic of China, and the other socialist countries in their relations with one another, does not lend any support to the idea of a natural harmony of interests among the peoples or the working classes. Socialist or proletarian states in their dealings with each other have displayed the same conflicts of perceived interest that states of all kinds have minifested in earlier periods.

The view that a certain section of society is naturally internationalist is plausible only when it is asserted before that section of society has achieved power. It is the elements of society which do have power that most closely identify themselves with the maintenance or extension of the state's power abroad. Those elements in society which do not enjoy power at home, are less concerned with the state's external honour and interests, and are natural dissenters from its foreign policy, and sometimes sympathisers with its opponents. But once they rise to power at home, they inherit the concern for the state's power abroad. The doctrine that peace will be established by the universal triumph of the true ideology does not take account of the argument Hegel made in his critique of Kant that it is the state *qua* state that is the source of tension and war, not the state *qua* this or that kind of state.

However, a states system which rested upon a single ideology, whichever this might be, and was free of the conflict of ideologies, we might expect to be more orderly than that which exists at present. The states system in the past, as Raymond Aron has noted, has undergone phases at least of relative ideological homogeneity, in the intervals between the wars of religion, the wars of the French Revolution and Napoleon, and the World Wars and Cold War of the twentieth century, which have been the phases of maximum ideological conflict. It is possible to agree with Aron that the coincidence of major wars and maximum heterogeneity of the states system is not accidental — not only because the successive ideological conflicts have been a cause of these major wars, but also because the wars themselves tend to accentuate ideological conflict, as each warring state allies itself with domestic factions within the enemy state.

These periods of relative ideological homogeneity, however, have been characterised by the toleration of ideological differences rather than by ideological uniformity. The wars of religion and the wars of the French Revolution and Napoleon, while superficially ending with the victory of one side, led, through a process of exhaustion, to compromises that made possible ideological coexistence, as the ideological conflicts of the twentieth century may also do. What we have in mind by a states system that is ideologically homogenous is one in which states are united not by a formula that allows different political, social and economic systems to coexist, but by determination to uphold a single kind of political, social and economic system. We have in mind, in other words, a universal Holy Alliance that is able to make a single ideology prevail throughout the states system as a whole, as such an ideology now prevails within the limited spheres of the American alliance system and the Socialist Commonwealth.

Such a system promises a high degree of domestic order because any challenger to the prevailing political, social or economic system would have to face not merely the state immediately concerned but the society of states at large: interventions of the sort whereby the Soviet Union has upheld challenges to the socialist system in Eastern Europe, or of the sort whereby the United States has sought to exclude the same system from Central America, could take place in support of the existing regime, with the difference that they would not be met with the condemnation or criticism of other states. The system also promises a high degree of international order; while conflicts might occur between one state and another, arising from clashing material interests or anxieties about security, ideological tension would not divide them. Indeed, the common interests of all states in defending the entrenched political, social and economic system would provide them with a strong incentive to moderate their conflicts of interest.

It may be doubted, however, whether world politics is likely ever to display the kind of ideological uniformity that would be necessary to establish or to maintain an alternative form of the states system such as this. If we assume that in the future as in the past there will be constant change and variety in the ideologies that are espoused in different parts of the world, then the attempt to remould a states system on principles of ideological fixity and uniformity is likely to be a source of disorder, and we are driven back to the principle that order is best founded upon agreement to tolerate ideological difference, namely the principle upon which the present states system is founded.

BEYOND THE STATES SYSTEM

If an alternative form of universal political order

were to emerge that did not merely constitute a change from one phase or condition of the states system to another, but led beyond the states system, it would have to involve the demise of one or another of the latter's essential attributes: sovereign states, interaction among them, such that they form a system; and a degree of acceptance of common rules and institutions, in respect of which they form a society.

A System But Not a Society. It is conceivable that a form of universal political organisation might arise which would possess the first and the second of these attributes but not the third. We may imagine, that is to say, that there might exist a plurality of sovereign states, forming a system, which did not, however, constitute an international society. Such a state of affairs would represent the demise of *the* states system, which...is an international society as well as an international system. There would be states, and interaction among them on a global basis, but the element of acceptance of common interests or values, and, on the basis of them, of common rules and institutions, would have disappeared. There would be communications and negotiations among these states, but no commitment to a network of diplomatic institutions; agreements, but no acceptance of a structure of international legal obligation; violent encounters among them that were limited by the capacity of the belligerents to make war, but not by their will to observe restraints as to when, how and by whom it was conducted; balances of power that arose fortuitously, but not balances that were the product of conscious attempts to preserve them; powers that were greater than others, but no agreed conception of a great power in the sense of a power with special rights and duties.

Whether or not the states sysstem, at some point in the future, has ceased to be an international society, it might well be difficult to determine. There may be acceptance of common rules and institutions by some states, but not by others: how many states have to have contracted out of international society before we can say that it has ceased to exist? Some rules and institutions may continue to find acceptance, but others not: which rules and institutions are essential? Acceptance of rules and institutions may be difficult to determine: does it lie in verbal assent to these rules, in behaviour that conforms strictly to them, or in willingness to defer to them even while evading them? Granted these difficulties, it has already been shown that there is ample historical precedent for an international system that is not an international society....

An international system that is not an international society might nevertheless contain some elements of order. Particular states might be able to achieve a degree of domestic order, despite the absence of rules and institutions in their relations with one another. Some degree of international order might also be sustained by fortuitous balances of power or relationships of mutual nuclear deterrence, by great power spheres of preponderance unilaterally imposed, by limitations in war that were the consequence of self-restraint or limitations of capacity. But an international system of this kind would be disorderly in the extreme, and would in fact exemplify the Hobbesian state of nature.

States But Not a System. It is also conceivable that a form of universal political organisation might emerge which possessed the first of the essential attributes that have been mentioned but not the second. We may imagine that there are still sovereign states, but that they are not in contact or interaction with each other, or at all events do not interact sufficiently to cause them to behave as component parts of a system. States might be linked with each other so as to form systems of states in particular regions, but there would not be any global system of states. Throughout the world as a whole there might be mutual awareness among states, and even contact and interaction on a limited scale, but it would no longer be the case that states in all parts of the world were a vital factor in one another's calculations.

It might be difficult to determine how much

decline in the global interaction of states would have to have taken place before we could say that they had ceased to form a system. If there is a high degree of interaction throughout the world at the economic and social levels, but not at the strategic level, can we say that there is a global system? Does a global states system cease to exist merely because there are some societies that are excluded from it? Even today in the jungles of Brazil or in the highlands of Papua/New Guinea there are societies scarcely touched by what we nevertheless call the global states system.

Once again, there is ample historical precedent for an alternative to the states system of this kind; ...as it was not before the nineteenth century that there arose any states system that was global in dimension. Does such an alternative represent a superior path to world order?

It has often been maintained that it does. A series of isolated or semi-isolated states or other kinds of community might each achieve a tolerable form of social order within its own confines, and a form of world order would exist that was simply the sum of the order that derived from each of these communities. At the same time the classic sources of disorder that arise in a situation of interaction between states would be avoided because interaction itself would be avoided or kept to a minimum.

This was the substance of Rousseau's vision of a world of small self-sufficient states, each achieving order within its own confines through the operation of the general will of its community, and achieving order in their relations with one another by minimising contact. It also entered into the prescription that Washington laid down for the United States in his Farewell Address: "The great rule of conduct for us in regard to foreign relations is, in extending our commercial relations, to have with them as little *political* connection as possible."[4] This for Washington was a maxim only for the United States, which was in a position of actual physical isolation from the powers that might threaten her. Cobden later transformed it into a general prescription for all states in his dictum: "As little intercourse as possible betwixt the governments, as much connection as possible between the nations of the world".[5]

Cobden believed in non-intervention in the most rigid and absolute sense. He opposed intervention in international conflicts as well as civil ones; for ideological causes (such as liberalism and nationalism on the European continent) of which he approved, as well as for causes of which he disapproved (such as the interventionism of the Holy Alliance); and for reasons of national interest such as the preservation of the balance of power or the protection of commerce. He rejected the distinctions John Stuart Mill drew between intervention in the affairs of civilised countries and intervention in a barbarian country, and between intervention as such and intervention to uphold the principle of non-intervention against a power that had violated it. He even opposed the attempt to influence the affairs of another country by moral suasion, and declined to sanction the formation of any organisation in England for the purpose of interfering in another country, such as the organisations formed to agitate against slavery in the United States. However, in Cobden's vision the promotion of the maximum systematic interaction at the economic and social levels was just as important as the promotion of minimum interaction at the strategic and political levels. Assuming as he did the desirability of universal pursuit by governments of *laissez-faire* policies in relation to the economy, he was able to imagine that the strategic and political isolation of states from one another might coexist with their economic interdependence.

A form of universal political organisation based on the absolute or relative isolation of communities from one another, supposing it to be a possible development, would have certain drawbacks. If systematic interaction among states has in the past involved certain costs (international disorder, the subjection of the weak to the strong, the exploitation by the rich of the poor), so also has it brought certain gains (assistance to the weak and the poor by the strong and the rich, the international division of labour, the intellectual enrichment of countries by each other). The prescription of universal isolationism, even in the limited form Cobden gave it of political and strategic non-interventionism, implies that the opportunities arising from human interaction on a global scale will be lost, as well as that the dangers to which it gives rise will be avoided.

World Government. It is conceivable also that a form of universal political organisation might arise lacking the first of the above essential attributes, namely sovereign states. One way in which this might occur is through the emergence of a world government.

We may imagine that a world government would come about by conquest, as the result of what John Strachey has called a "knock-out tournament" among the great powers, and in this case it would be a universal empire based upon the domination of the conquering power;[6] or we may imagine that it would arise as the consequence of a social contract among states, and thus that it would be a universal republic or cosmopolis founded upon some form of consent or consensus. In the latter case it may be imagined that a world government would arise suddenly, perhaps as the result of a crash programme induced by some catastrophe such as global war or ecological breakdown (as envisaged by a succession of futurologists from Kant to Herman Kahn), or it may be thought of as arising gradually, perhaps through accretion of the powers of the United Nations. It may be seen as coming about as the result of a direct, frontal assault on the political task of bringing states to agree to relinquish their sovereignty, or, as in some "functionalist" theories, it may be seen as the indirect result of inroads made on the sovereignty of states in non-political areas.

There has never been a government of the world, but there has often been a government supreme over much of what for those subjected to it was the known world. Throughout the history of the modern states system there has been an undercurrent of awareness of the alternative of a universal government, and of argument on behalf of it: either in the form of the backward-looking doctrine calling for a return to Roman unity, or in the form of a forward-looking doctrine that sees a world state as the consequence of inevitable progress. In the twentieth century there has been a revival of world government doctrine in response to the two World Wars.

The classical argument for world government is that order among states is best established by the same means whereby it is established among individual men within the state, that is by a supreme authority. This argument most commonly relates to the goal of minimum order, and especially the avoidance of war, which is said to be an inevitable consequence of the states system. But it is also sometimes advanced in relation to goals of optimum order; it is often argued today, for example, that a world government could best achieve the goal of economic justice for all individual men, or the goal of sound management of the human environment.

The classical argument against world government has been that, while it may achieve order, it is destructive of liberty or freedom: it infringes the liberties of states and nations (as argued by the ideologists of the successful grand alliances that fought against universal monarchy); and also checks the liberties of individuals who, if the world government is tyrannical, cannot seek political asylum under an alternative government.

The case for world government may thus appear to rest on an assumed priority of order over international or human justice or liberty. It may be argued, however, that the states system affords a better prospect than world government of achieving the goal of order also....

A New Mediaevalism. It is also conceivable that sovereign states might disappear and be replaced not by a world government but by a modern and secular equivalent of the kind of universal political organisation that existed in Western Christendom in the Middle Ages. In that system no ruler or state was sovereign in the sense of being supreme over a given territory and a given segment of the Christian population; each had to share authority with vassals beneath, and with the Pope and (in Germany and Italy) the Holy Roman Emperor above. The universal political order of Western Christendom represents an alternative to the system of states which does not yet embody universal government.

All authority in mediaeval Christendom was thought to derive ultimately from God and the political system was basically theocratic. It might therefore seem fanciful to contemplate a return to the mediaeval model, but it is not fanciful to imagine that there might develop a modern and secular counterpart of it that embodies its central characteristic: a system of overlapping authority and multiple loyalty.

It is familiar that sovereign states today share the stage of world politics with "other actors" just as in mediaeval times the state had to share the stage with 'other associations' (to use the mediaevalists' phrase). If modern states were to come to share their authority over their citizens, and their ability to command their loyalties, on the one hand with regional and world authorities, and on the other hand with sub-state or sub-national authorities, to such an extent that the concept of sovereignty ceased to be applicable, then a neo-mediaeval form of universal political order might be said to have emerged.

We might imagine, for example, that the government of the United Kingdom had to share its authority on the one hand with authorities in Scotland, Wales, Wessex and elsewhere, and on the other hand with a European authority in Brussels and world authorities in New York and Geneva, to such an extent that the notion of its supremacy over the territory and people of the United Kingdom had no force. We might imagine that the authorities in Scotland and Wales, as well as those in Brussels, New York and Geneva enjoyed standing as actors in world politics, recognised as having rights and duties in world law, conducting negotiations and perhaps able to command armed forces. We might imagine that the political loyalties of the inhabitants of, say, Glasgow, were so uncertain as between the authorities in Edinburgh, London, Brussels and New York that the government of the United Kingdom could not be assumed to enjoy any kind of primacy over the others, such as it possesses now. If such a state of affairs prevailed all over the globe, this is what we may call, for want of a better term, a neo-mediaeval order.

The case for regarding this form of universal political organisation as representing a superior path to world order to that embodied in the states system would be that it promises to avoid the classic dangers of the system of sovereign states by a structure of overlapping authorities and criss-crossing loyalties that hold all peoples together in a universal society, while at the same time avoiding the concentration of power inherent in a world government. The case for doubting whether the neo-mediaeval model is superior is that there is no assurance that it would prove more orderly than the states system, rather than less. It is conceivable that a universal society of this kind might be constructed that would provide a firm basis for the realisation of elementary goals of social life. But if it were anything like the precedent of Western Christendom, it would contain more ubiquitous and continuous violence and insecurity than does the modern states system.

Non-Historical Alternatives. We must finally note the possibility that an alternative will develop to the states system which, unlike the four that have just been considered, does not conform to any previous pattern of universal political organisation.

Of course, any future form of universal political organisation will be different from previous historical experience, in the sense that it will have certain features that are unique and will not exactly resemble any previous system. My point is not this trivial one but the more serious one that a universal political system may develop which does not resemble any of the four historically derived alternatives even in broad comparison. The basic terms in which we now consider the question of universal political organisation could be altered decisively by the progress of technology, or equally by its decay or retrogression, by revolutions in moral and political, or in scientific and philosophical ideas, or by military or economic or ecological catastrophes, foreseeable and unforeseeable.

I do not propose to speculate as to what these non-historical alternatives might be. It is clearly not possible to confine the varieties of possible future forms within any finite list of possible political systems, and for this reason one cannot take seriously attempts to spell out the laws of transformation of one kind of universal political system to another. It is not possible, by definition, to foresee political forms that are not foreseeable, and attempts to define non-historical political forms are found in fact to depend upon appeals to historical experience. But our view of possible alternatives to the states system should take into account the limitations of our own imagination and our own inability to transcend past experience.

ENDNOTES

1 I have discussed this doctrine in "The Grotian Conception of International Society," in Herbert Butterfield and Martin Wight, eds., *Diplomatic Investigations* (London: Allen and Unwin, 1967).

2 See Morton Kaplan, *System and Process in International Politics* (New York: Wiley, 1957), pp. 50-52; and Arthur Lee Burns, "From Balance to Deterrence," *World Politics,* 9 (July 1957).

3 Ibid.

4 This is quoted by Richard Cobden at the beginning of "England, Ireland and America," in *The Political Writings of Richard Cobden* (London: Cassell, 1886), p.3.

5 Ibid., p. 216.

6 John Strachey, *On the Prevention of War* (London: Macmillan, 1962).

Death in the Nuclear Age

Hans J. Morgenthau

It is obvious that the nuclear age has radically changed man's relations to nature and to his fellow men. It has enormously increased man's ability to use the forces of nature for his purposes and has thus concentrated unprecedented destructive powers in the hands of governments. That concentration of power has fundamentally altered the relations which have existed throughout history between government and people and among governments themselves. It has made popular revolution impossible, and it has made war an absurdity. Yet, less obvious and more important, the nuclear age has changed man's relations to himself. It has done so by giving death a new meaning.

Death is the great scandal in the experience of man; for death — as the destruction of the human person after a finite span of time — is the very negation of all man experiences as specifically human in his existence: the consciousness of himself and of his world, the remembrance of things past and the anticipation of things to come, a creativeness in thought and action which aspires to, and approximates, the eternal. Thus man has been compelled, for the sake of his existence as man, to bridge the gap between death and his specifically human attributes by transcending death. He has done so in three different ways: by making himself, within narrow limits, the master of death; by denying the reality of death through the belief in the immortality of his person; by conquering the reality of death through the immortality of the world he leaves behind.

Man can make himself the master of death by putting an end to his biological existence whenever he wishes. While he cannot live as long as he wants to, he can stop living whenever he wants to. While he cannot choose life over death when his life has reached its biological limits, he can choose death over life regardless of these limits. He can commit suicide; or he can commit what Nietzsche has called "suicide with a good conscience" by seeking out death, especially at the hand of someone else. He is capable of sacrificial death. In his self-chosen death for a cause in particular, on the battlefield or elsewhere, man triumphs over death, however incompletely. He triumphs because he does not wait until his body is ready to die, but he offers his life to death when his chosen purpose demands it. Yet that triumph is incomplete because it cannot overcome the inevitability of death but only controls its coming.

Man also denies the reality of death by believing in the immortality of his person. This belief can take two different forms. It may take the form of the assumption that the finiteness of man's biological existence is but apparent and that his body will live on in another world. It can also take the form of the assumption that what is specifically human in man will survive the destruction of his

---

Reprinted from *Commentary*, September, 1961, by

body and that man's soul will live on forever, either separated from any body or reincarnated in someone else's. This belief in personal immortality, in defiance of the empirical evidence of the finiteness of man's biological existence, is of course peculiar to the religious realm. It presupposes the existence of a world which is not only inaccessable to the senses but also superior to the world of the senses in that what is truly human in man is there preserved forever.

It is a distinctive characteristic of our secular age that it has replaced the belief in the immortality of the human person with the attempt to assure the immortality of the world he leaves behind. Man can transcend the finiteness of his biological existence either in his consciousness or in objective reality by adding to that existence four different dimensions which are in one way or another independent of that finiteness. They are different dimensions of immortality. He can extend his consciousness into the past by remembering it. He can extend his consciousness into the future by anticipating it. As *homo faber,* he embeds his biological existence within technological and social artifacts which survive that existence. His imagination creates new worlds of religion, art, and reason that live after their creator.

By thus bestowing immortality upon the past, man assures himself of immortality to be granted by future generations who will remember him. As the past lives on in his historic recollection, so will he continue to live in the memory of his successors. The continuity of history gives the individual at least a chance to survive himself in the collective memory of mankind. Those who are eminent, or believe themselves to be so, aspire to posthumous fame which will enable them to live on, perhaps forever.

The ability to remember and the aspiration to be remembered call for deliberate action to assure that remembrance. The assurance of his life after death becomes one of man's main concerns here and now. Man on all levels of civilization is moved to create monuments which testify to his existence and will live after him. He founds a family and lives on in his sons, who bear his name as he bears his father's. He leaves an inheritance of visible things not to be consumed but to be preserved as tangible mementos of past generations. Over his grave he causes a monument of stone to be erected whose durability, as it were, compensates for the impermanence of what lies beneath. Or he may even refuse to accept that impermanence altogether and have his body preserved in the likeness of life. At the very least, he will have pictures made of himself to perpetuate his physical likeness.

This concern with immortality in this world manifests itself on the highest level of consciousness in the preparation of man's fame. He lives in such a way as to make sure that his fame will survive him. All of us, from the peasant and handicraft man to the founders of churches, the architects of empires, the builders of cities, the tamers of the forces of nature, seek to leave behind the works of our wills and hands to testify to our existence. *"Roma eterna,"* "the Reich of a thousand years" are but the most ambitious attempts to perpetuate man in his deeds. The tree that he has planted, the house that he has built, have been given a life likely to last longer than his own. At best, he as a person will live on in his works; at worst, he has the satisfaction of living on anonymously in what he has created.

It is, however, in the works of his imagination that man conquers the mortality of his body in the most specifically human way. The artists and poets, the philosophers and the writers, can point with different degrees of assurance to their work and say with Horace: "I have finished a monument more lasting than bronze and loftier than the Pyramids' royal pile, one that no wasting rain, no furious north wind can destroy, or the countless chain of years and the ages' flight. I shall not altogether die...." In the works of his mind it is not just his physical existence, the bare fact that he once lived, that is remembered. Rather, what is remembered is the creative quality that sets him apart from all other creatures, that is peculiar to him as a man. What is remembered is not only the specifically human quality, but also and most importantly the quality in which he lives on as a unique individual, the like of whom has never existed before or since. In the works of his mind, man, the creator, survives.

Yet why are those works a "monument more lasting than bronze," and why can their creator be confident that "on and on shall I grow, ever fresh with the glory of after time"? Because the man endowed with a creative mind knows himself to be a member in an unbroken chain emerging from the past and reaching into the future, which is made of the same stuff his mind is made of and, hence, is capable of participating in, and perpetuating, his mind's creation. He may be mortal, but humanity is not, and so he will be immortal in his works. This is the triumphant message of Horace.

Our life, then, receives one of its meanings from the meaning we give to death. What we make of life is shaped by what we make of death; for we live in the presence of the inevitability of death and we dedicate our lives to the proof of the proposition that death is not what it seems to be: the irrevocable end of our existence. We search for immortality, and the kind of immortality we seek determines the kind of life we lead.

The significance of the possibility of nuclear death is that it radically affects the meaning of death, of immortality, of life itself. It affects that meaning by destroying most of it. Nuclear destruction is mass destruction, both of persons and of things. It signifies the simultaneous destruction of tens of millions of people, of whole families, generations, and societies, of all the things that they have inherited and created. It signifies the total destruction of whole societies by killing their members, destroying their visible achievements, and therefore reducing the survivors to barbarism. Thus nuclear destruction destroys the meaning of death by depriving it of its individuality. It destroys the meaning of immortality by making both society and history impossible. It destroys the meaning of life by throwing life back upon itself.

Sacrificial death has meaning only as the outgrowth of an individual decision which chooses death over life. The hero who risks his life or dies for a cause is bound to be one man, an identifiable individual. There is meaning in Leonidas falling at Thermopylae, in Socrates drinking the cup of hemlock, in Jesus nailed to the cross. There can be no meaning in the slaughter of the innocent, the murder of six million Jews, the prospective nuclear destruction of, say, fifty million Americans and an equal number of Russians. There is, then, a radical difference in meaning between a man risking death by an act of will and fifty million people simultaneously reduced — by somebody switching a key thousands of miles away — to radioactive ashes, indistinguishable from the ashes of their houses, books, and animals. Horace could say, thinking of the individual soldier ready to die, "It is sweet and honorable to die for one's country." Yet Wilfred Owen, describing the effects of a gas attack in the First World War, could call Horace's famous phrase "The old Lie," and beholding a victim of modern mass destruction, could only bewail the futility of such a death and ask in despair, "Was it for this the clay grew tall? O what made fatuous sunbeams toil to break earth's sleep at all?" The death of the Horatian soldier is the assertion of man's freedom from biological necessity, a limited triumph over death. The death of Owen's soldier and of his prospective successors in the nuclear age is the negation not only of man's freedom but of his life's meaning as well.

Man gives his life and death meaning by his ability to make himself and his works remembered after his death. Patroclus dies to be avenged by Achilles. Hector dies to be mourned by Priam. Yet if Patroclus, Hector, and all those who could remember them were killed simultaneously, what would become of the meaning of Patroclus's and Hector's death? Their lives and deaths would lose their meaning. They would die, not like men but like beasts, killed in the mass, and what would be remembered would be the quantity of the killed — six million, twenty million, fifty million — not the quality of one man's death as over against another's.

Of their deeds, nothing would remain but the

faint hope of remembrance in distant places. The very concept of fame would disappear, and the historians, the professional immortalizers, would have nothing to report. What had been preserved and created through the mind, will, and hands of man would be dissolved like man himself. Civilization itself would perish. Perhaps in some faraway place some evidence would be preserved of the perished civilization and of the men who created it. Nothing more than that would be left of the immortality man had once been able to achieve through the persistence of his fame and the permanence of his works.

And what would become of life itself? If our age had not replaced the belief in the immortality of the individual person with the immortality of humanity and its civilization, we could take the prospect of nuclear death in our stride. We could even afford to look forward to the day of the great slaughter as a day on which the preparatory and vain life on this earth would come to an end for most of us and the true, eternal life in another world begin. Yet a secular age, which has lost faith in individual immortality in another world and is aware of the impending doom of the world through which it tries to perpetuate itself here and now, is left without a remedy. Once it has become aware of its condition, it must despair. It is the saving grace of our age that it has not yet become aware of its condition.

We think and act as though the possibility of nuclear death had no bearing upon the meaning of life and death. In spite of what some of us know in our reason, we continue to think and act as though the possibility of nuclear death portended only a quantitative extension of the mass destruction of the past and not a qualitative transformation of the meaning of our existence. Thus we talk about defending the freedom of West Berlin as we used to talk about defending the freedom of the American colonies. Thus we talk about defending Western civilization against Communism as the ancient Greeks used to talk about defending their civilization against the Persians. Thus we propose to die with honor rather than to live in shame.

Yet the possibility of nuclear death, by destroying the meaning of life and death, has reduced to absurd clichés the noble words of yesterday. To defend freedom and civilization is absurd when to defend them amounts to destroying them. To die with honor is absurd if nobody is left to honor the dead. The very conceptions of honor and shame require a society that knows what honor and shame mean.

It is this contrast between our consciousness and the objective conditions in which we live, the backwardness of our consciousness in view of the possibility of nuclear death, that threatens us with the actuality of nuclear death. It would indeed be the height of thoughtless optimism to assume that something so absurd as a nuclear war cannot happen because it is so absurd. An age whose objective conditions of existence have been radically transformed by the possibility of nuclear death evades the need for a radical transformation of its thought and action by thinking and acting as though nothing of radical import had happened. This refusal to adapt thought and action to radically new conditions has spelled the doom of men and civilizations before. It is likely to do so again.